Howard, Leslie G.

The expansion of God /

The Expansion of God

LESLIE G. HOWARD

The
Expansion
of
God

ORBIS BOOKS

Maryknoll, New York 10545

The Catholic Foreign Mission Society of America (Maryknoll) recruits and trains people for overseas missionary service. Through Orbis Books Maryknoll aims to foster the international dialogue that is essential to mission. The books published, however, reflect the opinions of their author and are not meant to represent the official position of the society.

First published 1981 by SCM Press Ltd, 58 Bloomsbury Street, London WC1, England

U.S. edition 1981 by Orbis Books, Maryknoll, NY 10545

Photoset in Great Britain and printed and bound in the United States of America

Library of Congress Cataloging in Publication Data

Howard, Leslie G.
  The expansion of God.

  Bibliography: p.
  Includes index.
  1. Christianity and other religions. 2. Asia—
Religion. 3. Christianity—20th century.
I. Title.
BR127.H67   1981   261.2'4   81-4521
ISBN 0-88344-121-7 (pbk.)   AACR2

Contents

Introduction

Any introduction to this book ought, in the short space accorded it, to say more about how and why it was written than precisely what it is about. When I planned this study, I was not completely sure of all the answers to the questions raised by it, and readers in turn might lose something if they were to understand the meaning of the title and the drift of the argument perfectly in advance. Positively, however, I might say that I have written about the modern spiritual crisis with special reference to the contacts of Asian religions and cultures with Christianity, but if, as might be more appropriate, the theme were negatively defined, then it is not, as might be imagined, about Whiteheadian philosophy or theories of growth in some contemporary liberationist sense.

Looking back on writing *The Expansion of God*, the assumption of the task, finding the answers and making the connections, seems strangely inevitable. At times when I was tired of it, or felt it ought to be, as in any other century it would be, a subject for philosophers or mystics rather than the wordly-religious layman, it seemed that some movement within the collective unconscious demanded that the questions be faced, and offered the answers along with them to any diligent seeker. But this was, or was largely, illusory, for in fact there was nothing especially inevitable about the matter. It depended very much on a particular life-situation, a prior course of research, and residence and travel in Asia, which gave, beyond knowledge, sympathy.

Most books written on Asia and the modern spiritual crisis before the last decade, during which they became more propagandist in tone, were either uncompromisingly academic or written with a view to promoting 'global civilization', while importing to the West the 'spontaneity' and intuition of the East, in which the rationalizing West was regarded as somewhat deficient. This kind of writing was often American, and more deeply influenced by social and sexual undercurrents of American life of the time, with its 'melting pot' and its rising feminism, than by any profound feeling about Asia itself. Deep sensitivity in relation to Asia and its common life, as in Pearl Buck, was fairly rare. Even among anthropologists faced with a dauntingly immense task, the 'etic' approach (from inside) as opposed to 'emic' (from outside) ran the danger of a sympathy so uncritical that it could border on racial condescension in its unwillingness to admit values and imagination common to mankind, and helped perpetrate notions of an inscrutable East.

In contrast to this, I can perhaps claim a certain novelty of approach and certain advantages. It helps not to be associated with one of the more privileged Western nations, whose members are always rightly or wrongly suspected of carrying around a load of unacceptable cultural prejudices which, even if they renounce them, can cause them to be considered so odd that the international contacts still may not proceed much beyond polite exchanges to the real confessions. If, however, one can be identified with Ireland, the only European society with a colonial heritage and fractured culture, after the manner of so many Asian countries, one is more likely to take on the role of father confessor, and ought to be able to have greater sympathy with what is learned.

In my own case, there were a few questions concerning which I did not even need to learn very much beyond the historical facts. I recognized them immediately, knew the outlines of the problems and the structure of their resolution, from previous Irish research. The larger issues of the current spiritual crisis and the future of religions was, of course, more complex and in a sense a more personal issue – it goes beyond anything like anthropology – but that it could be a 'personal' problem helped. Unlike Northrop or Toynbee, I was not doing penance for 'imperialistic' religion by inventing a mystical substitute that was little short of a political policy, but living a real conflict between a part of myself which seemed Asian and another part more Western. Jung believed that serious contact between East and West, cultural or psychological, is potentially dangerous, even demoralizing. From experience I must agree that it can be very difficult, but the tension is one which underlies much Celtic writing, as in Joyce's *Ulysses*, where so many assumptions are implicitly or explicitly Asian, but the exacting structure indelibly Western. When this tension is actually directed upon the real Asia and the current Asianization of culture, it bestows, not only sympathy, but authority and ease in criticism. I am not so remote from the problems and complexes involved that I feel the need to be unduly tolerant to what I cannot approve.

Altogether then, though I have often been told that this book is 'a work of scholarship', it was never, despite its research, conceived as such. If the aim had been scholarly, I should have felt obliged to treat Hinduism in some detail from a philosophical standpoint and devoted more consideration to the psychology of Mahayana Buddhism. It is really a work of imagination and synthesis which needed to be written and inevitably would have been. It simply awaited the right time and combination of experience and then 'wrote itself'. It can at most be an introduction to what it implies of the theological anthropology and psychology which almost certainly will be fundamental to the religious statements of tomorrow.

Hong Kong, 10 September 1980

1
The Expansion of God

So fundamental is religion to individual feeling and social development that it declines only when it gathers unpleasant associations, is identified with decaying or oppressive establishments or imprisoning patterns of thought. The spiritual stirrings of the present time put paid to the view that science and progress are the end of faith. At the same time, while the revival of the religious impulse cannot be denied, its form is unusual and it is open to question whether much that passes for religion today is not closer to religiosity or doctrines of fate than religion in the classic sense.

In the West, religion used to be conceived of as the salvation of the individual soul, and in the East, as deliverance from the burden of reincarnation and individual identity. In any society personal faith and the idea of deliverance from the painful dichotomies of existence were normally paramount. In the contemporary West, religion is increasingly required to provide a trip, to 'expand' the consciousness. Mysticism, diluted, is expected to provide instant ecstasy or relief from the wear and tear of modern urban life.In the East, by contrast, there is a new emphasis on religious allegiance in terms of cultural and political identity. Neo-Hinduism and Neo-Buddhism are not deeply spiritual movements by historical standards, and the monks and nuns who immolated themselves in Vietnam did so for their country as much as for their good *karma*. In Japan, Sokka Gakkai aims to establish a new society and is politically orientated. In Thailand, resistance to declining fervour will be registered in the revival of temple arts, endowments of hospitals, and crash courses in modern politics for the monks.

Growing awareness of human rights and threats to the existence of nations newly born have brought the faiths of the mystical Orient down to earth.

The unity of East and West in religious change is only matched by the contrast of the roles and aims within the process. In the nineteenth century it was the West which so confidently offered to the East its historic faith and social criticism, while in the twentieth century it is the East which brings its historic faiths to the West, accusing it of materialism. But it is not a simple question of the West assimilating Eastern values and the East accepting those of the West. Americans suddenly fascinated by, for example, the theory of reincarnation and seeking reincarnation readings, are embracing with enthusiasm a belief from whose consequences the East has endeavoured to extricate itself, and it is obvious, sociologically, that Western acceptance of such belief is an adjustment to a world so unprecedentedly full of choices and variety that one life is not felt to be sufficient in which to realize one's potential. In the same way, Asia has not really gained much of the very real spirituality, even other-worldliness, of which the West is periodically capable. Despite its aura of mysticism, Asia has always shown itself to be very materialistic, and in some respects it has become more so in response to social change and the Christian missions, which emphasized a way of works in order to dissociate themselves from the social indifference of Asian faiths. The character and opportunism of missionaries in both cases has affected these strange cross-fertilizations, for the classic form of the religion concerned is far from always being the one carried overseas. Just as Western Christians have sometimes been appalled at the beliefs and culture which have travelled to Asia under the banner of Christianity, so today there are Hindus who regard Californians as the dupe of every mad guru or species of folk religion which their faith has to offer.

If one were to define the original feature of religious change today, it would thus be in the shift from the emphasis upon traditionally central qualities of any faith, like knowledge of truth, the experience of the holy, and the achievement of 'salvation', however conceived, to the incidentals, the fringe benefits, like harmony with nature, spontaneous life-styles, cultural participation, the kind of things which modern life seems to be so drastically taking away from mankind and which religions have either ignored or managed to lose in the process of their development. It is true that there is much talk of reaching the Ultimate, but on the whole it is an

Ultimate to be experienced here and now to enhance the present, sometimes in unspiritual ways.[1] The Buddhist knowledge of 'suchness', with its mystical independence of past and future, even made pop philosopher Alan Watts feel 'light' or 'jazzy inside';[2] its reliance upon the immediate justified a bohemian life-style. Vulgarizations are probably inevitable. More important is whether the new emphasis can be considered as marking the humanization of religion, or as only a symptom of a larger spiritual crisis.

Altogether it seems doubtful whether religion of the new kind is in fact becoming in any profound sense more humanistic, despite the greater emphasis on the human factor and the greater range of choice in religious forms. Novelty and formal variety are not to be confused with such a trend. Not only is the Asian 'no self' doctrine which underlies the majority of new mystical outlets no ally of either conventional individualism or humanism, but there is every reason to suppose that in the West at least, individualism is declining amid the advancing bureaucratization and computerization of society and amid the challenge to the family, which, as studies like Philippe Aries, *Centuries of Childhood*,[3] have demonstrated, has been a crucial factor in supporting individualistic feeling. The need of Americans to be individualistic in groups and their high susceptibility to all forms of religious teachers and appeals, suggests a certain loss of self-confidence, and it could be argued that attempts are being made to remedy the consequences of permissive upbringing and broken homes within the security of cults and the substitute father figure of the guru, much as culturally *déraciné* Asians find meaning in the participation mystique of Neo-Hinduism and Buddhism.

Harvey Cox seems to confirm this in his *Turning East*.[4] In his interviews, he discovered that the majority of those attracted by the East admitted that the desire for friendship and community had taken precedence over other ideological considerations, however important. The typical American 'East-turner' was middle- to upper-class, Jewish or WASP, rootless, homeless, and a victim of a permissive, consumerist ethic, which had left him avid for experiences, but so centreless that he was looking for security and the group, while remaining susceptible to doctrines of non-attachment and egolessness. These, though imperfectly understood, made some sense to his type of experience.[5] Humanism and individualism thus count for little with this group, while in Asia the 'social gospel' quality that has crept into Neo-Hinduism and Buddhism is more a concession to laity and the new urban man than an overwhelming conviction.

It is more likely that beyond the faddism, the new spheres of emphasis represent a collective intuition about the sort of issues which a new or renewed religion would now have to take into account in order to claim authenticity as a religion for the times. This is the symptom of a religious crisis which is perhaps better understood, if not so deeply felt, by those philosophers, historians and psychiatrists of culture, like Northrop, Toynbee and Jung, who call for radical religious restatement or a union of religions to secure the salvation of the new global society and the satisfaction of science. When the new mystic opts for an archaic mantra or outlandish diet, he is not just affirming the importance of technique as against, say, faith, but to some extent the need for a completely new approach to religion, something larger than simple reform. The very difference of the mode can be function enough in terms of a situation which seems to demand a measure of psychological and intellectual transcendence.

The fact is that, however psychologically and spiritually valid believers may consider their particular belief system to be intrinsically, they usually feel the style, the original apologetic, the framework of the doctrinal statement to be dated. Works like the Buddhist *Lotus Sutra*, for example, may enjoy a new lease of life in the hands of modernizing sects, but are no longer felt to offer, simply as they stand, a very obvious relevance to Japanese youth, when they dismiss life as nothing but suffering and passion. Likewise, the absolutes, the self-evident truths of law and reason as they appeared to the classical world, and against which St Paul formulated Christian doctrine, contain less meaning for us as that classical heritage declines and everything from relativity theory to Hindu mysticism jostles for attention. Rather than concern themselves with St Paul's vindication of freedom over against law, members of a modern society are likely to ask more radical questions, like why the deity who is said to have given the law needed to be male, or, in view of St Paul's concern with it, what greater function Mosaic law could have had in the development of human consciousness which would justify a revelation within such peculiar terms, so far removed from modern and Asian experience. Thus, a Jesus for today is required to fulfil more than the law and the prophets, which themselves need to be placed in a wider perspective. Contemporary apologetics for religion have to be extended to embrace the whole social, psychological and natural process in response to suddenly enlarged horizons.

Spiritual crises do not necessarily entail loss of belief as such, but occur quite simply whenever there is a breakdown of deeply felt belief, a loss of a sense of wholeness in what is believed. When Pope John XXIII embarked on his reform of the Catholic church, he claimed to do so in an awareness of a universal loss of conviction and intensity in religion, as in much else. It is not so much that in their rapidly changing circumstances, knowledge and uprootedness, people *cannot* believe in their various belief systems, as that they feel strain in doing so and grow apathetic, wondering why they should make the effort through all the confusion. The symbols, the reasons and pretexts for belief must change to generate the required energy; there must be a completely new beginning in which the new experiences of the world are assimilated and defined. Movements like the Reformation and Counter-Reformation in the West are obvious examples of the discovery of a new intensity and unification of experience following the disintegration of a whole social order and psychology, but the synthesis was perhaps less complete than the mediaeval one preceding it, while today the crisis is of more massive proportions due to the exceptional increase of knowledge and the acceleration of social change. The situation in which religions are at present required to frame their apologies is one in which the possibilities are a new universal faith, an ecumenism of faiths, or the move by one faith to restate itself in terms which can fulfil the highest aspirations traditionally contained within the others. Naturally the exclusivist position of Christianity ought to give it a stake in the last possibility, which historically speaking is the development most likely to succeed, even if total uniformity of faith would never be achieved (some local individualism would always erect a barrier).[6] Yet this interest is not especially apparent. It is Hinduism rather than Christianity which is currently aiming for spiritual and cultural universality, and with few exceptions, the theology of the mission field has been less interested in new directions than in representing the views of churches in the West. The concern seems to have been less to found the church of tomorrow in Asia than to graft Asian churches on to those already existing.

As I shall demonstrate, it is likely that this lack of ideological enterprise, so crucial a factor in the current spiritual crisis, is related to the relative failure of Christian outreach at the grass-roots level in Asia. However, it is also obvious that revulsion at the times can keep many blinkered. It is only too easy, in condemnation or complacent dismissal of current religious and ethical trends, to aver that situations like the present one have existed before and are part and parcel of a decadence which is doomed to pass. That is quite possible, but the religious and other trends will not pass before the message they disclose is taken to heart and they cease to be judged solely from their worst features. Every social breakdown obviously has its positive and negative side, and the negative is the more readily visible when the opportunism of the worst elements of a society manifests itself in crime and general abandon. There are, of course, parallels in the existing situation with the Roman empire and its breakdown of values. At that time there was also a loss of traditional standards and beliefs and a proliferation of exotic cults, though these eventually gave way to Christianity. To follow the theory of history in Spengler's *The Decline of the West*, we have reached once again the age of relativity, and hence of mere religiosity, because knowledge and change have disrupted order and certainties.

Yet against this determinism, it is also requisite to note with Spengler's critic Toynbee that the wheel which goes round also goes forward, and thus, that while history may repeat itself today, the situation is also unprecedented and therefore still requires answers. No belief, no apology, is valid simply because it worked within the framework of an allegedly similar past. The concept of an ever 'living' faith discountenances such an escape from the labour of originality. While the new experience of reality may not affect the intrinsic moral nature of humanity, it has changed needs, concerns, opportunities and sensibilities enormously, and in effect has separated us from our past and the sense of continuity with a historical process which most generations have possessed. We know and possess more facts and things than we can cope with in terms of most systems of education and summary, and even of life-expectancy. If in our laws and customs we are suffering, as some claim, from the weight of the past and limitations of freedom, many are also burdened by what Toffler would call 'over-choice' and 'future shock'.[7] The pattern of affairs may be familiar, but ours is a brave new world nonetheless. No religion can safely fail to acknowledge this, but conservative repetition or compromising drift are obvious temptations here as in most areas.

With Christianity, it is probably true to say that some justified resentment also needs to be overcome before current issues are seen in perspective. The religion has created values which can be used to its disadvantage. Protestantism, for example, through emphasis on tolerance and democracy, has helped to produce the situation in the West in which anything short of total exposure in education and media to every variety of religion and superstition can be attacked as a conspiracy against the achievement of wholeness. Children barely able to grasp the sense of their inherited religion can be represented as oppressed or deprived if they are not conversant with the less open-minded doctrines of Confucius or Mohammed. There can also be Christian resentment that religions like Hinduism, long content to be faiths of an exclusive society and disinterested in the hard labour of evangelism, should wait until the era of mass communications to assimilate the Christian hope of a world unified under God. Religions have always been arising, combining and falling apart, but concern with conscious change, the organized mission, messianism, either began with Christianity or were most highly developed within it. All in all, missions to the West and calls for an ecumenism of faiths or a new faith owe a great deal to Christian activity and ideals.

It is, however, unlikely that many of the calls to transcend Christianity would have occurred had its critics not been given scope by apparent failures within East and West to respond to specific challenges. Three rather sweeping objections, political, moral and scientific, have often been heard. Missionary outreach in Asia, originally tainted with imperialistic associations, can be considered largely unsuccessful and often culturally disruptive. Inevitably it has been argued that this undermines the faith's use and its claim to be a unifying and universal force. This is the oldest and most familiar of the objections. Morally, recent attraction to Asian mysticism, particularly in America, owes much to discouragement at the guilt orientation of a widespread fundamentalism which is not conducive to that self-confidence and creativity from which personal and social fulfilment arise. In *Modern Mystics and Sages*,[8] Anne Bancroft explicitly claims that modern youth is convinced that there must be more to religion than the moral life, being condemned and forgiven by a saviour. Granted, the modern West may be too materialistic and permissive for its own good, but religion must be more than a matter of saying 'no'. It must minister to the total person. The call is for a new life-style, more organic and spontaneous than rationalized, one which permits the individual to live in harmony with the natural world, from within outwards. Where doctrine and moralism are supreme, those who think in this way argue, it is more difficult to see things as they are in themselves.

In science, the new awareness of the interrelatedness of things (holism) and relativity theory brings alterations to our understanding of the individual and the world. The traditional dualism of the West against which Christianity is normally formulated, the belief that the individual is a distinct entity separate from the world, and hence God, stands to be modified by evidence that the organism is a field of energy continuous with its environment and a process continuous with the universe. It can be argued that these perceptions are in greater accordance with Asian monism (the doctrine of the unity of things) and the 'no self' mysticism which relates man to the One, denying his individuality as illusory. Asian mysticism, with its intuitions of space-time, the uncertainty principle and the limits of causal thinking (which depends on a linear perception of time and on which so many Western arguments for God in turn depend) bears a special relationship to the new knowledge. The world and matter can no longer be viewed in terms of substance, as in the Greek-influenced philosophy of the West; they must be seen as movement or event. In consequence they are not so much upheld by form or governed by some natural, absolute laws, but rather come under the single law of the whole. Quantum theory shows that the world cannot, ultimately, be understood apart from the observer who makes his contribution to what is happening, thus tending to suggest what modern psychology has also proposed, that a *completely* objective revelation of truth (such as Christianity might be thought to imply) is an impossibility.

The scientific objection, however, does not always carry as much force as some might hope. Most occidentals do not feel the attraction to Eastern beliefs registered by 'East-turners', so that the new perspective on reality is more likely to increase agnosticism about Christian assertions than to bring conviction that Asian ones are valid. If the West and Christianity have not been more devastated by the religious implications of the new knowledge, this has much to do with temperamental realism which remains – for all practical purposes – satisfied that the extremities of inner and outer space need not unduly influence our perceptions. The West will continue to assume that the conceptualizing of the intellect which commonly distinguishes sharply between individualism and the view of the world imposes its own laws, has its own reasons (as in mathematics) and as such possesses independent validity. When the East protests that the self possesses no substantial reality, arguing that it is the product of memory, the West is likely to reply that the self is rather the product of a sense of will which has been culturally discouraged in Asia. Though temperament obviously plays its part in forming these judgments about reality, this is rarely emphasized, and in the West less than in the East, which is why what can appear 'obvious' facts and examples to, say, missionaries in Asia, have seemed more like local obsessions to Asia, and not necessarily very nice ones at that. For example, it is possible to regard the missionary description of the transcendent God, separated from his creation and sinful man, as the concomitant of the Western imperial and apartheid mentality which has long separated humanity into white and black.

Such a situation might suffice to underline the importance, at least for Christianity, of reviewing cherished intellectual positions. But it will be assumed that the issue runs deeper, and that even while Christianity and the West can dismiss the Asian and modern dimensions consciously and on a practical basis, unconsciously, its troubled intellectual condition and its deeper urges suggest the need for resolution in the face of them. Moreover, only in facing the challenges involved can Christianity hope to perceive itself in a new light, not simply as a doctrine or institution, but more widely as the unique psychological and cultural development in human consciousness that it represents, making possible a requisite broadening of its apologetic. Here Christianity has a unique opportunity to rid itself of a long accretion of intellectual errors, increasingly acknowledged but rarely treated by its exponents, which have associated it with a static view of reality which can no longer be sustained.

However, it is undoubtedly in the context of its relative failure within Asia, where Christianity confronts a totally different mental climate, that the backlog of intellectual and psychological errors catches up most immediately with average Christian assumptions and demands new descriptions of the absolute, of good and evil, to replace those which have remained more Greek or mediaeval than Christian, while other elements of the religion were modernized. It is, in fact, peculiar how the plethora of modern biblical criticism managed to avoid fundamental issues in favour of secondary questions of textual analysis.

As matters stand, the once-powerful claim of Christian exclusiveness is compromised by mystical descriptions of the ultimate from theologians like Thomas Merton, too little differentiated from the Asian to appear significant enough to claim attention. More popularly, moral and practical descriptions of the faith given by missionaries often reduce it to mechanical rigidity at variance with the Asian spirit. Both these trends are the distant products of a questionable mediaeval view of what constituted orthodoxy. If Christianity intends to remain distinct, yet express its distinctness in terms of monism, rather than discredited dualism, in such a way as to fulfil and supply new significance to the positive aspects of the Asian faiths, then it must dispose of the image of the unmoved first mover, source of fixed forms, a description which derives from Aquinas, in favour of an absolute describable in terms of movement and activity, and in a certain respect 'growth', as in the philosophy of St Gregory of Nyssa, for whom the Godhead could be described in terms of an 'operation'.

Only with this can the Christian response to the world become more creative and hope to anticipate rather than merely pronounce upon developments. One reason why so many of the church's necessary and often sophisticated concessions in everything from Freudianism to liturgy have not been more effective is because they arose more out of external pressure than a 'prophetic' impulse within the church, and thus had the air of mere contrivance. The effect was rather like that given by those early Christian basilicas in Rome which have received so many renovations and decorations that they express nothing in particular, and are even vulgar. Just as a cathedral appears to best advantage when it is purely Gothic or purely baroque, the church is badly in need of a new purely modern or purely Asian teaching and style. No mere adjustment benefits a religion when it is prompted by times and secular pressure alone. From the historical viewpoint, religion can be seen to be the first impulse of culture. Once it no longer anticipates the developments of a society, but is carried along by it, a religion may be said to offer religiosity rather than religion if not a tired conservatism, as in some high churchmanship and fundamentalism, the 'mock Gothic' forms of theology. Such religiosity lacks even the thrill of exotic cults which supply the demand of the times for mere difference within a society which is itself declining with the religion.

For clarity and convenience, I shall assume that the gradual erosion of initiative in religion dates back to the era of Aquinas and the scholastic philosophers, who attempted to ensure that the church had a total authority over every aspect of life. The trap set was long imperceptible, and actually possessed even more remote origins in early Christian reaction to Montanist heretics and the blow this dealt to inspiration and futurity. The extravagant conduct of the Montanists and their distortion of the apocalyptic hope bred a profound rationalist reaction in which emotion was suspect (prayers and sermons were even required to be written), and the focus of community interest was transferred from the future to the past. The result was that when church doctrine was defined against Greek philosophy and the church was established under Constantine, Greek rationalism gained more authority over Christian experience than was appropriate, as did the Old Testament; reason and Jewish history were called upon to provide codes of civil and personal conduct according to immutable rational principles deemed to exist beneath prophetic utterances. At the same time, the prophetic view of God as 'jealous' and 'wrathful', primitive approximations to spiritual realities nonetheless essential to maintaining the dynamism and consistency of the faith, were replaced by a rationalized mathematical view of God as a withdrawn Creator of formal perfections. Greek-influenced doctrines of perfection and plenitude would in fact deny God even a will and desire of his own. Since it would be 'jealous' of God to deny existence to anything which might exist, goodness compelled him to create the greatest possible number of things, with the result that everything is necessary and nothing new. Even evil, whose existence in terms of Greek substance theory seemed so inexplicable that some denied it ultimate reality, could be considered necessary to enhance the perfections of the good God and the glory of virtuous souls.

In the evolution of Western society, not only did this intellectual position entail serious, unforeseeable consequences in relation to increased knowledge, but however logically satisfying it might have been to those craving an objective faith, it was psychologically inauthentic, and produced, according to Jung, a division in the soul which would be all too evident.

In the rest of this chapter we shall focus on the experience of Christian outreach in Asia, especially in terms of indigenization or lack of it. Adaptation to a culture obviously contains many aspects, philosophical, political, aesthetic, but by way of introduction and to emphasize the connection with contemporary issues, I shall stress adaptation to Asian philosophy and consciousness generally rather than the more practical issues treated later. Those who are more interested in a description of Asia or who would prefer to approach philosophical issues from the practical aspects may turn directly to Chapters 2 or 3. In this chapter I shall suggest that even sophisticated interpretation of Christian belief against Asian categories will be inadequate if it does not (a) take into consideration the Asian consciousness beyond the philosophy; (b) treat existing versions of Christianity as final and authoritative, rather than exploring Asian concepts themselves for the light they may shed on aspects of Christian doctrine, like the nature of evil, which in existing philosophy are not perfectly consistent.

II

If, as is generally accepted, it can be emotionally demanding for most people to live in foreign cultures over a protracted period of time, the experience is even more demanding when, as in all but distinctly modern missionary experience, the culture and history of the countries concerned were little-known factors. All criticism of Christian missionary activity and its results in Asia is bound to take this into account, especially if it draws comparisons with modern Asian missions to the West and their successes. The cultural and even physical disadvantages of the traditional missionary to Asia must be set against the information and means of communication available to the missionary from Asia; the natural conservatism of the East against the Western love of novelty. Thus, when one states that Christian missions have been a failure in Asia, the judgment is more qualitative than quantitative, and refers to the type of success as much as to any proportion of failure; complete failure is no longer in question.

Owing partly to the forces of change everywhere, missions have survived and even flourished, despite the decline of church influence in the West, which in the popular view has rendered them irrelevant. The fact is that though it may be difficult for the church to maintain worldwide growth or even numbers in proportion to the population explosion of the Third World, it is nonetheless advancing in and influencing societies where it was previously absent, or its influence was minimal. The growth of the church in Africa has been phenomenal (between 1900 and 1960, the Catholic population alone rose from half a million to twenty-five million); the extension and deepening of religious life in South America is notable. But in Asia, numerical growth is small; the church, normally a tiny fraction of the population, might hope for a two or three per cent annual growth-rate, though its moral and cultural influence upon Asian societies is often extensive, particularly through education and medical services.

Missionaries are needed even when they are not wanted. Whereas in Africa they may do a few years stint and even then leave evangelism to local people, within Asia they might still make it a life career, though theoretically, as in Africa, even they are co-operators. Missions have progressed through the stage of pioneering and benevolent dictatorship to paternalism, service and co-operation following social change. Missionaries, whether in a ruling or a serving capacity, need not be Occidentals, and so there are some Japanese Christian missionaries in Thailand, Korean missionaries in Japan, and so on. This being the case, I shall use the terms 'missionary' and 'mission' throughout the book in the broadest sense, to include people intent on furthering their religion in Asia, or any native church (like certain churches in Hong Kong or Singapore) supported from abroad as being within a 'missionary' situation. Churches of this latter kind will be almost identical in style and sympathy with the traditional mission, and in hostile regions they will be regarded, like individual Western missionaries, as 'destroyers of culture' – a term frequently applied by the Thais to missionaries.

Though the missionary need not be a 'destroyer of culture', obviously some have been, and the often unintentional role of mission schools in educating a Western élite to service a colonial administration cannot be denied. Among Catholics, the Jesuit and Maryknoll missions have displayed a fairly sophisticated approach to foreign societies, and among Protestants, to some extent the Overseas Missionary Fellowship and the Methodists have done so too. In recent times, bodies such as the School of World Missions, Pasadena, have contributed to the sociology of missions, and the Bangalore Christian Institute for the Study of Religion and Society to a theology of greater cultural relatedness. However, not only do these represent a minority, and not an especially influential one, but they still mostly perceive their work in terms of adjustment rather than the creative development as described in this book. The main burden of my criticism would tend to apply to the more conservative Catholic orders and Protestant missions, like those of the Southern Baptists and the Christian Missionary Alliance, who appear so strongly and ubiquitously represented in Asia; it would, however, be invidious to keep mentioning certain societies in a critical way by name, especially when only minimal research would make it clear to which groups one was referring. Besides, most missionaries are highly individualistic persons, who are perhaps best judged in their own right independently by any group whose policies they may well disregard once settled in an isolated station.

The conservatives rather than the liberals must receive most attention because they conceive their task in primarily religious terms, and in this they are closer to the new spiritual concerns of the West than the liberals with their rationalism, while in Asia, their iconoclasm, however resented, can be more acceptable to converts than the religious neutrality of many liberals. Christianity is always a disturbance to Asian conservatism, a call to a measure of individualism and change, whatever way, religious or social, it is presented, and thus it is only frustrating to learn that after becoming involved in new ways, Christianity is scarcely different from any other faith.

It is nonetheless true that speaking with or writing about conservative missionaries is complicated by the refusal of many to see beyond the purely spiritual factor in any religious situation. A few sociological facts in the patterns of advance and decline in Christianity just mentioned are, however, very clear. The Third World missionary whose work often advances on the socially conservative rural front will regard the setbacks for his religion in the West as the fruit of decadence, but this decline (relative though it is, for there are powerful movements of renewal, like the charismatic movement) reaches back to a failure of the religion to maintain a grip on humanity within today's industrialized, technologized urban society, and it shares this failure to a lesser or greater extent with the other Asian faiths. Religion aims to unify and concentrate experience, whereas the more developed forms of urban life tend to fragment and disperse it. This predicament can be transcended to advantage, as the urban diffusion of early Christianity testifies, but in the modern situation, where religion does not appear to have made a higher synthesis of modern knowledge and the new individualism (which owes much to Protestant religion), the fragmentation is exaggerated, the secular knowledge glorified, and all varieties of self-gratification or inclusive 'mystical' religions take its place. As the theologian Reinhold Niebuhr once suggested, the problem for churches in modern society is primarily 'relevance'[9]; there is a discontinuity between the very feel of the depersonalizing modern life-style and the feel of religion, and for many people this can be much more significant than loss of faith due to any specific discovery in science or psychology.

As regards advance, Christian missions thrive best where there is least resistance of culture and civilization, or again, when culture and civilization are weakened under the force of some upheaval or emergency, i.e., the crisis situation. Africa is obviously an instance of least resistance, even though this situation has begun to alter under the force of revived tribalism and the influence of Islam. It is not that in Africa there was no culture, nothing that could be called aesthetically and socially significant; plainly there was, as in Uganda, or among the Bantu of South Africa, but it was tribal all the same. Africa had no advanced priesthoods or philosophies, and aesthetically was emotional and expressionistic rather than involved. For this reason the culture and scientific knowledge of the missionary, even though it might not always fit comfortably within the setting, could not help but dazzle, while religion convinced in one of the classical ways. Like St Patrick, leaving the Roman world to challenge the wizardry of the Druids with the power of Jesus and reason, the missionary has confronted the witch doctor and has usually been considered the victor. The pattern is the same in Asia. In Indonesia it is the 'primitive' cultures of Sumatra and New Guinea which have been responsive to missions, not the Islamic and Hindu societies of the Indonesian mainland and Bali; in Burma, the tribal Karens rather than the majority Buddhists. The Philippines, the only Christian nation in Asia, would be another example of low civilizational resistance, though the country was also subject to conquest Spanish-style, and this accounts for the undistinguished quality of the country's religion, which has been imposed rather than assimilated. The church, then, can confront the witch doctor, and many missionaries of evangelical or fundamentalist persuasion (these perhaps inevitably constitute the majority) perceive their message primarily in terms of confrontation, but when they come against the Brahmin they usually fail. What he represents cannot be 'confronted' in the classical way that they anticipate even when, as sometimes happens, say, in Bali, elements of witch doctoring and black magic may exist beneath the more sophisticated veneer.

The crisis situation and its opportunities apply more to modern Africa and South America than to Asia, though to some extent they apply to Korea, the only Asian country apart from the Philippines where Christian influence is fairly strong. Particularly in Africa, missionaries, although often more favourable towards colonial authority and opposed to nationalist movements than their congregations have liked and justice demanded, were still broadly associated with the drive to human rights, the advancement of black status and the struggle against poverty in a period of massive change. Owing to the vastness of Asia and the complexity of its problems (none of them so markedly racial as in Africa), the church has been less intimately associated with the struggle for human rights, and more identified – sometimes correctly, as in Vietnam – with colonial establishments, so that to be patriotic was to be of a specifically non-Christian religion. In India, for example, it was Annie Besant and the Theosophists who were most concerned about the rights of Indians, even if the missionaries they opposed did more in terms of medical and practical assistance.

The third factor in expansion is indigenization. Despite many delays, setbacks and misunderstandings, indigenization, though far from fully achieved anywhere, has been given more scope in Africa and South America than in Asia. Indigenization can take many forms, and provided that it does not cover mere regression into the abandoned religion, the more forms the better. It may refer to church leadership by native people, church music, ecclesiastical design, marriage custom and ceremony. Sometimes one has to think of indigenization as adaptation (making the religion possible within a society); sometimes, and perhaps more often, as relevance. Obviously (or rather, not obviously to the least sensitive missionaries), festivals like Christmas and Easter will seem remarkably empty and incongruous if their presentation takes no account of season or local colour, as happens when a European white Christmas and frosty carols are imposed upon tropical society, thus involving the worshipper in a painful sense of discontinuity with his world. The negro spiritual is one form of indigenization, the concession to polygamy made by the Dutch Reformed Church another, and the Amerindian art of South American churches another. Today, indigenization in Africa is widely supported, especially among Catholics, but it is also controlled, whereas the three examples given arose more as the consequence of condescension or indifference towards native behaviour than from concern.

In Asia, indigenization has been slower to gain acceptance and is more controversial, due to the more complex patterns of culture and politics involved. Among conservatives there is the erroneous belief that the failure of the Nestorian and Thomas churches within Asia should be attributed to such compromise. Donald Hoke's *The Church in Asia*[10] makes out that Nestorian Christianity in China was a 'soft sell' which obscured the truths of sin and salvation behind practices and terminology which made the faith appear like a sect of Buddhism. But quite to the contrary, the trouble with Nestorian religion was that it was a hard sell, an overly ascetical version of Christianity centred on groups of hermits to the detriment of layman and congregation, an impractical situation in unascetical, family-orientated China. Against this barrier, attempts to describe the religion in Chinese categories are irrelevant. Such attempts were not, however, misguided, and were certainly preferable to the kind of identification with imperial power which modern missionaries would long suffer, sometimes justly. The point is, Christianity will always be compared to something, and it is better that that should be something inside the country than outside it. Moreover, it should be noted that anti-Christian Chinese literature during the eighteenth and nineteenth centuries consistently compared the religion with Buddhism, despite the Jesuit attempts to accommodate to Confucianism, to the detriment of Buddhism. From the rationalist Confucian standpoint, anything which spoke in terms of heaven and hell was Buddhist. I have made some comments on the Thomas Church in India in Chapter 6.

Another more recent line on indigenization in Asia, espoused again by Donald Hoke, and echoed by Michael Griffiths in *Changing Asia*,[11] is that missionaries can no longer be considered a causal factor in the Westernizing trend, if in comparison with traders they ever were; as the people have chosen against their past, the necessity for adaptation today is not strong. As will be evident, I am not at all convinced of the truth of this judgment. Hoke one-sidedly quotes the historian Arnold Toynbee on the tremendous Westernization of the world, ignoring his reservation about the assumption that in Westernization one thing leads to another,[12] and his anticipation of a reaction already indicated by such movements as Neo-Buddhism, Hinduism and the Western attraction to Eastern religions. In Toynbee's view, the Westernizing process is unnatural, and involves an excess of *yang* values which must produce a *yin* reaction; it has only occurred because the East does not like to protest and resist after the manner of self-assertive Western man, who took it by surprise.

As far as religion is concerned, it must appear that churches from the Roman to the Southern Baptist have been remarkably and even shamefully reluctant to allow freedom in the financial, intellectual or aesthetic sphere to the churches that they founded. One Chinese critic of my *Can There Be a Chinese Church?* asked how I imagined the Chinese could express themselves in view of what had recently happened to a leading Lutheran church in Hong Kong. It had planned to erect a new and larger church, whereupon the related American church, which was contributing, insisted on sending a representative to supervise the entire scheme and refused to accept any suggestions from the church council as regards its design or anything else. I had not realized that the situation could be quite so bad, since financial independence and rule by local clergy is theoretically an ideal acknowledged by the most Westernizing of missionaries, ever since Communist pressure imposed the Three Self Movement upon the church in order to ensure the autonomy of Chinese churches from mission churches. In any case, there is something suicidal in denying churches this freedom when it is so clear that even the mildest concessions to indigenization yield more response. In Taiwan, for example, the Protestant churches which draw most numbers and arouse most fervour are precisely those founded and organized by the Chinese, like 'The Little Flock' and 'True Jesus' churches, while in Hong Kong, even those churches most Chinese in appearance will show the largest congregations.

Practical indigenization is something which will recur throughout this book, but underlying it is the more philosophical issue. There is little doubt that the churches can indigenize if they so wish. Historically, Christianity is one of the most indigenized of religions (even though this is currently not so in Asia). That is because, as a historical religion, it has tended to take social change and difference more seriously than other faiths, though even these, as I have said, have been amenable to some change when forced. Hinduism and the Hinyana form of Buddhism in Thailand, both long considered monolithic, have demonstrated novelty in the face of altered social circumstances.

In Asia, however, something more than a random adaptation to local forms is required. Asian cultures, even those fractured and threatened by change, are peculiarly complete and enveloping in comparison with the more open and diversified Western ones, and thus Asian expectations for adaptation involve something more integral and psychological; Neo-Hinduism would even demand a complete assimilation. In consequence, if Christianity does not want its message to fall victim to an Asian syncretism, as it threatens to do in India, it must itself make an 'assimilation' of Asia, and undergo a creative **development** to produce a new theology, a new philosophy, a new aesthetic. Many missionaries would, of course, argue that Christianity is not only doctrinally exclusive, but culturally iconoclastic; their critics, like Northrop,[13] would agree with them and propose that it should cease to be so before it causes more trouble, joining in an ecumenism of faiths, a solution considered in Chapter 6. The potential of Christianity for the total adjustment in Asia, and what the churches do about it, will tell us much about the nature of the religion and also Asian faiths that has become obscured by custom and repetition.

At present, indigenization at this deeper level seems only to occasion distress to the average missionary, who perceives nothing but a threat to the faith. As one missionary in Bali, critical of my ideas, stated:

> Neither do I think theology changes or should change. Truth is not accommodating. Truth is absolute, is Christ . . . Christ will inevitably change our attitudes and nature – that is conversion – but he does not change our culture. Salvation is not in tradition, neither is Christianity a culture. One does not need to pass through Western and Greek and Jewish culture to find salvation. But in another way we have been born into the Kingdom of God and to the 'Culture of the Kingdom' which is universal and non-racial. That does not mean a universal Western church! It means traits, attitudes, thought-patterns and reactions all similar – dominated by love which modifies everything. . . .

Though the missionary in question happened to be a Protestant, it was evident from this and other opinions expressed that the concept of 'absolute' was the Catholic one that has entered into European thought since Aquinas. If God as the source of fixed forms has revealed a doctrine, the form through which it was revealed is necessarily as universal and axiomatic as a geometrical theorem (Greek notions of truth were based on geometry), and there can be only one way of expressing and understanding it, and nothing that can or need be added to it. Granted, notions of the fixity of God and his creation find support of a kind in the scriptural statement of James 1.16 normally translated to read 'The Father of lights in whom there is no variation or shadow due to change', but even assuming the correctness of the translation,[14] the real issue would be the consequences of the fact that while God is infinite, man is finite, and thus bound in some measure to experience his relation to God in new terms and terms of change, no matter how unchanging God may be. This is why there is no contradiction in other scriptural affirmations to the effect that God is the one who 'is, and who was, and is to come' (Rev. 1.8), who is to reveal aspects of his grace in ages to come (Eph. 2.7) and whose salvation is not only once for all, but eternal, continual (Isa. 51.6). Moreover, these statements are in greater sympathy with the modern knowledge which demands room for a degree of spontaneous and continuous creation in modification of traditional concepts of fixed immutable laws in a fixed creation.

In the rather specialized and obscure fields of 'process' theology, attempts have been made to assimilate modern ideas of change, but common experience in any case tells against the view that truth can be fixed and absolute. While they may have held a creedal essence in common, it is unlikely that Christians have ever perceived Jesus and his teaching in precisely the same way from century to century. It should be obvious that the Jesus of St Bernard and the Gothic cathedrals is not the same as the Jesus of the Puritans and Methodists. By being accepted, meditated on and acted on, truth in itself produces new situations which set the original truth in a different light. As I replied to the missionary critic:

> Every significant culture usually adds something to the gospel, at least in the sense of bringing to fullness something only implicit or little explored before. The Trinity is – if you like – an 'invention' of Greek theology. It is true that Christ spoke of the Father and the Holy Spirit, but the implication could only be realized by the Greek mind, which, unlike the Jewish, had the philosophical tools to assimilate and describe it. The very word 'Trinity' which Christians now use as though it came straight out of the Bible, only came to us from Greece. . . .

I could have added that where no such invention takes place there can only be a progressive narrowing, leading to social withdrawal. The missionary's 'culture of the kingdom' is liable to end up like the holy circles for prayer and Bible study which missionaries tried to impose on the South Seas, as a substitute for the dancing and singing they wanted to eradicate. Fundamentalists never seem to grasp the vital principle that historically the most religious societies, like Ireland, are the most culturally inclusive, rather than the most exclusive, and also so constituted as to allow reasonable scope to people not to be deeply religious if they do not feel so inclined. Fundamentalists also ignore the fact that in Asian lands the Western ecclesiastical idea of the tight-knit congregation or community would almost certainly require modification in a way that I shall indicate later.

The claim, 'One does not need to pass through Western, Greek and Jewish culture to find salvation', was, however, too controversial to ignore. Missionaries in Asia, confronted by the charge that Christianity is a Western religion, or if not a Western religion, one presented in Western terms, frequently counter that Christianity is an Asian religion founded by an Asian, and, with their 'axiomatic' approach, seem to assume that converts should realize this beneath the Elizabethan verbiage of the Book of Common Prayer or the sound of Victorian hymnology. If the Western 'tone' were all, maybe they should, but for many it runs much deeper than this. It is necessary to be clear that many actual or potential converts *are* being required to assimilate Western thought patterns and culture.

Klaus Klostermaier makes the point forcibly in his controversial *Hindu and Christian in Vrindaban*[15] and *Kristvidya*[16]. After much discussion with Hindus, he became convinced that unqualified missionary reference to 'Son of God', 'Kingdom of God' (which has specific political overtones in India), 'second birth' and remedies for human sinfulness, can give an impression of the content of faith far from the orthodox one intended. In many cases, what missionaries took to represent a wilful refusal of Christ's uniqueness was only a perfectly logical interpretation of his person against the *avatar* doctrine from which missionaries did not effectively know how to distinguish it. Their presuppositions derived from Western descriptions of Trinitarian dogma and their refutations of Hindu ideas were also those of Greek and Western philosophy, like dismissing Vedanta as pure pantheism, which technically it is not. Nothing was argued in terms of Hindu thought and nothing was allowed to fulfil Hinduism, yet when Klostermaier adopted this approach many Hindus told him that for the first time they had acquired an inkling of what Christianity and its claim to uniqueness signified.

Klostermaier, to elements of whose apologetic we shall now turn, is far from being the first to attempt description of Christianity within Indian categories. Notable Indian Christians, like Chenchiah and Upadhyaya, have attempted the same, but their knowledge of Indian categories was not always equalled by an understanding of the Western ones against which christology developed, and on account of this, the reinterpretations, though illuminating in the area treated, often fail to be either sufficiently comprehensive or fundamental in the face of the complexity – to some extent illusory complexity – of Hindu philosophy (see Chapter 6). Questions like the desirability of securing Christianity's exclusiveness after the manner of these theological indigenizers and the possible relevance of their conclusions to modern knowledge are not the concern at this point. I only want to draw attention to a few problems of reinterpretation and to affirm that, despite problems, reinterpretation is not only possible but makes the distinction between Christianity and Hinduism clearer, rather than robbing it of its force. This is particularly the case in relation to christology, which the Hindu mind almost automatically interprets in terms of the *avatar*, saviour figure.

By placing the emphasis upon the Absolute, and unity from the centre, Hindu monism tends to reduce the phenomenal world to an inferior or illusory status of only practical value, and not a world in which a divine salvation could be positively wrought. In this context, 'saviours' are either individuals who make concessions to limited, dualistic understanding, or persons about whom the ordinary individual suffers illusions and hence individuals without whom it is possible to reach the truth of the centre. According to Klostermaier, if Christ is portrayed in the manner of the missionaries, as a bringer of remedies, one who deals in good and evil, his *avatar* status is certified, as it is also by describing him and his work as a 'manifestation' of God. 'The Absolute cannot be worshipped, so we must worship a manifestation', writes Vivekananda.[17] Christ in Hinduism thus becomes an *avatar* by virtue of being worshipped, because whatever is worshipped cannot be the Absolute.

Four assumptions can be noted underlying the belief in numerous temporal or archetypal manifestations of the Ultimate which is opposed to a doctrine of incarnation. Though the terms and pretexts change, they entail problems common to most Asian religions.

(a) *The nature of God*, which in Christian doctrine must be at least in part personal, rather than impersonal or transpersonal as in Hindusim.

(b) *The Hindu concept of the soul* as a spark or part of God, rather than a created and individual spirit dependent upon God (in Buddhism, even this soul is an illusion, a no self within the ultimate).

(c) Related to (b) is *the contrast between Hindu monism and Christian dualism*, the emphasis on union over separation. Since, however, both religions acknowledge, in their way, a unity of things from God, and it is possible to describe Hinduism in terms of dualism (Sankhya philosophy) and Christianity in terms of qualified monism (Bishop Berkeley's 'immaterialism'), the issue is less one of philosophical terms and bias than a difference of religious doctrine as regards *creation* and the *nature* of divine subsistence within it. I have examined this problem, which hardly concerns Klostermaier since his theme is incarnation rather than general subsistence, later in the chapter.

(d) *The nature of good and evil* which, given the Hindu understanding of unity, are relativized in Asian belief, but which in Christianity, on account of the personality accorded to God and also Satan, have normally received an absolute status and been treated as practical realities.

Hindu philosophy postulates God as *Brahman* (according to the philosophical school partly or wholly ineffable to man) and *atman*, the 'soul' of man, completely distinct from the disposable or even unreal ego and body, which subsist through *Brahman. Atman* shares an identity with *Brahman* which can be mystically realized by those who turn from 'ignorance', but it still remains absolutely distinct from it. *Atman* can be considered as God immanent, but only in the most limited way, as a kind of subtle matter, such is God's transcendence. 'All beings abide in me but I do not abide in them', says Krishna, an incarnation of God, in the *Gita*, one of the leading Hindu scriptures. However, especially since the world tends to be seen less as the creation of God than as a physical emanation or mental construct of *Brahman*, there is a real sense in which, despite the distinction of *Brahman* and *atman*, the world is God's body, is himself.

Hindus thus feel that it is a limitation upon the Absolute to suggest, like the missionaries, that there could be a unique incarnation of God. God ought to be able to become incarnate through anything and anyone, and they believe that he has done this. There have been innumerable temporal 'sons of God', *avatars* who, like saints and reformers, periodically appear on earth to restore the balance of 'good' when 'evil' and ignorance prevail. They may temporarily proceed from God, like Krishna or Ganesh, or like Gandhi and Ramakrishna just be more God-like than normal people in their emptiness of ego and realization of their identity with the divine. When Christ said 'I and my Father are One', Hindus believe that he realized perfectly the identity of soul and God so as to be God. Theoretically, anyone could do the same, and like the other *avatars*, Christ only worked within the realm of *maya* (illusion and created things) and of *karma* (cause and effect) which stands over against the world of *Brahman*. Truly enlightened souls pierce the realm of *maya*, live beyond the law of good and evil and only deal in it, like Krishna and Christ, as a concession to the weakness of souls who, thinking in terms of duality, look to the help of gods. Christ thus becomes one of the temporal gods, a sort of *medium* of the divine through whom the being of God may be glimpsed by worshippers who merge their egos with him. St Paul is understood by Hindus to have achieved this union when he declared, 'It is not I who live, but Christ within me'. When missionaries speak of grace, it is realization of this sort to which Hindus believe they refer. Grace is something in which man rather than God takes the initiative, for the grace exists in the manifestation which attracts, rather than in any positive action on the part of the god. As Krishna says, 'None are hateful or dear to me'. However, in order to achieve union with the god, the devotee is required to deny himself (more an annihilation of the ego than its discipline), develop a new attitude and perform good works in the spirit of devotion (*bhakti*). When missionaries emphasize conversion, self-denial and showing the fruits of conversion in *good* deeds, this will again appear to associate Christ and his salvation with the *avatar's* function of assisting the salvation of the weak in terms of this world and their imperfect understanding of reality which divides everything into opposites.

What kind of answers can be made to these assumptions? Perhaps no Christian apologetic can ever completely answer them, for though philosophical reinterpretations are illuminating, they never completely break the closed circuit of Hindu thought, which is more a rationalized psychology than a doctrine in the Christian sense. A Christian apologetic would nonetheless have to maintain that the Hindu view, both of divine incarnation and divine indwelling in the believer, is very limited despite its possibility of variation; it describes a situation in certain respects the opposite of the one to which the missionaries imperfectly refer. The freedom God possesses under Hinduism to become incarnate through everything is simply akin to the 'genius', 'goodness', or good measure of the spirit, which a human may be said to possess. One could never truly say of the *avatar* 'In him dwells all the fullness of the Godhead bodily', for one can adore the *avatar* only as one who is in harmony with *Brahman*. God is too transcendent to be truly immanent, or by some accounts even to be able to do anything at all: 'Though I am the world's creator, know me to be incapable of action or change', says Krishna. God has not in the slightest degree created man 'in his own image'; he is usually considered so beyond all form that he cannot manifest or reflect himself within form.

In such a context, then, Klostermaier would maintain that the uniqueness of Christ cannot be most effectively described in terms of Sonship or Messiahship. More appropriate is the Word, the Logos of St John, especially since even in Hinduism, *Brahman* is sometimes called 'the indestructible essence of the *Word* manifest in the shape of things, the source of creation'. This Logos can be identified with the 'supreme issue' from Brahman postulated by Pancaratra theology and predicated to no god or *avatar*, since by comparison, avatarism would have to be regarded as simple inherence of spirit. Logos is the aspect of God through which creation and form,which for Christianity is the realm of dangerous freedom rather than illusion, were made possible and through which things hold together. Christ is the image of the invisible God in which man was created. He is also the illuminating Logos within the heart of men waiting to draw them back to God. Logos is the possibility of both motion out from God and return to God[18] the incarnation of God and the divine indwelling within man. The unique incarnation of Christian theology can be seen as the culminating point of a single centrifugal and centripetal movement by the supreme issue. Logos cannot be incarnated under any form because it is not a personal or impersonal principle, but person and principle together, and the freedom which the Hindu concept of incarnation allows within the finite would be transferred to the possibility that the Deity can dwell in individuals in the way the *avatar* cannot do.

According to Klostermaier, Kristvidya is of the nature of Brahmavidya; Christ is not 'outside' but 'inside' *Brahman*, and the affirmation of Christ that 'I and my Father are One', was *Brahman* knowing *Brahman*, and not, as is commonly maintained in advaitin terminology, *atman* knowing *Brahman*[19]. When St Paul affirmed that Christ lived within him, he obviously did not mean by this that he was or would become identical with God after the manner of Christ, but he did mean that he enjoyed an active experience of Brahman through Logos rather than passively merging himself with any temporal deity or gaining higher cognition of things temporal, as in yoga. Thus ideally the believer may repeat the kind of communion which *Brahman* has with *Brahman*.

On the other hand, once one has established this, it does remain in a sense true that Christ's work and his miracles lay within the realm of *maya*; even in the gospels they are described as 'signs', but when Jesus speaks 'openly and no longer in parables' of himself and his salvation, he is speaking of the real and transcendent sphere. None of Christ's judgments were made by purely objective criteria, but only in their relation to the Father who is pure Being, the Being that he mediates. If this is not recognized, then given the Hindu distinction between real and illusory, eternal and temporal, Christ and his work will be seen as related to and imprisoned in the temporal. Jesus will also be reduced to a remedy-bringing *avatar*, operating only within the opposites of good and evil.

Hindu philosophy is ontological (being philosophy), and does not start from the human and practical viewpoint of Jewish and Greek thought which, treating situations as they appear to be, describe spiritual affairs in dualistic terms, heaven and earth, good and bad. The suggestion that Jesus the Son was sent down to the temporal sphere by a good God to warn humanity against and release it from sins and make the world better, is language fit for an *avatar*. Strictly speaking (though not always practically speaking when it comes to bringing change to affairs) the Hindus are correct in hesitating to follow the Hebrew prophets, Aristotle and Aquinas in saying that God is 'good'. In an infinite deity, Being and attributes must be identical. God exists in and for himself beyond all laws of right and wrong, the 'I am who I am' who spoke to Moses. Goodness cannot be a quality he possesses among others, and Christians would have to say that God is thus defined only in relation to this finite world and ourselves, to make a distinction from all in man or devil that willed separation from God. Sin in Christian doctrine is, strictly speaking, less 'badness' than separation.[20] In Eden, Adam and Eve did not know what good was, nor did God explain it to them; rather, it was the devil who told them that they would learn the difference between good and evil. Only the forces of death and non-being impel the need for description. Thus, Christ did not in reality abolish sins or establish new codes of good and evil; he abolished sin in itself, which is separation. He did not effect salvation but rather *was* salvation, something which involves the believer in a realization rather than a remedy. He was sacrificer and sacrifice, a concept which could possibly be explained in terms of Vedic theology.

Yet even if translations of this kind are possible without prejudice to the orthodox christology upheld by most missionaries, they are not necessarily more than mere adaptation. Here is more of an intellectual adjustment than a confrontation with the Asian consciousness, and it is made within the context of a society for which the purely intellectual statement has never enjoyed the status it has in the West. It clarifies and vindicates Christian exclusiveness without according it a purpose beyond the nature of the God-realization offered: it is not an integral philosophy; it would not help to explain history, nature, the status of the Old Testament, and the faiths beyond Hinduism. It would tend to draw Christian philosophy away from the sphere represented by Aquinas, but does not place it firmly within the other sphere represented by the philosophy of Gregory of Nyssa which the relationship between Christianity and modern science, and Asia generally, would seem to demand.

The church has to accept the challenge that in many respects Christianity is a Western religion which is now obliged to become Asian in style as much as in theological categories, and to undergo a revolution as far-reaching as when it left its Jewish roots to contact a Gentile world, or opened the way to Christian art by opposing the iconoclasts. It will not do to say that Christ, humanly regarded, was an Asian, and the Bible an 'Asian' book. The New Testament may be fairly universal, but it is doubtful to what extent the same can be said of the Old Testament, or at least those parts of it that have concerned Western man and figure large in missionary teaching. The Japanese Christian novelist Ayako Miuro was first attracted to the Bible, not by the stories of prophets and patriarchs, but by the pessimistic book of Ecclesiastes, one of the books of the Bible most ignored in Western commentary.[21] Job, Jeremiah, Proverbs and Ecclesiastes are perhaps rather Asian books, but overall, though the Bible and the Middle East which produced it may be 'Asian' in relation to Europe and the Americas, and the Semitic spirit easily distinguishable from the European which has been formed by the more analytical and rationalistic Roman culture, it is still not very different. Like the mythologist Joseph Campbell[22], and almost any orientalist of note, we should affirm that Asia starts not at the Bosphorus but beyond Persia. Semitic man is Western man. This is not to postulate an 'East is East and West is West' view of affairs, to portray Asia and the West as simple opposites; however, very real psychological differences need to be fully acknowledged. Asian man is not accustomed to the sort of Western legalism and dogmatism represented by the Old Testament; rather, he has custom and opinions, even though these can sometimes assume the force of law for him. He is allowed a Taoist style, whim or abandon rather than individualism in the Western sense; he cultivates moods rather than spontaneous emotion; he prizes concentrative or 'one-pointed' perception over the dualistic, logical Western assessment of reality. His natural virtues are of a feminine rather than a masculine order; he prefers adaptation to confrontation, peace to justice.

Some of these differences are commendable, some questionable, some culturally influenced, and some apparently innate, but given their existence, the church, if it is to understand, communicate and transform, is required to go beyond adaptation in terms of custom or even theological categories, to a different level of consciousness. This is because Asia operates at a different level of consciousness and because interpretations of doctrine which do not take this into account are in danger of ending up as mere efforts at special pleading. One certainly feels this about the translation of biblical categories into Buddhist ones (like *tilakkhana, anatta, dukkha*, as introduced by Stanley Bishop and D. T. Niles).[23] It is obviously straining comparisons to suggest that Christianity understands the meaning of no self, no soul, and no being, because it is holistic, teaching that body and soul are one (rather than separate as in Greek and popular Christian belief), and that when one dies one dies wholly before rebirth to a new life. It is well known that Christianity is insistent on personal immortality, even though it has an unusual approach to this as a possibility. What is necessary is to have a feel for the vital issues and emotional field of the religion in the mind of its adherents and address oneself to that, rather as Kitamori did in *The Theology of the Pain of God*[24], which derives from a specific theological experience mediated through leading values of Japanese society.

It is, however, precisely fear of a new *consciousness* which arouses such resistance to the very idea of an Asian theology and church. The emotivity of African drum and negro spiritual seems Western and acceptable beside the thought of a celebration of the word through the elemental sounds of Japanese instruments or the lingering tones of Indian ones. There is something in us which shudders at the prospect of theology and ethics becoming subject to Asia's 'yogic', as opposed to intellectual treatment, which would be the inevitable consequence of the widespread acceptance of Christianity everywhere, save perhaps in dogmatic China. The idea that, like Gandhi, one might cultivate moral force more through example than through preaching, and effect change through group, meditational and passive means rather than through individual, planned and legal means, would seem shocking. So, too, given the ontological standpoint of Asia, might be the realization of Christian imperatives in terms of the way of things, of what is fitting and self-consistent, rather than as the arbitary commands or fixed natural laws they might appear to be.[25] This would not necessarily be contrary to what is implied in the New Testament (the matter is discussed in Chapter 7), though Augustine's 'Love God and do what you like' has always seemed too giddily liberated to the West which, lacking the interiority and self-discipline of the East, confuses liberty with licence.

Thus, despite the Christian cancellation of the law, there is something in the typical Western attitude which feels compelled to impose religion on society, exteriorize rather than interiorize it, reduce it to rules. Given the chance, many would cheerfully tear down 'heathen' altars and idols in the name of the laws of God or nature, close the local theatres and ban dances, as did some of the Victorian missionaries; or, like Anita Bryant today, they would demand that homosexuals should be put in jail; or, like the 'right to life' campaigners, protest that no one should be allowed the freedom of abortion. Western man has such little natural self-discipline that he feels that unless he is imposing or suffering a discipline, he cannot be in the right way; added to which, for the combative spirit of the West, somebody must always win and somebody lose. Teilhard was sure that in the confrontation of East and West, the West must win; anthropologist Mircea Eliade is sure the East will win. It is to be hoped, though, that neither will 'win' and neither remain completely unchanged.

This, of course, is to differ from those involved in the inter-faith 'dialogue', like Dom Aelred Graham[26] and William Johnston,[27] who, divesting themselves of the problems of christology and integral religion, postulate a worldwide perennial religion of God-mysticism, such as medieval philosophy and mysticism (though not the Bible) might support. However, we all require a measure of change, whereas this 'ecumenism' is doubly conservative, not only in its desire to leave Eastern and Western traditions more or less alone, but in its philosophical assumptions. The philosophical principles which allowed Aquinas his mystical beliefs could do with review in the light of modern concepts of being and reality, just as aspects of oriental mysticism can equally be questioned in the light of modern psychology.

The East certainly needed many of the ideas, both religious and secular, that the West brought it. At the same time, not only did the West need some of the unifying and psychological principles enshrined in the East, but its lack of them, which prevented the synthesis of post-Renaissance knowledge and individualism, was a major factor in its spiritual and intellectual decline. This decline has been accelerating since the eighteenth century (the major era of international missions), and is reflected in the loss of an integral philosophy, of a cosmology and trinitarian religion, without development or reinterpretation of which it could neither continue its own evolution nor communicate with Asia over religion, in relation to which it would appear merely imperialistic.

That the West could and should have developed some of these principles independently of and prior to its confrontation with Asia (in which case it might not have been such a confrontation) would have been neither impossible, seeing it is a question of consciousness, nor illogical, given the implications of Protestant interiority and individualism. Intimations of such a development were present, for example, in the immaterialist philosophy of Bishop Berkeley, which was almost ignominiously rejected. That it was so bespeaks a serious psychological and spiritual failure in Western evolution. Although in terms of the cyclical theory of cultures introduced by Spengler, the West (and the Christianity which underlies many of its assumptions) is theoretically 'doomed' to the pattern of development and decline it exhibits, nevertheless if Christianity is what it claims to be, it should have been able to transcend this tendency to entropy. It should instead have realized its implicit capacity for continuous creation and have arrived at some age of the Spirit in succession to those of the church and the book.

The question, however, is not simply one of philosophy, but of establishments and habit. For many, both Catholic and Protestant, the cost of change would seem too high. Too many long cherished claims and assumptions would need to be discarded, or drastically revised. Like St Peter denying the revelation that unclean animals could be clean, the revision required would seem to many too radical, even a denial of their beliefs. To take two very straightforward examples, Asian mission experience must stand as a challenge both to the Catholic concept of hierarchical authority and to the conservative Protestant attachment to the Bible as the description of man and guide to action in all possible matters.

If I were a Catholic, I imagine that my faith in the extent and value of the church's claims to authority and worldwide jurisdiction of church affairs might be rather shaken by study of its record in Asia. As far as can be seen, it has been precisely the church's inflexible attachment to this principle which has lost it most of its hard-won gains, especially in China. Despite the remarkable labours and achievements of individual men, like St Robert Nobili in India, St Francis Xavier in Japan and Fr Matteo Ricci in China, until this century, when its image improved, the Catholic record in the East appears unfortunate, a long study in misguided zeal. At times the record is so unfortunate that those disposed to supply spiritual as opposed to sociological explanations of missions have almost inevitably hypothesized that it was a case of the devil playing havoc with the church to prevent its advance. The main thing to recognize, whether spiritually or historically, is that in so many cases the church, rather than the field of mission, was the worst enemy.

Incidents like Jesuit meddling in the affairs of Siam, or the seizure by the Inquisition of the first Chinese bishop; the destruction of the records of the Thomas Church of India because it had never recognized Rome; or the disruption caused in the Nagasaki community when, after it had existed for two centuries as a persecuted lay church, priests arrived to demand allegiance to the Pope, were tragic enough, but the banishment of Catholic missionaries from China in 1787 was the worst. The rivalry of Dominicans with Jesuits was the immediate pretext. As is well known, the Dominicans envied Jesuit successes and their standing in China, and attempted to undermine their position by insinuating to the Vatican that the Chinese ancestral rights permitted to converts by Ricci, and imperially approved, involved an infringement of doctrine. In pure Confucian teaching it was reverence rather than worship or prayers that was offered to ancestors, but with time, superstitious reverence had crept in. It may thus have been that the concession to local custom which Ricci had sanctioned invited misunderstanding, though he had made it in good faith that no doctrinal infringement was involved, and if he was wrong, it touched only a minor point. Owing to the enormous distance of the Vatican from Pekin, the ensuing wrangle lasted for years and involved European popes, hierarchy and theologians who pronounced, regardless of the political and religious effect, on rites and philosophies of which they knew little and on situations of which they had no personal knowledge. The results were appalling. An emperor, alarmed and insulted that his decisions were annulled by foreign potentates and a young and flourishing church, plunged into persecution over a formality. If the Jesuits who were sworn to a special allegiance to the Pope had denied Rome its jurisdiction over the Chinese church, as have the Catholics of Communist China who have been obliged to live without contact with Rome, it would have been understandable. Here, if anywhere, was a case for extensive if not complete independence in the running of a church. Maintaining contact with

Rome, to request its permission for every move, was a weight round the neck of the missionary church from the outset, and when advice did come it was only to unfortunate effect.

The desire to control religious activity and doctrine rather than sometimes to leave events and the cause of truth to God, as Gamaliel and St Paul recommended, is not of course unique to Catholicism. China missionary Hudson Taylor had to struggle against remote missionary societies controlling policies and purse-strings in order to establish the principle of the China Inland Mission (now Overseas Missionary Fellowship) that the centre of a mission must always be where its work is. It is not my purpose to question the specific Roman claims to authority but rather to stress the consistent weakness of its refusal to set pragmatic limits upon that authority and to recognize that until these are made, it cannot hope to grow notably within Asia. In the vision of Ezekiel, the Spirit of God is seen to leave the Temple, the very centre of Jewish religion, when sin makes that presence irrelevant, the point being that not even the most vital religious focal points and authorities are absolutely indispensable. Thus, when authority cannot fulfil its function there must be grounds for considering its limits. I cannot help feeling that the Catholic church always vaguely realized this and that it is why so little interest was evinced by early missions to the Far East, as those like John of Montecorvino involved in them complained. Those who travelled so far were in danger of setting themselves up as another authority and challenging an ecclesiastical authority which over the centuries had settled rather complacently into forms more political than religious and more fitted to a European world than to any other. If anything, modern missions to the East were originally the outcome less of zeal than of a need to keep pace with the colonial expansion of secular society whose members priests needed to serve.

In very modern times the remarkable and uncharacteristic acquiescence of so many Catholics in 'dialogue' may well amount to tacit acknowledgment that Catholicism stands little chance of extensive growth in an Asia whose Christians find it difficult enough to swallow the concept of the Jewish vocation without additionally being required to accept the supremacy of a European authority in Christian religion. In addition to that, they have to realize that it is one of the paradoxes of Asia that though in many respects the people are socially more conformist than Occidentals, in matters of mind and religion there can be considerable freedom of choice and action. Pure Buddhism and the sects which have arisen from it demonstrate decidedly 'protestant' tendencies in terms of religious sociology. For Gandhi God was his 'experiment', and it seems unlikely that most Asians would be prepared to settle for less freedom for the inner man were they to adopt Christian faith.

None of this is said with the object of reassuring Protestants, because there is no less need for them to discard a few cherished assumptions. Many, especially of the Victorian missionaries, but also today, have behaved with a tactlessness as individuals which quite rivals the Catholic failure collectively. This is true even of leading figures of mission history, like C. T. Studd and Amy Carmichael, who outraged the customs of the countries in which they found themselves, preaching and singing in the open air while still imperfect in the language concerned and pressing tracts on unwilling recipients, the particular scandal in Miss Carmichael's case being that women who spoke and moved about with ease and insistence could only be mistaken for prostitutes. The picture is perhaps worse with Emily Whitchurch, the zealous undertaker of Hudson Taylor's CIM policy of opposition to Chinese religions through public burning of the idols and ancestral tablets of converts. While the discarding of idols was the natural corollary of conversion, the disposal of ancestral tablets (comparable to burning family photos and portraits in the West) was not; even less so was an exhibitionist way of doing it, to shouts of hallelujah and the sound of Victorian hymns.[28] This ceremony, performed by Westerners amid companies of rural Chinese who had never seen Europeans before or even heard of Europe, could only appear to be a full-scale war upon Chinese culture, especially as it was backed up by complete Puritan intolerance of all the art forms, like opera and drama. This was particularly absurd, since the dramatic forms, due to Confucian influence, were almost unrealistically moralistic. In his belated reconciliation with Christianity a minister's son, Lin Yutang,[29] could never quite forgive the missionaries who cut Christians off from their cultural roots by this means, Chinese culture being popularly communicated through visual rather than literary means. All things considered, the outrage at such aggressive missioning by Mandarins, who in the course of it rarely received the deference missionaries gave to their own social superiors, is hardly surprising.

It would be easy to pour scorn on, or at least write the comic history of blind missionaries, as Pat Barr has done,[30] but one has to recognize that even C. T. Studd (who left China for Africa) and Amy Carmichael (who left it for India) were sincere, that they did mature, and that they even had something of the religious genius about them. The question is rather who or what managed to make them quite so blind and insensitive. The answer was perhaps unconsciously supplied by J. Campbell Gibson in *Missionary Methods in South China*:

> The world of eighteen hundred years ago springs again into life and reality . . . The Chinese Dragon takes the place of the Roman Eagle; consuls, proconsuls, praetors, deputies, move across the scene in the persons of Chinese mandarins. Demetrius, craft maker of shrines, and Alexander, the provoking coppersmith, are our next-door neighbours.[31]

The missionary method was all too often an imposition upon persons and events of biblical parallels by people who refused, like C. T. Studd, to perceive the society in and for itself (in contrast to St Paul at Athens, he omitted even to visit the sights while in Pekin). They investigated neither the customs nor the beliefs of the people among whom they worked, and in assuming spiritual and moral parallels between different peoples, which as Christians and missionaries they had to, they assumed that *everything* was relevant. In this way they were hopelessly insulated against criticism, since if anyone opposed them, it only fed a martyr complex, or was attributed to evil forces on the basis that St Paul was a missionary, and if St Paul was attacked, therefore they had to be also. If the missionary did not like or understand anything, he could dismiss it with St Paul's 'their senseless minds were darkened'. Ironically, St Paul and the suffering apostle image seems to have been the greatest single hindrance to missionary attempts to relate to a society and culture in the way St Paul so obviously tried to do. In reading Protestant mission literature, Victorian and more recent, I have noticed that the insensitivity appears to be in proportion to the obsession with St Paul.[32] Olin Stockwell, Lutheran missionary and author of *With God in Red China*, is one of those who frequently quotes St Paul and exhibits remarkable blindness, as in his shock at the rejection and ingratitude of Chinese people who have been open to church influence. He cheerfully recalls 'the Western houses of missionaries' close to a high school or hospital which 'have usually been impressively built in Western style', as though the Chinese should be honoured to have access to these islands of Western influence.[33]

Having said this, I must also ask how much St Paul's famous descriptions of the pagan world in Romans 1 is helpful, and in what way and to what extent passages of the Bible relevant to mission should be used. Two points are very significant about Romans 1. First, though it is uncharacteristic of Paul to borrow (and I have never read of this in any commentary), the whole is remarkably indebted to the apocryphal Wisdom of Solomon, which expressed a Jewish attitude towards the Gentile world, and it is from this that the terrible indictment, 'full of envy, murder, strife, deceit, malignity. . .' derives. Second, it is adapted to the audience in so far as the terminology is Stoic in its emphasis on reason and nature and its concern with a decadence which would apply more to Rome than elsewhere. Literary indebtedness to Jewish polemic seems to have involved St Paul in a more impatient description of his position and that of the gospel's than he need have adopted ('For the wrath of God is revealed from heaven against all ungodliness . . .'), while the argument from reason and nature involves him in a judgment of men's beliefs which must now appear to us more Western than universal ('Ever since the creation of the world his invisible nature . . . has been perceived in the things that have been made. So they are without excuse . . . they exchanged the glory of the immortal God for images representing mortal man, or birds or reptiles').[34] It is well known that Western man has been deeply concerned with matter and the visible world, whereas traditional Asian spirituality has ignored it in favour of mind, and if that spirituality has a hazier or absent notion of the divine, it is precisely because it argues from the oceanic consciousness within and not from nature. Its attitude to images and idols is frequently different as a result.

This is not to say that Romans 1 is irrelevant nonsense, though with Aelred Graham it seems fair to say it does not qualify as the most inspired passage of the New Testament.[35] The main point is perfectly clear, and is not one most Christians would dispute: without God man cannot be truly righteous. He may turn to depravity, but even if he does not, he fails to live up to the best within him. This applies as much to Asian men as Western; after all, there are Indians today who worship God as a rat in rat temples, and even given Asia's different approach to the divine, they do not necessarily live up to the best within themselves. Over all, however, for those without much discrimination, a passage like Romans 1 could encourage a blind and impatient attitude towards the cultures and religions approached, and a confusion of the subtle idolatries of the East with the bloodthirsty Astarte condemned by the Old Testament, or the depraved cities of ancient Rome. The *mores*, especially the sexual *mores* of foreign societies, would be judged against Roman decadence. Naturally, the lesson is that the Bible, however much it may enshrine principles of universal validity, is not a guide to and description of every possible phenomenon known to man, and its truth has to be constantly reinterpreted. In effect the Pauline letters say so. 'Every scripture inspired by God is also profitable for teaching, for reproof, for correction and for training in righteousness. . .' (II Tim. 3.16), but the amount of reinterpretation required is not something that will be favoured by all members of the church.

Lest it be argued that the kind of missionary to whom I have referred is the classic fundamentalist, fundamentalist to the point of bibliolatry and hence unrepresentative, it should be realized that this approach was one with a larger error in which liberal missionaries have been involved, namely, the determination to translate any and every biblical truth, as they conceive of it, into terms of some concrete social programme, again without consideration of the milieu. There were missionaries like Harriet Noyes and Helen Barrett Montgomery bent on unbinding women's feet and emancipating them, regardless of whether it gave the impression that the church was composed of 'easy' women and that the religion was less a religion than a liberation movement. The excellent Sherwood Eddy of the YMCA, who so nobly grappled with the corruptions of Shanghai and the exploitation of children conveniently overlooked by more fundamentalist religionists, was another who threatened to make Christianity identical with socialism in an Asia for which – theoretically – religion, though primarily personal, must still be related to everything.

There is no need to decry the concern of such people, still less the practical morality of the Jewish vision from which it derives and which is a precious antidote to the sort of indifference which has afflicted India, and the materialism that has dogged China. The point is that Bible and Christianity cannot be accepted for less than they and traditional Asian religion are – namely an attempt to relate to everything – nor as other than a primarily personal possession.

As Western man reads the Bible, especially the legalism and historical awareness of the Old Testament, he reads it from the standpoint not just of the Jewish but also the Roman sense of law and linear history. However vaguely, Jewish history is part of his history, a whole Western concept of social emergence and fulfilment. For Asian man, who usually comes to it from the standpoint of cyclical time and psychological rather than social reality (attitudes best represented in the Bible by Ecclesiastes), the Old Testament will seem like patterns of *karma*, parables, lessons, an image of personal spiritual history and deliverance which St Paul (I Cor. 10.6ff.) and early Christians of the allegorical school of exegesis considered a legitimate manner of reading it, but not the unqualified prescription for social organization which so many missionaries have made it.

It is possible that within the Chinese setting, a rather communal, legalistic expression of religion comparable to that of the Pilgrim Fathers or the Anabaptists might be considered the indigenous ideal, as is suggested by the relative success of Pastor Hsi's 'Middle Eden' community, the Jesus Family in Communist China, or the Kingdom of God as conceived by the heretical Taipings. But in Asia beyond China and even within it, this could never be considered an acceptable version of the faith, though it seems likely that due to its highly scriptural orientation, this is the variety of indigenization most missionaries would prefer to see, if indigenization be considered imperative.

III

Religion offers a way of escape as much as an attempt at solution to the problems we have considered. To those who feel bound to tradition, the problems of East and West are purely religious ones. Either the world is merely stiff-necked and resistant to the divine, in which case success or failure do not count, or those charged with conveying divine truth were found wanting in the necessary spiritual virtues, or both. Sociological issues are either irrelevant, or would have been settled had there been enough attention to the divine will, and the same applies to philosophy. Even a historian of missions as sophisticated as Bishop Stephen Neill, who acknowledges the sociological dimensions in the failure, rather extravagantly sees many missionaries as having all but recrucified Christ.[36] Moreover, there is the one exception that seems to prove the rule. Though in countries like India and Siam, missionaries may have waited ten or twenty years for a single convert, the church in Korea, only moderately indigenized, is still a powerful church, counted in millions.

The trouble with this attitude is that while it cannot be entirely dismissed, it clouds the central issue, which is the very specific nature of the failure and its consequence in a resurgence of Asian faiths. Obviously, any church and mission is witness to shortcomings among its members which call for improvement, and every cultural and psychological issue that we have mentioned can in some measure be referred back to religious attitudes. *Religion* is at stake, but not simple *piety*. If sanctity and zeal alone could ensure success, it seems fair to say that Asia rather than Africa should have been Christianized, and Africa, which has suffered so much more from theoretically Christian rulers, should have been the critic of Western beliefs. Again, if it were simply a question of piety of application and spirituality of response, results should have been much more uneven and less predictable than they are. The greater response of Asian tribal peoples to conservative religion, and of the civilized peoples to a more indigenized faith, vindicates the sociological approach, while the great similarity of response in non-tribal Asia to all manner of denominations and evangelistic techniques by those concerned with conveying religious truth, unrelated to cultural ideas,[37] vindicates the assumption that a barrier of religious consciousness is not being crossed, possibly the same barrier involved in the current spiritual crisis.

Those inclined still to doubt this have only to work to the truth by a process of elimination. Despite missionaries like Francis E. Clark, who aided the colonial powers and feathered their nests, or eccentrics, like Griffith John and Wells Williams, who offended every Chinese notion of etiquette, 'wearing people down with the glorious Gospel', and confounding them with arguments into enraged silence, overall even the most sceptical must admit that the evidence shows that modern missionaries have been very giving of themselves. The Exleys,[38] who have worked with secular relief organizations, admit that religion seems to impart to missions a higher sense of dedication and giving. There have been quite enough of the heroic or martyr breed to found any number of churches if such sacrifice were the prerequisite of church founding, and those who maintain with Tertullian that 'the blood of the martyrs is the seed of the church' have to recognize that even significant churches, like the Early Irish, can be founded *without* martyrs. Judged by conventional standards of piety and doctrine, only certain shortcomings can have been in question, and it is doubtful whether they were so widespread or individually significant as to account for the situation. We may, however, give them brief mention. 1. The missionaries were of the type who, according to St Paul, can give their bodies to be burned yet not possess true love; 2. they did not mistake a vocation but mistook the time and place for its realization; 3. they overlooked the communal aspect of conversion and religious activity as understood in the New Testament and in Asia; 4. possibly, and most importantly, they accepted a vocation, but like St Peter in the face of the Gentile challenge, hesitated at the more novel implications of the call.

As regards the first possibility, it does seem that some missionaries, however well-intentioned, were and remain selfishly insensitive to the deeper feelings and needs of those around them. In *The Gist of Japan* the American Lutheran missionary G. B. Peery proudly describes how the missionary's house was 'a beacon light shining in a dark place . . . a little piece of Christendom set down in the midst of heathendom'.[39] In the home of the missionary there was not to be seen any taint of 'orientalism'; its furnishings were Western, its appointments were 'civilized', and altogether, it was kept inviolate from 'the subtle influence of heathenism which creeps in at every pore'. This is in notable contrast to the much criticized demand of the China Inland Mission that its missionaries live, dress and eat native-style, something which would surely have given Peery a breakdown, so trying does he portray life in his apparently comfortable surroundings. But it would be wrong to dismiss Peery's attitude as merely quaint or Victorian. It was typical throughout Asia, and in the circumstances it was not only foolish but unkind, carrying the implication, as such attitudes still do today, that the aesthetic and other values of the society are both irrelevant to Christianity and beneath the consideration of the educated Westerner. In the last century, however, missions in the Far East coincided with a period of vast change, upheaval and tension. For the first time in centuries the Chinese and Japanese systems displayed signs of internal decay as a result of population explosions and shifts in economic power, while the intrusion of the West and science, quite apart from the impact of missions, sent the societies into a spin in which the educated, like Sun Yat Sen, the Christian founder of the Chinese Republic, would be caught up in the painful counter-claims of tradition, revolution and nationalism. Until too late missionaries either failed or refused to recognize the agonies of birth and death in which members of the society were caught up. They did not try to minister to these problems, placing doctrines like incarnation and rebirth in the context of the society as converts and students of Christian colleges asked that they should.[40] For them the soul existed in a vacuum apart from these problems, yet independently of doctrine, ordinary love and concern should have shown them that this was not possible.

On the second count, missionaries may have been in the wrong place at the wrong time. This is possible even for those with a vocation. According to tradition, certain apostles, like St Thomas and St Jude, went East to Persia and India, but the majority voyaged West, and in Acts it is recorded that at one point they were specifically directed by the Spirit not to change direction towards Asia (that is, the Middle East) but to continue westwards towards Europe. They might easily have refused to heed this, and in doing so, missed the opportunity of contacting the Roman world which, owing to its vast social and ideological upheavals, was particularly receptive to Christian doctrine. Assuming that the missionaries of modern times did begin with some vocation, one doubts the timing and concentration of effort of their choice (or leading?) within certain political spheres. Granted that for European man to evangelize East Asia was an unfortunate development (the religion ought to have spread East through Persia, something which became impossible because of the Islamic persecution of churches, especially the strategic churches of North India and Kurdistan), nevertheless it seems lamentable that when missionaries did venture East, they assumed that they possessed 'carte blanche' to travel everywhere. One wonders, for example, why the China Inland Mission needed to be *inland*. Could not the missionaries have established strong congregations in port cities after the manner of St Paul on the Mediterranean, and let these congregations spread the word inland? Clearly only persons attuned to the ways of an imperialistic, self-imposing society would have thrust themselves upon shocked and bewildered rural people who had never seen and heard of European man, in the way missionaries were prepared to do. Furthermore, in so far as they reflected attitudes current to their time, are we not correct in supposing that they may not have lived up to the best of their vocation or even biblical example?

Third, it is possible that missionaries, both conservative and liberal, failed to address themselves to the communal spirit of Asia. Interpreting doctrines of conversion or moral responsibility in the light of the Western individualism natural to them, they rigorously demanded personal decisions and commitments before baptizing a convert or launching a church member into a programme, overlooking both the biblical sanction for group approach and the extent to which elsewhere people derive their identity from the group. When St Peter baptized the household of Cornelius, not all of whom could have been as religious as Cornelius, he did not make any detailed enquiry about their vocation; he does not even appear to have asked whether they wanted to be baptized. It was simply assumed that they should be unless they specifically declined.

I said earlier that Asia could be very individualistic in relation to religion, but it can happen, especially in the Chinese setting, that the individualism is itself of the group variety. When I read Rees' *The Jesus Family in Communist China*[41] as a child of the West I was appalled at the authoritarian narrowness imposed on all, children included, but on reflection I was bound to admit that this was authentically Chinese. In Asia, individualism is frequently unconscious; among the Chinese it has traditionally been conscious only among the very rich, as with the hero of *The Dream of the Red Chamber* (who is nonetheless considered weak-minded for it),[42] or among social misfits and rebels like the characters of *Water Margin*.[43] Even in Japan, which is more individualistic, the dedication of Samurai and retainers is akin to the marriage in which two become one flesh and mind; the retainer virtually ceases to be a separate individual. In this context of 'group think' it was surely ill-advised to operate in terms of Western individualism, although, given time, undoubtedly Christian influence would foster individualism.

Yet can we seriously believe that considerations like the foregoing cover the dismal picture and would have rectified it? The very fact that so many things were wrong in so many directions suggests that something very central was wrong, like the *one* thing that the rich young ruler would not renounce in the interests of discipleship. Fourth, then, missionaries may have failed to respond to the deeper implications of their vocation in Asia, and this is something which, if valid, I believe should be seen in the perspective of the modern spiritual crisis generally.

There were two ways in which the missionaries could have related to Asia. The first was a calculated way of straightforward adaptation of terms and customs such as was successfully practised by Ricci, making the religion approachable and leaving the native converts to solve any other problems with time. This approach would have been simply *wise*, and despite the missionary who accused my approach to missions of being carnal, the fact is that the gospels are all for worldly wisdom and shrewd investment. They record tantalizing sayings, like 'Be wise as serpents . . . and the Lord commended the unjust steward'. The other way, which need not exclude the first and might have given it more profundity, would have been more spiritual, addressing oneself in terms of the

Asian consciousness and religious experience as such. However, I am convinced that this would have first required a more satisfactory resolution of the problem of individualism as it had developed within Christian and Western thought. Without resolving the problem of the status of individualism and freedom as this developed after the Reformation and particularly after the eighteenth century, it proved more difficult to speak to Asia because either the religion would tend to impose upon it an individualism out of harmony with its society and instincts (the Protestant tendency), or finish evading, if not confusing, the issue of the personal in God and man, referring instead to a mysticism of union allegedly held in common by all religions (the modern Catholic tendency).

An individualism unrelated to any larger process and an unprecedented power over nature and society, which have become absurd and impersonal, lie at the roots of the modern anguish, inside and outside religion. Restating Christianity and individualism within the framework of Asian life provided a special opportunity to come to grips with both the modern alienation and the apathy of the East, but the opportunity was allowed to slip away. Missionaries sought lost souls more than they strove to realize the 'new creation'.

That there was some psychological barrier to be overcome, or that a divine lesson was not being heeded, is strongly suggested by a spiritual crisis and discovery made by Hudson Taylor and recorded for 17 October 1869, when at considerable length he wrote to his sister of his realization of the power of spiritual acceptance and not-doing. Exhausted in body and mind, insufficiently able to concentrate his mind on God and achieve power, serenity, patience or freedom from sins through prayer, resolutions, fastings or Bible readings, he suddenly discovered that faith and character would be strengthened 'not by *striving* after faith but *resting* on the Faithful One'. He also went on to affirm that his obsession with sins and failure was wrong, for the central problem is always sin and unbelief. Weakness could be overcome less by effort than realizing

> our oneness with Jesus. As I read I saw it all. 'If we believe *not* He abideth faithful . . . *I* will never leave you.' As I thought of the vine and the branches, what light the blessed Spirit poured direct into my soul. How great seemed my mistake in having wished to get the sap, the fullness *out* of Him. I saw not only Jesus would never leave me, but that I was a member of His Body . . . The vine is not the root merely, but all root, stem,

branches . . . and Jesus is not only that, He is soil and sunshine, air and showers. . . . No more can your prayers or mine be discredited if offered in the name of Jesus, i.e., not in our own name or for the sake of Jesus merely, but on the ground we are His, His members. . . . Faith I now see is 'the substance of things hoped for' and not mere shadow. It is not less than sight but more. Sight only shows outward forms of things; faith gives the substance. You can rest on substance, feed on substance.[44]

Taylor was not the first spiritually-minded person to arrive at such conclusions, but one of the first to realize them in modern practical terms. Freedom and power, even when deeply felt, were somewhat academic concepts, given little scope for expression, among the Catholic mystics, hemmed about by their monastic disciplines. Furthermore, they were not in Asia. There is a peculiar irony in this Christian approximation to the Taoist concept of *wu-wei*, 'not doing', the power of accepting and letting go, strength in rest, activity in action, existence through the ultimate, the truth not in the details but radiating from the centre. Granted, such truths are easier to formulate than to realize for man East or West, but Taylor's conclusions should have been his theological starting points within Asia. If this was a lesson which God was trying to teach him, it can only be said that it was not one that Taylor and subsequent missions learned very well.

If what Taylor had experienced was authentic, then there were at least two implications for doctrine which he did not begin to consider. By realizing that God was not just the vine to which he belonged but the surrounding nature as well, he had effectively returned to St Paul's holistic vision of the cosmic Christ. God is throughout everything, not just omniscient but omnipresent. If this is the case, then 'we also are his offspring', as St Paul said to the Athenians: *all* of us, believers and unbelievers. Thus, regarded from the mystical and psychological angle as opposed to the legal one, in which context we are St Paul's 'sons of God by adoption', we are children of God, and conversion is willing realization of the fact by the estranged. The second implication which follows from this holistic realization, especially if one acknowledges the Christian view of personality, is that the relationship of God and man must be one of co-operation and freedom, and that personality is an aspect of a dynamic process. (How this is so we shall consider later.) These are important considerations, ones which have to be felt and lived as much as intellected, but which, as will be seen, have facilitated mission encounter with Asia.

Taylor, however, seems to have exhausted the range of his insight as soon as he had achieved purely personal as opposed to philosophical satisfaction. He immediately mars his insight by stating that he is now free to ask anything of God provided that it is not contrary to scripture (as though scripture exactly covered every imaginable situation), limiting this freedom still further by indicating that God's will is absolute, a decision made for and independently of us, something we should seek out and to which we should submit. This, though a common, pious conclusion, based on the acknowledgment that God knows best, is not entirely supported by the doctrine of prayer. Not only does it limit God by suggesting that he can only ever offer two alternatives, but if it were invariably true, it would be liable to make us automatons, especially once one's identity with God became so total. If God has a fixed plan for us, and our own desires can never affect his decisions, then obviously there is not much point in speaking of a paternity-sonship, or of the freedom of God to make choices and man to have preferences.

Since it is obviously impossible to determine if and for what reason God was revealing something to Taylor to benefit his understanding of the missionary task, it is more profitable to approach the issue from the psychological angle, to concentrate on the fairly representative condition of anguish and failure which preceded the revelation, to see if the answer is relevant to contemporary anguish and missionary failure generally. Despair as such is a common enough phenomenon, and obviously there is a point at which an exhausted mind is ready to fall over into an opposite or complementary feeling or opinion, as happened in Taylor's case. It does not do so *necessarily*, as depressive and suicidal minds demonstrate, but it can do so if the mind is resilient and sufficiently anchored in its particular belief-system to be able to make creative sense of the transition instead of being drowned by it. Since the human mind is similar everywhere, this is not necessarily a religious experience, though it can be the vehicle of one. Sartre's atheistic view of life starting beyond despair, or even Buddha's illumination following his failure, are quite akin to this. Colin Wilson has given a lengthy existentialist analysis of modern depression and alienation from a non-religious angle, seeing it as an opportunity rich in creative possibilities for those few able to surmount it. In his opinion there is 'a margin of the human mind that can be stimulated by pain or inconvenience but which is indifferent to pleasure'.[45] As in crossing the sound barrier, there is a point at which laws of nature are reversed. If we can concentrate our will, and not revolt, as most people do, against the negative nature of freedom within certain circumstances which require primarily a change of attitude, then unprecedented invention, spiritual or psychic power is released. In the face of this portentous restriction, the only proper attitude, and one which overcomes, is the poet Rilke's '*dennoch preisen*', to praise or affirm nevertheless.

According to Wilson the pain threshold is the safety device for the human learning process. If, in our present state, our mind let in too much reality, we would be drunk and blinded, so we must be stimulated by pain and conquer reality by will. In the phenomonology of Wilson, which is turned upon the history of creativity and sexuality, reality is seen, almost theologically, in terms of an energy dependent upon the subject to will.[46] In religion, the doctrine of progress by pain is, of course, the teaching that 'the Lord disciplines whom he loves and chastens (or tests) everyone whom he receives', a text of which Toynbee made much because his *A Study of History* shows similar conclusions to Wilson's in its emphasis on the painful nature of the evolution of society and human consciousness.[47] Jung likewise concurs that individuation and spiritual growth are eminently painful. For those who cannot negotiate it, and even sometimes for those who can, the journey to God may be a journey into horror. 'One can love God but must also fear him' and 'the God who hears our prayers ... also does not hear our prayers'.[48] It is necessary to affirm beyond darkness and silence. At least one popular American religious writer, Merlin Carothers,[49] has recently taken it upon himself to correct average spirituality by suggesting that religion will indeed be little but discouraging to those who will not affirm nevertheless. His theology stresses Job's saying, 'Despise not the chastening of the Lord, for he makes sore and binds up; he wounds and his hands make whole',[50] and St Paul's 'In all things give thanks', a saying to which we shall have cause to refer again.

Despite the book of Job, we are, however, faced with the fact that the experience of darkness, despair, depression and alienation have been more pronounced among both religious and non-religious people during the last two centuries than previously. Hudson Taylor knew it, as did Simone Weil, who described it at length as 'affliction',[51] so did St Thérèse of Lisieux, who said that God had sent such dryness and darkness upon her that she feared that in discussing it she might blaspheme.[52] Kierkegaard almost equated it with the human condition,[53] Bonhoeffer considered the divine weakness or absence in *Letters and Papers from Prison*[54] and C. S. Lewis in *A Grief Observed.*[55] Modern missionary autobiographies, like Helen Roseveare's *He Gave Us This Valley*, may seem gloomy and even masochistic, full of fits of spiritual anguish.[56] On the secular front we need hardly mention the anguish syndrome in Beckett, Sartre, Camus, and a host of writers from Nietzsche onwards.

Up to a point there are, of course, medical and sociological explanations which it would be foolish not to take into account. Even Simone Weil admitted that 'uprootedness' such as produced by rapid social change can dehumanize people and plunge them into the unknown. There is no doubt that modern life is more stressful, hurried and artificial than most forms preceding it. But this is not everything, and Wilson derides the assumption that all depression is sickness to be cured by pills, or a spiritual limitation to be overcome by mind-expanding drugs. It is the mind registering a situation to which it sees no solution, but for which it should find one. In the same way, we might need to accuse those missionaries who refuse to acknowledge the church's failure in Asia, or who blame Asia for ungodliness, for not coming to terms with the challenge of their own darkness, the divine message which it might disclose.[57] Conventional piety interprets unanswered prayer as the answer 'no', or actual disapproval of sin, but the manifest faith and righteousness of many on whom darkness has fallen makes it as likely to be the God of Isaiah, who is like the eagle stirring up the nest, or the God of Bonhoeffer, forcing man come of age to realize the fact, to act and think freely. If this is something man unconsciously realizes, he does not seem to possess the ideological framework in which to realize it.

In the modern anguish syndrome, the unbeliever feels alienated and the believer helpless. In both cases the problem appears to be rooted in the unprecedented *individualism* or scope for individualism in modern man which tends to make the relationship to God, world and society more self-conscious and difficult. Unbelieving or half-believing man was previously secure within the bosom of some larger social whole which, like mediaeval society, thought for him, and when this broke down, science and philosophical dualism left him in a desert. Once the romantic novelty of his isolation wore off, anguish resulted. He desperately sought the cause and the group, the new society, Communism. Religion eluded him, and like Sartre he suddenly felt that, carrying the world on his shoulders as he was, if there was a God, it was intolerable not to be a god also. The recent post-Einsteinian trend towards a more holistic thought which affirms that, even if we feel isolated, we are in fact a necessary part of a completely interrelated web of being, must be a considered necessary and healthy modern response to the agnostic's impasse.

The troubled believer's position has much in common with the 'outsider's' in its 'Protestant' sense of isolation and responsibility, but here, to judge by the common symptoms, the tension centres upon the nature of freedom which the agnostic takes for granted. There is likely to be gloom, constant self-reproach and self-doubting, a desire to get power *out* of God in the way Taylor rejected. There is likely to be an obsession with scruples of the kind it took St Thérèse so long to overcome. Reading these brilliant but morbid and unsmiling modern testimonies, one is left wondering whatever happened to the Christian joy with which even the early martyrs were affected. Although they may have been a rather different religious emphasis, especially as regards life in the Spirit, as I shall show presently, the difference seems to be deeply involved in the very different historical sense of freedom and individualism. As long as man was the victim of social systems, like the Roman and the mediaeval, the plaything of nature and disease, he accepted the divine word simply, or else disobeyed it like a naughty child. His self-examination, his guilt, his repentance was not tinged with the neurotic considerations which have subsequently crept in. Only as modern individualism emerged did the response even of fundamentalists become more laboured and morbid. Only as man began to 'come of age' did he begin to see the stress – unconsciously at least – the purely individual factor, going on to reject these promptings as sin and to pay for them in feelings of unworthiness. The absurdity and inauthenticity of some of this unworthiness can be gauged from asides like Taylor's guilty fear that his plans for China might actually be too big for God, that he was asking too much of him. In this instance, because Taylor had been brought up to believe that God directs everything regardless of man, he was unnecessarily looking for a reason to be guilty, when as a born leader he instinctively knew what he wanted and what he could perform.

Part of the problem was that the reading of the Bible itself, which only became widely available to believers after the Reformation and the invention of printing, never became indigenized to the West like church ceremony and custom. A suitable way to approach it philosophically had never been discovered. It is small wonder that missionaries could not indigenize the faith in the East, for there is a sense in which it was never entirely assimilated to the West.

St Augustine and Justin Martyr were troubled that the epistles were not more like Cicero. One only needs to be conversant with classical literature to be aware that St Paul, despite attempts to write within the European style, was still Semitic. If Western man had had the kind of Bible he would have liked, it would have been something like the Orthodox liturgy, through which passages of the Bible and statements of doctrine are conveyed in neat logical succession, like a treatise of Aristotle. Western man, even when not introspective, is analytical, rationalizing, exacting. If the Bible places the accent on historical revelation, he demands that the Bible be chronologically precise, not as in Isaiah with the middle at the beginning or the end, the sort of habit the Bible shares in common with all scriptures from the Analects to the Koran. If he reads the Pentateuch, Western man wants to reduce its laws to a consistent rational principle; if he reads the Psalms, he wants to censor the occasional irrelevant barbarisms or be soothed by a regular flow of images, as in European poetry from Homer onwards, and not be disconcerted by its apparently arbitrary images and thought-connections.

It may be, as St Paul states, that the natural man 'hears not the things of God', but beyond all moral resistance, to Western man the Bible appears a somewhat capricious, disconcerting work which, if not read aright, far from achieving its spiritual purpose, can produce useless argument and doubts. From the very first the church fathers started worrying about harmonizing the gospels, anxious to reduce everything to scientific exactitude. Though such demands for consistency were not unreasonable, and the main tenets of the faith do demonstrate a certain logic, the danger was always the intellectualization of faith over its spiritualization, the search for 'gnosis' (knowledge) as opposed to a saving truth, the myth of the possibility of a completely objective revelation. The end-product of this trend is the identification of the mind of God with intellectual forms and deterministic principles, and an elevation of the abstract over the personal. This is explicit in scholastic philosophy, for reasons which I shall consider presently. In Protestantism, where the Bible was not reduced to philosophical principles, the assumption that it could be was still implied, which is why Taylor felt sure that the Bible must disclose the truth about everything and sometimes imposed what he thought it disclosed on China regardless of common sense.

It is, however, the privilege of scriptures to transcend the intellect for the life of the Spirit, and the Christian concept of prayer alone would suggest that God's will and word usually contain a conditional clause. God is portrayed as changing his mind, being moved by prayer in accordance with the persistence or number of those praying. The reason is that because God is good himself, anything he chooses to do will be good. He has, moreover, determined men's freedom, and this freedom cannot be lightly compromised, so that God only compromises it 'democratically' when man has reasonably demanded the intervention. Thus, to some extent, God's will is spontaneous. It shows a character and principles, but it is not a fixed law. God does not have one plan for people; he has plans and accepts suggestions.

Men of the West who, like Taylor, live by 'God's Word' alone, are liable to feel tossed about by it, particularly the Old Testament. They accept the Old Testament because Christ acknowledged it, and deny it because Christ denied it; obey some of it blindly, disregard other parts as cancelled or old-fashioned, rationalize other parts of it. One day the book condemns them, another day it forgives them. Not until modern individualism and the Protestant ethic developed was man so troubled by this arbitary 'foreign' quality of the Bible. If he could not agree with it, or reasonably apply it, it tortured him, he accused himself of pride and sin; or if he was less introspective, he took the liberal escape route and in rather cavalier fashion dismissed whatever did not immediately appear to agree with some arbitrary 'scientific' evaluation of biblical documents and history.

Spiritual darkness, frustration, failure, will always be the lot of those who allow themselves to be trapped, who cannot grow, who refuse to acknowledge their best instincts. Many modern intuitions are justified. It is, for example, quite right to feel that if there is a God, it is intolerable that we, too, should not be gods. Christianity *used* to claim as much by the doctrine of 'theosis' (deification), to which Byzantine theology still adheres. God became man to make man God. Jesus himself states, 'You are gods to whom the Word of the Lord came . . . all power is given to you. . . . I call you no longer servants but friends.' It is, however, true that where this emphasis is lacking and God is not regarded as omnipresent, or where his will is understood in terms of a fixed law corresponding to his own mind rather than in terms of principles and free choice, there is no room for growth, and God has become tied to a static rather than an active principle. To some extent Christianity is suffering from, and being accused of, the lack of features it has lost. The matter is, however, more complex than a need for restoration, for though to begin with the kind of ideas I have mentioned were present spontaneously in Christianity, at the level of intuition, even had they been retained, they would need to have become more fully conscious and undergone considerable intellectual elaboration. Nevertheless, had they been retained, the religion would have been better equipped to include modern individualism and the Asian consciousness.

As I have said, in early Christianity the problem of freedom and individualism, unity in diversity, was instinctively understood as an aspect of an undeveloped doctrine of the Spirit which was subsequently lost. In itself the belief in individual gifts of the Spirit within the body of Christ acted as a safeguard against the reduction of the idea of individualism so typical of mediaeval philosophy. Even to biblical man, as the theologian Friedrich Gogarten has pointed out, 'obedience' to God meant 'hearing towards', attunement to the infinite, to the true. Christian 'submission' to the divine 'will' is fundamentally submission to the imperatives deriving from the love and justice which Christ's teaching involves; it is not and never was submission to law in the Jewish or Islamic sense. In the words of St Paul, one 'obeys' truth or wickedness, and thus the high priests 'disobeyed' God in sentencing Christ, meaning that they obeyed wickedness rather than transgressed any specific written or revealed commandment of God or man. If Christian obedience came to appear akin to an Islamic submission to God and book, it was because Christian man formerly allowed himself to feel abjectly subject to fate; to flood, plague, famine and ignorance which with the advent of science and education he has in some measure been able not only to escape but also to control.

The psychology of classic evangelism is consequently feudalistic, less that of ruler and ambassador, as in Pauline imagery, than that of lord and servant or general and private. The characteristic of servant and private is that they await specific commands, and believers with such an approach will also regard the liberty of their faith negatively, almost exclusively in terms of a deliverance from sins rather than a release to fullness of personality. This attitude in itself must limit their sensitivity to the needs of self-expression in persons and cultures. It is with this submission in expectation of directives that so much of the missionary problem begins; this is how 'guided' souls, 'obedient to God's sovereign will' or 'awaiting God's sovereign power', as so much missionary literature states, nonetheless get themselves and the church drawn into situations so obviously unhelpful or even detrimental to them. Holding unreasonable expectations of divine guidance, and striving to emulate a biblical fervour, missionaries can suppress both their rational assessments of situations and their desires in relation to them as a mark of obedience to the divine will which they expect to direct them. When it does not seem to materialize, they force a solution by taking a biblical model, or are led by the surfacing voice of their own denied desires which are the more dangerous for never being frankly examined. None of this is necessarily like their model St Paul.

I remarked earlier that St Paul astutely centred his ministry in ports and key centres of the Roman Empire, but there is absolutely nothing in Acts or elsewhere to suggest that this was other than by shrewd human calculation. Although in Acts 13 it is stated that the Holy Spirit set apart and sent out Paul and Barnabas for the work, which constituted the first missionary journey, there is no indication that the route of their journey was decided beforehand. At any rate it was not preordained and enforced by the Spirit. Like Abraham, they seem to have set off without knowing exactly where the journey would take them other than where their wisdom in the light of truth suggested. That such was the case, and would always be so, is strongly indicated by chapter 16 and the second journey, where it seems that specific direction comes in negative form only.

> And they went through the region of Phrygia and Galatia, having been forbidden by the Holy Spirit to speak the word in Asia. And when they had come opposite Mysia they attempted to go into Bithynia, but the Spirit of Jesus did not allow them.

From this it is clear that the apostles went simply where they thought best unless otherwise forbidden by the Spirit, which subsequently they came to realize was driving them West into Europe. Again, in chapter 20, St Paul leaves Ephesus for Macedonia, but only because the uproar there impelled it, and there is no indication that he was specifically directed to go to Macedonia.

In his personal relations and desires, St Paul again exhibits considerable independence of mind. In Acts 16 Paul *wanted* Timothy to accompany him; there is no indication that God told him Timothy should. In Acts 15 Paul *thought* that it was not best to take

John Mark with them, though Barnabas wanted him to come. In I Cor 7.12, in giving counsel on marriage, St Paul says: 'I say, not the Lord.' Paul's desire to go to Rome to preach is entirely his own, and not God's leading, though he hopes that God may find a way for him to realize his desire: 'I long to see you ... I am eager to preach to you.' It would seem that Paul's wish was granted, though only through his virtual disobedience to the Spirit. In Acts 21, Paul stays at Tyre with prophets who 'through the Spirit' tell him not to go to Jerusalem, a warning reiterated by the prophet Agabus in Caesarea. However, almost in love with death, Paul proceeds to Jerusalem, where his arrest is the means of his being sent to Rome, to appeal to Caesar.

From such leads one would be obliged to say that Paul was a mixture of intelligent opportunism and wilfulness, the latter excused by the fact that it was essentially idealistic in nature, and thoroughly honest. In him there was none of the missionary who mistakes ambition or a desire to see the world for a call, or refuses to acknowledge that such elements (which are not in themselves evil) exist within the response to the vocation. One feels bound to conclude that the faith and fervour in which the church was launched should be compared (those informed of the current occult explosion will appreciate this) to the meetings of the coven in which a group comes together to raise power by psychological and physical means for the next quarter. The meetings in the Spirit described in Acts are almost certainly not to be thought of as meetings in which church leaders prayed for and 'received' detailed information as to how and where to found and organize churches in the way that missionary conferences today try to do, even if more and more time is given to discussion and the human element than formerly. Rather, the church sought to acquire power, altered consciousness and general attunement to the transcendent, and with this they erupted upon the world 'full of the power of the Holy Spirit' and full of 'discernment' as the moment called for it. But evidently they retained a good measure of individualism and independence, and St Paul is perhaps Bonhoeffer's 'man come of age' before the time; he certainly appears an example of St Augustine's 'love God and do what you will'.

If God's will is in certain respects expressed through *man's* will, how much of his character is mediated through man's character and growth? Without embarking upon some theological anthropology of Jew and Greek, I would argue that it should be understood as to a considerable degree so mediated. This seems implied by the Judaeo-Christian understanding both of creation in the divine image and the election of groups and individuals who are not always 'better' but more 'suited' to a task at a certain time. Very early in Christian theology, St Clement of Alexandria had deduced that, 'If anyone knows himself he shall know God', and, 'that man with whom the Logos dwells is made like God', but within the context of the highly rational and static Greek understanding of substance and the individual, such notions were hard to sustain then and later. Individuality was liable to be confused with the errors of passion and novelty, so that in Christian monasticism perfection was apt to be defined as suppression rather than expression of personality. Protestantism aroused rather than justified individualism, failing to supply it with an objective philosophical framework, and missionary disapproval of foreign customs, like Puritan disapproval of colours, was logical enough, given the persistence of classical prejudices. To have counter-balanced the new subjectivity, a monistic framework of thought would have helped, though to avoid inflation and to meet the challenge of new worlds in which Christ could be seen anew, a doctrine of divine movement or expansion was required. In its absence secular theories of evolution came to fill the vacuum and in modern times, philosophies of evolution, like those of Whitehead, Shaw and William James, which admit the religious factor, tend to pantheism and either state or imply that the process is one in which God has to perfect himself or man make him.

Yet a more dynamic view of God and reality would appear to be implied in early Christian doctrine and psychology. At the very least, in trinitarian language, Christ is always 'proceeding' from the Father, and though for specialized reasons Jung preferred the Quaternity image for God, he believed that psychologically the Trinity functioned as a symbol of growth. Moreover, modern Jewish thinkers, like Martin Buber and Erich Fromm, have recalled to Christians the origins of their notions of Deity and individualism in Semitic rather than Greek notions of activity and relation. It is not a substance which certifies the individual but an 'I' over against a 'Thou', while Deity is both a self-existent being and – towards man – a becoming. Not strictly translatable into English, the 'I am' of the divine name 'I am who I am' is in the so-called Hebrew imperfect tense of *ehyeh* 'to become', which implies past and future process as much as present being.

But ought we to say that God grows? Expansion might be the better word. Obviously, in terms of infinity God cannot grow and mankind could never increase the divine infinity, but in so far as God is love, there is a sense in which there must always be a creative 'reaching out', and in so far as it is believed that God has decided to realize himself in otherness and limitation, man is the condition of God's development. Man may be created in God's image, but it is he who is the necessary vehicle for its realization, the one who manifests within the material the greatest possible aspects of God's plenitude. Divine incarnation into the finite is not realized solely in the incarnation of Logos in a specific person, for in this it is seen as having only begun (Christ the image of the invisible God, the *firstborn* of creation. . . he is before all things . . . he is the head of the body, Col. 1.15ff.); it is reproduced and extended through the awakening of each individual soul who relates to God. The process is comparable to that of the artist or author who projects himself in his work, which is mediated through the unconscious that is larger than his conscious and publicly visible self. Through each individual and their reaction to him, it is possible for Christ to be reproduced and God extended. To the quality of any thing or person, God has purposed that the individual should add something. 'Your life is hid with God in Christ,' declares St Paul, but conversely, something of God's being is also hidden within us to be manifested. St Paul himself went so far as to suggest that in his own body he could add to Christ's sacrifice.

That the God who says 'I am who I shall be' is experienced in relation, and to that extent is always 'different', is implied not only by the curious statement 'the God of Abraham, of Isaac and of Jacob', but within the New Testament by the symbolism of the white stone to which Byzantine theology has drawn attention. In Revelation 2.17 it is stated that the believer will receive 'a white stone with a new name written on the stone which no one knows except him who receives it', indicating that in every divine-human relationship there is a 'different' aspect which amounts to an ineffable uniqueness. Despite this, the Christian presentation of Christ, especially as it would be interpreted against the static concepts of Greek thought and in its assumption of the possibility of a completely objective truth, has contributed to the psychologically untenable belief that Christ simply was and is a particular person who can be wholly described from the Bible and always presented to the world in exactly the same way. The Christ of the gospel says, 'He who has seen me has seen the Father'; the author of Hebrews writes of 'Jesus Christ the same yesterday, today and for ever'. But these statements would point to the fundamental principles revealed, especially the knowledge of God as love, and it need hardly be said that there is always something more to love. While there is no need to go as far as the subjectivism of the demythologizing school of theology, which tends to suggest there is no historical Jesus in the gospels, but only the preached figure moulded by experience of some saving realization, still the Jesus of John, though recognizably the same individual, is clearly different from the Jesus of Matthew. As Jung's psychology of perception has demonstrated, there is no such thing as a completely objective fact; there is *always* a subjective content to experience, quite apart from the fact that individuals choose to reveal sides of themselves to some and not to others.

Ironically, this feature of religious experience is rarely grasped by precisely those members of the church who emphasize the subjective dimension. For them the Christ of the gospels is so once and for all that the convert simply *renews* the realization of who and what that Jesus is. Missionary and convert are expected to speak the *same* language, rejoice in the self-same Lord. This is why the Southern Baptist or Christian Alliance missionaries (conservatives strongly represented in Asia) are neither especially sensitive to their audience nor usually willing to allow the convert much spiritual or cultural freedom of expression beyond spreading the Word to the next village. If God cannot be seen, however dimly, within man as well as in the Beyond, there is no particular call to respect the personality or the culture. Quantity rather than quality, reproduction rather than development, growth in 'grace' and morals rather than in self-knowledge or expression, is the implied aim. The Gospel, just as it is, is relevant in itself. Growth, however, is if anything from scratch and is total; this is not necessarily contrary to any 'orthodox' teaching, though how it came to seem so must be reviewed presently.

It is said that Jesus 'increased in wisdom and stature and in favour with God' (Luke 2.52), while Hebrews describes Christ as 'perfected in suffering' (Heb. 2.10). Christ is also associated with the historical and evolutionary process of society and world by being the historical and evolutionary process of society and world by being made the firstborn of creation, the head 'from whom the whole body ... makes bodily growth' (Eph. 4.16). These statements are usually passed over by the orthodox-minded, because the first two at any rate appear to support the old heresy of 'adoptionism', as opposed to Christ's pre-existence and trinitarian status. It is, in fact, possible, even likely, that before the first

Christians had fully considered the implications of their position and recalled the trinitarian possibilities within Jewish monotheism (the pre-existent wisdom of Proverbs and the 'Let us make man' of Genesis), they *did* regard Christ simply as 'chosen' and 'approved' by God, a being, like an angel more united with God in action (*homopraxis*) than in the substance (*homoousia*) which meant so little to Jewish thought. Nevertheless, quite apart from the fact that there is within the religious consciousness that which seems to demand incarnation and which certainly requires it if it is to avoid the harshness of pure monotheism, from the first the Christian position did imply a Trinity. Moreover, this can be rendered consistent with a doctrine of growth, *provided* (as in the original version of the Nicene Creed, which the Western branch of the church subsequently rejected) that both Christ and the Holy Spirit are seen as proceeding from the Father, not as in the Protestant and Catholic creed, where the Spirit proceeds from the Father *and the Son*. With some reason, Byzantine theologians claim that this appears contrary to the explicit statement of Jesus, 'I will send to you *from* the Father, the Spirit of Truth who proceeds from the Father' (John 15.26).

The philosophical repercussions of the difference are considerable. If Father and Son together are the cause, source and ordering principle of the Trinity, their persons become confused in that both are, or strictly speaking neither are, a 'Father', the initiating principle. The unity of the Trinity, which then becomes emphasized at the expense of diversity, ceases to be personal through the Father, and becomes impersonal through a shared essence, the personality of God, as in the philosophy of Aquinas, being reduced merely to the relationship in form between the members.

What this means is that God cannot really be known personally, that man is not a part of God and that individualism and freedom are not assured. Since obviously no one could know or be united with the divine essence, God must always be remote, unless one can know and exist through the divine *energies*, whose activity has been compromised in this treatment of procession. Since in this formulation Logos is part of the divine essence rather than the vehicle of manifestation in time and eternity which 'first-born of creation' implies, no one will exist through or have knowledge through this medium. Form, not Logos or Spirit, holds creation together. Because it in effect has a subordinate function, the Holy Spirit will not so much operate in the world, safeguard and stimulate individualism, as transmit knowledge of the impersonal principles or intellect of the divine being. Such a position is more or less that of Aquinas, and only in its dualism can his philosophy be said radically to differ from Hinduism, to whose concepts of God and man it is very close. Dom Aelred Graham argues that the mysticism of Aquinas, which permits only a negative description of God,[58] is what makes Catholicism (as opposed to Protestantism) with its theology of salvation a truly universal religion capable of dialogue. However, on the same grounds one could maintain that without the doctrine of procession, Christianity could neither assimilate the best of Hinduism, nor add to what is least attractive about that religion, like the world indifference to which it leads.

Critics of incarnational doctrine – and the contributors to *The Myth of God Incarnate*[59] wrote with an ecumenism of religions in mind – claim that incarnation excludes the possibility of moral dilemma and growth within Christ. This is quite a logical objection if one does not admit the procession of Christ from the Father, for then Christ would not be repeating in the temporal sphere his birth from the Father 'before all ages'. The Pauline statement that Christ was 'perfected in suffering' was obviously not intended to imply purification, but fulfilment and development within the existing human condition. The incarnation was not just a temporary change of status or an act of pity, but the acquisition of manhood, God becoming something he was not before. It would need to be seen as a continuation through a condensation of characteristics, of the manifestation of Logos which made creation possible, an expansion into the finite. Within Protestant theology, P. T. Forsyth's *The Nature and Person of Christ* would facilitate acceptance of this view.[60] Disposing of previous static concepts of God, Forsyth sees incarnation as the context of a dialectic of *kenosis* (self-emptying or self-reduction) and *plerosis* (self-fulfilment), maintaining that growth was assured by a kenotic ignorance at the human level of the divine incapability to sin. Divine attributes were not discarded but they were condensed; instead of being actual, they were made potential, so that Christ still struggles *like* a man, threatened by the question 'If you are the Son of God'.

As a point of cultural history, it could be remarked that Forsyth was a Celt, and in Celtic philosophy, which from Pelagius and Erigena to Duns Scotus and Bishop Berkeley is basically idealist, the emphasis is placed upon will and activity rather than intellect and knowledge, and a doctrine of divine expansion and self-reflection is implied.[61] On the whole, it seems true to say that if one were to locate the ultimate source of the modern crisis in religion and philosophy, it would date back to the mediaeval attempt, supremely represented by Aquinas, to fix and abstract Christian doctrine. Even the Protestant revolution never quite overthrew the values and categories of this system. Highly controversial among churchmen and philosophers during his lifetime, the fact that Aquinas was accepted by the church after it might need to be regarded as a sociological phenomenon, an assimilation of faith to the fixed feudalistic system.

The vision attributed to Aquinas before his death in which he perceived the insufficiency of his philosophy, which he described as 'straw', ought perhaps to have warned his admirers. Among the dangerous ideas of Aquinas we should notice here; (a) the identification of intellect and will in God and man; (b) the inferior or merely accidental status of individualism; and (c) the wholesale adoption of Aristotle's distinction of matter and form which leaves God as pure form and matter, separate from and over against an indeterminate potential substratum awaiting activation by form.

When intellect and will are regarded as aspects of the same thing, it follows that love, a function of the will, is not truly supreme in God and sin is not truly manifest in man, whose sins are merely ignorance, failures of the intellect. If the will is to be free, as Duns Scotus maintained in criticism of Aquinas, it must be autonomous and unrestricted. God must be free, and because he is being and goodness in himself, whatever he wills is inevitably good and cannot be subject to deliberation or self-imposed laws. As to man, if we assume that the ego is at all real, as Christianity emphasizes in contrast to most Asian philosophy, common sense is witness to what Socrates knew, that man often sees the right but chooses the wrong as an act of will; there is nothing to suggest that he would do right if he only knew and understood what was right.

In any case, in the philosophy of Aquinas, man becomes virtually a mechanical being; his individualism derives more from accidents of matter, or his position in space and time, than from any real difference of essence of character. Far from tending towards diversity and individualism, as we know from science that it does and gather from scripture that it should, creation tends only from the potential to the formal perfection in so far as that pertains to a class of beings which are similar in essence. Doing the will of God logically becomes a kind of calculated self-interest which God had determined. Scotus asked how, under Aquinas' system, if mind was merely the form of the body, immortality of the individual could be assured when the body dissolved. In the philosophy of Aquinas, only the Trinity possessed real individuality by virtue of the fact that God was *pure* form and a 'unique' *class* of being. By contrast, Scotus identified the individual with the real and maintained that there was always a difference between people and things because of a super-added soul matter, *haecitas*, which allowed all matter, primary and universal, to be related. This was a rather quaint solution to the problem, which could only really disappear with the Aristotelian orientations of Aquinas' system, and in Christian terms that was impossible. (The philosophy of Scotus, like earlier Christian philosophy, was influenced by Platonism, which still gave more room for Logos doctrine and individualism, though its dualism of matter and spirit threatened to distort Christian teaching.)

Worst of all, however, was Aquinas' portrayal of God's transcendence, which under Aristotelian influence became more or less total. God was pure form over against pure matter upon which he impresses forms attaining to varying degrees of perfection. This led to a thoroughly mediaeval, feudalistic and mechanical portrayal of God, not as continually involved with and sustaining and guiding the creation, but as the unmoved first mover of the sequence, a kind of emperor ruling a hierarchy of fixed forms tending towards fullness. Evil was easily tolerated and fate accepted since evil was not something active within the world, a canker in the bud, as is possible in a world described in terms of will and activity, but the merest absence of perfection or the perversion of a 'mutable good', a kind of minor mechanical failure in the machine.

Earlier philosophy from Clement of Alexandria onwards had a doctrine of Logos which applied not just to man but to nature, but if in this picture God has the omnipresence biblically attributed to him, it is hard to gather how it operates. Dualism seems inevitable, and as mentioned earlier, Berkeley would argue that matter so completely separate from God, even if we should see it as created *ex nihilo* (a principle which Aquinas conceded, though his philosophy speaks in Aristotelian terms of 'primal matter' as though it had always been there and was only moulded by God) would, in effect, constitute a rival God. Berkeley's immaterialism nonetheless found as little favour with religionists as with the sceptics for whom it was intended, basically because at the popular level, without an adequate doctrine of procession and the Spirit, the philosophy was likely to seem a form of pantheism, while dualism also appealed strongly to the Western mind and supported orthodox belief in the separation of sinners from God, heaven from hell. Teaching like that of the Byzantine church, which distinguished between abiding in God and merely existing through him, as is the case even with hell, was felt to be too subtle.

Matter remains a notable problem of Christian philosophy. Christianity uniquely affirms creation *ex nihilo*, denying Asian doctrines that the universe is the divine body or that it emanated from God. Emanation is used of the origins of the Son and the Spirit from the Father rather than that of man from God. At the same time many theologians affirm that in effect the world is a burning bush which is not consumed, that God 'fills' the world (Jer. 23.24), is everywhere, in the depths of the sea, in the depths of Sheol, etc. (Ps. 139.8,9). So if creation is not God's body, it is still one of his habitations. He is the life within living things, similar to life within the body, which although it does not immediately disintegrate upon death, is substantially dead without the 'soul' of its occupant.

Before it became clouded with Greek concepts of dualism, inert matter and form, the original Christian position would seem to have been closer to the Hindu one which postulates a 'gross matter' out of which the visible world and the body is made, and 'subtle matter' which pervades it. In Christian terminology this 'subtle matter' would be simply Spirit which, for purposes of conceptualization, we are obliged to think of as a kind of matter, or perhaps electricity, the white light of the mystics. This Spirit, however, is completely distinct from matter in the sense that while Spirit can affect matter and matter is dependent upon it for its continued existence, matter cannot affect Spirit; though they may be bound together like the skeins of one rope, gross matter has in no way evolved or emanated from Spirit, as would be maintained of divine subtle matter in Hinduism. One might say that the manifesting principle, Logos, offers its body *to* the matter which it has created to support it, but this does not mean that the *world* is the body of Logos. Only those committed to the life of the Spirit as such can be grafted on to the divine body. Hence for St Paul, while God's invisible nature is manifest in nature, Christ's *body* is composed of the church, those fully *in* the Spirit.

There are, however, places, moments and events, like the incarnation, when Spirit and matter are more closely harmonized in such a way that a general redemption of creation is envisaged. Here it is no longer a question of Spirit sustaining matter, but of matter acting as the vehicle for a manifestation of Spirit. It may be true, as even Asian philosophy admits, that the Tao that can be named is not the true Tao, that visible Spirit is not pure Spirit, but obviously the interplay of these forces is very difficult theologically and philosophically, and one is apt to confuse Spirit and matter, especially if one thinks of both in terms of energy, activity and light. When we 'look' at sub-atomic particles which in reality are not matter but dynamic *patterns*, and observe their creation *ex nihilo*, are we still observing matter, or in some respects Spirit, and if matter is not inert, but is ultimately energy anyway, is it not appropriate to call the universe the body of God?

Depending somewhat upon one's interpretation of creation, the position of Spirit's independence (as opposed to its identity or absence) is perhaps best judged against the psychological consequences which avoid two extremes of exploitation and indifference to which the others lead. The Christian doctrine of creation does seem to merit philosophical review. Creation out of *nothing* must seem dubious in that nothing outside an infinite God sheds doubt upon the infinity. The void itself would need to be created before creation began, and this may be the sense of the phrase. However, further doubt is cast on this formula by the Hebrew text which allegedly supports it. Genesis uses the Hebrew word *bārā'* for create, and the original meaning of this was 'to cut off'. The scriptural transcendence of God which the *ex nihilo* formula attempted to safeguard might be better affirmed as creation in terms of will and a completely new *kind* of life, as opposed to an emanation of Godhead. Such a creation could have been effected by separation and transformation of the divine energy into something else. The Hindu philosophy of Shamkara claims that Brahman hurled out *shakti* (energy) which, once separated from the divine consciousness, was blind energy still requiring to be moulded. This did not diminish Brahman, because where energy is infinite, one may deduct anything and the remainder is still infinite. If this is the proper intuition, in Christian terms it would tend to mean that matter, though not the *body* of God, was still so in a secondary sense; it is his 'flesh', his symbolic body, as the philosophy of Erigena maintained for different reasons. It also raises the question whether as *energy*, it could be eternal, something possibly suggested by the idea found in Christian cosmology that at the end of the world the elements are dissolved in fervent heat (return to the original energy?) and that God will create a new heaven and a new *earth*, as though material existence continues for souls unable to live in some seventh heaven, where the divine light is the only light. Whether the Christian 'end of the world' would be seen as applying to the certain death of this solar system and galaxy, or of the entire universe, is open to question theologically and scientifically, for the vastness and expansion of the universe possibly indicates its endlessness. The nature and meaning of anti-matter is crucial here.

Altogether, it seems that Christian cosmology should be seen as dealing with three rather than two levels of existence: 1. God in himself, the Trinity; 2. God manifest, Logos, the possibility of creation and the 'body of God'; 3. the material plane *pervaded* by God, the 'symbolic' body of God whose ultimate operations are obviously very akin to that of Spirit which sustains and works upon it. In terms of such a cosmology, the type of yogic mysticism which opens the pineal gland, sees white light and calls it 'God' or *Brahman* would have to be regarded as confusing the receptacle of the Spirit, the energetic substratum of the material, with Spirit in itself, and spiritual faculties of response with divine energy.

This, however, cannot always be considered worse than doctrines like the Western, which by limiting or abstracting the divine presence to the same degree that Asian doctrine places it everywhere, encourages an attitude of imperialism towards both the personal and material. This is the exact opposite of the Hindu approach which, by bringing the divine too close, finishes by denying persons and the material much significance *in themselves*. The separation of mind and matter introduced by Aquinas could only lead to Cartesian dualism and modern evolutionism. Where God and man do not co-operate, man imposes on nature, and as Seyyed Hossein Nasr indicates, when man becomes more materialistic, change, diversity and development in nature become confused with a metaphysically and scientifically controversial theory of evolution.[62] Morality and human progress – if it *is* progress, for there is much regression – becomes confused with the physical and psychological process of 'mutation' hypothesized but never proved by evolutionists. As Theodore Roszak says, if increasing numbers of people fall under the spell of the scientifically and philosophically unsound evolutionist theory of Teilhard, it is only because Western man has created such an appalling cultural disjuncture for himself that he wrongly believes that only a mutation could do something about it.[63]

As a determined biological operation, a spiritualization of matter into a consciousness universally converging upon a Christ Omega point, the fusion of the individual with God, Teilhard's kingdom of heaven may be considered a Western Catholic solution to the problem raised by Aquinas. However, it is not necessarily in harmony with the Bible or science, satisfactory to human liberty or dynamic in relation to Asian thought, except perhaps from some sentimental universalist standpoint. The idea that creation is fixed and that God withdrew from it (or, in the modern version, must force its evolution) was never attested by Christian doctrine, and any impression that it was results mainly from the scholastic emphasis on God as prime mover who set out natural laws, the expression of his intellect to do his work. This assumption was easily made on the Aristotelian presupposition, influenced by geometry, that since much of the Jewish law was not the outcome of a divine *way* of things, but an absolute impersonal law, God was the God of impersonal laws, not of creation and freedom in this world.

Today, with the advance of knowledge in science and psychology, a great movement outwards and inwards in awareness has occurred which requires a science of the levels of reality, of the micro-, macro- and meta-spheres. This latter sphere is the one against which Christianity with its emphasis on time is defined. Here it has become apparent how far 'fundamental' laws possess relative force and are dependent upon the operation of the larger reality, which must be understood holistically. We are aware that at least at the level of matter-energy, creation could be considered continuous and *ex nihilo* in the sense that new entities are formed which possess no pre-existing parts in the normal manner,[64] and that in the light of findings like the uncertainty principle, any determination of the world now seems to lie in the sphere of a predictable *probability* of events rather than a predictable *certainty*. Matter is not fixed but 'free'; not anarchically free (an atom of a certain class will remain of that class), but free to do many things which cannot be predicted.

Realization of the inter-connectedness of things, the dependence of the earth and solar system for its balance upon even distant galaxies, has reopened many closed questions, like astrology. Everything is relevant. Science is expanding horizons and awareness, is coming to recognize the value of intuition. Only religion, perhaps especially 'orthodox' Christianity, appears to remain closed, with the consequence that some persons, like Fritjof Capra,[65] have gone controversially far in portraying the universe in terms of the dance of creation and dissolution mystically attributed to Shiva, and proposed that modern science should be reviewed in the light of Eastern mysticism. But with its easy acceptance of evil through the union of opposites and its negation of individualism this approach offers an austere vision which would undermine the very real achievements of the West. As a corrective to it, and offering a more human if equally intellectualized interpretation, Harold Schilling's *The New Consciousness in Science and Religion*[66] reviews the same discoveries in the light of process theology, which is still largely ignored. It is 'ignored' because, as Hossein Nasr recognized, ever since theologians assumed that there were no metaphysical principles in the Bible which could relate to science, they have buried themselves in an existential religion which relates neither to nature nor to the new consciousness which it furthers only by 'demythologization'.[67]

In Schilling's interpretation there is only transformation and divine direction. We are not dealing with a God who has become a ruler to subjects in contrast to the equality and participation of the Trinity; he appears as king and judge only to those who resist the essentially free force that his being represents. In the New Testament Christ is the one by whom, in whom and for whom creation exists (Col. 1.15), the one who is reconciling the world to himself, a world which is groaning and travailing to bring forth the new.[68] This position is less evolutionary than transformative and on-going; there is no Omega point of maximum development, only the promise of 'a new heaven and a new earth', in the context of a life where new creation can already be experienced. St Paul states that we should 'in *everything* give thanks' and that '*everything* works together for good for those who love God'. This view takes life and nature holistically; one cannot overcome evil and misfortune by simply hoping for the good and fleeing from the bad. The *way* of things is good, not because evil is absent but because evil can always be transformed for those who work, like God, from things as a whole. It is out of the whole pattern that God moulds new possibilities and brings about good. These may be spiritual affirmations, but they harmonize with what is now observed of nature, the effluence whereby it produces the new, abundance and variety, and also its 'morality', since this happens in large measure through mutual aid, symbiotic co-operation. Nature changes for good even against man's destructive work upon it, yet at the same time it is largely manageable and predictable by man. By every implication the man-nature relationship should be co-operation and not hostility.

With such considerations in mind, Schilling thus proposes that we describe God as 'source, guide and goal' of all that is, a 'living' God, participating in the world.[69] Though he is not the sole agent of creation, it is still through him that all comes to pass. He is ultimate sufficient cause, turning possibility into actuality; he is also the guide and end, the continuing source of nature's existence and development. God offers a lure, a persuasion, acts as the principle of concretion, is both the 'control' and 'efficacy' of occasions. The flow of events is produced by a combination of efficacies and causative drives arising from the interaction of two subjective aims, God's and nature's (in the sense of general pattern, not determination) which give ultimate and proximate causes to affairs.

I need not say more, since process theology, which is related to the revolutionary but obscure philosophy of Whitehead, gets very complicated and would seem unlikely ever to achieve much popularity. It is, however, noteworthy as an important reinstatement of the belief in divine immanence, though I believe that this aspect of Christian doctrine and the mechanics of transformation could be more satisfactorily expressed in Asian categories, as we shall see. Concepts like immanence and divine indwelling seem almost impossible for Western man to realize philosophically or practically, hence even process theology has fallen into the old Western either/or as opposed to the Asian both/and, heretically making God entirely immanent and in no way transcendent. It offers a form of pantheism or panentheism, so that Schilling describes God as the 'infinitely relative',[70] and Edward Schillebeeckx describes God as no longer 'wholly Other' but 'wholly new', always beyond us and different, and thus never – essentially – knowable.[71] Christ becomes identified with a natural *principle* called cosmic Christ, though this is not the cosmic Christ in any trinitarian sense. While in this way the orthodox Trinity is discarded, there is insufficient recognition of the contrast of finite and infinite which is *basic* to religious feeling, even to Hinduism with its *atman* and *Brahman*. Even in its weakest formulations, trinitarian dogma allows this essential religious distinction.

It will, however, be objected that there is little point in mentioning orthodoxy when the ideas considered, however reasonable in the abstract, would violate orthodoxy in practice. Others will also argue that there is no explicit sanction for such ideas in terms of revelation, and that so serious an issue might require more than the deductions or obscure texts used to support it. These objections can be challenged, perhaps especially the second charge. It is true that some orthodox assumptions about inspiration, personality and ethics would undergo modification, but more as a result of regarding them in a different light than through cancelling them out in the rationalist manner of theological liberalism. I shall return to this point in the final chapter. As for revelation, it can be argued that in so far as a revolution of consciousness can be a matter of revelation, it is anticipated in the Bible, where it can be found as an aspect of messianism.

Jews and Christians all have their different ways of interpreting the times of the Messiah foretold by prophets like Micah and Zechariah. For Jews, prophecies like 'the law shall go out of Zion . . .' refer to future events, while Christians see statements like 'I will write a new law in their hearts' as fulfilled in their faith; yet others postulate an earthly millennial kingdom to follow the age of the church. It is not my purpose to argue the interpretation of these texts in terms of dispensational ages, but two points should be noted. First, the prophecies of a 'golden age' can never be taken as other than forecasts. They can be accepted or rejected at will; but unlike much 'prophecy', which was a forthtelling, they bore an exclusively future reference and aimed to supply a glimpse of society and religion different from the existing society and religion, whose law was considered an absolute. If we keep that in mind, among these forecasts we shall find at least one which cannot be considered as fulfilled in any way, Jewish or Christian, yet which is so concrete that it cannot be symbolized away, like the ideal temple of Ezekiel, or reasonably referred to some heavenly state (by the time of the prophet concerned the Jews had a developed notion of heaven, and much of the prophet's vision takes place there, so that what he forecast, he expected to be realized on earth). The prophecy in question is from Zechariah 14.20f.

And on that day shall be inscribed on the bells of the horses 'Holy to the Lord', and the pots in the house of the Lord shall be as bowls before the altar, and every post in Jerusalem and Judah shall be sacred to the Lord of hosts . . .'

The situation envisaged is surely one in which a revolution of consciousness has occurred and a new sense of the holy has dawned such as neither Judaism nor Christianity has ever realized, nor really could, given the present dualistic bias of their thought. The psychological mechanics of the realization (though not the content, which refers to the sacred and the personal in a way that Zen would not acknowledge) are Zen-like and similar to the thought contained in 'before Enlightenment, chopping wood and carrying water; after Enlightenment, chopping wood and carrying water'. The world itself has not changed, but is seen beneath a different light; in the prophetic instance the ordinary has become holy, activity ritualized, and religion has become of the heart. This is not, for example, how Catholics at this moment would care to think of the distinction they draw between the altar and the rest of the world. The original Jewish idea of the holy depended upon a sense of distance and unholiness which would suggest pure dualism to the ordinary mind, even though, as we have seen, this was not positively affirmed even in the Old Testament. It is not enough to dismiss this prophecy by claiming that it represents a sublime situation which God has brought or will bring about in individuals. It is total, and at any such time as it were to occur, it could not simply be an individual spiritual event; in order for it to be understood and lived up to at all, a complete philosophical reorientation would be required.

Here, then, from within the Bible comes the possibility of what may be called an 'Aquarian' gospel for the new age,[72] which at the same time is a prescription for change which need not, perhaps cannot, be produced by revelation. It can hardly be objectively and personally revealed, and in so far as it has been suggested in Logos doctrine, it could not be fully assimilated to consciousness before the present. For one thing, it involves recognition that Christ is not just the person of Christian doctrine or the impersonal principle of divine beings in Asian mysticism, but both; someone and something seen through everything. Paradoxical though it may seem, the church in Asia could not avoid developing this aspect of doctrine, if only to keep intact the fundamental doctrine of Christ's person, so foreign to Asian thought. The Jesus people, who even now are trying to enter Asia, not only pose a danger of confusing devotion to Christ with a Western personality cult, but by over-emphasizing the person, they compromise the divinity in terms of the *avatar, bodhisattva* figure, which Asians commonly set up *against Brahman* or the void.

The letter from the Bali missionary which I mentioned earlier struck me as being intelligently and succinctly representative, and makes this point quite clearly. It shows how the expectation is always that when problems of communication arise, one need only go to Jesus; the fact that God has apparently not given answers to failing missions, and that he is far from giving an automatic answer to the prayers of even the most devout, is never taken as a challenge to think for oneself or to see another aspect of God. It is always assumed that God will eventually reply or tell someone else, the converts if not the missionary, and that when he does reply he will inform his people what to *do*. It is assumed that there is no realization beyond the most conventional (awareness of his goodness, his power) to work upon. Thus:

The truths (Christ) presented and elaborated were to be contextualized by us, interpreted into action which is appropriate to time and place . . . (indigenization) calls for a sovereign move of God by his Spirit, for which we should all pray. What is needed is a renewal of the Spirit. . . . From this central point changes emanate and a growing impatience is evidenced with extraneous meaningless patterns [I am not clear what this means and hope the correspondent did not refer to the ceremoniousness of Asian life and the convolutions of Asian art.] This is not a censure on you for tackling the problem from outside. If anything, it would be a censure upon leaders. Truly Christ-centred spiritual men, sensitive to the Holy Spirit, should be trying to tackle it from the inside. . . . I long to see an outpouring of the Holy Spirit upon a group of Balinese who have no Christian patterns yet taught them, who by direction of the Spirit and the Word might set up their own ways. . . . Why should we teach them?

In reply I answered:

I think (the carnal approach) is at any rate sometimes legitimate (for religious people). Even St Paul talks of regarding Christ from the human view first as the necessary introduction to the spiritual. . . . Guidance is an awesome subject. There are many pitfalls even for the best, and for this reason I feel that you may be asking too much of people to expect that conversion and a meeting with Christ would resolve all these cultural problems. It is for us with Christian history behind us to help direct and think for them as well. If God really exists through all things, he must speak both directly and/or through scriptures, events, friends, art, and is not obliged to speak to us under any one form, though from weakness we might like to think so (many have been left in darkness, etc.). So will you tell me that the poor weak converts of Bali, raised to every ceremony, are to have no alternative ceremonies, no 'aids', no customs, are not to be allowed the spirit of litany with which even the Western church has helped the weak overcome the horror of silence, and the monologue in the dark. When God does not speak from a particular place, the 'out there' of the imagination, it may be necessary to find him everywhere and anywhere, God within us, God among us. I think that an Asian theology, less likely to sunder sacred and profane, would clarify this principle. Besides, it is elaboration, not simplification, which is typically Asian, and I think it is wrong to believe that all the Asian church needs to do is to see and meet Jesus. . . . It must be freed to discover and show him through everything and not just through the medium of that emphasis on personality and conversation which seems in itself a limited, rather Western view of Jesus. Jesus also 'fills the heavens and the earth', and like St John, if we simply assume that we can lie on his breast and talk, we may come up against the shock with which Revelation opens, that he is also a blinding light and a consuming fire, not just a 'friend'.

So it is, I believe, an aspect of any Christian movement in Bali that it should involve an aesthetic flowering, a 'remythologization' of the world of denied gods with a whole world of the Spirit and angels. . . .

It must be admitted that the church in Bali, or the prospect of a church in Bali (most Christians on the island are Chinese), is a subject which it is especially hard to review dispassionately, since it involves such impossible alternatives. The one certain fact is the exceptional beauty, homogeneity and continuity of the highly artistic culture and life-style of Bali within a setting of natural beauty. It is something which most people would wish to see preserved at almost any cost. The culture is threatened by Westernization and has long considered itself threatened by Westernizing Christianity. Aesthetically it certainly is by the plainness of Dutch Reformism and evangelical dullness; to observe a church in all its stark Protestant functionalism cannot but seem a scandal in a land where practically every door is an object of carved beauty. Also threatened is the Balinese sense of harmony with nature, moon and the stars, which the West has lost and could well rediscover. The celebration of full moon in Bali, which is particularly impressive, is heralded in the afternoon by an incredibly rapid transformation of the fields into seas of billowing white streamers, while down every road and pathway the women, bedecked with garlands and in bright dresses, come bearing on their heads tiers of baskets filled with temple offerings.

But all is not sweetness and light. By any standards the society is seriously deficient in basic virtues, like honesty, reliability and tolerance, and it is in certain respects petrified and held in thrall by a sinister undercurrent of superstition and black magic which no one who spends sufficient time there can fail to notice. Liquidation of rivals and enemies with assistance from black magic, or else bribery with the appropriate authorities, is a frighteningly regular occurrence. So is a variety of cruelty to animals, and pretty flower-strewing ceremonies to placate evil spirits, a practice which ensures the tiresome deceitfulness and moral cowardice of so many of the inhabitants. Altogether, local imagination is curiously black. The art is frequently lurid, and certain of the exhibits in the art gallery at Ubud, the artists' colony, with their pictures of Krishna devouring souls, or snake gods crushing victims, are among the most sickening I hope to see. I was assured that they reflected local feeling authentically and were in no wise the product of drug hallucinations, as I had imagined; and in view of the rather degrading forms of worship, like that of the snake at the beautiful rock temple of Tanah Lot, this must be the case.

So it is that this is no land of the noble savage; if anything, it is nearer to the classic missionary concept of 'heathen darkness'. Christian converts, though possibly encouraged to greater dissociation from the culture that is strictly necessary, stand in serious danger of family and tribal disownment and even persecution, and so intolerant is the atmosphere of the island that Christians other than the Chinese and town-dwellers are practically compelled to live in a ghetto region at the far west of the island. Thus, one can neither wholly accept nor reject Bali society, and the imagination required of church and missionaries is of the very highest. So I should regard it as quite a test case for the church in Asia.

IV

Keeping briefly at the practical level, we may turn to the Korean exception which proves the evangelical rule. In excess of four million of South Korea's thirty-one million people are of Christian affiliation, and the Protestant majority among these shows a ten per cent annual increase in their membership. The first feature to notice about this church is that originally Korean Christians chose Christianity and even went in search of it. In 1777, a group of Korean scholars studied Ricci's apologies for Christian religion and, duly impressed, sent one of their number to Pekin for further information. This scholar, Lee Seung Run, brought back relevant books, and a Catholic group was formed on a lay basis. Though ten years later, when there were four thousand Christians, the Catholic church, alarmed at this liberty, intervened in the person of a Chinese priest, Chou Wen-mo, to establish the faith on formal lines, this unique venture automatically dissociated Christianity from the common charge that it was an intrinsically foreign religion introduced by foreigners and politically suspect people. Catholicism in Korea would be dealt a blow from which it has never quite recovered by the persecution of 1864, but the independent nationalist bias of Korean Christianity would also be a feature of Protestantism which entered upon the opening of the Hermit Kingdom to the world in 1885. Not least responsible for this was the influence of the former China missionary, Dr John Nevius, who had been considered a bit of a maverick (because of an excessive concern with Chinese demonology) rather than the far-sighted person he was. The famous 'Nevius method' adopted by churches after 1890 involved a system of self-support, self-government and self-propagation by local people; also, churches were to be built in local style, a principle usually ignored for lack of missionary encouragement, but a step forward. The main result of Nevius' influence was obviously to render the independently-minded people largely independent of missionaries, at any rate until the Korean War and American influence. The national image of the church was further enhanced when under the Japanese occupation (starting in 1906) it was prominent in resistance to Japanese attempts to foist state Shinto upon the conquered population.

If Korean Christianity is nationalistic, it is because Korea has always been caught between the political and cultural crossfire of China and Japan, knowing both the meaning of dependence and borrowing, of independence and initiative. Korea has never felt ashamed of borrowing and has even affirmed its independence in so doing. The acceptance of Christianity appears to be an instance of this. As regards the kind of revivalist religion which took root, it has to be born in mind that as East Asians go, Koreans must be seen as a rather inspirational people, if not actually a religious one. Were the fact not known, it might be deduced from the 'sincere' as opposed to merely opulent quality of its Buddhist art, in contrast to many of its Chinese models. Furthermore, the exceptionally free and inventive quality of some Korean dance recalls the inspirational trend in the culture which derives from the strong legacy of Shamanism. Whereas in China Confucianist rationalism and Buddhism had tended to modify these more 'primitive' religious urges, in Korea they were preserved. The country, though witness to a developed and beautiful civilization, has nonetheless been quite culturally informal in contrast to its neighbours, for whom its people were always 'the country cousins'. This being the case, prayer-power and revivalism of the Welsh or New England variety, entailing hours and even nights of fervent religious activity, has never appeared the oddity or burden it could seem elsewhere in Asia, in cultures more formal or less intense.

Having said this, I do not think that churches and missions should assume from these facts that what exists or has existed necessarily represents the best possible item. Furthermore, René Monod's *The Korean Revival* (which treats of the revival, starting in 1906, under the Japanese invasion and the more recent one dating from the Korean war) could prove misleading on several counts.[73] For a start, it describes traditional Korean life as 'primitive', which is far from the case, for the country even had the first printing press in the world, before England and Germany. Observing that revival is now hitting the Third World rather than the West (Uganda 1929, Formosa 1945, Indonesia 1965), the book confuses depth of religious fervour with Christian growth, of which it even seems to make that the precondition. This is not at all evident; Indonesia and Taiwan are very far from showing a Christianized society or an indigenized church today. Worst of all, like too much American religious literature dealing with overseas areas, it reads like a tract against world communism and even gets a word in for the need to have Americans in Vietnam. Obviously, Christianity has its controversy with the Communism which has usually opposed it and denied it basic rights, but one can question how much the churches either helped their reputations or fulfilled their possible duties towards Communist populations by adopting this line of protest. National churches have to be adjusted to live with the circumstances in which they found themselves, and cannot be turned into satellites of the US, constantly looking to it for protection or being used by it in less than religious political arguments. Under the Carter administration and its plans for troop withdrawal, the South Korean church, for all its history of national independence, has been wailing like a host of lost Americans. This lesson should have been learnt from the Formosa story, in which American Christians lobbied for Chiang Kai Shek and his mostly greedy, corrupt henchmen (especially over American aid), doing so because many Nationalist leaders were nominally Christian. This unfortunate partisanship only brought the church into disrepute, and made things more difficult for those under Communist rule.

For the critically-minded, there are chinks in the armour of this 'ideal' Korean church. I would not want to minimize the notable achievements of the church in education and medicine, but as often happens with churches of a revivalist tendency, common social justice gives way to religiosity, denominationalism to the essentials of the faith. Remarkably, there are eighty Protestant theological colleges, while – I am told – lepers still lie around the streets in a country with a poorly developed sense of welfare and democracy. Many Christians feel that those of their number who have rallied to the support of the imprisoned dissident Kim Dae Jung are quite wrong to do so. Furthermore, it must be realized that although the church is traditionally independent, it is not sufficiently indigenized. The failure to achieve a truly indigenized church within so nationalistic a society is almost certainly the cause of the success of so many quasi-Christian sects, most notably the now famous syncretistic 'Unity' religion of the Rev. Moon. Schechter's *The New Face of Buddha* mentions a syncretistic tendency which has left some Catholics combining Christian funeral rites with offerings to ancestors on Buddhist altars.[74] One of the reasons for the brake upon the indigenizing programme can be found in the economic hardships, especially during the 1920s and following the Korean war, which, by upsetting the self-supporting scheme, tended to throw the church back on missionary influence and foreign support, especially American. It has never quite escaped from this, as is clear from the massive Billy Graham Crusade of 1973 and its follow-up.

Not everyone can be satisfied with a fundamentalism divorced from culture and philosophy, nor is the liberal rationalistic trend, espoused by a minority, a real solution to the longings of the essentially imaginative Korean soul. As early as 1936, the conservative *Journal of Theological Instruction* maintained that the Korean theological task was to help realize an age of the Spirit which could free Christianity from enslavement to institutions as in the Catholic tradition and to the book as in Protestant history. The otherwise conservative religious journalist Kim Jae Jun has deplored the fundamentalist contempt for Korean history and tradition, and one of the leading branches of Korean theology is at present concerned precisely with Koreanology, belatedly relating Christianity to cultural and religious insights of the past. As an example of this new concern, I could mention a devout Christian Korean I met in Hong Kong who had taken very successfully to treating and often curing supposedly incurable patients by acupressure and certain ancient remedies, in the belief he had a vocation to do this following his own cure from an illness for which

Western medicine could do nothing. He personally believed that the church had been wrong to ignore all Asian beliefs, like the Yin Yang philosophy, with its emphasis on the whole man, on which his treatment is based, and he believes that they could be reviewed in a Christian light. My personal conviction is that they *must* be. I shall turn to this presently.

In one plan for a book on Christianity and world religions which I abandoned in favour of the present work with its emphasis on missions, I had outlined ideas under the headings:

> India: religion as mysticism
> China: religion as politics
> Japan: religion as aesthetics

I still believe that these generalizations are valid, but if one were to add a section on Korea, it would need to be on religion as religion, or religion as magical power. The churches cannot afford to overlook such associations, and have done so at their peril, or at least severe disadvantage. For example, as far as China is concerned, there has been no sect or religion, including Buddhism, which has not at some time had a political twist, since the fundamental question of Chinese philosophy has not been an abstract one, as in the West, but how to achieve the best possible society. Religion always carries a solution to the social problem, even if only the *laissez-faire* one of Taoism. Undoubtedly, the kind of Christian religion the Chinese most wanted and needed was a socially aware one on the lines of the historic Moist philosophy, once the rival of Confucianism and the doctrine closest to Christianity in spirit. As it was, missionary Christianity, with its exclusive emphasis on soul, only backed up the tottering system of popular Confucianism. As the leading layman, L. H. Lee, complained in 1948, 'There has never been a clearly defined theory, practice or experiment by and for Chinese Christians as to what a more abundant life, the brotherhood of man or the kingdom of God would mean.'[75] Chinese Christians, he considered, might make better parents or children, but not new men of the world, after St Paul's example, or new citizens of his country. Without this change, Lee protested, there could be no new China, for man realizes salvation as much in relation to society as to his soul. It would be foolish if conservatives were to dismiss such a judgment as mere liberalism and compare it with the social gospel in the West. It must be evident to any observer that as Christians, the majority of Chinese

Christians still lack the civic sense which was so shockingly absent under Confucianism; Lee's protest is valid for the simple reason that, given Chinese thought, the Christian notion of salvation would have to be consciously worked out in family or social terms if it were not to be a refined Confucianism or form of Western individualism.

Because of its incurable rationalism and less than purely Christian dualism, in the West life is life and religion is religion, the affair of the worshipping congregation. It is sacrament, Bible reading or prayer meeting, and because it is, Christians feel an affinity for the revivalist and rather conventionally pious Korean church. But while sacrament, Bible-reading and prayer could never be ignored or discarded, the assumptions that the holiest persons are always necessarily those most involved in such activities, or that such activities are the exclusive expression of faith, are not entirely justified. With these assumptions, the church cannot hope to get far in an Asia where everyone chooses their own way, like the Hindu way of *yoga* or devotional *bhakti*, or good works, or intellect; nor can it relate to a way of worship in which some are chanting while others are meditating. The individualistic West expresses its devotion corporately, the 'impersonal' East more individually by offering the expression of a temperament or talent; this being the case, if the church of Japan or Bali wants to go (and appears able to go) the way of aesthetics and dance, it would not seem to be the duty of any church to stand in the way by arguing that the Koreans like church groups.

In conclusion, we may return to the theme of Koreanology and the opinion of the doctor that Yin Yang theory needed to be reviewed in a Christian light. The average missionary would tend to consider the wish for such a harmonization a luxury or a dangerous extravagance. From almost any other informed standpoint, it is an imperative. Indian mysticism raises the problem of monism, the nature of the unity of things and human identity within it, but apart from Shivaism, its mysticism tends to emphasize voidness and stillness, and the fundamental contrast in its metaphysics is between Being and Non-Being, not action and inaction. In the modern exchange of the symmetrical for the asymmetrical worldview and ideas of substance and form for energy and motion, perhaps Taoism and Zen with their dynamism and paradoxes exhibit most harmony with modern science, some of whose truth can only be intuited. 'The stillness in stillness is not the real stillness. Only when there is stillness in movement can the spiritual rhythm appear which pervades heaven and earth,' and 'The this is also the that, the that is also the this' are the kinds of picturesque statements in which the ineffability of some modern knowledge could well be expressed. Moreover, in so far as some of the practices and assumptions of Yin Yang were incorporated into Taoist yoga and alchemy, it is also relevant to issues of modern psychology and the Jungian theory of individuation. Despite its incomplete, experimental nature, Jung's interpretation of Christian symbolism and world mysticism has become common dogma to most groups of the Aquarian frontier and most intellectual elites, except the French, who prefer rational and socialist explanations of religion, and ecclesiastical circles, which have a remarkable blind spot where the implications of Jung's work for theology and missions are concerned. Those few clergy, like Morton Kelsey and Dr Leslie Weatherhead, who study it, appear to find it either Christian or useful to Christian therapy.[76]

Jung's developing theory of individuation drew added confirmation from alchemy and *The Secret of the Golden Flower*, a text describing the yoga of a Taoist sect in which he saw manifested and controlled the processes of the psyche which he had observed in the dreams of patients, or creative and spiritual people, working their way towards wholeness. In such essays as *Christ a Symbol of the Self*[77] and *The Answer to Job*,[78] Jung threw out a revolutionary challenge to Christianity, arguably the old gnostic challenge, that God is not necessarily good and redemption is not a dualistic deliverance from evil to perfect good, but the difficult achievement of wholeness (whose advent is heralded by dreams of drawings of an Asian, mandala-like nature) through a harnessing of the two forces popularly regarded as good and evil. Whether it is the golden flower or the philosopher's stone, whether it is the Taoist adept releasing his higher self from matter, or the alchemist producing gold from base metal, the essential idea is the same. The psyche insistently seeks and finds the deity in matter, especially in ages of decline when the gods seem remote. Thus, in the gnostic vein of myth, the Light Man, an aspect of deity, who wandered in the *pleroma*, was tempted to earth by evil matter (the creation of a bad god), where he shattered into pieces. Here below, he must be released by a redeemer, or the more superior kind of individual within whom the shattered deity dwells, and in releasing the light, the individual can redeem himself, is himself the redeemer.

A traumatic vision experienced in youth and the dreams of his Christian patients convinced Jung that God includes everything, and whatever the conscious may assent to intellectually, the unconscious, as it works towards harmony, corrects, and thus Christ appears in situations or in disguises, like the green gold flesh of the alchemist's vision, which assimilate to his good and spiritual side the dark and earthy side which is lacking in the conventional picture. Christ, like Buddha, by his very humanity and also by his perfection, does not necessarily suffice the psyche as the hidden deity or the Anthropos figure of world myth who, like the Light Man, exists throughout nature.[79] I shall return to Jung and the natural gnosticism of the psyche presently.

Yin Yang theory is popularly associated with Taoism, but it predated it and was the product of the sage Fu Hsi (800 BC?) and the centuries preceding Confucius and Lao Tzu. Taoist mysticism sought basically to transcend the endless process of becoming, being and passing away which Fu Hsi demonstrated. Since the Taoist philosophy of Lao Tzu was reacting against a spectacle of war and rigid patriarchy, it drew upon earlier matriarchal religion and posited a womb-void as source, commending a kind of gentle woman power as the best way to survive in a troubled age. It is questionable to what extent Fu Hsi would have been satisfied with this, for his system, while making for the equality of opposites in the sense of their necessity to the whole, evinces a certain preference for the Yang 'positive' principle, and when worked out in physical and psychological terms, the prejudice appears not without all justification.

In Yin Yang theory, everything which exists and occurs is theoretically divisible between the polarities of positive and negative, masculine and feminine. The male is positive, active, bright, dry, good; the female negative, passive, dark, wet, cold, bad. Day is Yang, night is Yin, fire is Yang, water is Yin, and then, by extension, centripetal motion (movement to the centre) is masculine, centrifugal motion (movement away) is feminine; downward (concentrative) movement is Yang, upwards (dispersal) is Yin. Nothing is absolutely one or the other principle; there is always a little of each in everything. Constant change is in process, like that which takes the world from night to day, summer to winter.

In contrast to Western thought and even to much Indian thought, which has a clear view of substance, things are differentiated not by *essence* or form but by motion, by the way they *act*. There are two important consequences: nothing has any final identity – a common conclusion about things in Asian thought – and everything is part of a whole. This contrasts with the Western system, in which everything is an individual entity and matter is differentiated from the immaterial and from mind.

It was stated earlier that what is required today is a new science of the levels of reality. The intuition of Western philosophy that things do possess an identity, that they belong to a class and possess some formative principle (like the carbon molecule which always remains a carbon molecule whatever it 'chooses' to do), was not wrong; yet at the same time the Asian intuition that the universe is ceaselessly moving and changing is also valid and, depending on one's view, perhaps more fundamental: in the spiralling patterns of Yin Yang and of altering density the universe moves from matter (Yang) into energy (Yin), energy into matter. While the theory of no identity can be questioned (sociologically there is something very Asian in a vision of the world as a factory of busyness, packed with anonymous, disposable workers), more significant is the Asian understanding of the essential interrelatedness of things in the physical realm and the union of opposites there and in the operation of the psyche. In these realms, Yin Yang theory can no longer be ignored. Certainly it cannot be dismissed as superstition, as it has been by China missionaries since Hudson Taylor, who brought back T'ai Chi T'us (the disc diagram of the Supreme Ultimate with its double helix formation) as souvenirs to scandalize eager audiences.

Yin Yang theory was always regarded as indispensable for Asian knowledge in connection with acupuncture, acupressure, judo, yoga and macrobiotic diet, which aims to maintain health and cure illness by adjustments to the chemical balance of the body as it understands it. The Asian doctor, unlike the Western, would not consent to those operations and drug remedies which treat a part of the body in isolation and run the danger of side effects, or treat the symptom rather that the cause, which is frequently tension, poor exercise, or diet. The nerve 'meridians' postulated by Yin Yang theory run right through the body, so that a headache, for instance, might be cured through the fingers.

Acupuncture and acupressure have been proved to work in many cases, though the precise mechanics of their working is still uncertain. Macrobiotic diet, the staple fare of the long-lived Zen monks, which is believed to immunize against most ailments and is alleged to cure such incurable diseases as diabetes, VD and simple schizophrenia, has been explained by research. Yang foods have been discovered to be those high in sodium (Na), Yin foods those high in potassium (K). The proper proportion of Yin to Yang in diet should be 5 to 1, but in many foods, mostly the sugary, watery or very hot ones, the proportion is very much higher, as in the orange (570 to 1) or the potato (512 to 1). Disease and vulnerability to disease have a special association with constitutions and diets too high in Yin, and a more Yang diet (i.e., mainly cereal with some fish and fowl) is advocated to restore a healthy balance, though naturally a diet too high in flesh and Yang can in turn produce disorders and the fierceness noted in some men.

Obviously the principles involved are not entirely foreign to the West, though in macrobiotics and Asian medicine they receive their fullest exposition. Snake bites are cured by snake venom; immunization against disease is effected by injections of the dead virus. Altogether, the basic patterns of physical reality to which, today, the Taoist and Shinto intuitions can be seen to relate, are (a) the positive and negative polarization of energy in magnetism and electricity; (b) the function of the spiral helix in movement and emergence, and the ultimate structure of things from genes to galaxies; and (c) as regards matter, the tendency of these asymmetrical polarities to be involved in a mirroring activity at their centre giving rise to the phenomenon of enantiomorphism, which is represented by the double helix of the Taoist symbol.

This introduces us to the paradox in respect of asymmetrical (as opposed to symmetrical) objects of complete distinctness within identical pairs (like the sameness yet non-transposability of left and right hands), a paradox which assumes importance in dealing with ultimate problems like matter and anti-matter and the ability of the universe to include the opposites.

Today, as far as Christianity is concerned, the difficulty with Taoist philosophy arises over the scope of its doctrine of inclusion, the way in which, for example, its principles are applied to the moral sphere and the ultimates of life and death. The result is that good and evil are declared *relative*, being born and dying purely *natural*. To be appreciated, happiness is assumed to require sadness, and beauty to require ugliness – that is, if 'appreciation' is indeed of value, since the philosophy strictly aims at transcending the relative world and entering the formless womb-void of Tao, which is everything: good, evil, and beyond it. Morality in the normal sense can hardly be said to exist, for one can arrive at goodness by exhausting evil, and peace by exhausting passion. It is even said that there is no use in protesting against a corrupt and evil political regime: the more it is propped up, the quicker it will fall, since one extreme must always give way to an opposite tendency. There is no room for the concept of an incurable evil.

It is possible to counter this problem, as theologians have tended to counter similar, if less developed, theories in the West, by denying the logical connection between the merely physical realm (which is presumed to be fallen) and the moral realm. Others will maintain that there is a sense – the ontological one which was mentioned in connection with Hinduism – in which it can be said that only God, who is pure being, is real, and if we hold to him who is good by the fact of his being, we transcend the moralist's concern with good and evil. However, we are not speaking, as in Hinduism, of a disturbance within the divine body for which we are responsible and which we must overcome, but of the total way of things, the materialization of the spiritual and the spiritualization of the material, and all the opposites, directly attributable to nature and God, which would make what is subjectively experienced as evil positively necessary. Moreover, neither the logical nor the transcendent rejection of the problem explain the *psychological* evidence from the process of individuation which challenges them, a matter which I shall consider presently.

In the circumstances, it might be better to inquire whether the Yin Yang process does not provide a theological clue as to how the universe remains open and creative, accommodates variety and mitigates evil in the way proposed by Schilling earlier. Assuming with Duns Scotus that God is the principle of love and free-will, there must be choice and change even in a perfect world; there must be good, better and best. Logically, then, in Eden, before the Fall, there was still a garden to be 'tended', still the alternation of day and night; though presumably, instead of being the harbinger of the death-sleep of this world, as Origen emphasized, night was for the ecstatic dream of Adam, which was Origen's hypothesis. The error is always to imagine, as does Toynbee in his otherwise brilliant application of the Yin Yang philosophy to patterns of history, that Eden must represent the state of blessed passivity (Yin), and that though logically the perfect world and perfect God cannot admit Satan and evil, evil was in fact necessary to arouse God and the world to activity (Yang), to let creation continue; evil and opposition is really the possibility of things ever going 'from glory to glory', in St Paul's words. Still, given an Eden where growth and change are implied by the description of the primal couple as 'gardeners', not happy idlers, who could therefore have altered the pattern of things by, say, the selective breeding of plants, it is unreasonable to assume that theologically or psychologically an identity of goodness with inaction and fixity of form was intended here. Logically, again, in the new creation, the second Eden envisaged in Revelation, immortality and perfection are not incompatible with a world where trees bear different fruits for every month of the year, thus presumably shedding their leaves. The point is, there is opposition and opposition, change and change.

Most opposition and change plainly does not require something considered evil (whether in some objective or subjective experiential sense) in order to have meaning and operate. Hot and cold, bitter and sweet, red and green, are all opposites in some way ultimately resolvable in physical terms, but no one needs to be sickened by one of the pair in order to be able to prefer the other. In Taoism, *all* the opposites of life will seem as natural to the enlightened man, but it is only the Asian value necessarily set on endurance, and the distrust of ratiocination, which has not permitted the universality of feeling about the irreconcilability of some opposites to become a metaphysical problem. Seeing that so much opposition is painless, it is necessary to inquire whether what for Christian doctrine are results of the Fall (evil, ugliness, death) should be seen not as natural complements of goodness, beauty and life, but as possible oppositions able to become attached to an originally 'biassed' oscillatory process so as to appear essential.

How might this occur? From a scientific perspective, is it even a sensible speculation? At the present time, no one could really be definite, but the answer, if there is one, is most likely to come, not from further penetration into the microsphere, but from more extensive research into the activity and properties of electricity, unexplained features of ultra-violet radiation, the Kirlian effect, and what Russian scientists have tentatively called 'bioplasma'. Bioplasma, or the 'counterpart body of energy', possesses features which recall the psychiatrist Wilhelm Reich's controversial theory of the orgone energy and static electricity which he endeavoured to prove was not identical with electro-magnetism but within and beyond it. Apart from their alleged functions in sex and nature, the important thing about static electricity and orgone was that they are not bipolar but each displays two functions, attraction and repulsion. Orgone in the body is unipolar, yet according to circumstances, able to attract or repulse. In short, beyond, beneath and pulling at matter as currently known, there may be another 'substance' more subject to will; indeed, phenomena of ESP can hardly be explained without such a hypothesis.

Even without a theory of orgone, the question of the claims of bias over opposition seems legitimate both in terms of the popular application of Yin Yang (like the 'equality' of forces in macro-biotics, which in its 1:5 ideal ratio implies a bias of sorts), and in its modern scientific formulation. Whatever the Taoist and the derivative Shinto system may hold with regard to evil and the negative aspects of life, its own traditional description of the universe as a Yang positive, which contains positive and negative, makes it clear that total equality of forces, whether viewed ethically or not, is never in question. The One which unites everything is a One with a necessary bias; in the scientific formulation of the theory, the structure of the universe is asymmetrical in favour of life. In terms of physics, the universe is seen as matter within whose limits, envisaged as a clockwise spiral, there emerge the electrical and magnetic polarities. Existing within an asymmetric universe, these can be conceived as the properties of either one of two possible enantiomorphic helices.

One of the advances in quantum theory came in 1956, when some Chinese American scientists, influenced by Taoist intuitions and sceptical of the Western theory of the symmetrical universe, disproved the universality of the law of parity and went on to the discovery of spatial asymmetry in some elementary particles. From here it was an easy leap for those favourable to Taoist intuitions optimistically to maintain that the whole universe is asymmetrically structured in favour of life. The point is relevant on account of the problem, or rather threat, of anti-matter, which can annihilate all matter it contacts. An updated Taoist vision of the universe would insist there must be a distinct difference of structure between the electrical and magnetic type of polarity which can exist within the 'positive' helix of this universe and that which would prevail with matter and anti-matter. The existence of an enantiomorphic matter does not necessitate equal existence of an enantiomorphic anti-matter. The asymmetrical structure of space-time itself would militate against simultaneous existence of what would be two helical members of an enantiomorphic pair; one would be constantly eliminated. The Tao symbol, when viewed in its constituent parts with its two spirals, demonstrates the principle involved. Both spirals must move clockwise if viewed from the front, or counter-clockwise if viewed from the back, in both cases implying that two opposite-handed structures would be unable to exist simultaneously (see fig.). The Tao notion of inclusion projected on the universe

is thus total as regards *possibilities*, but not total as regards *actualities*, and hence it is not necessary for anti-matter to exist. In so far as it exists as a possibility, it is continuously eliminated; if somehow it did actually exist, it would do so to our total elimination.

Asian scientists are thus tentatively optimistic about reality. As the universe for them is inherently asymmetric, they charge Western scientists who postulate anti-matter from the existence of anti-particles as persistently thinking in traditional symmetrical terms. The yang of matter would have to have its yin somewhere, but it does not have to have it in any absolute sense. But Western scientists, always as concerned with the 'theoretical component' as with visible reality, are only prepared to associate the visible asymmetry of things with characteristics of entities in space, and refuse to discount the possibility of a completely opposite space-time and all that it implies. There is, moreover, the apparent action of black holes and cannibal galaxies to be explained, and hence, asymmetry is something Western scientists would prefer to attribute to this galaxy and to its fortunate preference for life over death rather than to the entire universe. Moreover, as was seen, Asian scientists doubt, but have to admit to the *possibility* of anti-matter; their optimism is challenged by the picture of reality which allows for an uncertainty principle and the behaviour of subatomic particles, like the neutrino, which are able to generate either left- or right-handedness in contrast to the apparent right-handed bias noticeable elsewhere, as in the protein helix.

Perhaps the question of asymmetry and anti-matter, which stands at the frontier of physics, can never be resolved, or will be settled by some compromise between asymmetrical and symmetrical world-views, the one perhaps seen as the ideal pattern or the rule of a part like our galaxy, the other the apparent reality. Since the question lies at the frontiers of science, it can only be at the frontiers of theology, but even so, it raises the question of how it could be *both* something and 'nothing', and how it could appear in a divine universe without God being directly responsible, a problem which Greek substance-theory could never satisfactorily resolve.

What if evil runs through matter and is especially manifest in the activity of anti-matter, possible from the start but in fact unnecessary? We can envisage anti-matter as having originally been nothing but a mirror image, a shadow of reality constantly 'eliminated' by it, a 'nothing' in terms of substance, but later rendered a 'something' affecting matter purely by a will which generated in it a contrary activity, a pull in the other direction. Was creation intended to operate on the 'growing' asymmetrical principle? And then, following some catastrophe, did it become subject to a law of opposition and symmetry (in contrast to one of exchange and degree) which may eventually entail that dissolution of everything into energy anticipated biblically as the end not only of the world (II Peter 3.10) but the very heavens, though the full force of this shock is still absorbed and delayed by the law of asymmetry operative within our sphere of the universe? Despite attempts to justify Shinto insights in terms of science, one might feel that biblical ones are as good or better, with their picture of a universe which is not co-aeval and ever-changing but created perfect and 'delivered to futility' (Rom. 8.20), in the last resort unable to permit the coexistence of good and evil. Of sin, it is said that 'when it is full grown it brings forth death' (James 1.15), and if, as we have suggested, the ultimate nature of God and man is describable in terms of will, and the nature of matter is now seen to be of a kind that can be subject to intention, this could well be a statement of more than spiritual facts.

Evil considered in terms of motion, identity through a possible but unnecessary withdrawal into isolated selfhood, nothingness, the eternal Luciferian fall symbolized by the 'bottomless pit' would solve one of Jung's riddles posed to church doctrine. Once Christianity can approach Taoist and Asian mysticism in a larger scientific perspective, and Christian philosophy divests itself of the theory of Tatian, Basil, Augustine and Aquinas that evil is either a substance or ultimate nothingness,[80] it is in a better condition to answer Jung's serious charges against it on psychological grounds. Jung's position is that evil is real, necessary and ineradicable and that the greatest, most outrageous effects of evil, such as have been exhibited in oppressive rule, wars of religion, Nazism, etc., are the consequences either of believers trying to be too good, or unbelievers projecting the evil in themselves upon groups or classes, the blacks, the Jews, etc. What is required is the acknowledgment and acceptance of evil, as the structure of the psyche and its symbols demonstrate. According to *The Answer to Job*, the Anti-Christ of Revelation is a terrible psychological necessity, a future likelihood in consequence of Christianity's splitting God and the soul asunder into good and evil.[81] History *will* get worse in terms of tyrants and popular delusions and produce an Anti-Christ, who is already coming to birth in the collective unconscious and even the unconscious of Christians, who either assimilate Christ to their shadow self, or reproduce the myth of the dying king and the young child, showing that they realize the limitations of their faith and that they anticipate a new one. In short, 'the Christian God-image cannot become incarnate in empirical man without contradictions'.[82] Christ is the world's best archetype of the Self in the sense of completed *man*, but cannot assimilate to the God *imago*, for though it goes so far as to redeem the animal side (in Revelation Christ becomes the *Lamb* of God), it seems to be too 'perfect' to integrate the shadow, the fount or representative of creativity and the instinct which easily runs to evil; the anathemas and allegedly irritable tone of the Epistles bespeak the tensions of being too filled with light and love. Jung's findings on the psyche and its essential unity do not permit an escape by the suggestion that the unconscious corresponds to 'the flesh' or 'fallen nature', which is dragging down some redeemed or rational conscious. For Jung, as for St Paul, everything is in some sense 'fallen' or 'saved', so there have to be other solutions.

In Jung's psychology the psyche is divisible into elements, such as the ego, the conscious, the unconscious, the *anima* (the feminine component in men) and the *animus* (the masculine component in women), the *persona* (the social self), the shadow (instinctual and suppressed self), and the Self, the ideal totality. All of these elements are animated by 'complexes' and symbolized in culture and dream by archetypes, a sort of imprint around which symbols like gods, witches and wizards, variable according to the society, gather. The mind is in a lesser or greater state of disharmony with itself, conscious against unconscious, and personal unconscious with collective unconscious by which it can be invaded or obsessed. The goal of the individual self is the Self; the components of the mind are in quest of a higher form of the original remembered wholeness, one in which the ineffable Self struggles to be born and to assume its role of unifying and regulating the interaction of conscious with the personal and collective unconscious. This drive to effect an at-one-ment involves a painful quest which can only be effected through religion, though common experiences, as of marriage and sexual relations, approximate to it in so far as they help to integrate *animus* and *anima*. Other experiences may equally jeopardize the quest, and disturbed or dangerous persons, like Nietzsche and Hitler, are those whose development, being uneven, suffers serious 'inflation' of one component at the expense of another, occasioning obsessions, will-to-power and paranoia.

Whether or not individuation corresponds to conversion experiences of the classic Christian variety is controversial and beyond our scope here – clearly elements of individuation are involved – but according to Jung, a disciplined mysticism was the surest way to wholeness, though each discipline held its dangers. Eastern mysticism runs the risk of inflating the unconscious, and Western forms of mysticism of inflating the conscious; by its easy acceptance of the shadow, Eastern religion suffers little of the demonic struggles of the Western variety which has such difficulty with repressed contents, but as the cost of acceptance is total identity with the unconscious, the East suffers defects in imagination, will, and even positive goodness, because this requires some help from the conscious, and because the shadow, as in criminals, can even have its *good* moments – a point we must remember in judging its role. Alchemy exteriorized the mental processes of individuation in terms of a necessary myth, the transformation of base matter into gold, but the stages of transformation are universal to spiritual experience. First, the alchemist attempts by washing and cleansing to reach *prima materia* in which 'the spirit of nature' exists; then, by further processes this substance disintegrates into *nigredo*, which has 'the blackness of death'. The alchemist then works at it, preferably with a soul friend of the opposite sex, until it bursts into colours, the *cauda pavonis* (peacock's tail), before achieving the gold of *prima materia* resurrected. Examination of conscience, death to self and the dark night of the soul, the struggles of second birth, the new life of transformed relations and the realization of the beatific vision of God have parallels here, while practices like the co-operation of 'brothers' or 'sisters' are indications of the way in which the *animus* and *anima* undergo integration. This is a perilous, painful journey for which the right words would be 'take up your cross', because the cross is a symbol of centring and because it involves a sacrifice of the egotistical conscious self to the greater Self which struggles to be made conscious. This can only be achieved through the dangerous integration of the shadow, dangerous because one must be divested of the artificial control of the *persona* and confront the primordial images which engage a conflict, as of the feminine with the masculine, and the masculine with the Self, to which in turn they must be subordinated. But here the real problem begins. What shall we call evil, and what is happening to the shadow or matter?

The gnostic heretics condemned by Jung in so far as with their emphasis on knowledge and identification solely with light, they arrogantly confused mere ego with the Self, regarded matter as a snare. The mediaeval alchemists, like the Taoists, more optimistic, worked to transform matter and even held to a belief in the redemption and reintegration of Lucifer, their version of the fallen god. But either way, deity is sought and symbolized in matter, and Christianity seems to differ from this Western and Asian mysticism in its limitation upon the control or reintegration of matter and shadow. Despite their great force and humanism, these Christian symbols, the most complete in terms of *what* they symbolize, remain incomplete in important ways. Neither the God *imago* nor the self's image of the *anthropos* entirely satisfies. 'The totality of the Trinity is a mere postulate', claims Jung.[83] The natural structure of the *psyche* and the pattern of individuation demands not just a Trinity but a Quaternity with God the Mother, or some physical aspect, while an incarnation of God the Son in the flesh is no satisfaction to the Self either, in that the natural symbol of wholeness persistently demands embodied Anthropos, the 'universal man' of myth, not only a redeemer. (Jung appears ignorant of instances where, as in the Irish Catholic poetry of Joseph Campbell, Christ is consciously and without apparent sense of contradiction, realized as nature, his hair the stars, and so on.) History has proved Jesus to be too perfect and bodiless (sexless?) in relation both to man and eternity to be able to prevent the mystical self-deification of gnosticism (Jung was concerned at the way in which man rather than God is taking the centre in modern mandalas) or to prevent the God *imago* from producing its shadow which is Anti-God, Anti-Christ, to exhaust the world and dying civilization with the evil it has repressed. The only hope of avoiding the coming breakdown of civilization and religion may be the essentially pagan, yet psychologically necessary worship of matter through the Virgin, the late declaration of whose assumption and 'immaculate'' nature within Catholicism Jung regarded as a wise reaction from out of the collective unconscious to the loss of faith and the increase of materialism. Disregarding all conventional theological interpretations, he saw this solution as anticipated by the self-divided St John of Patmos, who introduced the sun-woman into the book of Revelation.

Without wishing to discount Jung's important discoveries, we ought to acknowledge this bias in man and his experience. Subject during the whole of his life to exceptionally vivid and expressive dreams, Jung was personally prejudiced to believe in the good and evil of God, allegedly projected in the dreams of others, because of his bizarre childhood fears, as a pastor's son, that God would test him and make him blaspheme the Holy Ghost. This crystallized in palpitations and a terrifying, almost Shivaite-like dream vision in which God dropped faeces over a church. In his last work, his autobiography, Jung remarks that it was strange that he never once considered until old age the possibility of deception in this dream, or that the devil might have been deceiving him.[84] This is all the more surprising since as one of the intellectuals most instrumental in reintroducing astrology to the West, and using the horoscope for psychological analysis, he did not perceive the classic opportunities for deception in aspects like Moon conjunct Neptune square Sun conjunct Uranus. As a child, Jung began early to think of Jesus as the 'dark' lord of the graves, the man-eater whom he later associated with the phallic deities, Telesphoros, Osiris, Hermes, etc., whose erect phallus decorated the graves of the ancient world. Later, his garden at Bollingen contained phallic sculptures of his own composition. This, and the obsession with earth gods, and a sort of Pan-Shiva consciousness, is again explicable by his horoscope with late Capricorn and its ruler Saturn exalted in the sign rising, and opposing the Sun in Leo, the sign of exhibitionism. Jung's Christian patients and associates, who would not have had such planetary configurations, were, however, culturally sophisticated, intellectual people, who like students and many intellectuals, compensate the mental life, at least in dreams, by a more physical life.

Such an 'explanation' might modify the problem, but it does not make it go away. I believe that the more serious distortion is connected with a confusion throughout Jung's work of God's 'dark side' in Judaeo-Christian tradition with the chthonic (earth) deity theme of world myth. This occurred through failure to acknowledge that the Judaeo-Christian contrast is not simply between good and evil – which would tend to entail a substance theory – but between new and old, and also a refusal to distinguish the *possibility* of God being evil, which theology ought to recognize, from the *necessity* of God being evil. Jung himself admitted that if God required him to commit murder, he would not do it, thus betraying his fundamentally moral position.[85] For Jung, a good-evil God effectively means one who, like Shiva, would combine the elements of the ascetic and Pan as opposed to the simple virginity of Jesus. One returns – almost – to the old Freudian problem of repression, the association of sex with the Devil, who in mediaeval imagery assumed the form of horned Pan, the god of sex. Up to a point, the difficulty must be admitted. An idolatry of St Paul, whose attitude to sex I have considered in Chapter 7, is one factor; statements like 'you have crucified the flesh with all its desires' are open to morbid interpretation and indeed, may be unwarranted constructions by a late and very repentant convert upon Christ's call simply to *bear* the cross, or the yoke (identical with the Indian 'yoga') of the gospel. While a measure of asexuality is always essential to safeguard spirituality, in practice sex is the weak link in Christianity, as in the other 'higher religions', especially Buddhism. The absence of any real *rite de passage*, coupled with the later marriages and longer educations of modern civilization, often lies at the source of the smoking, drinking and anti-social behaviour in the young which preachers can unthinkingly attack. The tendency to exclude eroticism and all depiction and mention of the sexual members in Christian culture (as in Buddhism and Confucian culture) has also been unhealthy. While I should regard Hindu worship of the Lingam as wrong because of its grossly inadequate image of God, one can appreciate Gandhi's surprise at missionaries who found the rites and symbols of modern Shivaism intrinsically obscene. Obviously, just as the cross does not only represent an instrument of execution to Christians, so the lingam is a symbol that does not only represent sex to Hindus. Sex ought to have been more fully integrated to life, though because of the association of reproduction with mortality, which is universally experienced in terms of guilt, a certain shame (which the Bible acknowledges) will always attach to nudity. However, reflections like 'not that we would be unclothed but that we may be further clothed. . . .' (II Cor. 5.4) are merely cultural, and take their source in the values of the desert and the Bedhouin swathed against the sun.

Basically, Judaeo-Christian views about the flesh are paradoxical. The fact that God is supplied with a gender and 'moves upon the face of the waters' (feminine) in fact associates him with sex. Salvation has to be achieved by Christ in the flesh, and even St Paul counsels husbands to love their wives as they love their own flesh. Yet at the same time, like the world, the body is 'this body of death', condemned to futility. We have seen how this may well be a statement of fact. It does not mean that matter is intrinsically evil, as in gnostic thought, or alien, as it became in Catholic philosophy; rather that it is neutral but susceptible to the influence of good and evil which are describable in terms of will and motion rather than substance and intellect. While it is still 'upheld' and acted upon by the good, matter is effectively dominated by the 'pull' of evil or death. Forms of material and psychological trans-formation are thus not really the issue here. Though they are meaningful and certainly possible within a limited sphere, they do not necessarily hold good for the larger process, and it is important to recognize that all systems, including the Jungian, which place illumination within the individuation process, are based, as in conventional Taoism, on a cyclical rather than a progressive view of reality. Even for Jung, the self-transforming soul only peram-bulates around reality. In the pattern of divine becoming, as death itself has to be discarded, life and ultimate change will need to depend pre-eminently on Spirit.

Apart from the possibility of some healthy subconscious attempts to integrate sex more fully to life, I do not believe that Jung's Christians were necessarily contradicting their own faith when they 'alchemized' its symbols, but only registering where it had gone emotionally and intellectually wrong in recent centuries. Uncon-sciously, we could equally see them as recognizing the psychologi-cal impossibility of dualism and reinstating the forgotten doctrine of *theosis* (divinization), which neither Protestant liberalism nor fundamentalism could accommodate. Under the influence of Prot-estantism they had realized the meaning of individualism and the supremacy of will, but knew that it must be compensated by the objective parallel in doctrine and science if they were not to fall into the alienation, absurdity and anguish which has come to characterize modern thought in the face of heightened self-aware-ness and dissolving levels of reality. In so far as *they* are the divine body and the world is a vehicle *for* redemption, they rightly 'alchemized' the Christ-figure.

We are now in a better position to see why the Trinity should not be a masculine and feminine Quaternity, why God the Son is not a universal man in the sense of Anthropos, and why God and

Jesus have no shadow. The Trinity is not a Quaternity towards us within the finite, precisely because we are (or rather are potentially) the other part of God. *We* are matter and feminine, *we* will be *eros* and *anima* to God, the wife, the bride about whom he is 'jealous'. In terms of infinity, God too is feminine, as is hinted by Isaiah (42.14). However, because, as we have seen, life must be right-handed if it is to continue, and must have a bias, and because the nature of God is describable in terms of will and becoming, which the psyche automatically represents with masculine symbols, then from the human standpoint God must be represented as masculine. Jung himself ought to have known this, since he had established that of necessity the psyche subordinates the feminine component in both sexes to the masculine in all true spirituality. Man is the possibility of woman's spirituality, or, as St Paul said, 'Man is the head of woman'. Modern feminist philosophy is quite naturally atheistic in origin, and Mary Daly's announcement that the woman's movement is Antichrist and Antichurch, is theologically and psychologically appropriate.[86] Any Antichrist would have to declare for absolute equality, as against the principle of bias, in sex as in most other things, arguing for the divinity of human nature just as it was rather than within God.

Because of the fact of bias, as person and principle Christ had no need of a sexualized and universal body, like the mystical Anthropos. Christ was designated the head; we ourselves, if our consciousness and theology are properly adjusted, constitute the body. This is also why there is no psychological necessity for the worship of the Virgin who, as 'friend of sinners', could even be regarded as compensating the mentality of those too will-less or sensual to consider themselves the body of God, the temple of the Holy Spirit. Indeed, the danger, as among matriarchal people like the Celts, is that one will finish by merely worshipping self and matter, albeit in a refined form, through Mary, who cannot even provide the theological satisfaction of being God.

Which leads to the shadow. The fact that the shadow of criminals can disclose a good side in compensation of the bad shows us how intangible are the contents of this source of instinct in comparison with, say, *animus* and *anima*. It can include any repressed content or any other thing. I suggest that its most 'natural' function might be to relate us to others and the world, to be always more than we are, bestowing a capacity for imagination and projection, such as lay behind Yeats' doctrine of the mask. Artists, it is admitted, always have strong shadows. God has a shadow in the sense of capacity for otherness, as it is being realized through man and the finite, but he did not choose or succumb to evil in the sense of losing hold of the centre or being selfish, which must be possible within any free situation or existence in love. To possess a shadow in the sense of capacity for otherness is different from its gratuitous use in terms of negation and an absolute and dynamic withdrawal into nothingness, which is the opposite of divine expansion. This, I believe, is how the problem of evil would need to be approached. God is not evil, nor in contrast to God is evil nothing, the mere 'privation of good'; there is still *an identity through action* and an infinity which is derivative.

If evil is neither simply non-being, the privation of good, nor being in Jung's sense, where evil (confused with the sexual life-force) is considered essential, then it is anti-being, active death. As such it cannot be assimilated to life, nor can any moral declension, whether anticipated by Jung or by the apostles, be laid at religion's door. To maintain our Taoist imagery of the dynamic universe, if we envisage incarnation as the end of the spiral of the spiritualization of matter (or rather of the closest approach of Spirit to matter), what follows is the spiritualization of the material, and the previous acceptance of evil/death would be complemented by its successive exclusion. This assumption is virtually explicit in a remark by St Paul which Jung did not fail to notice, but which he simply interpreted from the psychological standpoint of 'God's' alleged growing consciousness: 'the times of ignorance God over looked, but now he commands all men to repent'. In Pauline doctrine, Antichrist is not a figure of vision but the natural corollary of the teaching. God alone is 'restraining' the forces of evil which such a figure will unleash. One reason why to St Paul's eagle eye no one can be holy enough would be because now God cannot 'include' evil as he did formerly; to sin now in these 'last times' of progressive spiritualization is to be susceptible to, or even to align oneself with, *death.*

This does not mean that there is no sense in which a shadow is to be assimilated, since strictly speaking nothing is wrong in itself unless it is action outside God, or 'All things are lawful, but not all things are helpful (expedient)', as St Paul puts it. Christians are presumed to overcome darkness with light, evil with love, not by simple rejection and contention; even the archangel Michael is offered as an example of one who did not presume to dispute with or pronounce upon Satan. When it comes to acknowledging one's own capacity for evil, the shadow is certainly to be assimilated to consciousness and the activity put into evil is to be sublimated fruitfully. The simple fact is that there is a great difference between using one's weakness and identifying with one's demons. Even in Asian mysticism, particularly Tibetan mysticism with its gods of wrath, adepts who identify themselves too closely run the risk of madness or 'possession', and it would be misleading to maintain that the assimilation of evil there only produces tranquil souls who do no harm, as was supposed to be the case with those who followed the way of the Golden Flower. Behind its 'selfless' control, militaristic Zen has been a vehicle of cruelty, while the haunting images of Tibetan mysticism with its demonic figures contributed to the oppression of the traditional society because the people were in awe of the deities with whom their religious leaders identified themselves. The sometimes sinister quality of Taoist bliss is quite honestly reflected in incidents recalled in John Blofeld's *The Secret and Sublime*[87] and should make Christians involved in dialogue hesitate to identify Tao too easily with God, individuation with conversion and white light with the coming of Spirit.

Enough has been said to give an indication of the challenge of Asian and modern thought to missions and the traditional claims of Christian doctrine. It should at least be clear that radical and meaningful restatement against them is quite possible, that they are not necessarily a threat but an ally in the arrested development of Christianity and even of the West. The value of this approach ought to become even clearer in successive chapters, despite the difference of starting point and emphasis; but whether or not the understanding of Christianity and Asia involved amounts to authentic progression, to Jung's evening knowledge, or a combination of both, is a question which every reader must decide for themselves, whether or not they appreciate the significance of 'evening knowledge' in the technical sense.

2

Interpreting Asia

Perhaps because Asia is so vast and requires so much time, travel and study to absorb, those disinclined to idealize it and portray it as everything that the West is not (a common trend) are tempted to say that it is essentially all the same. The result is seen in works like Steadman's *The Myth of Asia*[1], with its special pleading for a denial of the differences within Asia and an approach to Asian wisdom like that of Aldous Huxley, who makes out that Asia offers a 'perennial' philosophy in harmony with the best Western insights, if only we make the effort to realize it.[2]

In this chapter I shall try to outline what appears to be the most salient characteristics of Asia, especially in their bearing on religious and moral self-expression. My assumption will be the 'anthropological' or 'autobiographical' one that personal and social experience must colour even the most seemingly universal terms and symbols of any religion. The archetypal, as Jung well realized, is only an imprint which gathers similar *types* of associations and provides similar types of problems and practices; things that are similar do not necessarily bear the same meaning. When the archetypal is not in question, there is even less reason to assume parallels.

How, for example, should the Hindu term *samadhi*, which is commonly rendered 'highest bliss', really be translated? Is the cool, calm deliverance in meditation from the torment of life and heat which it implies comparable to the warm, passionate, almost sexual connotations of 'bliss' for those who live in less torrid Western climes? The word 'religion' gives problems. In Sanskrit, whose demise it has survived, it was signified by *dharma*, which equally indicates 'duty', 'justice' and 'law'. Modern cross-cultural use of the word 'philosophy' is not much better. Although, like Christianity, original Buddhism received a philosophical description once it had been established, how correctly is it ever called a 'philosophy'? Not only does its underlying intuition about things deny those dimensions of reality within which philosophy is generally believed to have meaning, but the tendency in the West to regard Buddhism primarily as a theory of the illusion of self and world, and as such, as a rather sad, pessimistic doctrine, itself reflects a Western tendency to regard religion in terms of intellectual or emotional propositions. This is not to say that many Asians, especially the Japanese, have not taken the same view and registered the same negative response. However, that may not be the case for most Asians, any more than for the Buddha, who was less interested in propositions then perceptions.

The controversial Indian writer, Nirad Chaudhuri, an agnostic, basically unsympathetic to Hinduism and Buddhism, has described these faiths, as have certain anthropologists, as religions of the *senses*, sense-bound escape routes from the sense-misery of Asian man.[3] If this is true, as I think possible, it is something missions need to take into account. For a large section of Asian humanity unable to grasp the no form, no self-knowledge of the Buddha and the gurus, ultimates count less than the feeling of having the goal in sight. And this goal of deliverance from the misery of the senses appears possible in the context of the more rarified objects of sense, the pleasing and convincing sights, sounds and smells of the temples: sandalwood incense, for example, even provides respite from mosquitoes. By contrast, as the philosopher Alan Watts remarks, modern Christians leave their bodies at the door of a church,[4] and Joseph Needleman proposes that some of the attraction of Eastern religions to the contemporary West is the religion of the senses and the body that they offer.[5] I am inclined to agree with this, not least because wheras church Gothic formerly appeared to me to be slightly chilly and antiseptic, since living in Asia, I have found this style, which missions have transported East, almost irrelevant. The richer colours and more solid forms of most Asian temples, even when not to one's taste, express a warmer, more holistic vision of things than the Gothic, with the underlying dualism of its conception.

Experiencing and feeling is knowing. Asian religion is always stressing that, but even those who defend the Asian world-view take the implications little to heart. I was appalled but not very surprised to discover that Alan Watts, one of the most influential exponents of Asian religion in the West, had never in fact visited Asia apart from a few holidays in Japan and a stopover in Sri Lanka after most of his books had been written. Though Watts is more lucid than many orientalists, numbers of whom have as little Asian experience or less, it was apparent that no one who had really experienced Asia could have written of its religions as he did. Less known, but much more authentic, is John Blofeld, who has lived in Asia and whose *Compassion Yoga* (a study of the Chinese cult of Kwan Yin) beautifully conveys the spirit of the faith involved.[6] There is a melancholy poetic flavour to this account, which properly belongs to the subject and is something felt in much Chinese literature.

Naturally, it is possible to live in Asia and never experience it, as happened with certain culture-blind missionaries like Griffith John, and the founder of Theosophy, Mme Blavatsky, for whom Asia presented itself as the pretext for promoting some Christian or anti-Christian idea, not something to be appreciated in and for itself. But this is probably not so common a situation as is generally believed, and in most cases of so-called blindness, it is rather that the expatriate is confronted with such a multitude of impressions that he is lost for any adequate response. Portraits of missions and missionaries, like those by Pat Barr[7] and Paul Varg[8], which make them out to be comical or intolerant, overlook the possibilities for purely hysterical love-hate reactions, which were inevitably provoked at some stage in even the best-intentioned, especially in the pioneering days, by the heat, noise, dirt, disease, dialects and sheer immensity of Asia. It was thus easy for people like Carol Hollinger, for a long time a university professor in Thailand and author of the ironical *Mai Pen Rai Means Never Mind*,[9] to grow sceptical of purely academic, objective records of Asia and Asian beliefs. A writer needs to take his own and others' subjective reactions into account as the most honest, rounded way of dealing with the subject. Certainly, in reflecting on the subject of religions, I have learned the limits of my tolerance and goodwill, and while criticizing the intolerance of certain missionaries, I am forced to realize that my own reaction to foreign cultures and faiths also cannot agree with, say, those Catholics of the post-Vatican II dialogue who have resolved only to say nice things to Buddhists on the basis of abstract principles established by clerical professionals in Council in Rome. I have never forgotten a court case in Hong Kong which dealt with a particularly gross case of police corruption to the detriment of innocent people at which one of the witnesses, a pious Buddhist police officer, refused to give testimony because Buddhists never speak ill against anyone. Though Buddhist prophets against injustice are not unknown, at any rate in Japan, this indifference is in fact the common practice and is illustrated with almost comic verve in the Koshin at the shrine of Nikko, a wood carving which shows the three monkeys who hear no evil, speak no evil and see no evil. The police officer was in no way an exceptional or unrepresentative Buddhist, but given the nature of the case, his views were especially memorable to those with differing concepts of justice and responsibility.

The point is that religious traditions take a lot of practical understanding. Scriptural formulations may mean something quite different and be realized within ordinary life in quite different ways from those in which they are comprehended by persons of other cultures. Through visiting Israel I discovered that it was possible to have new perspectives on the Old Testament, though I am satisfied that biblical literature is fairly transparent and that the difference between character and cultural style among the Jews has never been very wide. This is more than can be said for other scriptures and cultures. At first I was rather impressed with Lao Tzu's 'Truly, humility is the root from which greatness springs. . . . Only he who was willing to give his body for the sake of the world is fit to be entrusted with the world . . . to bear the calamities of a country fit to be king of the world.'[10] Reading *Tao Te Ching* as a scripture, as readers are encouraged to do, this seemed quite Christian until one reconsidered it in a purely Chinese and Asian context. It is possible that Lao Tzu meant precisely what he said. Obviously, his words are in harmony with a theme of the book, which is that 'nothing' is the useful basis of everything, like the emptiness of the pot and the hub of the wheel, but Asian argument is rather opportunistic and has little of the rigour of Western argument, so a literal interpretation can be questioned. We could as easily be dealing with a type of '*Koan*' (reason confounding argument) made with the object less of giving a positive value to service or defining how and by whom society should be run, than of undermining the authority of the ruling powers on the basis of accepted religious notions. The standard interpretation of Lao Tzu in the West is politically that he taught *laissez faire*, whereas it is more likely that he sought excuses for anarchy. Even if there was no ground for this interpretation from popular myth, which portrays Lao Tzu as insulting even Confucius yahoo-like, the thesis could be supported by the nature of Chinese life, criticism, and the historical context of the writing.

Approaching the matter in terms of Chinese life, one notices how little sense is made by the advocacy of humility, for in Chinese life, people of talent and merit almost as a matter of course are made to take the lowest seat whether they volunteer for it or not. This is not done to test or prove those people, nor, incidentally, does it have the effect of producing great leadership. One of the greatest weaknesses of Chinese society derives precisely from a suppression of originality, often so severe that initiative, the capacity to deal with any emergency, such as Taoist-influenced martial arts would require, is what is most lacking in the society, So great can the Chinese communal sense be that a jealous, inverted pride can raise itself against anyone of originality, to make him less than the multitude. Recently, for example, I attended a Chinese opera which was considered to be a cultural event of some note. The opera blended the old Chinese form with new Western ones to produce a wider dramatic and symphonic rendering of an ancient musical form. It was an impressive achievement and may well become an art form of the future. The programme was filled with pictures and biographies of the opera stars, conductor and director, but the actual composer, the true original, was only accorded a name in small type at the back.

Incidents like these, and the fact that practically all traditional Chinese criticism was indirect, incline me to suppose that statements like the one quoted above do not represent so much a positive valuation of service, as a typically Asian *argumentum ad hominem*, a basis for undermining the pretensions of the powerful. Rulers are strong, but since they are not morally strong enough to suffer what they would cheerfully and rightly impose on anyone else, they are unfit to rule. Everyone is equal, and no one has the right to claim superiority on any grounds. The period at which the philosophy of Lao Tzu was composed was one of great unrest, tyranny and civil war. The response in Lao Tzu's case was the conservative one of woman's power and womb-consciousness, which the society, reacting against the power of its mediums and priestesses, had not long previously overthrown. Yin Yang philosophy preceded Lao Tzu by centuries, and it is possible that at least parts of his version of the philosophy, like some Zen statements, should be considered a scriptural spoof, or a form of political subversion in a religious guise, one that expresses a popular

Chinese view at that.[11] Communism would not have been possible had a large section of Chinese society not always believed – very differently from India and Japan – that short of work and material gain, everyone is, or ought to be, completely equal.

Even Asian philosophy has its context. Because of its frank attachment to the historical principle, the sociology of religion, which was pioneered by Max Weber, has been applied much less to the East, despite Weber's studies of Brahmanism and Confucianism, than to the West and Christianity. Asian religion is regarded as being essentially 'natural', 'timeless' (like the allegedly 'timeless' primitive art which, however, as Malraux demonstrated,[12] is not impervious to change) and so is much less studied in terms of the human factor. In any case, it has been relatively immune from examination. The anthropology of Asia still has many lacunae, and there is scepticism about the possibility of ever knowing Asia culturally.[13] Apologists for Asian faiths see its religion as involving a *technique*, a knowledge of oneness empirically verifiable by anyone and beyond all sectarian ways to its attainment, Hindu, Buddhist, or Taoist. Yet it should be obvious that the void of Buddhist meditation has a white-magical whiteness and goodness to it which could not be predicated of the nothingness envisaged in Shamanistic banishing rights (of which it can be considered a philosophical refinement) or the sorceries of Casteneda's Don Juan. Almost certainly the easy acceptance of Buddhism in the northern countries of Nepal, Tibet and Mongolia is attributable to the measure of relief it brought from black magic without completely upsetting the authority of priests or shamans, who could simply change the terms of their doctrines. From reincarnation, which is an extension into time of Shamanistic metempsychosis, to the doctrine of no self, which is a refinement of the shamans' self-sacrifice, the connections between yoga and leading concepts of Hinduism and Buddhism cannot be overlooked.

From the sociological standpoint, it is open to question whether the mystical identity of *atman* with *Brahman* described in the Upanishads and which in a psychological perspective points to total identification with the unconscious, is not more the expression of a pious wish than a reality, being a prescription for self-inflation. Certainly, the Upanishads are suspiciously confused as to whether *atman* is identical with *Brahman*, or everything is totally identical with *Brahman*. Considered from a historical perspective, the lives of gurus seem likely to have contained a good deal of psychological self-inflation masquerading as philosophical profundity, and for good sociological reasons for this which we can understand. The role of even the world-renouncing ascetics as a status group cannot be disregarded within the context of a society so frequently overrun that it was obliged to be satisfied with purely moral victories. The later Upanishads mark a radical departure from the Aryan Vedas, in which the deities are perceived mainly in transcendence, and the date of their composition coincides with a waning of Aryan power and a resurgence of the native peoples and their yogic cum shamanistic religion. Never an especially warlike people, the native population can be seen as challenging the Aryan authority and caste claims which made even those of Brahmin caste gods, by means of an equalizing mysticism, a mysticism which the Aryans had to absorb if they themselves were not to lose status. The epic *Mahabharata* offers the standard portrait of the Aryans as demi-gods striking down the demonic forces who represent the native population, but centuries later, in mediaeval myth, Krishna, originally the friend of the Aryans and a god, pays homage to the yogis as to gods when he comes to earth to fight the demons, even though he is still a god. This, it seems, shows the secret desire and social motivation which underlie much Indian 'oneness' mysticism; it represents the desire of conquered peoples to be treated on equal terms with Aryan gods and Brahmins.

Historically, what has been called the natural or perennial religion of Asia, underlying Hinduism, Buddhism and Taoism, should probably be seen as a development of the mysticism of matriarchal religion. This in turn arose as a reaction to Father God religion when it was believed (as suggested in the Bible and world myth generally) that the Father God had withdrawn himself. This natural mysticism of oneness reached its apogee and most extreme expression in early mediaeval India with Vedantism and the pure philosophical monism of Shamkara, for whom everything was *Brahman*. This corresponded to the triumphant consolidation of Hindu society over both the aristocratic pretensions of the conquering Aryans and the socially divisive influence of the Buddhists. The difficult philosophy of Shamkara was subsequently modified into a qualified monism, as in the philosophy of Ramanuja, as the society reacted to new religions, like Christianity and Islam, and attempted to break free from the new rigidity of Brahmin-ruled religion once this was freed from the old Aryan and Buddhist challenges.

'Natural religion' is the illusion of the East and its defenders, as 'natural law' is the illusion of many Western Christians and of

Greeks before them. Its leading assumptions are: first, that there must be some ultimate religion, because opposites are reconcilable, and second, that this natural mysticism emerges everywhere, even in hostile climates, as happened with Cabbalism within Judaism, and the mediaeval mysticism of Meister Eckhart and Nicholas of Cusa within Catholicism. However, as I indicated in the previous chapter, the fact that the world is composed of opposites, as in electricity and magnetism, or that waves and particles do contradictory things in sub-atomic physics, is no guarantee that all opposites can be resolved; if anything, the supposed universality of the mystical experience is really one of a recurrent historical situation or personal dilemma. Whenever history becomes unbearable, as in the era of the Black Death, men turn inwards from disease, dirt and poverty. They may also do so whenever the mother element in religion or personal experience is strong, as in the late mediaeval period with its exaggeration of the cult of the Virgin, or as happened with Bishop Berkeley, whose concern with philosophical monism could be accounted for by his early formation and the influence of Celtic matriarchy.

None of this is said with a view to reducing the whole subject of religion to agnostic relativism, nor do I mean to imply that Asia's natural religion has no significance at all beyond the psychological, and that only the Father God religions of the West can maintain any claim to religious insight. I shall consider the question of truth and religious exclusiveness in Chapter 6; at this stage it is important to note that religion and culture are never 'natural' and 'timeless', as may sometimes appear: they are always to some extent historical, biographical and personal.

With this in mind, I shall briefly describe what seem to me to be some of the more salient characteristics of Asian religion. Leaving aside most of the judgments made by academics, travellers and missionaries, I shall try to see it basically in terms of psychological types and dispositions. Among the academics, it was Jung who first did this seriously in the essays comprising *Psychology and Religion: West and East*.[14] If his pioneering work has not been more followed up, that is doubtless because it rather supports the pessimistic belief that 'East is East and West is West'. For Jung East and West demoralize one another with their views of will and grace, and in contact they usually stand to lose what is best in both traditions. This is not exactly good news to missionaries of the various faiths, nor to those universalists, like Hocking, Northrop and Radhakrishnan, who wish to unify the world in one all-embracing mysticism.

Jung's prime assumption, which I believe to be right, is that the West is extravert and the East is introvert. He affirms this in terms of the general *style* of the culture and people concerned; obviously he does not claim that all Occidentals are natural extraverts and Asians natural introverts. In fact, I believe that the Chinese are relatively extravert, and that it is this which sets them apart within Asia, although the aesthetic and religious trends in Chinese society are more introvert and within the Asian pattern.

Those familiar with Jung's theory of extraversion and introversion will be aware that objectivity, empiricism, the rule of fact, judgment from the material aspect are predominant among extraverts, whereas subjectivity, the personal impression, philosophical idealism, psychic and aesthetic reality count for introverts. The extravert has little interior life and is alienated from himself, regarding introspection as morbid or narcissistic, and finds his expression and security in action and the domination of the external world. By contrast the introvert enjoys, or at any rate 'undergoes', a rich internal life, often manifesting an indifference towards action and the external world, regarding the extravert as rather crude and insensitive. The attitude is philosophical or religious rather than scientific, since by preference the world is not analysed in parts but grasped in its wholeness. Within Western tradition the extravert/introvert polarity is reflected in the philosophical debate between nominalists and realists. Plato's belief in the reality of pre-existent ideas is typical of the introvert conviction that there is nothing in the world that is not first in the mind, whether of the subject or of God. More typical is the extravert Aquinas, who wins the day, with his 'nothing in the mind that was not first in the senses'. This empirical attitude will not do as a belief since the mind does not come into the world as a *tabula rasa*, and it can only understand the world in terms of certain predetermined patterns of mental response. This is why, in ultimate terms, the intuitions of the introvert mind, like that of the Yin Yang, can be more scientific than those of mere empiricists, even if the latter are better equipped for scientific research into the intermediate levels of reality.

On the basis of his theory, Jung maintains that Christianity is the natural Western religion, to the extent that there is a Christian cast even to Western materialism and atheism. Christianity is eminently extravert with its view of man as essentially an unworthy nothing, and God (like matter) conceived as completely other, bestowing grace upon man and imposing laws or evangelistic missions with which to dominate societies and individuals. Consequently, Western man cannot really understand Eastern religion, though its anthropocentric basis may attract his humanism; his desire for its knowledge is only another manifestation of his acquisitiveness, much as evangelism is of his imperialism. If Western man desires Eastern values, there is only one place for him to seek them, and that is within himself, the aspect of himself that he has long ignored.

This judgment involves a rather extreme interpretation of Christianity, perhaps itself a rather Western extravert one in view of the fairly introvert cast to much New Testament writing. However, the interpretation cannot be dismissed, and it must be obvious that if revelation strikes individuals of an extravert type, the faith will assume an extravert colouring, just as, if it is delivered in words, it will be refracted through a given language. This does not cast aspersions on the integrity of the religion, or limit the possible development of its meaning.

One of the more helpful insights to arise from this treatment of a religion relates to the vexing problem of intolerance within Christianity, which has long been felt, especially in Asia, to compromise its message. To follow the Jungian theory, the extravert fetish of *completely* objective truth (which is a psychological illusion, as I suggested in the previous chapter) tends to accompany an attitude that makes every other opinion a heresy and a challenge. As a result of an extravert obsession with bare facts, the unconscious colouring which must always surround a fact, having been denied, is emotionally transferred to the intellectual formula which attempts to order such facts. Truth no longer speaks for itself, but is surreptitiously identified with the individual, who ends up apparently defending the formula but in effect defending his threatened personality against evil enemies. This is how absurd contentions arise between sects like Strict and Open Baptists. Differences of opinion and doctrine, which derive less from fundamentals than from differences of temperamental or intellectual approach, become wars in which the saints of God struggle with the forces of evil. Similarly, on the political and missionary front, when colonized people, like the Irish or the Indians, have shown the least resistance, they can easily be pictured as insane rebels or enemies of truth, although they may have suffered enormities from the imperial power concerned. Of course there is another side. By contrast, as a result of the fetish of pure subjectivity, the introvert mind may run to the other extreme, as among the Hindus, and perceive something in every point of view as part of a greater whole, reducing truth to a relativity which threatens science, and all too often avoid bad action by doing nothing at all.

So it is that the East counters the West and its objectivity with the authority of subjectivity and, in the case of the mystics and philosophers, identity with the collective unconscious. Eastern man can be as alienated from the world as Western man from his inner self. Eastern man, according to Jung, is spiritually caught in the bind of total identity with the unconscious to achieve harmony, just as Western man to be good can be caught in artificial dependence upon a grace deemed wholly external, both inadequate responses to the fact that the unconscious is basically an unreliable factor which responds to no one at will, but seems more likely to co-operate when minimal conscious effort is put forth. Despite Western tendencies to doubt or deride the ineffability of the classic Asian mystical experience, Jung believed that it was authentic, while doubting whether it deserves the mystique which it had acquired. 'Since we cannot attribute any particular form to the unconscious, the Eastern assertion that the universal mind is without form, seems to be psychologically justified.'[15] The unconscious is, however, the birthplace of forms and hence of the Asian belief in archetypal gods which arise from the void. For the East, void is form and form is void because thought has reality which can only be compared to the reality accorded to matter in the West, so that Asians are quite prepared to admit the simultaneous existence and non-existence of their gods. Everything depends on one's approach.

Nonetheless, it will be observed that no Western introvert (e.g. Plato) has gone as far as Asian man in denying his ego and form, although there is a kind of heterodox materialism and scepticism which could be compared to the Western variety. Jung himself was surprised at the apparent lack of 'egocentricity' in the East, the looseness with which the introvert ego is attached to the mind, compared to the West. There is a disposability about the Eastern ego which has no comparison in the West; rather the Asian concern is with states of mind. To this problem Jung had no answer, and it constitutes the weak link in his whole argument. It is possible that had he not been so hostile to Freud he might have had resort to Freudian notions of woman's oceanic feeling and the sexual qualities within mystical experience, thus proceeding to the belief, which I would maintain from experience, that the East is not only introvert in relation to the West but is to some extent feminine, demonstrating the generally lesser female assertion of self and will. Where in Asia society is not so introvert in comparison with the West as in China, it is still feminine in relation to the West. It should also be noticed that Jung associated the 'introvert-feeling' type among introverts mainly with women, though he did not jump to any conclusions: for example much of the literature and customs of Japan, like moon- and flower-viewing, could be explained in terms of the introvert-feeling type.

To see Asia as 'feminine' would be an important step, not least because it implies possibilities of marriage and individualism rather than mutual hostility or respectful toleration between East and West. It is, however, necessary to be wary of such generalizations because they are more emotive and less exact than the distinction between extravert and introvert. The 'femininity' of Asia is manifest from country to country in many and differing ways. I should also stress that what I am describing is not to be confused with the features of societies of 'matriarchal' background like the Celtic or Tahitian, where women may resemble men and men women in more physical ways (though there are traces of this, most notably in Cambodia and Tibet). Rather, throughout the whole society what by Western standards would be considered the feminine element is exaggerated; one very obvious example is the Asian attention to detail and the love for small objects, flowers and scents. In the main, this is a psychological phenomenon, though it is not absent at the physical level, as any book of Asian sexology will show. In East Asia, the men have poor beards and possess that extra sub-cutaceous fat which in the West is associated with women. Many gestures, like a tendency to move the eyes rather than the neck to secure another view, and a disposition towards nervous laughter, will appear feminine traits by Western standards. Asian women simply exaggerate common feminine traits, either in the direction of submission and 'butterfly' gestures, or, less commonly by adopting matriarchal behaviour; their motives are highly materialistic and they jealously safeguard possession of persons and rights, unnaturally projecting the mothering instinct upon marriage and the world.

Paradoxical though it may seem, it is precisely this feminine bias within Asian society which has contributed to the more absolute nature of authority and patriarchy in the East in comparison with the West. To the West, the ruthless demands for obedience, made for example, by the samurai upon his retainers and their abject submission to these demands will seem merely irrational to the West. The fact is that the tendencies in Graeco-Roman thought which set up authority and the male as representatives of mind over matter, reason over emotion, put limits upon that rule. Despite the principle of bias considered in the previous chapter, at least in popular understanding, Asian mysticism can only undermine all rationalizations of authority; however, since there will always be authority, it will always go to the strongest. Asian rationalizations of authority exist in the Indian Code of Manu and Confucianism, but they carry less weight than the Western ones and have never prevented might from carrying the day in the form of tyrannical matriarchs, or even servants, if possible. It so happens that men have tended to win the day more often. In popular Asian lore and in the theory of the physiognomists, very powerful or very rich men usually possess bullish or even big, piggish faces, and certainly among the Chinese and Japanese at least, I have noticed a tendency towards a thick-set frame among those with authority, and this 'piggishness' in the self-made rich. Anyway, bullish and big-limbed men are about the nearest Asia comes to masculinity as the West understands it; the rest, those who are obedient, are more feminine and have recourse to the ways of intrigue and subversion rather than moral or physical confrontation, in relation to those who presume upon them. In less secular India, the parallel phenomenon is of fussy haughtiness and ill-temper met with moods and indifference, but the general pattern in Asia is otherwise.

The femininity of Asia is chiefly manifest in a habit of submission to individuals and by extension to fate at large, although in this respect the natural disasters which overcome humanity in Asia have to be taken into account. Even though the warrior knows the samurai is wrong, he still does his bidding because he is sworn to him for life, a projection upon a person and a career of the essentially female desire for the perfect union, the indissoluble monogamy. Even though he knows the father is unjust or wrong, under the Confucian code the son is still not to remonstrate, thus giving, in the Western view, further grounds to the bully. To a considerable degree, this self-control is only tolerable because of the very distinct hierarchical system (a projection upon society of divisions and distinctions not permitted intellectually and mystically) which gives considerable scope to the frustrated individual to vent spleen on immediate inferiors (elder son on younger brother, wife on daughter-in-law, and so on, down to the various untouchables of Asian society whom it is not necessary to address or reply to with any of the common courtesies). Even in modern Thailand, which is a kinder, less authoritarian society than many within Asia, there are quite a number of people who on account of their status do not warrant being addressed as Mr and Mrs, or need to be asked or thanked in the way conventional to the West.

Not surprisingly, within such a system Communism has held no uncertain attractions (Mao's horror at the overweening contempt of his social superiors is crucial to understanding his communist and egalitarian sentiments), and is even seen by many Buddhists as more logically fulfilling the theoretically egalitarian vision of Asian mysticism. However, because of its relation to native 'femininity', the Asian communal spirit can be an uncertain possession. It is true that Asians like to work in units and are genuinely loyal within them (even though economic and geographical conditions have sometimes demanded wider co-operation), but just as the solidarity of women may quickly break down upon the intrusion of a man into the circle, novel situations can upset the communal goodwill. This appears to have occurred most recently in the Cambodian anarchy. The real value of the group is as a certification of the individual, who by himself feels himself a nothing. Missionaries stressing the individualistic quality of Christianity rarely grasp this, and it lies at the root of that incongruous situation in which missionaries invite Buddhists to save the souls their religion denies, only to find resistance to Christianity from Buddhists who assert the identity of their nation and *society* with their religion, a form of identity they do not wish to lose.

The traditional virtues of Asia are thus on the whole feminine, even 'masochistic' ones, which relate to the emotions and self-image rather than to the will and society. There is some similarity here to the statement of St Peter (I Peter 2.18), 'For one is approved if, mindful of God, he endures pain while suffering unjustly', but in this case the idea refers to situations which cannot be changed. Because of its sense of history and Christianity, the West has tended to believe that things can and should be changed, whereas the East attributes misfortune to bad *karma* and sees events in terms of eternal return rather than linear development. It may be true to say that the best and the worst of Asia is epitomized in its women. Much of the greatest Japanese literature has been composed by women: many of the typical arts and crafts of China have come from female hands. In India, though their contribution has been less cultural, Indian women are generally felt to represent the more human aspect of the national character. On the other hand, ruthlessness and demonic evil of the kind associated in the West with men like Nero and Hitler seems to be the possession of women, as with the Empress Wu and Empress Dowager Tsu Hsi. Missons have intuited the crucial importance of women in the life of Asia, but one may still ask (as I shall in another chapter) whether giving Christianity a feminist accent and appeal has been to its advantage.

Extraversion and introversion, masculine and feminine; these appear to provide basic psychological distinctions between the West and Asia. In addition to these differences, and sometimes in consequence of them, I shall note a few further characteristics relative to my theme which seem to distinguish Asia absolutely from the West. It must be stressed that my judgments are personal, and even when they are of a critical nature, I do not mean to suggest that Western solutions to similar problems are always superior. Sometimes I am judging with reference to Christian values which the East does not possess and the West has misapplied.

One of the first things that strikes me about Asia, especially having established its introversion, is its remarkable lack of any 'psychology' and analysis in the Western sense. It is true that in Japan the literature can manifest profound psychological insight, but as in yoga, it tends to analyse only to reduce or annihilate. A common resolution of psychological problems is further descent into one's void, or lamentation at one's total uniqueness and alienation. A sense of purpose is lacking, and society hinders any genuine resolution of problems, so the Japanese history of easy suicide is quite understandable. Japanese psychiatrists have observed the need for a different view of the ego before they can even apply Western psychology to much effect.

Asia is generous with sympathy and concern for the sick and obviously troubled, unlike the West, at least within specific kin and interest groups, but this is psychologically a sympathy without penetration and does not extend to neurosis and the more subtle forms of suffering. It is basically of the practical variety, from long vigils at a sick bed to generous gifts, or the silent commiseration Pearl Buck so much appreciated. It is the sympathy of the mother for the child rather than of the doctor or the priest for the individual, and when it comes up against problem cases, it is more likely to aggravate the trouble than relieve it. Psychology is in effect forbidden to Asia because of its low view of the ego, whether in its own right or in relation to the whole mind; it is further ruled out by the ultimately 'irrational' ordering of social relations, which is nothing but a pecking order. By tradition, social relations are highly codified and organized, but they concern roles which are hardly defined in and for themselves, except possibly in the Indian Code of Manu. That is to say, they exist like the Confucian Code, to satisfy an ideal for the whole of the society to the detriment of the individual, so that the reverence that wife or son pay to father or husband is a training in the duty everyone owes to state and society. The kind of Christian requirement that father respect children, husband respect wife, and master respect servant, though theoretically covered by the concept of *jen* (reciprocity), is given too little scope to be meaningful. That being the case, no individual problem or condition can really merit examination in and for itself, nor can anyone really claim the protection, respect or privacy from society which their vulnerability may demand.

In India and Thailand, depending somewhat upon the class, children can be petted and spoiled and even exhibit a mildly precocious air, which develops, however, into subtle individualism. The picture is quite different in East Asia. One is amazed again and again at how blindly and insensitively teachers and parents can overwork their children into breakdown or suicide (six-year-olds doing homework till midnight), or achieve the same effect by frightening them with failure, or impelling them into careers for which they are obviously not suited. Senseless cruelty masquerading as discipline and just punishment are all too common. Further down the road from one address at which I lived in Hong Kong, passers by were amazed to discover a terrified six-year-old girl strung from outside of an eighth-floor balcony in retribution for not having honoured her family with better school grades. One professor I know used not only to be beaten by his father for minor faults, but afterwards was forced to kneel all night to meditate upon his wickedness. The irony is that the same parents would never have praised their children's success and good deeds. Apart from some first-born sons spoiled to ruin by doting mothers and sisters, most parents, even those innocent of all cruelties, will not reward their children with generous praise for examinations passed and duties done, a point which makes Chinese and Japanese parents the despair of their child psychologists, who attribute the all-too-common withdrawal symptoms to discouragement. 'I think my father was pleased with me,' one girl said to me after securing a commercial qualification. 'When I told him I had passed, his face changed.' In the bad old days it used to be the same in the professions; apprenticeship in everything from the stage to the kitchen involved submission to every humiliation, privation and cruelty.

Inevitably, things can work the other way, and within Chinese and Japanese life, sudden gruesome manslaughter of parents and employers, who may finish chopped to bits or mangled by supposedly dutiful offspring and employees, is fairly common.

Eccentricity and obsession are remarkably widespread throughout Asia in consequence of the denial or humiliation of authentic individualism. I think of Indian and Chinese girls I have either personally known or heard about, who against all family advice and commonsense have pursued unlikely men everywhere, ignoring every rejection, gripped by a mixture of passion and mystic fervour. Again, there will be young men who may follow young women round every street, or kneel in the street before their house with offerings of flowers or presents every day for a year until the woman, if she is an Asian, delivers them to the police or sues them, where an Occidental might try to acquire the services of a psychiatrist.

The massages, hot baths and various yogas of Asia are not fortuitous local customs; they are means of physical relaxation whereby, as with drink in the West, psychological problems can be temporarily dissolved. Sometimes I sense that frustration is the almost permanent condition of East Asia as, to a lesser extent, 'Angst' is in the modern West, and if the literature were anything to go by, there could be no doubt. The West has its Othello-like tales of frustration, but these refer to highlights of a life, not its normal condition, whereas the Asian spectacle seems like a nightmare, pure irrational *samsara*. In traditional Chinese literature and in modern Japanese literature, oceans and deserts of suspicion, resentment and hatred come to alienate even the closest relatives and friends. The lack of privacy, small dwellings and over-population of the habitable areas of Asia undoubtedly play a part in the situation, robbing many of the desire to relate, and promoting again only the desire to escape. Moreover, in contrast to the West, many are better equipped for escape. Though they may not achieve the 'bliss' of the mystic and his capacity to meet all situations evenly, they can make their mind go blank, dissociate themselves more easily than Western man. Even laymen, with no mystical leaning or trainings, will say that to go to sleep immediately, or ignore noise, rush and pressure, they need only to control their mind to go blank. This must be the case, or the noise, crowds and pressure of parts of Hong Kong, Tokyo and Bangkok would be the undoing of many more persons than it is.

It can be argued that cutting off the root of thought, as opposed to reforming the problems, is little better than taking opium or drink, but reformers, and especially religious reformers, have probably not taken the Asian desire and capacity for escape sufficiently into account. It is certainly a factor, as we shall see, in the alienation of many Indian and Japanese Christians from the idea of church and church community. Release and salvation are always assumed to be either in the person, or beyond him in the desolation of mountain, cave, island and temple. Society, associated with pressure, is not the place in which to achieve salvation. Its constant distractions are in any case hostile to the prayer and meditation of the discursive variety favoured by the West, nor, for those for whom thought is an added burden, are they felt to be a very attractive mode of release. It is for this reason that the mantras or contemplations suggested in works like Dechanet's *Christian Yoga* have proved quite popular with Indian Christians.[16]

According to the Hindu philosopher Radhakrishnan, who was anxious to relegate Christian dogma to an expression of Western organization, it is organization and efficiency which distinguishes West from East.[17] This is only partly true, for obviously Japan, like all military societies, has always been highly organized, and so too has China, periodically, in a bureaucratic way. However, it is apparent that the basis and notions of organizations are radically different. It is not, as might be supposed, that Western organization is purely the result of science because until recent centuries, Asian knowledge and know-how rivalled and occasionally outdid Western, even in the smaller kingdoms, like Korea, where the printing press first began, or Cambodia, where hydraulics systems were so advanced. It is especially in areas like music, or the involved novel, as of Balzac, that Western sophistication is most evident. The Western conquest of harmony and orchestration is less 'scientific' than the expression of *willed* organization; so too is the modern novel, over whose organization Asian novelists – and there have not been so many – have had such difficulties.

By tradition, organization in India, which was mediated through the caste system, was, ideally, 'natural'. It was made in the image of the body, with intelligence and spirituality giving initiative at the top, and strength and material activity lower down, but since reincarnation was relied upon to secure this, and history witnessed illicit cross-caste unions, the system has not worked according to theory. In China and Japan, where there is a certain attraction to figures, and in more recent times, to the computer, the systems have been more abstract, impersonal. Nature offers a framework of reference for the philosophers, but often the rule of numbers could be substituted for it. The social systems have worked tolerably well, but whenever they went wrong, like a failed computer, they kept repeating the same mistake *ad nauseam*. The human factor was hardly considered in the breakdown, the object being simply to reimpose order and to get the machine going again, with a few knocks if necessary. Revolution or total social collapse rather than reform has thus been the factor in change. In the West, something of this automatism has been demonstrated, though for different reasons, by the Latin countries, and was a factor in their loss of intellectual leadership to the 'Teutonic' lands after the Renaissance. Northern Europe prized the masculine value of reason as before, but under Protestant influence more in conjunction with will and imagination. At its worst, it degenerated into mere conquest of man and nature, but obviously the modification of organization by reason and will and the justification of initiative has been an advantage to civilization.

The low value in Asia set on pure reason, the obsession of the Greeks, can be put down to environmental causes, like nature (which is irrational) and education, but it is likely that other factors, such as the 'feminine' cast of Asian thought and the structure of its languages, play their part, for the matter is more than one of value. The Asian mode of reasoning is very different from that of the West, and despite the practicality, the handy gadgets and nimble ways, by Western standards there is little sense of the logical or even of the obvious and the probable. For some Occidentals, reasoning with Asia will seem like dealing with the normally practical housewife whom no amount of logic can convince and nothing draw from familiar ways of doing things if her mind is set against it.

This is perhaps most noticeable in Japanese society because of its apparent commitment to change and its love of novelties. It is at first hard to believe that in past centuries the Japanese preferred to starve rather than consume available buckwheat when the rice crop failed, or that even today, after two thousand years, rural people still suffer winters in flimsy houses modelled after the styles of the Indonesian and Pacific regions from which their ancestors hailed, rather than adjust their architecture to the extremes of Japanese climate. By tradition, the seasons were fixed to dates which required the wearing of specific kimonos, and if the seasons proved unreliable, etiquette demanded shivering or sweltering in the prescribed kimono regardless, just as today the heating and air conditioning of most offices and transport systems take no account of actual conditions. The obvious in this case is defined by a romantic sense of duty and tradition.

The tonal languages and scripts of East Asia are responsible for a lot of confusion in other areas of life; there is more spontaneity and initiative among the Indians who, because of the influence of Aryan languages, maintain a hold on analytical thought which contrasts with the awkward system of tones in the speech and the fixity of pictorial concept in the script which inhibit flexibility and analytical self-expression, especially among the Chinese. The main thrust of Chinese languages, which in construction emphasize nouns rather than verbs or adjectives, is directed upon hitting the right tone level between identical words of dissimilar meaning, rather than refining shades of meaning. The rigidity of thought this tends to impose will be gauged by the foreign visitor when, having obviously finished his meal, he says *madang* (bill) to the waiter and, wallet in hand, is obviously waiting to pay, only to discover that the waiter can be relied upon to look as amazed or confused as though asked for a ticket to the moon. He will not calculate, as would a European, that 'madang', like 'rose', 'rose' and 'rows' in English, can only ever mean a certain thing among a limited number of meanings, but will wait for the correct pronounciation or even try to speak in English on the assumption that the person before him must be speaking English. It is the same in Japan, though there is not the problem of tones. George Mikes has written wittily at some length about the problems of communication and the exasperating assumption that imperfect Japanese must be English.[18] It is sometimes worse in Thailand, where the tonal problem recurs. To give only one example, I stood very 'obviously' as a tourist with photographic equipment on one of the main roads which lead to Wat Phra Keo, which is the temple of the Emerald Buddha, the main sight of Bangkok, and hailed taxis to take me there. In reality I wanted to go to the National Museum, but already suspected that anything less than the main sight would be too sophisticated a demand. Even when I pointed ahead and marked the Temple from a map, still I was greeted with looks of complete bewilderment and was even asked if I wanted to go to the cinema, as though this was likely for a tourist loaded with map and camera in the middle of the afternoon.

Sometimes the obvious is avoided as a matter of etiquette. Occidentals can at first be surprised at visits and conversations the aim of which may be some favour or personal enquiry, which seriously begin just as it is thought they are about to terminate. In this case there is deliberate avoidance of directness, but usually the obvious is avoided through sheer failure to perceive it. Frustrations and misunderstandings of this kind have made me more sympathetic towards the seeming bigotry of at least pioneer missionaries, whose witty or bitter accounts of frustration should perhaps be seen as their only outlet against the impossible demands of politeness and self-control constantly placed upon them. The American Arthur M. Smith's *Chinese Characteristics* (1904) is cited by Paul Varg for its implications of missionary prejudice. Smith asks the average (uneducated) Chinese his age.

> He gazes vacantly at the questioner or asks in return 'I?' to which you respond 'Yes, you'. To this he replies with a summoning up of his mental energies for the shock. 'How old?' 'Yes, how old?' Once more adjusting the focus, he inquires, 'How old am I?', 'Yes', you reply, 'how old are you?' 'Fifty-eight', he replies with an accuracy of aim, his piece now being in working order.[19]

This may be condescending, yet having, like a lot of other people who are not missionaries, experienced the same kind of difficulties or worse, and sometimes among the not so uneducated, I recognize one has to smile sometimes to survive the frustration. It is not, in any case, a matter of suggesting that Orientals are stupid; on the contrary, the IQ of Asian children in America is usually found to be equal or superior to that of American children, but they are hampered by archaic values which discourage direct and independent thought, and as Smith himself realized, especially languages and scripts. That has virtually been admitted by Communist China, which is simplifying Chinese script and encouraging the use of Roman letters. This is a great aesthetic loss, but that is another matter. As it stands, the Asian mentality is the monolithic one. Romantic Orientalists hostile to Christianity, like Blofeld and Keyserling,[20] may emphasize the flexibility of Taoist and Buddhist philosophy, while even Carol Hollinger, mentioned earlier, may extol the wonderful improvisation of the Thais ('Red for Go and Green for Stop', as he entitled one chapter),[21] but in fact the Asian mind knows only one way of doing things when it comes to essentials. The all-important factor is life in society and the group, and it has to be borne in mind that Taoism and Buddhism are not really part of society but a form of monasticism, and Taoism especially was long regarded as a protest tradition, even a way of eccentricity.

Although it is possible that Asia may become more direct with time, it is possible that pure logic may always elude her. We must consider this point next. The West is intellectual, the East aesthetic; the West is logical where Asia looks. The East prefers vivid illustrations, parables and metaphors to logical arguments. Asia manifests a certain horror or disregard for the intellectually abstract. India has employed logic in its philosophy only to argue for the absurdity of intellection. Only efficient Japan has manifested some respect for the neatness of a logical argument; overall, logical and abstract thought counts for little. One Thai Christian, Chad Saiwan (see Chapter 5), goes so far as to suggest that missionaries might have had more success, albeit perhaps a dishonest one, if they had not argued for God from doctrines and notions of cause and effect, but just seduced the mind with the pretty illustrations by which the Buddhist monks impress the ordinary people. In the East necessity is aesthetic and seeing is believing, which is why the ultimate is identified with the seen and felt, the 'white light' of the enlightened mind. Logical consistency of the Western variety is little respected, given this view of truth. It was a surprise to some that Dr Suzuki, the famous exponent of the functional, Zen form of mysticism, should privately have been a Buddhist of Pure Land persuasion who hoped for a happy heaven. Asian rationalism is a doubtful possession. Conversation can shift from the scientific to the I Ching or palmistry; Chinese students who profess to rationalist or agnostic views may put up a God of Money poster for New Year; Asians who describe themselves as atheists very often mean no more than that at the time of speaking, the idea of God does not seem particularly real to them. Within the stream of consciousness all can be true.

The appeal of Eastern religions for certain groups within the West is their inclusiveness and 'realism', their disinterest in the abstract and faith in the Greek and Christian sense. The only faith required by most Asian religion consists in techniques for disclosing reality as it lies beneath forbidden or forgotten territories of the psyche. Northrop's *The Meeting of East and West* makes an intellectual distinction between the Western concern with the 'theoretical component' and the deduction without which Christian philosophy and modern science would have been impossible, and the Asian concern with the 'aesthetic continuum', the underlying mental substance of things, the stream of consciousness, the pure white light of void which lies beyond the intellectual process (this light of energy is actually produced by the opening of the pineal gland, and can be considered equivalent to the ultimate substance of things).[22] There is a kind of ultimate scientific sense to the Asian emphasis; it belongs with the intuitions of modern psychology and the science of relativity.

Another feature of Asia which no one concerned with religion can fail to remark is its materialism, which can be pronounced even in so spiritual a country as India. The imperialistic 'masculine' West is acquisitive: it desires money for power and show, but Asia presents a different and more feminine picture. It desires money out of a sense of insecurity, not only for the practical necessities of life, against which it can never have enough insurance, but also to secure its identity. Money is a kind of substitute individualism, the excuse for an ego, or for imposing oneself. The most self-abasing, kow-towing Mandarin, the slave of his Emperor and his parents, enjoyed unbounded authority as bestower of favours. The necessity to be a big soul or a big mind was obviated or compensated for by the possibility of being a big spender. The Western cult of genius has no equivalent in Asia, and at the same time, while Buddhism inculcated a certain notion of 'holy poverty' in those countries like Thailand and Japan which historically took the religion with some seriousness, elsewhere religion or ethical systems, like Confucianism, despite a certain emphasis on thrift and frugality, raised no particularly strong objection to the acquisition of wealth. Because of the essential wealth of Asia, it has always shown accumulations in rich hands beyond the dreams of Western avarice.

In Asia, life is bounded by money to an incredible degree. The nearest approach to the Asian situation is found within the Latin countries, like Italy and Brazil, where what in North Europe and America is rightly expected to be free and the responsibility of civic authorities, like access to a beach or a lift, is subject to toll by some firm or landlord, who then insults the public by spending the proceeds on showy trivia, or the most expensive items on a menu. In such countries, privilege and respectability is not identified with character and talent, but solely with wealth. It is interesting that militaristic Japan, the most 'masculine' country in Asian terms, has been familiar with values which have a Teutonic ring, so that even among aristocrats money need not be absolute, and courage and honour could be independent of possessions. There is even an expression 'the gods laugh at those who pray to them for money'. By tradition, India and China would scarcely understand what that meant. In India, even the 'poor' follower of the princely Krishna accepts that the Shivite worships an ascetic god who is looked to for bestowal of wealth and success. Such are the fundamental paradoxes of Hinduism, for where everything is illusion, everything is as good as real, and where cash is denied as merest matter, it can end up being worshipped as the highest god.

Since Asian materialism is born of a feminine fear rather than a masculine affirmation, it can be as limitless as the sea. Perhaps only in this light can one grasp the terrible rapacity of which Asians are capable; one thinks of the Indian officials today who seize relief donations intended for victims of flood and famine, or the fabulously wealthy Chinese who, at the turn of this century, with their barns bursting, were content to let the peasants eat the bark of trees. Money catches most of Asia in a vicious circle. So greatly is the commodity worshipped that nothing can be achieved, nothing acquired, no respect gained without it. The best are obliged to join the rat race in order to survive; in order not to be bought and sold by corrupt officials and misapplied laws; in order to be educated or to pay the exorbitant fees of doctors. Those who do a good turn simply from their heart are regarded as fools, or with suspicion, as were some of the Taoists who gave away *objets d'art* and other articles free. 'What do they want?' is the unstated question, and the poor response of some Asian societies, especially the Chinese, to mercy missions and the free medical services of missionaries must be put down to this factor.

In a moment of discouragement, one religious worker whom I know complained that his helpfulness and the good turns which he had done to Chinese associates, both secular and religious, did not meet with gratitude or even common loyalty. The answer was, of course, that sadly, providing financial assistance and throwing parties like a man of the world is much more appreciated than the best of good turns, which to the touchy and insecure will even be conveniently dismissed as condescension. Traditionally, Chinese society held that one should do almost anything rather than request assistance, so there is lingering prejudice against acknowledging assistance proffered even when it was virtually requested. Favours requested or given are, as far as possible, not made to appear as such, and normally involve the giving of presents and financial agreements. Maintaining status is an imperative, and poor families may even end up enslaved to creditors, with their daughters forced into prostitution in order to be able to pay for banquets and functions which they cannot afford and which will be attended by many people whom they hardly know. This is an appalling abuse, and one is amazed that missionaries who emphasize contextualization, if not indigenization, fail to inveigh against such empty materialism in sermons and in their evangelistic outreach.

Overall, materialism in Asia would appear to enjoy the same status as violence and lust in the West. Religion has greatly suffered because God or the gods are assumed to be so easily buyable. This is very much the case with the Hinduism of South India, where, as Hindus will frankly admit, the priests can be very greedy and encourage the wealthy to acquire merit by building unneeded temples and making gurus pampered millionaires, while the misery of the masses, easily dismissed as the fruits of bad *karma*, goes unrelieved. Buddhism, though a more modest religion, less open to hypocrisy than Hinduism, has not been without infection from the same vice. The ordinary worshipper might find barriers to his entry into devout circles of Chinese Buddhists, if he did not possess sufficient means, since some of these circles are little better than Freemasonries for businessmen. In fact, in recent times the wastage of wealth by the rich on prestigious but unneeded temples in Thailand has come under scrutiny, as well it might be a land where there is no welfare and no assistance towards the exorbitant cost of medical care.

Neo-Hinduism and Neo-Buddhism have shown a certain contempt for the 'lower' Christian way of action in contrast to contemplation. Here Asian religion shows that it remains essentially monastic, a way of withdrawal for which religion and worldly activity are mutually exclusive to a degree unrecognized in Western and Christian religious belief, where God himself is considered to be active. A further consequence of this belief in withdrawal towards a divinity who is a motionless centre is that the famed spirituality of the vast mass of Asia is closer to the power-conscious self-help religion of magic, and deals in psychic reality rather than spirituality in the Christian sense, though undoubtedly here too the femininity of Asia, its natural intuition, cannot be ruled out. Dreams, feelings, omens, telepathy, spirit communication, numerology, palmistry, all have more significance for the average Asian mind than the Western (see Chapter 6).

Justice is also more easily compromised by this otherworldliness. It would not be very original to say that Asia is distinguished from the West by its concept of justice. 'Oriental despotism' and the arbitrary administration of justice by one person, often in camera, has been a cliché ever since the Encyclopaedists of the Enlightenment, yet its extent and nature still need to be stressed, particularly in the context of religion and missions. In India the problem has not been so great as in East Asia, and was rather one of religious attitude. Law in India was administered by king and advisers, or groups of village elders, and their task was almost sacramental. They increased their *karma* if their judgment was wrong, and if it could be seen to be wrong, they themselves would theoretically be punished. Punishments of the guilty could exceed the crime in modern eyes, and they included torture and mutilation. However, since Indian law was simply a development from Indian concepts of social *dharma* (duty), Indians were not especially litigious. Life was full of religiously sanctioned injustices which were attributed to fate, like the status of the widow, who was an outcast of her family, obliged to consume one meal a day and sleep on the floor, a plight from which many escaped by suicide. In China and Japan, injustice has been experienced as something more purely human, so that at the beginning of the novel *The Scholars*, the Mohammedans must suffer torture because, although the mandarin has passed a wrong judgment on them, he must not lose face by changing it.[23]

Justice always demands a rational world-view, a clear notion of the divine, which the Asia of the Hindu myths and the novel *Journey to the West*, a famous mythical account of the discovery of the Buddhist scriptures, for the most part lack. Emphasis on the stream of consciousness has tended to produce a kaleidoscopic nightmare in which unjust judgments, cruel parents, unwanted offspring, merciless landlords happened like earthquake and flood, and like earthquake and flood had to be suffered or else transcended. Since this was understandably too hard for many to accept, the response would be that of either cunning or revenge. Monkey, the very figure of Jung's trickster,[24] is omnipresent in Asia, from India and Thailand, where he is Lord Monkey, a deity who helps save Rama against the forces of evil in unusual ways, to China and Japan, where, as in *Journey to the West*, he takes on heaven and Buddha in the most irreverent ways possible. In the *Journey* particularly, he is amusing, but there is little attraction about him. Opposed to all authority, he is no Robin Hood for robbing the rich to pay the poor, but one who rights wrongs more by accident, or for fun, or because he is bludgeoned into it, than from altruism. He expresses the basically impotent Asian concern to be free, to upset the applecart, to regain face through cleverness, to be strong. The purpose of *The Journey* is really to persuade readers of the futility of looking for justice in our world of illusion from which it would be better to escape.

More serious, but hardly more attractive than the antics of Monkey, is the East Asian vengeance tale in which, since God is less trusted than under the Hindu system to give everyone their just reward in the end, man performs justice instead, or even regards himself as the instrument of God to perform vengeance. This is another leading theme of East Asian theatre and art. *The Orphan of Chao* is one of the more famous Chinese dramas of revenge;[25] *The Soga Brother's Revenge* is a familiar theme of Japanese storytelling and art.[26] In China, vengeance is more likely to be pursued individually or nationally. Revenge under the old Japanese system was more involved than the Chinese and required retainers to avenge their lords, right or wrong, almost indefinitely. The most sinister aspect of this custom-become-attitude was its inevitability. Anger did not subside with time, even over a generation, and children could suffer for the parents, servants for the master. Under the Gang of Four, I was impressed by the political vengeance theme of Chinese films, like *Princess Saiseze*, and I think it not impossible that, had the Gang of Four not been displaced, their eventual aim would have been vengeance on Victorian imperialism wrought a hundred and fifty years later, if need be by marching on to the West by the million. The long pursuit of personal vendettas, over misunderstandings as much as over proven wrongs, is undoubtedly the least happy feature of Asian life, and energy that should be put into righting genuine wrongs is wasted in trivial ways, which make for the hyper-tension, the strokes and various nervous ailments to which East Asian society is so prone.

Friendship can survive the effects of materialism and injustice, and no account of the salient characteristics of Asia would be satisfactory which failed to mention the singular care with which most Asians cultivate and cherish personal relations. Asia demonstrates neither the reserve of Western man and his 'good fences make good neighbours' nor the informality of regions like the Pacific and Caribbean. It is simply a paradox of Asian civilization and an expression of its feminine values that beyond its impersonal religions and the barriers set up by its materialism, the priority given to the personal, even the sentimental, has made friendship into a true Asian humanism. The memory of Asia is long, with the consequence that 'out of sight out of mind' does not usually apply; letter writing is a sacred duty; everything from anniversaries to favourite recipes are remembered as a matter of course. Friendship can be regarded as something fated, which may be continued for ever. In *The Way of the White Clouds*, the German Buddhist, Lama Govinda, describes how when he and his wife leave Tibet, their servant on their journeys carves them a tablet and prays to be reborn with them to serve them again in a future life.[27] This is explicit and dramatic, but it is not essentially untrue. Moreover, since friendship is frequently regarded almost in terms of kinship or marriage, and therefore in the Asian perspective of devotion and service, the individual is in danger of being pampered and at the same time having considerable responsibilities placed upon him not to hurt feelings or disappoint expectations. The strict Hindu tries to perceive God in everyone; the rest of Asia is inclined, at least sometimes, to see something of the divine through the human. In the event, one senses that within the course of some encounters and friendships there is a trace of 'Waiting for Godot', the unconscious expectation of Asian religiosity that enlightenment may be reached through human communication.

The theory of the guru and the chela (disciple) is precisely that divine knowledge can be conveyed directly through the soul friend. Western readers are likely to be familiar with the theory in its more extreme manifestations, as conveyed by writers like Alexandra David-Neel[28] and Lama Govinda,[29] but it can assume a secular form, or is perhaps the spiritualization of a common pattern of deep attachments which develop between teacher and pupil, master and servant. Whether as a religious or cultural pattern, this seems to be a dimension of Asian experience which eludes the average missionary whose life stories have little to compare with those of secular writers like Pearl Buck,[30] or Lafcadio Hearn,[31] when it comes to faithful servants (Pearl Buck's secretly followed her to Japan) or other dependents. The missionary so often imagines that he comes to preach faith to multitudes or to rectify social evils, and is so inured to expectations of opposition and frustration, that he simply addresses people, rather than contacts them and illuminates them like the guru. He assumes that his cross must be the opposition he sometimes justly arouses, rather than the cross of responsibility which involvement in sensitively balanced relationships like that of guru and disciple must entail, for needless to add, the arrogant and even ruthless ways in which guru and Zen master can treat their disciples, exploiting their trust, could not be justified from Christian values even with enlightenment in view.

Readers may have noticed a certain correspondence between the characteristics of Asia listed here and Buddhist philosophy, which declares that the evils of mankind lie in clinging and craving to persons and things and which sets wisdom and salvation above reason and logic. Buddhism as a religion is inevitable and lacks the surprise element of Christianity. It does not explore those aspects of life and human nature which cannot be readily observed and named, especially through introspection. The association of the ego with clinging, craving and suffering is justified in terms of Asian psychology and the 'feminine' society which, possessing little ego and suppressing what it has of it, causes itself suffering by substituting material craving and emotional clinging for authentic willing and self-affirmation.

Buddhism is the religion of Asia in the sense that it puts a name to the leading characteristics and mental conditions of its people. Until Christianity, Theosophy and Gandhi came to disturb its caste system., Hinduism was a provincial religion, the religion of a society, the spirit of which Buddhism distilled and universalized at the very high price (to all save monarchs in search of a social order) of denying God and human identity. Outside India, it was the monarchs or emperors of Ceylon, Thailand, Cambodia and Japan, who to a greater or lesser extent appropriated the divine role, while the existing religious traditions which were assimilated to the new faith restored a tenuous sense of soul, identity and heaven to the masses who wanted it. Though Buddhism has provided a distinctive and elevated moral code (abstinence from killing, theft, alcohol, unchastity), I still wonder how far it may not be responsible for the Asian sense of drift, illogicality and nothingness. It seems more likely that Buddhism has only sanctified and refined the necessary indifference of Tibetans to harsh conditions, or the drifting, dreaming disposition of the nomadic Thais, rather than actually producing those traits in them. Buddhism perceives life as so many states of mind, even moods. Jung considered that the West did not so much need Eastern wisdom as to discover or rediscover within itself the area of mind in which Asia deals. Personal experience of Asia leads me increasingly to realize how little Asia possesses culturally in the specific way of the West, that is to say, as the expression of will and deliberate originality. Malraux claimed that (assuming, presumably, that our childhoods were rich and introvert) the Orient is our childhood and memory.[32] This may be true. At any rate, to my surprise, what I had imagined about the cultures and mood of India, China and Japan from little information proved to a remarkable extent to be justified. In Japan I felt that I had recovered something forgotten. The poetry of

things Chinese is something I felt I had always known, to the
extent that I sensed a rapport even with *The Dream of the Red
Chamber*, which is more than one could say for many Western
novels. Nepal is the nearest I have come to Tibet, but there and in
North India I have visited temples in Tibetan style, and in the
fiercer, darker aspects of their somewhat baroque art, one feels
affinities to the black magic of Crowley and the dark poetry of
Nazism. Much of Asia that is presented to the West in the guise of
high philosophy is a matter of simple intuition and the spontaneous
or concentrated perception of the child and artist; they involve the
powers which all excessively rationalist educations temper. History
and philosophy are not the only keys to understanding what is
probably most essential about Asia. To do this, it is necessary to
look within.

II

Of course not everything can be known about Asia by looking
within, any more than Asia can be explained by Hindu-Buddhist
philosophy. Even the most cursory survey requires special consideration of China, which is different because of its relative alienation
from Buddhist ideals. This has been crucial for China, especially
within modern times. Where Buddhism is well entrenched, if the
character of the people is at all secular, as in Japan and Thailand
(in contrast to Burma and Nepal), there is considerable openness
to change and modernity because the religion encourages drift and
living in the present. Despite the rationalism of Confucianism and
the dynamism of (philosophical) Taoism noted by the Communists,
the indigenous beliefs of China which rivalled and modified Buddhism managed to place China on a very conservative axis indeed.
There are probably two main reasons: first, that the beliefs and
philosophies which Confucianism finally supplanted have in common an inordinate concern with society and social harmony rather
than with the individual situation, as in Buddhism, and second,
that as a society China has had an overwhelmingly peasant con-
stitution and has demonstrated the usual characteristics, like conservatism, obsession with class, organization, bureaucracy, and a
horror of nonconformity. As a result, religions have tended to
succumb to government control, with Confucianism the philosophy
and the religion of the élite (in so far as temple cults of Confucius
evolved). In this way neither Confucian rationalism nor the char-

ismatic (prophetic) element of Taoism nor the personal element of Buddhism would have much scope for changing things.

It is unlikely that any civilization has gone so far in limiting religious freedom as the Chinese. The extent to which religion was politically controlled is quite remarkable, and must be taken into account by Christian commentators assessing Red Guard persecution of Christians and the Communist refusal to acknowledge the right to proselytization as an aspect of religious toleration. Taoist and Buddhist priests, for example, were not permitted to train a neophyte until he was over forty, or to ordain more than one man, lest religion become too powerful and too many individuals be drawn into 'unproductive' occupations. Ordinary citizens were legally forbidden to pray to God on the basis that going to him for supra-human justice might only encourage political rebellions on earth. Thus, as much from sociological as from temperamental reasons, Chinese religion was liable to be characterized by a very formalized observance punctuated by fits of revivalism, often of a political-'messianic' flavour.

Confucianism can be considered a religion only in so far as it supported the rites which universally involved ancestral worship. Otherwise, it was not religious, nor was it mystical save for the vague concept of *li*, the duty and righteousness which informs the social conduct laid down, and which is defined in terms of cosmic harmony. The most sublime element of Confucian ethics, a negative formulation of the Golden Rule, 'do not do to others what you would not wish them to do to you', has inevitably been the least influential. It points to an interiority, a quality of criticism which the system with its stress on obedience and organization tends to play down. Not that Confucian philosophy itself is especially organized; like certain passages of the Bible, it is seemingly contradictory or paradoxical, a characteristic which in the case of the *Analects* is often attributed to the Master's tendency to adapt a truth to the level of his pupil's understanding.

The peculiar effect of the Confucian value system as popularly mediated has always been to mix grave formalism in certain fixed areas of conduct with a peculiar naturalism. Whole areas of Chinese character held in check neither by a more comprehensive philosophy or by an introversion of the Indian type emerge in terms of pure unselfconscious temperament. Whether this is pleasing or disconcerting will depend upon the individual personality, which may be vigorous or apathetic, pleasure-seeking or studious, but will be accepted in any case with fatalistic tolerance wherever it does not conflict directly with the system of duties. Later Confucianism described character or temperament mechanistically in terms of proportions of '*chi*' or material energy, and this was certainly true to things as they had been made to appear.

Philosophical Taoism (religious Taoism was the Chinese response to Buddhism and absorbed higher elements of primitive Chinese religion) gave scope to precisely the element in Chinese temperament which chafed at the artificiality and injustice of those Confucian rules which tended to hold it in check. Theoretically, the philosophy taught the mystical unity of everything in the Tao and the notions of identity and balance already alluded to in Chapter 1. In the hands of artists, disillusioned scholars and politicians, it became socialized into a doctrine of retreat, return to nature, comedy, free expression, self-indulgence. Popular Taoism likewise could supply gods and techniques to the outcasts of the Confucian system, the secret societies, bandits and prostitutes.

Buddhism, the foreign faith, entered China in an age of agony (the Three Kingdoms and Wei Period of the third and fourth century), when withdrawal held a definite appeal for all classes and conditions of men. It was never completely at home in China despite several centuries of considerable influence and its inspiration of some of the greatest Chinese art. Though China received the easier Mahayana version of the faith with its emphasis on ritual and on grace mediated by *bodhisattvas* rather than salvation by personal effort, it was still too ascetical as regards family and food; furthermore, the doctrine of reincarnation held little appeal and was considered irrational by the educated. Chinese and subsequently Japanese Pure Land Buddhism, which emphasized heaven, and Ch'an or Zen Buddhism which sought enlightenment in the here and now, both represented attempts to avoid the principle of reincarnation. Buddhism ceased to be a major force among the educated after the twelfth century and the assimilation of some of its ideas to Neo-Confucianism. After this time, its main function, apart from satisfying popular spirituality, was as a justification of individualism and a kind of feminism, since the way in which Buddhism elevates pity as a virtue has always made an appeal to women in the Far East through its contrast with the hard and automatic rationalism fostered by Confucianism. All the major Chinese novels represent individualistic and sometimes feminist critiques of the corruptions and severities of the establishment. Given the individualistic and 'feminist' presentation of Christianity in the last century, in sociological terms it was natural that some of the most zealous converts, the 'Bible women', who instructed and evangelized in the villages, should have been former Buddhists.

So it was that Chinese religion remained in a dialectical tension between the way of rules and action and the way of no rules and inaction, in which enlightenment of the Asian variety became confused with liberation from convention, as the lives of many drunken and abandoned Taoists demonstrate. The Chinese soul would be a peculiarly divided one: on one side a rationalist and moralist, on the other side of a nature-lover, a Bohemian, with little or no chance of resolving the two, especially since Chinese society, sensing its safety and identity to be in numbers, has endeavoured to present a front of togetherness which is either fictional or only realized – if at all – at very high cost. The majority of Chinese in fact appear to suffer constant emotional repression. Recently, one Chinese actor actually remarked he had chosen his profession because then he would be free to be natural and give vent to his feelings; Chinese business, which is extremely demanding and tense, gives little scope to emotions beyond the negative ones of envy and resentment, and it would be hard to account for the native love of shouting and deafening noise, and the penchant for anti-social littering, which the Communists have tried to curb, without some theory of serious repression or resentment.

Altogether, what really separates China from the rest of Asia psychologically is its greater extraversion, though it remains Asian as far as 'femininity' and general response to life is concerned. By extraversion I do not refer so much to the energy of the Chinese, which makes them the most industrious people in Asia, as to the greater importance attached to the objective fact, the environment, the doctrine. This is not always to the advantage of the famed Chinese humanism. As in the West, and particularly in France, a country which has certain affinities with China, noble words are in constant danger of being confused with noble deeds, and reorganization of structures and the environment of being confused with change of heart and social change in depth. Like its Latin counterparts, Confucian bureaucracy soon became more a system of rules for the rich and powerful to catch out those below them when they felt like it than something promoting a universal and impartial efficiency after the manner attempted by more miltaristic societies, like the German and the Japanese. The philosopher Chu Hsi sounds impressive when he declares love to be the principle of things and the basis of social relations, but one wonders what relationship this bore to the corrupt society which bought and sold women and children and practised the most hideous systems of punishment and execution, and how far his ideas were meant to reform any of this. Like 'liberté, egalité, fraternité,' such things can belong more to the sphere of rhetoric than to that of practical ideals. Later Confucianism had much of the philanthropist who loves society without loving anyone in particular. As Wang Yang-Ming wrote, 'The sage regards the world as one family and the country as one person. As to those who make a cleavage between objects and persons and distinctions between the self and others, they are small men.'[33] And clearly those Confucianists like Chang Po-hsing, who opposed Adam Schall and the Jesuits, did think them small men and attacked them with bitterness over the depravity and socially subversive mixing of the sexes in church, an ironical and rather hypocritical charge in view of existing attitudes towards prostitution and concubinage, though logical to those who rate conformity to custom as the prime virtue.

Like the Western extravert who possesses little interiority and projects his complexes and imperfections upon others and finds security by imposing himself (for example, the English talking about the funny men who begin at Calais), the Chinese have usually been xenophobic (the only exception was during the T'ang dynasty), regarding their neighbours as barbarians fit only to be subdued and Sinified. However, it is probably true to say that this suspicion has been exaggerated by the repression of the emotions and imagination of the individual countenanced by the society. Only in this context can one hope to understand the fevered imagination of those attacks by mandarins on Victorian missionaries which no amount of missionary folly and misdeeds could justify and which precipitated the Tientsin massacre. Most famous of all was 'The Death Blow to Corrupt Doctrines' of 1861, which attributed to Catholic priests and Protestant missionaries alike almost every imaginable depravity and cruelty, including the gouging out of the eyes of the orphans they tended and use of the sexual organs and fluids of converts for the dark purposes of their religious ceremonies. The remarkable thing is that such nonsense was believed and roused the public to frenzy. Even today, however, one notices that in business and other scandals, particularly religious ones, as broke out in 1978 in Hong Kong over the finances of a Catholic school, the bigger the slander, the more it stands to be believed. There are parallels in the religious history of basically rationalistic and materialistic France, and it seems almost as though religious scandals provide the populace with a catharsis, an alternative spirituality of protest, in which the demons of imagination are exorcised at the expense of the innocent or perhaps the weak.

Commentators on Chinese affairs, religious or otherwise, tend to be either all for the Chinese or all against them. As might be imagined, I am unable to be either, and feel a certain affinity with the position of the author of *The Dream*, who portrays his society as truly Yin Yang, a tissue of curiously cruel acts and deeds of great generosity and self-sacrifice, and otherwise evinces great respect for native aesthetics, awe for the numbers and immensity of China, love for the underlying poetry of the society, and yet a certain alienation from many national values in theory and in practice. With this in mind, I shall mention a few characteristics related to our subject which seem to be points of difficulty or friction in contact between Western and Chinese, Chinese and Christians.

Almost everyone, the Chinese included, is agreed upon the decided pragmatism of China. The Chinese mind is supposed to bend before any wind, like the bamboo, without breaking. This is the way in which historically the people are believed to have withstood the revolutions and natural cataclysms which have periodically overtaken them. But pragmatism is not just learned; it is an acknowledged feature of the extravert mind, which is not the sort to cry much over spilt milk or hold out unnecessarily against the crowd or the age, as the introvert sometimes has to do in order to survive. The disconcerting thing about Chinese pragmatism, however, from the standpoint of ideologues like Communists and Christians, is its typically extravert inconsistency. It is hard to judge where, if anywhere, the centre of affections and self-interest lies. In one generation and one place the Chinese may hold to tradition against modern and Western inroads with almost blind romantic defiance, and in another generation and place, throw away tradition without apparent regret as an impediment to self advancement. The difference between Taiwanese and Singapore Chinese in this respect is instructive. Overseas Chinese attach no value to nationalist and cultural concepts of China, yet turn unpredictably romantic, especially about the sacred land of China or themselves as a race; thus Indonesian Chinese long settled in Indonesia may leave everything to go to die in the land from which they or their ancestors emigrated. The most Westernized Hong Kong citizen may suddenly declare himself 'pure' Chinese.

It is well known, and a tragedy of Christian missions, that many Chinese at least appeared to enjoy being in the vanguard of Westernization only to change their tune with the rise of Communism, denouncing foreign influence and the association of missionaries with imperialism. Chinese history ancient and modern is full of such seeming reversals of favour (seeming so, at any rate, to foreign eyes, which may not be able to discern the eternal China beneath the changes). At all events, the church is obliged to ask itself what the Chinese want. If it fails to indigenize, it can be accused of encouraging disloyalty; if it tries to encourage indigenization in Hong Kong or Singapore, it runs the risk of being accused of not being realistic and relevant. The consistency of the introvert societies, like Japan and Thailand, which simply state their hostility to Western religion, is really much easier to cope with.

Faced with Chinese changeability, moralists, and even Sinophiles, like Bertrand Russell, have been inclined to accuse the society of cowardice.[34] The respectability traditionally accorded to just running away lends some weight to the charge, but I suspect that the question of face is more important. Like the rickshaw men of Hong Kong who recently told those interested in their profession and the construction of their carts that it was 'shameful' to be involved in rickshaw business today, tradition, aesthetics, count for nothing if one is not respectably in fashion. Western mockery of Taoist superstition disposed of Taoism among the educated much more quickly than any philosophical objections. Then, too, the Chinese have been amazingly accustomed to repress and silence their feelings and opinions, and they believe, with the false objectivity of the extravert who attributes everything to environment, that they are the product of society alone and have duties towards society. This being the case, they are scarcely conscious of the ethnic feelings which may at any moment overcome their Westernization and send them in another direction. It is this lack of interiority that causes them to project the Chinese spirit in themselves upon concrete things, like the land or the masses. The marked Westernization of Singapore Chinese – more pronounced than in Hong Kong, apart from political authoritarianism – is a mark of self-confidence and ambition, almost a situational ethic. While the Chinese are together, they feel they have an identity, whatever their style, but one could predict that if they were threatened by political neighbours, their host country or Communist China, they would quickly alter. The strong pressure on Malaysian Chinese to conform to the host society encouraged many to become communists. The Chinese abroad have always displayed the greatest reluctance to become assimilated to non-Chinese political ways.

It seems that what the Chinese want most essentially is to have face and belong, to be of a Chinese group whatever the style or ideology. However, as their occasional regrets and prejudices reveal, they would certainly prefer a Chinese style provided that it did not conflict with material and social ambitions, as it sometimes does. Because it recognizes the need for ideals and naturalness of expression, the church is therefore still obliged to encourage a measure of indigenization.

Another factor which may strike the foreigner forcibly about the Chinese scene is the matter of humour and the related question of face. The absence of the more socially significant forms of humour, like high comedy and satire, must almost certainly be accounted an element in bolstering the national conservatism and resistance to change. Humour can contribute to the revolutionary mood, as did *The Marriage of Figaro* to the French Revolution, but the nearest the Chinese come to such comedy is in the lampoons which appear once the revolution has started. In this disposition China contrasts strongly with Japan which, despite its even greater formality, has at least periodically criticized customs and rulers on stage or in art, while in fiction it shows an ironical sense of humour which would be unacceptable to Chinese society and its developed sense of 'face'.

Chinese humour is mainly of the extravert, slapstick, levelling sort, of which England has had quite a variety. Someone bumping their head is funny on stage, in story, or even in life. More commonly, again as in English humour, there is the anecdote 'I'll tell you this story', or 'I know a person who. . . '. In this way the possibility for subtle, psychologically penetrating, or even very spontaneous humour is avoided. It is important for the foreigner to realize this, since so poorly do the Chinese take the suggestion of personal slight, whether intended or accidental, that to make an error of humour might prove the end of a good friendship or even invite dangerous enmity. I have much sympathy for a Taiwan missionary who told me that one of the most difficult things to accept with grace was the almost total suppression of a sense of humour required of him.

No one enjoys criticism or being made a laughing-stock, but it is hard for the Occidental mind to appreciate how little ego (and it is this, not pride) the average Chinese possesses, and how extremely vulnerable this ego is. If the extravert is someone who has little ego in the sense of self-possession and awareness, the Chinese extravert also has a 'feminine' sense of nothingness or inferiority.

At the same time, if 'hell knows no fury like a woman scorned', it can sometimes happen that the same applies to a Chinese criticized, perhaps especially when the criticism is just, or when criticism is only suspected but the impression is enlarged by imagination. Until I had had more experience of the weaker, less attractive side of Chinese character, I doubted Victorian missionary Griffith John's complaint about the mandarins. 'It is impossible not to displease them. To preach is to insult them, for in the act you assume the position of a teacher. To publish a book on religion or science is to insult them. To propound progess is to insult them. . . .' Even to nurse the sick or assist orphans was to insult mandarins, John claimed, since they alone were supposed to organize relief and charity.[35]

Such behaviour must have been very hard to bear, especially as with all people who lack a broader view and whose responses are automatic, dictated by book or custom, etiquette is one-sided, and the Chinese who will not brook the slightest murmur of disapproval or tolerate the least breach of behaviour, can be breathtakingly rude in situations or to persons not covered by formal etiquette. I leave aside the barging and pushing, the disrespect for queues, which is a result of Confucianism having pre-dated buses and post offices. After writing a book on the Chinese Church, I myself was told, by Christians, not to presume to talk about the Chinese and to get myself back to my own country, and my writings have been banned from many religious bookshops as though they were pornography. One Chinese woman, evidently more influenced by Confucianism than the Bible, insisted that if I were really a good person I would never criticize anyone (Confucius taught that the virtuous man corrects only himself, never others, which is certainly face-saving). Though appalled by this behaviour, I can still smile at it, not having given my life to missions, but such attacks and ingratitude towards missionaries, not all of whom were vicious, must have been a hard cross to bear in a far land.

Not surprisingly, in view of what has been said, there is a Chinese proverb, 'If you want friends, don't enquire too much about them'. Real friendship is probably harder to establish among the Chinese or with the Chinese than in any other Asian group. Not only is it potentially dangerous to the kind of sensitivity described, but native pragmatism tends to limit relationships to the wide circle of family and clan members, and to business associates with whom there is usually too much duty or tension involved to allow the pleasures of friendship. This may not apply so much to those under twenty-five today in Hong Kong or Taiwan; there is a certain openness, though age and duties still threaten to invade this liberty with time, and even with a meeting of young people I have noticed tensions and jealousies because of real or imagined differences in social – basically financial – status.

It is in this context of traditionally limited friendships that one has to understand Matteo Ricci's final judgment of Chinese society as 'a desert of gentility'.[36] In the fashionable circles he knew, and to some extent in the less fashionable circles he did not know, the greater part of social calling was occupied with exchanging empty pleasantries and going through elaborate ritual gestures, like pretending to dust the visitor's chair. In one of the passages of Chinese prose which comes nearest to satire (chapter 53 of *The Dream*), the author exposes the stream of meaningless exchanges and time-wasting costly entertainments. Even today, especially at festival times, it seems that many Chinese never really talk to their friends because they are too busy giving presents to one another, treating one another to gastronomic feasts and playing mah jong. The tremendous pressure within a limited time (the Chinese are always working) to meet, greet and treat the widest possible number of clan and business associates has placed severe restrictions upon the cultivation of depth, psychologically and spiritually. As in France and most peasant-formed societies, there is a horror of solitude, inactivity and boredom. Such is the pleasure to please and serve the group that it is amazing how the early Jesuit missionaries managed to contact and convince so many fashionable members of Pekin society.

Inevitably, however, there have always been two kinds of religion in Chinese society. There has been the social, ritualistic variety which was and is almost wholly pragmatic, placating spirits and asking favours of ancestors and the heavenly bureaucracy rather than seeking any personal communion with divinities, and there has been the religion of withdrawal and dedicated groups or secret societies, such as the early Buddhists, the Taipings, the Boxers, and the Jesus Family. This division usually corresponds to one between urban and rural Chinese, since rural man usually has more excuses to avoid the social round. From the Christian standpoint it would be hard to see how Chinese secular life could be easily reconciled with even a conventionally devout religious life as in other societies, and on the whole, Chinese Christian life in the cities has usually been undistinguished and unsatisfactory, as in Shanghai. There would be more heat and fervour, if not always more light, with the rural societies.

III

With this in mind, I shall round off these observations on the Chinese difference with a few comments upon its distinctive Christian theology. In comparison with Japan and Korea, China (whether mainland or overseas) showed itself slow to produce any distinctive or indigenous emphasis; indeed, only in the last decade, with the work of the Taiwanese, Dr Chou Men-hwa, *Preface to Establishing Chinese Theological Thought*, has any conscious effort in that direction been made.[37] Dr Chou is, surprisingly, a Southern Baptist; previously appeals for such a theological emphasis came from liberal missionaries in the 1930s, but the author does not get much further than suggesting the possibility of paralleling some mainly Confucian categories with scriptural terms. The value of this identification has by now been considerably diminished since for too long too many Chinese Christians, like the woman who thought no good Christian ever criticizes anyone, have unconsciously and uncritically interpreted Christianity in Confucian terms; they have sometimes done so to the point where they have a faith which is almost more Jewish and limited to the family, than Christian and related to society. There is also the problem that the kind of national schools of theology, like the German, which Dr Chou would emulate, require theology to be worked out against a conscious and cultivated national complex or subjectivity. Japan and Korea possess such a complex, but the 'extravert' Chinese, emphasizing the objective fact and playing down the personal, does not – at least consciously – and therefore identifies Chinese ideas with Confucianism or Communism, more often than not rejecting these Chinese ideas totally when he accepts Christianity. This attitude is severely literalistic; much Chinese Christianity, like English Puritanism, has been convinced that it was literally following the Bible that it was never aware of the elements behind the literalness which made its faith distinctive.

Dr Chou's approach has been countered by the theology of incarnation put forward by Dr C. H. Hwang. He feels that it is undesirable to Christianize any culture, as can be seen from the results of the Emperor Constantine's attempt to do this in Europe (I think Hwang has confused indigenization with *imposition* of religion and the consequent *syncretism* which sullies the faith).

Hwang regards life as a stream of events or a patchwork of historical and social situations into each of which Christ and his teaching must be incarnated and contextualized. The church does not look merely for 'contacts' with a religion or culture, with all the weight of rigid formulations that these seem to invoke, but tries to perceive, interpret and realize God's will in all ideas and events which come along.

The emphasis on social environment to which this theology leads is undoubtedly needed in the overseas Chinese context to counterbalance the obsession with the local and family group, but the philosophy is over-idealistic (who but saints can hope to 'incarnate' Christ everywhere and always?). It is also intellectually frustrating in its refusal to see to what extent it is in itself an interpretation through Chinese values, which could be more powerfully and effectively channelled within a specifically indigenous theology. Apart from the very Chinese emphasis on the practical aspects of religion and on action (almost Chinese hyper-activity in the circumstances), there is a rather Taoist strain answering to Chou's 'Confucianism' when it comes to questions of continuous creation and the transcendence of events, albeit by reference to Christ as opposed to Tao. Another Chinese element is the equation of God, man and nature implied, which opposes itself to the conventional Western God, church and world.

Perhaps the most significant element in Hwang's argument lies in his refusal to be slavishly tied to the biblical text. This leads to one of the more distinct features of Chinese Christianity in recent times, at any rate within Protestantism, which has probably been the more dynamic force. For many Christians, unswerving adherence to Confucian principles or to Mao's *Little Red Book* could be exchanged for an adherence to the Bible. Sometimes, indeed, this adherence was so unswerving that the new faith was one of Jewish legalism and politics, while the spontaneous 'Taoist' side of the national character was given minimal scope for integration. This dubious strength of Chinese Protestantism could not, of course, be duplicated in modern Catholicism, where authority attaches to the church rather than to a book, and although the average non-reading Chinese might prefer authority to take this distant form, the implications for non-Chinese power have been controversial.

The problem of biblical literalism dates back to the 1930s and what may be called the rural revivalism of the mainland. In their anxiety for outreach, Hudson Taylor and the CIM had contacted as many regions as they could, founding but not confirming and educating churches. These congregations subsequently languished beneath the rule of ill-trained pastors and their often illiterate, superstitious flock; occasionally, with typical peasant disregard for the sacred (compare the casual Latin treatment of churches where people can eat sandwiches, breast-feed children or chatter while others hear Mass), churches were used as part-time stables or even brothels. Meanwhile, most missionaries, unable to cope with the variety of rural dialects and peasant character, concentrated on the cities and the middle class. Protestant Liberals, more concerned with Christian social duties and the Communist challenge, made some outreach to the country and sponsored agricultural projects. They were, however, poorly equipped to negotiate the realism to which the Communists appealed or to confront the superstition, the very marked fear of *kwei* (bad spirits), to which fundamentalists with their world of warring angels and devils could address themselves. It is hard today to envisage the polarity of liberal and fundamentalist opinion which prevailed in missions during the 1930s. Subsequently, opinion has become more relative; the late Bishop Pike was interested in spirits, and Dr Leslie Weatherhead allowed that some instances of alleged demon possession in China may have been genuine.[38] Likewise, representatives of the fundamentalist or conservative standpoint, like Billy Graham or Dr Coggan, would not dream of attributing most mental illness to demonic forces. However, Sung Ju-un (John Sung 1901–1944), the son of a Methodist minister who aspired to be an evangelist but had his faith shaken by liberal views at Union Theological Seminary, resolved all his problems by attributing liberal teachings to demons. The college, taking alarm at his opinions and apparently erratic emotional responses, sent him for psychiatric examination. Sung escaped from the hospital, and undeterred, on his return to China, went on to become the most famous of Chinese evangelists to rural China and overseas Chinese groups, stirring languishing congregations with the fear of God and calls to second birth. Since ignorance was the chief problem with rural congregations, he instituted the most rigorous and thorough Bible training courses, and delivered marathon sermons lasting hours as he expounded biblical texts. At the same time, his alienation from liberalism was such that this study was permitted no contextualization and he preached as though the misery and problems of China did not exist.

Similar emphasis is found in other noted evangelists of the 1930s and 1940s like Wang Ming Tao (though he was finally imprisoned by the Communists for opposing the Government and the co-operating liberal Three-Self Church) and Pastors Lee Han-Wen, Andrew Gih, and Timothy Dzao. It is remarkable how little these men actually had or have to say. Pastor Gih's *The Church behind the Bamboo Curtain*, written from Taiwan,[39] is little more than a reiteration of familiar biblical texts with a series of black-and-white comparisons like 'Christians believe in God, Communists are atheists'. To understand such writing and preaching, apparently blinkered to events and subtle distinctions, we must see it in the context of a society where there is often complete ignorance of Christianity along with very imperfect Chinese translations of the Bible, which may require a pastor to simplify and repeat the text over and over again.

John Sung as such is a phenomenon which it would be foolish to accept or dismiss too easily. Many Chinese today regard him as little short of a saint, attribute their spiritual beginnings to him, and only wish for others of his kind to come to revive them and modern China. My own feeling is that the imperfect vessel is getting mistaken for an ideal in default of more examples, and as it works out, this contributes to continued misconceptions among missions about indigenization. Leslie Lyall's biography of Sung, *Flame for God*, is unlikely to commend him to most Western readers, of whatever shade of religious opinion.[40] Though Sung spoke much of full dedication and service and the wholeness of second birth, his own religion was rather one-sided; it radiated no Christian serenity or graciousness. His self-dramatizing behaviour could be insulting to the point of spitting in people's faces or climbing on altar rails. I do not mean to prejudice even the most fundamentalist belief about evil powers in suggesting that Sung's emphasis on demons almost certainly has some bearing upon his own unexorcized demons and unresolved conflicts, which are suggested by the bizarre nature of his youthful spiritual battles and his tragic early death from cancer.

Sung's development shows great contradiction and repression. His father, a devout bully with whom he often came to blows, must have confused him in his view of God. Pastor Sung's arbitary betrothal of his son to a girl at an early age placed him under a terrible strain when as a student in America he fell in love with another girl whom he knew he could never marry. It is clear that Sung felt it hard to be accepted by God because his own volatile temperament, unacceptable to Chinese norms (though not un-known among the Fukienese), made him associate grace with a peace and perhaps a social smoothness of which he was incapable. Hence the terror and the emotions aroused by every new or un-accustomed religious idea, for everything upsetting the equilibrium must be evil and outside grace. This also accounts for the confusion as to whether he was converted in China or America, for he too readily associated conversion and conviction with any kind of great emotional upheaval. It must be emphasized that revivalism East and West is not easily compared, since the Chinese, being so re-pressed, are not only extremely susceptible to emotionally charged situations but are also consummate actors who can feign tears and emotions to an extent unimaginable in most Western countries; the nearest comparison is with the Italians, who are often in danger of failing to realize when they are acting.

Genius is often close to madness, as the lives of artists show, and to say that Sung was unstable is not to discount his religious vision. It does seem likely, however, that he represents a case of danger-ously forced development, a classic instance of the religious person who wills and believes himself to be holier than is acceptable to his unconscious, so that the latter takes revenge in fears and obs-essions. It is not impossible that at a deep level, like Luther, Sung may have hated God (and his father) and the demands he appar-ently made on him, but unlike Luther, he never realized this and so never overcame and transformed the hatred. There is something excessive and unnatural in his throwing overboard his American diplomas (he was a Doctor of Chemistry and had claimed to be guided to study in America). He may have consciously believed that it was his heroic duty to renounce his family for God, and refuse to support its members financially by the fruits of academic success, as being Chinese they desired and expected, but uncon-sciously he may have felt rebellion against both the endless de-mands of the Chinese family and the God whose vocation appeared to pose serious spiritual dilemmas to these claims. Only a mixture of Chinese literalism and absolute self-control could perhaps have produced quite the interpretation of Christian vocation and the emotional solution at which Sung arrived. One feels that a little more compromise would not have made him a lesser man or a lesser Christian.

Yet maybe this judgment is in itself too severe, and possibly beneath his 'fool for Christ' mask Sung was a wiser, shrewder man. Not all China is composed of elegant mandarins and butterfly women; its peasants, like peasants everywhere, could be rude, harsh and grasping, and in Sung's time most were illiterate and hopelessly ignorant. These people needed a 'direct' approach; they also needed to memorize Bibles, since many could not afford them, while others would one day have them ripped up and destroyed, as happened under the Red Guards. Furthermore, whether he realized it or not, Sung must have seemed like a Taoist crazy or a Ch'an master, shocking people into enlightenment by shouting at them or knocking them over. Seen in this light, he may have been the prophet, the man of the moment.

The greatest danger is to institutionalize Sung, seeing him as an example of indigenized Christianity, as conservatives like to do, because of his extreme emphasis on the Bible. Indigenized theology, to merit the name, requires self-consciousness and a breadth of application in the biblical message, and Sung had neither. But for all its imperfections, Sungism undoubtedly had an effect. Chinese Christianity appears more vital in Taiwan and Singapore, where his influence was felt, than in Hong Kong, where Christian witness is still mostly limited to education. However, it is revivalism of this kind which encourages Dr Stanley Mooneyhan, President of World Vision, to speak of the need for a 'New Testament aggressiveness' from the Asian church.[41] Apart from the fact that even St Paul at his most vehement was not as aggressive as Sung, whatever Chinese needs may be, aggressive Christianity is not what non-confrontationist Asia requires; Asia is already tired of it and it is a factor in Asian resistance. It is wrong, then, to look to the Chinese as the new Puritan, the new ally in reaching a lethargic Asia. It is disturbing to see how Michael Griffiths of OMF rather takes the Chinese side against other Asians, maintaining that they work for their money and hence deserve what they get abroad. This judgment can be questioned: the Chinese, who are very business-minded, cannot resist a gamble or a chance to raise prices, and the way in which they can send land prices soaring in foreign countries, or alter working hours and customs (they tolerate no tropical siestas), has been regarded with some alarm by host countries whose attempts to place restrictions on Chinese ambitions sometimes appear necessary.

Notwithstanding these negative reflections, the outlook is far from completely gloomy and there are positive things to say. In 1920, the former Buddhist Ching Tien-ying founded the Jesus Family, in the wake of the Shantung revival and the creation of the indigenous (Chinese organized) 'True Jesus Church', and by 1949 this had developed into 140 communal groups in eight provinces. The Jesus Family proved that evangelical faith could be combined with practical action and concern. Ching promoted agricultural schemes which reaped bumper harvests, permitting the communes to support not only themselves but the surrounding poor and to give relief, particularly during the famine of 1942. As the Family knew no central control and refused to build churches, worshipping instead in the central building of their commune, they adjusted more easily to Communist rule and appear to have received more toleration.

There are many aspects of Jesus Family practice which deserve comment, but more important for our study is Ni To Sheng (Watchman Nee, 1903–1974), another Bible teacher and evangelist, the founder of 'The Little Flock Movement' and author of the controversial *Re-thinking Missions*.[42] Nee was the grandson of a Congregational pastor and the son of a customs official, but the main family influence appears to have been his mother, which was not unnatural, since his native province of Fukien had always been quasi-matriarchal.

The emotionalism and independence of Fukien, the skill of its people at language and literature within a China more adapted to business and mathematics, are factors to be taken into account in considering both the penetration of the church within that region and certain characteristics of Nee's thought which reveal an uncharacteristic degree of independence and also introspection in comparison with his evangelist contemporaries. However, this does not mean that his work is un-Chinese. It is more Chinese than Sung's.

In his home, at Trinity College in Fukien, and later in Shanghai, Nee had been initiated into the nationalist ferment and the problem of the anti-Christian movement (1918). He had also witnessed the evils of Shanghai, against which the church seemed helpless. All this crystallized in the foundation in 1926 of the indigenous, independent 'Little Flock Movement', though its principles were not fully worked out until *Re-thinking Missions* in 1938. This manifesto radically asserted the sovereignty of the local church, denied the value of all denominations – they were dismissed as scripturally unwarranted – and maintained that the church in China must return to more apostolic patterns. Following Nevius, Nee revived the principle of self-support, self-government and self-propagation. Later, the Communists would demand nothing less, though they eventually ruled out propagation. Missionaries, many of them deeply attached to denominationalism, and unable to appreciate the offence this gave to Chinese 'one family' ideals and the confusion to which it gave rise in a situation where churches were further divided by dialects, took alarm and opposed Watchman and his followers, only driving many Christians into his group. It is almost certain that the extent of opposition prevented the indigenization from progressing from organization to style, as Nevius proposed; the churches of the 'Little Flock' would continue to look Western and their hymns sound Western, while the more original insights of Nee's theology would be obscured by the defensive, careful presentation.

I had often heard Nee's theological writing praised, but at first sight, I found it very dry in the manner of Chinese classical writing, by which he was influenced at an early stage. Soon, however, I was impressed by the quietly revolutionary nature of his thought, in which one can perceive the beginnings of a shift in psychological emphasis towards the reinterpretation of Christianity outlined in the previous chapter. The failure of Nee's admirers to recognize this reminds one of the Western dispute over the nature of Bonhoeffer's theology, in which conservatives fail to see the originality perhaps because, as with Nee, they are misled by the biblicist tone and the emphasis on obedience. Nee's attitude to obedience is influenced by his training at the hands of Victorian missionaries as well as his embarrassment at his own originality, and this gets rather in the way of the realizaton of freedom which he glimpses and which any Chinese theology would need in order to counterbalance the extremes of native authoritarianism.

In *What Shall This Man Do?* Nee begins to exalt the personal aspect of revelation suggested by St Paul's 'it was the good pleasure of God to reveal his Son *in me*'.[43] Even the Bible, he maintains, must not be exalted above Christ and inward knowledge. Although he allows salvation to be realized in objective events, doctrine, according to Nee, is the formulation of knowledge and experience that cannot and should not be conveyed in wholly intellectual terms as objective facts. (It should be noted that his refusal to sanction the republication of his own highly systematic *The Spiritual Man* derived from his somewhat Zen-like belief that true faith is of the Spirit, and that anyone who supposes that it can be intellectually grasped is lost to the workings of the inner man and the Holy Spirit alike.) He demonstrates that psychologically and biblically the most important thing is to believe in Christ, not in what he has done. Here he opposes any presentation of Christianity which would say (like Sung) that Jesus effected certain things and the individual must believe them or else. Where people have no clear view of Christ's personality and nature (as would happen in mission areas), this is a fraudulent approach. Normally, knowledge of Christ and self puts the events of salvation into proper perspective in due course. Nee agrees that this happens not least because of the nature of grace, and stepping in where Augustine and Calvin feared to tread, he speculates from his evangelistic experience as to who God has elected and why he has given them grace. God, he says, does not save the good or the bad, but only the honest. Those who say they are disinterested in God and do not want to be saved, and even those who say they cannot believe in God, may well find him. Conversion is never a human achievement; it has to be realized, and those who say that they 'cannot' be good, or 'cannot' believe, are precisely those most susceptible to change and being acted upon. In the same way, once begun, Christian progress is never towards a far-off goal; it is rather a matter of seeking God's standard.

> You advance spiritually by finding out what you really are, not by trying to become what you hope to be. . . . It is when you *see* that you are dead you die, when you *see* you are holy you become holy. The end is reached by seeing, not by doing or working.[44]

This is very Asian, and a whole doctrine and discipline of seeing could easily be developed from Nee's thought in this field. However, according to Nee, honesty and seeing are virtues often lacking among Christians; he instances the Christian pastor (Sung?) who never cared for his family but made out that he had rejected them all for God.

Nee has much to say about the church, which he interprets as an aspect of the divine desire for incarnation. The church is at once being transformed into *one* person, the extended Christ, yet working towards diversity, in such a way that he is convinced that by some psychic force (he does not use that term) the members really do suffer or receive blessings according to the actions of groups within the body whom they may not even know. The church has a high role; its principle in this world is 'to restore to God his own omnipotence'.[45] Overall, the existence of the church leads to an expansion of God (again, he does not use that term), for the human experiment will mean that omnipotence will be morally greater than in eternity past:

> Because there will be a possible limitation. Man will still be able

to disobey, but will never choose to do so. The separate, created will of man will be wholly set for God. This . . . will be the glory of God.[46]

As I remarked, there was little or nothing consciously aimed at indigenization in this theology, and it remains for others to develop it, fit it into more specifically Chinese categories, and integrate it to art or liturgy. If one were to look for a specific model for an indigenized Chinese church, it would undoubtedly be among the heretical Taipings who, with nothing but a Bible and the leadership of a mentally disturbed but gifted man who declared himself Christ's younger brother, established a new religious and political community. As is well known, the community eventually became a revolutionary body which spread havoc across China, during the 1840s and 50s, and prejudiced the authorities against Christian ideas by spreading distorted versions of them before the new missions really entered the country. At the same time, it anticipated many socio-ethical changes which would subsequently overcome the country. The doctrinal and revolutionary extravagances are irrelevant to the style of the first manifestations of Taiping religion, which merit re-examination. One notices the emphasis on the Spirit (normal with those who strongly interiorize religion), on the Ten Commandments, the group, the confessions (important as a psychological release in Chinese society because of silent resentments and the acceptance of slander), the writing down and ritual burning of prayers, the religious poems.

It is true that the Taiping rebellion originated among the Hakkas, who again, like the Fukienese, were semi-matriarchal and somewhat alienated from Confucian norms. Nevertheless, the appeal of the movement was widespread and lends further support to Dr Yang's thesis that despite the rationalism of the élite, historically the Chinese have shown themselves far from irreligious, even if they have never been among the most deeply spiritual of men.[47] The problem of Christianity in China is that it has usually been on the one hand too individualistic to form a model for the religion of community and withdrawal, like that of the Taipings and the Jesus Family, and on the other hand, too personal and unaesthetic to satisfy the average Chinese demand for a rather formalistic religion.

3
The Chinese Setting

Soon it will be possible to fly direct from London or New York to Beijing (Pekin) and penetrate China from the centre, but like many people in modern times, my first contact with Chinese life was to be through the more hybrid world of Hong Kong. In a sense, this was as representative a place as any other to begin, because strictly speaking, there is no longer any 'Chinese setting' to write about as there is a Thai or Japanese setting. Despite the glories of the Tang and Ming, China before the foundation of the Republic in 1911 was always more a civilization than a nation, which is why it was so vulnerable to Western and Japanese imperialist encroachment. Today, the civilization, in so far as that could be designated Confucian, has been either discarded or severely modified, and the nation in the sense of the Chinese people has long since broken its borders. Like the Jews, the Chinese are found everywhere. Thus one can only speak of levels and intensities of Chinese consciousness as one finds it not only in China, of which I shall give some impressions later, but in Taiwan, Singapore, Hong Kong, and even further afield.

When I first came to Hong Kong, I was shocked and disappointed, and the magnificent setting could not make up for it. At first I could not even perceive how and where any Chinese consciousness existed. Like an increasing number of people, especially artists and architects, I had expected a much less Westernized city, by which I do not mean that I expected traditional China, but at least a city in which some blending of East and West had occurred, as in Hawaii, or one in which, as in the San Francisco Chinatown, traces of the past would be more evident in architectural forms. Of the buildings and high blocks of which the city in its all-pervasive materialism boasts, scarcely any came above the average and could not be seen anywhere. In literature, drama and art, I found a cultural desert where the confrontation of cultures seems to have exhausted both sides and brought them to the most insipid forms of self-expression. The only place where anything like a real Chinese culture could be found was in the homes of a select company of rich, who live gracefully and own priceless collections of Chinese art, or else among the ubiquitous working population, in whose apartment blocks, resettlement areas and shops, icons and lucky posters will bespeak centuries-old folk religion. But for the rest, the businessmen, and to a large extent the professional classes, there is a dreary capitulation to the functional and to everything Western – often, for want of better example and experience, the worst of its kind.

The problem can perhaps be seen at its most acute in the religious sphere, in the temples and churches, which are fairly numerous. Usually, when I arrive in any foreign place, I am keen to visit and photograph the religious monuments, because it is here that the history and the spirit of any people is most distilled, religion being the first impulse of all cultures. But when one looks at the temples in Hong Kong – and tourists are apparently not expected to, since there are no adequate directions for reaching even the largest and most interesting – they are untidy and ill-kept in comparison with temples in, say, Taiwan. No matter how many people go to pray for luck in them at festival times, they suggest that the spirit has gone out of local inhabitants, for when the spirit is strong there is a sense of style and order. It could be said that the traditional religions were dying, but if that is the case, there are plenty of the conventional signs to suggest that the newer, and in certain respects fashionable, religion of Christianity has more life. Again, one finds no real style. It is true that a few churches show modest incorporation of Chinese elements, but they do so in no significant way; none of the mystery which characterizes Chinese religion is retained, nor is anything of the drama which characterizes Christianity added. Not only has the religion produced no new style; it can hardly be said to have produced new values of a kind to suggest that it has been taken creatively to heart. While Chinese Christians are probably more conscientious and public minded than their associates, it cannot usually be said that they think more deeply. If anything, their views are rather confined and predictable.

Church leaders, only too glad to count numbers and see lives well lived, might not think that these things mattered, and certainly they could plead the pressures and limitations of Hong Kong life as an overcrowded colony living on borrowed time, were it not that other Chinese settings show the same sort of picture. Nevertheless, though the situation is far from being untypical of overseas churches founded in the Victorian era, from the standpoint of the artist or the sociologist, it does break all the historical rules about religion and raises many questions.

It is certainly quite out of harmony with Chinese treatment of novelty, religious or any other. Here matters are quite plain. It is a principle of Chinese social history, as of Chinese art, that progress and innovation are never absolute, but involve a going back on the past and a process of sifting and transformation. This is the significance of Mao Tse Tung's 'Let the past serve the present.' It can well be asked if a church which ignores such principles can ever hope to be truly Chinese. Again, to quote Mao on the acceptance of foreign ideas generally:

> Our policy is to learn from the strong points of all nations and all countries, learn all that is genuinely good in the political, economic, scientific and technical spheres, and in literature and art. But we must learn with an analytical and critical eye, not blindly, and we must not copy everything indiscriminately and transplant mechanically.... What we must study is all that is universally true, and we must make sure that this study is linked with Chinese reality.[1]

A good deal of Christianity in the Chinese setting does appear to savour of mechanical transplantation.

At first, these problems of aesthetics and religion were not something about which I theorized in anything like historical or sociological terms, although I was reasonably well equipped from previous studies to do so. Since it seemed that I was fated to live in Hong Kong, I began rather with protests against the situation, and practical suggestions to interested groups for improving it; it was only through defending my position that any theory of, for example, religious indigenization emerged. Despite its value as a record of Chinese, colonial and ecclesiastical attitudes, and as giving clues to the remote origins of thoughts underlying this book, I shall not supply a history of controversies and experiments in which I involved myself. I shall only deal in some of the main conclusions, especially those which have some psychological or sociological bearing on the religious theme, since my first conclusion is precisely that information about Chinese culture or religions is no longer the problem. There is almost too much information, and so many summaries that one would hardly care to add to them. Missionaries in the Chinese setting today are not usually uninformed about the culture, even when they dislike and oppose it, while others, far from being unwilling to enter into serious intellectual or aesthetic relation with it, feel that the problem lies not with themselves but with the Chinese, who lack sufficient pride in their heritage. Missionaries, however, rather like the academic world generally, have not adjusted to the transitional features of the times. They study the history of a nation when they should be studying the shape of history, a culture when they should be studying cultures. The result is that their adjustments, if they make them, will be to classical expressions of a religion or culture, while their refusals to adjust may be made in the belief that since the classic expression of a religion or culture is passing or deceased, all attempts to relate are doomed. These views suggest academic rather than practical appreciation of human realities, something which has always been anathema to the Chinese mind, which sets much store by intuition and feel and is much more aware of the ebb and flow of events.

II

In order to understand Chinese life in any setting, one is obliged to study the history, the art and the leading literary texts (not just the philosophers but the leading novelists and poets, like Wu Ching Tzu, Ts'ao Hsueh-Chin, Tu Fu and Li Po, who represent more popular views) and then either forget them all and trust to 'feel', or remember what one can, with the object of appreciating the extent to which the Confucian philosophy never really was a humanism or rationalism in the Western sense, but was also considerably dependent upon intuition. Undoubtedly, Confucianism, whether considered as a philosophy or as a life-style, constituted the binding element in Chinese society, even though with its subjective views of justice, coupled with its indifference to extra-familial duties, it bred enemies for the establishment in terms of the regionalism and the secret societies which periodically toppled dynasties and fomented the Taiping and Boxer revolts.

In so far as Confucius, then Mencius, then Hzun Tzu, placed great stress on education, the investigation of phenomena, fulfilment achieved within social relations and truth capable of realization by man, it is possible to speak of the Confucian tradition as rationalistic and humanistic and psychologically 'extravert'. But two important considerations intrinsic to the system and Chinese thought-feeling cut across all this. The first is quite simply the status of introspected abstract principles, like *li* (duty, religion, and many other connotations), *yi* (righteousness) and *jen* (benevolence), which are repeated again and again within the philosophy like words of mantric power. The great error in tackling these is to assume, like the Enlightenment philosophers who portrayed Confucianism as a deism or a cult of reason, that one is dealing with intellectual principles or cardinal virtues as the Greeks might understand them. From the way these principles work and the way Chinese people think, influenced as they still are by Confucian values, it should be clear they are closer to complexes, and sometimes virtually interchangeable psychologically with archetypes as they would operate in Indian myth; if they are not interchangeable with these, it is only because 'intellectual' considerations have been allowed with time to modify the sort of feelings they represent. Principles, Confucian or most other as Chinese people tend to apprehend them, can refine, grip, animate or enslave, as can only the archetypes when they are manifest as forces invading the conscious. Chinese life has many examples of people zealous and sometimes hopelessly eccentric in defence of some supposedly rational principle. Psychologically speaking, the Chinese principle, like *yi*, is something gnostic, more like the archetypal *sophia* or wisdom than the Greek reason. There is, after all, no classical Greek sense of *telos* or purpose in Confucian thought; indeed, Chinese language is such that it is not possible to proceed from describing something as 'good' to describing it as 'a good', an object to which something might tend in fulfilment. The first interest of the Confucian gentleman was to *be* good rather than to *do* good. Moral character can be seen most essentially to consist in such harmony with oneself and the universe as will produce correct attitudes and choices; the precise results are of much less consequence, which is why the possible injustices of the Confucian family system, or the cruelties of society or the mistreatment of animals, are either secondary or ignored. A traditional Confucian might say that these would involve problems of *li*, changing values, whereas getting in harmony with *yi* or mystical virtue, which gives rise to values, would be more important. Confucian *jen* or benevolence thus approaches the mystical and has a kinship with the *bodhisattva* ideal of Mahayana Buddhism, where the god who loves without object is more by way of an inspiring light than an active helper. Likewise, attachment to *li* or duty has often justified animation by feelings of vengeance so intense as to suggest kinship with the archetypal buddhas of wrath. Little attention is paid to the lower expressions of any principle even when, as in the case of vengeance, it is considered perfectly acceptable, and this leads to the second significant feature of the culture.

Despite the emphasis on practical affairs and the investigation of things, there is nothing especially 'realistic' about Confucian thought, which is idealizing and remarkably exclusive of the barbaric. Even in Taoism, which like Indian and Japanese religion accepted the union of opposites, the pain of opposition, the horror of the evil or the ugly, which is aesthetically realized elsewhere, is muted; for Taoism, negative elements are a pretext for some artistic mannerism. The terrible is not a reality to be overcome; it can hardly be said to exist. This marks an advance in optimism relative to Asia, but not necessarily in terms of human understanding. Chinese concerns, even when dressed out in philosophical terms, end up being nothing if not basic. There is little encouragement to development in depth, little possibility for critical understanding. Idealized realism describes both the philosophy and the art; one sees nature and society as it should be rather than as it is. It is not 'reason' which gave to the Confucian gentleman his eighteenth-century character, but acceptance of the world as the best of all possible worlds, and his optimistic prejudice that man was born good and became evil by merest accident of training or environment. Present in Confucius, this optimism is most developed in his successor Mencius, who may have overstated the case for human perfectibility in order to lay to rest rival trends of thought, like the pessimistic legalism which the Confucian revolution had overcome. Anyway, this was harmonious with Chinese feeling, and it still echoes in much Maoist thought about man and his possibilities within society.

When these two features of the traditional culture are recognized, it is easier to understand not only the Confucian thought and some of its apparent contradictions, but the complementary relation of Buddhism and Taoism to it. For the average Chinese, whether scholar or layman, philosophic Buddhism never held much weight, and it penetrated the culture, as in Neo-Confucianism, only where it could give greater depth to already existing belief. On the one hand, it is possible to portray Buddhism as an alien faith, and in many ways it is so; yet purged of its more demanding or fantastic aspects, there is a Buddhism which bears a relation to Chinese character rather like that of Anglicanism and its 'empirical' theology to the English mind, engaging respect even while it is little practised. If nothing else, Buddhism represents an intensification of depth in relation to the introspective current within Confucianism, while the nature of Chinese language alone, pictorial and unanalytical, encourages sympathy for the 'seeing', the immediacy, the ineffability of Buddhist perception. In this respect Buddhism is not, and never was, alien in the way that Christianity is.

In the same way, when the subjective element of Confucianism and the affinity of its 'principles' with 'complexes' is acknowledged, it will be easier to grasp the sneaking sympathy which cultured Chinese, desiring change, have had with Taoism and even its more obscure alchemical forms, as in *The Secret of the Golden Flower*. When it is realized that the 'morality' of Confucianism is never psychologically far removed from the management of complexes, it will be appreciated that a system of taming the unruly archetypes and stilling the mind must assume authentic religious significance. The ethics of Western man are much more influenced by considerations of both intellectual reason from the Greeks and numinous authority from the Jews, who were original in the extent to which, psychologically speaking, they let the conscious and the exclusive super-ego, rather than the inclusive unconscious, be a medium of truth.[2] The result is that the interval between human and divine, and good and evil, is perceived as being that much wider and more difficult to resolve. In turn, for Chinese people, a religion like Christianity is likely to register as a form of obsession with Jesus, useful for ordering other obsessions, depending somewhat upon the individual's temperament.

Philosophy, as I have stressed before, has never been very important for Chinese people, and Confucian, Taoist and Buddhist doctrines have at times been regarded as highly antagonistic. Yet at other times, as religions, all three have been practised simultaneously and been made to appear similar, which in a way they are in their use of recognizable, psychological and aesthetic dispositions. Chinese philosophy thus remains 'symbolically' significant; its study is relevant to religion and life in terms of form. An uneducated Chinese with no understanding of the Confucian theory of *li* or Taoist aesthetics could still judge certain specimens of Christian art or passages of the Bible as barbaric because they come in a form and treat of a subject-matter which historically the

Chinese mind has been disposed to ignore. One can be Confucianist in belief, or practice, or style. Today, it is often only the style which remains, a fact which church study and apologetics never seem quite to grasp.

Since even philosophy is felt to be ultimately reducible to practical schemes for the acceptance or formal embellishment of common realities, popular religion tends to be still more basic. Buddhism may have changed the calendar and modified views of the after-life, but it has scarcely touched Chinese eating habits or treatment of animals, and altogether it is seen as yet another form of investment.

Where religion is the subject, once again Confucius undoubtedly struck the authentic note: 'While respecting the spirits, to keep aloof from them may be called wisdom', and: 'Absorption in the study of the supernatural is most harmful'. When his disciple Chi Lu said, 'I venture to ask about death', he was answered, 'While you do not know life, how can you know about death?' The notion that death itself might supply clues as to the significance of life did not trouble Chinese humanism. It is not even clear whether Confucius believed in God, though as he remarked that he had often prayed without success, accused 'Heaven' of trying to destroy him, and maintained that whoever offended Heaven could pray to no one else, one should probably assume that the abstract 'T'ien' carried over some anthropomorphic associations in his mind from the earlier Chinese concepts of a supreme deity, and that his attitude towards a supreme deity was typically Asian: namely, not so much agnostic as profoundly pessimistic.

Religion can be a powerful presence, as the red incense-laden gloom of the temples with their rich murals and elaborate images testify, and a part of the Chinese consciousness is undoubtedly away on the mountain tops amid pine forests, looking at the cloudy void of Taoist vision. On the other hand, the careful commercial mind of the average Chinese has little intention of getting lost there, and leaves it to priests, artists and mediums to probe the greater problems.

On the whole, the popular religion is disinclined to believe that there are many problems, as to a remarkable degree the beyond is envisaged as an idealized prolongment of earthly life, even of the class system, since the gods operate like a civil service. If a good deal of Indian religion has never left Harappa, much Chinese religion has never left An-Yang and the royal tombs with their offerings of utensils for the use of the dead. The funerals of the religiously inclined are still surrounded by much burning of paper houses, cars, tables and chairs. One of the most powerful traditional objections to conversion to Christianity has been fear that Christian children will leave the parent a hungry ghost without ritual food offerings, and recently in Hong Kong, the number of converts to Catholicism has been swelled by elderly persons who, accepting with native realism the *fait accompli* of changing times and faith, frankly admit having joined the religion for its promise of a beyond where one is not dependent upon unreliable children to be fed. This fear is, of course, more pronounced in elderly women than elderly men, because by custom, the securing of salvation and benefits has devolved upon the woman, who has charge of the domestic altar and the religious education of children. It is not exactly that Chinese men are sceptics – they can be, but theirs is usually a mixture of scepticism with fitful belief or superstition – but that in a society where material success and the protection of the family enjoys almost sacramental status, it is enough that the paterfamilias attends to his career.

As a consequence of this situation, the Chinese Buddhist and Taoist priest is often less of a philosopher or an ascetic lost in meditation than a confidant of women and a general diviner, though, of course, many fortune-tellers and mediums are independents. Much Chinese religion outside the home would thus be considered akin to spiritualism or white witchcraft in the West, and one of the benefits of reading Chinese poetry, like *The Songs of Ch'u* with their spirit journeys, is to realize how much of Asian Shamanism remains within the imagination and popular custom. Even in artistic theory, the emphasis on portraying the bones and 'skeleton' of objects, a tendency which has militated against fleshy eroticism, derives from the old pre-Taoist Shamanism with its nightmares of sacrifice, in which the adept must imagine himself a skeleton, his flesh torn from him by the spirits. Popular and magical Taoism has thus been (and is) vastly more important than the philosophical Taoism now familiar to the West. In Hong Kong, amongst those who are religious, the eight fairy immortals are still quite widely revered. The birthday of the Redwood fairy draws crowds at the Wong Tai Sin Temple, and new moon brings devotees to consult the medium at the Monkey God temple.

Nevertheless it would be wrong to over-emphasize the practice of religion. Though most people are registered as Buddhists, there are numerous heretics, unbelievers and materialists, while Taoism is perhaps rightly regarded as the religion of the poor and the cranky rich. Some people occasionally burn joss-sticks to 'God' independent of all cultus; some, if asked their faith, will reply 'I am Chinese', which indicates that their devotions are limited to ancestral cult, or possibly, that they have intimations of some mysticism of community. I have observed that being Chinese does constitute a sort of religion for some people, comparable to the ancient tribal beliefs which perceived even immortality in collective terms, the 'was gathered to his fathers' of the ancient Semites. It remains true to say, however, that most people, even the purely secular, usually have a kind of reserve belief in 'fate', like modern Hindus who have lost their faith. The nature of Asian hope lies not so much in the working out of any general or particular divine purpose through events, as in the rewards which must eventually accrue to patience or virtue, if only through the boundless possibilities of life, in which Asians are inclined to think that anything can happen. It is a case of 'everything comes to him who waits', or, 'something has to happen in the end'. This attitude accounts for the continued lively interest in all varieties of fortune-telling, dream interpretation, geomancy, phrenology, numerology and the Chinese almanac, and it may be recalled that for all his scepticism, Confucius had great reverence for the I Ching. Ensuring that the right *fung sui* (wind and water interaction) prevails in an office or dwelling is of enormous importance. Almost any setback in life is liable to be placed at the door of bad wind and water as it attracts ill luck from evil spirits. Many Christians, perhaps especially Catholics, would not reckon to live in a place, or be married at a date not deemed auspicious by a fortune-teller, despite ecclesiastical opposition.

Though I have made a different assessment of the Asian occult in Chapter 6, basically I see the Chinese variety as dangerous because of its lack of all hold on the objective, 'scientific' element, with the result that the client is constantly the prey of frauds, or ruthlessly accurate psychics. So-called palmists, for example, supply intricate information from the hand which the lines of no hand could reveal, and which could never be traced to a text-book of palmistry. As I write, one educated Chinese I know is undergoing psychiatry following the suicidal urges set in motion by a palmist's forecast that he was about to die. Numerology, on which much so-called Chinese astrology is based, gives an illusory impression of objective authority to a people whose talent is more mathematical than linguistic, and whose plans and arguments are based on the ten ways, the hundred opportunities, and so on, a point which has been lost on missionary preachers, who have rarely used the biblical numerology in the elucidation of their arguments.

Thus it is important for religious commentators to note not only the superstition but the chauvinism which keeps these interests alive, considering that if there is anything in, say, astrology, undoubtedly the Western form is more efficient, and currently enjoys some support from the findings of scientists, statisticians and psychiatrists. However, I have heard it said by Chinese that the Western system, like Western medicine, is not to be trusted; this contrasts with the more open attitudes in Thailand, where I have heard local fortune-tellers denigrated and Western astrology and palmistry frankly praised. Anyway, it is clear that 'Western' religion is often viewed in much the same light. 'Most people in Hong Kong are very busy, and as the Chinese already have their religions anyway, they do not feel they can spend the time learning Western religion', as one young man said to me.[3]

'Western religion' first came to Hong Kong in 1842, soon after the foundation of the colony, but its function at that time was to serve expatriates, and its wider influence was felt mainly in education. The church schools tended to provide bilingual clerks for the colonial administration. Christianity helped to form an elite corps, and in Hong Kong the religion has remained solidly middle-class (over 80%, I was informed), but it was not purveyed by an elite corps anxious to come to grips with Chinese life, as was the case with the originally successful Jesuit mission to Peking two centuries before. Until after 1945, and the massive influx of refugees from China which raised the population from 600,000 to over 4,000,000 by 1975, there was no major evangelistic thrust, despite the frequent use of Hong Kong as a regional base for missions. The colonial authorities disliked the idea, local Chinese remembered the humiliation of the Opium War which had ceded Hong Kong, and the missionaries were more interested in mainland China. After 1945, the church was granted extensive freedom in the operation of education, hospitals, recreational centres and other welfare concerns by a government somewhat overwhelmed by events, and the result was 432,500 Christians (59% Catholic, 41% Protestant) by 1972. Obviously, some of this religion was nominal, and the 12% annual growth rate of the 1960s declined to 3 and 4% in the 1970s. The belief that 10% of Hong Kong is Christian is probably illusory, since many believe that the population of Hong Kong considerably exceeds 4,000,000, and that for various social and political reasons, the true figure is ignored.

Habit and crisis have always been two very important influences in the growth patterns of Chinese churches. Whereas in some cultures familiarity breeds contempt and the church school in particular acts as an inoculation against the religion among the Chinese, who tend to be xenophobic, to realize that Christians are normal people and that Christian life is feasible, attendance at church school can be a significant experience leading to a genuine if not enthusiastic conversion. Crisis and/or loss of identity is another factor. The Communist riots, political upheavals and economic insecurity of the 1960s in Hong Kong produced exceptional interest in religion, absent in the more secure and more culturally nationalistic 1970s. For the Chinese, religion is deeply involved with identity. In Thailand, for example, where the churches include many Chinese, one factor assisting conversion in an otherwise highly conservative people is a certain willingness to dissociate from the Thais and their Buddhism.

The post-1945 situation thus presented the church with great advantages, but there have been serious disadvantages as well. Given the nature of Chinese society, its group orientation and reverence for age, the best approach is not to aim first for the individual and the young, though educational and welfare work in Hong Kong encourages precisely this. It is preferable for the quality of church life, and for getting to grips with Chinese culture and society, that the group, the family and the elders are brought in first. Lone individuals or youths can easily be 'persecuted', or at least demoralized, by family opposition, while their openness to Western ways may only alienate their elders, or as often happens, itself wear off with time. Moreover, school religion, which is limited by law from treating the more doctrinal aspects, and may be tailored to examination requirements (doctrine classes are optional, though expected of those attending church schools), easily gives rise to misconceptions; children may finish well informed about St Paul's missionary journeys but have no clue concerning the religion's doctrine of creation, or they may imagine that Mary is an aspect of God. Moreover, since church schools offer superior education, and the churches did the work of a government taken by surprise, they came to be government assisted and fee-paying, with stiff entrance requirements. This made the church a party to assisting the children of the prosperous, rather than the needy, and to supporting a rat race which has children taking examinations in kindergarten to qualify for entry to superior infants schools, and suffering nervous breakdowns at ten in trying to enter select senior schools. This situation has obviously concerned many thinking missionaries and clergymen, but it is only part of the unacceptable conservatism of a church tied to a government's apron strings.

The excessive gratitude with which some missionaries look upon the Hong Kong government for bestowing on them the influence they enjoy is almost disturbing, and the difference has been exaggerated by politically unsophisticated fears that any social criticism is tantamount to returning Hong Kong to China. Many people genuinely believe that it was out of some English Christian charity that Hong Kong sheltered the millions of Chinese refugees which it did, and not with an eye to political necessity and their economic value both to the colonial establishment and the big business interests represented especially by the refugees from Shanghai. These last helped to build up the modern booming Hong Kong, but only by perpetuating many of the old evils of Shanghai; it is the big business interests which the Hong Kong government has consistently supported (usually against greater public interest), and until recent (post-1974) years, when local corruption and exploitation became internationally famous, against all common justice.

While for the purpose of encouraging investment the super-rich went virtually untaxed[4] and there was a chronic shortage of hospitals, while the prosperous gambled fortunes away and denied their sweat-shop workers statutory holidays and compensation for accidents, one could still read and hear priests and missionaries saying how relatively *good* the government was. For a long time this puzzled me, until I realized that to some extent, especially among the Catholics, conservatism was the price paid for influencing the government in the Legislative Council towards puritanical laws on off-course betting (the fabulously wealthy Jockey Club has a monopoly of on-course betting and is too powerful to be opposed), prostitution, abortion and homosexuality. All these were more or less illegal (as of 1978), though since then there has been some evolution, and proposals for changes over abortion. Given Chinese values, the police corruption, the role of the triad societies and Hong Kong's situation as a port city, nothing could have been more unfortunate and conducive to crime. Triads and the police have grown rich on protection rackets and blackmail, and with prostitution completely illegal, it has been easier to corrupt and bully young girls into the oldest profession. Undoubtedly, as in Bangkok, legalization would have been the lesser evil. It is true that the churches are far from being exclusively to blame: there is a Confucianist tendency to moralize and regulate, which is next to fundamentalism, and the Hong Kong Christian Industrial Committee, among others, has consistently opposed such Puritanical laws; however, church responsibility cannot be overlooked. Idealism has triumphed over realism and charity; children have been maimed for life as a result of unsuccessful back-street abortions, and homosexuals, if unfortunate enough to be working-class, have languished in jail for behaviour not necessarily reprehensible by traditional Chinese standards.[5] There is much more moralizing about the evils of sex than about the bribery, the property rackets, stock market fiddles, cruelties to children, neglect of unsupported sick and elderly, and the conduct of civil servants who, to gain promotion, lie to government about conditions. And it is not as though the Chinese people are unable to see through this. Commenting on the levelling off in conversion figures in the 1970s, a recent television survey mentioned that in the working classes, conversion patterns were proportionate to Chinese feeling that the church was working for and identifying with the people. Preaching and specific doctrines had little to do with the matter for ordinary people, who were more swayed by good examples, and although it was recognized that the Christians had long been involved in worthy activities, they were also felt to have been so in identity with the establishment, whose wrongs they ignored rather than with the people and their true needs. Certainly, like many Christian laymen, I have long been surprised at the lack of support of the former China missionary, Urban Councillor Elsie Elliot, who is celebrated as the one-woman opposition party to the mountains of corruption and miscarriages of justice which have characterized Hong Kong life and the occasionally serious opposition to her from church leaders.

Hong Kong is expanding and changing so rapidly that it is difficult to evoke its atmosphere and make prophecies about it. The new relationship with China; the greater prosperity and security of the people indicated by the less compliant shop assistants; the 'softer' youth; the scholarship grants which begin to release students from parental dependence and reverence for teachers, are already producing changes in this physically and psychologically over-intense colony, which perhaps appears most Asian at night, when the blaze of lights blots out its architectural mediocrity and there is some mild diminution of the humidity and the exhausting, almost numbing, noise and bustle of the streets. Many young Chinese growing up in Hong Kong today refuse even to think of the future. Some have begun to think of Hong Kong like a national identity, and in the eyes of the Mainland refugees who cannot stand the competition, and overseas Chinese who find the inhabitants rather less than typically polite, such thinking appears justified. To the expatriates, many of them necessarily British but many also Americans, Hong Kong can never be home: it is rather a place where they pass an often neurotic existence, somewhat like life in a hotel suite. Against the high level of nervous and marital breakdown which expatriate life entails, one psychiatrist, not very realistically, proposed that each family should own a yacht in order to escape regularly to such peaceful undeveloped beaches as remain. It is true there is something about the colony which is suffocating, spiritually and otherwise.

If all this sounds unflattering, I should say that I am not unaware of the unique problems of Hong Kong, and know enough about Chinese people and culture not to take the city and its obvious defects as representative. I have also been fortunate to know many Chinese who have risen above it and represented the true virtues of their race. On the other hand, I do see Hong Kong as a painful exaggeration of the Chinese weakness of materialism which afflicts Christians like the rest (though they are usually more honest and scrupulous with it). The tendency of Chinese, whether Christian, Buddhist or Communist, always to regard affairs from the material view, and to sacrifice the romantic for the real, leaves me with more empathy for Japanese and Thai society, though I find both mostly inferior in terms of the aesthetics and sense of gracious living which is hard to overlook in assessing any country.

In contrast to Hong Kong and its purely selfish materialism, the People's Republic of China with its 'doctrinal' and socially orientated materialism must obviously appear more moral, even while its official 'faith' is atheism. I cannot hope to supply any integral portrait of China, but only a few possible correctives to Hong Kong and other overseas images of China, especially religious, which colour world religious views generally. I have long been sceptical about the reports of China from religious observers, like Asian Outreach, which, alternately gloomy and optimistic, portray the country as steeped in atheism and every oppression, or else hungering for the Word and undergoing secret revivals. I am not accusing Hong Kong missionary organizations of distorting truth and inventing sources, but I am suspicious of an unconscious Chinese tendency to embroider and mythologize, especially when they have some passionate political or personal interest. Christian reports of the supposed execution and tortures of Watchman Nee are a case in point. There is no question that Nee, who died in jail in 1974, was victim of a shameful outrage of common justice. He was jailed on absurdly false charges in 1956, not released at the end of his sentence in 1967, and forbidden to mention God in letters explicitly, but he wrote letters until the end, and it helped no one to have it said that his hands had been chopped off and his eyes gouged out. Many Hong Kong Christians hold strong opinions about China, but refuse to visit it when they have the opportunity, and this is a pity, especially when many ordinary Hong Kong citizens are going safely to visit relatives there.

Having been refused entry earlier, I went to China in 1978, and it was obviously changing. It was not comparable in style and feeling to countries of the Soviet bloc, and it is apparent to citizens and visitors alike that it is not at all what it was under the disgraced Gang of Four, in which a spy system left friends feeling threatened by friends, and everything down to Beethoven subject to censorship. Now there is much more freedom of expression, and even visitors are invited to make criticisms and suggestions.

When one enters other Communist countries one senses a certain gloom, while sullenness and resentment often prevail even among so-called 'comrades'. Current Chinese Communism is rather more sunny by comparison. Old magazine pictures which revealed workers, their faces cracking with smiles as they wielded hoe or factory lever, were of course unnatural, but moderate cheerfulness is certainly quite common and not forced for tourists. Now that it is possible to wander through streets and fields to gain personal impressions without being followed, it is obvious that the Communist way of life is not privately experienced by most as an intolerable burden, even if it can sometimes be frustrating and 'everyone has their own opinions', as one girl put it. Among some there is an impassivity, a vacancy of look or automatic response, which is vaguely troubling and may hide something, but expressions of absolute resentment or dejection seemed absent. Granted, if one wants to paint a negative picture, misery exists in some places. The recent descent upon Pekin by protesting, half-starved peasants from Shantung province, who were dressed in tatters, would not have occurred otherwise, while China has made no attempt to hide its dissatisfaction with the high crime rate, the theft and incidence of rape in Wuhan province. These trouble spots, however, only remind us that China is not just a nation but a continent, with different races, dialects and material resources which no amount of attempts at social uniformity can hope to stamp out, and in any case complete uniformity is not the intention; regional cultures are mostly protected. At all events, my point is that boredom is likely to be a greater enemy than dejection.

In 1978, when it became easier to leave China, thousands of legal immigrants began to flood Hong Kong, embarrassing a government which had only just solved the problem of illegal immigrants. I feel sure that when it does not involve people anxious to join relatives, this immigration is mainly the result of the limitations rather than the hardships of Chinese life. Unless one has special reasons, like alleged religious persecution (which again is a somewhat regional phenomenon),[6] or one is a landlord's son (they are paid 70% of their rightful income, an issue just being reviewed), there would seem little ground for leaving. Accommodation can be poor and shabby in China, but there is nothing to compare with that of the poorest in Hong Kong, the corrugated shacks or rabbit-warren-like rooms of the tenements with twelve or so bunk beds. Medical care is universal, and one does not see the sick or crippled (often victims of bad midwifery) evident in the slum regions of Hong Kong,[7] nor the very old working. Nor does anyone appear overworked. Life is easier in China for both workers and students; there is less cramming study, no requirement of four or five A-levels, less push and hurry. Work may be hard, but it is leisurely, and the cyclists, with whom even the bumpy country roads are usually full, do not pedal at a furious pace to their destinations. In Hong Kong Saturday is a work-day, and for many Sunday, too, but in China the weekend starts on Saturday afternoon, when people crowd the shops in the cities.

Thus, there is reason for many to be content, especially as it is still apparent that China was once very poor. The intense and varied cultivation on every side is modern, but back from the roads and sometimes incongruously flanked by Stalinoid functional buildings, stand the picturesque but obviously once poverty-ridden brick villages, recalling scenes from Pearl Buck's *The Good Earth*.[8] The poverty which still threatens is symbolized by the bicycles which carry bales of hay and other burdens which elsewhere would be transported by lorries. Lorries appear to serve mainly military purposes, and empty military vehicles seem to ply the roads everywhere.

Notwithstanding humanitarian attendance to fundamentals, life must be rather dull. Leisure and sports facilities are kept to the minimum and are often primitive; standards in concert music, Western and Chinese, are high and performances can draw crowds, but theatre seems rather artificial and limited; shortage of electricity can make for dull evenings even in cities, and the telephone and television, which all but the very poorest shack dwellers of Hong Kong take for granted, represent the ultimate of luxury. Stores are shabby, and despite the Chinese love of clothes, these are uniform and almost uniformly shabby, though brighter, more varied designs are now reaching the shops. In life or on the media, romantic interest is almost nil.[9] Food, too, must often be poor for this race of gourmets. Only in tourist restaurants is there cuisine of a standard equal to that in Hong Kong. Though I had heard them praised as superior to average fare, hotel meals left something to be desired, while some of the fruit and vegetables sold in shops and markets appeared of inferior quality. Thus this is a spartan country, with little room for the fastidious and demanding. Though such people might be found in Pekin and Shanghai, generally they do not exist. Not only was the flight or execution of the privileged extensive, but China has been too long cut off from the world. Films, television and magazines have given Hong Kong Chinese of all classes a strikingly different face. Self-conscious style is largely absent, tourists are objects of wonder, and the poses and expressions of the art and light music currently in favour all belong to the 1920s and 1930s. Marxism may be committed to history, but behind everything the manner is that of the 'timeless' peasant.

Atheism is the official 'faith'. Theoretically, religious practices are tolerated but may not be propagated, because it is hoped that religion will dissolve with time. In reality, toleration depends upon the time, the region and local leaderships. As is well known, especially under the Red Guards, Christians and other suspect persons, both religious and secular, were given short shrift, if not actually persecuted; scriptures, prayer books and images were taken away, and churches and temples closed. Twelve years later, the abuse of liberties by Red Guards is only just being openly criticized in wall newspapers. No doubt it will eventually be assessed in purely political terms in China, as in the world. My own view is that it represents a perennial feature of Chinese life, especially in relation to religion. In one large temple I passed a group of boys who were throwing various projectiles and booing at a large image of the Jade Emperor. There is no question that had an official been near or had one reported it, they would have been punished, for religion apart, the public monuments of China do not exist to be vandalized. The real problem is, however, twofold and psychological: on the one hand a projection onto any deity of an unresolved hostility to authority, and on the other, the frustration of a type of materialistic mind before the mystery of the infinite. France, with which I have compared China, shows these same traits to a high degree, from the mediaeval fools' feasts celebrated in the churches, to the modern anti-clericalism and the rude, almost childish behaviour of those who smoke in cathedrals, talk loudly during prayers, or clamber round altars. This behaviour, as Jung pointed out, is Trickster and Monkey in purest form; in both France or China it is irritating, because one always suspects that the mockers are not really willing to change things (like the French, who hated Catholicism but failed to turn Protestant), or if willing to change, are party to schemes so abstract and mechanical that they leave individuals wishing to affirm themselves in this way.

I was anxious and curious to learn whatever I could of the religious situation at first hand, but it is impossible to gauge the representative value of what I learned, whether about religion or anything else. Everyone said that there were Christians in Pekin, but because of the appeal of ritual to Communists, 'Christian' usually designates Catholic only, and it is well known that even under the disgraced radicals, a pretence of liberties caused a show of tolerance in the capital. In Canton the Catholic cathedral has been closed since the Red Guards, but is it not a museum, school, or art workshop like many temples, so that visiting Catholics are told that it has been, and could be, used. The same applies to the cathedral at Shanghai, which requires renovation and repair, but may now be re-opened.

While I was walking in a park (not in Pekin), a Chinese, speaking excellent English, introduced himself to me. He was thirty-five, he had been born in Shanghai, and had been a teacher there and elsewhere. He asked me my nationality. When I said I was Irish, he replied that he expected I was a Catholic. I said that as it happened, I was a Protestant, but automatically asked whether he was a Catholic. I did not expect the affirmative I received, its genuineness underlined by repetition of some sentences of the mass in perfect Latin. I asked him whether he knew that the mass was now said in the vernacular. He did, but was not aware of later news like the deaths of two popes and the election of a Polish one. He had not been to mass for years. I asked whether there were not house masses and meetings where he lived. He said that there used to be, but not after the Red Guards; in any case, thirty years of isolation is a long time for a small church like the Chinese, and many older members had died. I asked whether the Protestants did not meet in houses, this being easier as they did not celebrate mass. He believed that they did to some extent, but not much. One might pray with a friend or two on an irregular basis. It seemed that the designations Catholic and Protestant had ceased to mean a great deal between believers. How easy was it to recognize and meet other Christians? Obviously there were less problems if someone had stayed in one place since 1951, but many young people had not, nor had he. One certainly did not go around advertising that one was a Catholic; one would only confide the matter to people whom one knew very well. Under the Gang of Four life could be terrible because everyone was so afraid of one another; they confided practically nothing about anything and limited conversation to the merest small talk. A year ago he would not have dared to talk to tourists like this.

How was it he had done relatively so well in the teaching profession? Might not knowledge at least of his Catholic origins tell against him? Naturally he had not troubled to find out precisely where he stood, but he reckoned that if religion was not associated with notable class origins, if one did not campaign against the law, and one's talents were sufficiently needed, it would not count too much. On the other hand, if only because of his age and lack of notable political commitment, he had not risen, and could not rise further. The kind of person who would do so, or become a guide today (a desirable occupation), would be chosen from among the younger group, under thirty, who would be more indoctrinated. How much did he feel Chinese people really believed atheism? This was hard to answer. Foreign people, particularly Americans, give direct answers revealing their thoughts and emotions. Chinese people conceal them much more, so it is difficult to know what they believe without knowing them well personally. They may have religious thoughts because even today, when they get older and no one cares much what they believe, they may go to the temple or search out family Buddhas, even instruct grandchildren. What about religious radio broadcasts? He rarely heard these. Anything on short waves, as from the Philippines, gave poor reception in most places in China, but religious and other broadcasting from Hong Kong could be heard clearly enough in the surrounding Kwantung region, though he had never heard rumours of the intense secret religious life sometimes reported of that region. He himself liked to listen to the dance music which was received clearly from Japan, but even this was not always clear, and there was not too much opportunity. No one would listen to radio excessively, for obvious reasons.

Life in China was not terrible; school life, whether as pupil or teacher, had not been duly arduous (he even called it 'cosy' in its way), but he did not always want to live there, and like thousands at present, had filed for emigration and now had good hopes of rejoining relatives in America. These were the main points. There was a limit to how much I could ask in the time, since politeness required that I should show interest, not only in a subject, but in the person, and it would have been unfair and frightening to demand very exact information for the purpose of writing. He said good-bye before we reached the entrance-exit of the admission office as though he did not wish to be seen with me. Perhaps China was still not quite as free as even he felt in the new flush of liberty.

Our guides, theoretically much indoctrinated, were rather enigmatic, but allowed considerable freedom of expression and were almost infected by the same liberty in stating their own opinions. One felt a little sorry for them, separated as they must be by experience from the mass of people, and caught between the nutcrackers of Chinese obligations and Western challenges to their belief system. One could understand their anxiety to visit this strange West that kept visiting them. They can expect many awkward questions and affirmations about human rights and religion, at least from Americans. One girl insisted that materialism only makes for selfishness, as in America, and that what people need is God. Another woman, evidently a disciple of Edgar Cayce, was so thrilled with the Chinese that she would insist that she was Chinese in a former reincarnation. 'Reincarnation?' repeated a guide. She carefully wrote this down on a slip of paper which she passed to him. He concluded that she must be a Buddhist, and rather more than that, I suspected.

Least spontaneous and informative was a short, cheerful, fairly intellectual-looking young toughie, who despite a fair command of English, stumbled over monotone speeches and descriptions he had unsuccessfuly tried to learn by rote. He was evidently one of the young breed of interpreter linguist I have just mentioned, who get the best jobs. Another guide was a bright young girl with an initially impersonal air, which broke down on acquaintance. She thought life was better in China today than formerly, and wanted to know about Taiwan. She seemed disappointed to learn that life was better there, too, now there had been land and other reforms. I asked if she had read the long-banned *Dream of the Red Cham-*

ber. She had, and had greatly enjoyed it. I did not enquire whether she had read the notorious *Golden Lotus.* She believed that there was no God, and that one went into the earth at death. Superstition was for the old. She may not have been telling the truth. After I had correctly guessed that our reincarnated Chinese was a Capricorn, the subject turned to astrology. Not wishing to be accused of superstition, I mentioned the new scientific and statistical evidence for astrology. I need not have bothered. Our confirmed atheist now performed a somersault and whispered that young people in China were becoming interested in these subjects again (is this true?), and asked both to have her fortune told (even though I had spoken only of psychological types) and for me to write up a summary of traditional astrological assignments for her.

One guide, whose manner swung between breezy familiarity and rather haughty airs, seemed fairly well-informed and opinionated about religion and was anxious to sell the idea to sceptical audiences that there was religious liberty in China, and that any closed churches were closed only because there was no one to attend them. After all, there was open practice of Islam in recent times, and the old, the main practitioners of religion, were unearthing their Buddhas, so that there was nothing against Christianity if it wished to manifest itself. As a more recent and more Western religion, it had naturally stood less chance than rival faiths. Taoism was China's native religion, but it did not deserve the name of religion because of its lack of organization, its absurd belief in immortality through medicine, and its shameless borrowing from Buddhism.

Some of us had this guide and his stock of presumably representative Communist views on religion one evening over a banquet. Altogether it was mildly harrowing. The feast lasted two and a half hours and we were seated near the door trying to ignore gusts of freezing air reaching us with the platters born in from across the bridge of the ornamental garden outside. To my left was an extravagant Chinese American covering his offences to good manners with self-mocking apologies and endless raising of his glass. Main butt of his humour was the commissar to his left, a man of machinal manners and an unsmiling vacant expression, occasionally relieved by sharp movements of the eyes. He was a master of many 'dialects' but gave the appearance of not knowing English until wild statements from my left registered expressions of moderate alarm upon his face.

Conversation was difficult and lapsed, for few of us seemed able to say the right things. I expressed the hope that Tibet would soon be open to tourists. Glances exchanged between guide and commissar, the former winced and looked impatient. An innocently frivolous suggestion that I should guess or inquire the astrological assignment of our guide (Scorpio) led to extreme misunderstanding. A member of a government department of an Asian country which liaised for religions turned to the subject of religious liberties again and also to Taoism, insisting it was an authentic Chinese religion. As regards liberty, we were told again that it was no problem, since it affected mainly the old, though when we asked if there were regions where not just the elderly might be religious, we learned that in the Western regions towards Tibet and to some extent in the North and historic Buddhist areas like Honan, people sometimes showed a religious disposition. As to Taoism, its religious nature was strenuously denied; we were given the standard Communist evaluation that it was only a superstitious system for gaining physical immortality. I saw fit to point out that really there were three kinds of Taoism, the philosophical (as of Lao Tzu, which the guides seemed not to have read), which offered mystical transcendence; the popular, which hoped for pleasant immortality as a spirit by merit; and the monastic, the kind of which he referred and which attempted to gain physical immortality by technique. These distinctions were dismissed on the remarkable basis (evidently an exaggeration of the opinions of the rationalist Hu Shih, who has greatly coloured Maoist opinion) that China never had any religions at all, only philosophies, as of Confucius and Mo Tzu, and that religion, in the sense of belief in a God, entered from India with the Buddhism which infected the land with superstitions and caused the invention of Taoism. I protested that some would say that early Chinese philosophy reflected rationalizations of early state religions, while Taoism was a refinement of an earlier shamanism, and since this had been dominated by female spirit mediums, philosophy and religious Taoism both in their ways represented a rationalist and patriarchal reaction. Scorpio, who did not understand the word 'shamanism', said such accounts of Chinese thought were unknown to Chinese scholars. Anyway, he continued, all faiths like Taoism must decline where people have enough material wherewithal. It was observed that when people have enough material wherewithal, interest in religion often increased, and someone else unwisely enquired whether China was not showing the kind of voluntary return to religion observed among Russian youth. Our guide's fist clenched, and his jaw tightened. 'We would do *nothing* like the people of the Soviet Union,' he hissed. Let Russia return to Christianity, the religion was only the same as the Buddhism discredited beyond recall in China. The comparison of Buddhism with Christianity raised objections: but the fact that it taught heaven, hell, merit, etc., was seen as sufficient grounds for the claim. Rather peevishly, I asked to what extent our guide had the right to speak with such authority, seeing religion was not officially studied in China and the only faith taught was atheism. This really aroused ire. Cheeks flushed and face trembling with suppressed rage, he told me that he knew whole passages of the New Testament and had read some of the Old Testament as well. Where? In college in Pekin, of course. Considering his age and the reported decision of colleges only that year to resume the study of religion for historical purposes, the admission was perplexing. Maybe he had read the Parable of the Unjust Steward which proved Jesus dishonest, or the Parable of the Talents which proved him a bourgeois capitalist, as in one book a Communist sympathizing friend in France had once shown me.

The tirade was continuing. Our guide's grandparents had been pious Buddhists and God never did anything for them when they needed it. He did not help them when drought and famine came; he did not put a roof over their heads. God never did anything for China, and if he existed, he would only help those who help themselves. I reflected that really orthodox Buddhists would never ask Buddha for miracles anyway. I also thought of the Victorian Baptist missionary Timothy Richard, who, when the drought came and his converts grumbled, made them pray for rain, and rain allegedly fell on that one village, but Richard, not presuming upon miracles, committed himself to attacking the sins and ignorance of Chinese life which made people victims of nature. Refraining from the direct criticism that the Chinese only think materialistically, I began a trifle facetiously to inquire whether it was reasonable to charge God with not putting roofs over people's heads. I was interrupted by someone who put the matter, if not at a more practical, at least at a more existential level. Religion was not simply a matter of acquiring material benefits, or forming concepts of God, but of setting oneself in relation to mortality and one's destiny, whether or not it would have significance in terms of love, and perhaps when Scorpio had attachments, children. . . . The mention of marriage seemed rather inappropriate; our guide's whole style suggested that it would be unlikely. Yet perhaps the argument had been appreciated and the message taken, for when the Commissar absented himself, the guide was suddenly more relaxed. He thanked us very much and told us that it was very interesting. My analytical frame of mind is not such as to give much credence to talk of 'the inscrutable East', but for one moment I felt the force of the expression.

III

The gulf which divides mainland China from Hong Kong is a large one, but the religious interest is to bridge it from the Hong Kong side, in the realization that sooner or later the mainland, however altered under modernization, represents its destiny. It does not represent this for the middle class, which will increasingly make an exodus, but it is within this class that Christianity is most entrenched, so that any philosophical or cultural relatedness needs to be between the seemingly hopeless alternatives of popular religion and Communism, a real test. Complicating the matter are the many missionaries and Chinese Christians who either do not believe in 'indigenization', feeling that the gospel offers relatedness enough, and the others who desire it, but in highly academic ways, like intensive study of Taoism, or total revision of scriptural translations and religious terminology, which is undoubtedly necessary but is very much work for the long term within situations of great uncertainty.

It was probably helpful for my understanding of the factors involved in this bridging work that I began with aesthetics and the problem of incorporating Chinese design to modern work rather than questions of faith. One comes to realize how, apart from the fact that religion is more fundamental than, and socially antecedent to, movements of art, attitudes to it engender the same sort of emotions and belong with the same social trends. One is more aware of how what are often called 'doctrinal' grounds for objections to any Sinification of the church, at least from the Chinese, can be influenced by quite different considerations. Two things seem particularly noteworthy, both with reference to imitation in life and art. With things Chinese, it is the first step which counts. Though subject to many subtle variations, Chinese painting can scarcely be said to have innovated very greatly beyond the T'ang in terms of subject matter or even style. Radical innovation would be regarded as the expression of an unacceptable individualism, an affront to the masters from whom one had learned. The cult of elders and teachers has always inhibited originality, and this attitude is duplicated in religion. Doctrine has been something passed down from adept to disciple, and thus there seems little question that Christianity, once accepted in a given form, no matter how inappropriate, is liable to be faithfully followed in that form unless the same people who gave the faith, in their role as teacher, take some initiative in adapting the form. Modifying this characteristic and constituting the second point, is imitation at the social rather than the individual level. Like all colonized or culturally over-shadowed peoples, the Chinese have desired to equal or excel those who have overcome them, and thus one finds patterns of ardent and arbitrary attachment to Westernization sometimes compensated for by some equally arbitrary traditionalism. The average Chinese artist today, even without commercial pressure, will imitate Western design rather than imitate or incorporate Chinese, and may even prove quite hostile to suggestions that Chinese motifs be more visible in public monuments or hotels, or the fashion industry in Hong Kong. He may maintain that one is condescending to or exploiting his culture, encouraging people to come look at Hong Kong like a romantic curio, rather than the smart cosmopolitan city, the equal of a New York, that it should be. At the same time, the same person may prove a vehement advocate of, say, the movement for secondary school instruction in Chinese language, on the grounds that speaking English is a cultural deprivation. One finds these contradictions with religious questions. The same Westernized Christian who will not countenance Chinese music in a service, may stop his ears against ecclesiastical disapproval of the ubiquitous gambling, and waste considerable time and money at Mah Jong, because, being Westernized in so many other ways, he would consider it anti-social to refrain from such activity with friends.

If one looks at Westernization within Asia in a wider perspective than that of colonial Hong Kong, with its middle class which can only look forward to emigration to the West, and its working class which can only expect eventual absorption to China, a distinct pattern seems to hold. Whether or not there is actual colonization, one can expect, as in India, Indonesia, Japan, etc.: first, conflict, as the native population shows itself suspicious and hostile; second, enthusiastic acceptance, as foreign education becomes a fashion, with sometimes slavish imitation as national characteristics are deemed backward or peasant-like; and third, reaction caused by exhaustion, disillusion and nostalgia. At this last stage, the old, reassessed with the objectivity of the new, is increasingly restored and modifies the new. Hong Kong in the seventies began to show signs of this reaction in a minor key in the new craze for Cantonese popular music, Mandarin classes, the increased temple visitation noted at festivals in 1976 and 1977, and the new crop of Buddhist schools. The phase of maximum attraction to Christianity, in so far as it is seen as a Western religion, has probably passed. The end of the process of Westernization is one in which the native religion, always the first to come and the last to go in any civilization, can be expected to benefit, as witness Neo-Hinduism in India or Neo-Buddhism in South East Asia.

There can be much chauvinism or even intolerance in such movements, but up to a point one has to sympathize, since many of those Asian societies, few of which have much to compare with *secular* cultures in the West, have very little to show once their religion has been undermined. The spirit of, say, Thailand is mainly distilled in its beautiful temples and related art and dance. Modern Bangkok without its Buddhist monuments would seem like a poor imitation of an American boom-town, so if the church cannot assimilate or transform the cultural forms, short of losing all identity to the West, the people might as well keep their religion.

When I made this last statement in *Can There Be a Chinese Church*? it caused offence to some people who rather lifted it out of the context of the argument. What matter if people lost their culture, what matter if cities looked ugly? If one had Jesus one had everything, they reasoned. In a way they reminded me of an ardent Buddhist who, in response to my horror at the filth and pollution marring a scene in the New Territories, exclaimed, 'But Lord Buddha is everywhere. If you knew that, the scene could not be spoilt for you.' On reflection, I feel that the appropriate reply might have been, 'If it was *God* you saw through the scene, you would consider it an offence.' The point is, one does not necessarily 'have' Jesus as it were in a corner. He *is* reality, and hence, though certain areas of reality are more important than others and will concern some persons more or less following their temperament, nothing can be irrelevant to a Christian perception. Thus it is arguable that a programme of conversion whose effects will not be to involve at least persons of a certain temperament in cultural transformation as their main concern can scarcely be considered authentic. In effect, this judgment has been anticipated in Chapter 1 with its understanding of individual fulfilment, but in terms of practical policy, one must speak rather of indigenization, and to this I shall turn briefly next.

Indigenization, or the process of adapting the message and forms of any creed in ways more meaningful to a given environment, is a process common to all religions and societies. Judaism, exclusive though it was, would never have survived or given birth to Christianity if it had not assumed new forms of self-expression, in Babylonia, and within the Greek and Roman empires. St Paul, though he abandoned attempts to compromise with the dilettante philosophers of Athens, secured the internationalization of Christianity by initiating the trend towards using Greek terminology to expound religious truth and showing favour towards certain Roman values as regards church and social organization. The development and spread of mystical Sufism was the condition of Islam's acceptance within regions like Indonesia. Buddhism was a failure in China until it dropped some rules and became considerably Sinified in its forms. Indigenization is not the same as accommodation or the syncretism by which a religion loses its identity or effective meaning. Here again the pattern is quite clear. Hinduism within South East Asia, as in Cambodia and Indonesia, was adapted and assimilated to both local cults and Buddhism until it ceased to exist as anything meaningful in its own right. Much of Catholicism in Brazil, or parts of the Caribbean, has become virtually indistinguishable from spirit cult and voodoo.

The main dividing line between indigenization and accommodation is between a religion attempting to express itself within an alien culture and introduction of a religion closely associated with, or imposing itself in a distinctly political way, so that matters of spiritual self-expression are not paramount. By its nature, indigenization is never total. The retention of some uncompromisingly alien elements to Buddhism, like its ascetical alienation from the Chinese family system, was almost an advantage, a challenge, and certainly a reason why some of the most individual art and literature was made under its influence. At the same time indigenization aims consciously or otherwise at a certain wholeness; it favours the philosophical interpretation, offers a new theory of society, makes its own aesthetics, and as such, is both more far-reaching and broad-minded than what is called 'contextualization', which is establishing points of contact with a society in terms of its more specialized vocabulary, its forms of address, its eating habits or whatever.

'Contextualization' is about as far as most Protestant missionaries venture today in a century which follows upon an imperial era which sought to Westernize, and within a church with a more recent legacy of aggressive neo-orthodox theology from theologians like Karl Barth and his mission interpreter, Hendrik Kraemer. These writers invented a theory of revelation and proclamation as total shock and disjunction with the world and even common reason, such as to discourage any attempt at indigenization. Kraemer, who laboured not very successfully in Bali, would never brook the least compromise with the surrounding culture. The aggressive Barthian approach to life can only really be understood in terms of its deliberate challenge to a form of accommodating, rationalizing theology, which in Germany failed miserably in its relation to the causes of two world wars.

In mission circles indigenization is often regarded as a form of defeat. Either the missionary must be watering down the faith in the interest of numbers, or the convert is seeking a way of worldly compromise. What is so rarely grasped – one probably needs to have suffered some cultural disjunction to appreciate the issue – is that ideas, especially of the spiritual kind, just do not readily sink into the mind and possess it, unless they are conveyed in forms close to native thought and imagination. Victorian hymns from far away, like 'Fight the good fight', which may be fun to sing in a Hong Kong church choir, ring a lot less true in situations like the Red Guard persecution, when the 'fight' actually has to be fought. At such times, like the Greek church under Turkish rule, one needs hymns and liturgies one can call one's own and which resonate within as the expression of the community, in order to survive. Just as pain does not cease to be pain because one believes in God, so grace does not necessarily abolish the confusion of crossing cultures and speaking and believing in unfamiliar ways. As Simone Weil, the French Jewish convert to Christianity, put it, 'A change of religion is for the soul like a change of language for a writer. . . . Except in special cases the soul is not able to abandon itself utterly when it has to make the slight effort of seeking for the words in a foreign language.'[10] Though from ignorance of Asian religions and their popular practice, Simone Weil probably exaggerates the extent to which they provide spiritual sustenance and teach belief in God, her point, which is similar to Toynbee's on the dangers of 'schism in the soul', [11] must be taken, and having suffered quite enough from some of these cultural disjunctions, I am sympathetic to the thesis for which she is celebrated, that déracinement (uprootedness) constitutes one of the crisis features and is a curse of our times. Wherever possible one should aim to transform and fulfil. Not only does this appear to be harmonious with gospel intentions (Matt. 5.17), but it is probably true to say that the alternative will, in all save exceptional cases, be failure. Either indigenization, as in some of the Indian churches, will proceed in an unsupervised way little removed from syncretism, or there will be no response at all, as in East Asia where, historically, the most successful missions were the culturally sensitive ones of the Jesuits to China and Japan. In China today, following a century of modern missions, there is probably only one half of one per cent which can be called Christian, and less than that figure in Japan.

Naturally, dangers exist with indigenization as with everything else, and my own criticisms of traditional philosophical formulations of Christian doctrine in Chapter 1 could be taken as an argument against the policy. The philosophic Hellenization and Romanization of Christianity may have seriously distorted it. Yet if it did, it did so because it attempted to fix its own interpretation down to the last supposed implications of the religion for science and ethics, for all time. There is, nonetheless, such a thing as a provisional truth, a correct partial truth in terms of a society, a race, an era and the available knowledge, and every effort should be made to find it. Implications of a faith which may appear perfectly obvious later can sometimes only be realized after progress though a whole series of partial formulations. Certainly it should be clear that I consider that the substance-theories of divinity which colour our creeds were not so much inappropriate deductions from hints within the original Jewish teaching which gave substance little attention, as incomplete and insufficiently subtle ones.

Though particularly vital where philosophy is concerned, the same need for many formulations will apply to most aspects of indigenization, including the visual culture, which in a society like the Chinese so visually orientated, and in Hong Kong where the people are so indisposed to read anything except newspapers and gossip magazines, is far from irrelevant. I am unable to accept that, for example, a church wholly in Chinese design, as was the ancient chapel of the Jesuit house in Pekin, marked a capitulation to 'paganism'. Despite the extremely Chinese appearance even of the altar, the chapel was not filled with pictures of Christ or Mary indistinguishable from Taoist deities, and I should regard it rather as the first step towards a new Christian art which did not have opportunity to develop.

The belief that capitulation is involved in such ventures signifies the existence of several things in the minds of those protesting against it. It may proceed from a belief that all art is itself a sort of paganism, which is so unreasonable there is no point in even discussing it here; it may imply that there is a form of Christian art with which the person is familiar, like Gothic or Byzantine, or Free Church plain, which is so perfectly Christian that all other kinds must be somehow 'wrong', an opinion born of merest habit, or it may signify that the culture itself is felt to be an insufficiently perfect medium, and that to use it is to limit the message. This is the only meaningful objection. Christianity is often regarded, even by those who are not Barthians, as making for a radical disjunction with whatever is, rather than the harmonies they assume Asian art to represent, hence Chinese art is too familiar, soothing, or insufficiently dramatic to be true. In so many words I understand the objection, even though it can be argued that the harmonies of Asian art themselves only represent the solution to a sensed disjunction of sorts. This notwithstanding, the greater disjunction one senses on entering any church, English or Chinese in Hong Kong, is the radical one with practically anything associable with life outside; one feels in a sort of ghetto or limbo in which it is even hard to focus the mind, especially if, as I once witnessed, a solemn faced choir trips out to sing in Chinese 'Washed in the Blood' to the tune of the bawdy 'In the Quartermaster's Store'. This does not so much mark a holy rupture with the society as it represents a radical identification *with* a Mid-Western American one, which if it occurred on the Mainland, would not unreasonably entail charges of foreign sympathies, or as used to be said of being 'running dogs of the imperialists'. Even at the risk of 'paganism', some identification with the society one wished to transform must be preferable.

Moreover, any Christian disjunction with the environment can only truly be appreciated when that environment is taken into account. It is only by attempting to render Christian concepts adequately within a Chinese style that one can appreciate the real points of difference and what areas to emphasize or alter. It is probably quite true that the higher expressions of Chinese culture are too harmonious to contain what, to its eyes, would be the barbarisms of Judaeo-Christian vision. Rather than dismissing Chinese culture outright on that basis, more profit is likely to accrue, at least to those of us for whom even mystical urges cannot blot out a strong vein of eighteenth-century feeling by facing our demons and admitting that were it not for our Christian educations, we too might incline to the same response and then enquire why this is so. Hard as I find it to appreciate some Jewish aesthetics – the abrupt transitions and arbitrary images of much Jewish poetry usually dismays me – I feel I have gained much by setting myself the exercise of perceiving Christianity as an educated Chinese might perceive it, and of asking questions like to what purpose any divine revelation should proceed through the more 'barbaric' medium of Hebrew desert experience than the more civilized one of, say, Greece.

One is likely to conclude, not only that civilized societies, like Greece with its slavery and China with its penal tortures, may hide a viciousness which the barbaric society does not possess, but that certain barbarisms in the vision or the laws, though not in themselves or presently to be justified (the fundamentalist error is to do this), protected, before the time of overt formulations, concepts of indispensable ideological or psychological value. Considerably different though his interests and avenues of inquiry were, like the Harvey Cox of *Turning East*, I find my mind more rather than less clarified about many facets of the Judaeo-Christian vision and its purpose through setting it against the Eastern one. But, it must be emphasized, such profit is likely to be won only through a fair degree of initial cultural acceptance and a certain effort of imagination or feeling, that is to say, a process in which intellect is not sole judge, nor the critical faculty wholly shelved in identification either.

IV

In conclusion, then, I shall endeavour to outline where it seems to me that Christian self-presentation fails to make the intended impression. Since in this field criticism itself is likely to miss the mark if it is not constructive, I will lay down some practical alternatives. These key points for any work of indigenization, though made with reference to Chinese society, I take to be more or less relevant to all Asian settings save India. Since some philosophical perspectives on the Christian presentation of truth were considered in the first chapter, one need only refer here to a few leading areas, like preaching, visual culture and church organization. Since I am not a church leader (one discovers that involves a special temperament!), or if I were, would only wish to be involved with indigenization sufficiently to stimulate the creativity of a congregation, my concern is not to be dogmatic, but only to provoke thought among those whose task it really is.

Preaching is the most obvious place to start. There is no need to substantiate the claim that a good deal of preaching and evangelism in Hong Kong does not hit the mark; unbelievers are little affected and believers often bored by it, even when it comes from Chinese preachers, for these may exaggerate the failure of Western mentors. There is no harder subject to treat unless those criticized are at least sympathetic to the idea of indigenization, since it is too easy to hide behind the belief that one must be dealing with spiritually unresponsive souls; as the gospel is assumed to be 'final' and universal, it ought to be transparent to everyone. This is not necessarily a reasonable assumption, and if Acts supplies us a picture of a proclamation which always engages a lively response, even when it is not always successful, there are good reasons; the time was ripe for the message, the existing culture enjoyed sufficient unity through Rome to minimize possible problems with regard to terminology of address, and where it did, the apostles adapted or could rely on the assistance of converts from among the Jews and 'God fearing' Gentiles within the Jewish communities of the empire, to transmit the message.

> It was the presence of this prepared elite that differentiated the missions of the apostolic age from those of every subsequent time and makes comparison almost impossible.[12]

It is easy to forget this obvious fact. Points of contact and even suitable audiences need to be sought out. If the apostolic task was more physically demanding, the modern missionary task is more intellectually demanding.

In Hong Kong, the preacher can be undecided about his message, even as to whether he is evangelizing or instructing. Evangelization in any typical sense is ruled out by the Hong Kong situation, in which street rallies are more or less banned, and there is a shortage and unavailability of large meeting-places for such purposes. Evangelism may thus be limited, when not to sermons, to odd occasions, or the distribution, by the fundamentalist wing, of alarmist tracts which string together texts, usually quite without comment, like 'Repent or perish'. Presumably something of the message gets across, since a Chinese youth once remarked to me above the noise of a motor-cycling fiend, 'Him hell angel, send him to Jesus.' On the other hand, it does not always do so, and a quite intelligent young woman I know, subject to some Christian influence since church school, was quite surprised to learn that Christianity was meant to be historical and true and not just a psychological myth after the manner of Mahayana teaching. At that rate, one can hardly believe that an intensification of evangelism would serve the purpose some missionaries imagine; indeed, those church leaders who considered my suggestions for indigenization close to science fiction, since even a lot of the right theological terms have either not been discovered or are not used, had their point. How, indeed, should one address the Chinese audience?

Questions of vocabulary apart, to begin with, it is probably necessary to dispose of the idea that simple belief and unbelief in relation to the given doctrine constitutes the main problem. It is, for example, quite true that the Chinese, especially the men, can adopt an uncompromisingly rationalistic line towards what many would dub Christian superstition, but they usually do so only like the late pagan philosophers who cited Plato and Aristotle against early Christians while they dabbled in cults which those they cited would have disdained to acknowledge. What is signified by 'reason' and 'superstition' to the Chinese, I shall deal with presently, but the chief barrier with which in all but exceptional cases preaching and evangelism is confronted, is the psychological resistance to any 'dynamic' world view. Even the convert suffers from this. For the Chinese it is hard to assimilate that any action or belief on his part could assume great significance for God himself or society. From physiology, traditional values and social situation, every inclination is towards acceptance of whatever is. As a group or a nation, one might hope to change things, but Christian aspirations to change lives, transform society, or express oneself more fully, ring hollowly; some may dream of wealth, but most are not permitted larger ambitions than to survive and be comfortable. Where, as in the past, a Christian value judgment runs counter to the will of elders, to whom all honour and gratitude is due, there is a measure of conflict and challenge, but not otherwise. Unless, say, they were of Hakka or Fukienese origin, the average Chinese do not excite or enthuse easily save at certain fixed places and occasions, like the theatre, which act as safety valves for emotion. Passion and excitement, which in just causes at least, are regarded as something almost virtuous by Occidentals, are usually perceived as nothing but marks of desperation or that lack of reason which traditional philosophy rated so highly. This reacts on the understanding of matters like prayer and grace among believers and unbelievers alike. With what some would call the strength of the weak, the Chinese who believe in bending like the bamboo before the breeze have little respect for the iron instruments which snap under stress, as they sense may be the case with hulking great Americans almost tearfully witnessing to how grace supported them when they broke. It is fairly natural to Western man, with his extraverted perceptions and philosophies of purpose, to think of God as the source, something larger than himself, and to direct prayer outwards, but to the more introspective Asian vision of reality as a continuum, unsupported as this is by any teleological philosophies, the impulse is rather to identify with the 'reality' and draw upon it from within oneself.[13] 'I don't believe in God, I believe in me', as one young Chinese put it. To be calm, to trust in one's recuperative powers, is seen as virtue. One must be reasonable and avoid superstition, unless one is too uneducated.

What does this mean? The Mandarins consulted the I Ching, and the Communists have not stamped out a trade in almanacs. The reasonable, as we have said, is not necessarily something purely intellectual, nor is it 'natural law'; rather it is what makes for clarity, for system, and what may be controlled. A good deal of so-called magic, as in divination and geomancy, can be controlled. Forces which may or may not be set up by Christian prayer are suspect, like the varieties of Taoist and Buddhist magic that received little toleration from authorities. Superstition is whatever cannot be fitted into the system or measured, and which comes from afar, like certain doctrines of Buddhism and Christianity. I think that a few sentences from a long letter to an English newspaper summarize and give the flavour of what I have been suggesting. The letter, of a rare fluency, was written in the wake of some admittedly extremist Catholic correspondence on the various sex laws.

If it (homosexuality) occurs as instinctive behaviour in animals, which it does, then it is natural, whether or not the correspondent finds it personally distasteful or religiously unacceptable, but he returns to scripture, the last refuge of those who refuse to think. The Bible, for this obviously is the only holy writ of concern to him, is a document recording the mythologies and superstitions of Judaeo-Christian faith. It should not be law in Hong Kong. Condemnation from the pulpit is one thing and legally sanctioned persecution another. . . . We poor colonials are allowed freedom of religion, but unfortunately never freedom from religion. The law is even more reprehensible in that it stems from the religion of an imperial power and is in no way native to Chinese culture. I am not a Christian, but would not see the correspondent sent to jail for attending church, but he would have people imprisoned for simply being what they are.

In fact, the writer's 'reason' was no more thoughtful than the fundamentalism it opposed, as it overlooked the extent to which the law concerned is retained by Chinese demand, rather than by any united Christian one, and also, the extent to which the Chinese, if not himself, have often refused people the right to attend church. But this disposition to consider oneself the voice of reason against all prejudice and to dissociate being from doing in moral issues, as in the last sentence, is typical.

What the preacher is faced with in the Chinese audience is a spectrum of opinion and feeling which ranges between the picturesquely superstitious and the highly rational, at least in the sense of an empirical practical spirit. It is possible to protest that one cannot hope to address people across such a spectrum, or belittle the problem by suggesting that everywhere an audience is composed of such contrasts, so that one says what one would say anywhere. It does seem, nonetheless, that there are comparisons to be made with societies of predominantly peasant values or the Latin societies. I have already alluded to this in Chapter 2. Certainly, in the Latin societies one does find that the modern religious writing tends to set up a unique balance of the scholastic with the simple. One thinks, for example, of Paul Claudel's vision in Notre Dame of the 'childhood' of God, and St Thérèse de Lisieux's way of childlike devotion, as this contrasts or interacts with thought like that of a Maritain or Simone Weil. Moreover, if they have contact with it, Asian people are particularly responsive to this strain of writing. Paul Wu claimed that Christianity only became real to him after a reading of St Thérèse's 'little' way, and the Japanese Catholic novelist Shusaku Endo was influenced by this French tradition when he wrote Wonderful Fool, about a sort of saint whose saintliness is disguised beneath clownishness.[14] Why it is that Latin and East Asian peoples who, on the one hand, love philosophical jargon to describe mystical concepts, on the other hand may display a certain childlikeness towards the same mysteries, I am not quite sure, but one must simply register that a Franciscan 'little flowers' trend exists. The Latin synthesis of this scholastic-simple strain of the peasant society comes in Guareschi's comic but very penetrating Don Camillo and Peppone, where the priest is caught between the claims of a Communist rival and the Christ who regularly speaks wisdom to him from the altar. In

Thailand, Kukrit Pramoj was so struck by this series that his *Red Bamboo* endeavoured a transfer of the situation to a Thai village, with an abbot caught between a socialist troublemaker and an oracular Buddha – an awkward transfer in so far as the Buddha, having reached nirvana, cannot strictly be allowed to speak.[15] The main point, however, is that he was so struck. The East Asian thought world is one of rapid transitions between reason and a world of ghosts, serious reflection and humorous release; it is an intensely physical world where it is quite legitimate to think of the simplest moral conflicts in terms of devouring dragons or angels delivering demons a hearty wallop over the head. Metaphors, or the lower expressions of more weighty truths, are rarely in question, for a thought also possesses its reality as a thing. One must take the comic truth along with the serious one, the child with the adult, and all in close up. There is little sense of the horrifying infinities of Germanic or Indian imagination.

Bearing this in mind, it seems that there would be good reason for preaching to focus on Christ as truth or as the creative Word which, as we saw, Klostermaier, if for different reasons, considered so important for the Indian setting. Originally I had thought that, because of its appropriateness in relation to the Asian interiority, there should be more emphasis on God as Spirit, but not only would it be doctrinally confusing not to begin with Christ, but God as Spirit is rather awesome, and many Chinese Christians find the local Pentecostalism quite frightening. Yet as we have seen, if one speaks simply of Jesus, an overly personal or historical presentation also has its drawbacks, as it is wrongly thought to mean a personal manifestation of divinity over against the essentially impersonal ultimate represented. If one starts personally, save with highly emotional Chinese who usually compose the evangelical wing of a church, the Chinese mind and values are such that one finishes with something impersonal. The natural drift of the Chinese Christian is towards a kind of liberalism, which by a subjective process reduces the gospel to an objective moralism. If one starts with the creative Word, one can embrace a continuum that can be objectively described, and with teleological implications to dissociate it from simple complexes, yet also something that may be introspected. One would have to trust in God and the workings of the psyche that this would be realized not as something impersonal but personal and also as conveying grace. Although I take grace to be a complex of factors, something neither wholly exterior nor interior to man, it is probably best that in order to prevent such a kind of mental disorientation, one starts with the interior aspect from which Asians are disposed to regard it, if only the better to perceive its creative independent quality.

Needless to say, a lot more work needs to be put into the psychology of specifically Christian thought and conversion patterns, and before that has happened, one hesitates to speak of what vocabulary should be used in these areas. Logos has often been translated Tao even by those unsympathetic to indigenization, but the highly feminine nurturing rather than creative associations of the latter must shed some doubts on the advisability of its use.

In a society so little disposed to read as the Chinese, and with versions of the Bible so poorly translated, the educated often prefer to read it in English. Plainly the transposition of religious truth, especially through visual images and liturgy, is a matter of no small concern. To the average Chinese, the absence of art, or its presence in inferior Western forms, must be eloquent, while the lack of festivals or their celebration in anything approaching Chinese style, which would have groups banging drums and cymbals in the street, or setting up flags and pendants, must make the religion seem rather anaemic, especially in Asia where there is no doctrine or idea which does not achieve some visual or ritualistic equivalent. Even Christmas, which the Chinese rather like, is celebrated by many churches with meagre decoration and ceremony, the carols mostly sung, English fashion, after rather than before the event.

Naturally, when one speaks of 'indigenization' in this realm, one is caught between the claims of the higher kind which entails formulation of a style and iconography, and the lower more practical kind, which must address itself to the need of ordinary churches simply to acknowledge local colour and motifs. Even if the higher form could be a costly delicate affair which must remain a distant ideal, it is nonetheless best that to avoid errors in the lower kind, one keeps it well in view. Certainly, at the present time the problem is not that Christianity 'needs art'; there have always been occasional efforts to produce that, and most people are familiar with Mary rendered like some place maiden in the style of Chui Ying, or the Sermon on the Mount done à la Chu Yu. What is necessary is a total aesthetic and culturally sensitive notion of the function art should assume within a particular society. A revitalization of Christian art, as of Christian theology, might not be unconnected with what will evolve within Asian Christianity. In India, much of the aesthetics is an extension of yogic visualization; in East Asia, it is more by way of a meditation on the Taoist opposites within nature, or those aspects of reality which could assist an enlightened 'seeing'. In the West, Catholic art began with didacticism, the simple need to portray the main events of the faith to the illiterate; in Greek churches the icon was an ideal image, a presence partaking of the new creation as understood against the Greek view of incarnation and the possibilities of matter.

Since Asian art, and particularly Chinese art, is highly stylized, the purely didactic functions of art, if they are needed, would be limited; most people have vague notions of the Christian *story*, and if portrayal of fact were all that was necessary, an unfamiliar realism would be called for, but it is something closer to an art of Christian archetypes and psychological states which is required, particularly if the object is to distinguish a Christian from a perennial mysticism. In Buddhism, only nine major incidents and even fewer gestures or *mudra* were selected; development is rather one in depth and subtlety than simple variety. For these reasons, images like Christ ascending or in judgment would be especially helpful, both from the standpoint of stylization and as a counterbalance to that mysticism which places more stress on dissolving and dying than reintegrating and reviving and on the feminine rather than the masculine. The favourite gods tend to be female, like Kwan Yin, goddess of mercy, and Tin Hau, Queen of Heaven, who accept rather than make any demands. The historical refusal to acknowledge the full masculine function in spiritual development has, as we have seen, assisted instead a despotism of emperor, husband and father, which compromises freedom and individuality.

The Greek doctrine of the icon probably has more use in justifying art to those who fear idolatry than supplying an aesthetic apart from the function of its hieratic style as a link between Western realism and Asian stylization. Basically, the Greeks, like the Indian Protestant mystic, Sadhu Sundar Singh, would maintain that a right to art, against the earlier commandment, is signified by the incarnation. This, in its humanization of God, no longer involves the risk entailed before it of portraying the divine barbarously and inadequately, while as to possible idolatry, homage to a Christ image is at least devotion in the right direction, and little different from that which people give to the representatives or even paraphernalia of power.

Iconography becomes an important issue when one considers the need, first of the Asian home with its family shrine, and of the church building, often only a room or a hall within a building, to possess an adequate and appropriate focal point. I should think that for the former this should be a red-backed Christ 'icon' and for the latter a large Christ image, like the Buddhas of a Buddha hall. The matter is really indissociable from that of liturgy. For one thing, certain church leaders concede the desirability of some family devotions because religion by tradition is domestically conceived, and because it seems to me that the ghosts of ancestors are never quite laid to rest for some, unless one can substitute a form of rite or blessing for the homage and offerings some make at the ancestral shrine and God-shelf.[16] I fulfilled a request to supply an idea of what I meant by this and wrote it with the thought of how it would translate.

As I had hoped, it went well, getting very close to the feeling of the earliest Confucian rite. As regards orders of service, modern and Chinese needs, not to speak of the physical exigencies of church halls, require a more flexible structure. The Chinese either do, as in some Catholic churches, or would like to, mill about and wander in and out at will, again rather like the Greek Christians at their very long services. The language of orders of service, like the Roman mass and the Anglican Series 3 communion, may have been modernized, but they still retain far too much finicky ritual and the old almost exclusive emphasis on repentance. What is needed is a simple, if hieratic, ritual and a liturgy with more contemplative and theologically educative substance, a communion with more of the 'prophetic' reminiscence and expectation with which the last supper was originally instituted. The altar for this could well be an ornate table, specifically carried in and set out as part of the rite. I envisage a church without seats, save for the elderly and infirm or mothers with children (people would sit on mats or cushions, as in the Japanese No Church meetings), and a platform for choir and 'orchestra' playing local instruments and music.[17] No Asian church can completely rule out the possibility of masked drama and dance, which is such a feature of Asian religion, and is not by its nature difficult to assimilate, in that it does not, as in the West, present problems from any incongruous sensuousness.

Altogether, the decoration and liturgy of an Asian church should possess a more portable quality. Not only would this have cost benefits and facilitate experiment, at least with interiors, and it allows the church to move on to the street and the park if it so wishes, as the Taoists would do at, say, Ghost festival, when tent-like temples are set up, offering an overwhelmingly mysterious impression from what is little more than a movable table-altar, a wealth of ornate drapes, icons and incense burners. Not even the Free Churches need be exempted from change. Often the dreariest part of the churches, the pulpit could be a podium of Chinese design, flanked by red calligraphed screens decorated with individual Chinese words or scrolls. Lantern shades and lecterns are also opportunities for highly ornate work, the latter in wood.

A Hong Kong architect, interested in but critical of my ideas, felt that, especially when I touched on the question of architectural plan and exterior design, I was setting decoration far above exigencies of plan. He made the important point that in future, as land and construction costs soar, and temples which the churches could transform fall into disuse, it will become a matter of practical necessity to think in terms of structures and rituals in relation to them, which will be closer to traditional Chinese patterns. It is true that I had been much influenced by the East-West churches of Hawaii with their basically Western plan and Asian decoration. I was never greatly concerned by details, only that Western Christians should do almost anything to encourage Asian Christians to find their own solutions.

Actually, this is not so easy an aspiration to entertain as it sounds. Although there is unlikely to be any specifically racial condescension to Chinese, the average Chinese Christian is prone to be regarded as a bit of a naughty sheep, especially under the ubiquitous American influence, which seems to project upon church organization a good deal of the ruthless policing techniques of the American business world. There is little freedom.

These matters of church policy lead to the last point I want to make about indigenization. Latecomers can be denounced from the pulpit regardless of the loss of face involved for them and the fact that the actual time when services begin should take into account the Chinese custom of arriving late. I have known of eager souls who have offered their time and energy (there is not so much of it left free in Hong Kong) to distribute literature or visit, only to be refused on the basis of some positive or negative ratings which record that they had missed choir practice or a Bible class.

If one wanted to be unkind, one could say that the Hong Kong view of what constituted a good Christian was formed, if not by the standards of American business, by the prejudices of monastic and lower-middle-class piety; only the daily communicant or the zealous quoter and distributor of scriptural texts is really accepted. As to sin, with church-school girls often required from modesty to cover their arms, if sex is the problem, the earth may as well come to swallow the believer. In fact, sex is only infrequently the problem, the chief one being deception. One can hear of church treasuries rifled by the devout, bribes taken by lawyers supposedly helping their churches over contracts, and other similar happenings. If the Chinese take all the structures and demands laid upon them, it is perhaps because to be presumed upon by every authority is a simple hazard of being Chinese, and anyone who becomes Christian can hardly be unaware of the demands upon them, to judge from the drilling and grilling of catechists. Catechism, at least for would-be Catholic women (for men, things are easier), can extend over two years or more if they are felt to be deficient in knowledge or the right attitude. If anything vaguely approaching the demands made on Asian catechumens today had prevailed in earlier times, it is doubtful whether a Christian church or civilization could ever have come into existence. In 1978 I wrote of some abuses in this area, including the tests and humiliations inflicted on one catechumen, a highly educated society woman who, as a former sceptic, for the sake of her family, consented to the Catholic rather than the Protestant instruction she would have preferred. I would never have imagined that the saga which began in 1975 would still be continuing into 1980 with the woman still not received into the church. I vainly imagined I had exposed a case of priestly folly which had extended to refusal of baptism for the woman before a serious operation, and later refusal to pass her at her classes because she asked too many questions which one Chinese priest angrily denounced as 'pagan'. But those priests, both Western and Chinese, who were involved, refused to be shamed in the matter.

What has happened in Asia represents an extreme reaction to the rice-Christian phenomenon of the imperial era, and it has been aggravated in recent times by the American tendencies already mentioned. Here, the object seems to be to raise spiritual power by rooting out every conceivable cause for sin through the presence of undesirables. Asian churches, however, are not so liable to be rocked by heretical movements and permissive troublemakers as the more volatile American home churches, so the problem is rather to avoid breaking the will of the individual altogether. A lot of the trouble is that the larger churches are becoming more and more like businesses run on committees, statistics, tests, and 'counselling', which sometimes get a bit close to keeping tags on people in a society where privacy is particularly valued[18]; if the spirited, intelligent individual falls foul of this machine, there is little that can be done about it.

Since the running of any large concern in the pressured world of Hong Kong and Singapore is a serious undertaking, one could forgive some of the inevitable failures if the new bureaucracies actually did their job. As it is, in the churches as in the government departments, committee talk is too frequently a substitute for action. As I pointed out to a group of Hong Kong clergy, it was unfortunate that with so much time spent on ecumenical committees, experiments such as I promoted to design Christian 'icons' in Chinese style should come against the problem that one cannot even calligraph a phrase like 'Son of God' on the icon because Catholics and Protestants do not have an agreed word for 'God' – they do not have common words for Christian, church or saint either. Yet despite the fact that it gives to the large number of barely literate the impression that 'Christians' worship various gods, no one seems particularly troubled by this bizarre anomaly.

Altogether, then, though naturally I have stressed negative factors, the churches perform a 'good' job in the Chinese setting, but that goodness retains a conventional caste; it is scarcely creative. It may be that the inevitable limitations especially of life in Hong Kong are to blame, yet in view of the tremendous obstacles that have been overcome, often with great originality and flexibility in the secular sphere, it is not unreasonable to expect that this might be reproduced in the spiritual sphere, so that there is no ground for complacency.

4

The Japanese Setting

To a considerable extent, Tokyo, when I first saw it, was the East I had wrongly imagined Hong Kong would be. Despite the industrial ugliness, the post-war jerry building and the undistinguished setting, it still has the character of a place related to its past in a hundred ways, from the ubiquitous courtesies to the little shrines down side streets, the fox graves and traditional wooden houses. Besides that, superficially it is appropriately inscrutable or impenetrable to the outsider, partly as a result of the language barrier – Japan was never colonized and obliged to speak English or French, like much of Asia – and partly as the result of an elegant efficiency which is un-Asian, or the most perfect expression of Asian tendencies, depending on one's view of the Zen and warrior discipline from which it derives.

More even than India, where misery detracts from the dream and artistic conservatism leads to monotony, with their variety and their rather bold, affirmative style, Tokyo and Japan possess monuments and a sense of history and continuity of the kind that in the West may only be felt in Rome or Nuremberg. The Westernization is profound, but it has a Japanese twist. On the whole, it has a mechanical orientation and was originally made possible by the fascination of the strong military section in Japanese society with foreign gadgets and although it is impossible that contact with the West and with Western science should have had no effect on customs and philosophy, as the Japanese originally hoped, all things considered this effect has probably been limited.

It need hardly be stated that certain supposedly Western features, like the very 'liberated' cinema, which is not especially typical of Asia, must be placed in the context of the nation's own considerable tradition of erotic writing and entertainment. Japan remains Japan.

Furthermore, it is important to see the country in and for itself as a very distinct culture. Though I know educated Europeans who are unable to distinguish even between Chinese and Japanese art, to the trained eye they are very distinct, as are the entire cultures of the two nations, and it is important to guard against the line of thought represented by Sanson's *Japan: A Short Cultural History*[1] and Hendrik Kraemer's *World Cultures and World Religions*[2], which seem to suggest that it is impossible to understand Japan without consideration of Chinese history and culture. This is rather like saying that mediaeval France should not be studied in its own right, but only explained in terms of the Latin language and culture of its universities. It is true that Buddhist civilization came to Japan from China, but it was adopted and modified by the native Shinto for reasons of politics and civilization and not accepted for purely religious reasons, as in China. It is also true that Confucianism came from China, but it operated within a very different context of class, family and ancestral cult. Unlike Chinese society, whose Confucian examination system (when not compromised by bribery) made for a degree of class mobility and meritocracy, Japanese society was aristocratic and fixed. Prime loyalty was given to resident lords, not clan heads and temporary officials, and the family was a limited entity, a three-generation affair, not an extended unit with members worshipped for generations. It should also be noted that Japan did not borrow Taoism from China, though a few Taoist ideas percolated through; the country simply remodelled Shinto and refined China's Ch'an Buddhism into Zen. Altogether, the culture and art shows little or nothing of the Chinese sense of flow and life prized by Taoism. Much of the art has a feeling for the asymmetrical, an awareness of the disconnected, the isolated detail, which is psychologically significant and is not Chinese. It is, of course, symptomatic of the highly introvert, privately individualistic quality of the Japanese mind, which is more evident from its literature (e.g. among the moderns, like Mishima and Kawabata).[3]

One sponsored study of the modern church in Japan laments the dearth of source material, but maintains that Japan presents such a hopelessly chaotic, muddling picture, with so many exceptions to every rule, that satisfactory generalization becomes problematic.[4] My feeling is that the exceptions, the fads, the cliques, odd movements in religion and art, can all be attributed to the periodic surfacing of the irrepressible personal element of the introvert character within a society of fixed forms which gives it little scope. The introvert mentality always appears to have difficulty in making simple, primary affirmations, and expresses itself instead in subtle variations or opposition. In the West, the introvert is frequently the artist who protests against the status quo. In Japan, it could be argued that because of the stiflingly fixed and developed forms in which Chinese culture reached the country, the protest has been institutionalized and that Japan, never able to gain a creative centre, affirmed itself negatively. The result is that its art especially can be described as a series of opposites to Chinese norms: Chinese elaboration is answered by simplicity; the grand scale in architecture by the small; poster colours by sober colours; Chinese pictorial emphasis with sculptural emphasis; the neatness of the Chinese scroll with the Zen ink splashes. I recognize that these and other opposites could be accounted for by the material poverty of Japan in contrast to China, with its sumptuous styles, or by the influence of the military at the expense of the aristocracy, yet all said and done, there does seem to be some element of negative affirmation.

Owing to the developed strain of subjectivity and individualism within Japanese life and culture, it might at first be imagined that the church would not be quite the outsider it has been, but be included among one of the expressions of subjectivity, especially since Japanese religion as such has been witness to much variety and heresy, more so than is common in Asia. Yet this is not at all the case, because Christianity has fallen outside the dialectic of social harmony and subjective right and its synthesis, 'Yamato spirit', as Japan has traditionally seen it. Moreover, its presentation has normally only had serious appeal for classes of people in major social transition or individuals allowed extensive subjective rights, namely, the daimyos and their followers of the sixteenth century, the declassed samurai of the nineteenth century, and students and academics within this century.

Political unity, homogeneity of culture and submission have always been Japanese fetishes, politically sometimes with good reason, psychologically with rather less. Originally much of Japanese society appears to have been a matriarchy, and such societies tend to be divided and anarchic. Division from any cause is something Japan could never tolerate because of the material poverty of the terrain, its proneness to natural disaster and its vulnerability, like that of all islands, to colonization. When patriarchy took over, it did so with remarkable compensatory emphasis on authority. With time and colonization, the society was again in danger of division because of a lack of racial homogeneity, the population being composed of Koreans, Chinese, Ainu, Indonesian, Polynesian and perhaps Russian groups, all of whom left their mark on the interesting complex of national myth. Through the Buddhism adopted by the Emperor Shotoku in 538 and the Confucian bureaucracy and titles imposed upon the restless aristocracy of clan leaders, attempts were made to achieve political and ideological unity. This was only partially successful, though Buddhism was taken seriously. However, it is worth mentioning that given the period and character of Japan, which in the West is often associated with cruelty and intolerance, despite crop failures, high taxes and the drift of the poor into a serfdom lasting into the nineteenth century, the age of Buddhist ascendancy was formally a mild one in which barbarous punishments were disapproved of and the death penalty was rare.

Still, the lords of the outer regions continued restless and the Confucian system of government was not readily adaptable to Japan, nor was the substitution of traditional clan tenure with small land-holding, imposition of which bred resentment because insufficiently good land was available for distribution to individual aristocrats. The aristocracy around the Emperor increased in refinement and decadent effeteness until its military supporters, who were despised under the Buddhist value system, swept them away in 1185 in a gory revolution which put paid to the old humanity for good. Subsequently, the military imposed upon the society a culture predominantly of the sword as opposed to that of the chrysanthemum, to use Ruth Benedict's familiar comparison.[5] That is to say, judo, karate, and later the austere elegance of the tea ceremony overtook the world of literature, art, scented love letters and moon viewing, famous from the writings of Sei Shonagen, Lady Murasaki and Kagero Nikki.[6] The best that can be said for the new system was that it tended to efficiency and honesty and a high sense of duty, though the sense of justice was poor and there was no mercy for the powerless, who could be struck down on the instant at the least suggestion of rebellion or complaint.

Once the military had gained ascendancy, the ideal of unity was postponed for further centuries while war lords, most notably those of the Taira and Mini Moto Clans, rivalled one another for the supreme authority, the Shogunate. The prospect of unity and peace only came into view about the time of Christianity's rather notable success and the reign of Shogun Ieyasu Yokugawa (1598–1618). Though the ruthlessness and massacres of this brilliant organizer, an unlettered and unstable man, can never be justified, the deed of exile, the persecution and tortures which he vented upon Christians and which his son continued must be seen in the context of an unfortunate plot against him by three Christian daimyos and the inexcusable leanings of Franciscans towards Spanish imperial interests, because of their rivalry with the more successful Jesuits. Though Spanish overseas ambitions posed little real threat to Japan, given the national insularity and still vivid memories of the terrible Mongol invasion, Ieyasu brooked no chances.

The hypocrisy of the Shogun in relation to the Christians is nonetheless seen in his boast that the secret of his political success – which was total ruthlessness – lay in his adherence to the principle 'requite malice with kindness'. That he should be able to think this way reflected the twisted values of militarized Buddhism, which could overlook the cruelty of its forms of combat to declare that the true enemy was self, so that in beating others the individual should only think he was subduing his own self.

It is quite clear that this self was the one which sensed any pity or justice. The real reason for the persecution of Christians was probably revealed by Hideyoshi (Ieyasu's predecessor who had himself instigated a temporary persecution), who in writing to the Viceroy of Goa, claimed that in Christian countries 'there is no respect for God and Buddha and no distinction between sovereign and ministers', and described Christianity as 'unreasonable and wanton'. The power of authority in Japan was so very extreme that the slightest gesture of independence or claim to freedom of opinion contrary to accepted rule was regarded as an intolerable insult to those in authority.

Unjust and presumptuous though authority in ancient Japan could be, it is arguable that it was accepted with marked submission (revolution of the Chinese variety has been rare) because authority and unity was also necessary on the psychological front. As I have already said, Japanese introversion is not of the intuitional type, which Jung believed could sometimes be attributed to Israel and its prophets, but of the more feminine, feeling type, which is quiet and withdrawn. Everything points to this designation, the tranquil nature cult of Shinto, the great sensitivity to atmosphere, the famous Japanese 'amorality' which disregards absolute standards in favour of what 'feels' right and wrong (shame rather than guilt, ritual defilement rather than sin) and the whole symbolic, suggestive poetic drift of the literature of the art. This highly aesthetic-emotional character is in constant trouble from a sense of nothingness and lack of structure, and this is something which historically the Japanese system has both exaggerated and resolved in such a way as to make the society one of the most self-contained and 'artificial' in existence.

It will be recalled that the more gregarious Chinese were theoretically united by *jen* (humanity), which could justify collective revolution, if not personal rebellion. The more aristocratic Japanese system discarded this in favour of a semi-religious concept of *on*, unconditional indebtedness towards emperor, country, parents, for the simple fact of existence, and to relatives and friends for favours. At least as far as emperor and parents were concerned, the debt could never be fully repaid. Thus, no one could ever really enjoy the right to protest against a wrong, nor was there even an individual experience of a completely individual wrong. Four basic spheres of interest and activity were recognized: *cho* towards emperor and superiors; *ko* towards parents; *gimu* towards family and friends; and *giri* towards the world and one's own name, honour and face. The duties were normally considered in that order. Many of the great incidents of Japanese history and literature are concerned with the clash of duties; heroes and ordinary individuals alike are constantly unable to act in conscience or pity because of *gimu* or *giri*, or are left with hopeless choices between *ko* and *giri*, *gimu* and *giri*, etc., often leading to despair or suicide. Samurai masters might demand the execution of the subject's relatives in battle as a test of loyalty; mother or father might demand the divorce of the son's wife without explanation, or expect their offspring to acknowledge blame for crimes which they themselves had committed. All these injustices were expected to be taken without murmur, just as the soldier was supposed to pretend he had eaten when deprived of food. Those who did feel personal wrongs or fall on the side of pity were judged to have the 'virtues' of thieves and criminals, those who *freely* gave or took loyalty.

It is in this context that one has to understand the criticism of Christianity as wanton, immoral and unpatriotic. Christian virtues, whether of self-sacrifice or mercy, did not enter the scheme of values. The Japanese system could be regarded as a secularized Buddhism in which the individual has no meaning or identity separated from the one, in this case represented by the nation or family group with self-control and mercy, subject to technique and calculation rather than freely given. In the demands upon the individual made by traditional Japan, the Asian tendency to avoid the obvious and practical reaches its highest point. During the Tokugawa Shogunate (1618–1867), the era of greatest isolation and discipline, a complaint by peasants to the Shogun of ill-treatment or tax extortion automatically entailed the death penalty for the plaintiff, whether the plaintiff was pronounced justified or not.

Hara-kiri (ritual disembowelment) could be instigated over the least loss of face, like misreading an official missive. Even in the Meiji times, other horrors were regularly enacted, like teachers losing their lives in saving the emperor's photograph from school fires (in wood-built old Tokyo, fires were common) or committing suicide if they failed to rescue it. It was even possible for fathers, like Count Katsu, to hold a sword over their offspring while they were undergoing an operation, threatening them with immediate and honourable death if they dared whimper. The rest of Asia knows nothing comparable to this, and it sets the Japanese apart. The feeling of separation is quite conscious. The Japanese regard the Chinese, for example, as inferior and undisciplined. Asians themselves, like the Thais who suffered the bridge over the River Kwai, tend to dismiss the Japanese as dangerous if efficient zombies.

But every system, even the most exotic, makes some kind of sense when seen and experienced from within, and certainly the Japanese have been far from regarding themselves as inhuman and unnatural. They reflect that they did not, like the Chinese, bind their women's feet, a terrible ordeal that caused the death of many girls, nor did they make their men eunuchs, another cruel operation, and they demanded instant decapitation upon disembowelment to avoid the lingering tortures common in the Chinese systems of punishment; moreover, what tortures the Japanese came to practise were of Chinese rather than native origin. Even the treatment of POWs during the last war must be judged in the light of the remarkable hardships their superiors inflicted upon Japanese soldiers, who expected of POWs the same endurance or even willingness to cover the shame of capture by the suicide they themselves would normally practise.

Faced with the inhuman demands and suicidal urges of traditional Japan, rather glamourized today and in attenuated form perpetuated in the examination system and the requirements of some companies, one is obliged to go further than explanation by a psychological type. Several factors must be born in mind. As a historical phenomenon, the severity and ideological force of military rule is partly attributable to the extent of the upheaval following 1185. This decimated so many men that beyond the terror it inspired, it made possible the notable subjection of women, who were previously more socially involved in everything from literature to warfare, on the whole with civilizing effect. Yet elements of matriarchy would always remain in Japan (the degree, for example, to which the Japanese wife would hold the purse strings might seem surprising), and it is in any case very easy, according to Jungian theory, for the introvert type to be mother or wife-dominated, since the more vulnerable sense of objectivity and form is in danger of being lost to an identity with the oceanic consciousness of the woman.[7] This may help to explain how a great, confusing contrast had arisen in the rearing of the Japanese child within the patriarchal system, a rearing which, though modified since the last war, still inclines to the old pattern. On the one hand, an early and full identity with the mother would be encouraged, and to begin with, she indulged and spoiled the child, especially the male child; on the other hand, she left herself open to hostility by teaching unquestioned and absolute submission to the distant and punitive father, and thus received the hostility which would normally be directed towards the father as a simple rival to the child's affections. In consequence, the mother could often be slapped and abused by the five- or six-year-old, who was allowed a rather dangerous measure of cruelty towards the primary object of love.

At the same time the mother could be cruel in her way, not only in her demand of submission to the harshness of the father and the system to which she would deliver the child at seven, but also in the way she would tease and frighten the child with threats of abandonment and talk of its unworthiness. In this respect the rearing recalls the ways of the matriarchal society. This society, basically egalitarian, does not tend to respect the individualism of the child and will usually try to level or ridicule its pretensions, especially of the male child where it is tied to the idealizing factor of the *anima*. As in Ireland, where by hampering integration of the *anima* a residual matriarchal element in the rearing has made for great personal insecurity and excessive touchiness in all points of honour, by school time the male was and often still is ready to fight and avenge honour on the least pretext and was in awe of all rebuke by authority. Ruth Benedict quotes Markino Yoshio and how when he was young and poor, he suggested to a missionary that he would go to America. The missionary, rather uncouth, sneered, "*You* go to America?"[8] The reaction was almost hysterical; Yoshio claimed he would rather be dead. Temper, lying, murder itself, he insisted, would be more excusable than the unforgettable wound inflicted by the sneer of an 'insincere' person. It is super-sensitivity and internalized hatred of this kind which accounts for *hara-kiri* and the other forms of self-punishment. Japan has never accepted the idea that one is insulted only if one thinks so; if society insults the individual, then he is insulted, since society is the form and conscience for the mind. Indeed, as Benedict observes, there is no Christian belief that 'What comes out of a man defiles him'; it is society which defiles.[9]

Service, attachment to society and a cause alone provide self-justification. Japan, like its former ally Germany, could almost be described as an army in search of a cause, and modern nationalism and its extreme dedication to the emperor marked an attempt to supply this when the Meiji reforms overthrew the Shogunate and made inroads into traditional patterns of duty.

All educations which at first spoil, then drop and ignore the child, make for harshness and repressed resentments. The Arabic world is the most notable example, but Japan is no exception to the pattern. It is, however, rendered more complex by the matriarchal element. The original identity with the mother would be transferred to emperor and society and historically to the feudal lord, where sometimes there were homosexual overtones. Loyalty is hardly the word to describe what is involved. Much Japanese martial and social behaviour can be described only in terms of blind and total identity with superiors. The emperor is noticeably co-aeval with heaven and earth, in themselves seen as more or less eternal, another concept suggestive of an inclusive perception of reality, de-differentiated and orientated on the mother. According to the Japanese psychiatrist, Kenji Ohtaki, because the West has an id, an ego and a superego, it takes its conscience seriously and is easily rendered neurotic, whereas the East, or Japan, more feminine and mother-formed, has only an id and a superego, and is more prone to psychosis. Certainly the response of Yoshio to the missionary cited above borders on the psychotic, as did the behaviour of Mishima and the subjects of his fiction, like the monk in *The Temple of the Golden Dawn*. As to superior moral feelings, in Japan they are less realistic than narcissistic, related to the superiority of the Japanese way generally.

Christian analysts of the Japanese experience need to be aware of Dr Maloney's judgment that in Japan anyone who is defined as psychologically disturbed or ill, is so in relation to the society, and the psychiatrist, far from releasing the patient from inner bonds and social claims, strives to tighten them, thus encouraging not maturation but regressive tendencies, and the desire for return to the womb and identity with the mother, which is the basis of the ego-denying social system.[10]

Consequently, spiritual problems also tend to receive the same treatment.

For Japanese belief, the original innocence of man, the Buddha seed of pure consciousness waiting to be rediscovered, is the time of identity with the mother and the original purity, is seen as clouded over, affected not, as Western Buddhists imagine, by logic and reason, but by the trammels of social demands which upset the harmony, the only harmony of which the society is able to conceive. Though the nationalism and secularism of Japan has long disposed it against Buddhism, much as with China, its education and social demands have made it Buddhist in feeling despite itself. 'You can appreciate how enormously satisfying it is for me to discover at last, through full realization, that just as I am I lack nothing,' wrote Yaeko Iwasahi to her master after she had achieved the enlightened knowledge that self is nothing and being oneness.[11] The problem of the ego and of form is not so easily resolved, and much of the sharpness which attaches to everything from Japanese architectural forms and the metallic ring of precise Koto music is, I believe, an attempt to overcome this formlessness with a clarity of structure and impression, though preferably by suggestion or with the help of symbol.

The Japanese search for clarity of expression has never been helped by the Chinese forms which the country has adopted, nor by its own demand that structure be intrinsic and suggested rather than completely realized. However, the belief of the West that Japanese culture is classical and the architecture functional may not be correct (though the military, like military everywhere, may have favoured functional forms). I believe that any 'classicism' represents an attempt, paralleled within politics, to 'establish' an order notably lacking from the anarchic inner life. Some proof for this comes from the fact that it was not rationalism, functionalism and disapproval of the imagination in the Western sense that underlay the original Zen simplicity, for even Zen archery was designed with the magical warding off of spirits in mind.

The effort to achieve a measure of design and wholeness is a Japanese obsession. Taken individually, many Japanese *objets d'art* are simpler and cruder than the Chinese equivalent, but it is the ensemble which impresses, as does the total rhythm in the tea ceremony. For this reason I believe that Japanese literature and music are much surer guides to the Japanese soul than the art. It is the most extravert cultures, like the Italian and Chinese, which excel at the more superficial and sensuous practice of art and distil their spirituality within it.

Anyway, the military leadership of Japan would appear to have profited from the sense of nothingness, imposing itself and rigid structures by way of compensation. Often lost and confused, the individual would cling to the system which in its totality provided identity and structure even when wronged, like an ill-treated wife clinging to a bad husband for the security of marriage. Exploiting and exploited could be joined in respect for the Yamato spirit, and for the Emperor, symbol of the whole, upon whom was projected the 'pure' love and reverence which could not always be honestly mustered for the sometimes tyrannical father and husband. 'Exploitation' is perhaps one of the key words of the Japanese experience. Keyserling suggests that the Japanese way is less one of imitation, as is frequently maintained, than of exploitation, as in *ju jitsu*, where the every strength of the opponent is used to defeat him. This is an important observation with rather sinister connotations.[12] At any rate, one suspects an unusual amount of psychological presumption and exploitation by the great upon the small in Japanese life. The outsider, like Keyserling, or even St Francis Xavier, who thought the Japanese the best people in the world, may well be impressed by the qualities of the ordinary people and the cultured and efficient life style; they may be impressed to the point of making apologies to the society and considering all criticism exaggerated, but disillusion may follow upon more experience with the leadership. Keyserling found them rather cruel, and the first Jesuit missionaries certainly lived to discover how cruel those they had admired could be. This harshness may be less evident in the de-militarized Japan of the present, but in a country of so much courteous humility, one wonders at the narcissism or arrogance of company executives who expect inferiors to come to the station to bid them elaborate and emotional farewells when leaving on a routine weekly business visit. Doubtless, however, they would excuse it as a way of keeping up the Japanese spirit and contributing to the social order.[13]

Given the Japanese mystique of power and authority, it is defeat and change of power which produces in them the greatest shifts of consciousness, political and spiritual. During the last war Japanese POWs usually felt so humiliated by their situation and so awed by their conquerors that if they did not commit suicide they made a *volte-face* and turned into supporters of America who would be loyal to the death. Similarly, there was a period under the Meiji reforms when it was seriously proposed by the members of the Ihowara embassy to America and by leading intellectuals that Christianity should become the state religion because Western knowledge generally had proved itself victorious. There were identical proposals after the Second World War and the MacArthur administration, but as soon as Japan recovered its self-respect and culture again, getting the foreignness of Christianity into focus, the religion waned and the churches, so full of enquirers in the late 1940s, were emptying by 1951. When Christianity first came to Japan there was something of the same pattern. The religion impressed people when the Jesuits answered the arguments of the fractious and unpopular Buddhist priests won over daimyos, but when it was disapproved of by authority, and martyrdom did not lead to further victories for the faith, its image rapidly became tarnished in the public mind.

Thus there have always been three major possibilities for the church in Japan. First, when permitted, its evangelism might catch the wave of social change and be declared a national faith; second, it might identify with or give identity to a specific class whose activity would then become dominant; third, its presentation would so change to match the Japanese spirit and psychology as to take a natural place within its subjectivity and gradually transform the society from within.

The first possibility owes more to Japanese proposals by both Christians and non-Christians than to missionary ambitions (many Protestant missionaries oppose the idea of national churches); because it was the expression of shock and defeat, it fell foul of the irrepressible Japanese spirit. When Catholics re-established contact with the hidden Christians of the south in the 1870s their interest was to re-educate them to a more perfect Roman and Western model which offended many who already felt martyrs to the faith, and was no encouragement to nationalistic Japanese to join them. At the same time, during the era of Meiji reform, Protestants (evidently unable to believe the biblical dictum that the leopard does not change his spots) took Japanese Westernization at face value and as inevitable; and when interest was shown in their faith, made no preparation for the nationalist and cultural reaction which followed. In default of a missionary religion or a Japanese one addressing itself to the psychology of the whole society (Buddhism was in abeyance and Shinto without theological sophistication), it was almost natural that the Emperor should become the new symbol of wholeness and a Shinto influenced by Christian theology rather than Westernized Christianity should take precedence.

The identification of the church with a class in Japan has been the consequence of an inability to grasp the mentality as a whole and address its problems. The first missionary to Japan, St Francis Xavier, who arrived in 1542, did address himself to the poor, as did his immediate followers. This was in accord with evangelical imperatives, and the history and patterns of church growth indicate that in so far as the church confronts social classes, it is best for it to begin with the poor. During the 1570s, and especially after the inspection of the Jesuit Visitor, Valignano, who impressed upon missionaries the importance of identifying with local ways, attention switched to the daimyos (feudal lords), who were expected to bring their subjects with them into the faith.

The missionaries with their Latin and martial background appreciated the martial skills and values of the class. They themselves came to dress like Zen monks, or even nobles, worshipped in chapels close to Buddhist style and taught the people to respect their rulers. According to the Franciscans who arrived later, the wooing of daimyos and samurai was at the expense of the poor and downtrodden, contempt for whom they duplicated. Franciscan criticism, however, was interested, and the Jesuits were trusted and popular. Nevertheless, one of the effects of the new emphasis seems to have been an exaggeration of disciplinary ideals among the rank and file of converts. Assuming the ethics of the superior class, they submitted themselves to violent penances and, as at the reckless celebration of the canonization of St Ignatius, exposed themselves to martyrdom to a degree which made the missionaries themselves quail. While it is impossible not to admire the valiant efforts of the Jesuits to come to grips with Japanese language and culture, their identification with the aristorcracy probably went too far, as did also their promptings of rulers to force the conversion of subjects and their toleration of the subsequent destruction of Buddhist temples and property, because the Buddhists were in disfavour among many feudal lords. The most damaging effect of the association between Christians and the daimyo class during a civil war was, of course, that at the end of the war the Shogun imposed loyalty on rebel lords at the expense of Christian subjects. Less partisanship might have modified the persecution when it came, just as less sympathy for Spanish imperialism by Franciscans might have outweighed its political pretensions.

By contrast, in the 1880s and 1890s Protestant Christianity became involved with a class more by accident than design, though with hindsight the association must appear inevitable. Practically all the leading names of early Protestantism in Japan, like Kanzo Uchimura, Nishima Yoichi Honda, Mashisha Uemura, Danjo Ebina, Horomichi Kozaki, and even the socialist-minded Toyahiko Kagawa, were of samurai class or higher: Uemura was a relative of the deposed Shogun's family. Only Gumpei Yamamuro, founder of the Japanese Salvation Army, came from the people, though in fact his family was a rich farming one, albeit fallen on hard times at the time of Yamamuro's birth, and he was educated to Confucianism and Chinese classics in the most traditional and respectable way.

The influence exerted by the church on the samurai class had three major causes. First, toleration of Christianity was limited until 1912, and evangelism was either restricted or forbidden, which meant that initially Protestant influence was mediated through colleges of education and the printed word: upper-class Japanese frequently attended Western and Christian colleges. Second, the samurai class, losing status to the commercial classes under the Meiji revolution (or imperial restoration) which deposed their old master, the Shogun, were looking for new causes, ideas and leadership, and mostly desired the modernization of Japan. Numbers of them had actually contributed towards the Meiji revolution, though most held back from association with the merchants who had been enriching themselves while they themselves were forbidden to trade under the Tokugawa regime.

Third, the highly doctrinal and unaesthetic presentation of Protestantism could only appeal to those with a certain degree of education, and its severely Victorian Puritan tone would prove acceptable particularly to those raised in a harsh school. These men regarded Christianity as a fulfilment and transcendence of the harsh Confucianism they knew, much as Christians saw the New Testament as a fulfilment of the Old.

Because of the deep prejudices against Christianity bred of more than two hundred years during which it had been outlawed and vilified on notices at every crossroads of the police state which Japan had become, it was in one sense a blessing for the church that its first defenders were men of status and education, not easily cowed by authority. On the other hand, their experience and values were scarcely representative enough to reach the vast body of people. It must immediately be stressed that Japan has been very markedly two nations: aristocracy and the rest, town and country; much more so than in traditional China where any family might rise and where, as *The Dream* shows, social ignorance or dirty talk could be tolerated in a way that would be unthinkable in aristocratic circles of Japan. The dance and music shows the difference; though they are united by a refining stylization, there is a contrast between the sedate and melancholy, even tragic style of aristocracy and the rollicking, half-drunken earthy mirth of the other, some of it like Celtic wake games, betraying the frank interest of a once-matriarchal society in fertility. If a very separated aristocracy is drawn into a new religious movement, what usually happens with the passing of time is that members look up to 'the quality' and confuse respectability and deference with real virtue, as in late-Victorian England, the final product is a hopelessly sedate, middle-class church. This is especially true of the modern Kyodan (Church of Christ). The sermons are frequently so intellectually sophisticated that the ordinary person cannot understand them, and the style so sedate that no ordinary soul could identify with it.

This is not said in criticism of the first Japanese Protestant leaders, who individually were very great men, but rather against those later missionaries and Japanese Christians who, when full freedom was granted to the church, did not enlarge its evangelistic thrust and alter its style. Kagawa at least had enough vision to complain about this, and insisted that the church must try to reach the rural and industrial areas if it intended to reach Japan at all. Most of the early Christians were only equipped to communicate with university students or, like some of the aristocratic saints of Christendom, tackled religion in terms of a heroic sense of honour and self-sacrifice which again ordinary people could not be expected to emulate.

This was true even of the saintly Kagawa, the man so devoted to the people that he would share his bed with beggars. His cruel childhood experiences at the hands of his foster-mother and school friends early provoked exceptional distress and conflict, while his Christianity caused him to be disinherited; in his fictional autobiography he describes the hero undergoing agonizing and hysterical conflicts to the point where he decides that to be Christian he will live as one dead, for in that way he will be able to repay or avoid the obligations of *ko* and *on*. The intensity and heroism may be of the kind with which churches are founded, but it is not what always makes them grow and relate to society.

A further problem raised by the alliance between the church and this somewhat feeble class was the opposition to the Imperial Rescript in which most Protestant groups and subsequently the Catholic authorities came to be involved. When in 1887 the Imperial Rescript apparently extended religious liberty, the church rejoiced, but the possible threat from the new state Shinto and its imperial status was heralded when Uchimura refused to bow towards the Rescript as was customary when it was read (since the text was felt to represent the Emperor). This act of defiance led to his dismissal and prompted general Christian opposition to bowing to portraits and to school visits to historical and religious sites. In turn, this raised new official opposition to Christianity as an unpatriotic religion.

Sympathy, both human and Christian, must go to Uchimura for refusing to give such excessive honour to any human authority, yet at the same time, mission leaders who supported his stand raised no similar objections to bowing to the American flag, or singing the hymn, 'I vow to thee my country, all earthly things above', or crowning a Pope who is theoretically 'servant of servants' – all practices questioned in modern Christianity. Given all this, along with Japanese reverence and the Japanese disposition to bow to everything, it is questionable how much the vulnerable church was advised to oppose the Rescript. Might not Uchimura's stand have been influenced by his class's resentment at the new Emperor's attitude to the samurai? Anyway, Kagawa, whose orthodoxy and sincerity were impeccable, stated another view, maintaining that Christians would have been justified in performing most of the usual reverences to persons and towards historical sites.

II

If we are to see how Christianity has addressed itself to Japanese society and to review any developments in that direction, we must first consider briefly Japanese national religion and spirituality.

Japanese religion has great diversity and to some extent originality, though as the native intellectual disposition tends to be scholastic and analytic, this originality is often one of speciality and technique. Few societies, ancient or modern (America is perhaps the nearest comparison), have gone so far to produce religion to fit a need or a social mood; the adaptation of pacific Buddhism to military ends is perhaps the most notable example, but by no means an isolated one. Impermanence and a rejection of a mono-lithic form is almost basic; even in the original religion, Shinto, the shrine of Ise had to be built and demolished every twenty years, while the practice of Zen recommended the destruction of Buddha images if they proved unhelpful. 'Religion was made for man, not man for religion' might be the Japanese motto, though since pray-ing for material benefits, especially financial, was frowned upon in all save 'floating' populations, like actors and prostitutes who had their shrines, 'salvation' or 'enlightenment' has never been far from sight.

Shinto was little removed from Shamanism, though as it comes into historical view, its sun-worship was evidently providing some measure of spiritual unity for animists, ancestor-worshippers and others; it offered a rather charming and comprehensive body of myth, had a priesthood and cultus, and was related to the imperial house. Its main temples were and are set in imposing natural surroundings with pines and cryptomerias, reflecting the profound Japanese affinity with nature and their association of things spiri-tual with it. This, Kagawa claimed, missonaries had ignored to their disadvantage, and he himself, like many Japanese, admitted to preferring the Gospels to St Paul because of their more mem-orable references to nature and the emotions (missionary teaching was usually highly Pauline and doctrinal). Washing, sweeping, polishing all had their part in Shinto ritual, which strongly em-phasized the need for cleansing, a symbol of the generalized good-ness (or just mirror-like openness to truth) which is prized by Japanese to the present day.

Influenced by Siberian and Polynesian myth in accounting for the existence of Japan, the religion has a fairly strong sense of creation (though not of a Supreme Creator) and of the eternity of spirits (*kami*) and Spirit, which exists throughout matter. This was something which Buddhism could never quite eradicate, so that there was always a vague theism and belief in eternal as well as self-made Buddhas. Shinto belief that on death everyone could become a kind of god also diluted Buddhist beliefs in reincarnation, so that the accent came to be upon attaining enlightenment in this life or gaining a heaven in the next, and indefinitely postponing nirvana. Many Japanese, however, do hold to belief in reincarna-tion, and this was especially true during the early Buddhist period.

Shinto is said to be emotional and aesthetic, a ritual rather than a doctrine, with what doctrine it does possess stolen from Buddhism and Christianity. No doubt this is true, but scholarship has probably failed to note the historic direction of religion by charismatic authority, which in more matriarchal times would have been represented by prophetesses who, with the greater freedom accorded Japanese women in modern times, have again been in evidence in the new religions. The patriarchalization of Japan and the ritualization of Shinto is suggested by the way in which Ameratsu, the Sun Goddess, hands over authority to her son, who institutes the imperial line.

The formal acceptance of Buddhism by the emperor and court of Japan in the seventh century must be regarded as in large measure a political decision and a decision for greater culture. Buddhism brought with it not only a plethora of North Indian and Chinese scriptures, to which the Japanese soon added, but Chinese civilization and the Confucianism on which Prince Shotoku reorganized the country. Shinto was never positively rejected, but fell into abeyance among the educated, its deities described as Buddhas. The terrifying and amoral aspects of Shinto gave way to a rather more rational view of life and conduct in which man was no longer at the complete mercy of nature and supernatural forces, but responsible for his salvation. It is important to grasp that, quite exceptionally, Buddhism appeared to Japan as a *humanism*. There were two main reasons for this. First, Shinto was so full of the invisible and awesome that the manifestation of the Buddha image was itself a humanistic affirmation to an aesthetically minded people like the Japanese – who were perhaps so immersed in aesthetic and ritualistic aspects that they never fully grasped its doctrinal import. Second, because Shinto arrived in company with Chinese philosophy and laws, it became confused with them, again making for a humanistic emphasis.

The earliest form of Buddhism in Japan was patronized by the court and the élite only, based on the Chinese Three Treatises, Mind-only philosophy, which was in turn derived from the philosophy of the Indian Narguna. It was too abstruse for a society which desired a religion of faith, intuition and aesthetics. Later, during the Nara period, 'Flower Garland' (Kegon) Buddhism made a somewhat wider appeal and nearly became the state religion. This sect taught the interrelatedness of all things, as in a flower garland, to the Lotus throne of Buddha; its scripture, the *Sutra of the Golden Light*, like Shinto, emphasized healing, and also wisdom and the uses of discrimination (usually looked down on in Buddhism), by which the individual could tell the difference between right and wrong. A Japanese concern with sincerity, and perhaps also Nestorian influence upon later Chinese Buddhism, led the court to practice *keko*, open confession of sins. As the court was never especially ascetic, confessions were usually long and interesting.

After 770, the emperor, afraid of the power of Buddhist monks, moved to Kyoto and supported the puritanical Tendai sect founded by Saicho on Mt Hiei. This sect followed the *Lotus Sutra*, which democratically promised salvation to all, though unlike the ambitious court monks of Nara they emphasized the superiority of the monastic way to gaining it. However, in time Mt Hiei would produce political and soldier monks sufficient to threaten first emperors, then shoguns, until it was rased by Odo Nobunaga in 1571. When it proved too puritanical for the court, Tendai was overtaken by the esoteric Shignon Buddhism of Kukai, a prodigy who composed *The Indications*, a work which reflects the Japanese intellectuals' un-Asian concern with logic and consistency. Imploring the aid of all Buddhas to help him perceive some unity amid the tangle of doctrines confronting him (by this time there were about 8,000 scriptures), he ranged the major Buddhist sects and other philosophies, Taoist and Confucian, into ten manifestations of one truth in which the Shignon version of Buddhism rated the highest. One of the reasons it did so was because, denying the consciousness or emptiness theories, it allowed the harmonious coexistence of mind and matter throughout eternity.

This faith was esoteric, that is, its authority lay beyond scriptures or supposed revelations to the historical Buddha (as in Kegon and Tendai); it was a revelation of the cosmic Buddha Vairochana. The aspirant might attain to an understanding of this revelation only through the aid of a master. So unspeakable were the mysteries involved that only art could suggest them or ritual bring one into tune with them. The point was that since the Buddha, the world and mortals were composed of the same six elements, correct movements might have universal and helpful vibrations. Shignon helped foster the great flowering of Heian culture and art by its declaration that everything beautiful was related to Buddha. In her famous *Pillow Book*, the court woman Sei Shonagen describes a pilgrimage to Hasedera (like Shinto, Shignon was and is a religion of pilgrimage) and writes of her first glimpse of the altar.

The sight was so strangely moving that I wondered why I had allowed so many months to go by without once coming here

... in this terrifying furnace of light (the altar was lit by innumerable offering lamps of pilgrims) the Buddha flashed and sparkled with the most magnificent effect.[14]

So carried away was she by the beauty of sight and sound that she grew irritated at the interruption of her religious thoughts by a less than handsome sutra recitant. However, she later corrects herself for such 'blasphemous' thoughts at worship, reminding us that self-examination never completely disappeared in this religion of beauty.

What are almost certainly Christian-Nestorian elements in this faith must be noted. Kukai 'baptized' Saicho into knowledge of it upon his return from China. Some of the ritual gestures and objects, like the bells and goblets, are suggestive of celebrations of the mass. In the scriptures of this sect, which despite its esotericism inevitably came into being, the emphasis on faith and repentance is pronounced, and there is an evangelical feeling that 'today is the day of salvation'. For example, we read 'Once you fall into hell, repentance is of no value ... however much you may lament and be tormented, there will be no one to help you. ... Do your best while you are on this earth.' According to Kagawa, garbled passages of Genesis were inserted into some Shignon scriptures.

Shignon Buddhism suffered an eclipse after 1185, when Buddhism finally democratized itself to reach the people in earnest, and also to reach women, who were usually declared not to possess souls or to be in need of further reincarnation, preferably in masculine form, in order to be able to practise the faith with effect. The trend had really begun within the Heian era with the priests Kuya, Ryonin, Ippen and especially Genshin, but Heian Buddhism had paid no more than lip service to the *Lotus Sutra's* claim that there was only one Mahayanist way to salvation; they had made it sectarian and associated it with class. Among the reformers, the new object of devotion was Amida, the Buddha of Boundless Light, who ruled in the Western Paradise and who had vowed to save all beings who would call upon his name in faith. Formerly Amida had been only one object of contemplation in the devotion of monks, but now the reformers told the individual to rely on him in faith, which was again a shift from the emphasis upon reliance on one's own works to become a Buddha. Kuya, 'the saint of the streets', introduced the people to Amida by ringing a bell, dancing in the streets (dancing was a feature of Shinto) and singing simple hymns.

He never fails
To reach the Lotus land of Bliss
Who calls
If only once
The name of Amida.

The people were invited to concentrate on Buddha and abandon themselves to the same dancing and chanting.

After 1185, this almost revivalist faith gained ground as people ceased to believe in themselves and one another and turned from a religion of 'self help' (*jiriki*) to a religion of grace or 'other power' (*tariki*). The movement is perhaps comparable to the considerable Buddhist defection to Christianity in Cambodia at the onset of the troubles which led to Communist rule. Comparisons with Christianity must, however, be made with care because in theory (though not, it seems, in practice) the love of Amida for mankind and of the soul for Amida was not understood to be a real love, after the Christian pattern of a redeemer's love, but part of a universal illusion; like talents and temperaments, love might thus be used to exhaust and overcome it. Nevertheless, under the influence of the monk Honen, who raised the *Senchakusha* scripture above all others, Amidism became even more 'Christian', a kind of monotheism and deliverance from hell by calling upon the Blessed Name. Genshin had taught that by fear of hell men were turned to good. Now, hell's terrors, already so manifest on earth, were brought vividly before the people, some of then fainting with terror like New Englanders at the meetings of Jonathan Edwards.

The religious art of late Heian and Kamakura (early feudal) Japan is significantly baroque for Asia. The screens depicting Amida's Paradise, or his appearance over the mountains, or on the clouds of heaven as he comes to deliver the believer, almost certainly relate to Christian ideas and images which did not receive the same doctrinal and artistic emphasis in the Chinese Buddhism which borrowed them, because of the more peaceful social situation of China and its less frankly emotional treatment of religious and artistic subjects. The portrayals of hell were also remarkably vivid and gruesome, concentrating on physical rather than mental distress, and the power of this art during the period is suggested by the famous 'Legend of the Hell Screen', told in different versions till modern times.

Shinran, Honen's disciple, denied practically all the Buddhist scriptures except those referring to Amida's vow, and produced a

Lutheran revolution not only by taking a woman to wife after a long inner struggle, but by declaring that salvation depends on faith alone and not on conduct. Religion became a matter of intention. One called on the name but in true faith, with a pure heart. As regards marriage, most sects, Buddhist and Shinto, subsequently followed the anti-ascetical revolution, in defiance of all custom and vows. This was in fact the best solution, since Buddhist monks had become notorious for visiting houses of ill repute. As to the rest, though Shinran personally believed in the need for good works and a good life – he did not take a wife easily – he leaned to the view that faith alone counted to the degree that even the greatest sinners could be saved. Some understood this to mean that one could sin the more that grace might abound. In time, his teaching brought Amidism into disrepute as a soft option, simplistic and automatic, a faith for weak people and prostitutes, like the characters in Fumio Niwa's *The Buddha Tree*.[15] Nevertheless, Shinran was very influential, to the point that most Buddhist temples not dedicated to Amida fell into disrepair or ruin. Reaction was inevitable. It came with the fiery Nichiren, who disliked the *Senchakushu*, and while maintaining the emphasis on faith, declared the *Lotus Sutra* the only true gospel. To faith religion he added prophetic zeal and obligations, emphasizing self-sacrifice and perseverance. His sect remains very influential, not least because he interpreted the Buddhist scriptures and prophecies to give Japan a prophetic role as harbinger of true Buddhism. A member of the lowest caste, he criticized rulers both for social injustices and for tolerating other sects. There was a strong militant, almost Islamic, quality to his religion.

The 'liberal' reaction to Amidist pietism began with the monks Eisai (1141–1215) and Dogen (1200–1253). The new feudal and military elite could hardly do otherwise then welcome such a functional version of the faith as Zen, when so much of the popular religion implied a condemnation of the conditions they had produced, even if it did not actually suggest that they were prime candidates for hell. Eisai brought Zen (Ch'an) and tea back from China because Ch'an was the only form of Buddhism he found still active there, but he seems to have known where to introduce it and how to adapt it. Eisai founded the Rinzei school of Zen, which helps to bring the individual to enlightenment in the here and now through the *koan*, an absurd problem which is not amenable to a rational solution but exhausts or shocks the disciple into knowledge. Introspection is active, and knowledge may come in the form of action, slapping someone or screaming, and not through the intellect or scriptures. By contrast Soto Zen gave room to scripture and intellect, albeit with Dogen's proviso 'stay on top of the Lotus (sutra), don't let it get on top of you'. Its main discipline, however, was *zazen*, the passive sitting still and meditation which conveys enlightenment if practised long and rigorously enough.

Because of the emphasis on technique rather than creed, it is with Zen that modern Christians, especially Catholics, have had a dialogue.[16] Some have even been initiated into it to acquire the sensation of enlightenment. Nonetheless, this is another example of rather élitist interests on the part of the churches, for this is minority religion, and it is controversial how far Zen is the mystical summit and summary of Asian aspirations, as its Japanese and Western apologists maintain. Undoubtedly Eisai and Dogen were religious men, though the practices they introduced led to scepticism or religious indifference in their followers. 'Great is mind. Heaven's height is immeasurable but mind goes beyond heaven. . . . How great the primal energy . . . Of all the things that heaven has created, man is the most noble. . . .'[17] These and other rhetorical passages from Eisai are clearly those of belief and a mystical temperament, while Dogen, though less mystical, appears almost superstitious about the power of the historical Buddha. What Zen appears to offer is a heightened sense of the real, a purified consciousness like that of the child who acts and sees naturally, stands up and falls down easily instead of awkwardly in ways dictated by reason, fear or custom. Such oneness with nature and ordinary consciousness is not at all similar to the Indian mystic's more inclusive philosophical, religious and even 'biological' sense of oneness with whatever the mind suggests of the worlds of gods and men. It ignores the mystical colours and great archetypes; it does not see things through the white light of spirit or void which binds together all things. It does not even see things with the fresh clarity of spring, but in the soothing, dull light of evening and autumn.

Later Zen designs would acquire a disconcertingly drab 'granny' quality, the style of vulgarly obvious china pieces and flowery wallpapers in the West. When realized in architecture as in the simplicity of the Katsura villa, any attractiveness depending solely upon the small scale and use of wood, Zen has helped to launch upon the West the functional unspiritual ugliness of the architecture which plagues us. An un-Asian realism was the greatest discovery of Zen. As the only true object of veneration became the master, his portrait became more and more real, and this contributed to the trend begun in Heian literature of making the individual an object of psychological analysis, despite the philosophical prejudice against individualism.

Yet love of any variety, human or theological, was extraordinarily lacking in the system, and Zen appears as cold and impersonal as the metalwork of the period. It was even cruel, an extension of Japanese child punishment and teasing. One head of a monastery remarked to Dogen, 'Formerly, I used to hit sleeping monks so hard that my fist just about broke. Now I am old and weak, so I cannot hit them hard enough. Therefore it is difficult to produce good monks.'

Though never influential as a faith, Zen has affected all society through the cultural forms it imposed or purified, like tea ceremony, flower arrangement, *haiku* (a short verse form), Noh plays (adapted from Shinto), generally marking an alliance of aristocratic fastidiousness with rural simplicity to the point of pretentiousness (a blank wall or an ink splash was called artistic; so long as a name or concept could be attached to it), while the use of asymmetrical design was taken to the point of eccentricity as in the Hiunkaku Pavilion at Kyoto. In everything, modernity with its impersonal unspiritual, quasi-sophisticated style was anticipated.

The martial arts of Zen are famous, and the monks became so adept at them that they precipitated the decline of Buddhism. Even today, judo, karate, fencing, sword fighting, sumo wrestling remain a fundamental aspect of Japanese culture. A mystique still clings to them, as when major companies expect employees to engage in martial gymnastics in their free time to increase their health, loyalty and efficiency. Wonderfully crime-free though Japan is – even in Tokyo, inns and hotels do not need to be locked at night – the result of so much martial training in combination with the other patterns of duty has been to produce a society dangerously full of repressed violence, which erupts in public demonstrations where demonstrators and police can nearly murder one another. It need hardly be said that a Christian criticism of Japan would need to take the country's 'Buddhist' leisure activities into account.

Opposition to Buddhist politicking under the Monoyama and Tokugawa regimes aided a Shinto and Confucian reaction which accompanied an artistic revolution away from simplicity towards the sumptuous (as at the shrine of Nikko) or the fantastic (as in the productions of Kabuki theatre). Neo-Confucian philosophy, so helpful in establishing an ordered, unified society, became more prominent, and when combined with martial values, produced the famous 'Bushido' (the way of the warrior), a faith, a religion of aristocratic honour and honesty, though not of great humanity. Neo-Confucianism also swayed towards Shinto because its ideas of Supreme Ultimate and soul found more support within that faith. Also, with the rise of the wealthy but severely restricted merchant class, which had little scope to spend its money outside the 'floating world' of theatre and mistresses, a non-monastic, non-moralistic, this-worldly faith was required. Shinto answered to the demand.

Some forms of neo-Confucianism and Neo-Shinto were crypto-Christian, and though in the case of Japan the blood of the martyrs had not been the seed of the church, its influence would nonetheless help 'to put down the mighty from their seats' and contribute to the overthrow of the Tokugawa regime which had persecuted it. Neo-Confucianism was divided into various schools.

The rationalist pro-Tokugawa Shushi school was anti-Christian, but the Classical and Oyemei schools, which emphasized will and emotion, interpreted neo-Confucian philosophy in ways resembling Christianity; this made acceptance of that faith by the Samurai easier after 1853, and contributed to the Meiji revolution, many of whose leaders were Oyemei Confucianists. The founder of the Oyemei school, Toju Nakae, took a monotheistic line, declaring belief in the Fatherhood of an infinite God, and used the word 'Deus', the old Catholic word, to describe this God. It is even possible that he was a Christian, for on the persecution of the Christians he resigned an official post and was known to avoid all shrines until he was thirty-nine, when he paid respect at Ise, possibly in the manner of those hidden Christians who pretended to worship when demanded. His disciple, Kumazawa, was imprisoned and under suspicion for his opinions, presumably because of their similarity to Christian ideas. Soko Yamaka, founder of the classical school, and Juisai Ito tended to develop Confucian ideas of *jen* in terms of Christian love and liberty. The result of this emphasis was to lead on the one hand to the charitable works of the peasant sage Sontoku Nisomiya, who did so much to relieve the poor and famine-stricken in the early nineteenth century, and on the other, to the rise of independent Samurai who, interpreting *jen* in a more purely Confucian and Christian light, made justice as they saw fit or sacrificed their lives to protest, and generally aroused the opposition to the Tokugawa system which finally triumphed.

A word must be said about the 'New Religions', which are sects or heresies, mostly of Shinto, but sometimes of Buddhism and

Christianity. These movements first arose during the last century, partly as a response to the new emphasis on charity alluded to, partly in response to Neo-Confucian and Western challenges to traditional religion, and nearly always as a means of achieving physical healing and acquiring some of the earthly benefits which Buddhism and Bushido had gone to excessive lengths to despise. If Protestant Christianity was the religion of the Samurai, practically every new religion would be founded for the people by some poor or outcast individual, or a more prosperous person who had lost status or suffered tragedies. The message, however innovative, would usually be very simple, like the revelation to Miki Nakayama, foundress in 1838 of Tenrikyo, who proclaimed the fatherhood and motherhood of God and the consequent need for all men to unite in one big sharing family. The socio-political, healing and artistic activities might prove more complex. Tenrikyo is missionary faith with an overseas following, bases in Singapore and California and forty churches in Hawaii. Members give impressive concerts and dramatic performances related to Gagaku (old court music) and Shinto themes throughout the world.

Konkokyo, Tenrikyo and Omoto were early arrivals, but the new religions (there are hundreds of them, many with only a few thousand members) only became significant after 1939 and the repeal of the 'Religious Bodies Law'. After the defeat of World War II, the same need for identity which produced the state Shinto of the 1880s led to a new spirituality. Sokka Gakkai (Value Creating Society), a version of the fanatical Nichiren sect devoted to the Lotus Sutra, is the leading new religion. It counted 9,000 members in 1950 and allegedly 15,000,000 by 1974, which if true makes it the fastest-growing religion in the world. In 1958, the present leader, Daisaku Ikeda, instituted a programme of dramatic mass-meetings and sports clubs to attract youth, and in 1959, launched a political party, Komeito, to usher in the Golden Age which the sect anticipated. Evangelists have reached the coal miners, farmers and fishermen, hitherto well outside the churches.

Rissho Koseikai and P. L. Kyodan have also been successful. Buddhists no less than Christians have been alarmed at the success of these religions, taking exception to some of the aggressive evangelism and brain-washing techniques, which in this decade have been limited by pressure of public opinion. A Christian new religion is Ikuro Toshima's Genshi Fukuin (Original Gospel Movement), which counts 45,000 members and is a kind of Zen Christianity that apparently denies the Incarnation and describes Christianity as a Hebrew and Oriental religion whose true teachings can only really be grasped by Asians. Jesus was a man whom the Spirit of the Christ (Messiah) seized, dissolving his ego. At his death, the Christ Spirit took wing to God. The Logos is the God-principle dwelling in men because of Jesus. God can only be worshipped as Spirit in spirit, not as the person Jesus, or in any external way. Accordingly, members pray with Buddhist techniques, are baptized in rivers, worship on mountain-sides, walk on hot coals and pass into ecstasies, as they strive to rediscover the original emotional import of Christianity obscured by official Japanese and Western Christianity.

Certain factors are significant in the new religions. Official religion, Buddhist and Shinto, is elitist, and in the hands of clerics or theologians, as in Japanese Christianity. While it is true that these religions have cults of founders and leaders to whom they may be abjectly submissive in satisfaction of traditional feudal spirit, the layman is deeply involved in evangelism, counselling or welfare, and at that level, may work on equal terms with those he would otherwise hold in deep respect socially. This is a legacy of Nichiren's egalitarianism. Second, the traditional guru-disciple relationship of Zen is often maintained and called a *sensei-deshi* ('parent-child') relationship. Each member is accorded a parent or elder brother in the faith to whom his personal problems are brought, and later, he becomes such a parent. I take this to be a typically introvert and private way of religion; although it grew into private confession, the early Celtic Christians possessed the same arrangement, contrary to the more communal practices of Southern Europe. Third, organizationally the Japanese love for the small intimate group, as in the tea ceremony, is respected.

The organization of a new religion is usually a complex of cells which meet individually to discuss problems and suggest policies. This is important in view of the fact that, in contrast to China, Japan has not known the religious fraternities and secret societies among the laity which would be the prototype of the church group. Religion is so personalized in Japan that even when sympathetic to Christianity Japanese have been exceptionally unwilling to attach themselves to a church as such, and would probably be less willing to join new religions were it not for the organizational forms.

Fourth, there is a rather unaristocratic emphasis on joy and fulfilment, for lack of which the founder of Sokka Gakkai criticized the sombre churches. Granted, if Japan had been a less persecuting, more tolerant society, the churches might not be carrying such a weight of melancholy minority consciousness, but the point must be taken. There is no need today to retain dull, Victorian hymns or to outdo Japanese gravity while the new religions work themselves into a lather, beating Suwa drums in the spirit of the people.

Fifth, there is the evangelism. Sokka Gakkai especially borrowed many ideas from American evangelism and Billy Graham, sponsoring everything from mass rallies and home visitation to religious journalism and the wooing of top people, and required every convert to make three more members. Inevitably these methods, like the American ones, caused as much opposition as support, and those Christians (mainly American) who believe that all Japan needs is mass evangelism, would need to take account both of the opposition and the many and subtle differences between the American and Japanese forms. American-style evangelism has definitely not worked. In ten years from 1957 to 1967, when there were intensive efforts at mass evangelism beginning with the Bob Pierce Crusades, coming to a climax with the Billy Graham Crusade and supported in the interval by the labours of evangelist Dr Ahura Hatori, it has been estimated that an exceptionally low 10% of those who made decisions progressed to baptism and church membership. Moreover this is not to consider the usually high rate of Japanese defection from church membership. Personally, I feel that the mass meetings encourage a mindlessness in the Japanese akin to German *Hitlerjugend* rallies, especially because of the low value placed on individualism and choice. Japanese mass rallies, though they can lead to requests to sign a pledge, do not exactly evangelize and call to individual decisions, like the Billy Graham meetings, but rather affirm a togetherness in those who have already made a decision and like to see numbers, while such impressive shows of numbers convince the sceptical that the promised kingdom is coming. It seems unlikely in view of Japanese temperament and training, that authentic personal decisions could normally be made in such an atmosphere, and criticism of the new religions often relates to cases of individuals who, influenced by private traumas, like examination failure and divorces, sign on and are then pressured to stay when they have second thoughts. If religion is subject to much calculation in Japan, it is because the intense inner life is vulnerable to illusions and because anything involving responsibilities is liable to be taken very seriously.

Finally, in any case the salvation and conversion involved are quite different. Adjustment of mind is the real end. Salvation and heaven in the here and now exist for those able to realize the no-self and bliss at the centre of things and willing to build the new Jerusalem of welfare and aid on earth. Beliefs are simple and pragmatic, though sometimes made to appear sophisticated; thus Sokka Gakkai borrowed its notions concerning 'truth, beauty and goodness' from neo-Kantian philosophy, effectively substituting 'usefulness' for 'truth'. Though they tend to foster good personal morals, there is rarely anything deeply challenging about these faiths. They are neither as strict as the old discipline (Bushido, Zen) nor as inclusive in their demands on all aspects of life as Christianity. There is more common generosity than formerly, but not in the disinterested Christian way in which a Kagawa, the Salvation Army or the German Midnight Mission dealt with outcasts or embarrassing problems like prostitution and alcoholism, or even the way in which the Catholics attended to the orphans. Good works, as with those of the Mormons in the West, tend to be limited to the group or laid at the door of politicians. There is more individuality of organization than before, but no real doctrine of individualism. Many of the new religions are nationalistic, seeking to reply to the noisy welter of American missions which still subtly identify Western habits with *Christian* beliefs; hence, converting Americans has become a prime concern. Japanese church leaders are weary of the nation's one-people view of affairs which, projected on to other societies, causes them to identify every American action from Hiroshima to Vietnam and brothel-visiting with Christian decisions and behaviour. The theologian Watanabe, complaining that the churches are too easily dismissed as hypocritical, noted that what the Japanese did in Asia is dismissed simply as having been cruel, but if the Americans do the same in Vietnam, it is said to be the height of hypocrisy. At least, he remarked, such twisted thinking shows that the Japanese associate Christianity with high standards.[18]

Japan has been called the land of happy atheists. Certainly there has been a good measure of Communism, and much formalism (it is common to be married by Shinto ceremony and buried by Buddhist rite), but no society could be called irreligious which had produced Amidism and Sokka Gakkai, and the atheism is frequently one of mood only. Irreligion must be seen in its social context. At home and at work, Japanese life is often still so extremely demanding, a crushing pattern of duties and a rat-race (despite the wealth of the country, there is no real welfare system, so everything must be worked for), that any regular church attendance or church work will appear a terrible chore when no self-advancement is in view, as may be the case in the new religions. The churches stress 'dedication', and to a Japanese, that is a serious matter, especially as the churches tend to deny him the freedom he would normally take to chop and change from church and denomination as befits his mood. The church leader Uemura (see below) insisted on young clergy staying for long terms in a single parish, and not flitting about as they liked to do. Yet the old Shignon love of pilgrimage and the faddism of new religions is more typical, and perhaps greater freedom is called for, especially as the high mobility of the sympathetic professional classes militates against regular membership. It also has to be realized that for many, to be free of all further commitments beyond family and company, is an object in itself. Hard though Japanese life can be, it is freer than formerly, hence leisure and pleasure is the religion of many; though this may not be very noble, its causes must be understood and should not be confused with total religious insensitivity. Japan has never been the most religious society in the world, but at the very least it was and is full of religiosity.

III

While it might be possible to describe patterns of defection from the church in Japan – the fact that members rarely enter with their family, and hence suffer more pressure to leave than to remain seems crucial – it is much harder to speak of patterns of entry. The fact that every known form of evangelism has been tried on Japan, with none showing more success than another, would indicate that something is wrong either spiritually or culturally. It is impossible that one method should not be more successful than another, unless the religion in itself is missing the mark culturally and psychologically wherever it strikes, as would seem to be the case.

We shall turn to Japanese theology presently, but first a few points of incompatibility and failure should be noted. For a start, it even seems likely that neither Protestantism nor Catholicism in their present forms are especially helpful to Japanese Christian needs, and Uchimura's foundation of the No Church Movement and Kagawa's avoidance of denominational tags is quite understandable.

Catholicism, which, apart from its political associations, has held some appeal for China, would probably be less suited to Japan than Protestantism, as indicated by its growth patterns and undistinguished theological record. Granted it was successful under Xavier, but at that time it was indigenized and existed in a more authoritarian age; perhaps, too, like early Buddhism in Japan, it was never completely understood. No converts apparently read or possessed the Bible. Today, the values of such a monolithic church, especially one owing allegiance to Rome, are not particularly Japanese. Even state Shinto existed to serve specific needs, and the 'irreverent' disposability of its main sanctuary is the very opposite of Catholic reverence towards altars and holy things. So, too, is the Zen tendency to smash idols. One could hardly imagine Catholics smashing crucifixes and images of Mary to improve their spiritual perception. That is much too Protestant.

By contrast, while Protestantism may appeal to the distinctly 'Lutheran' quality of Japanese intellect and spirituality, it is completely irrelevant to its studied ritualism and aestheticism. Many Protestant missionaries would not dream of permitting converts to use incense or visual aids, even if the intention with the latter was only to smash them. One missionary, who has done excellent work with orphans, told me that they would never consider the use of even a cross in church. Very few churches bear any relation to national designs, and certainly make no concessions, inside or out, to the nature cult usually associated with holy places. Although the great systems of theology appeal only to intellectual élites, the church member is usually catechized and sermonized through them, whether he likes it or not, while the Zen quality of the gospels, with their paradoxes, parables, shock statements and poetry (which the Japanese rather like), gives way to sweeping Pauline or prophetic schemes and constructions which are less favoured by the audience, even when they are understood.

The astonishing number of denominations and missions (many of which European Christians will never have heard of), with their poor ecumenical record, are also a confusion and scandal. Japan may have many new religions, but these exist to serve a need, a mood, and supply an alternative to Protestant denominations, engaged in intellectual arguments over how to baptize persons or what constitute the functions of a deacon. Despite a few concessions by the church leader Masahisa Uemura to major festivals, like the New Year, the church calendar does not take Japanese festivals into account, nor has it introduced any new festivals. Japan is the most festival-ridden country in the world, and scarcely a day passes without some region celebrating a colourful ceremony; bear, dragon and frog festivals, giant ox, heron and doll festivals, festivals of light, of rice harvest, of the feudal warriors, of the fishermen, and many more. Many are related to shrines, while some, like the English May Day and maypole dancing, have lost their significance and are simply pretty. Either way, however, they constitute a vital aspect of popular life. Christian communities, especially the rural and working-class ones, need either to Christianize or con-celebrate festivals (provided Shinto ceremony is not demanded), or invent new and mainly light-hearted alternatives.

This leads to the difficult and delicate point to which I shall devote the whole final section, that Japanese Christianity is altogether too puritanical, especially sexually. I am not entirely blaming the churches, which obviously feel obliged to maintain high standards; the fault lies with Japanese society, which can sometimes be well criticized in this area. Yet if the unusual Japanese disposition and situation is understood, a more tolerant and understanding line would seem appropriate.

Those few points would seem to indicate that an indigenized theology is of little value unless it is of a practical sort. The Japanese church has gone further than most Asian Churches in producing one, albeit not always intentionally. Again, this applies more to Protestantism than Catholicism, which until the 1930s was immersed in problems of form and organization, the foundation of dioceses and seminaries. After World War II it turned to establishing a basis for dialogue mainly with the mystical traditions of the country, essentially an elitist interest. A leading Japanese novelist and Catholic, Shusaku Endo, betrays the problem of being Catholic when he describes the faith in moral and existential terms rather than doctrinal ones, demonstrating the incurable 'Lutheran' element of the native spirituality.

Protestant theology could be regarded as officially represented by the United Church of Christ, an ecumenical amalgamation of churches founded in 1941 which in 1972 claimed 40% of Japan's 723,000 Protestants. (The number excludes sects and heresies, and it is not to suggest that Japan is secretly Christian to indicate that the small figure is not representative of the larger number who either accept or are very influenced by Christianity, but do not choose to be church affiliated.) The style of this church is Presbyterian-cum-Lutheran, its theology 'neo-orthodox', that is to say, much influenced by the Swiss theologians Barth and Brunner. The origins of the church can be traced back to the Yokohama band of students of the 1870s; the other major trends go back to the Kumamoto and Sapporo bands who stand at the source of the Congregational and No Church movements respectively.

The limited tolerance for Christianity in Japan and its relatively late beginnings, in Victorian missions, had important effects. The impetus for church organization was at first governed by the recipients of the message, who were usually careful of their relations with authority and desirous of a national church and theology. At the same time, the date of arrival coincided with both the revolution of liberal theology, which encouraged an intellectual yet subjective approach to religion, and the proliferation of American sects.

The result was that between 1870 and 1900 Japan was visited by an exceptionally large number of groups, which led to denominationalism. Relations between missionaries and converts appear to have been exceptionally bad, or else the discord was more frankly voiced, because of Japan's non-colonial status. Uchimura's 'I have hated the rude and proud manner of some foreign missionaries' seems typical of many early Protestants, and his No Church movement arose from the infuriated disgust at all denominations which he first felt under the Methodists who, when they discovered that some Sapporo students had been baptized Anglicans, awkwardly demanded the return of 400 dollars given towards a church building which the students had also supported with Anglican funds. Understandably Gumpei Yamamuro, later the founder of Japan's Salvation Army, was so frustrated when Baptist missionaries refused to baptize him despite all his piety that he ran out into the rain and declared himself baptized by God.

What is thus most distinctive about Japanese theology is its subjectivity; this is not necessarily a pietistic subjectivity, but a thoroughgoing philosophical one, mixed with considerable scepticism over the institution of the church. Accordingly, much attention is focussed on the most objective events and duties of the faith, the first and last things (creation and apocalypse), the scope of incarnation and Christian socio-political movement. There is a major division between those who stress social action; and between those attaching importance to church structures and those allowing the church no real objective function at all.

Because of the Japanese concept of the coaevality and the eternity of matter, the doctrine of creation and purpose has always fascinated thinkers, as it did Shimita Nishima, one of the first Protestants, so eager to acquire knowledge and modernize his country that he stowed away to America to study theology. Unfortunately, in the 1880s the missionary labours of Germans like Wilfred Spinner and Otto Schmiedel brought Darwinism and a liberal theology which took evolution too uncritically. The influence of these missionaries seems to have been remarkably negative. Many Japanese Christians were disappointed with the faith they had just received and which they had been taught perhaps too literally; many abandoned it or were plunged, like Yumanuro, into severe religious crises. The Kumamoto band, led by Hiromachi Kozaki and Danjo Ebina, turned liberal; these leaders both denied the infallibility of the Bible and the latter denied Christ's divinity as well, since he believed rather simplistically that incarnation must compromise the infinity of God. His objections to orthodox faith generally suggest not so much conviction in terms of liberal theology as an inability to transcend Buddhist and Shinto categories.

Since the Congregationalists and the Unitarians (who sympathized with them) denied so much that was deemed essential to the faith, they turned to accommodation with local religion and nationalism. There was talk of a nationalist theology. Zenji Iwamoto and Yasu Togawa spoke of 'Buddhistic Christianity' and Kaiseki Matsumura of 'Confucian Christianity', while Ebina identified God the Father with the father god of Shinto, aiming at 'Shintoistic Christianity'. All of these theories brought authentic indigenization of Christianity into disrepute, allowing it to become confused with syncretization. The aim was less to convert than to make Shintoists better Shintoists. Liberals also directed their idealism towards socialism. The first Socialist Democratic Party of Japan, organized in 1901, was largely sponsored by Liberals and Unitarians. The drift of this party towards materialism (for which religious members were not wholly responsible) and the local opposition of these Christians to the main-line churches unfortunately alienated many Christians from Socialism and reform generally, and settled the churches into the middle-class views and ways which, despite the efforts of Kagawa, they have never quite left.

Theology of this liberal kind, which thrives to this day, may be called 'Jesusology': dedication to Jesus as a teacher or perhaps a new *bodhisattva*. It is some of the most radical theology in Christianity because it is not checked by the historical or sentimental considerations which prevail in the West[19]. Seiichi Yagi, *Formation of New Testament Thought*, aims to go beyond Bultmann's 'demythologization' by suggesting that there is really no kerygma (gospel proclamation) at all, but only an existence in love. Nobuo Odagiri, Buddhist-like, does not deny Christ's divinity, but denies his identity with God *qua* God. Christ is Son God, or God the Son, rather than the Son of God. The affinity with Shinto need hardly be stressed. Sakae Akaiwa's *Exodus from Christianity* marked an attempt at 'liberation theology', the separation of the religion from the evils of church authorities. It is Jesus the man who draws out our humanism, not Christ as God, and he denies Christ's divinity. Kanzo Tagawa, *A Phase in the History of Early Christianity*, maintained that Mark had no christology and was written to oppose the Jerusalem establishment's picture of Christ. Toshikazu Takao, *Basic Intentions of Jesus*, claims that Jesus was the friend of the revolution, an ordinary person who inspires us to ordinariness.

Such liberalism has its message first to liberals, the illogicality of whose position is exposed by the more logical Japanese theses. A Jesus without divinity or uniqueness to support his claims has a limited or confusing message to non-Christian societies. Liberalism has no mandate to found or use the services of a church structure when Christ can only be ranged alongside the Buddhas. At this point the church and its structure and disciplines, devoid of historical or mystical purpose, becomes, if not a form of oppression, the cause of needless division within society. Conservatives are also condemned, at least indirectly, by the Japanese response, not only in their indifference to the social problems liberal theology tried to tackle, but also because that Zen-like radicalism indicates how little conservative preachers must have entered into the national culture and philosophy so as to redefine the faith intelligently. Many of the ideas involved are neither original nor always wilful 'heresy', but unconsciously Buddhist or Shinto. Conservatives can also be seen to be wanting – in their inflexible, unrealistic approach to the profound Japanese subjectivity – in interiority itself. Once Christianity was introduced, it was unreasonable to expect the Japanese would accept ecclesiastical and biblical authority. The introvert always relates to ideas and grasps the sense behind forms, laws and words in such a way that adherence to authority will always be personal.

Because of this Japanese disposition of thought, the mainstream theology of the Yokohama band and the Church of Christ theology tends to be 'neo-orthodox', that is, philosophically rather than literalistically orthodox. The problem was that though Japanese Christianity might be intrinsically neo-orthodox, when finally this group latched on to the Barthian revolution of the 1920s, which most completely justified their position, they did not seem to recognize how much its theology came packaged with a number of cultural and religious prejudices of rather less use. Most obviously, there was Barth's intransigent opposition to Christian cooperation with culture, which has poisoned church and mission policy throughout this century with Westernizing trends. Much influenced by Romans, Barth unreasonably emphasized St Paul's statement that 'the natural man hears not the things of God', which should be set against others. Missions and churches which hold this view will take no care to relate the gospel to cultures and situations, almost throwing it in the face of society and assuming negative reactions to be the sign of its holy unacceptability.

Yet in a sense, attachment to Barth's theology was a form of indigenization, though not of the total sort which reaches the larger forms beyond a few individual traits of culture. Barth's militancy and iconoclasm in itself appealed to the military instincts of the Japanese soul. His suggestion that God should be God and that his word was always a surprise and offence perhaps satisfied 'Zen' feelings about the irrationality of spiritual knowledge, while the massive metaphysical system underlying the surprises was sufficiently complex to occupy the traditional scholarly interests of the religious professional, who normally eschews the way of action. The view of the church propounded was also satisfactorily functional. The iconoclastic effect of Barthian theology might have been modified by the dialectical theology of Brunner which was also popular. He accepted the promise of the prophets and its fulfilment within the church in a way which did not limit the essence of religious truth so much to the paradoxes of Christ and St Paul; he allowed that natural theology existed (i.e. that God lights everyone that comes into the world and that everyone may have some knowledge of God, however dim), and this led him to a broader view of revelation and the church's relationship to culture. However, rather ironically, when this theologian who had so criticized Barth came to Japan and taught at Tokyo Theological Seminary during the 1950s, he confirmed theologians in Barthian exclusiveness by suggesting, rather absurdly in view of the church's failure in Japan and the communication gap between clergy and laity, that the problem was lack of humility on the part of the Japanese and unwillingness to conform to the ways of the church.

Before Barth and the Japanese Barthians there was Masahisa Uemura (1858–1925), at once evangelist, theologian, social worker and ecclesiastical professional. He shared the common early Protestant detestation of denominations and subservice to missionaries, insisting that any missionary work which he furthered should be independent of overseas churches, but always insisted on working within a church framework, however ecumenical. A pious

Shintoist in youth, he had been impressed by the doctrine of creation and was converted through the Rev. J. H. Ballagh in 1873 while taking English lessons at the Shubu-kan in Kanagawa. He joined the non-denominational Japan Church of Christ (founded in 1872 by students), which united with the Presbyterians in 1877. He graduated from Itchi Theological Seminary in 1878, was ordained and soon engaged in the parish missionary work that always concerned him. He helped translate the Old Testament and founded the Tokyo YMCA, and later, the Tokyo Union Theological Seminary.

Religious journalism first brought Uemura into the limelight with the famous Ebina-Uemura debate, in which he defended the divinity and redemptive work of Christ and opposed excessive religious accommodation to the age. The occasion of the debate was the Japanese Christian Evangelical Alliance's bid to evangelize Japan, which fell foul of the greatly varying beliefs and methods espoused by different church groups. Uemura himself was hostile to techniques of mass evangelism and thus for better or worse set evangelism on a more personal and also a traditional and doctrinally conservative basis, though he himself was far from being a quoter of texts and was concerned to indigenize theological terms. He also declared that the church alone was the kingdom of God, so that this kingdom was not something to be realized socially or individually. In this way he rejected both the liberalism of Ebina and the individualism of Uchimura.

From church organization it was a natural step to systematic theology, and Uemura's disciple from Tokyo Theological Seminary, Tokutaro Takakura, was the first to take it up with his *Evangelical Christianity* (1947). The discontinuity between the kingdom of God and society recognized by Barth was emphasized; there was even a battle between the orders and not an evolution towards goodness or a process in which the church helped to fulfil the aspirations of a given society. Faith and conversion was always a crisis, a bolt out of the blue. Christ's message shocks and surprises rather than fulfils; spiritual knowledge relates, rather, to realization of the metaphysical scheme behind all events which makes for personal salvation rather than any visible redemption of man and society. Since liberals opposed the teaching of the Second Coming, Takakura espoused it and placed ethics and philosophy within that context, greatly influencing Japanese churches. Subsequently, the Kyoden's shaky socio-political convictions would be summarized as 'works of love made in eschatological hope', in effect, actions made less in terms of any eternal principles or existing political ideologies than of the 'opportunism' of an ethics of the interval.

This eschatological dimension was enlarged by Kumano's *Eschatology and the Philosophy of History*. The emphasis was on the separation between world views and philosophies and faith-religion. Christianity has only faith-ethics for between the times. All ethics, Kumano claimed, have more or less the same religious content, and all religions the same ethical content, but in Christianity there is no assumption that moral imperatives can be fulfilled naturally. In the course of making some important distinctions, he defined freedom as not imminent to the being, but an attribute of the relationship to God.

Enkichi Kan, an Anglican, began as a leading exponent in 1930 of the social gospel theories held within the Student Christian Movement, maintaining the immanence of God as life power and the possibility of salvation only when the individual finds a place in the society built by those whose minds are one with the divine will. However, abandoning the social gospel in the wake of the controversy of 1932 which brought an end to the SCM in Japan, he made a *volte-face* to become the most Barthian of scholars, declaring Brunner (who gave some room to natural theology) to be logically right, and Barth (who did not) to be right in practice. Kurada, Mujamoto and Nabayane were other leading Barthians who increasingly emphasized biblicism over against historical criticism, social gospel and indigenization.

Within the official churches, but showing a different trend, were Seiichi Hatano and Kazoh Kitamori. In different ways, both expressed a more emotionally and aesthetically Japanese-related theology, starting from existential considerations of love and freedom. Both were opposed by the professional theologians, so I shall place them with the next group. Of the Barthians it could be said that they never saw the wood for the trees; their theology was mostly a search for the basis on which to found a church, and on which to define this against the fissive tendencies of extreme liberalism rather than in relation to Japanese life generally.

Kanzo Uchimura, founder of the 'No Church' movement, said 'I hate theology', and accordingly, he disliked the official churches. A born rebel, while at school he had prayed to the Shinto gods to punish the missionaries who taught him, and he thought little better of them after conversion. 'No Church', however, was an invention of his later career. Originally he passed through the Anglican church and American theological colleges, and only in

1894, after his dismissal from Tokyo First High School over his refusal to bow to the Imperial Rescript and a career in religious journalism, did he start the home-based Bible studies which grew into No Church. According to Uchimura:

> The truly Christian temple has God's earth for a floor and his sky for a ceiling, its altar is the heart of the believer; its law is God's Word and his Holy Spirit is its only pastor.

Uchimura's position was close to that of the Quakers, or even the Blue Domers; the Japanese desire to worship close to nature is apparent, though Muyokai groups do worship indoors. Members of the groups met and meet anywhere, in houses, halls, factories, to engage in Bible study and prayer, and they sit on the floor on mats. Officially there were no sacraments, but Uchimura himself would sometimes baptize or administer communion if he thought it would be helpful. He led meetings, but others were invited to offer comments and prayers. The Bible teacher was considered equal to a bishop. Uchimura considered he had gone beyond Luther and aimed for the style of 'the sanctified Confucian teacher' with disciple groups.

In view of his marked originality, it perhaps needs to be stated that Uchimura was deeply religious and not just a faddist. His greatest religious experience seems to have occurred not at conversion but later in America when, like Luther, he realized that he could not be saved or freed from guilt apart from grace. His distress and his refusal of salvation through the self would seem to indicate how little even conservative theology, which aims at clarity and directness, had genuinely clarified itself in the minds of those accustomed to Buddhist and Confucian notions to this effect. Theologically, Uchimura was neo-Orthodox without being Barthian; he eschewed all theology, to study the Bible simply from the text and search for the existential meaning. The result was sometimes a rather Japanese tendency to espouse causes and fashions, like pacifism and the doctrine of the Second Coming (which he finally decided must be taken literally) and he influenced Japanese theology considerably with his discourses on this theme. His individualism and that of his followers, who regarded society as simply a collection of individualists, nonetheless tended to militate against any concerted social action and a grasp of the dynamics of social change.

Although it was assumed that group consciousness alone could ensure orthodoxy, obviously the free-wheeling use of scriptures had its effect. Disciples like Watanabe, Maeda and Fujii Sekine divided over the meaning of church and Bible. Some thought the destiny of No Church was to become a church. Overall the effects were positive, leading to the study of hermeneutics (interpretation) and the necessary translation of Christianity into existential categories. When Watanabe disagreed with Uchimura over Darwin and the theory of creation, instead of pressing his point of view in the Western way, he was stimulated to query how the Bible generally was to be interpreted and how to reconcile conflicting points of view wherever possible. As in the 'false' argument of faith against works, Watanabe doubted whether Christians were usually called upon to take one point of view; he felt they should think dialectically, finding the truth within heart and conscience. The 'doctrine of the scriptures' requires that we should ask what the author meant, what the church canon meant and what is relevant to the interpreter in any given question. Theological interpretation, however, must take preference over historical criticism. Buber-like, Watanabe believed that the Bible in its entirety must be allowed its numinous 'Thou' power. Another disciple, Miss Tamiko Okumura, produced a rather Japanese and aesthetic argument for the authority of the Bible from its structure and arrangement; she perceives a specific kind of religious 'Gestalt', but the title, *An Essay on Biblical Interpretation: Basic Theory for the Morphological Interpretation of the Biblical Canon*, bespeaks Japanese Christianity too well.

Seiichi Hatano attacked Barth and put Christianity into more existential categories. He came to Christianity through philosophy and acquired the conviction that the good elements in the Western philosophy which he attempted to convey to Japan were fundamentally Christian. He also believed that without love, human life is an irreversible drift towards death. He described how different qualities of love characterized different stages of life: natural life was dominated by desire, cultural life by *eros*, religious life by *agape*. In this latter stage there is a future which saves the present from slipping into the nothingness of the past.

Kazoh Kitamori, more popular and influential, described Christianity in terms of the love and pain of God. Speaking in terms of the early post-war sense of drift and disillusion, he emphasized the non-committal quality of much Japanese life and culture, especially as suggested by Zen art and poetry which makes restraint and indifference *iki* (sophisticated), and involvement such as Christianity demands and God experiences *yabo* (uncouth). In traditional

Western theology God is characterized as angry over sin, and Christ is the intermediary who suffers, but Kitamori emphasizes the pain of God, suggested in Jeremiah and Isaiah, which occurs when God loves and desires to reach those estranged from his perfect nature. God the Father is neither unaffected by evil (as in some Western descriptions), nor merely sympathetic to man (as would happen in Buddhism or some liberal theology, where without wrath there is no dynamic of love but only a passive sympathy). Pain is the synthesis between God's love and wrath; pain is the swallowing of a just wrath. Human pain is a symbol and reflection of God; the transcendent pain of God is seen as immanent in the painful reality of existence.[20] This somewhat evangelical critique of Japanese drift and Christian universalism was severely criticized by theologians who considered the argument too neat and popular, for there was a popular appeal in the emphasis on pain which is almost a virtue in the Japanese mind, while in drama the tragic hero is one who overcomes his just wrath.

Toyohiko Kagawa (1888–1960), a prolific author and the founder of the Kingdom of God movement, who based his entire views on Christianity simply as an expression of divine love, was similarly criticized by liberals and conservatives, and this hampered the effectiveness of the evangelistic efforts to which he strove to rouse the church. His superiority to his critics is proved by his opposition to Japanese militarism which meant that he was imprisoned during the war, whereas the Barthian theologians, ignoring their mentor's own opposition to an identical German militarism, took a conveniently nationalistic line.

Credally orthodox though he was, Kagawa was philosophically very eclectic, borrowing ideas from everywhere. He paid tribute to the religious traditions of Japan which had influenced his youth: the Shinto which had taught him reverence and love of nature, the Buddhism which gave a sense of the transcendent, and the Confucianism had inculcated a sense of moral standards. Like Gandhi, he was influenced by Tolstoy to take Christian pacifism very seriously, and as a preacher and social reformer working in the worst slums, he suffered much for this.

More revered outside Japan than inside – at any rate among the theologically sophisticated – Kagawa exceptionally combined the religious scholar with the man of action. A student of Tokyo Presbyterian College and Kobe Theological Seminary, where he became disillusioned with missionaries, in 1928 Kagawa founded the 'Kingdom of God Movement', following the International Missionary Council of that year in Jerusalem. The Movement aimed to reach a million souls and also to improve Japanese social conditions, which at the time were blighted by rapid industrialization. Kagawa had already espoused the cause of labour and had been imprisoned for it, and he encouraged the Co-operative Movement among farmers and fishermen as an answer to encroaching Communism. Kagawa was accused of preaching a social gospel by conservatives, though he denied this. 'Such a social and economic movement as this (the Co-operative Movement) is not the whole of Christianity. God's love is revealed not only in the social order but in the life of every individual.'[21] However, he maintained, the social oppression in slums and the poor rural regions of the times was such that the Japanese could not be satisfied with a purely individual gospel. 'Unlike Buddhism, the religion of Jesus teaches not only grace for the individual; it also postulates the Kingdom of God. Christ revealed not the God of creative but redemptive love . . . Christ is able to save society as well.[22]

Kagawa was influential not only in pioneering much social reform but also in instituting the Sunday school (which was popular enough to be imitated by Buddhists) and the 'Friends of Jesus' societies, groups which were sometimes attached to and sometimes a substitute for churches, especially in rural areas, where they combined Bible study with education in rural and social improvement. It is possible that they were more sophisticated than effective, for Kagawa's own literacy classes for slum dwellers could become surprisingly erudite and even include philosophy, while he was unable to address the rural people in the local languages still in use, something which has been found to reduce the impact of any outreach anywhere.

Finally, I must mention the inter-religious dialogue which dates from the 1960s and Matatoshi Doi's *The Theology of Meaning: An Introduction to the Theology of Mission (1963)*. Doi has been influenced by Tillich and the theology of the ground of being which, despite its much-needed treatment of the religion in terms of depth psychology and cultural forms, is the least distinctively Christian of modern theologies because of its over-emphasis on ontology. Whatever Doi, as director of the National Christian Council's Centre for the Study of Japanese Religions, may have intended in fostering dialogue with other faiths, the love affair of the young generation of theologians with Tillich's ontology, which facilitates the dialogue, has let loose a flood of subjective religion, archetypal Christs, Zen, and Amidist parallels. The modern situation is very confusing. As Fr Gabriel Furuta puts it, Even when they (the Japanese) accept, they do not understand what we are speaking about. Christianity has come to a point, historically speaking, when teachers do not know what they preach.[23] With good reason, the theologian Tetsutaro Ariga, *The Problem of Ontology in Christian Thought*, stated that Japanese theology needed to de-emphasize ontology (being-philosophy) in favour of more emphasis on hatology (doing theology). It is, of course, quite true that once one starts talking exclusively about the ground of being, ultimate concern and subjective truth, one may as well become a Shintoist or Hindu; only Christian prejudice on the one hand, or a type of Japanese anti-logical reasoning on the other, can ignore the fact. Most of the church's losses in Japan are said to arise because individual converts become so unclear about the difference between Christ and the Buddhas that they see no purpose in offending their families by continuing to be Christian.

There seem to be two issues for the church here. First, the traditional Japanese attitude to truth, and second, the need to objectify the essence of Christian truth without undue recourse to the historical and doctrinal schemes which do not belong to Japanese tradition and seem either to confuse or make little impression. The Japanese who accept Christianity and do not understand it are basically people who are looking for anything which 'clicks'. Although they may 'feel' the religion is true, they are not looking for truth as such, have not been encouraged to look for it, and have never had many philosophical guidelines in that culture to help them ascertain it. They are *all* objectivity, as when they apply themselves to science and the computer, and *all* subjectivity, as when they think. The question of truth was solved in Heian, Japan, with its diversity of religion sects. In *The Tale of Genji*, Genji discusses with his mistress the art of the novel, defending it with a religious parallel against the charge that perfect and imperfect are set side by side:

> But even in the discourses which Buddha in his bounty allowed to be recorded, certain passages contain what the learned call Upaya (adapted truth), a fact which has led some superficial persons to doubt whether a doctrine so inconsistent with itself could possibly command our credence. . . . We may indeed go so far as to say that there is an actual mixture of truth and error (in the scripture). But the purpose of these holy writings, namely the compassing of our salvation, remains always the same.[24]

With this kind of reasoning, it might not matter who and what one worships, as long as one experiences the feelings presumed to be those of salvation; even the Hindu concern to avoid the influence of demi-gods or deceiving gods is lacking. The unstated Japanese creed is perhaps 'beauty is truth', or some such aesthetic formula.

Whether the average Japanese, like many people of aesthetic inclination, *cannot* grasp philosophical arguments or *will not* (Japanese illogicality in the face of the best arguments emotionally repellent to them is well known) is open to conjecture. Theologians are left with the reality that Japanese who do not belong to the intellectual elite (and some of those who do) seem exceptionally unadapted to negotiating conventional doctrinal arguments. In the circumstances, instead of redoubling theological efforts, might it not be better to abandon them and encourage an aesthetic solution? Intellectual simplicity and aesthetic power (a traditionally favoured combination) are what is required. The question of the necessity of doctrine could be reduced to the affirmation (on the basis of the kind of arguments given in Chapter 1) that since we are a part of God, and God is ever active, it must matter quite considerably what we do and believe if the body is to function well. The implications of Jewish history and St Paul's doctrines could be summarized in terms of an original form of mandala and the production of a new style. The theology of Chapter 1 can certainly be reduced to the type of schemata used in mandala of the Shignon variety. A 'proof' of Christian experience ought to be realizable in terms of a new integrated style. The psychological and metaphysical problems of Japan are written everywhere across the national art. The indecision between decoration and realism and the poor integration of them, the value attached to incomplete, ugly or morbid portrayals of the human body (which, though justified by the sage's inclusion of ugliness, reflect evidence of psychological disturbance) everywhere betray the divided mind, for which the mystical acceptance of the opposites is often little better than a repression or new confusion. To those who would say that Japanese art is already beautiful, one can only reply that one could imagine it *more* beautiful. The Christian experience requires aesthetic expression of the kind which rendered Shignon and Zen doctrine intelligible. Christianity must have an emotional approach, but one which is also capable of objectification and illuminating relation of doctrine. The achievement of style may well equal that of intellectual apologetics in other societies.

As we have seen, much Japanese theology, however original,

does not serve its purpose of enlightening the church or relating to society. Its bankruptcy was painfully evident in its refusal to oppose Japanese militarism and the evils of modern Japanese life. Lack of communication between clerics and laity has become notorious. The Japanese novelist Ayiko Miura, a convert to Protestantism, recalls how while she was in hospital and newly converted, with feelings of evangelical fervour, she invited a minister to the ward to preach to the patients. In the event, the visit proved embarrassing to her and everyone; as soon as the minister had departed, the patients were looking in amazement and asking what the man was talking about.[25] McGavren's study of church growth recalls the incident in which a Japanese film star, convalescent and feeling the need for a spiritual anchor for her life, invited a Christian and a Tenrikyo sect leader to explain their religions to her. The Tenrikyo leader entered informally by the back door, helped in the house doing simple things and giving a simple exposition, while the Christian, as though representing a foreign religion, entered formally by the front door, offered no assistance and delivered a learned exposition. The actress concluded that Christianity was a sublime faith but too difficult for her to understand, and opted for Tenrikyo instead.[26]

While it is true that no one style, social or intellectual, could hope to satisfy everybody, and that if the church were too informal it would doubtless be accused of foreign vulgarity, church leaders do not appear flexible or audience sensitive, and what is psychologically obvious escapes them. When I was last in Rome with a couple of Japanese friends who were not Christians, I was asked to explain the sights and monuments. I began by doing so, but after a time gave up when I saw that their relationship to the sights was purely aesthetic and emotional. It was no use telling the history of Santa Scala or Luther's famous reaction to it when they were so intently absorbing the crucifixion paintings in and for themselves. Every Sunday in Japanese churches, Mr and Mrs Shimoda listen with the traditional reverence for scholars to smart young men back from Switzerland, California, or Tokyo Seminary, where they missed the rat-race by studying hermeneutics, holding forth on Barth, Brunner, Bultmann, Bonhoeffer or some modern liberation theology. It is not surprising that the Spirit of Jesus sect, which preaches simply and to the working class, is the most rapidly expanding of the Protestant churches or that of the Tokyo churches examined in Lee's *Stranger in the Land*, the most ritualistic Protestant church was the most popular and thriving.[27]

Much thought needs to be given to Japanese ritual and worship, especially if the theology were to be put on an aesthetic basis in the way just proposed. It is, moreover, in this area that in relation to the church at large Japanese Christianity could be most futuristic. The church organization which so many wish to see functioning in the spirit of the 'priesthood of all believers' could be seen simply as a group of persons, united as in a tea ceremony, to perform rites. The rites, however, unlike all those preceding them, would serve a general and psychological function rather than a religious one. For example, one would use incense, not as in Catholic or High Anglican rites to 'cleanse' the altar in preparation for receiving the material elements of the communion, but simply to evoke the divine. Likewise, the various reverences, without which no service could be Japanese in spirit, would not be towards cross, altar, or elements, or if they were, would be less gestures of respect towards those objects than a means of physiological arousal to achieve a general sense of reverence. The altar or communion table should be dispensable: erected, dressed and taken away before the congregation. I am much in favour of some use of the gong or drum, with which monks emphasize statements or rouse the wandering.

I believe that this demythologized, or rather desacralized, ritual is neccssary not only in Japan, where it would be agreeable to 'Zen' feeling, but elsewhere. This is for several reasons. It helps to deliver the church from the superstitious accretions of past rites, while it also delivers it from the mere functionalism of modern Protestantism, which does not engage the individual's deeper mystical feelings, his body or his artistic talents. It is precisely the highly contrasted alternatives of Catholic mediaevalism and Protestant rationalism which have helped many in the West to explore Eastern religions, and perhaps like a witchcraft, more for their mystery than their message. Moreover, this ritualized religion would more clearly demonstrate the new type of open theology, redefined in relation to Asian thought, which was elaborated in the first chapter. That would be the case especially if, as the theologian Friedrich Gogarten has maintained, 'obedience' in scripture literally means 'hearing towards': an attention or leaning of the will rather than blind total submission, as in Islam, and worship must be conceived as mediating between the divine will and human desires, as a means of purification, clarification and reverence, St Paul's 'seeking to know what God desires'.[28] This is perhaps best achieved not by endless expositions of scripture or prayers for guidance, but by first setting the mind in tune with the infinite, stimulating appropriate religious thoughts and receptivity.

In terms of Japanese life, such proposals must in any case seem appropriate for two reasons. First, religion and worship is commonly associated with festivals and shrine visiting; consequently, because the church group and its ceremony are so unfamiliar, these will need to be thought of as a modified and more intimate form of festival ceremony. Second, the price of land in Japan, which now makes it so difficult to found new churches in certain areas and forces meetings to be held in homes and halls, also makes it desirable that any ritual be related to this state of impermanence.

If God could be known solely by ritual, Japan would have known him long ago. Some Japanese rituals are among the most impressive in Asia or anywhere else because of their elegant co-ordination (elsewhere in Asia rituals are often disorganized and confused) and their strongly vibrant quality in which the infinite is suggested, especially in the elemental music. Though I am for invention rather than mere imitation, I feel that it is a pity that Japanese church ritual and hymnology lie so completely outside this tradition, and this should be remedied. (Happily, there are at least a good number of Japanese-composed hymns, which contrasts with the Chinese situation.) I realize that to Japanese ears there is some music which would have such precise social and historical connotations that it would not be desirable to use it in a Christian ceremony, yet speaking from the standpoint of an outsider I would imagine that something like Gagaku Etenraku could well be used in Christian services in Holy Week (it almost sounds like the beginning of an Asian passion oratorio), and Aizu Bandaisen, which accompanies a folk dance, possesses a quality of solemn elevated joy one might associate with Easter Day.

A trait which strikes me about much Japanese custom, from Gagaku music to Noh play dance and Kabuki dramatic sequence, is the monotony and also the slowness. Though in modern times Kabuki drama has had to be shortened to avoid excessive monotony, the repetition appears consistent with the introvert culture which seeks fixed forms, and also the purely magical or shamanistic current in Japanese religion and culture which requires concentration. (Japanese scholars have been some of the foremost researchers into Western witchcraft, and the 'primitive' aspect of Japanese culture, as in the chorus sounds of Noh, relates to the magical tradition.) This being the case, it can also be suggested that litany should feature prominently in any Japanese Christian ritual: not, of course, the conventional mediaeval sort, 'from battle, plague and sudden death, Good Lord, deliver us', but the more poetical and druidic variety, as of St Patrick's Breastplate, which is at once an act of dedication and a banishing rite. Rural and more superstitious congregations might find this very helpful, and it could be a means of committing verses and events of scripture to memory which might otherwise seem tedious work.

Christian festivals should be respected as festivals and well celebrated. Since many Japanese are willing to celebrate Christmas, Christians ought to celebrate it joyfully and lavishly, making its meaning clear in the process. (At present some denominations discourage its celebration and merely raise holy hands against the commercialism, as though Christmas really meant nothing and shops, rather than Christians, had invented it.) I further fail to see why certain biblical episodes, like Job and Daniel, have not been translated into the wide variety of dramatic and dance forms of festivals in notably Christian areas, like southern Kyushu. However, any use of these forms, especially dance, would need to be introduced very casually. As soon as there is a suggestion that people are doing this for witness as opposed primarily to self-expression, the requisite naturalness is somehow lost.

So far, I have said nothing about church decoration and architecture, basically because I am not sure what is best. I am not enthusiastic about Zen simplicity and emptiness, but this is probably best for all crowded and smaller settings, where plainness has a calming effect. The saying, 'You do not know what beauty (*kekko*) is until you have seen Nikko', would suggest that the ornate style of that shrine is more popular than anything of which official Zenified taste approves. The rule seems to be that sumptuousness is suited to festivals, big occasions and big places, while simplicity is for small occasions and small places. A large Christ image in a focal position (like a Buddha image in a Zen hall) would be preferable to a large cross or crucifix above an altar. This should not be interpreted as an attempt to flee the serious meaning of the cross, but to supply the correct focus for a more archetypal theology and ritual, which must necessarily have before it the image of the completed man to which the experience is tending, rather than the human Christ of a specific moment, as on the cross.

When it comes to social witness, the Church of Christ particularly seems to have lost itself in theoretical debate about whether change should be evolutionary or revolutionary, spiritual or material. Practically speaking, the best thing seems to be to pronounce on social issues in the name of a Christian individualism. It has been stressed how a poorly integrated personality lies at the heart of the nation's moral problems and makes for the presumption of the powerful and the weakness of the led. Social policy in Japan is influenced by a very low sense of individual worth. The average Japanese is not especially wealthy, despite the nation's enormous wealth; in income per head Japan comes twenty-first in the world, not second or third; that is to say, it ranks below most Common Market countries. The fact is that the major companies simply 'own' their employees, who are given bonuses and perks like trips to the sea or night clubs, and the welfare and security which society does not provide, rather than a substantial salary. Small and medium firms and industries, which are numerous, nearly all pay badly. The national government can justify mean policies by traditional feudal and spartan values, and as a result a wealthy country has poor housing, poor and expensive food, constant urban traffic jams and shocking overcrowding on inadequate transport services, all of which create daily trials. Social opportunity is almost nil; anyone who can win in the rat race (which in the educational sphere has become so intense that it is sapping the physical strength of the youth) enters a promising firm and is almost never fired, rising steadily in status; the rest stay in the circumstances in which they were born. Many have tried to escape social inevitability by fleeing from the countryside and the tyrannies of rural fathers, only to discover new pressures with the freedom of the over-populated cities. Uncontrolled industry has polluted and pock-marked the land; city planning is poor, and even today safety regulations and compensation for accidents in industry and construction leave much to be desired. The average Japanese is remarkably honest, but ironically, society and the powerful are influenced by an unscrupulous mafia.

Thus it is that anyone anxious to find abuses beneath the calm and slick surface can find them everywhere, and to an exceptional degree, the abuses appear to be born of wrong attitudes towards the individual and not simply accidents of the capitalist system; it seems unlikely that socialist or Communist reforms could bring radical improvements: the people would still be cogs in a machine. In the circumstances, an authentic religious criticism of the society automatically becomes a social one.

IV

There remains the problem of sex, which in mission circles is likely to be ignored if not actually condemned. Uchimura had three wives; the second died and the first he divorced, to the scandal of church associates. Uchimura discovered this first wife, a former student of the Christian Doshisha College, to be trivial and wilful; she deserted him to return to her parents some months after their marriage. Very much in love, he pleaded with her not to leave him, but she insisted, and upon her return Uchimura felt so wounded that he could not bring himself to live with her any more, and against all advice divorced her.

By Catholic and some Protestant standards, Uchimura's subsequent marriages amounted to living in sin. However, this position must be seen as typical of Japanese and Asian Christian attitudes generally, especially those of India. At various times both Catholic and Protestant missionaries have been shocked by the way in which Christians who assumed they had reason to be divorced and remarried would live together openly if no church would recognize their union.

It is not that Asians, Christian or otherwise, tend to be more sensual and promiscuous than Western man. If anything they are less so. However, their attitudes are more femininely pragmatic and subjective. A marriage which is no longer felt to exist does not exist, and 'irreconcilable differences' and mental infidelity may be taken as seriously as physical infidelity in the West, or more so. At the same time, physical infidelity need not always be taken so seriously where the action involved is understood merely to satisfy a physical need; thus the Japanese wife, who holds the purse strings, has traditionally given her husband money to spend in houses of pleasure. Naturally, she has not always done so happily and willingly, but neither partner to the marriage would necessarily consider that this amounted to infidelity, which is seen more as a state than an act, especially as there still is, I believe, a widespread custom for wives to cease from intercourse at middle age. What the Japanese wife really dreads is to be ignored and to be insulted because the husband is away from home excessively, whether in the company of a mistress or in the pursuit of some pleasure. As the Japanese do not tend to entertain at home, this might make her rather lonely or condescended to by other women.

On the whole it could be said that Japan and Asia do not experience sexual guilt in the Western and Christian way at all;

indeed, it would be almost impossible for Asia, with its different psychological structure and evaluation of the ego, to do so. It is, of course, erroneous to say that no guilt is experienced, for some guilt in this sphere is universal; however, the pretext and expression are different, and sexual guilt is more general and unconscious than personal and conscious, a matter of shame rather than a sense of specific wrong-doing. This may be the shame of the prostitute who, while not experiencing guilt at furthering her career, nevertheless senses shame in relation to her body (Japanese prostitutes have frequently been considered very modest), or the shame of the many men who used to attend the notorious Yoshiwara with basket hats to shield their faces. Although social rank played some part in the shame of men, the evaluation was essentially emotional. There was a 'bad feeling' about the matter but no sense of offending laws of God or man.

The Western sense of will versus desire (or 'spirit' versus 'flesh'), which derives from a masculine, patriarchal, and to some extent Greek rational world-view, does not enter the picture. As Jung had it, masculine ideals tend to the achievement of perfection, an almost intellectual value, and feminine to wholeness; if too uncritically applied, both bring psychological and moral problems in their wake. In the more feminine world view, emotion and desire are always more or less natural, and the sexual function is less a chosen pleasure or an object of sacramental reverence than a natural function, to be allowed its due.[29] If excess and lewdness are the dangers for the West, a merely automatic and clinical use of sex is the danger in the East. Thus it is the 'Christian' West which has an aesthetic view of the body. There is nothing of Michelangelo or Titian in the art of China or Japan; the erotic art is merely obvious or crude, even obscene, suggesting that despite the emphasis on wholeness, the body was dirty or unacceptable.

Differences of these kinds (and there are more) have important consequences for the churches which they badly need to recognize. In the section of Japan in his *Urgent Harvest*, Lyall remarks that the lapses from the Japanese church are frequently caused by sexual problems.[30] It is the only Protestant book I have read which mentions the point. The Catholics are more realistic about the situation (securing husbands for Catholic girls is a major and difficult task for priests in that woman-dominated church), but they are not in a position to compromise much, because of the current hard line on birth control and abortion which runs completely counter to Japanese tradition and present political policy. All the same, unrealistic attitudes towards Japanese sexual problems and pressures probably constitute one of the chief barriers to church affiliation and keeping it; the church seems too holy to join or to remain in. When I think, for example, of how remarkably pragmatic by Western standards a Chinese Christian like Dr K. L. Ding of the Hong Kong Christian Industrial Committee can be, I realize how much more unacceptable to Japanese the perfectionism or prudery of missionary attitudes must seem. Dr Ding, otherwise a fairly conservative Protestant, has suggested that prostitution in Hong Kong should be legalized because with the shortage of women it is inevitable that men will require the services of prostitutes, and has recommended that abortion should be on demand. While I could not entirely support this kind of reasoning, the approach of the church probably needs to be more realistic in relation to both Asian psychology and the social situation.

Perhaps the first thing to grasp is that Japanese belief has always maintained, and custom to some extent proved, that individuals should be able both to indulge and deny themselves. Less naturally controlled than the Asian, not even the permissive Occidental really believes this possible, while the religious Occidental may defend personal morals more than practically any other article of faith, because he rightly senses that for the extravert mentality, purity is the condition of feeling anything spiritual at all. He is also more concerned than the Asian with achievement of an objective perfection rather than a subjective wholeness, hence for him the familiar pattern of repeated sin, confession and recourse to grace, makes a sort of painful sense in comparison with the Asian demand for total and immediate resolution, or else sufficient temporary compromise along the way to self-improvement. Religious imperatives are one question here, the psychological bias involved another. Doing right for the sake of being right and keeping the church happy is unlikely to be considered a good by Asians when it is felt to be at the cost of inner consistency or the happiness of immediate associates. As I have remarked, wholeness rather than abstract perfection is the Asian ideal, and it may well be that if it is possible, Christian notions of moral perfection will have to be restated in terms of a psychology of wholeness. Traditionally, Japanese have believed that true strength was displayed in the ability both to cultivate *and* deny the senses.

Psychology apart, Japanese society, perhaps more than any other in the world, proves Aldous Huxley's disturbing thesis about correlations between permissive morals and the repressive society, puritanism and democracy. Just as drunkenness remains to this day the accepted avenue of release and protest (if one wants to criticize others, the politest way is to get drunk and shout abuse), sex remains the leading consolation – and more. Like religion, it is a means of expressing the ego. It is because the vulnerable ego is often deeply and sensitively involved that it is hard and sometimes dangerous to engage in criticism. It would doubtless be true, but also a trifle facile, to maintain that if the individual Japanese began to rate moral courage over the physical and asserted himself more, the dignity he acquired would have a good effect on his personal morals. The fact is that whatever the individual does, he will still live within a society which imposes traditional values and modern pressures which will inevitably modify all the judgments and demands made by the churches. Christian influence has led to a reform of some of the worst abuses relating to prostitution and the status of women generally, but the legacy of centuries will not be undone in a day.

The basically militaristic values of the society have discouraged, and still discourage, any deep family ties. So intense is involvement in corporation life that on being asked their names many Japanese give the name of the company, the family being an afterthought; it is thought proper to spend even leisure among business associates. Traditionally, as sons were compelled into matches they did not want, and were forbidden to take second or third wives for love as in China (because the women's right derived from the original matriarchy of Japan), they engaged in more clandestine relations with mistresses and prostitutes. Business custom and high mobility perpetuate old arrangements even today, while the militaristic pressure to be 'masculine' (which the obsession with violent sports constantly implies) does not encourage refined feelings towards women. The hero in Japanese drama, as in most Asian theatre, should ideally be rather soft and slightly feminine. In practice, toughness is associated – not without reason – with badness. In real life, however, and among actors, such grace is often homosexual. Homosexuality has always been freely accepted, almost more so than in any other society since ancient Greece. The relative idealization of such conduct in Greece appears to have been duplicated and has even given rise to a distinctive literature.[31] Today, the Japanese Gay Liberation movement must be understood essentially as a movement to free the homosexual for a homosexual identity as opposed to the traditional obligation of bi-sexuality.

Traditionally, women in Japan have not been permitted the same sexual liberty as men. The average woman makes a modest girl and a faithful wife, but the society has always reckoned that within her limitations she was to be allowed sexual fulfilment. Wives, often abandoned by husbands for distant posts on government command, were positively enjoined to engage in '*plaisirs solitaires*' and were provided with instruments to heighten their pleasure. Lesbianism was common, and sometimes encouraged, while extra-marital affairs might be indulged depending upon the class, the region and the period.

Altogether there is little encouragement to other ways. Like French literature, Japanese literature is often exquisite but rarely edifying. The first and greatest piece of national fiction, *The Tale of Genji*, is a vaguely Buddhistic record of the elegant conquests of an all but incurable seducer. But in any case, it is likely that the Japanese are just more highly sexed than other Asians. If this is not always more apparent, it is because (apart from the striptease which they invented and which can be regarded as the rejection of inhibitions and formality by an inhibited, formal people), it is 'behind the fan', subtly expressed rather as in the suggestive art of rococo. In Mishima's *Forbidden Colours*, it might at first be hard for readers to grasp just what sexual intrigues are afoot.

Despite all this, it would be wrong to suggest, as certain authorities have done, that the Japanese have never had morality, sexual or otherwise, and that this is the land of happy atheists and happy immoralists. On the contrary, Japan has even known the most extreme forms of Puritanism, like the kind which caused the wives and daughters of the Samurai to be guarded by servants and forced to sleep uncomfortably with the legs together, lest there be the slightest suggestion of indecency. The founder of Bushido was all in favour of sexual abstinence, and imposed this on many of his followers, while various Shoguns pronounced against any consorting of the military with prostitutes. We have also seen that in the early Buddhist era and during the Amidist revival, confession of sins, including sexual sins, was required. Yet all these tendencies were really 'patriarchal' or Chinese impositions upon the basically matriarchal amoral values of the original society. By its devaluation of will and reason the matriarchal society takes everything, good and bad, into its womb consciousness. Polynesia and the pre-Celtic societies of Ireland exhibit the same trend and show similar sexual customs, like the right to abduction by stealth, which in Japan meant that in certain regions unmarried girls long retained the right to receive a lover secretly by night. This matriarchal heritage was easy to perpetuate because of the feudal values which made social duties the highest good. For example, it was not evil for a girl to become a prostitute or someone's mistress, but only to refuse to do so if her family desired to place her in such positions to support them.

Two major attitudes towards sex are to be noted in Japan, the pragmatic and the neurotic. The first takes the line (most nearly represented in the West by St Augustine who said that prostitution was necessary, like the sewage system of a city) that needs are best satisfied lest worse result. This line is common to all Asia, especially traditional China, which, in contrast to Japan, has greatly deromanticized love and has believed in family and brothel.

'Neurotic' sex is well represented in the famous novels of authors like Kawabata, Tanizaki and Mishima (a homosexual).[32] Here the characters engage in unconventional conduct because their self-image and situation is itself so unusual that sex has become a medium of perception and development. The peculiar loneliness to which everything in Japanese life and temperament inclines cannot be ignored either. As sex appears such a sensitive area in the search for identity in Japan, in these cases redemption for the self rather than from guilt is, or seems to be, the true problem and the angle from which religious criticism (or in individual cases counselling, if it is not a bit faddish) would need to be pursued. Moreover this unconventional behaviour must be distinguished from purely decadent behaviour of which, despite the Tokyo fleshpots, Japan has possibly less than the West. To the average healthy missionary, Japanese complexity may well appear exasperating, needing to be shaken up and put in order quickly. However, this is probably an impossibility, and it is unlikely that a thriving and sophisticated Japanese church could avoid carrying a few 'bad' experimental Christians (like Barbey D'Aurevilly, Jouhandou, and so on, in French Catholicism), especially if it wanted to include artists. Perhaps it is already too late to raise the question of how churches should respond to Japanese morals. By now the church is assumed to be a sexually intolerant place to which a sexual problem cannot be brought, or in which it cannot be worked out, as in some of the more broadminded churches of Europe and America. Those who become Christians are for the most part those who have never suffered great sexual desires, problems or pressures in the first place.

Probably the first thing to recognize is that Japanese society (its leaders rather than the individual) has been primarily to blame for what Christians would disapprove, and criticism usually needs to be made first of the values which disregard individual freedom and dignity. Kagawa, who did so much to lessen the abuses of traditional prostitution, admitted without sentimentality that many of the prostitutes were good women, who had been forced into the profession, or entered it to support sick relatives.[33] The values of Japanese society past and present are not Western ones, and must be judged accordingly. Not only is respectable shock inappropriate; so too is the idea that St Paul saw it all and knew it all from Rome. For example, it would be wrong to imagine, as does some popular and conservative Christianity in Asia, that male and female homosexuality is automatically an expression of decadence. There is certainly a type of sordid and violent inversion which is the product of decadent societies, and within those societies persons will 'exchange' heterosexual for homosexual relations (which is what St Paul refers to), but this is not necessarily typical of the average homosexual. Inversion, though sometimes innate, quite predictably occurs within certain types of child-rearing patterns and cultures, of which Japan happens to be one. Much could be said on this controversial subject currently much debated among Western churches, and some mention of it is made in the concluding chapter. Suffice it to say here that those churches who take a theologically and psychologically conservative line and try to force or hurry cures, marriages, or total abstinence upon homosexuals, need to be very sure what they are doing, since the record for cures is so low that they must be responsible for the problems they may cause for all concerned (one thinks of the suffering the cure-all Protestant marriage caused the wife of novelist André Gide). Altogether, the problem of inversion is not so pressing as other sexual issues which relate to the counselling of adolescents and the married. Mission churches are usually stricter than most Western churches, but sermons, evangelism, or confessionals which directly or indirectly make an issue out of masturbation (for example, the Southern Baptists sermonizing, 'God knows your secret sins') are ill-advised and only trivialize the idea of sin in a society where the very concept of sin is questioned. East Asian reaction is liable to be one of amazement that Christians can seem so unrealistic or hypocritical, and the effect of attitudes in this area could lie at the root of the old slander, so widespread in China, that missionaries must be severely perverted and harbour evil passions for children and the like. Almost certainly, too, this emphasis has helped keep lots of otherwise sympathetic young men who have passed through mis-

241

sion schools out of the church and made it a church of women. Pearl Buck tells of a student of a Christian college who lost his faith after returning home to the Chinese setting in which the morbid guilt to which he had been trained suddenly seemed so unnatural.[34] In the East masturbation is considered a natural function, a phase, and resentment is felt at efforts to impose guilt. That is not to say that traditional Western attitudes are entirely wrong; the greater sense of ego occasioned more awareness of motive and responsibility for sexual fantasy, even prior to Christian times. Nevertheless, Western and Christian attitudes to this subject have no conclusive biblical warrant, and religion has been trivialized by an over-emphasis which too often has made deliverance from sin nothing more than deliverance from adolescent habits.[35]

Again, the churches probably need to be rather lenient over divorce, especially with converts. Where the individual was under strong pressure to marry against his inclination, or has maintained a mistress over a long period (this would usually apply to the rich or the older generation), probably the happiest and most honest solution for all parties would be a new beginning with a marriage of true affections. Where this was impossible, then the affair might need to be tolerated (much as the Catholic church used to tolerate such affairs, or as some Protestant churches in Africa tolerate polygamy in certain circumstances). The point is that it is one thing to be repentant and make good resolutions on one's own behalf, another to do so at the expense of others, like St Augustine, who dismissed his mistress and tried to ignore a son in order to be able to lead a perfect celibate life. While it was not a matter of church ruling but of Japanese arrangements, it would clearly have been much better for Kagawa had he been raised by his natural mother rather than his father's wife. Since Japanese churches have been so influenced by Brunner, they might usefully refer to his rather liberal interpretation of marriage.[36]

In a society such as the Japanese, where a degree of flexibility is required, the most important thing would seem to be that the church leadership should offer good examples. The main concern should be less to purge congregations of every suggestion and taint of sin than to ensure that bad conduct is not positively encouraged by presumptuous leaders. I am not, for example, sympathetic to the kind of line taken by some American churches, which tolerate divorced priests or lesbian priestesses. This is confusing enough for Americans, and would be worse for mission churches. But all excessive Puritan zeal to impose standards, whether inside or outside the church, is surely misplaced. Mission history from Africa to the Pacific is too full of the accidents of such zeal, some of which, like prohibition laws in America, increases the very evils which it seeks to eradicate. Zeal is never a substitute for wisdom, nor revolution for solid growth and a natural evolution.

5

The Thai Setting

With Thailand we enter South East Asia. Here Chinese influence, which was so crucial for the development of Japanese society, is less prominent than the Indian with which it is blended, and is to be found more in the aesthetic than the philosophical sphere. It is a curious blend, as the very landscape seems to mark out Thailand and South East Asia down to Singapore as an extension of China (Phuket is virtually Kweilin in the tropics), and among a race so physically akin to the Chinese as the Thais, the austerity of the monks, who go barefoot and eat one main meal a day, comes as a surprise. Comparisons are not perhaps the right approach. Synthetic though it is, South East Asian culture has very distinct elements, each of which requires to be seen by and for itself. Of few nations in the regions would this be more true than of Thailand, the extent of whose capacity for local transformation can be gauged from the way in which the Indian epic of the *Ramayana*, so basic for its art and drama, has quite lost its Indian reference and become popularly confused with the dynastic saga of the national monarchy.

At present, then, Thailand is culturally the most homogeneous of the culturally chequered South East Asian countries. Historically, other regions never achieved the same confident synthesis as Thailand, or if they did, have seen it dissolve, as in Indonesia, under the forces of Islam, colonization, and extensive Chinese immigration within recent centuries. If one were to define the precise quality of Thai and South East Asian culture, it would perhaps be the supremacy of form in every area of importance

244

including that of religion; the danger is that this form can be emphasized at the expense of content. The questing intellectualism of India is largely absent, as is the sturdy 'substance' of Chinese culture in everything from the 'realism' of Confucianism to the bold reassuring outlines of traditional village and temple. Form is supreme but shapes nothing very substantial; local temperament, imported philosophy, and the need to achieve unity among a diverse tribalism, has made the form achieved through strategy or play, almost too delicate, often tied to no real principle but the dream. Far from being assimilated to the consciousness as in South India, the jungle profusion (what is not flat rice paddy is often forest) seems to encroach upon it, rendering its objects and gestures still more vulnerable. From Thailand to Bali the music 'shimmers' and dies upon the air, less langorous than the Indian, less affirmative than the Chinese to which it owes so much. In Thailand the people laugh; they also burst into tears rather easily. There is something vaguely oppressive about the Thai scene, like that of South East Asia generally. The beauty which is almost too exquisite seems threatened by some corrosive jungle void or culturally antecedent demonology, and though there can be a strong sense of community, there is little sense of home, the physical aspect of which often receives rather makeshift attention. One reason for this is the rather romantic bias in the value system, which is at its most obvious an obsession with personal rank (almost more important than class status); the consequences of this bias is a rather contemptuous treatment of ordinary existence, an all-or-nothing view of what constitutes success and the good life, as when contemporary films show enterprising country boys married into urban wealth. The life of the privileged classes, which has always been delectably elegant, seems to remain the only significant model of style and organization.

Dwarfed by India and China, Thailand and South East Asia have not always received the attention they deserve, whether culturally or politically. We can be amazed at the opposition and indifference historically encountered by Sir Stamford Raffles, founder of Singapore, when he pressed the purely strategic value of the region for British Imperialism, yet even today, when the area makes news, scholarship lags behind, and what little there is of it inclines to be merely factual and tedious. Thus, the many tourists now invading the region find venerable Thailand described as little more than 'the land of smiles' or 'the land of the elephant kings'; my own original starting point was not much better. I can still recall the excitement and relief of arrival.

If one flies into Thailand from, say, India, the contrast is extreme. From the dust bowl of the Hindustan plains and the sombre world of Indian mysticism and physical misery, one reaches the green, well-watered, *klong* (canal) – divided rice paddies of the central Thailand plains and touches down at Dong Muang airport where the elegant scurry of airport hands, defying the often muggy heat, bespeaks a different world. Already it seems to promise the East of worldly delights, of luxury, the dance, and self-conscious attention to social forms.

To some extent this promise is fulfilled, though sprawling, boomtown Bangkok with its ugly mediocrity, incredible traffic jams and dangerously petrol-polluted air could at first disappoint the most optimistic. Bangkok used to be beautiful and was dubbed the Venice of the East before granite, concrete and steel, intractable materials, inimical to the delicacy of most Thai design, took precedence and the muddy substratum demanded expansion outwards rather than upwards. The chaos and poor planning of post-1960 Bangkok is also an insistent reminder of how much Thai society is still rural, for much of what is wrong with the city is a consequence of the country suddenly come into the town. Vehicles can be driven like bullock carts, offices and dwellings are thrown up, knocked down, altered and extended in the casual way of the prefabricated Thai village houses, while what is sometimes rightly attributed to corruption and inefficiency in the realm of planning and construction is sometimes only improvisation, a perpetuation of the old easy-going Thai attitude towards organization and authority. Until the 1960s, many parts of Thailand, especially the Communist-infiltrated North East, whose population is more Lao than Thai, lived a life of village independence without significant contact with government.

Traditionally, Thai society was to a considerable degree the feudal two-nation society with aristocrats (who were often also the bureaucrats), scholars and military men (these last remain influential in everything from politics to the hotel industry) at the top of the pyramid, and the mass of peasantry, rice growers, fishermen and foresters at the base. No colonialism disturbed this edifice by producing either a new middle class or the self-criticism characteristic of nationalist resistance movements, and today complacency is probably the greatest single threat to Thailand. Exceptionally for Asia, the Thais were too adept at diplomacy to be colonized. In consequence, the middle class, composed of merchants (often Chinese), middlemen, money-lenders and wealthy farmers, is of fairly recent origin, a product of modernization and economic change within South East Asia generally. Both traditional upper and lower classes tend to abhor this class, which has introduced competition and bleeds the peasantry, especially in the North East, making the task of rural reform and combatting Communism more difficult.

Like most people of nomadic origin, the Thais are not especially materialistic in motivation and are inclined to suspect those who are. This does not mean that they are indifferent to worldly goods or pleasures (especially today and in the cities), only that they are less enterprising than opportunistic. They make the most of things, but things must be given them. At worst, through some popular understanding, or misunderstanding of Buddhist fatalism, they may even regard any loss or misfortune in others as nothing but an opportunity given them. It remains true, nonetheless, that achievement of status, knowledge or simple contentment have been more important than straightforward financial gain, as proverbs like 'In youth acquire knowledge, in old age money' testify, while even today, gain is so unimportant that in bargaining, Thais will settle on a price, then refuse to sell if they have decided they dislike the customer – a disconcerting practice against which visitors are warned. Thus, while corruption (which originates in the low salaries of civil servants) has always threatened Thai organization and the new rich are becoming very unscrupulous,[1] the ordinary Thai appears somewhat indifferent and usually honest where money is concerned. After all, honesty is a cardinal demand of Buddhist ethics, and Thai society is one of the most orthodox Buddhist societies in the world.

Such a judgment is official and subjective. It was King Mongkut, who reigned from 1851 to 1868, and was a reformer and intellectual (despite the erroneous portrait in *The King and I*) who began the modernization of Siam and reformed Buddhism, setting monastic teaching and discipline, especially in the royal monasteries, on its current severely Hinyana doctrinal basis. Thai Buddhism always had been and still is – popularly – a mixture of elements with a good Mahayanist strain. King Mongkut, very tolerant towards Christian missions but opposed to Christian doctrine, took alarm at missionary charges of Buddhist superstition and aimed to set the faith on an intellectual and scientific basis by returning to the earliest, most rationalistic Buddhist texts. In this he was astute, for by making the same charges, missionaries in China destroyed practically all religion there among intellectuals, delivering the society to materialism. The monarch's act may be compared to that of Colonel Olcott, the Theosophist, in Ceylon, today another orthodox 'Buddhist' land, when he reduced Buddhism to a few leading ideas and helped restore Hinyana Buddhism in a country where it often degenerated into spirit worship.

Orthodoxy or rationalizing attitudes have never been typical of the Thai way of religion. The poor cohesion of this society, as of all societies of nomadic origin, the lack of institutions, the artistic disposition to concretize and adapt rather than to experience and conceptualize, have so far militated against dogma and favoured the syncretistic approach. Another vital fact not to be overlooked is that only after the reform of Mongkut and the translation of the Bible into the vernacular, did Buddhist leaders see fit to translate the Pali canon. The situation was thus similar to that of traditional Catholicism and its use of Latin, and contrasts with Mahayana Buddhism in China and Japan, where scriptures were early rendered in the vernacular.

Buddhism itself was originally accepted and has been allowed to form values largely because of the suitability of its doctrine of impermanence to the intrinsic nomadic temperament. The Thais are as curious as their Chinese cousins are incurious; they love change and excitement. If a harvest fails or they feel bored, many will pack up the prefabricated Thai wooden house, put it on a boat and go seeking new territories, neighbours and adventures. While this is sometimes a matter of 'politely' or even selfishly getting out of difficult relationships, there is no doubt that they move because they bore easily. Even the Siamese who were presented to the French court under Louis XIV, when Versailles was considered the centre of the European world, soon became bored and wanted to move on. In Thailand governments and officials come and go with alarming rapidity; it is almost a game. The latest fashion in clothes or disco hits can be assured a delighted greeting among those financially able to indulge such pleasures. Life is *samsara*, impermanence, save for those perennial themes and symbols, Thai nationality, the monarchy, the *sangha* (the order of monks) and the village *wat* (temple) which is the hub of all social life. Symbol and style, as in Thai dance, the things that can be interiorized, count more than organs of power.

The main body of Thais migrated from Yunnan, South China, to present day Thailand around the twelfth century AD, following earlier migrations from Northern China. There are still Thai-speaking peoples in China today, but because of their love of freedom and nomadism, the Thais were never in harmony with the Confucian and fixed peasant values of China, and Chinese imperial expansion in the South had forced them out. The religion they carried south with them was influenced by Mahayana Buddhism. Elements of ancestral and Chinese spirit worship blended with existing South Asian animistic beliefs in the *phi* or bad spirits.

The early Thais ('free people', the name readopted after the revolution of 1932) did not really 'conquer' Siam – they had never been an especially warlike people, nor had they realized the unity necessary to military genius – but settled in sparsely inhabited regions, establishing their position negatively in revolt against the Khmer rulers who at the time held nominal claim to the area. It was from the Khmers, with whom there was some intermarriage (darker-complexioned Thais tend to be of Khmer or Malay descent) that the Thais first learned the Brahministic rituals and lore, like the ploughing ritual, water festival, astrology, and of course the *Ramayana* epic, which is so fundamental to their dance and drama. They were also influenced by the cult of the god-king which modified their own more democratic view of kingship.

It was, however, at the first Thai capital of Sukhotai (founded 1238), when Thailand was establishing an international position, that the saint king, King Tiloka (reigned 1441–1487), managed to impose the doctrine and art forms of Hinyana Buddhism with help from Ceylon. Had it not been for a desire for new beginnings, the popular attraction of the frugality of Hinyana monkdom as opposed to the extravagant Mahayana priesthoods of their neighbours and the fear of the *phis* which the revered monarch opposed, it is unlikely that so naturally religious a people as the Thais would ever have adopted such a rationalistic, almost 'atheistic' form of belief in an Asian world where Hinyana had been progressively rejected in favour of the more mystical Mahayana.

As matters stand, Thai religion is a curious mixture symbolized by the Shrine of Buddha's footprint where pilgrims can ring bells to make themselves heard and welcome in the god Indra's heaven. Images of Buddha are found everywhere, like crucifixes and holy water containers in Ireland; one can even sign cheques in the shade of bronze Buddhas prominently displayed on the counters of city banks. Yet outside the same bank will usually be the exquisite little spirit house set on a pedestal with clinking wind chimes and little offerings to placate the spirits who may have been disturbed and offended by the erection of the building.

Most Thai Buddhism ought perhaps to be called folk Buddhism or Buddhist animism. Pure Hinyana is practised and understood in perhaps six elitist monastries and by a few intellectuals. For the masses, Buddhism is essentially a social affair, like Shinto in Japan, something against which the main stages of life: birth, marriage and death, are registered. The deeper religious convictions are often animist. The Prime Minister, General Kriangsak, has been known to pray before spirit houses before political consultations. Even today, businessmen in Thailand would hardly dare set up a major office without satisfying employees that the spirits had been ceremoniously placated, as few would work for them otherwise, or if they did, would attribute the first setbacks to bad spirits. Ordinary misfortunes are often attributed to spirits fed the wrong food or drink, or whatever tale the local sensitive trumps up. One need not be superstitious in Thailand, but one must be pragmatic. The guardians of doctrine, the monks, of whom there are 20,000 with whatever degree of conviction, bless homes, buildings and enterprises in accordance with these popular and mostly pre-Buddhist beliefs. The average Thai is a heretic in terms of Hinyana, and when not an animist, a Pure Land Buddhist without the name, who does not hesitate to ask the Buddha's blessing on everything, though his belief in Buddha signifies little more than assent to the notion that Buddha was somehow supremely 'enlightened' and triumphant over the universal law of *karma*. In *Mai Pen Rai Means Never Mind*, Carol Hollinger quotes a society woman who told her that she regularly prayed to Buddha to let her be born Thai in the next reincarnation, though such identity orientation would be the very negation of the no-self doctrine.[2] 'It's terrible,' one evidently orthodox Buddhist said to me; 'they all talk as though Buddha were God and even ask him to send the rain.' Even the wretched kind of taximan cum pimp who asks you, 'Do you want girl or boy?' as you get into his cab, is likely to have a Buddha pendant or sticker to protect him against the high accident rate.

Buddhist ethics and the social etiquette of non-involvement they encourage count much more than Buddhist philosophy and mysticism, and in this, Thai society differs radically from that of India, where the average educated person is aware of the distinction between popular and philosophical religion. Of course there are monks and laymen who are dedicated to understanding fully *dukkha* (suffering), *anicca* (impermanence), and above all, *anatta*, the problematic 'no-self' doctrine, the truth that all pain and evil derives from the grasping activity of the soul, which considers itself an independent entity as opposed to the drop in the ocean it is or needs to become. But no-self and nirvanic dissolution as such means little to the average Thai, whose education in the concept is unlikely to amount to more than the practical exhortation which derives from it, namely, that one should cling to nothing in life as permanent. In *Buddhadhamma for Students* the monk Buddhadasa goes so far as to maintain that this not-clinging comprises the central idea of Buddhism.[3] Not surprisingly, then, when I have asked about no-self doctrine on the assumption that the men (who are normally expected to spend some time as monks learning doctrine) will know about it, my question has been greeted with surprise, shrugs or statements like 'the priests just taught us to be good people' or, 'Buddhism is terribly difficult', perhaps implying that Christianity by contrast was too simple. In short, what is considered in the West to be most essential and typical, may be about as relevant as the philosophy of Aquinas to the average Catholic.

The point at which Christians would probably find the Thais most doctrinally Buddhist is in their uncritical, literalistic acceptance of reincarnation and in relation to the idea of God as creator or purposer of events. The literalism with which the doctrine of *karma* is popularly taken is extreme, and arguably beyond the legitimate bounds of orthodox Hinyana teaching which, as King Mongkut explained to missionaries, teaches that life transmigrates rather than individuals (he completely denied the validity of the Jatakas).[4] The influential dramatic literature abounds in tales of innocent persons wronged and heroically bearing wrong because of some presumed evil in former lives. The conservatism and fatalism which this teaching instils, at least among the rural peoples (revolution, democracy, etc., tend to be urban forms of expression), can hardly be overestimated. The monks who to some extent benefit from the hierarchical social order and are content to have the women who feed them (though not hand them the food for fear of pollution) kneel before them, would seem to have some responsibilities in correcting popular belief, but in this case social convenience is probably confused with a policy of 'kindness' towards ignorance.

As regards the Deity, the Thais have an expression for 'God', 'Phra Tham', which refers to a vague pre-Buddhist speculation concerning a deity who formed matter and then withdrew from it.

However, Buddhism has almost completely obliterated reference to him. Buddha or Indra or Vishnu may be 'God', but all these are simply existents of uncertain origin, and having an origin, are not eternal, but themselves subject to transmigration and nirvanic dissolution. Here there is a marked difference from myth and religion in India, China and Japan where creating, purposing eternal gods are assumed by some sects and traditions. As it has developed, the Hinyana tendency has been to 'tame' the more vivid local gods, to include them if necessary, but to denigrate and humanize them rather than include and exalt them as in Mahayana. Educated Thais regard this as a mark of sophistication, proof of the religion's 'gentleness' in comparison with the 'wrath' and 'jealousy' of the Jewish usurper God. The wider implications of the 'jealous' policy are overlooked. People who 'buy convenience' for fear of local spirits will readily give and take bribes which, for a law like the Jewish, are sinful; moreover, talk of a 'gentle' people and a 'gentle' faith rings hollow when one thinks of the crime rate and the sheer war-zone condition of roadways in Thailand which seem to result from the prevalence of buying rather than earning driving licences.

Western admirers of oriental religions have sometimes waxed lyrical in admiration of the profundity of Buddhism, its transcendence of the anthropomorphism to be found in popular religion and Christianity. However, this overlooks that for Thais, *peng eng* (of itself) thinking is almost a quirk of the South East Asian attitude. When Henri Mouhot discovered Angkor, and enquired about its origin, some Cambodians replied, 'It built itself', while others equally improbably said, 'The "king of angels" (i.e. 'God') built it'. One can see here the bewildering tendency to attribute nothing to cause and effect, or superstitiously to shift the responsibility for almost any phenomenon to some spiritual force. Both attitudes are deeply embedded in the temperamental disposition of South East Asians, with its alternation between cheerful scepticism and profound reverence. Either way this *peng eng* thinking, when projected upon the divine, should not be seen principally as some sophisticated expression of a 'mind only' doctrine or a mystical realization, but rather as witness to the extremely feminine and unmechanical-minded nature of the people.

Under the modernization programme of King Chulalongkorn (reigned 1868–1910), it was a problem to get Thais to study any industrial or technical work. Because they preferred to travel West to study languages, literature and art, Europeans were reluctantly imported to make up for the technical deficiencies which resulted.

At a deeper psychological level, *peng eng* undoubtedly reflects a degree of obsession with the mother, and the desire to regress if not to the womb, at least to childhood. It is well known that in certain matriarchal and primitive societies, birth is not thought to be purposed. The father is not assumed to be in any way responsible for the birth of the offspring; everything is *peng eng* from the mother. Thailand is, of course, neither primitive nor matriarchal, but the feminine sensibility is such that it is considerably influenced and orientated by the concept of the mother – the monk is considered a 'mother,' nature is consistently referred to as a 'mother' – and the idea of deity, of cause and effect, is affected in consequence. As in Ireland, another mother-formed country whose pre-Christian myth knew no creation stories, there is an air of surprise, almost of childish wonder before even fairly common events and doings, which sometimes breaks through even among the sophisticated. As in a Beckett drama, Thailand offers a comedy of non-connections.

In addition to all these tendencies, it must also be noted that, as the theologian Kosuke Koyama has pointed out in his essay, 'Will the Monsoon Rain make God Wet?', even by Buddhist standards there is something peculiarly Buddhist about the very climate and situation of Thailand.[5] In harmony with the Buddhist view, Thailand is a land of the regular cycle, the absence of all cataclysm, where the fruit drops from the trees. Nothing is further from suggesting the God of earthquake and flood, or of struggling creation. In the case of the Buddha and doctrinally orthodox Buddhists, however, I feel that there is a further explanation for this virtual 'atheism'. Some orthodox monks do go as far as identifying *karma* (cause and effect, especially as manifest in reincarnation) with God.

At this juncture it would seem appropriate briefly to recall the main tenets of Buddhism, in order to establish its influence on national character. The four noble truths of original Buddhism are:

1. The truth of suffering: all life is sorrowful, birth, decay, death, reincarnation (this last is controversially taken as self-evident).
2. All sorrow is due to craving (desire).
3. Craving can only be stopped by bringing an end to all desire.
4. This can only be achieved by moral disciplined conduct culminating in the meditative life of the monk.

These root beliefs, born of Indian sorrow and weariness, are pragmatic and realistic rather than logical or philosophical in content. To deny self or soul because one cannot see it or feel it at all times, is unsatisfactory metaphysics by many standards. Subsequent philosophical commentary on Buddhism obviously encountered enormous difficulties explaining how one could feel sympathy and charity for all sentient creatures or strive to attain nirvana while combatting emotion and desire. 'We must also know that hearing is a mental state, otherwise we mistake the hearing as "I" hear. . . . It is of extreme importance to realize that when we hear or see, it is the mental state which hears or sees.'[6] Identity with the unconscious (as opposed to the ego) is thus total. It sounds like a dangerous prescription for total dehumanization, though of course since the human element *cannot* be denied, the unconscious works overtime for the conscious and loves and feels without apparent motive and object. Certain modern Thais who do not grasp this psychological point have been led to believe that the pure materialism of Communism fulfils Buddhist aims. Anyway, in Buddhism the Indian doctrine that there is no final self or soul because everything is God, or because it cannot be observed, has become a refusal to acknowledge anything but flux and the eternity of matter. Everything, the mind included, is illusory, merely a cluster or aggregate of things, all dependently originated; all emphasis is on transitory phenomena, and there is no adequate explanation of the meaningful repetition of forms and the similarity of persons within the essentially chaotic nature of the universe postulated.

The fourth truth involved the Noble Eightfold Path, the assumption of right views, right intent, right speech, right conduct, right means of livelihood, right endeavour, right mindfulness and right meditation. Subsequently, these conditions led to a proliferation of rules, especially with regard to the conduct of monks, which is being much pruned and adjusted in modern Thailand. For example, no longer are monks expected to walk through villages with eyes lowered against women. The demand of 'right meditation' alone tended to ensure that religion was essentially monastic. The interest of the laity would be less in achieving enlightenment than in obtaining 'merit' for heaven or a good reincarnation. This was especially true of the women, who have been the chief pilgrims and effective supporters of the monks in Thailand. Buddha was definitely suspicious of women, as being creatures at a lower level of reincarnational experience, and he opposed the orders of nuns which became such a feature of Mahayana Buddhism. In Hinyana Buddhism, a woman needs to be reincarnated as a man before she can hope to achieve enlightenment. Thai Buddhism possesses none of the female deities of Mahayana; its art has a decidedly 'protestant', rationalist flavour – fantasy and the feminine ideal are reserved for paintings of the *Ramayana*.

So it is that for the laity the cardinal precepts are those relating to right action binding on all Buddhists.

Do not take life.
Do not steal.
Do not engage in illicit sex.
Do not lie.
Do not take intoxicants.

Failure to live up to any of these precepts is sin in the sense of sin against oneself rather than God or man, and for this the individual will always eventually pay. Thus, given Hinyana 'atomism', the sense of responsibility can be quite limited. By denying a real inter-relation of things, the religion encourages the Thai belief that if one releases a caged bird at a temple one has done *good* (gained merit), even though the bird was caged to be released, while if one takes indirect revenge on political rivals through friends or hired assassins, one has not necessarily done *wrong*. This is especially the case since the *Dhammapada* (a famous Buddhist treatise on ethics), though full of the highest ideals, proclaims that the righteous man will criticize no one but himself and his own deeds,[7] thus ruling out a truly connective, social morality and its guardianship by prophetic denunciation.

Moreover, human nature being what it is, the average Thai in many cases frequently disregards the five rules and believes that they can only apply to the monks. This is especially the case with the first and fifth rules, which many observe only during festivals or in retreat. Thus, most Thais are not vegetarians (understandably, considering that only monks exempted from most manual labour could find the energy to work on a diet of rice and vegetables, especially the polished rice of recent times), while many Thai men, being of mercurial temperament, have a certain weakness for the comforts of strong drink.[8]

All this tends to mean that Thai life and values, apart from being coloured by a notion of life as impermanent, are more strongly influenced by a Buddhist etiquette and the incidental teachings of Buddhist ethics as conveyed at the temple or in myth, literature and theatre. Thus they have been deeply formed by the approved ethical qualities of *karuna* (compassion), *metta* (loving kindness), *mudita* (emphatic joy) and *uppekka* (equanimity and non-attachment). To be worthy, one is required to be *akkodhana* (free from anger), *na paritassati* (free from worry), *anusada* (free of arrogance), and perhaps above all, *santo* (calm or serene). On the whole, morality is associated with serenity and the cool heart. In Carol Hollinger's *Mai Pen Rai*, her friend Khun Amorn considers that the 'cool heart' behind his merriment has prevented his taking bribes and being corrupted by the corrupt members of society with whom he has to associate.[9] Frequently, in praise or criticism, the Thais will say that someone has the cool heart; in such a permanently hot country, coolness is next to virtue.

In addition to these prized virtues, three other Buddhist-related but also ethnic traits should be noted. These are the beliefs that first, life should be *sanuk*, that is, a play which should be done with a smile and with as much pleasure as possible (with many interludes for a dance, a song and a joke); second, that life should be *saduak* (convenient), done with the minimum of fuss and trouble but not forgetting others; third, that life should be *sabai* (easy), as comfortable as possible, a somewhat tropical and languid value. But all these values are taken seriously and contribute to the notable politeness, tolerance and easy-going charm of the country. It is a society in which it seems almost normal to make oneself pleasant and helpful and to avoid retaliation and complaint.

The question obviously arises, how genuine are these attitudes? Because of the national capacity for drama and imitation, the charm might be easy to simulate. Before acquiring a balanced new perception, foreign observers may at first be highly impressed, only to suffer terrible disillusion over the depth of underlying hypocrisy.[10] Obviously it is not possible or healthy always to be charming and demure. There has always been an underlying strain of violence in Thai society manifested in the obsession with every form of fighting and competition: cock-fighting, fish-fighting, kite-fighting, Thai boxing, sword-fighting. These witness to hidden desires to protest against injustices and a hard fate. Against this, there is something to be said for prophetic protest and St Paul's counsel to be angry, but not let the sun go down upon one's anger, especially as the Thai heart is simply not cool. The demeanour is composed until some sudden passion overpowers it, and things are said and done that were never intended, so that even murder may result, while when it comes to death or the major crises of life, even the best Buddhist can usually be counted upon to let the personal factors predominate, lamenting and wailing fit for an Irish wake.

Paralysing complacency is another danger. Thai values, though genuine, are essentially negative (not angry, not impatient, etc.) and are rooted in no positive moral dynamic or view of self, so that not even an emergency easily stirs the individual to great effort, or making improvements, whether on the social or the individual level. Too often, 'Mai Pen Rai', which at first is a tonic to the over-civilized, will be found to be an admission of the lack of all initiative or of courage to protest against obvious wrongs. Buddhadasa recommends that those who pass an examination should not get carried away and those who fail should simply consider it part of life. However, deliberate indifference of this sort leads to the shoddy work and low academic standard which threaten the life and integrity of the country. This is why bureaucracy is so often muddled and Bangkok floods with every heavy downpour.

Given these reservations, the fact remains that there is a strong vein of spontaneous and disinterested kindness in the Thais which few could deny. It is just that it is much less evident among those in authority and these impulses are likely to flourish within certain recognizable situations more than in others; they soon come up against force of custom, in which there is no Christian concept of reciprocity, of helping one's neighbour or society – freely if need be. From an impulse of pity, the good person will certainly help those in distress – witness the generally superior Thai treatment of the East Asian refugee problem in comparison with neighbouring states – but there is no sense of obligation, indeed, not even if they are paid to do so. Thus, for those of us surviving members of one of the all too frequent coach crashes there, neither the police nor the bus company saw, after twelve hours, any obligation to get us to our destinations or back to our homes. We stood in no relation to them and probably had bad *karma* anyway. Granted, there is a Thai saying, 'Never trust policemen or *likay* actors', but the concern of the police with regularly saluting one another at intervals rather than actually doing anything for us is not unrepresentative of larger trends.

Ties of duty in Thailand are hierarchical rather than reciprocal, regardless of whether – in terms of this existence – deference is deserved. The system of priorities constantly produces corruption, as when the medical service is compromised by the students' 'duty' to cheat in medical examinations in order to fulfil obligations to parents who paid for studies, and teachers who taught them (whether well or indifferently). In *Mai Pen Rai*, Carol Hollinger paints a dismal picture of well-meaning dishonesty in academic circles.[11] Moreover, even when the individual does act from pure generosity, or *bunkhun*, goodness as of mother to child, unless the recipient is a beggar or some member of a floating population, custom is such that giver and receiver will automatically enter a kind of patron/client, superior/inferior relationship of duty, *kreencaj* (consideration) or even *kreengklua* (respectful fear); in this the 'client' is virtually expected to repay the assistance in some form sooner or later, although the giver is assured of religious merit. Thus, there are no Christian attitudes, like 'Give freely' or 'Lend, expecting not again', except perhaps in crazy ways irrelevant to civic responsibility, as when in the famous *Wetsandon Chadok* story of Buddha's previous life, the Prince gives away his two children to a shrew who wants to make them slaves.[12]

In short, then, morality will be constantly modified by that uncritical devotion to family and authority which the gospels do not commend but which is so widespread in Asia. Theoretically the system is akin to the Japanese, with its cult of the small family and its sense of unlimited obligation to that and to king and superior authorities. In reality, however, the system has always been much milder and open than the Japanese; certainly within the family there has been a greater sense of reciprocity, as when parents have genuinely made sacrifices for the education of their children or have checked their impulses to beat and scold them (which is considered inferior, uncontrolled behaviour). Apart from expecting an allowance from children who work in the cities (whether it is needed or not), the biggest obligations which rural parents place upon (male) offspring is that they should enter the brotherhood for a specified season. In this way, parents acquire merit as well as their son and escape hell. (The consequence for Christian missions and Christian identity among the youth need not be stressed: this explains the low adolescent response in church schools in comparison with other regions). If anything, it is the teacher who has received the reverence and possesses the authority reserved elsewhere in Asia for parents, especially in all branches of the arts. Dancers who do not observe the teachers' ceremony are still believed to court damnation,[13] and no actor would perform without first making prayer and offerings to the spirits of living and dead teachers.

With so many customs tending to make charity interested, it is in their kindness to children and animals that, by Asian standards, the spontaneous generosity of the Thais is most obvious. But all evaluations of the moral ethos have to be set against the total social picture, and even the possibilities for demoralization in the Buddhist fatalism, to which the Thai spirit mostly responds with an impressive optimism, a bold face set against a world that offers few prospects. Life expectancy stands at around fifty, and though in comparison with much of Asia, Thailand is a land of plenty with fruit dropping from the trees so that no one positively starves, still many will go short because the rainy reason will bring floods and the dry season destroy crops. Competition in work can be stiff and job satisfaction is probably minimal. Many Thais work unacceptably long hours; for major businesses and government agencies there is an eight-hour day and a five-day week, but outside this sector almost anything goes. Children frequently work in defiance of the statutory seven years of primary education, as inspectors are notorious for their indifference – which seems all the more scandalous in a society so formally obsessed with paperwork. It is within this social context that we must see the Thais curbing anger and impatience, moderating their criticism and natural satirical verve. This is not wholly from fear of retaliation or from indifference but, as in modern Thai literature, which can be highly moralistic, from a genuinely philosophical or non-judgmental attitude towards others which admits 'it could be me'. This is very marked in sexual relations, in which the race has long been noted as being relatively free of jealousy and reluctant to stigmatize persons; for example, there are no distinctions of legitimacy and illegitimacy among children. Criminals, too, are usually given the benefit of the doubt and rarely serve their time, but are saved by regular pardons from the monarch or on Buddha's birthday (14 May).

However, as we have seen, there is more than ethics to the religious life of the people, though with its many facets from animism to meditation united by a Buddhist philosophy few really understand, the precise quality of Thai spirituality is hard to define. The air of imminent revelation, the Himalayan consciousness which broods behind Indian temple and icon, is absent, as is the colourful gloom and mysterious distance in Chinese religion. The Thai temple, decorative and sometimes colourful to the point of gaudiness, is always simple in plan and never awesome, though the bold outlines of its central massive Buddha image convey peace and an impressive concentration. Again, the exquisite mural paintings which have adorned the more prosperous temples seem more poetic and fantastic than strictly religious. The fact is that in Hinyana, with its emphasis on interiority, there is little attempt to objectify the belief system, so that the temple functions primarily as the symbol and centre of the community which makes merit there, in any way from meditation to sticking gold leaf on images. In a sense it is not 'essential'; people admit one could be a good Buddhist without attending the temple, a belief with consequences for the Thai Christian's attitude to church.

If religion were to be defined largely by a sense of the numinous, then for Thais spiritual feeling is concentrated in three areas: the spirits and local gods, which are feared in some places and placated nearly everywhere; the monarch, who is revered as a kind of Pope of the faith and Buddha-to-be; and the monk (*bhikku*) who, though not enjoying the status of India's deified gurus, is nonetheless considered a bearer of merit and (despite the Buddha's disapproval of *siddis*, psychic or spiritual powers) sometimes a force of virtue against malign influences. As I shall discuss the spirit cult later, I shall concentrate only on the two latter here.

Because of its artistic legacy, as at Angkor, the Hindu-Mahayana cult of the god king is better known and understood than the role of monarch in Hinyana, as in Ceylon and Burma (historically) and in Thailand (currently). Hinyana kingship traces its origin to notions of universal monarchy first exemplified by Emperor Ashoka of India (reigned 274–234 BC).

In this tradition, whose complex lore in relation to Thailand is treated at length in Tambiah's *World Conqueror and World Renouncer*,[14] the monarch is lay head of the *sangha* (monkhood) by a voluntary submission on its part and is purifier and guardian against heresy. At the same time, because of an Indianization or Hinduization of Buddhism which caused Buddhists to associate monarchs with Indra, the god of justice, the king, regarded as a Buddha-to-be, can, like the Buddha in one of his previous incarnations, according to the Jatakas, assume the rule of conqueror and warrior in furtherance of the good; his residence is a Mount Meru, a symbolic imitation of the Hindu-Buddhist centre of the world. Thus without being deified like the kings of Java and Cambodia, the monarch is still a virtual deity. It is he who approaches the nation's Emerald Buddha to change its vestments seasonally; he who presents their robes to the monks at the Kathin ceremony and throws lustral water over the heads of the faithful at festivals. Excluded from the skies, God is enthroned on earth, and the traditional paraphernalia of monarchy, the ornate barges, carriages and thrones, have the numinosity appropriate to this virtual deification.

The Thai obsession and identification with monarchy has been extreme. In the context of a 'karmic' society where one's status is fated, as the drama and literature adequately testify, thwarted ambition, dreams of a better life, desire for a more just society, are all projected upon monarchical figures who command, punish and enjoy the best. Given the atomism of Hinyana, one could even contend that its late-formed doctrine of kingship made it psychologically possible for the masses. The king is permitted the emotion, the anger, the punishment which the faith otherwise discourages (and criticizes within Judaeo-Christian religion). The king is so 'holy' that even today criticism of him is regarded as little short of blasphemy – it is not really permitted anyway – but this is not so fortunate for the social system as in comparison with Judaism, where blasphemy is referred to a 'perfect' God. It is not that the recent kings of Thailand have been bad; if anything, the reigning monarch King Bhomipol is positively enlightened in his concern for the people's condition, but as even sophisticated Thais will admit, when public attitudes to monarchy are of the Thai variety the possibilities for conservatism and corruption are enormous. While a monarch is on the throne for the people to identify with and to make the symbol of their nation and their soul, the same royal umbrella which protects the *sangha* will protect many aspects of the social system from criticism, since attacks on all but the most obvious and extravagant abuses of power, such as occasionally lead to a sentence, are apt to be distorted and dismissed as attacks upon monarchy. The extent of the psychological problem can be gauged from the fact that one hundred years after the death of Rama IV, *The King and I*, an absurd Hollywood musical not worth the serious attention of serious people, is banned as a gross insult to monarchy and Thai people alike, and can even be used by nationalists confronted with international criticism of the dangerous extent of Thai corruption as proof that the outside world is full of liars who do not know the facts.

I first personally experienced the mechanics of this familiar phenomenon the day I complained to a representative of a government department (actually the same as accused by Dr Elizabeth Langley) about the stream of inconveniences and misinformation to which I had been subject, a situation rendered worse by the fact that it was even insinuated that I was somehow to blame for my troubles. (Like the Brazilian murderer who held God finally responsible for the death of his victims, the Thai tendency on being discovered is to blame the offended party who, by being deceived, must have the worse *karma*.) It signified nothing to the representative that I did not blame him personally; the hysterical response was, 'But you have blamed me – O my King and my country. I believe we have a good king and a beautiful country, the most beautiful in the world, and all you want to do is to come here and criticize them.' This was mean; in some situations it could be sinister, and any judgment of missionary bitterness with its sometimes wild attacks on Buddhism would have to take into account the possibilities for paranoid feeling in such a social climate. Buddhism, benign though it is, is not invariably willing to give the benefit of the doubt or to appreciate good intentions.

Below the monarch is the monk. Though not revered like the king, he still receives considerable homage, especially from women in whom this patriarchal religion engenders more metaphysical anxiety. While the monarch could be considered guardian of the national soul, the monk both gains and bestows merit, especially in relation to his family. Poor families cannot always afford to release sons for even the temporary novitiate, but most strive to do so, especially since failure to do so advertises lack of merit and the brotherhood is the surest way for the intelligent boy to rise in society. If there is linguistic or intellectual skill, the youth may eventually arrive at the Bangkok Buddhist university, Mahachula-langkorn, where he may establish important social connections, even pursue a career as a 'society priest'. On the whole, however, monks, though somewhat sheltered, will not live in especial luxury, and if city-trained, are more likely to return to the native village to assist in modernization and the work against Communist infiltration than other bright pupils. Set on a pedestal, the celibate monk is revered as almost super-human, is sometimes believed to possess virtuous or magical powers, and is considered to be of the 'third sex' (this refers to the mean that they are expected to cultivate: impassive, expressionless, neither masculine nor feminine, though it sometimes reflects the repressed homosexuality of the over-mothered son). In certain respects, like the sovereign, the monk is the denied self deified. He is of the people and his status bestows status on relatives. The situation is comparable to that of nineteenth-century Ireland, where social deprivation and the aspirations of ambitious mothers placed the priest on a rather impossible pedestal.

II

It might seem from the foregoing that Thailand, despite its modern trappings and love of novelties (it was first in Asia to install television) should perhaps be called 'modern' with certain reservations. Its retention of spirit worship and its understanding of *karma* alone entail attitudes and institutions which give the society a conservative, ingrown character, and even the designation 'free' (Thai) people refers more to independence from other people than positive democracy. On examination, modernization in Thailand would seem to owe more to pragmatic or casuistic acceptance of the politically inevitable and a certain illogicality towards Buddhism than a definite will to change.[15] Since the race is religious, one could argue that it would take the adoption of another faith rather than secularism to achieve the conditions for real modernization, but whether or not the idea is valid, in its cultural self-containment and its reception (though not its treatment) of Christianity, Thailand can be compared with that other Asian country so associated with modernization, Japan. Both countries have appeared singularly resistant to missions and are proportionally among the least numerically Christian in the world – 0.5% are Christian in Japan and somewhere between 0.4 and 0.5% in Thailand. Again, it is noticeable that according to most commentators, no single form of evangelism has been found to be more effective than others, thus indicating a serious and very basic communication gap which goes beyond simple aversion to the faith as such.

Before we even consider mission history, two oversights can immediately be noted for what might be considered their extreme obviousness. First, the mistaken emphasis in presentation. The almost complete failure of the early Jesuits to convince the Siamese (in comparison to their much-persecuted but relative success among Vietnamese Buddhists more influenced by Confucian rationalism) ought to have warned their successors against the logical and intellectual exposition of the faith to which they have always held. The Thai evaluation of life is primarily aesthetic and emotional, not practical and intellectual, and to begin from objective proofs for a Creator as opposed to making an existential appeal or offering aesthetic persuasion (one thinks of all the 'pretty' picture-book lives of Buddha and the doctrine) would be quite inappropriate. By implication this is borne out by the statistical findings of missionary Alex Smith (see below) on patterns of response among persons in the Uthai Thani area of central Thailand. Although this is not a case of an outstandingly successful mode of evangelism, because those interviewed were not usually converted by any one means (they had suffered saturation treatment), it is still noticeable that many had been influenced by Christian hymns in indigenous music and were more impressed by films (visual aesthetic appeal) than radio and tract material (more argumentative 'intellectual' treatment).

Second, the same statistics indicated that meetings in the local congregation were five times more effective than general religious conferences or rallies in conversion patterns. Though the author fails to draw the full significance – it might be too painful to admit, given his somewhat narrow theological line – the finding points up the highly social and group-orientated nature of religious feeling. We have seen that for the Chinese, religion has been family-based and to some extent a question of Chinese identity; with the Japanese, religion has been more purely individual, often a way of establishing a measure of individualism and liberty within a rather limiting society. For the Thais, Buddhism is associated, not only with national identity, but with group solidarity, a life-style, and Christianity could not be otherwise. The temple has never been a purely religious institution, nor the monk a wholly religious figure. The temple and its grounds was the village centre, the place of litigation, the school, the theatre, the hospital, the advice centre, a games centre for the children, or just a place for meeting friends, and apart from a transference of much medical and educational service elsewhere, that is how it remains in Thailand, and in other orthodox Buddhist countries like Burma and Sri Lanka. The monk is far from being purely religious in function. Most of Thailand's leading linguists are monks who may even be seen interpreting at the airports. Currently, many are working for the government in furthering agricultural and educational projects. The only comparison I know would be nineteenth-century Ireland, where the priest and the priest's house was the centre of all community identity, information and activity. Buddhism always has that quality of 'holy worldliness' which the theologian Dietrich Bonhoeffer said that Christianity needed to acquire or rediscover.

Thus, it is unreasonable to imagine that the average Thai would or could adapt to a faith, especially in the fundamentalist mould, which reckoned to improve the shining hours with a regime of Bible study and prayer meetings only. If the church cannot offer a whole alternative life-style, both religious and secular, making the building and its surroundings a place where the people can come to chat and perform theatricals without specific religious reference, then it is largely wasting its efforts and certainly not beginning to provide a more abundant life for its converts.

Many 'Thai' Christians, certainly from the more dynamic and faster growing part of the church,[16] are not in fact ethnic Thais, but Chinese, as they have always been since the days of the early Jesuit outreach in the former capital of Ayuthia, where Chinese merchants had already begun to install themselves. The Chinese are the largest single ethnic group within Thailand, currently comprising about three million, and if intermarried Chinese and their offspring are included, up to 14% of Thailand's population of over forty million is Chinese. The present royal family of the Chakri dynasty is of Chinese descent. The purest ethnic Thais are found on the central plains. Among many ethnic groups with greater or lesser sense of Thai identity are the Lao, the Lisu, Khon Muang, Pak Thai and the Malays (in the far south this sense is very poor). The babel of customs and tongues has long been as taxing for missionaries to negotiate as for the government, which has tried to insist on the use of Thai language. The number of Chinese dialects in use (Fukienese, Cantonese, Hakka, Mandarin, Teochiu, etc.) has in itself been daunting, and has been a barrier to personal contact and to the creation of a sense of unity in the churches. From the purely political angle, King Rama VI's pronouncement that to be truly Thai was to be Buddhist, can be understood as part of a desire and a policy to establish a basis for national unity. In fact, religious solidarity does not work because, for a start, most Chinese Buddhists remain solidly Mahayanist; their sons make no merit during adolescence and their monks have nothing to do with the ochre robes of the Thai monks and their morning food-begging ritual; less abstemious, they dine instead in their own Chinese-designed temples. Some of the Malays are so ardently Mohammedan that they do not wish to belong to Thailand, and sympathize with the Communists, while the Northern Lisu, who are Buddhists-cum-animists, consider themselves nothing but Lisu. So it is that Hinyana Buddhism and appeals to conform to it has only confirmed 'pure' Thais in their sense of a need for identity as Buddhists; the more success the church enjoys with ethnic groups, such as the Chinese and the Lisu, the more danger there is that the religion will appear foreign or divisive, like Islam in the South.

Sometimes from common prejudice, sometimes with reason, the Thais have been hostile to the Chinese. The Thais are not alone; Tibetans, Koreans, Indonesians and Malays, an incredible forty per cent of whose country is now Chinese, have all been embittered by what they regarded as economic exploitation by the Chinese. The Chinese, like British imperialists in Africa, have never seen the point, because to them rewards are due to those who work – and the Chinese do work. They consider they have brought, if not civilization, at least greater organization to the countries they settled. The point is, however, that they also flaunt their wealth and dislike mixing, and the economic power they acquire can reach a level at which it becomes a political and cultural factor affecting the total life-style of peoples with different values, and not a matter of simple rewards for hard labour. The most reasoned and sustained objections proceeded from articles composed by King Rama VI in 1914 under the title 'The Jews of the East', which naturally enjoyed widespread influence because the king had written them. King Rama highlighted the Chinese sense of family and racial identity, their tendency, in his view, to exploit, especially financially, all those outside the racial fold. He also noted the pronounced materialism of the Chinese, as of the Jews, and their ultimate loyalty to a land other than that in which they lived. I personally feel that it is not so much that the Chinese are like the Jews as that they are the people most like the Jews within an Asia far removed from any kind of Judaeo-Christian attitudes. As I said before, I find many Chinese characteristics and values almost French.[17] However, the important thing is that in South East Asia the Chinese are widely *thought* to compare with the Jews, with all that implies for their appreciation of biblical ideas. In the circumstances, it is unfortunate that, under the highly fundamentalist influence of Southern Baptists and others, missionaries have taken a pro-Chinese rather than a tactfully neutral line,[18] and in their theology have emphasized the Old Testament, Jewish and Puritan work-ethic values rather more than is considered necessary or normal among most Christians. These, then, have constituted rather obvious barriers to any mission work.

Because of errors of this kind, I shall have to spend rather more time on the current presentation of the Christian faith in Thailand than on the history of its propagation, which is not particularly helpful for understanding the present situation. There is not, for example, the intellectual and theological theory which attaches to the church in Japan, nor is there the drama of Jesuit entry into China, or the confusion of the Protestant entry into China with imperialism. Many of the results and records of the early period of Catholic missions were lost, along with monuments to Thai civilization, when the old capital of Ayuthia fell to the Burmese in 1767.

I have already said that Jesuit intellectualism found little scope in Thailand, and was even a barrier. Other handicaps would be the more inflexible use of Latin than was the case in China, and failure to gain royal support. In China, Ricci had been able to work independently of imperial approval; given the coexistence of Confucianism, Taoism and Buddhism, he had never ruled out the possibility of the adoption of another faith, and as he gained increasing converts and influence among mandarins, Ricci hoped to be able to present the faith to the emperor. In Thailand, where in the seventeenth century Buddhism was the sole faith and the monarchy still literally a god whom the common people might not look upon and be permitted to live, toleration of missions was practically irrelevant when not accompanied by positive approval of the faith. If a monarch did not actually adopt the faith, then the religion could only appear illegal to the majority of people, and as in fact happened, its influence, as might be expected, was limited to the foreign residents – mainly Chinese – and tribal people and took the form of good works, involvement in hospitals, charities and education. King Mongkut, who was revered as a god, though he terminated the traditional status of monarchy, voiced the typical monarchical attitude when he remarked to a missionary, 'What you teach them (the people) to do is admirable; what you teach them to believe is foolish.'

European contact with Siam arose as a consequence of the Portuguese conquest of Malacca (1511) and the desire to increase trade and possess rights of harbour on the route to Malacca. Portuguese overtures were eventually rewarded by rights of trade in the then capital of Ayuthia. The first missionaries were probably two Dominican friars who entered in 1555/6 and were well received by the people. As a result of disputes between Muslim merchants and the Portuguese, Fr Jerome was murdered and Fr Sebastian wounded by Muslims when they presented the faith to Buddhist monks. King Maha Chakrapat and the nobles offered apologies and protection which led to the entry of further missionaries; their work appears to have been wiped out in the Burmese attack on Ayuthia in 1569.

After 1569, there seems to have been some activity on the part of Spanish Franciscans, and according to the Spanish ambassador to the king of Cambodia, Diego Beloso, in 1594 they and their converts suffered sporadic persecution, the reigning king, King

Naresuan, being described as a tyrant and oppressor. In Thai history, Naresuan, the Black Prince, is regarded as one of the greatest heroes because he delivered the country from its old enemy, the ever-predatory Burma, and the Cambodians who raised the land, capitalizing upon the national distress. The fact that the Spanish missionaries had entered through hostile Cambodia would largely account for the short shrift given to the missionaries, though persecution by nobles cannot be ruled out.

Under King Naresuan's successor, missions and missionaries were better treated – quite well in the circumstances. When in 1624 the Spanish attacked the Dutch, who were under royal protection as a counterbalance to Portuguese and Spanish influence, and were requested to return prisoners and property, their captain, Don Fernando de Silva, spoke in defiance of the monarch. The Spaniards were attacked and defeated by the King, who allowed Spanish and Portuguese priests to negotiate in favour of those captured, and on behalf of a Fr Cardin who was accorded protection and permission to commence a ministry. This ministry flourished, and subsequent toleration was sufficient for the 'Société des Missions Étrangères' to adopt Siam as its centre of activity and training for South East Asia. However, the toleration of King Narai was misunderstood and even presumed upon by the politically-minded.

King Narai (reigned 1657–1690) presided over one of the most glorious periods of Siamese history, during which the country was at the height of its wealth. The capital Ayuthia, which the monarch transferred to nearby Lop Buri, was described by Europeans as grander than London and larger and more populous than Paris (it had over one million residents), while the standard of living and hygiene among the mass of people were superior to both European capitals. Narai's problem was the balance of power among the traders of Portugal, Holland and France. Moslem Indians had been given power on the coast which rankled with the Dutch, who successfully blockaded the Chao Phraya river in 1664, demanding trading privileges and extraterritoriality. Alarmed by this show of force, but equally anxious not to displease the new power in the East, Narai decided that he had better cultivate relations with the Dutch enemy France. As early as 1662, when Bishop La Motte Lambert had arrived in the capital as Vicar Apostolic to Cochin-China, the monarch had made enquiries of France, shown interest in the scientific knowledge of the Jesuits, and asked whether the Bishop rated his religion more highly than that of Siam. Like China at the same period, Siam considered itself the centre of the world, so that the king would have found a superior religion hard to imagine. Though the bishop had the tact not to answer the question too directly, and simply gave some facts about his faith, it seems likely that he had misinterpreted the question to imply greater interest in the religion than it did; he also ignored the strong political reasons against conversion, even had the king been interested. The fact that in their struggle for power the Moslems had begun to press their own religious claims on the king would make any Christian claims, however disinterested, seem political, especially in view of the unedifying squabbles of the theoretically Christian traders. Besides, the monarchy was obliged to safeguard national unity. It is true the king was sympathetic and tolerant; the Bishop was donated lands on which to build a church and school, and complete liberty was accorded to missionaries to pursue their work. The king even requested reports on Jesuit sermons and educational practice, but he was probably more concerned to be kept informed of Western ways. At any rate, when in 1685 the Chevalier de Chaumont arrived as an ambassador of Louis XIV, who sought an Asian ally and his conversion and on being presented to the monarch, broached the topic of a royal conversion only to be rebuffed, it suddenly became clear that there had been a serious error in reports to Europe. The king replied he had never considered the matter and that his own people did not understand this faith, so it was thus not fitting for him to be converted; he also distrusted the intentions of Louis XIV in the affair and felt sure that the diversity of religions existed because whatever God there was, had intended it.

The mistrust of French intentions was not entirely misplaced. In the history of missions, since the Crusades the French had had the worst reputation for mixing missions with politics (practically all the worst clerical abuses of extraterritoriality in China would be French). Having failed to arrange a conversion for the Jesuits and Louis XIV, at the behest of the royal adviser Phaulkon the Chevalier made a treaty to leave behind French troops to train Thais. Constant Phaulkon was a Greek adventurer who had also fraternized with Jesuits and become a convert to Catholicism for political reasons. He had risen from cabin boy, to trading officer, being befriended by the merchant and interloper George White; later, after being shipwrecked, he became friends with a Thai ambassador in the same plight. In 1680 he was appointed assistant royal treasurer. Further privileges had aroused the envy and suspicion of nobles, especially when he assumed residence in what was virtually a palace.

At first, Phaulkon had advised the king well, if out of self-interest against the Moslems, Portuguese and Dutch, but when the English, jealous of their trading rights and of Phaulkon's position, threatened Siam, he tried to sway the king towards France and Catholicism. When the Catholic policy failed, aware of the opposition of local nobles and the merchants of imperial nations (in the Thai phrase, feeling himself 'between a tiger and a crocodile'), he built up personal support with French aid. At first this policy worked, as when Phaulkon put down a rebellion against Narai by Moslems incensed at European rights; however, the French soldiery made a bad impression on the populace and the increase in their number under Des Farges in 1687 did not improve matters. In 1688 Narai fell ill, and a noble, Phra Petraja, led a nobles' rebellion and was installed deputy king. This caused Phaulkon to bring the French troops out. Only the sudden death of the king prevented an open clash, and led instead to Phaulkon's execution following torture for alleged treason; it was said he aimed to cede Siam to France.

Though Phaulkon was an object of jealousy and the victim of exaggerated allegations, it says much for Thai tolerance that there were no further recriminations beyond the banishment of French troops. The priests remained, and although some missionaries and converts were temporarily jailed, Phaulkon's family saved their lives and retained their religion and some of their privileges. This would never have happened in eternally intolerant Vietnam or in most other places in Asia at the time. Nevertheless, it was a turning point for missions, as King Phra Petraja and the nobility expressed open contempt and opposition for everything European, and king and nobility had serried ranks. This contrasts with Japan, where even after persecution, Catholicism and the philosophy it inspired drove a wedge between Shogun and Samurai. This ultimately led to the modernization of Japan. In Thailand, modernization, though later encouraged and to some extent assisted by Protestant missionaries, would nonetheless come about through the initiative of the pious King Mongkut. Christian missions were not totally eclipsed after King Narai, but did not become a vital issue again until the nineteenth century and the Bangkok era. Ayuthia was cruelly sacked by the Burmese in 1767, with great loss of life and appalling destruction of Thai culture with vital historical records. Today, Ayuthia, like some Babylon, has only a few arches and a massive Buddha to attest to its former greatness and in 1776, when the half-Chinese soldier, Phya Taksin, Siam's saviour in its darkest hour, became king and moved to Thonburi, opposite Bangkok, the church, like the whole country, had to start all over again.

Persecution of the church, such as it was in Thailand, was chiefly manifest in the period between 1778 and 1878, the year in which the edict of religious toleration was passed. Kings, nobles and laymen were to blame for persecution rather than the religious establishment and even today, discriminatory pressure upon converts in remote rural areas will come from embittered village elders or parents rather than from monks, since as I have remarked, monks and religion are 'people-ridden', and it is the people who take the initiative. They are also less informed of the laws of toleration than the monks. In 1769 and 1782, King Tak Sin suffered spells of insanity in which he declared himself a god. Numbers of missionaries and converts, unable to acknowledge his divinity, were sentenced to death, but in 1782 the king was himself sentenced to death in the course of a palace coup, whose instigators declared him insane. Under King Rama I, who was also half-Chinese and founder of the Chakri dynasty, a period of intense cultural restoration began, and in view of recent events and continued Burmese harassment, political centralization was taken seriously. Buddhism having fallen into a rather decadent state, the scriptures were revised and annotated for more effective usage. The attitude which King Rama VI would enunciate over a century later was 'to be a good patriot, a Thai must be a good Buddhist'. The last formal persecution of Christians took place in 1869, when two Protestants were executed by the Prince of Chiengmai; like Tak Sin, he had also declared himself a god with powers of life and death over all.

Protestantism had entered Siam in 1828, with the colporteur and roving evangelist, Friedrich Gutzlaff, more famous for his work in China, and the Rev. Tomlin of the London Missionary Society. Because of the language problem, the vulnerability of missionaries to tropical diseases, and the opening of China, missionary defections and turn-over were rapid, and serious outreach only began with the Presbyterians and the Rev. Daniel McGilvary, who worked in Siam from 1858 until 1911, reaching his main centre, Chiengmai, in 1867. Other notable early missionaries were Daniel Beach Bradley of the American Board, who worked in Bangkok from 1835 to 1873. He introduced the printing press, publishing the country's first newspaper, *The Bangkok Calendar* in 1844, and also pioneered in smallpox vaccination. He was enabled to meet

King Mongkut after the monarch suffered a stroke, which required an operation upon his mouth. The Rev. Stephen and Mrs Mattoon opened the first Presbyterian church in 1848 in Bangkok, and also the first school for women. Trusted by the monarchy, Mattoon was appointed US Consul in 1856. The welter of missions and missionaries who subsequently descended upon the country (today there are more than thirty denominations, plus sects like the Seventh Day Adventists) met with rather less trust and gave a poor and confusing impression to this unity-minded country.

The Catholics who, as in Japan, had converted people to a catechism and a Latin mass and had not used the Bible, encountered little of the Protestant problem of communication, that of translating the Bible along with the more extensive exposition of doctrine this entailed. Moreover, after Catholicism had rejected St Augustine and the superstitious theory of certain damnation outside baptism at the Council of Trent, it was not constrained by quite the same degree of urgency and consequent cultural insensitivity which afflicted the extreme fundamentalism of missionaries like Gutzlaff. These evangelists, almost more Augustinian than the Catholics, worked at such a pace that they seriously mistranslated the scriptures and preached irrelevantly. Leaving aside the ludicrous mistakes easily made in speaking a tonal language like Thai, they failed to realize that even the use of the word 'love' (*khwam-rak*) could suggest evil and weakness in the context of a vocabulary heavily coloured by Buddhism. To this theoretically 'no anger' society, the expression 'wrath' of God was also open to shocking misinterpretation, making God appear another of the angry and self-deluded *phis* to be placated. 'More haste, less speed' was a saying which early missionaries did not understand, but in the long run it was nineteen years before the Presbyterian made their first Thai convert, and another year before they made a second.

In his reflections on the Thai situation in *Waterbuffalo Theology*, the Japanese missionary and theologian Kosuke Koyama considers that if McGilvary's account of his preaching in *A Half Century among the Siamese and the Lao* is accurate, it is hardly surprising there was little response.[19] He managed to say everything calculated to mislead, quite misrepresenting the Buddha, who cannot be said to have groaned under any burdens of guilt or have been troubled by 'sin', at any rate consciously. In his anxiety to duplicate Paul at Athens and to say what he said, McGilvary managed to overlook how St Paul himself changed his emphasis and terminology according to his audience, though Koyama does concede, as I think we must, that McGilvary's task was intellectually more problematic than St Paul's. At least St Paul worked within the framework of a Roman world with some degree of cultural and linguistic unity.

In the event, McGilvary ended up as 'apostle of the Lao' and the tribal people rather than of the Siamese – a common pattern. His most significant achievement was perhaps to help establish the Edict of Toleration from King Chulalongkorn in 1878. According to this,

> It is strictly enjoined on Princes and rulers and on relatives and friends of those who wish to become Christians that they throw no obstacles in their way, and that no one enforce any creed or work which their religion forbids them to hold, or to do such as worship and feasting of spirits or working on the Sabbath day. . . .

Buddhism nonetheless remained a virtual state religion, since the monarch was legally bound to be a Buddhist, and government officials were required to attend Buddhist ceremonies. Notwithstanding this, the toleration bestowed was extensive, and one can only wonder why, if converts today are harassed for not worshipping *phis*, etc., in the way claimed by Alex Smith, formal representations are not made. After all, even St Paul laid claims to his rights of Roman citizenship. One suspects that a touch of martyr complex, a need always to feel that life is a struggle, may have prevented certain missionaries from taking the obvious course of action.

Even before the Edict, there had been many changes under King Chulalongkorn's father, Mongkut. Deeply pious, he had spent twenty-seven years as a monk, studying Buddhist scriptures and going on pilgrimages, in the course of which he learned intimately of his people's condition. It was thus improbable that late in life he would wish to change his faith,[20] and though he liked to discuss Christianity and Western knowledge with missionaries, he resented the forceful demands of some that he make this change. He employed Mrs Leonowens (of *The King and I*) expressly to have someone who would not tutor his children in English evangelistically, or from the Bible, as apparently Beach Bradley had done when teaching the language to this royal linguist and universally curious man. However, King Mongkut was impressed by Christian morality (since Buddhism is often regarded as a morality, Christianity is often considered the same) and he gave missionaries land and opportunities for labour. He himself laid the foundations of democracy, arranged for the election of judges, set up embassies and welcomed technology, and altogether promulgated five hundred laws instigating the reform of Siamese life, which before his reign had fallen to very low levels in inefficiency and corruption, causing grave peasant discontent. His son, Chulalangkorn, known as 'the Emancipator', enlarged the programme, abolished slavery and forced marriages (though not polygamy), set up model schools, hospitals and the postal service, travelled abroad, and encouraged Siamese to do likewise in the interests of increasing their education. Strongly influenced though these policies were by missionaries whose charitable works Chulalangkorn encouraged, obviously the churches received minimal popular credit for stimulating these reforms in comparison with elsewhere.

In the first part of this century, the church still made little headway, especially under the force of a nationalism which had three main pretexts. First, there had been the loss of Thai territories in Cambodia and Laos during the late nineteenth century through pressure from French colonialism, which had originally taken as its justification the admittedly disgraceful persecution of Vietnamese Catholics; these losses continued to cause suspicion of all foreign motives. Second, there was the nationalism of the English educated Rama VI (ruled 1910–1925), who tried to compensate for his marked Anglicization by cultural nationalism and for his extravagances (he left the Treasury in debt) by favouring devotions. This monarch made himself spokesman for the view that Buddhism and nationalism were synonymous. Third, there was the nationalism which gave rise to the revolution of 1932 and the overthrow of absolute monarchy. In the aftermath, fears of internal and external threats to the structure of the society which owed so much to monarchy occasioned another brief period of suspicion in which all non-Buddhists were informed that they might lose their government posts, and certainly could not expect promotion. As the government has always been a large employer, defections from Christianity were noted. This, however, tended only to affect the nominal, church-school educated kind of Christian, and a compensating effect of the Thai revolution was to make the church more independent and national. In 1934, an independent Thai church, the Church of Christ in Thailand, was founded. It achieved financial independence from overseas, and united most Protestant sects, though it was basically Presbyterian. This long overdue improvement would be somewhat offset by the invasion of new American denominations and sects following World War II. By

1945, the churches had still only reached twenty of the land's seventy-one provinces. Thailand, as Siam became in 1932, had been almost abandoned as a hopeless case by missionaries, until the closure of China in 1951 led the Overseas Missionary Fellowship and many other groups to direct attention there. The 1970s have been the single greatest decade of growth, particularly after 1973, when the then Prime Minister, Thanon Kittikachorn, requested a group of religious leaders to help solve his country's problems. Recent years have produced very new attitudes, and we shall consider a few of these next.

III

Not only Buddhists but Thai Christians have seen missionaries and their message in a rather different light from the one intended. The casual reader of Saad Chaiwan's *The Christian Approach to Buddhists in Thailand*[21] might wonder if the same religion and endeavours were under discussion as those that figure for example in Alex Smith's *Strategy to Multiply Rural Churches*, which, like a good deal of mission writing, has a vaguely self-righteous tone, as of the martyr battling against all odds. Smith's book concludes with the statement 'it still requires dogged determination to find receptive peoples'. . .[22] and he claims that church and missionary 'will press on until they hear the Lord's commendation, "Well done, thou good and faithful servant".' It is possible that Mr Smith would consider Mr Chaiwan full of ungodly complacency or bitterness in the face of the urgent task – opinions will always differ. Anyway, Chaiwan notes the following errors of policy and presentation: an excess of denominations and missions fostering unedifying petty charges that everyone else is a sort of heretic; poor relations between native ministers and missionaries, who virtually 'hire' the former and treat them as inferiors; Christian love little better than condescension; the demand for excessive repudiation of ancestors on the part of the Chinese and addressing Thais in unfamiliar and difficult ways; not reiterating things; not choosing vivid similes and analogies or using picturesque language in the accustomed way; and needlessly outraging most treasured values, say by taking life too easily (I am not clear what this refers to – perhaps the hunting expeditions one reads that some American missionaries have engaged in).

I mention this criticism partly in defence of my own, for when it comes to describing some aspects of missionary activity in Thailand, it is hard not to lapse into fashionably witty and unkind treatment. While I would question the policies of missionaries in the Chinese and Japanese setting, I still feel sympathy for the complexity of their task; it can be appreciated that missionaries fear suffocation by a society which has not always treated them well, which can maintain a certain distance from foreigners, and which discourages Western individualism. By contrast, Thailand offers a freer climate and has shown unusual tolerance to missions, yet it is here that missions in Asia possibly reach their nadir. Granted, the toleration has often represented little more than cheerful opportunism – the Thais have had little of the Japanese pride when there has been a question of getting something like science or medicine free – while their rejection of the message has often been due, one suspects, to little more than sheer lethargy. Nevertheless, one still feels that almost anyone could have 'sold' the faith better, enjoyed more success and won more affection. Certain aspects of the record here are quite baffling,[23] and one can only try to account for it in terms of some Western extraversion and insensitivity.

Catholic missions retain a basically élitist approach, but stock 'Aristotelian' arguments have given way to a presentation of the faith in specifically Buddhist or existentialist categories. A missionary priest fairly prominent in the organization of mission work in East Asia told me that he was privately rather appalled by what was being done in Thailand, especially by Jesuits. He felt that just as certain Jesuits had made pronouncements on socialism and trade unionism, only to by-pass the workers and the shop floor and speak with union leaders, so in Thailand they discussed refinements of Buddhist philosophy with monks who had not the slightest interest in converting, while they ignored the problem of relating theology to the broad mass of people.

Fr Marcello Zago of the Oblate Fathers of Mary Immaculate, who is not a Jesuit, puts a rather different view.[24] He acknowledges that there is so much animism, Hinduism, etc., beneath Thai religion that there is a good case for relating theology to the assumptions of this popular religion, but he still rejects such an approach. Most Thais like to feel themselves Buddhist, even to believing that one cannot be a true Thai without being a Buddhist – which is a great hindrance to missions. He claims that, as sayings like 'Hell is in the breast, paradise in the heart' suggest, there is enough interiority in the Thais for them to be responsive to the general idea and expectations of Buddhism, even while failing to grasp the full doctrine. Moreover, the fact must be faced that monks and laymen who reject the faith will interpret Christianity within Buddhist categories, describing Christ as *arahant* or *boddhisattva* and his sacrifice as renunciation of the self or even punishment and self atonement for sins in past incarnations. The educated Buddhist sees Christianity as a religion of faith as opposed to effort, one of rites as opposed to inner development, its materialistic view of salvation focussed on an illusory happiness of heaven, with a materialistic conception of divinity to match. Since 'person' is not distinguished from individuality, the personal quality of deity, so important in Christianity, is regarded as an inferior selfhood, attachment, egoism, an evil. To imitate Christ's good works has value, but attachment to him would drag one into more reincarnations. Converts and others who can transcend this thinking, claims Fr Zago, have been found first to have been deeply affected by Western philosophy or education.

In these circumstances, Fr Zago believes that one is required to present the faith both existentially, as a fulfilment of the higher aims and expectations of the society generally and to some extent within Buddhist categories, and critically as a modification of these. I think that the churches are bound to agree with this, though it could be questioned whether Fr Zago has found adequate theological and psychological perspectives.

Fr Zago feels that the Christian *kerygma* (proclamation) should start existentially with man and his adequacy and anxiety, not with God or God's separation from man through original sin, since God is problematic and sin is considered to originate only within. More pertinent is the fact that Buddhist man does not, and usually cannot, fulfil Buddha's precepts, or even understand them. As in Buddha's own time, so in the modern ferment everyone has to choose a guru and decide whether he can honestly be believed and followed. Even Buddha demanded that they should do that. Christ is thus presented primarily as a teacher who acted in the unconditioned state of perfect liberation turned towards the absolute and who, by following a mean of conduct in connection with the existing law, emphasized its interior content. He did not *find* a path like Buddha since he always possessed it (see his childhood discussion in the Temple), and he was admired for teaching which he had not learned (Luke 4.16). Christ *chose* detachment and poverty (Phil. 2); he was not required to practise it. His deeds and miracles were not an expression of attachment to the material, but can be shown to be the result of detachment from the world and from passions which allowed him to act in a disinterested way, while his culminating act showed his detachment even from his own life. His resurrection signified not merely more material living, but victory *over* evil passions and the world. Jesus indicated both the goal of the spiritual journey and the path of its attainment, which is God. God is describable even in Christian terms as truth (*sacca*), immortal (*anatta*), absence of misery (*niroddha*), the wholly transcendent (*lokuttara*). God thus becomes *both* nirvana (described positively as opposed to negatively) and the existential search for the absolute in doctrine and life. Putting aside difficult concepts of God like those of Creator and providence, one can declare the Absolute as Father, as the mystery hidden for centuries which Christ alone could reveal since he was the one person uniquely in harmony with the Transcendent. The kingdom of heaven can then be within us, as the Absolute was within Christ. God and his relation to Christ is thus introduced through the polarity of immanence – transcendence.

Even though Christ is seen primarily as teacher, Fr Zago still feels there are grounds to call men to decision. To realize the unconditioned, we must still be converted in the heart and be reorientated, for more is involved than doing good and avoiding evil. The pre-condition of necessary conversion is willingness to follow Christ, who alone can be the perfect guide. Only by following his example can definitive awakening be achieved. We do not increasingly free ourselves from Christ, since he does not do away with personal effort and does not take our place; however, the more we advance, the more we realize that the two are becoming one, in the Pauline 'It is no longer I who live. . . .' Following Christ, as in Buddhism, demands self-renunciation leading to purification, but though commandments or precepts are a condition and a means, positive charity is superior, since in itself it eliminates the passions. That is why God, our liberation, is called love. Conversion transcends both ethics understood as behavioural change based on selfish motives and legalism or purely external fulfilment of laws.

As far as it goes, such adaptation is reasonable enough, but it fails in two related particulars. First, in its limited sense of what constitutes existential anxiety (an inability to fulfil Buddhist precepts) and secondly through its basis in catechismal instruction. Its focus is altogether too religious, too idealistic. Most Thais give little indication of a concern to live up to Buddha's precepts, provided that they have time and money enough to make merit, and most have not taken the decision to receive Christian instruction. Like many people, however, they can be troubled by death, impermanence, lack of direction, and so on, and do not always feel their religion answers the heart. The poet Suntorn Phu writes:

O pagoda, strongly built, only to fall in ruins,
I regretfully look on you with tears in my eyes.
In this way, what name and what fame
Will not pass away before our eyes?[25]

Thai literature, and I would judge, Thai life, is full of such sentiment and indirect questioning of fate.

Fr Zago's argument also assumes a formal catechismal teaching. If only the New Testament were to be used in evangelism, all might be well. However, if converts are to open the Bible and read of divine creation, and a God who smelt the smell of Noah's sacrifice with pleasure (rather like a *phi*) and who smote the Egyptians in his wrath, they are going to feel mystified, if not cheated. Granted, even St Paul said that the law was only a schoolmaster to bring us to Christ, and theologians since his time have explained these images as conditioned by man's early ignorance, or God's revelationary concessions to man's early ignorance. Nevertheless, this in itself says much for the nature and purposes of God, and means that the issue of history and the scheme of salvation in the faith cannot be passed over lightly. Moreover, why not talk of divine 'wrath' against wrong provided that God is not thought to rage out of control? ('Displeasure' might be a more appropriate word.) At least in the Indian source versions of *Ramayana* there are examples of the wrath of gods and yogis which are much less edifying than the biblical ones. Furthermore, though I personally am inclined to believe with many Protestant theologians that Christ did give precepts (*sila*) for interior realization, rather than absolute commandments, one doubts whether many Catholics or fundamentalist Protestants would agree with this line (we have seen the rigid and literal way in which, for example, the divorce issue, the nearest the Gospels come to a rule of conduct, has been treated).

The Japanese Protestant theologian Kosuke Koyama has considered some of these difficulties.[26] He rightly perceives that one of the greatest problems is Thai *vocabulary*, which is very heavily weighted by foreign terms borrowed from Indian Buddhism. These can cause aspersions to be cast even on words like love. He wonders whether one can genuinely say that Christ was the only *arahant* (perfected one) who, out of 'infinite mercy' for the race caught in 'craving', suffered and died to 'instruct' the way from *samsara* through the *dharma* (duties and teaching) to nirvana-heaven. Instead of speaking, as do some missionaries, about 'salvation through the blood of Jesus', which confuses those being taught to regard shedding of blood as sinful on any account, he prefers to describe the 'content' of *dharma* as sacrificial death.[27] Koyama concludes that although the apostles risked using loaded pagan words, like '*logos*' (word), '*sōtēr*' (saviour), and 'metamorphosis' (transformation), the value gap was not as large and potentially as confusing. His theological solution is rather Barthian, in a Japanese way, with Christianity emerging as the iconoclastic negation of the Buddhist way: a series of oppositions like 'cool *arahant*, hot God', Buddhist apathy and transcendence of history versus Christian concern and historical involvement. Of course, there must be some direct negation of this sort and most Christians would share Koyama's horror that the evils of the world should be attributed to the affirmation 'I am', as opposed to the results of 'I will'. All the same, such complete opposition palls in the end, and it is impossible for there to be no points of contact.

In the realm of the psychology of the Christian approach to Buddhism, Koyama is full of invaluable criticism and suggestions, some of which I shall mention. By contrast, his complete theological iconoclasm seems unnecessary. If he is so troubled by vocabulary, why does he not suggest the wholesale imposition of new Christian terms on the language? After all, the English language has recently and meaningfully acquired the French originated 'existentialism' and 'structuralism' to convey philosophical ideas, and Thailand's Buddhist vocabulary was in any case originally Indian. So perhaps '*agape*', '*logos*', etc., should be offered just as they are.

Koyama does not agree with Zago's line in discouraging undue emphasis upon God as Creator. He points out that the Thai response is likely to be mostly one of unspoken criticism that it does not greatly matter who created the world, seeing that it is not a good one in which everyone would necessarily like to live. I feel sure that this is important. Here is one area in which the existential treatment and psychological dissection of Thai and Asian attitudes can begin in depth. It just is not enough to state that the world is imperfect because of man's sin. Doubtless it is, but there is a certain feminine, emotional Asian resistance to the easy dismissal of suffering this makes possible, though it may require long experience of Asia, or less robust health than the average missionary is officially required to possess, to appreciate the matter.

There is something debilitating and demoralizing about the crowds, the suffering and often oppressive humidity of much Asian climate and the torments of nature (mosquitoes, cockroaches, etc.). Men often wish to escape from such an environment, especially when they are also borne down by life's troubles. This is not a good world, obviously proclaiming God's power or goodness, as St Paul thought it did (Romans 1), and even if man had sinned, there comes a point where he feels that the punishment, if it is that, far exceeds any crime of his. Never have I heard so many people say, as in Asia, that they hated God or thought be was cruel, nor met so many people indifferent to life, wishing it was all over. One educated Hindu woman told me how once, on a pilgrimage to a temple, she had suddenly been so overcome by heat and the sight of so much suffering that she was torn between a violent desire to scream blasphemies to God and to try to dissolve once and for all into annihilatory peace. The Asian problem is the problem of Job, of not spoiling one's chances by blaspheming; many Asians appear to manage this by avoiding the issue of God altogether, in a sort of negative piety. This spiritualistic atheism is perhaps also fostered by the prevailing climate. The more dynamic religions enjoy a certain association with dry climates or mountain air, as in Israel, Tibet, Mexico, desert Arabia; saturation humidity decreases efficiency – physical, mental or spiritual; it can strike the body like a malarial fever, imprisoning the individual in the darkness of the material, cutting off the sense of spirit. The Buddhist emphasis on withdrawal, calm and deep breathing, or, as in India, Shamkara's philosophical relegation of all truth and reality to the subject alone, must be seen in this light. Certainly I can testify that, with my low toleration of humidity, at the breathless onset of a monsoon I have sometimes been almost paralysed with feverish exhaustion. If this coincides with illness or depression, one can feel so oppressed, so unable to reason, that one is ready to die. In such situations, St Paul's 'when I am weak I am strong' will seem less meaningful than his 'pressed beyond measure'.

Historically, the Thais, who are more optimistic, more healthy and enjoy a somewhat better climate than the Indians, did not solve the problem with so much mystical silence or by declaring God both good and bad, but made Buddha good and the *phis* for the most part bad, and though they follow Buddha, many probably believe more in the *phis*. The world is definitely a bad place. Two things seem necessary to make Christianity and the doctrine of creation credible in Asia, or even to people in the West who, depressed with the world situation, believe with Turgenev that 'the most terrible thing is that there is nothing terrible'. First, an emphasis on spiritual evil even over and above one on original sin and purely human responsibility for sin; second, a doctrine of divine love and atonement along the lines of Kitamori's interpretation, which Koyama commends. In the first instance, the idea of Christ's miracle of stilling the storm could be considered a potent reminder of the fact that nature is not as God intended, and that we can just as well see the Devil and all his works manifest in it as the goodness and creative power of God. Even in the creation story, on the second day God does not say that his creation is 'good', as other days, perhaps because evil forces were thought to have entered at this stage. Secondly, as Koyama realizes, God must be seen as love first, not as condemnatory justice with a secondary element of conditional love. He describes how he came to realize Luther's Westernness when he was interpreting the story of the Syro-Phoenician woman to Thais in a Lutheran way.[28] For Luther, Christ appears to reject the woman's request, by providing an 'Anfechtung' (a divine or demonic assault upon man), a test of faith, a rejection foreshadowing Christ's own desolation on the cross, and he uses 'doubts, turmoil, panic, despair' to describe the emotions in play. Without denying the truth of this interpretation, Koyama felt that there was another less metaphysical aspect, that of the mother's need and the increase of faith and humility within her, things which the Asian mind would see first. Faith growing through need and natural love rather than faith given despite divine testing and assault upon the consciousness seemed the more appropriate starting point. Assault religion belongs with the Western mentality. (It could be mentioned that Jung insisted on the shock nature of much Western religion and attributed the appeal of the Tarot cards with their 'hanged man', 'falling tower' and 'judgment' pictures to the difficulty which the extrovert mind has in reaching the depths without being propelled into them by such vivid images.)

Koyama also feels that Kitamori's understanding of the atonement as God striving with God, love against perfection and justice, and receiving into himself the pain of accepting the sinful, is more psychologically helpful than the purely legalistic or 'penal' Anselmian approach which influenced Luther. Here again one is inclined to agree, indeed, a purely penal description will only logically hold in the context of absolute dualism and where only 'masculine' feelings are attributed to God. If one postulates the unity of things and identifies Christ with the Logos through whom the now sinful physical creation subsists, one can appreciate that Deity could be involved in a sort of conflict, specifically between the demands of an exclusive perfection (the Father) and an inclusive toleration (the Son), justice and compassion, which would place the whole notion of Christ's mediation in a more awesome mystical light. Divine love is not solely fatherly love in terms of the perfect and worthy, but compassion (Heb. *rachamim* from *rechem*, womb), the motherly impulse to accept the helpless anyway. The belief that God the Father did nothing but separate himself from Christ who had 'become sin', letting him endure all the physical and mental suffering, while he felt nothing but satisfaction of his just wrath, seems neither fair nor consistent with the idea of the ultimate unity of the Trinity. For extrovert Western man, who needs violent images, one can imagine that the mental picture conjured up of Christ as it were standing in the way to ward off his Father's sometimes Zeus-like wrath had a sobering effect; in Asia, where man seems less in control of his destiny and is inclined to blame God for even being born, such assault imagery will rarely convince people that God is any kind of concerned and approachable Being, no matter how true it may be that divine perfection separates God and man. The picture will need to be more positively loving, and Shusaku Endo's recent *Life of Christ* suggests that Asia might be more interested in the femininity of God and calls attention to the 'motherly' feelings of Jesus.[29] Though, as I have just indicated, this would not be impossible, and represents a dimension ignored, because of the usual linguistic and anthropological misunderstandings, it is obviously dangerous to the psychological structure of the religion unless one places it within the kind of larger theory introduced by Kitamori.

It seems unlikely that the missionary, Alex Smith, would agree with all this However, before we consider his approach, we might consider two further observations by Koyama. He sensed the crucial role of 'neighbourology' in Thailand, the need to meet people and relate to them individually, rather than just to feed them ideas and faith. Without being a missionary, I had grasped this point before even reading *Waterbuffalo Theology*. It is striking how important the personal touch is in Thailand despite the cultural stress on non-involvement. Guide books even warn tourists not to be shocked by the personal questions they will be asked, like 'How much did your shirt cost?' or 'Where did you buy your watch?'

While it is true that some of this enquiry is merely aimed at assessing the stranger's status in order to decide what role and duties a relationship might require, much of it shows genuine curiosity. Indeed, the perennial danger of Thai – Western friendships is that the greater Western disposition to involvement which draws the Thai from the underlying hedonism and loneliness of his *sanuk* (non-involvement) society, arouses an intensity which few persons of any society could reasonably respond to for long, and ends with an embarrassed retreat of both parties, the Westerner relieved, the Thai crushed. Even if this unfortunate situation is not produced, the stranger is still required to relate in a very *specific* way, since unconsciously, relations will be made to approximate to some standard pattern: parent-child, teacher-pupil, neighbours, lovers, etc. Some missionaries understand this, and accept the peculiar responsibility which friendships entail in the context of the highly individualistic, non-involved social etiquette, but probably most missionaries, more interested in 'movements', numbers and revivals, do not. The Western kind of impersonality is of quite a different order from the Thai. It is more likely to be that of what Koyama, quoting the theologian Emil Brunner, calls 'legalistic man':

> Between him and his neighbour there stands something impersonal, the 'ideal', the 'law', a programme, something abstract which hinders him from seeing the other person as he really is . . . the other man is only a 'case'. . . .[30]

Of course, this type of missionary will insist that he loves souls, is bringing the living Jesus to them and doing good works to exemplify the fact, but souls mean little, and Jesus hardly comes alive to the imagination where people do not live and interact first. Legalistic man, too busy to act as guru, too remote from the culture and society's problems to act as real counsellor, too jealous of chastity to risk sentimental feeling, can finish with a heart as big as a shrivelled nut, and a vision which goes no further than his nose. Such people are of the kind who arrive at Bangkok Airport to remark, as they remarked to Koyama, that Thai Buddhism was nothing but the invention of Satan.

Happily, by no means all missionaries are like that, but there are enough to make a disconcerting presence. Their only hope of success at mission work, short of terrorizing souls, is to be extremely patient in a way that is temperamentally uncongenial to them. Certainly it is possible to work with large groups and in terms of movements rather than individuals; sometimes, as with tribal peoples, it may be unavoidable. However, as one veteran missionary informed me, it takes a very long time. After ten years in a district the missionary will be fluent, and the people will have just about accepted the concept of a creator God which will have been often repeated to them. After fifteen years, when the missionaries may be thinking about leaving, the people will have overcome the etiquette of detachment sufficiently to accept them as part of the scenery and want them to stay. After eighteen to twenty years, when the missionary is resigned or despairing, the people finally absorb the notion of a redeemer God and results begin to show. This must be correct, because in one recent anthropology I read, after putting together my own impressions, I found that the author was disappointed because, after living six years in Thailand, he had not been able to establish one single deep friendship with a Thai. The pace of rural South East Asia remains very slow and unmotivated, and those who want dramatic results would need to go elsewhere.

Alex Smith's *Strategy to Multiply Rural Churches* is influenced by, though less sophisticated than, McGavren's *Understanding Church Growth*.[31] 'Growth', in the sense of rapid multiplication of converts and strategic church planting, is the new American Protestant fetish. Many liberals dislike its evangelical emphasis on outreach at all costs, while many conservatives are suspicious of a possibly 'unspiritual' emphasis on human calculation and techniques which its advocates have tried to cover with a rather apologetic, pedantic emphasis on supposed scriptural precedents. As will be clear from this book, I have no doubt that a good technique and wise and flexible policies can do much for a mission; McGavren's line is a fine antidote to current defeatism or the woolly kind of spirituality which makes waiting for 'guidance' into what is obviously an excuse for total inaction. On the other hand, many of the ideas involved appear to relate better to the semi-Christian Western, African or South American situation than to the non-Christian Asian one, while the wider concept of church also seems questionable.

Smith's view of the Thai missionary situation is introduced by a lengthy, controversial description of the church and its vocation, and it is clear that regardless of the perspectives and experience of history, he will be content with nothing but a restitution of the first-century church, even insisting, 'In each local community, God's will is that the local community be the full expression of his worldwide church in miniature.' Smith realizes the need to supply an alternative society for isolated or uprooted converts, but thinks exclusively of new identity in terms of a super-religious other-worldly church group, compensating for its social unrelatedness by emotional intensity. We are informed that in a parable (not stated, perhaps because it is to twist the sense so much) Jesus gave a clear command to missionaries, 'Occupy till I come', and he admires the eccentric inflexibility of the Japanese soldier who endured twenty-nine years in the Philippines' jungle until he was told the war was over. This indicates the militaristic theology and programme represented by Smith: he praises 'aggressive evangelism', 'blow by blow' treatment of subjects, etc. . . . God is goal-orientated and intends everyone to be 'reached', and to demonstrate his power, churches must be constantly planted, so that apart from worship and fellowship, 'total mobilization' for evangelistic purposes should be the object of church and converts, who must be trained, drilled and tested to make evangelists. Personally, I fail to see how this extreme emphasis on evangelism tallies with St Paul's mention of evangelism as a gift and role for some, or St Peter's milder stipulation that the ordinary Christian should only 'be ready to make a *defence* to anyone who calls you to account for the hope that is in you'. The emphasis further contradicts McGavren's insistence that it is vital not to practise salvation evangelism in indifferent societies or those with high resistance, lest rejection becomes total, or they spoil the dynamic of the message by casual and misinterpreted knowledge. As things are, Thailand is already being flooded with millions of 'pieces of Christian literature' and with radios mostly open to gospel broadcasts. When such outreaches are ill thought out, they have been known to do much harm.

Psychological and cultural problems are swept aside because Smith affirms that the gospel message is the invention of 'our supra-cultural Lord' who, knowing sin was everywhere, knew the message could apply anywhere. Cultural relatedness is reduced to whatever clues idioms or scraps of information one can glean from the culture to prove a point or draw a parallel. God 'prepares elements, incidents and illustrations in each culture as germane seed for comprehending the gospel'. In other words (and this is typical of many missionaries), one does not waste time reading the *Ramayana* or modern Thai novels, watching theatre or films to get the 'feel' of the society, and to comprehend the psychological structure, but hurries through, looking only for a phrase or an anecdote often taken out of context, which can be strained into some holy meaning. If population growth, literacy rate, flora and fauna and such miscellaneous facts and figures could constitute 'knowledge' of a country, Smith, like many missionaries, has it and can convince himself and readers of the fact, but it is not this mere information which is needed.

There is no danger of progressing to greater relatedness than this since the quality of 'stewardship' is defined as 'simplicity with discipline' and a life-style which is not 'extremely aesthetic' (i.e., puritanical, functional, and definitely not Thai style). Furthermore, one would gather that there could be little or no room for religious pictures, images and the like since the Old Testament (especially the Decalogue) stands on an equal footing with the New Testament as a direct revelation of God's will, despite St Paul's view of the law as a schoolmaster and his drift from the Decalogue ('Judge no man according to his use of a sabbath day'), or the historical drift of most churches from the prohibition of images. This Old Testament emphasis nonetheless explains the extreme authoritarianism of Smith's organization of affairs, his circle's harsh treatment of erring members and his surprise at Thai dependence upon the church leader for any and every decision. Christians, he claims, must recognize that God alone holds all rights, title deeds and copyrights to everything in every department of his life. There is, of course, a general Christian obedience to God, but I suggest that the attitude indicated here closes the door on real growth and discrimination, and frustrates the kind of purposive freedom in divine and human relations to which I alluded in Chapter 1, making men a kind of holy robot, if not actually easy prey to religious fanatics and cultists. Quite often 'God wills' can be psychologically interpreted as the 'I will' of the leader into whose power and inspection the whole life and possessions of the follower is delivered.

Rather surprisingly, from what I know of the interdenominational OMF missionaries whom I have met or read of, Alex Smith belongs to this mission rather than the Alliance Church, and traces post-war rural Thai work through his experiences and the mission. I hardly recognize his picture. The story tells how progress was made in central Thailand from work in two main fields, first among lepers, who, already outcast from Thai society, were more willing and able to suffer 'persecution' and perhaps Westernization too, and second, through churches related to mission hospitals, the members frequently drawn from patients and hired staff.

The starting point was when OMF missionaries, expelled from

China, descended upon Thailand so shocked by recent experiences that they expected the second coming any time. They saturated their adopted areas with literature, open-air meetings and house visitations, and kept open house. They also gave English classes, and 'we chat, sing, tell Bible stories, use gospel recordings'. As the story is told, the youth were very interested but then drifted away: if they showed interest, they were opposed by parents; if they were baptized, they did not attend church regularly and with enthusiasm, or left for work and education in other regions (this mobility is a major problem of all Thai missions). By 1955 there was more response from the Chinese than the Thais. Another way of telling the tale, one suspects, is that the curious Thais revelled in all the funny pictures, gadgets, homes, and ways of the missionaries, but soon got bored in the usual style, especially as the missionaries got to know everyone in general, but few, if anyone, in particular. This made them suspect, especially to the older and more conservative villagers. A Miss Harris, who took much trouble over a few students and wrote letters to those who had left the district, was much more successful.

The early setback led to a decision to do what had always been needed: to concentrate on smaller groups at a more personal level and let these spread the Word. Actually, the missionaries felt 'guided' to do this. If they were, they nearly spoilt the new programme by making group life so intense. They kept examining and digging up the roots of each life to see how it was doing, and pressed for aggressive evangelism. From 1955 to 1960, the clinic church at Uthai Thani grew from eight to seventy-five members as lepers received treatment, physical and excessively spiritual, at clinics, and families of the patients were drawn in. In the early 1960s, family interest led to active (aggressive) evangelism towards husbands and wives, as these would bring a whole family unit into the church. In 1962 there were seventy professions of faith, with seven couples, but this was raised to fifteen couples in 1965. In the 'strong growth movement' of 1967 and 1974, a multiplication of clinics and an influential villageman's introduction to the more responsive Lao people in nearby Barnrai brought some long-desired expansion. 1960 to 1967, however, had showed a decline. Leadership, or necessary education for local leadership, was deficient, while poverty favoured the old enemy, mobility. Added to this there was a spate of 'spiritual conflict'. When the buffaloes died and the crops were ruined, and there was legal trouble over rebuilding the church, some could take no more and Satan became active. Attendance dropped, evangelism declined and a few people lived in sin. A flare-up of ungodliness led to severe disciplinary measures.

It is not hard to see what went wrong. Even before trouble struck, the life of the congregations, half of them sick people, the others mostly poor and hardworking peasants, wanting only some relaxation in the evenings, was over-intense. It knew no diversions, no theatre, no jollity, but only the severest regimes of Bible study. People were expected to memorize and comment on the Bible, make open confessions of sins and engage in more or less compulsory extempore prayers, disciplines which would tax and horrify even the average Western Christian, who would never tolerate it. All the time the individuals were being sifted and tested as potential evangelists and examined for their spiritual growth, and they were subjects of Smith's extensive log and statistics. Small wonder there was rebellion. Accustomed to the gentle chidings of the 'mother-like' priest or even his jollity – though not exactly impressed by such behaviour, I think of the monastery yard games of young monks I have seen, or the humorous improvisations which punctuate even the reading of the Great Birth – the people began to feel themselves imprisoned, used by the well-meaning but hard missionaries and their hard God. I dread to think what the severe disciplines might have entailed, considering what has been known sometimes to have occurred in the South Seas and Africa when there was any suggestion of sex. What would it matter whether members had 'domestic problems' or not, or if the wife was frigid or let herself go, giving herself a bloody mouth chewing betel, or if the husband had deserted (which is easy enough in Thailand)? In this closed world there are no extenuating circumstances, no needs or weaknesses: 'We call sin, sin'. I realize that no church can overlook such conduct completely, especially if leaders are involved (which was not the case) or the congregation is incited to such behaviour by some members (again, not the case), but in infant churches and in Asia, a tactical error is involved when an issue is made out of it. Any kind of public loss of face is more or less unacceptable to Asians and may be resented for a lifetime, while harsh Puritanism in infant churches ensures massive defections to sects and cults which, it is hoped, will be more tolerant. That happened in the South Seas in the last century. The Thai Protestant Church, small as it is, has already suffered considerable losses to Mormons and Jehovah's Witnesses, who, significantly enough, make more converts from the Christians than from the ordinary population. There are, of course, other factors than the sexual. Mormonism offers a more total life-style than the holy huddles of the kind I have considered which refuse to acknowledge that some people are just more religious than others and that religious development cannot be forced.

Nevertheless, backsliding followed by the growth period of 1967 to 1974. It was surely not quite so unforeseen and amazing as is suggested. After ten years, as even Smith acknowledged, the surrounding people had grown accustomed to the missionary presence, while the expanding clinic services engendered goodwill. Even if feared, missionaries were trusted, and the basic gospel truths, endlessly reiterated as Chaiwan recommended they should be, had eventually begun to make some impression – enough for the message to be carried with some degree of accuracy beyond Uthai by more mobile members of the community. As to the Lao of nearby villages, it is a sociological commonplace of mission history that the tribal Thai peoples are more responsive, so it is surprising no outreach was actively attempted earlier in this direction. With these people the chief problem would not be apathy, but the *phi*. Lao response to film evangelism was encouraging, but it is scandalizing to learn that this evangelism was conducted in the grounds of a Buddhist temple. Even if a village man had proposed it and the monks accepted it, it was still an act of presumption and tactically wrong; since no Christian would like Buddhists to interrupt their services or use churches as an evangelistic pitch, obviously the missionary will seem beholden to and inferior to the monk in matters of tolerance.

Numbers of families, some of them extended families, in the region, showed interest and were converted, but the *phis* began to be angry at the local response, and according to Smith, even killed off some believers with sickness. One convert, Mrs Siang, whose family was much attached to the *phis*, was suddenly possessed during counselling by a spirit, who mocked Smith and the mission and took two hours to be exorcised.[32] However readers may choose to interpret these and other stories of 'demonic activity', it is certain that some of the rural people are unacceptably and degradingly subject to rule by their *phis* and that terror of them is one of the leading barriers to accepting the gospel and carries much more weight than any loyalty to Buddhism. It is also apparent that unless a whole family is converted together, much trouble can result. In their fear members of the family can be very intolerant, mocking the individual convert, boycotting them or even driving them from the village. In Ban Jan, a Christian wife was severely beaten by her husband for attending meetings, and withdrew when he threatened to murder her (tribal peoples are known to murder wives rather easily in Thailand!). On the whole, opposition was not met by martyrs' determination. In any case, ultimately Asians do not possess much personal ego. In religion *à la* Smith there is no accompanying social gospel, so no satisfactory accommodation to nationalism. Asians will die for the nation or a group cause to which their identity is tied, but religion of this kind gives no grounds for sentiments like that of the hymn, 'Let me carry your cross for Ireland, Lord'. When accused of disloyalty to family or lack of patriotism, the persecuted Asian crumples up and gives up. Besides which, since according to one statistical survey only one in four had been influenced to conversion by the idea of Christ's love, and in another sample, 22.6%, and in another 48% had been frightened into conversion by the Christian hell portrayed in posters or sermons, the quality of the response is perhaps not so surprising.

IV

Everything but the obvious. This might sum up the procedure adopted by Smith and so many missions in Thailand. 'Expansion growth', 'Bridging growth', 'Recycling Lessons', 'Goal Orientation', 'Strengthening Seminars', 'Pilot Projects', 'Lay Pastoral Training', 'Prayer Cells', 'Instruction and Nurture' classes, 'Concentration of Witness', 'Campaign Approach', 'Conversion Dynamics'. What a church, and how unnatural and impersonal it sounds! Smith is against those missions (mainly Catholic) who would like to substitute some species of Christian rites and blessings for *phi* worship and agricultural rituals, or who try in any way to accommodate to local needs and culture.

So many things do not ring true and seem forced. The first time I ever visited Thailand was during water-throwing festival, and as I stood by the Chao Phraya river trying to avoid getting squirted with coloured water from a group of young passers-by, a man, observing my discomfort, asked as though in apology, whether I knew that the day was a holy day and whether I was going to go to the temple to pray. Surprised, I replied that for me the next day was a holy day. It was Easter Day, and then I would go to church to pray. I do not know whether I had completely grasped the man's meaning or whether he grasped mine, but such an encounter in itself would suggest that if one spoke fluent Thai and was looking for opportunities to 'witness', with religion so commonplace and conversation so informal, opportunities would not be lacking. Thais introduce religion into conversation almost as easily as the Irish, while to ask a middle-aged woman about the location of a Buddha or temple, or about Thai painting, seems almost guaranteed to engender an animated response. One thus suspects that if, for example, Christians had set up some alternative to spirit houses outside their homes, or worn unfamiliar medallions in this land where everything is a subject of comment, given Thai curiosity, they could have begun to spread the Word by ordinary conversation and gossip alone. They could then have gradually followed it up with literature or picture books, or invitations to concerts of religious music, for the Thais adore these and love playing the native instruments. In Asia, where there is much feminine curiosity and natural religious or superstitious impulse, 'aggressive evangelism' is irrelevant and offensive because the normal practice is that one searches out the monk or yogi whose 'evangelism' would be simple exhibitionism, an invitation to curiosity.

As in Bali, the artistic talent of even untrained persons can be quite remarkable, so one is left to wonder why sick lepers were not given 'projects' like making illustrations from the Bible or – more ambitiously – painting the church walls with Bible pictures, rather than having their heads stuck in a Bible. Had they felt more involved in this way, they might not have acted so stupidly and absent-mindedly over their Bible lessons. When they did 'backslide', the 'occult' argument, as of Watchman Nee, that the health of the church depends on the attitudes of all its members might have been more stirring and convincing to the Asian group mind, deeply affected as it is by the 'psychic' factor, than appeals to the wrath of God.

This leads to the important point that both the concreteness and 'magical' aspect of local faith have not been adequately considered. Faith declined when the buffaloes died or when members fell ill, and not under the onslaught of intellectual doubts about the Bible. Moreover, it is precisely against these common ills that rural Thais in particular reckon to protect themselves with medallions, merit offerings, tattoos, etc. But material affairs were largely ignored and most visual aids rejected in the name of the laws of God. It was felt to be enough that Western medicine was being used to cure the sick, but this somewhat austere and spiritual approach can be challenged in the context of this society, which mixed the practical and aesthetic so oddly. Would it be so wrong to supply medallions, pendants, etc., if that helped to serve as a concrete reminder? Those conservative Protestants who reject this are obliged to account for the fact that even St Paul is portrayed (Acts 19.12) as having risked distributing blessed handkerchiefs and aprons among the sick whom he was unable to reach personally. If the people are really as terrified of the spirits as I have described, and if by temperament they must visualize and concretize everything, in a certain' type of mind, would not, say, throwing holy water at unholy places or possessed people for protection amount to much the same thing as more abstractly 'surrounding oneself with prayer'? Indeed would not its very reality engender more faith?

If the congregations were widely dispersed and weak on literacy and Bible learning, and there was a serious shortage of adequate leadership, one solution would have been to have given them psalms and litanies full of edifying biblical references to sing and recite (as did the church in early centuries). If some litanies and a minimum of ritual were permitted, even leaders of less than perfect education or spiritual development could be safely left to lead a small congregation in chanting, and the honour of this leadership might promote more responsible behaviour. In any case, the litany is almost ideal for Thai society, accustomed to lengthy and repetitive sutras, like the Japanese, especially as it can be adapted to home use, since devout families reckon to have morning prayers before the family altar. Despite the fact that ancestor worship is not the problem it is among the Chinese, home worship must be taken seriously on several counts. First, because (as I have said) the family shrine is important to the devout; second, because it might help to keep families together in a country where rather thoughtless attitudes to domestic duties, or even casual desertion by a partner, are easy; third, because despite Alex Smith's hopes, a very intense church group life is not a strong probability even for a much more Christian Thailand than at present exists. Even in Ireland, a very religious country for modern Europe, church activity outside Mass is, and always has been, minimal, but counting the rosary at home has been very important, and the church is currently trying to restore it to promote deeper spiritual life amid change. This pattern of little life among church groups is common to all basically introvert cultures, and the ideals of the early church must be seen in the context of the common Mediterranean emphasis on 'solidarity' and 'fraternity', somewhat at the expense of the individual.

Church architecture and decoration are more problematic. There can be no question that they are important because of Thai conservatism and love of cultural homogeneity, and I was impressed how Holy Redeemer Church, the one church in Thailand in authentic national style, is well known by people who know nothing about churches. Certain churches, like the Church of Christ at Sam Yek, or First Church Cheng Mai, or Mater Dei, Bangkok, bear some vague relationship, modernistic or otherwise, to Thai design, but are not nearly so advanced as Holy Redeemer, which is a very welcome change to the gloomy functionalism, inferior Gothic, or colonial flavour of most other churches, even if the imaginative interior has not achieved quite the right synthesis.

Certain problems are very pressing in all such experiments. First, imitation of the Thai religious building by small congregations is hampered by financial considerations; although in poor rural areas one can expect temple interiors to be shabby and plain, strictly speaking the more authentic the building, the smaller or more shuttered the windows are likely to be, and the more the interior needs to be brightened by the almost obsessive yellows and golds of the Thai style: gold lead, gold paint, bronze images, gold cloths, which can be expressive enough even in substitute forms. Although the Thai window of the temple and palace, and to some extent of the home, was made with ventilation for a humid, monsoon climate in mind, in comparison with the houses and open air temples of Bali, it tends to leave the person feeling rather boxed in, separated from nature rather than communicating with it. This feeling, which in traditional design is heightened by the gold and black of lacquer screens and sutra boxes, is duplicated in the modern functional, air-conditioned urban architecture in which one is almost imprisoned from the light and feel of the day. The division is worth noting, however, because it effectively means that those who can only afford a hall do not have to feel that because they cannot afford the exterior, they need not experiment with their interior.

Thai architecture is a mixture of Hindu influenced fantasy held in check by Hinyana rationalism. It used to be less gaudy than it became in the Bangkok era under Chinese influence, and the softer outlines and more sober colours of the traditional temple, as at Wat Phumin, will hold greater appeal for some and appear more appropriate to the total style. It is because Thai architecture is basically adjusted to the medium of wood, and, as I have said, holds together two possibly incongruous tendencies, that the traditional art has proved so difficult to translate into viable modern forms, or even to set beside other forms. The confusion of the summer palace complex at Bang Pa-In anticipated the more vulgar confusions of modern Bangkok. The difference between the painting, with its fantasy, and the sculpture, which is almost Greek, is also very wide and makes it difficult even for modern revivalists of Thai style to grasp Thai art in its totality. As a result, the problems for imaginative church design are multiplied, and considerable assimilation to the original temple form seems essential if indigenization in this art is to be attempted at all. On the other hand, though Holy Redeemer Church has a highly conservative design, I dislike the mere omission of all conventional pattern and ornament from the exterior, i.e. doors and gables. A Christian substitute could surely be discovered. Controversially the cross has been more or less omitted from both exterior and interior in concession to the Thai aversion, born of familiarity with images of serenity, to crucifixes and symbols of torture. Instead, the interior has a huge image of Christ the King in blessing, which is impressive in itself, but out of harmony, as is also the continuous stone frieze, with the rest of the Thai design of the altars and chapel. The Christ image is of a kind of rusted bronze instead of the necessary shining gold or bronze, and is inappropriately expressionistic.

Aesthetically speaking, the cross has no natural place within any Asian art unless it is set within a circle or mandala, because of the universal sense of rhythm and lack of angularity in Asian art. Religiously speaking, the absence of the cross or crucifix probably does not matter provided that the Christ image, as an image of completion, has the imprint of the nails in the hands, symbolizing that completion was achieved through sacrifice and within the material realm. It has to be borne in mind that the earliest Christian images of Christ were not of the crucified but of the Good Shepherd; the symbol of the cross is of late derivation. Incidentally, the bright colours and mosaics of the Ravenna basilicas which contain this stylized shepherd image could serve as some kind of guide to decorating the Thai church, where there is a demand for bright colours. A Thai church would need to be empty, that is to say a hall (though preferably pillared to relieve the monotony, if the hall were particularly large); the focus of interest would be a large Christ image behind a portable and ornate wooden altar at one end. The walls should be patterned or hung with pictures rather than left plain, and if possible, the walls, at any rate of the largest churches, should be painted with religious murals preferably of parables or prophetic visions rather than realistic or historical scenes which are stylistically more problematic. Given the current revival of interest in Thai temple and traditional painting and the new artists it is producing, the matter should be taken fairly seriously.

So far I have said nothing about music because in this, at least, certain churches, especially in the north, have been served with native composed hymns arranged for Thai 'orchestras'. However, this was due more to insistent Thai conservatism and the conversion of a Thai actor who was skilled in music and composed many hymns which proved popular, than to any prompting by missionaries. It is far from being a general phenomenon. As to further acculturization, Smith speaks of the use of 'skits' (sic!) on biblical themes in Thai style. (Whatever that means, I have not read or heard of it elsewhere.) Some theatrical adaptation of tractable biblical material (like Esther, Daniel) is probably desirable, and ought not to be excessively difficult to manage, since most children have been drilled in Thai dancing at school. In Indonesia, the Catholic church has quite successfully annexed the art of puppet shadow theatre (which also exists in Thailand) in preference to the dance drama, apparently because of the great technical skill required for classical dance forms. However, whereas Indonesian dance is rather difficult to master (a Balinese dancer who kindly tried to demonstrate some basic movements to me could not get me through the first arm moves), Thai dance is more Neptunian; the popular, simplified forms call for only a certain facility with the swimming muscles which most Thais possess, being swimmers from an early age.

As Smith's comprehensive statistics and commentary omitted an explanation of the low membership recorded of those between twenty and thirty, it perhaps falls to the layman rather than the professional religionist once again to fill in an anthropological gap and conclude with a footnote on personal morality. This is harder to assess than in the case of Japan, since in contrast there is a greater gap between theory, which is very idealistic, and practice. Modern Thai novels, which mostly have a limited circulation and are not always very socially representative tend, like the novels of Dokmai Sod,[33] to be highly moralistic, even prudish, and while there is something of a trade in blue films in Bangkok, Western films like *Emmanuelle*, which was filmed in Bangkok and at Doi Lithanon National Park, are completely banned.

The Thais are neither the most nor the least sensual peoples of Asia, though as a fairly handsome race with an air of tropical langour, they may give the impression of sensuality. Traces of a stylized eroticism in the painting and the banter of the unpuritanical *likay* theatre might enhance the impression, but appearances must not deceive. Sensuality, such as has periodically troubled Indian and Japanese society, is less the problem than the disposition, encouraged by Buddhism, to avoid deep involvement and to distrust women and love as karmically bad. The result is that while the sexual morals are in theory practically identical with those of Christianity, the basis for maintaining respect or fidelity is subtlely undermined. Desertion, especially of wives by husbands, is very common. At Thailand Theological Seminary in Chiengmai, I was told that at the attached Piyat College, something approaching 90% of the pupils had no fathers by adolescence, when they most needed them, because of desertion. They had been raised by mothers without any notable legal or financial redress against their situation; it was also felt that most of the psychological problems of young Thais were due to this type of irregular upbringing.

The Thais seem to 'drift' into sexual trouble, as they do into debt (they are great gamblers) and much else. In some respects they are positively careless of themselves. The notably high numbers of prostitutes (some sensationalizing reports claim as high as one in ten persons in Bangkok) is commonly attributed to the problems of deserted rural wives. Many unemployed girls, it seems, take to prostitution nearly as easily as men in the same situation drift into the monasteries, where in recent times some have been disgracing the *sangha* with their drinking and womanizing. But it is not only a question of the path of least resistance where prostitution and other sexual relations are concerned. Loneliness is another factor and is perhaps the consequence of an underlying hedonism in this *sanuk* society where so often nothing too onerous is performed even for friends. Whereas, however, by tradition there was in Thailand's close-knit communities a certain unity in hedonism which determined that a miserable neighbour was best helped before he infected everyone with his gloom, today, this has often given rise to crass indifference among the uprooted and young population. Moreover, frightened as the Thais are (and with some reason) of burglary and violent crime by night, they dread solitude, marvel at foreigners who travel or live alone, and hence have become much less particular about how or with whom they drift into personal relations.

In recent years, the influence on Thai politics of the military, with their ultra-realistic attitude towards prostitution and morals generally, especially under Japanese and US influence, has changed urban morality somewhat, making for more nights out on the town, at least by businessmen. Otherwise, for women and the rural population, morals are more strict.[34] By general consent, the Thai woman is an enigma. In many respects Buddhism despises women, but the same society has always respected the mother, and as in Japan, has accorded women more power than superficial appearances might suggest. Thus, it has been frequent for Thai fathers to bequeath cash to the sons, but land or stock to the daughters – who thus enjoyed opportunities for business – on the basis that the latter were less footloose and fun-loving than the boys. Many Thai wives, like Japanese wives, also look after the cash and thus regulate the husband's pleasures somewhat. Customs vary, of course, between region, class, and ethnic group, and the variety is registered in the women, who can be perfect models of charm and elegance, or assume, especially in the lower classes, the rather pouting manners of a despised race, though perhaps nowhere have so many nodding violets gained so much authority in major businesses without the aid or style of women's liberation.

Some of the confusion in the female image rubs off on the children, particularly the male who, as one has heard from Thais, tends to look down on women as 'weak' or 'unreliable', and uses and abuses them, or else imitates them in a whole variety of ways, from the monks and leaders who are supposed to 'mother' the people and the *khon* actors who play women's roles to perfection to the large minority of transvestites and homosexuals. In many respects, inversion in Thailand, as in Indonesia, has been a response to traditional sex segregation, the weak or absent father model and the sometimes too pure or dominating image of the mother. This is perhaps why missionary condemnation of inversion as decadence can be greeted with such incredulity; indeed, within South East Asia no Islamic or Christian influence has occasioned the people to regard the subject as an appropriate one for moralizing,[35] probably because there has never been a question of public nuisance; the violence and open immodesty of Sodom finds no echo within the social history. Inversion must simply be seen in the context of the social tendency to guard female virtue. An exaggerated type of Christian emphasis on female purity has sometimes produced similar effects in European countries like Portugal.

Inversion and Buddhist prejudices aside, it does seem that Thai culture feminizes almost everything it touches (apart from the style of some of the military). The degree to which it does so is enough to arouse the curiosity, and I am almost certain that in the future, the feminine quality of the race will be partly explained by the Thai Buddhist custom which causes a pregnant women to purify herself and her offspring by abstaining from highly flavoured foods during pregnancy. As tests in Canada and France are now proving that women who desire a male child should adopt a savoury diet and avoid a sugary one, it is possible the Thais have almost over-feminized themselves. The manifestly greater energy, and even virility, of the military is certainly due to the obligation upon them to eat unpolished rice as opposed to the unsatisfactory polished fare of the majority of this major rice-producing country.

Regardless of possible medical perspectives, missions currently operative in Thailand represent rather muscular Jewish and Roman virtues within a decidedly 'feminine' culture which raises certain questions of ethical policy and priorities. It is plain from Smith that OMF policy at any rate, is, to found a strictly Puritan-revivalist community, a kind of austerely moral culture within a society which does not possess any kind of prior basis for so doing, like, for instance, the Confucian-influenced Chinese communities. Thailand is actually so far removed from the Puritan spirit that even to describe a person as 'serious' is almost insulting, because to be kind and polite requires a touch of lightness; like much of South East Asia, Thailand's culture is not very analytical or scientific, but aesthetic and experiential, a fact exaggerated by the poor literacy rate. Within such cultures as that of Italy, morality is historically a matter of learning and experience, and as with Benvenuto Cellini, a less than perfect moral conduct and culture may still be accompanied by a deep and even perceptive spirituality; I suspect that the reason is that wherever social custom is very fixed, as in Thailand, or the weight of political authority particularly strong, sexual adventure becomes an important mode of self-affirmation and initiative, whereas virtue may be too close to a general timidity to be worth much to God or man.

Bearing this in mind, it would seem that the church has two leading models for development. Either, like Smith, it can demand the constant correction and perfection of all members and continually sift out the chaff to have that perfect purity without which those with revivalist beliefs maintain no blessings or extension can be expected, or else take a somewhat more Catholic model and work to have a nucleus of devout persons, while carrying a lot of 'passengers' and tolerating weaker souls within an outer circle. Not only can excessive perfectionism be turned against the weak till they become too discouraged to be questioned theologically, but within an exotic culture in which missionaries are frequently making errors of communication, even well-justified criticism may finish with negative results, like those which roused the Anti-Christian movement in China.

There ought perhaps to be a third possibility more closely related to Thai custom, with a 'monastic' practice which contrasted with ordinary lay observance, the 'monasticism', like the Thai variety, being of the open kind, not involving irrevocable vows or excluding the layman from adolescent and/or periodic involvement. There would be several advantages to such a system. (*a*) If associated with baptism or confirmation (as youthful retreat often is with the coming of age in Thailand), it would be a useful substitute impressing the importance of the ceremony more clearly on the mind, especially if, as at the adolescent novitiate, there were pleasant, *sanuk* associations, some travel and celebration and family merriment, rather than exclusively solemn and holy performances. (*b*) The type of social customs and obligations which do not tend to make for sabbath orientation in Thailand, as in Asia generally, could be partly replaced by retreat. (*c*) Organization of this kind gives some scope to the Thai 'moodiness', which can no more be expected to produce the completely regular spiritual response than any other. It is true that there has always been a touch of mediaeval man in the Thais, a sort of Lent carnival syndrome which has him making merit for three months in a monastery, only to return gratefully to the world to get drunk, and this is not to be encouraged. On the other hand, it is clear that the native temperament is volatile by any Asian standards, and thus will always demand a pattern of alternating intensity and relaxation which the sober Anglo-Saxon evangelicalism that holds such sway in the missionary churches does not tend to appreciate. A few lapses of personal morality may need to be tolerated in members, especially when too wealthy Westerners, pouring into Thailand, commit much greater immoralities and many Western churches, rightly or not, do baptize, marry and bury alcoholics, the divorced and others, while church dignitaries are quite able to tolerate the less-than-perfect morals of Christian notables like the Kennedys. In this situation, the Puritan missionary is obviously inviting the resentful response, 'Go and preach to your own people', or worse still, stands to create the impression that the native is despised and is never quite good enough for the perfect white missionary. Furthermore, it is unreasonable to be too strict in the context of an unofficially polygamous society in which the laws do not accept adultery by the husband as a ground for divorce.

The object is not to preach the permissiveness of some Californian churches, nor am I suggesting that Thailand raises grave problems of personal morality, like those of Japan, or classically, Christian Jamaica.[36] However, the country is not Puritanical or in any way extremist, and is never likely to become so. Church history is consistent in certain lessons, and one is that the personal morality of Christianized peoples is modified but never completely altered; the same patterns of behaviour, the expression of a temperamental and physical type remain. Thus, Italy has remained sensual despite St Paul and Catholic marriage regulations, and Tahiti is still notorious, despite the religious fervour of the majority of its people and the efforts of singularly misguided Victorian missionaries to punish sexual misdemeanours.

Where radical changes seem to have occurred, as in the behavioural patterns of the once-permissive and semi-matriarchal Celtic realms, a Puritanism may exist, but if this change has not been accompanied by an in-depth examination of the psychology concerned, it will be shifting the locus of the problem, so that it emerges in alcoholism or violence. The same process has occurred in Africa, where an over-zealous missionary Puritanism, anxious to abolish polygamy and African customs, left central Africa with an unprecedented problem of prostitution, when thousands of dismissed wives were left without a home. Abuses of this kind are not likely to overtake missions in Thailand, but given the good many missionaries really do, it would be tragic if no lessons were to be learned from the weaker aspects of missions.

At this stage in history, Thailand and missions within it are threatened by the surrounding political situation. In the circumstances, it is not the most opportune moment to train often reluctant converts to the pinnacle of evangelical perfection before they are allowed to influence their society more widely or the churches speak of their faith in a wider framework. One hesitates to speak of crises, since American missions have exhausted the term within an Asia not given to dramatic statement, but slowly and relentlessly an internal crisis in building up within Thailand, where it is popularly registered in the increase in crime and violence, though there are other factors, like the attitudes of youth and students, competition, materialism. The old fatalistic order is breaking up and can never be completely restored, even among the rural peoples who have now been introduced to television. If one were to speak from a purely political standpoint, ignoring all religious claims and imperatives, one might say that Thailand needs some Christianity, if only to help absorb the shock of change and to provide an alternative current of thought, a loyalist opposition, before serious internal disaffection arises. There is no doubt that so far Buddhism has been a positive unifying factor, but Hinyana can only embrace a very narrow range of thought and social institutions. The complacent assumption that the Buddha who helped in the past must do so in the future may meet an unexpected reversal. There is nothing in the local situation to support great optimism, and there is always a first time for everything.

6
The Indian Setting

To an unusual extent, the Thai setting seemed to question the value of missions. On the one hand missions undoubtedly have a poor capacity to relate, but on the other hand, there is a degree of lethargy among the people themselves, perhaps to be described in terms of the 'mudswamp' imagery which the novelist Shusako Endo directed against Japan,[1] the people of the 'mudswamp' being those who could distinguish every flame and avoid every challenge. In such a setting, the failure of missionaries may be not only cultural but also tactical, because they persist within societies when their talents might be of more service to people elsewhere. In this chapter I shall try to examine the meaning and purpose of missions today and their ideological relation to other faiths, and to review the sociological conditions of mission growth. First, however, we need to consider the situation in an Indian setting alongside that in other Asian settings. This forms a natural introduction to the topic of mission exclusiveness, which is so radically changed by the Hindu inclusiveness.

If I had not started with 'humanistic' China, I would have begun with 'metaphysical' India, because it is obviously the major source of the whole mysticism of withdrawal and the doctrine of nothingness so fundamental to Asian religions and so intimately related to the Asian introvert and feminine sensibility. However, since I am ending with India, it seems more appropriate to broach the subject by calling attention to the hidden Western face of India which Chaudhuri so stressed throughout his *Continent of Circe*.[2] Though they are not completely typical of Hinduism, it would certainly seem unlikely that the Divine Light Mission and the Hare Krishna movement would have enjoyed the success they did in the West if there were not points of contact. To begin with, Hinduism, in contrast to the more or less self-contained culture of China and its satellites, derived its primitive *form* from the West, from the Aryans, however much native belief, yoga and ritual overtook it. Some early Vedic hymns are Pindaric or Druidic and scarcely Indian; epics like *Ramayana* and *Mahabharata* are more Indian, but still 'Homeric', and recall the wars and aristocratic (or caste) values of the early Aryans. Hinduism thus retains worldly, priestly and fundamentalist currents (the latter represented by the 'back of the Vedas' of the Arya Samaj movement) and a sense of ego and a concern with form which the Buddhist and yogic reactions would tend to dispense with. India is thus not completely foreign or 'inscrutable' to the Occidental, nor the West to the Indian.

To the Western enquirer, Hinduism, especially that branch of it which teaches a doctrine of evolution as opposed to a theory of cycles, is much more positive, even scientific, than the Buddhism which has sometimes appealed to those in the West who desire a rationalist spirituality, or cannot abide the 'idolatry' of Hinduism. Hindu religion permits larger scope to the individual than its doctrinal statements might suggest: a fraction of the original self lasts within God for ever, and the reincarnational status that one receives, the mantras, yoga, gods and scriptures that one chooses, are all adjusted to individual need. There is also a certain glamorizing of failure and the drop-out psychology (in the Vishnaite cult, as opposed to the Shivaite, poverty and set-backs are almost a proof of divine favour and testing), and this appeals to those who are the accidents or critics of the American rat-race and materialism, which, insufficiently criticized by the churches, is a distant result of the Puritan work ethic. Hinduism also tolerates much religious dualism and devotional faith (*bhakti*), despite the monist assumptions of its classical Vedantist philosophy. Western man can relate to all this.

In effect, some of the *bhakti* religion, and especially the poetical theism and Shiva worship of the Tamil regions, border on heresy or misunderstanding of Christian doctrine.[3] This is especially true of the philosophy of Madhva. These heresies made strides in the eighth century and afterwards in the southern region of India in which the Church of St Thomas had flourished, and at a time when it was beginning to fall into decline. The 'good' and loving side of Shiva, telling believers not to fear and forgiving their sins, succeeds to the original devil side of the destroyer god (though it does not cancel that out), and is curiously Christian. The same is true of Madhva's restoration of the Aryan wind God, Vayu, to act as a kind of Holy Spirit to his theology. The legend of Krishna, which is extremely composite and evolved over many centuries, has plainly absorbed Christian and other philosophically serious elements into what was originally a body of sunny pastoral tales which surrounded a Pan-like fertility figure.

Christianity is not 'new' to India as it is to, say, China; the trouble is rather that it has existed there in hidden or misunderstood forms, or in Islamic interpretation. It is doubly misunderstood, since in so far as there can ever be said to be an orthodox Hindu tradition, a classical statement of belief, it lies with the Upanishads and the Vedantic philosophy which includes to monism (like that of Shamkara), and not the Samkhya philosophy of early Hinduism, the *bhakti* tradition and the philosophy of Ramanuja, which are more dualistic. These traditions, though popular and widespread, are less acceptable to the intelligentsia, who in any case realize that they represent compromises with Hindu monism rather than pure denials of it. Moreover, in any classical view, there are three aims in life, *kama* (love and pleasure), *artha* (power, success) and *dharma* (virtue, legal and moral order); the way of the sage lies in the transcendence of all these aims to the realization of divinity throughout everything. Because of this, Christian love of God and divine love for man, or Pauline attempts to achieve righteousness in relation to God, would be considered secondary, inferior concerns, and though most Indians would be too polite to say so, the Christian concept of making peace with God vaguely resembles getting right with the goddess Kali by animal sacrifice if one cannot stand the vegetarian discipline. Inferior people get right with God, superior people realize him or it within themselves, and the integral, almost biological nature of Christian salvation, which requires both a psychological *and* a physical resolution, is not appreciated, if indeed it has ever been adequately represented.

Of course, the seeming irrelevance to Hinduism of sin and emotional attitudes is another feature which appeals to the antinomianism of modern Americans. The irrelevance is, however, more apparent than real, as partisans of both modern antinomianism and missionary fundamentalism need to realize. Leaving aside misdeeds in the supposed determination of karmic status, ignorance and sin are presupposed in the theory both of the present inferior age, the Kali-yuga, fourth in the moral declension from the golden

Devapara-yuga, and in the theory of moral evolution in Neo-Ve-
dantism. What India has tended to do – and this is very Asian –
is to perceive sin in the Christian and Western sense, in communal
and social rather than highly personal terms. Naturally, the individual has his experience of sin, but it is the generalized one of the
introvert and relates less than in the West to the infraction of a
particular law. Traditional Indian law, like the Code of Manu, and
caste laws were often of such an arbitrary taboo nature that it
permanently discredited law in the eyes of intellectuals. The Pauline aim and situation with its precise reference is unthinkable, but
guilt may be experienced over an inability to fulfil self-imposed
standards, or remorse may be suffered at the consequences of
wrong attitudes. One can regularly hear Hindus say things like, 'I
shall never forgive myself for not being kinder to my late sister
when she was ill.' 'I can never forget how I was so selfish that I
refused to help my neighbour when he was in trouble.' Sin, rather
than sins, is the problem, and conservative missionaries probably
need to reflect on the psychological difference between the treatment of the theme by St Paul and by St John in I John, before they
despair of relating or accuse Hinduism of having no awareness of
sin. I would question the theses of some Indian theologians and
missionaries that the moral must have supremacy over the metaphysical in Indian Christianity. Equality would seem sufficient and
more natural in the circumstances.

The real problem for the scholar and missionary is to decide just
what Hindu religion *is* and what is the most fitting way to approach
it. Should it be approached philosophically, anthropologically,
psychologically? For example, an apologist for neo-Hinduism may
inform us that the Hindu creation myths and the vast scale of their
years, their millions and billions, are proof that the yogis knew the
facts of science before the time, knew better than Moses and his
seven days. Another will inform us that the myths are precisely
myths, that their time-scale is not literal, but a technique of exaggeration devised by yogis to boggle the mind in order to arouse
revulsion at the thought of reincarnation. And so on. The opinions
and variations on every subject and sect appear as endless as
the Hindu beyond itself, and the outsider, even the Hindu, can find
himself battling Proteus or the many-headed Hydra in search of
truth:' Not this, not that, nor both, nor neither.'

It is easy and tempting, at least for the Westerner, to think of
Hinduism simply as polytheism in the Indian style. In reality,
'Hinduism', like 'Christianity', covers differences as large as those

between Catholic and Quaker, to which the ecumenists, and the Neo-Vedantists like Vivekananda and Aldous Huxley, give the appearance of a greater unity than is the case. There is the social and ritual tradition which derives from the Aryans and the Vedas, the mystical tradition of the forest ascetics, the first gurus, who reacted early against the priests and composed the Upanishads. There are the six systems of salvation, or six philosophical systems, leading to enlightenment through the intellect; the most important of these are the Sankhya, Yoga and the Vedanta, the last of which arises from commentaries upon the Upanishads. Shivaism and the cult of the Great Mother, which coloured mediaeval faith and flourished in the Tamil and Bengal regions respectively, are survivals from the earliest pre-Aryan culture. Vishnu, less of a fertility god than Shiva, emerged as a universal god around the beginning of the Christian era, assimilating the native boar cult and Varuna, the Aryan god of justice, and was worshipped more in central and northern India. Brahman derived from Prajapati, 'Lord of Beings', an archetypal *anthropos* figure, and was more a philosophical concept than an object of worship. Brahman, Shiva and Vishnu, though often portrayed as a Trinity in scholarship and occasionally in art, were never worshipped as such; the connection derives from Aryan worship of trinities. Brahman was little worshipped; Vishnaites and Shivaites each claimed supremacy for their own god, and displayed serious ideological and ethical differences.

Others trust in local deities, saints or gurus, to lead them towards salvation. Undoubtedly yoga and guruism are the most authentically Indian. The philosophy, social ideas and art forms owe a good deal to the West, to Persia and Greece, which contributed an impetus towards formalism in relation to the jungle-like profusion. Yet there is a kind of unity between even the myth and the more sophisticated philosophy, an *attitude* which makes Hinduism what it is.

The jungle of Hindu myth is distinctive, and contrasts with the patterns of good rewarded and evil punished which Confucian and Buddhist editors stamped upon most popular legends or China and Thailand, or the sense of what is aesthetically and socially fitting, which colours the legends of Jàpan. Hindu myths (as distinguished from the more rational epics) mainly treat of the wars of gods and demons who, playing virtual football with the universe, are born and die, expand and contract, divide and coalesce, become human and animal to achieve their end. Little distinguishes the two sides morally (though the incarnations of Vishnu demonstrate a certain concern with order and morality), and reward and punishment has little rhyme or reason. Thus yogis may fast millions of years to exact one boon from Brahman, while Putana, the child devourer, is translated straight to heaven for offering her breast to the baby Krishna whom she had intended to devour after failing to recognize him. In her introduction to *Hindu Myths*, Wendy Doniger O'Flaherty maintains that all the Indian myths are different yet all alike;[4] they celebrate a belief in the boundless variety of the universe and affirm that everything happens simultaneously and anything is possible. The universe is closed, a world-egg of energies, constantly re-arranged in the most unlikely forms, a process in which even the gods are scarcely immortal or personal, but differentiated from man only as symbols through which a unity of the self with the self and with the whole is glimpsed. Psychologically, everything is an eternal alternation or conflict between Eros and Thanatos, desire for the flame of fire, creation of order out of chaos, and desire for dissolution or reabsorbtion into the ocean, the world of womb. If this description is valid and may be considered fundamental (beyond incidental, cultural influence, such as the war of gods and demons as a reflection of Aryan native struggles, the ebb and flow of life as a mere reflection of the yogic breathing), then the myth ties in thoroughly with the subjectivism of the philosophy.

A good deal of Hindu philosophy, from the Upanishads onwards, is taken up with disproving the reality of the ego on the basis that forgetfulness of self in sleep, intellectual and physical activity, indicates that there is no such entity. Here echoes of the Shamanistic denial, or rather *annihilation*, of the self (the gods tear the Shaman to a nothing) is combined with the Asian introvert obsession with the unconscious at the expense of the conscious. If one cannot see or feel something as a fact *all the time*, then it cannot truly exist; it is only a mode of consciousness, the only existent. Nothing, not even God, can strictly be an object of faith; an entity is not abstractly real, nor can it be a real item certified by God's perception of it, as in Bishop Berkeley's immaterialism, where the park does not cease to exist when we stop looking at it, because God is still looking at it. Read in conjunction with Hindu philosophy, Berkeley's Christian immaterialism brings into relief the underlying 'prejudice' of Hindu thought, which is that God and man are so ultimately identical that God cannot be an Other who takes a pure initiative, springs a surprise or does a new thing. The only surprises God springs lie in the undiscovered region of the mind's capacity for symbolic formation. Brahman may 'play' at creation, but does not really have a creative purpose towards man or world, an attitude which arguably betrays the foundation of the thought in a type of psychological regression. For the devotee, it is enough to realize that God is 'there'; to realize that one exists in God is itself conversion and favour. The purest expression of this Vedantic[5] thinking would be Shamkara's monist philosophy, most famous for its doctrine of the Maya, the illusion, which constitutes the world. In this philosophy everything is God, who is realized from an entirely subjective view. Ultimately tables and chairs, heaven and hell, exist for the subject who thinks that they exist. The reality accorded to the world is relative, and practical. So long as there are finite individuals, we are obliged to treat the world as real, one in which it can be said that the Creator God (Ishwara), the mode of infinite Brahman, is knowing an object as real. But from Brahman's standpoint the world is neither Being nor Non-Being nor both, nor neither; everything is identical with him, though not his infinity. From the human standpoint this means that every impression and affirmation is nothing but a point of view, and religion is realization of a centre, of being itself.

Psychologically, like the myths, this can be regarded as the purest elaboration of consciousness acknowledging the unconscious, and simply regarding all the beauty and ugliness, good and bad, of what Christianity might term the images of the unregenerate unconsciousness or collective unconscious as the truth. There is really no answer to this extreme subjectivism. The only possible reaction is a large degree of acceptance, playing the game and trapping the subject within it, arguing from the subjective position and revealing its inadequacies rather than denying it entirely, because of course it is not completely wrong. Notwithstanding, the possibilities for 'madness' are extensive, as can be seen from even the idolized Ramakrishna, who could be sent into trances of God-realization by almost any person or object. As he wrote:

> Who cares for bread and clothes? Millions come and go every minute. Who cares?. . . (Like all gurus, Ramakrishna did not lack life's necessities). . . . Go beyond law, let the universe vanish and stand alone. I am Existence-Absolute, Knowledge-Absolute, Bliss-Absolute, I am He, I am He.[6]

Then there was his disciple, Vivekananda:

> All the thieves and murderers, all the unjust . . . the wickedest, the devils, all are my Christ! I owe worship to the God Christ

and the demon Christ . . . She my Saviour whose street-walking is the cause of the chastity of other women.[7]

Clearly, there is a vast difference between claiming that the world exists through God, or is in some sense his 'body', and declaring that it is identical with God.

Not all Hindu philosophy is so extreme, nor are its effects so unfortunate. The determination to perceive God anywhere can give Hindus a kind of God-intoxication which Christians too often lack. Sheila Cassidy, searching for the cross in the cracks or beams of prison walls and doors in the Chile where she struggled for human rights,[8] is a 'natural' Hindu, but she is as exceptional within Christianity as her commitment to a truth of both inner and outer value is exceptional among Hindus, for whom *darsana* (inner vision) has been taken to excess. The Hindu subjectivism (or idealism, philosophically speaking) is of the most radical kind. Its concept of God and humanity depends ultimately upon a limited psychological empiricism (or even a psychological fixation) which leaves no room for individualism or revelation in a Christian sense; free will, as Ramakrishna logically asserted, is itself an illusion: 'One enjoys freedom when one realizes that God is sole actor. Trouble comes of the notion, "I am a free agent".' Thus, philosopher and *bhakti* alike end in a total dependence upon deity and archetype, there is little scope or need to correlate the philosophy with reality and the development of life and society which effectively results from the actions of free individuals. It is true that Sri Aurobindo and Neo-Hindu apologists would seek to correlate the faith with science and evolution, but intrinsically, when they turn outwards, their system is deterministic and group-related as it must be, the product of a 'gnostic super race' and social conditioning. Hinduism appears to demand that Christianity should deal with a narrower field of reality than that whose existence it recognizes, and to redeem less than it believes is possible, to be satisfied with 'realization' and 'adjustment', as opposed to creative change.

This was apparent right from the first major ideological reaction to Christianity, which derives from Ram Mohan Roy, founder of the Brahmo Samaj theistic reform movement. Roy criticized precisely the concept of divine revelation and intervention; also atonement, by which the scheme of salvation acquires concrete, physical dimensions, pointing to a redemption of world and matter and not just the mind. Brahmo Samaj, which, under Protestant influence, sought to abolish Hindu 'idolatry' for theism and which reverenced

Christ as the supreme teacher of good precepts, initiated a standard Indian view of Christ, heard again in Gandhi, for whom Christ was detached from all religious and historical associations to emerge as the teacher of peace. Brahmo's own attacks upon conventional Hindu worship prompted the Neo-Vedantic reaction, which justified a variety of devotions provided that they pointed to the largely-forgotten realization of the divine oneness of traditional philosophy. The prophets of this reaction, Ramakrishna and Vivekananda, sought to extend this inclusiveness to world religions, which were portrayed as essentially an awakening to the light of 'God' within, but Neo-Hinduism was only really popularized and related to modern philosophical and spiritual trends by the philosopher-statesman Sarvapelli Radhakrishnan. Radhakrishnan, however, deeply influenced by Christianity and strongly opposed to its doctrinal claims, gave a new dimension to Neo-Hinduism as he attempted to include something of Christian dynamism and scientific evolution within a complete reinterpretation of Shamkara for the modern world. He spoke of religion supporting diversity and realization of the ideal possibilities of life and insisted on the integral nature of religion, its involvement of the whole person. The synthesis, however, is achieved by inverting the principles of the essentially closed system of Hindu philosophy. Whereas formerly mind and matter were over-active and in need of stilling to achieve harmony with the divine centre, activity is now more acceptable since Brahman is described as the all-active principle, a complex of processes *eternally* bringing forth the new, while persons and things are real as functions of Brahman, differentiated by the structure of the functioning. Under this new system God can do practically anything, but never have *one* specific purpose or be involved in a single process of becoming, if one can even speak in such terms, since creation was produced out of a surfeit of joy only (the refined version of the 'play' theory). Hence it is man rather than God who has the purpose, which is realization of the organic unity of the whole and the conscious change or evolution which is actually imperative because God, who is too absolute to be revealed, *must* include and 'save' everything. The human realization of these truths is through 'intuition', of which Radhakrishnan makes much, since without it no intellection or activity is possible. This means that behind the humanism and individualism, the supremacy of the unconscious is restated, to the ultimate detriment of values.

In Hinduism, one must possess either a consciousness or an

unconscious; God must be active or inactive, and man likewise, but never both.[9] There is a special irony in the Hindu rejection of a Christian 'exclusiveness', since the entire Hindu response to life is based on an exclusivist thought process which quite naturally expressed itself in concrete terms in the exclusive caste system.

Most Christian apologetics and efforts at indigenized theology have been in reaction to Radhakrishnan's treatment of Hinduism in the light of Shamkara's monism and his instrumental theory of world religions ('all creeds have only an instrumental value'). This has not always been a happy result, as works like Mark Sunder Rao's *Ananyatva* might suggest.[10] Preferring to speak of 'non-otherness' in divine-human relations, as opposed to non-duality, he acknowledges Christ's humanity and human individualism, but less as something of intrinsic value than as an eternal aspect of reality, an experience to be lived through and surrendered in *bhakti*-like dependence upon the divine infinity. Life and religion thus loses its personal force to become mainly 'societary' in nature. Surjit Singh's *Preface to Personality* is more satisfactory.[11] This criticizes the inconsistencies in Radhakrishnan's acceptance of individualism and a monism which does away with values; aiming for a better synthesis, it portrays Christ's sacrifice as the denial only of an absolute value placed on individualism within an organically united world. The danger in these interpretations of limiting a Christian view of personality is as great as the limiting of Christ's divinity in Kalagora Subba Rao's portrayal of Jesus as the supreme guru, or Chakkarai's as supreme *avatar*. Among theologians, perhaps only V. P. Chenchiah, in his *Rethinking Christianity in India*, transcended polemics and mere adjustment to get to the heart of the matter by emphasizing that Christianity is about 'new creation', an increase of the Spirit, and is as much biological as psychological, integrally true.[12] Even though his description of Christ's coming in terms of *shakti*, or 'new cosmic energy', was controversial, he was on the right track. The Indian church, however, is still trying to find its path.

II

By 1975 there were fourteen million Christians in India, 2.6% of the population, and around three million of these have apparently been added to the church since 1960, since when, after centuries of dormancy and poor response to missions, it has begun to show significant signs of growth. The Hindu population dropped during the same period by one million. 55% of Christians are Catholic, 10% Orthodox and 35% Protestant, a large proportion of these belonging to the ecumenical churches of South and North India. Most Christians are still concentrated in the south, where by the fourth century AD there was a flourishing church allegedly and quite possibly founded by the apostle Thomas. By the fifteenth century there were 200,000 Christians of Nestorian allegiance. These were discovered by the Portuguese, who forced Catholicism where they could, causing a reaction in which many appealed to the Patriarch of Antioch to secure full communion with Orthodoxy. This Thomas church subsequently underwent a variety of transformations and splits under Anglican, Orthodox and Evangelical influence. With the decline of missions (only Commonwealth missionaries are now admitted to India, and only for essential jobs), it has finally developed the mission consciousness it so remarkably lacked.

Indigenization as such has never been a problem with Indian Christianity; the question has been what to indigenize. It is notorious that all ideas, customs and faiths assume different forms and are assimilated to mother India. Even the English dress suit was accorded an Indian design as soon as it appeared in India. The more obvious problems of Westernization, the conflicts of old and new which have been set in motion elsewhere by religious and scientific missions, have not rent 'eternal' India, and if the contemporary Protestant church, especially in North India, has such an incongruously Western face, that is only because for so long it was the property of Western people and outcasts who, like the untouchable in Mulk Ananda's classic novel of that name, was enthralled by whatever was *not* Indian, and any religion willing to accept him, if only in the back pew. The aim of the Indian lower classes is always social acceptance, which is why today in the aftermath of colonialism there has been such a rash of unsupervised indigenization. Ceremonies surrounding marriage, for example, have become increasingly Hinduized, and the local fortune-teller is consulted for an auspicious date. Women wear the Shivaite spot on the forehead. Luke and Carman's *Village Christians and Hindu Culture*, which treats of rural Christians of South India, deserves to be read as a corrective to recent church growth success stories which appear to owe more to the contact of evangelists and uprooted Christians with the new urban populations than that with rural groups.[13] In rural India, syncretistic confusion reigns, and only those actually born into the larger traditional churches or higher Hindu castes might be said to be technically orthodox in relation to their respective faiths. In the low caste villages, full of poverty and ignorance, worship of local deities and devils is often more prominent than that of Vishnu, Shiva or Kali. These local ceremonies are often compromised by low caste Christians, and their association with animal sacrifice has led to strange misinterpretations of doctrine by semi-literate evangelists, like maintaining that Jesus was sacrificed to appease Satan's wrath.

The handicaps and misunderstandings seem endless, but they mainly come down to the fact that, as the authors admit, 'the Christians have such a low wall of protective Christian "culture" around them that Hindu influences penetrate easily'. To begin with, missionaries have given far too little thought to doctrinal vocabulary, so that the message has never been perfectly clear. Bishop Appasamy's attempt to indigenize theological terms may have been well-intentioned, but it was careless.[14] To suggest that Jesus was the one and only *avatar*, and that Christians offer him *bhakti*, was an almost impossible contradiction in terms, if not heresy, and could be compared to explaining Christianity to the radically monotheist Moslems by saying that Jesus is the Father, or Jesus is Spirit. Missionaries have further offered a salvation which, is too radically individualistic and iconoclastic for the uneducated Indian's group mind and aesthetic consciousness. Plainly, in a society where only 34% are literate and many churches could not bestow literacy even on members, the refusal of pictures and rituals by Protestants is absurd. At worst, idolatry of Jesus images is better than compromise with local demon gods, and at least there is something to show to enquirers, who ask converts where their new gods are. As Hinduism thinks of everything, all church customs down to the smallest have needed systematic attention, and that includes the beauty spots which South Indian Christian women desire to wear and often do. It is hard to grasp why Christians should not wear a spot of a different colour from the Shivaites, or perhaps paint instead a tiny red cross, which some Russian Orthodox have on their foreheads at Christmas.

On the other hand, it must be admitted that on the Catholic front, recent attempts to render the liturgy more Indian and build churches in a more Indian style have not always met with favour, and it is ironic, considering how far since the seventeenth century Catholics have admitted caste distinctions to their congregations as a result of the influence of de Nobili, that they should insist on a church looking like a church, i.e. a European church. This is also strange in view of the very Indian feeling of some of the Catholic churches of Goa, which date from earliest Western contact.

In this particular case, it may be that this conservative protest is a genuine but unfortunate attempt to save a Christian witness and identity within a situation which Western advocates of change understand insufficiently. In order to be a distinctive Christian community in India, the churches have needed either the authority of an Indian tradition, or an authentic christology, with all that would imply for its social and aesthetic forms. Until the St Thomas churches were rudely awakened from their tropical torpor in 1502 by the Portuguese, who were soon demanding their 'conversion', they effectively possessed an authority of tradition, an apostolic tradition which might be considered comparable to the authority some Hindus have accorded the Vedas. This had given them a stake in history and a kind of social status, without which it is doubtful they would have lasted so long. Yet it was precisely in this faith that they were attacked and demoralized, first by Portuguese (who inexcusably destroyed most of their invaluable records, leaving us with lacunae on the St Thomas tradition), and later by Victorian Protestants, who accused them of ritualism (they addressed an invocation to the saints before communion) and immorality (though this ran counter to most earlier reports which portrayed them as high-minded if nothing else). In default of tradition, theological freedom to construct an Indian christology was required, but missions were hostile or indifferent to it, and imposed doctrine on Western lines. The Hindu tendency to equate God with simple being was and remained central to the philosophical problem, whereas Christianity requires being to be connected with action, becoming and the historical; this is also associated with the problem of defining the status of the personal. The average Hindu perhaps thinks of Brahman as transpersonal rather than impersonal, and associates personality in God or man with limitation. The Western presentation of christology, however, mostly by-passes these problems by speaking in conventional religious terms derived from dated and static Greek concepts of substance and personality; we have noted from Chapter 1 the kind of confusion which results. Caught between the nutcrackers of the inclusiveness of resurgent Vedantism and the exclusiveness of Western orthodoxy, confused Indian churches opted for the Western difference. The current theological situation, more open though it now is, is comparable to that of Japan; basically it is 'Neo-Orthodox', something which favours the native subjectivity and dislike of literalism, but other-

315

wise keeps theologians in the shadow of Western trends, in which they are irrelevantly learned, while they relate cautiously to Hindu philosophy (or rather aspects of it, since they have no total view) without much compensatory relation to the people or problems of India at large.

The fragmentation and demoralization of the Thomas church is thus much to be regretted, though as a church it cannot be idealized. It long suffered three major handicaps. (a) At an early stage it was severed from its mother church, which with or without St Thomas must have been the Syriac-speaking church of Edessa and the churches of Mesopotamia. By 345 they were suffering such problems of leadership that the Syrian church sent out clergy to impose some order, but after the fifth century, with the decline of Rome and Persia, the sole contacts with the West until the Portuguese were Nestorian merchants, often refugees of persecution, who changed the church's doctrinal colour. (b) The liturgy remained Syrian, and although Indian priestly feeling, and perhaps the desire to possess an alternative to the Sanskrit of the Hindu elite, kept the Syrian language within the church, this was contrary to the policy of the mother Eastern churches and inappropriate to the larger Indian situation. (c) There was wrongful assimilation to the caste system, with members of different castes attending different services. This trend first became fixed in 878, when a charter of Ayyan King of Vened accorded the Christian communities extensive rights and privileges, involving a controversial acceptance of and acceptance by the Hindu establishment. Not only was this inadmissible to doctrine, but it was a tactical error, in that the later appeal of Islam and Gandhism to millions of Indians lay precisely in its attack on the caste system. By failing to tackle this issue, Christianity lost not only the element of challenge but also its main chance to bring a clear, practical alternative to Hinduism; iconoclastic, dogmatic Islam, which contained a promise of freedom, also smashed down temples and idols and wrought widespread destruction, inoculating many Hindus against monotheism and religions of dogma and the will. Although India tamed and modified even Islam with time, the memory remained and Hindus automatically equated dogma with violence and intolerance, and easily associated Christianity with the same stream of thought, since modern missions arrived along with imperialism. It is perhaps useless to argue that the identification was unfair, that the Crusades and the Inquisition and all that is most intolerant in Christianity can be traced to compromise and the contamination of its ideals in its own struggle against Islam, or that the first Protestant missionaries to India were obliged to bless British imperialism, since otherwise the East India Company, troubled by the democratic potential of missions, refused them access (the first English missionary, William Carey, was obliged to enter under Danish auspices). The fact is that the damage has been done, and in trying to take account of the Christian message and its contradiction by many Christians, Hindus have evolved their own interpretations in which Christ is seen not as fulfilling or transcending the Old Testament, but contradicting a Testament in which the more progressive elements are overlooked at the expense of the more intolerant, which are less universal and fix it within the conditions of an era.

Despite the outreach of some Catholic orders and individual Protestant missions, the result of all this, as the agnostic Chaudhuri has observed, is that the churches have almost lost the basis for an evangelistic position because they are content to do little else publicly than affirm that they are not intolerant or inflexibly dogmatic. Having properly rejected the old Christian imperialist criticism that Hinduism is merely superstitious, nothing but cow worship, poverty and dirt, and hence wrong (the kind of *prejudice* many Hindus equate with dogma!), the new style is to discover 'points of contact', say between messiah and *avatar bhakti* and pietism. All of this can give a confusing impression to the average Indian Christian, especially when debates become rarefied with frequent quotation from fashionable modern academic theologians. Reaction was inevitable. One finds it, for example, in the American-trained Strict Baptist evangelist Vankateswami Gupta,[15] who, as a former Hindu, goes to the other extreme, reducing Christianity to the simplest 'one wayism', the negation of everything Indian. He denounces most Indian Christians as unrepentant and unregenerate, and modern Hinduism as being little more than a means of corrupting Western spiritual values in preparation for the false religion of the Antichrist. Neither of these two positions appears especially sensitive to the real needs of India, and the causes of existing attitudes to Christianity.

In Chapter 1 I pointed out that at least some Hindu resistance to missionary 'one wayism' was the result of a genuine incomprehension of Christian categories. There are other factors. One is obviously that the geographical, ethnic and linguistic diversity of India, and its historical vulnerability to invasion, has called for tolerance and the inclusive view. Consequently, any new doctrine is required to display adaptability and tolerance, and to have policies which will ensure that Christianity has not always shown such a character. Missionaries have sometimes been more interested in souls than in the whole man, while some of the criticism of Hinduism, particularly of the caste system, was simply a matter of the pot calling the kettle black. Indefensible though the system was, especially towards untouchables, imperialism and the imposed system of land ownership were the factors which bestowed unprecedented rights upon the wealthy and prevented what opportunities for inter-caste movement there were, thus emphasizing some of its worst features.

On the practical side, Christian missions undoubtedly gave to Indian consciousness a concern with moral and individual responsibility which its mysticism had ignored and broke down many cruel superstitions like those surrounding pregnancy and widowhood; yet these were matters of emphasis or particular custom. A general presentation of Christian ethics had to await the non-Christian Gandhi, while a general presentation of Christian religion in terms of Indian life was never achieved. When not saving souls, most conservative missionaries committed to evangelism (many missionaries just did good works and otherwise lived fashionable lives within colonial circles) were content to leave society to its colonial reform. K. T. Paul felt that some good could come out of Indian nationalism (its fulfilment would gradually disentangle Christianity from politics) but saw British imperial influence on India as providential.[16] The educational missionaries, Alexander Duff, John Wilson and William Miller (founder of the famous Madras Christian College) regarded the substitution of Western culture for India as preparation for the gospel.[17] Nicol MacNicol told Hindus that they must make an absolute choice between Christian doctrine and Vedanta;[18] this might be compared to requiring Christians to burn Plato and Aristotle. On the Catholic side, the brilliant Brahmabandhah Upadhyaya was soon in trouble with priests and peasants in his attempts to establish a monastic order along individualistic Indian lines and to indigenize theological terms (which, as a Brahmin, he did better than most even if describing the Trinity in terms of *sat-cit-ananda*, 'being-knowledge-bliss', was controversial). Opposition became so intense that he decided that Christians must support national independence in order to achieve freedom to express their views. Even by 1942, the Poona conference of the Indian Christians Theological Association (Protestant), while demanding greater involvement with Indian life, pedantically suggested only such changes in forms and terms as would make the gospel intelligible. This favoured bureaucratic rather than visionary reinterpretation.

Inevitably, then, the gratuitous issue of church aesthetics has scarcely been in question. By national standards, the San Tome church in Madras, which enshrines the supposed remains of St Thomas, is positively antiseptic. Psychedelic colours, murals, images, the exuberant profusion which expresses the Indian sense of dream and wonder, are absent. Churches possess neither the intimacy of the small or the grandeur of the large Hindu religious edifices; neither their light nor their dark. They possess a European indoor as opposed to an Indian outdoor orientation; they have none of the informal, organic plan: alcoves, halls, shrine rooms, open areas, which permit different functions and observances, religious and secular concerns to be casually pursued in different sections. Perhaps the only positive feature of ecclesiastical mock-Gothic (and other yet worse styles in India) is the aerial aspirational effect given by the spire as against the heavy, graceless, earth-hugging tendency of much Indian design, suggesting a resignation towards nature and the ugly, an inability to raise the soul which, of course, mission theology would wish to challenge. This, however, is a small advantage, and I have been appalled when after traversing Delhi, or sightseeing in holy Varanasi (Benares), and experiencing the dirt, the misery, the superstition, the heat and the human intensity, I have come across a church, like the Anglican church at Varanasi. Unlike the temples, it is far from the crowds and surrounded by a virtual park, chill, colourless, rationally austere, redolent of former privilege, something from the world of Jane Austen in the middle of the world of Gandhi. It seems to mock the very Indians entering it. Not only socially and aesthetically inappropriate, colonial church architecture suggests the formal highly organized sense of church community, that concept of church against which, influenced by the Hindu stress on individual initiative and effort in the mystical quest, practically all thinking Indian Christians from Sundar Singh to Chenchiah have revolted.

My idea of a Christian church-temple would be one in which there was a main hall with an altar for formal (Sunday) services, a variety of airy rooms, one for individual prayer and meditation, another for talks and recitation (one envisages marathon scripture recitations which visitors could enter and leave at any time), another for impromptu music (psalms and hymns to sittar), a gallery with mystical pictures to dream in on hot days, and an open area for meeting people, selling religious items, and children's play.

Since in any case no missions can hope to reach all India or make all its congregations literate, to make churches open places where the faith can be casually heard is really its only hope. To some extent, the Christian Ashram movement founded by Jesudason, with its simple life and works of charity, aims at something more identified with the people, but whereas many Hindu ashrams are located near or within temple grounds, Christian ashrams are not likely to be attached to the church in such a close physical or formal sense.

So it is that while acculturization in terms of ritual forms and church designs is no more than a church's debt to its members and society, in India, where no evangelism can be complete and people need to come to the church, such adaptation is inseparable from evangelism. However, despite this, the aesthetic dimension has been the last concern of a mission unable to decide on its priorities, caught between those like Dr Ida Scudder, who in the face of such obvious need have substituted Christian 'aid' for evangelism, and those like Vankateswami Gupta, for whom the emphasis has been mainly on preaching, or a somewhat conditional and selective aid. I shall not digress on to this large and serious issue except to say that the alternatives should not be so sharp. I am personally sympathetic to Mother Teresa's policy, which reserves preaching and advice for certain classes of people, particularly the wealthy, the educated, and those in positions of responsibility. In the case of the sick, dying and obviously deprived, with whom she deals, Mother Teresa aims only for 'a baptism of love', not wishing to secure conversions out of a sense of gratitude and duty. A modicum of privilege attaches even to religious choice and responsibility, and to theology even more so; within the context of much of India, the theology of the epistles, however necessary for Christianity, must seem as gratuitous as fine art, and the same naturally applies to Hindu philosophy.

Most Christians have been especially reluctant to be accommodating towards aesthetics in India for fear of the least taint of 'idolatry', that subject which is the target of so much evangelistic preaching. The concern is little justified because of the psychology of Indian belief, and one may well ask whether an evangelism which seeks to focus sin and arouse guilt in that area can touch the raw nerve at which evangelism aims. Certainly it can be more misleading to speak of modern Hindu 'idolatry' in the same breath as the Baals and Astartes of the Old Testament, even though the vestigial symbolism of some of the gods, like the blood-filled skulls of Shiva, indicate a less respectable past. A substantial number of Hindus cannot be accused of idolatry in a conventional sense because they do not sufficiently know what they believe and do not conceive of the divine in Western and Semitic terms. Many will readily adhere to one god one week, or one philosophical conception of God another, depending on what is most helpful in concentrating the mind on ineffable realities or the God beyond the gods. With Hindus there is a good deal of the Athenian 'to an unknown God' or the Vedic scepticism with its 'None knows whence creation has arisen, and whether he has or has not produced it. . . . He only knows or perhaps he does not know.' A European or a Semite may think of Krishna in fairly concrete terms as a god, an idol, a distinct individual, and undoubtedly *some* Hindus also do, like Catholics who believe all the stories of the saints, but for many other Hindus Krishna's historicity is irrelevant; he can be worshipped in any form, as a father, a lover, or even as a baby, and is assumed to be only one of the many incarnations of Vishnu, who in turn is a major 'aspect' of 'God'. One can be Hindu and believe in a Creator God or none, that the world is real or unreal, that God is good, or good and evil together. The real belief is in the unity of Being, the great Unconscious identified with God, into which the Indian appears able to dip in meditation and reverie with a facility almost unparalleled. In this Unconscious, a god is simply an archetype. As a guru remarks in Brent's *Godmen of India*,[19] an inanimate object like a chair can be one's guru or god if it concentrated the mind, and certainly many Hindus though they would not go as far as that, believe more in their guru than in Krishna or 'God'. One could even call Hinduism guruism.

St Paul who believed that the devil could appear as an angel of light (II Cor. 11.14) maintained that the gods of the heathen were demons (I Cor. 10.20) and that the myths and genealogies of the Gentiles were not only unhistorical but foolish tales (I Tim. 1.4). I would not deny that many of the ancient gods appear malevolent, if not positively demonic; moreover, there is little reason to dispute that many Greek and Hindu myths are both unedifying and unhistorical. Yet beyond this, some of them incidentally reflect primary psychological truths (like the Oedipus myth), while some gods are truly archetypal. Thus Venus is obviously a symbolic epitome of beauty and feminine aspirations, and for this reason she is constantly recreated in dream and in art (Botticelli's Venus) long after she has ceased to be worshipped. Venus, Mars, Mercury and so on can never be entirely denied and will never die.

Because of Indian introversion and the nature of its religious iconography, the archetypal element is very powerful. Thus while some forms of Shiva worship, especially the early forms, have been little better than a Satanism, and certain gurus, especially those proclaiming themselves divine, could be regarded as agents of the demonic, for many Hindus, especially those accustomed to believe that God is everything anyway, accusations of idolatry and appeals to relinquish it can only confuse unless they are well and precisely defined. Complete rejection of the gods is likely to seem either impossible or a prescription for terrible barrenness. It might be compared to descending upon Bavaria and preaching against its fantastic art and the spirit of the fairy tale which underlies it, or again, accusing of idolatrous waywardness anyone who feels an affinity for the *quality* of Neptune suggested in Holst's *The Planets*. I have known Indians who do not personally worship or believe in Vishnu, Shiva, etc., yet at the same time feel that they cannot deny that he is something, some part of God or themselves, and cannot help responding to the iconography. They could not reject idolatry if that required a total denial of his reality, a complete wiping out of the Hindu reference, and while they might remove his image from the family altar, they would not wish to indulge in those ceremonies of smashing or burning idols in which some conservative missionaries still rejoice. The educated Hindu situation in this respect is similar to that of the Greek pagans who, haunted aesthetically and otherwise by gods in whom they scarcely believed, showed a slower pattern of conversion to Christianity in comparison with the frankly idolatrous Romans. In fact, reading writers of the Neo-Hindu reaction to Christianity, like K. M. Panikkar one cannot but be struck by a degree of resemblance to Porphyry and the values of the late pagan reaction to Christianity which was compounded of an almost nationalist feeling against the invasion of a foreign religion and a profound aesthetic nostalgia, which would only be resolved when the church reluctantly allowed its reluctant converts their icons.

Despite the appeal of the baroque sweeps of the philosophy, there is much I dislike about Hinduism. I have not dwelt upon that, solely because missionaries have overdone and misplaced criticism. There is much which bespeaks darkness and degradation, and is almost sinister, like the worship of snakes, monkeys and rats and the excessive devotion offered to manifestly unworthy gurus. Yet when one has said this, India is vast and varied, and one is still forced to recognize not only that India has a special psychological relationship with the symbolic, but that Christians need to acknowledge that in the absence of an alternative Christian symbolic formation, at least some of the symbols are the only possible ones. Faced with the conventional scenes of Indian tropical beauty, lapping ocean waters, waving palms, scented air and the call of nocturnal creatures beneath an obsessive full moon and brilliantly starry skies, I have been surprised how even for me this was the night of Brahma and the dance of Shiva celebrated in Indian art and its haunting national music. There are scenes, particularly in the central hill regions, which so suggest Israel that one almost expects a biblical episode to be enacted before one's eyes, but basically God in the Christian sense appears absent from India, not having penetrated it concretely in aesthetic terms, or spiritually by association in a symbolically forceful sense. Jesus, even the Jesus of the desert (and how perfectly the stark Palestinian scenery is the backdrop of the temptation and passion), is still too human for India. To enter the tropical night and be clothed with the mystery his kingdom proclaimed, he must become also the *Lamb* of God, the *Lion* of the tribe of Judah, the messianic warrior on the white horse, the forms under which he is portrayed and even worshipped in Revelation, yet which have so little impinged upon Western consciousness.[20]

In Hinduism, the association of 'God' with nature is suggested by a series of most improbable incarnation tales (Vishnu becomes a boar, a lion, a fish, to save the world) and also in the underlying savagery of the original Shiva, but in Christianity the kind of images mentioned should be thought of more as aspects or epiphanies of God, a reminder that the human incarnation, while conveying what is most essential about God, cannot reveal him in entirety. The Trinity *is* God as the mind of a person is the individual, but God also exists through his creation. There is no need for incarnation in bestial form when it involves so great a limitation of the essential nature, but as an addition to glory or to proclaim the redemption of nature this aspect must be recognized. Anyway, a Christian Indian spirituality could not afford to overlook such imagery. Shiva worship and imagery are very special. Whatever the origins, I take the Shiva of mediaeval iconography to be an image of the soul, especially the Asian soul, so tormented by life and nature that it is bound to seek God principally within, and to overcome life with a kind of crazed will to joy within acceptance of natural forces. This is represented by the calm dance against which worlds are born and fall while the god declares 'fear not'.

The Shiva image, whether represented as ascetic or dancer, be-speaks 'resolve' and will, or as near to it as India comes, which is why it cannot easily be dismissed.

The absence of a real value based on will, save perhaps the resolve to escape existence, accounts for much of the confusion in the Hindu doctrine of the divine, and is another reason why charges of idolatry fall on deaf ears and Christians who pursue it only become lost in the labyrinth of Indian argument. It is little use declaring that there is only one God, or that God is a Trinity, or that God is good, or God is love, for Hinduism appears to have a reply to every statement. Hindus will agree that there is only one God, but he is through everything and everyone, so that idolatry merely refers to the wrong *kind* of worship; counter that God is not one and all but is a Trinity and Hindus agree that more essentially he is a Trinity, Brahma, Vishnu, Shiva, a matter of names only; insist that the Trinity is not ineffable, illusory or simply moral in the Hindu sense, but a creator, and they will agree that God is a personal creator, Ishwara, according to one's scriptural sources and attitudes to matter. Protest that God should be love and goodness and not a devouring Kali or destroying Shiva and they will retort that some people do worship God as pure love or pure goodness, but that these destroying images are only similar to those of the Hebrew prophets who declare that Yahweh has come to slay and destroy or to scourge and test. This comparison can be seriously questioned because there is a great difference in quality between the irrational blood-lust of the skull-rattling Kali and the demands of Yahweh for justice. However, it is really the question of will that is at stake.

In discussing the doctrine of God's two faces, his good and evil side in Shivaite religion, one Hindu protested that of course God was good and evil together; it was obvious that he was creating evil floods, earthquakes and famines all the time. It struck me as significant that God was conceived as continually 'creating' evil rather than permitting it, or else like a Satan 'performing' it on people. I knew that 'creating' was intended. The Asian, and especially the Indian understanding of cause and effect, can be quite peculiar, due, I feel, to the extent to which the irregular motions of the unconscious are permitted to invade the conscious. Earlier, I cited Vivekananda who stated that the street-walking of the prostitute was the *cause* of the chastity of other women as though chastity could never be chosen or willed. In Hindu doctrine 'God' is conceived as having either merely set things in motion (in which case evil is a matter of illusion or subsequent accident), or as indwelling and constantly creating nature. This creation, however, is not really one of will and design but an urge to plenitude (reflecting the Asian value of desire for wholeness), which necessitates the myriad forms of the myriad worlds; alternatively, this desire for plenitude can be regarded simply as *lila* (play),[21] so that almost logically (especially in psychological terms because of the opportunity given in wholeness doctrine to regression) some of the early cruder myths even portray the world as being produced by Brahma's pleasure in relieving himself. The distinction between God as *creator* and *sustainer* of the universe does not effectively exist, is not psychologically understood, even if some scripture could be adduced to support the idea. Such thinking perhaps provides a root explanation for Indian inefficiency; it is the reason why making plans and declaring policies which come to nothing are confused with actually performing them. God, identified with the totality and the continual presence of the unconscious, is seen as always active everywhere, yet because the unconscious is the only model for God, the activity predicated of him is also unconscious. It will be recalled how Jung's own controversial and bizarre identification of the God of Job with evil was derived from God's supposed lack of true consciousness shown by his uncontrolled need to boast and rave which was, Jung felt, resolved mythically by the promise of a messianic incarnation to improve, or render conscious, the God image.

While I do not accept, like Jung, that God is both good and evil, that evil is possible for God's being or potential in anything he sets in motion, and that God is therefore indirectly responsible for the evil that exists, I think that Christians should admit that it was a horror at this thought and a desire to 'absolve' God from such responsibilities which caused mediaeval philosophy so impossibly to deny a substantial reality to Satan and evil, with all the awkward philosophical and social consequences which followed. If God is love, which is a free principle (and it must be recalled that when Hindus describe God they do not necessarily admit that he is love – the standard description is *sat-cit-ananda*, 'being-knowledge-bliss'), then evil, or the wrong choice, is potential but is deliberately refused by an act of will. In so far as God 'risked' creating a free mankind for his own pleasure (though notice the distinction between conscious pleasure and unconscious play), he shares indirect responsibility for the evil and suffering possible, so that perhaps we should take seriously the disturbing statement in Genesis that

God 'repented himself' over having made man. Whether God is imperfect in the sense of having made a mistake in creating a world, which he knew would fall is an issue to which we may return later.

In the Judaeo-Christian view, the 'evils' of earthquake, flood and famine are to be seen either as scourges and warnings (if an accredited prophet makes that interpretation) or as ordinary, even necessary events (at least within this existing fallen creation) which appear as evil because of human failure that could be overcome or ignorance about God's control of the world. Thus to take an obvious example, while earthquakes are necessary for the balance of nature, if misguided politics and economics did not cause people to live in danger zones, or more people were open to the divine guidance which warns them to vacate areas at the proper time, these earthquakes would not be a scourge. Statements like Amos', 'Does evil befall a city unless the Lord has done it?' (Amos 3.6) and Isaiah's 'I form light and create darkness, I make weal and create woe' (Isa. 45.7) have been used by Hindus and those thinkers, like Jung and Toynbee, who have been influenced by the East to present Yahweh as a 'two-faced' Shiva. Although the Jewish idea is akin to the Hindu one, namely that what is happening at any time is 'done' or 'created', it is because of the larger Jewish assumptions concerning a divine 'management' that this near-equation of sustaining with creating is philosophically permissible in a way the Hindu one is not. God not only sustains, but freely chooses also to permit and use evils contrary to his nature, for a greater good, a form of sustenance which is 'creative' in its operation upon the future.

It should be added that the way in which Christian understanding associates God so closely with will is one reason why it is essential that he should be described in masculine terms and why to speak of his 'anger' and 'hate', though only analagous and not to be understood in the crudely human sense of early Hebrew or current Hindu understanding, should not be regarded as complete misrepresentation either. God is not just 'masculine' ('Elohim created man in his own image, in the image of Elohim created he him, male and female created he them' makes this fairly clear), nor does he rant and rave, but he does will, feel and choose. Furthermore, quite apart from the socio-historical conditioning which feminists stress, the structure and functioning of the psyche and individuation is such that the spiritual person is forced to associate God predominantly with the masculine as he does. That is why, as world myth shows, one must either have a male Creator God or no creating God at all, describing everything rather improbably as 'of itself'.

There is no need to go further into metaphysics at this stage. My aim has been to emphasize that if there is an Indian idolatry in the Christian sense, it is one of the excessive reverence that is bestowed upon the passive undiscriminated 'Godhead' of the unconscious. This throws up its anarchic myriad things and reveals the human and divine potential rather than their actuality, which will be a union of a redeemed unconscious and conscious (obviously the conscious, rational ego is not perfectly good by comparison) to the willing of the perfectly good.

It thus seems likely that any evangelism needs to arouse the subject to a greater awareness of the ego and his free agency. This cannot be normally achieved by conventional sermons, mass rallies, or school religious instruction; it needs the teacher and the group meeting that can be witnessed everywhere in India, in temple, hall and park, in which by an opposite progress the guru talks, argues, or tricks the members out of their normal sense of reality and confronts them with the beyond. Instead of delivering the direct message leading to appeal, there should be the *sruti* (scripture), *yukti* (reason) and *anubhava* (reason) of Hindu argument; one needs to perambulate round and round the subject with proverbs, parables, and potted psychology, spiralling into or suddenly dropping within the centre, especially since, as I said earlier, sin (perhaps the sins of omission rather than those committed) is to be taken into account. It is noticeable that the successful guru-type South Indian evangelist and healer, Sadhu Joseph, does not make the repentance of unbelievers a condition of healing.

Needless to say, however, no missionary could hope for a single formula for conveying Christian truth when the anticipated end is 'realization' and wisdom rather than truth and knowledge. The evangelist can only become aware of the sensitive area produced by the religious concerns of the region, caste or prevailing type of worship as the discussion proceeds. He has to 'go' with the discussion and give out from his own awareness. Because he wishes to emphasize individualism, he should respect in audience and church whatever individualism a society recognizes. Among other things, this means that doctrinal exclusiveness must not be confused with one way of being or doing things. A Hindu can go to God by a chosen discipline, yoga, mantra recitation, musical or artistic devotion, deeds of charity, scripture study, philosophy, etc., and his choices should not be restricted if he becomes a Christian.

Practically all Indian Christian thinkers, and the best Christians, like Sundar Singh, have shied away from mere church; its organization and its regularity stifled them both spiritually and as individuals. The fact that church organization has this effect is rather unfortunate, not only because where the organization is firm, message and aid are more effectively spread, but because in India with its manifold problems, establishing good models of organization seems close to a virtue. Yet I understand the hesitation. The church structures and the purposes they serve can be so far removed from Indian norms and feeling, that joining and continuing to belong to a church must often seem comparable in Western terms to being required to accept Mormonism and all its obligatory meetings, preaching and literature pushing. The more culturally de-Westernized I become, the more I appreciate how closely the Pauline system we inherit was approximated to Roman values and how this largely necessary adaptation would be interpreted from Augustine onwards to support a thoroughly mechanical rather than organic view of man, sin and society, in which everything is subordinated to the good running of a machine. If the contradictions inherent between Christian individualism and the system's almost military style were not apparent earlier, it was because of the very novel egalitarianism of the community before God. Today, however, when egalitarianism has been secularized and almost abused in parts of the West, and in India where the forms and feelings which underlie its structures are very different, the consequences for the individual are more apparent.

In the West, church organization is precisely something organized by man under God. In India, any organization is likely to be seen as intrinsic and, like the traditional caste system, waiting merely to be realized. One would not mobilize groups for preaching, literature pushing, etc.; one would simply discover who possessed evangelistic talents or whatever and encourage them to use them. Like the Indian who told me they went to a certain church because they could relate to the altar there, the church is a place before it is a community. The true introvert type is always alone even in the crowd. He has little or no 'esprit de corps'; he merely identifies with people of the same type. Famous statements like 'by oneself is one purified, by oneself is salvation made' are perhaps less doctrinal affirmations than experimental observations. That is how things feel. Thus, 'church' will probably need to be understood primarily in some oceanic or organic rather than mechanical or political sense, may even need to approximate to the idea of a society of natural specializations which the Hindu structure attempted but failed to realize because it placed all responsibility upon birth and refused to give room to change.

Without permitting considerable liberty in terms of self expression and degrees of involvement, the church is unlikely to deploy the talents or receive the loyalty it desires, because Hinduism is too religiously and culturally rich, and for all its scandalous weaknesses, allows every dog his day. In South India, even the untouchable can annually achieve grandeur at Holi festival, arrayed to dance the part of gods. The secret of the nominalism of which conservatives complain, perhaps excessively (for every religion has 'passengers' and no one is consistently spiritual throughout life), lies here, in the frustration of such individualism and diversity as Indians know.

Indian Christians must also experience some strain if they honestly try to reject the occult to the extent required of them by rationalist Catholics and fundamentalist Protestants. It has always struck me that, like Joseph in Egypt, a missionary to India might need to be an interpreter of dreams and omens to secure a hearing. Few might agree, though the controversial Catholic prophetess Jeane Dixon says as much.[22] Her vision of the apostles caused her to feel that St Thomas may have been the apostle of India because, falling, as she believes, under the sign Scorpio, which is more inclined than most to the mysterious and the occult, he was better qualified to deal with the all-prevailing Indian psychism. If anything, beneath its extravagancies the apocryphal lore of St Thomas suggests that this could have been the case.

In this difficult area, definitions are important. The term occult can denote a whole variety of things. It can mean (a) witchcraft, sorcery and spiritualism, which of course are ruled out in Judaeo-Christian thought; (b) so-called divination, as of the I Ching and Tarot Cards, and the sortilege practised in temples of East Asia, which depends on nothing but the subconscious reaction of the subject to images and cryptic messages; (c) psychic powers or ESP, like clairvoyance, telepathy, mind-reading, aura-reading, water-divining, dream interpretation, faith healing, etc.; (d) rejected 'sciences', like astrology (which has both opposition and support from biblical sources), palmistry and physiognomy. Though the elements in them are far from being equally valid or useful, I should regard (c) and (d) as worthy of at least investigation, if not actual use, by sympathetic church members, especially in the Asian context. I shall give reasons in due course. There is nonetheless a huge prejudice against such tolerance, less on specific scriptural grounds than from the general feeling that in the case of (c), no purely mental gift is likely to be natural or morally neutral, so that premonition, healing powers, etc., must proceed directly from evil spirits if they are not positively bestowed by the Holy Spirit, and that in (d) 'fortune telling' rather than legitimate characterology is involved. Such thinking does not carry much conviction in Asia. First, psychic tendencies are sufficiently common for a clear distinction to exist between the 'spiritual' and the mundane, the cultivated and the naturally spontaneous kind. In India, moreover, people who in England or America would never expect to anticipate visits, accidents or telephone calls, suddenly find themselves doing so. There is nothing spiritual about this; it is just an aspect of thinking. In the West the poet Tennyson is a good example of a person with natural psychic powers (like healing) without any kind of religious reference (he was agnostically inclined, and half afraid of his gift). My feeling is that when people claim that the Holy Spirit gives them gifts, they mean that a latent gift is powerfully aroused in them for specific use. In 'fortune telling', Asian thought has always recognized that it is impossible to draw an *absolute* distinction between characterology as in astrology or palmistry and fate as such, because to define a character is to indicate a type of fate, even if one denies the possibility and desirability of knowing the future exactly. If a person is born with, say, Virgo rising, or has the hands of an artist, he or she is unlikely to become a truck driver because they will do everything to avoid it.

But why is it important to take the psychic into account? For one thing, the concept of fate and occult characterology is the nearest Asia comes to the kind of ego identification and sense of life organization that Christianity emphasizes. These forms of conscious structuring provide the counterbalance to introverted values for the individual. India virtually expects that the holy man should be able to read and pronounce upon the individual, to give the 'sermonettes' in between the kind of prophetic utterances for which Jeane Dixon has been criticized in the West. In the illogical, unhistorical East, this is the equivalent of the logical or historical prophetic proofs for Christianity in the West. Where formal religion is a dead subject and glances like water off a duck's back, the occult always has an audience. Every Hindu is willing to discuss his fate, and the astonishment I have caused, the barrage of enquiries I have had from even the less religious Thais if I have guessed someone's birthday to be, say 5 September (even if it was in fact 6 September), or guessed their physical weaknesses, is something that the Christian missionary, struggling to communicate, might well envy. Moreover, strange as it may seem, I feel sure that only by accepting some astrological explanations of life and character can the church hope seriously to refute the unacceptable and tragic Indian doctrine of reincarnation which holds everyone, including many Indian Christians, in thrall, and feeds every injustice and feeling of resignation. Anthropologically, reincarnation may be nothing but the patient Indian extension of the Shamanistic metempsychosis, or even of the Indian perception of life (Swami Prabhupada has described our journey from cradle to grave as being so many 'reincarnations'), but in the popular mind it is reinforced, as it is somewhat in the West, by the psychic and introvert person's sense of affinity with persons and places, or with deceased persons whom they may resemble physically, or whose destiny pattern they may share. Especially for those who accept astrology, it may seem an empirical fact that a bad horoscope is a bad horoscope and that there must be a reason why some persons toil to the rhythm of their progressed 'bad' stars, or go from fortune to fortune with their 'good' stars. John F. Kennedy and Marie Antoinette had 'bad' horoscopes and they came to violent ends. Is it *karma*?

Lives leading to disaster and horoscopes which point to it are perhaps the easiest to explain. Given a doctrine of divine prescience, one can say that the stars reflect rather than cause what one will do, like the frivolous acts which ruined Marie Antoinette and the recklessness of Kennedy, who went to Dallas despite warnings. More problematic, however, is the observable distinction between consistently fortunate and unfortunate lives, clearly due for the most part to external circumstance or inherited temperament, and the tendency of opposition and restriction to follow cycles, which astrology appears to anticipate and confirm. Is this *karma*? Jeane Dixon would say yes, but in a general rather than the particular Indian sense.[23] God 'reincarnates' 'spirit', ideas and purposes, not souls, weaves patterns through history of which only certain people, astrological types, are able to take up the threads. If those elected to particular purposes fail in them, obviously it will go harder for those who succeed to them and who have to make up the historical failure. This metaphysical dimension apart, certainly those who have studied astrology will find that the physical and psychological similarities between people, attributed to reincarnation, are most satisfactorily accounted for in this way, though

Indian astrology has obscured this by attempting to describe caste types rather than intrinsic personalities. Unrelated people of similar appearance or characters can always be traced to identical sun or ascending signs, and these character types in themselves will tend to produce similar destinies. In France, André Barbault has interestingly traced the similarities and development of themes in art, literature and philosophy to distinct patterns of astrological inheritance, thus giving some weight to Dixon's view and accounting for experiences of the *déja vu* variety.[24]

Of course, it is one thing to approve astrology in theory, another to approve its methods and uses equally, and I have grave doubts about the Indian system and its uses, as about the related interests of the Thais, for whom government and business is practically – and not so successfully – run by the stars. The more authentic Indian occult 'science' is probably palmistry; this appears superior to the Western variety and Cheiro's famous system derived from it. Cheiro supported palmistry on biblical grounds (the much amended and disputed Job 37.7); Jung and Jeane Dixon insisted upon the medical value of palmistry.[25] The theory of serious palmistry (as opposed to the gypsy variety) is that in some ways the nerve patterns of the mind are joined to and printed on the hand; also that subconsciously, as premonitions suggest, everyone in fact knows their destiny, which is manifest in the hand. There is nothing psychic or magical about the practice, though it occasionally happens that palmists with psychic tendencies additionally receive vibrationary impressions from the hand, while all palmists need a touch of intuition to synthesize the data. Lines, stars, squares in certain positions can only ever mean certain things. Interestingly, Indians, professional or otherwise, who have read my palm have said the same things, and I am rather impressed at the degree of agreement with the data of my horoscope, which seems to support the idea of the unity and 'scientific' basis of such studies. I cannot speak for the Thai system, which is derived from the Indian and has admixtures of the Chinese, which appears less scientific and closer to fortune telling.

III

The diversity and inclusiveness of Hinduism (or rather its modern capacity for inclusiveness, for it was not always like that)[26] highlights the exclusiveness which attaches to Christianity and which is less favoured today in a world of global consciousness. In the rest of this chapter I shall consider the problem of mission ideology and Christian exclusiveness in this context; however, it should be remembered that this is less an issue than relevance for most Hindus (apart from a few embittered intellectuals, like Radhakrishna and Panikkar). Asia also has exclusive religions (Islam, Sokka Gakkai, Communism), and has too little sense of history and the control of events to be concerned with furthering global consciousness. Some of the fabled Asian tolerance amounts to the admission of little more than exhaustion and incomprehension where religion is concerned; in more tangible realms of life like politics it is less in evidence.

In Asia, Christian exclusiveness is challenged less by ideology than implicitly by the apparent irrelevance of Christianity. This irrelevance matters more in an Asian context than in that of Western secularism, since Western man is a creature of fashions and was a materialist before Christianity was born, whereas Asia is more intrinsically metaphysical. By now, it will perhaps be clear that underlying the problem of Christian missions is the fact that Asia does not seem to possess the metaphysical problems of the West, to which Christianity has so long addressed itself. The sense of guilt, anguish and curiosity about life, so developed in St Paul, but fairly typical of his time and of leading Western minds since, is absent, depending as this does on a good measure of ego-consciousness, and delight in knowing, willing, and doing. Despite the Indian yogis, the Asian mind is practical, taking life as it comes; not metaphysical in this intellectual or emotional sense, or perhaps just more able to repress such tendencies if they exist. At the same time, even the most practically successful Asians are remarkably prone to scorn life, retire, or even commit suicide, in the face of frustration, humiliation and conflict. Despair rather than anguish is the keynote. Denying the self is almost irrelevant. The problem is that of affirming it, and the same often applies to rejecting the world.

What this would seem to suggest is that missionary Christianity, though demanding, will need to become less argumentative and doctrinal in emphasis than existential, a simple confrontation with basic human need, the experience of hardship, illness, death; it will need to put more stress on deliverance and love as opposed to judgment if it is not to seem cruel, and will need to become a teaching rather than a preaching religion. One of the most important forms of evangelism would be to present a convincing criticism of other faiths. Asians are highly conservative and turn modern, if at all, for pragmatic reasons rather than out of conviction. Because of this, most people are not *looking* consciously for answers like Western man, but need to be convinced that the old vague systems, which appear to have worked well enough in the past, no longer work and need to be changed. Often there is no – conscious – sense of what 'I' should do; the question is what is best for society. Most Asians do not want or expect to get right with God, or to meet Jesus. The idea seems absurdly egotistical; most want what the evangelical wing of Christianity has always detested, namely 'religion', but that does not mean that they are not susceptible to a more personal faith if they are allowed to enter by that door. Because of the nervous disposition of many Asians and the association in many minds of religion with social and cultural identity and honour, evangelism should be pursued in a low key. I personally received a letter from an overseas Chinese who informed me that I had 'converted' him and that he wished to become a clergyman. The letter mystified me, as I could only recall having spoken with him over a meal about ideas already germinating in my mind which I wrote up later. As I do not normally consider myself good at it, my aim had not been persuasion, and I can only imagine that I had resolved some long rankling problems of cultural honour. I suggest that this is often a need of many persons subject to Christian influence in schools and so on.

Today, however, any evangelism is felt to require much justification, and since Harnack, liberal Christians have cast doubts upon the church's commission 'Go into all the world and preach the gospel'. The culturally disruptive effect of some missions, the feeling that perhaps any claim to exclusiveness was a side-effect of Ptolemaic as opposed to Copernican world-views, and the need for global harmony, has lent weight to these attitudes. Theosophists, philosophers, historians and sociologists, incline to ecumenism of religions, or the establishment of a new one, as proposed by Hocking, Northrop, Cantwell Smith, John Hick, Toynbee, etc.[27] Purely theoretical or historical understandings of Christianity have led to the controversial identification of the missionary concept with a conquest mentality, with imperialism and even the despoliation of the environment, Western tendencies which are felt to need modification in the light of Asian passivity and its sense of wholeness. Implicit in this critique is the questionable assumption that religions serve a social function rather than impart civilizing urges as a fringe benefit, a fact which only Toynbee grasps.[28] Social or invented religions, like the monotheism of Pharaoh Akenaten, second-century Roman imperial religion, the theosophy of Mughal Emperor Akbar and modern Theosophy, have either a very temporary or a very limited social appeal, and depending on the circumstances of their origin, may defeat their stated purpose by becoming political to the point of persecution. Higher religion depends upon a spontaneous burst of pure inspiration (the Hebrew prophets) or mysticisim (Upanishads), or a development out of existing tradition, like Buddhism from Hinduism and Christianity from Judaism.

Hocking and Toynbee[29] maintain that within an equality of religions, the right to evangelism should be maintained, though apart from placing a value upon diversity, they virtually undermine the religious basis for it. The question 'Why missions?' raises two issues, the practical or social and the religious. On the practical side there is little reason to oppose missions. As even the Exleys consider,[30] there are great benefits on the philanthropic front, probably more than from any secular aid bodies, and also – provided that the missionaries are not fanatics or culture destroyers – society and international understanding are helped by contact between representatives of one foreign culture with another on a basis which is not political or commercial. The point is that outreach in itself is a positive value, especially in Asia.

In suggesting that Christian exclusiveness and missionary zeal has been the inspiration of the crusades and of every intolerance, writers like Radhakrishnan and Aldous Huxley are being unfair, as are the advocates of global consciousness in stressing the negative side of missionary aggression as against the positive side of Asian passivity. The opposite of outreach is in fact secrecy and withdrawal, like that of Asian doctors who discovered herbal and other cures to various diseases but hid their discoveries within their families for generations, capitalizing upon their knowledge rather than revealing it for general human benefit. At first, all outreach will appear strange, if not offensive to this type of mentality, though under Christian influence Hindu and Buddhist leaders have now conceded the failures of their respective faiths and societies in terms of practice and practical concern. The social evils of Asia have been particularly acute, so that in reply to Radhakrishnan's charge that Christianity leads to intolerance, one can only say that if Christianity is the great enemy, with the friends which Asia offers, there would be little need for enemies. Leaving aside the seemingly endless evils of India, the corruption of its rich, the sickness, the child labour, the millions of beggars, their offspring crippled from birth in order to make them look pitiable, the tortures and murders inflicted by the Hindu Palavas on the Buddhist Ceylonese, there are the 'crusades' of the Buddhist countries. Burma, so Buddhist that it would not use the silkworm, tried to decimate the Thais; Vietnam offers a long history of every intolerance and torture; Cambodia one of every slavery and oppression; in Japan, Buddhist monks made war on the authorities and on one another. In 'tolerant' Bali, black magic and even murder is alarmingly rife. None of this proves that Christianity is the true faith, but it should cause us to hesitate before blaming intolerance and aggression upon its exclusiveness.

The religious aspect of missions is more problematic. While some objections have been raised to all missions, the new Asian ones as much as the traditional Christian ones, the issue is not so much whether a religion should promote missions, since practically all faiths, even Asian faiths like Buddhism, have at some time demonstrated some missionary activity. The question is to what extent a religion like Christianity, feeling itself to possess 'the truth', has the right to lay claim to it in absolute terms and press those claims anytime, anywhere. All true statements appear to be 'the truth' to those proclaiming them, but are they the whole truth, the only truth? Is this claim a psychological or cultural illusion, which if pressed can only be psychologically and culturally damaging? Ought not the modern aim be to promote diversity and encourage the best possible practice of an existing faith? Obviously, there is no solution; there are only pointers to some. All religions require faith, and no one can hope to prove conclusively that one religion is right or that relativity and inclusive tolerance in the long term would have the desired effects for knowledge and social harmony, that its proponents allege, but I feel that at least it can be stated that the Christian claim to exclusiveness is not unreasonable, the product of culture alone, or intrinsically harmful to society.

In the trend of thought begun by Hocking's *Rethinking Missions*, religions are seen as the expression of a particular culture and adapted to its needs. Had Christianity gone East first rather than West, Christ would have become a *bodhisattva* and not the Son of God, as elaborated in Greek theology. Religious conviction is culturally determined. If one is born in a Christian country, one is likely to be Christian; if one is born in India, one is likely to be Hindu, and in both instances to believe that one's faith is more right than another. More recently, Toynbee, Huston Smith and John Hick have added to this position with the reflection that since

God is love, he would not leave other societies in ignorance, and that a unique revelation was hardly geographically feasible or desirable before today, so that it is unlikely to have been intended.[32] In any case, religions are very similar in essentials; thus, while Buddhists and Hindus tend to an impersonal ultimate and Christians and Mohammedans to a personal one, the Buddha Amida or Shiva are addressed like a Christ or Allah. This relativist position is akin in spirit to the Hindu parable (sometimes attributed to the Buddha) of the blind men who felt the elephant. By touching its trunk, its legs, its belly and its tail, each pronounced it a different creature, though it was still an elephant, and fell to unnecessary arguing. As we search for truth, we should realize that every man sees his part and calls it true, whereas all are right and all are wrong. This conclusion is, needless to say, perfectly satisfactory if one believes that the elephant was important as a concept only and not something to be examined in terms of what it could do for the men, or be made to do for them, like carrying them somewhere. In that case, a sufficiently true description would be necessary and even some argument justified.

Like this parable, the 'ecumenical' arguments would seem highly questionable, if not sophistical. The identification of a religion with a culture occurs only after it has been accepted, and like Christianity and Buddhism, accepted often outside the society of its origin where it confronts and is rejected by religious establishments. It is wrong to confuse the process of filling a socio-spiritual vacuum with the belief that a religion is the *expression* of a culture. Italian Catholicism is extremely Italian, and Catholicism in many respects still excessively Latin, yet perhaps few peoples could be regarded as less *naturally* Christian than the Italians. In the same way, Chinese Buddhism has become very Chinese, but the religion is far from being the most natural religious expression of the people, who might have been more content as Jews, keeping a rigid law and believing themselves a chosen race. If anything, peoples do not simply choose their gods, but ultimately accept at a given time what they think they ought to in conscience, or must out of superstition. It is careless of Hick to suggest that Yahweh might have been mediated as God the Mother, had Israel been more matriarchal.[33] The prophets inveighed against those who prayed to the Queen of Heaven, while in matriarchal Tahiti, final honours went to a male Creator God. Precisely why a given society accepts a particular religion cannot be known; there is always an X factor as in a love affair, though certain conditions are more or less favourable, like crisis, cultural collapse or the discontent of a class.

This leads to the important point that there are no grounds for assuming that if Christianity had been taken East instead of West, Christ would have become another *bodhisattva* or *avatar* in any Christian theology. Where Christianity was carried East at a very early date and isolated, as in South India, Christ retained his unique status for centuries, though this was apparently explained in terms more Nestorian or Monophysite than Chalcedonian. Moreover, the saviour figure and his status enjoyed an influence in Asia disproportionate to Christian numbers. The 'monotheism' of Amidism and still more of mediaeval Tamil Shivaism are indebted to it, which is significant because it reminds us that similarities of religious tradition are not always spontaneous, even though an Asian idolatry of the unconscious is loathe to admit that external influences play their part and is inclined to emphasize spontaneity.

This is crucial in any consideration of the relationship of christology to the *bodhisattva* or *avatar* figure. Radhakrishnan waxes almost lyrical about the similarities between Christianity and Buddhism, particularly in the deeds and parables of Buddha and Christ, which are variously attributed to borrowing on the part of Christianity or the similar content of all religions.[34] Neither historical probability nor recent scholarship (Radhakrishnan's sources are mainly Victorian) permit such confidence, especially given the problems of dating anything reliably in India prior to the mediaeval period. For example, it is unlikely that Buddha, who was born in Nepal and preached in the Hindustan plains, walked on the waters of many lakes, and considering that the early Hinyana scriptures show him so opposed to the Hindu miraculous, it is unlikely that he anticipated the feeding of the five thousand by the distribution of cake to his disciples. The Buddhist parables of the mustard seed, the lost son and the sower derive from third-century Persian missionaries in Asia, and the famous vow of the *bodhisattva* from the *Vajradhavaja Sutra*, in which a saviour will suffer to deliver the world from misery, can be safely assumed to derive from the same source. Whether the doctrine of the *avatar* or even the Bhagavad Gita was influenced by Christianity is controversial, but the *bodhisattva* of later Mahayana Buddhism must be seen as an attempt (one which the churches of the Sassanid and Afghan region resisted before their demise at the hands of Islam) to accommodate Christ. While the concept of the *avatar* was prior to Christianity, we can be almost certain that its theology and multiplication of saviours was a consequence of Nestorian missions between the third and seventh centuries. For example, the ritual and saviour symbolism of Tibetan Buddhism, so late to develop (seventh century), certainly shows similarities to Christian practice as a result of a known Nestorian expedition to that region. Had the Mediterranean church desired to make Christ an *avatar* once it had broken with Judaism, the means were at hand, for despite the excessive reverence currently bestowed upon the Bhagavad Gita, it is not so very different from the vision of the Great Mother at the conclusion of Apuleius' *The Golden Ass* in which the deity, like Krishna, describes herself archetypally as all the gods and incarnations of the gods, known under many names but essentially the same.

The fact that Asia was so influenced by Christian principles prior to modern missions must in itself indicate a measure of dissatisfaction with what it has possessed, and this must be set against the argument that individuals naturally hold the faith of their society. Because of the materialism of the West, Christianity once established has usually been the simple alternative to irreligion (though one must not forget witchcraft). Asia, more religious, has had more options (even China had Taoism, Buddhism, Confucianism and Islam), but has not necessarily been content while conforming in its conservative way. Watchman Nee recounts an incident from his ministry which is far from being untypical of either missionary experience or Asian literature. He tells how one of his converts as a boy of twelve went to pray at a temple with his mother and was so overcome by the ugliness and dirtiness of the god that he prayed and dedicated himself to whatever God there was. He said that he 'met' Christ thirty years later but was 'touched' by God thirty years before.[35] Missionaries like Isobel Kuhn have always met individuals who recalled how their grandparents who never really believed in Buddhism had awaited the other god who never came, or themselves had the same feeling. In *The Dream of the Red Chamber*, both the hero and the Princess Ancestress in desperation address prayers directly to God rather than to the Taoist and Buddhist gods, though the princess, being of the Imperial House, had the right to address heaven (if it can really be called 'heaven' in the understanding of the Chinese philosophers). The prayer has a spirit close to that of the Psalms. 'Mighty Heaven, I, the unworthy head of the Jia clan, humbly lay myself at your feet and implore mercy ... I implore protection. Punish me and spare them. Turn their sorrow into joy. ...' In *The Scholars* a grateful father offers thanks to 'heaven' in personal terms. Arguably, what such incidents refer to is a 'natural religion' beyond local tradition, or, as St John writes: 'God lights every man that comes into the world.'

If this is true, it would dispense with Toynbee's sentimental argument that no God of love could do other than distribute revelation throughout all peoples and religions.[36] This will not do, since it is a Christian privilege to assume that God is love, whereas Hinduism might teach that God was beyond quality or was good and evil together. It is also a Christian privilege to assume that God is interested in what humanity does and is concerned to reveal himself.

Biblical tradition does not allow, nor can history be said to encourage the view that God has revealed himself everywhere. If he has, one can only marvel at the divine inefficiency, even allowing distortions of human imperfection. Mohammed at first wondered if his message had not come from Satan, and the principle of Holy War in Islam, which has been the death of millions of Christians and Hindus, hardly recommends it as a revelation of divine love; Buddha countered the extravagant polytheism of Hinduism with complete agnosticism towards God and denial of a Creator God. Confucius experienced a sense of vocation and was morally noble, but felt unable to describe God, and suffered such anguish that he wondered whether God was not trying to destroy him. The early Taoists were theologically eclectic, but were dangerous when it came to revelation and innovation and literally killed themselves with immortality pills.

Northrop would suggest that just as the new physics can contain logically contradictory propositions, so we should be able to assimilate the contradictions of the world's theology.[37] Radhakrishnan would speak of the merely 'instrumental' value of all creeds in relation to religion.[38] But not only is religion not pure physics, but the creeds do not even suggest the possibility of dynamic opposition and complementary views such as theoretically polytheism and monotheism might offer, since with Buddha even the concept of God or with Confucius of being able to know God is at stake, while mention of 'instrumental value' only begs the question. It assumes the existence of a 'self-realization' to which everyone aspires, while ignoring that some instruments must be presumed to be better than others for achieving this realization. On the whole religious ecumenists are driven back to the theory of a 'perennial philosophy', whether one speaks in terms of reaching it through Northrop's 'aesthetic continuum', Radhakrishnan's intuition, or whatever. Mysticism, union with the ineffable, the revelation of the God beyond God, becomes the true religion. Since the aim of this mysticism scarcely answers to the needs and feelings of the majority, who prefer personal immortality to dissolution in the eternal ocean, this faith has the quality of a 'gnosis' for the few whose negated individualism may even be compensated by a sense of composing the elite of all religious persons, tolerating the illusions of conventional belief. Moreover, there is something within the human spirit which must always balk at the view that the white light of void is preferable to the colour spectrum, contemplation to creativity. Purpose is not so easily dismissed.

Currently, a Christian, as opposed to a mystical, solution to the question of religious diversity needs to be phenomenological, based on an understanding of specialization and growth in life, though here one can only hint at the form of the solution. The alternatives presumed to exist for modern Christian apologetics are to accept that all religions are wrong, at best mere 'natural' religion, or else to believe that all (higher) religions are ways of God of more or less equal value, 'revelations', regardless, it seems, of whether adherents themselves would call them revelations in the Christian sense. Scripturally it can be questioned whether the former, more orthodox view, enjoys any more mandate than the latter. In Isaiah 45, a position somewhere between the two seems implied, as when the prophet announces that Yahweh has declared Cyrus king of Persia, his anointed one, to be the deliverer of Israel. 'I call you by your name, . . . I gird you, though you do not know me.' Historically, Cyrus was a Zoroastrian. While this declaration would seem to invite others like, perhaps, 'Behold Confucius, or behold Honen my servant . . .' there would nonetheless be a difference between God declaring his will for a society and performing it through individuals and positively revealing *himself*, which it is not suggested he did to Cyrus, and perhaps could not have done without misrepresentation. The real significance of the (seemingly) arbitary election of the Jewish people and Yahweh's revelation of his complete transcendence to them (crudely understood in dualistic terms, as statements like 'as high as the heavens are above the earth, so are my ways above your ways', would be) is that God is *not* within man in the sense of identical with the unconscious and the chaotic images produced by it, which are everywhere in world religion. The religious experience, though not necessarily identical with individuation, like it, must begin at a specific point and arrive at one, involving and animating different elements along the way. Any revelation of God is also a veiling, in so far as it is mediated through the agency of a culturally determined personality or society. Accordingly, to distribute revelation simultaneously among peoples, as opposed to using the most suitable or transparent medium to animate and eventually coalesce other elements into a new order, would tend to exaggerate difference, prevent recognition, and by producing so much variety, confuse deity with the chaotic mass of timeless archetypes constantly thrown up by the unconscious and the chaotic images produced by it, which are everywhere in world religion. The religious experience, though not necessarily identical with individuation, like it, must begin at a specific point and arrive at one, involving and animating different elements along the way.

When Christianity maintains that the various expressions of the higher religions are 'wrong', it means, or should mean, that they are wrong chiefly in terms of their ultimate framework of belief, since obviously, in terms of morality or spiritual techniques or aesthetics, they may be perfectly correct or even superior. For Christianity, possibilities for nearly everything exist, but only within definite regions and time spans. History is full of creative people who might have been more fulfilled in an earlier or later periods because their vision could never quite fit prevailing philosophy or existing information. In aesthetic history, the great flowering of Indian art under the Gupta required the influence from Greek form which acted as a kind of male logos to the female eros of Indian imagination to produce a new thing. Likewise, as regards religious diversity and Christian claims in relation to it, which for better or worse have come to involve a degree of Western and masculine imposition upon the Eastern and the feminine, it might be necessary to speak in terms of something like the operation of 'collective individuation' and the imperatives of 'integral truth'. As a religion, Christianity is a process in which both a constant pruning and grafting on takes place in relation to itself and ideally other faiths to achieve the most integral truth. Other religions offer truth, but not necessarily the most integral or dynamic truth possible; and before a modern existential Christianity shelved the issue, it always was a claim of the religion to the amenable to descriptions which showed it both subjectively and objectively true. Granted, modern scientists might question the relationship of Christian dogma to scientific reality, a point to which I shall return presently, but obviously the same solution could not be predicated for, say, Islam or Buddhism. Islam is iconoclastic towards any opposition, and is not amenable to the sort of rendering in the light of new knowledge or Taoist insight given in Chapter 1. Buddhism is more tolerant, but it cannot accord a reasonable status to form, patterns of recurrence and many human realities; it includes everything in a womb-consciousness, but is otherwise very limited.

Classic Buddhism and a good deal of Hindu mysticism must, I feel, be judged primarily in psychological terms as a rarefied form of 'cure' for human distress, superior to, but akin to the recommendation of cool colours and positive thinking to soothe frayed nerves in the West. In so far as this distress is compounded of guilt, it is arguably escapist in comparison with Christian belief; there is something suspicious about claims like that in the Taittiriya Upanishad (*Taittiriya* 2.8–9) that the enlightened soul, having realized oneness, will not need to be worried about whether he has been doing right or wrong. The problem may be larger than 'ignorance' after all.

Occidental seekers who have lived by inordinately extravert, materialistic standards experience the novelty of Asia's profound introversion in religious terms, while missionaries who have eyes only for the associated ritual, see idolatry and the works of the devil, thus also according it a more purely 'religious' status than it often deserves. Extravagant assertions to the effect that Asian religions are nothing but masterpieces of Satan, withholding men from God, serve little purpose, not only because they ignore how all religions, including Christianity, can be subject as much to evil as good influence, but because like all blanket assertions, they trivialize the serious truths they try to defend. Thus, although classical (Hinyana) Buddhism appears sane, rational, and devoid of the 'demonic' elements of some of the later Tibetan and Nepalese (Mahayana) Buddhism, it does seem possible that its 'cures' could become somewhat like a drug, and its beliefs and exercises atrophy a sense of the divine. I am not so impressed by the Buddhist serenity as religious observers, like Thomas Merton and Dom Aelred Graham, who pay flying visits to the East. Leaving aside tales which leak out of the beating of monks or of their achieving ecstasy through drug abuse (this was recently a legal scandal in Hong Kong), meditation can render some monks zombie-like or quietly ironical and resentful as they force their minds to accept their improbable world view. It is not easy for anyone to observe sea and mountain and discount deity altogether, and so, just as the atheism of scientists in the West often makes for a tiresome arrogance, so the virtual 'atheism' of Hinyana monks and Zen Buddhists (the degree varies greatly with the individual) makes for a kind of facetiousness. Nothing will convince me that Dr Suzuki was not a Zen wit who personally detested Christianity, but made game of Merton's gullibility.

The essence of the Christian objection to Asian mysticism as an experience is probably captured by Professor Zaehner in *Drugs, Mysticism and Makebelieve*,[39] where he discusses similarities between the vision of a dissolving relativistic world in Bernanos' sinister novel, *Monsieur Ouine*,[40] and Buddhist mysticism; he perceives a 'Satanic' quality in both visions in so far as by Christian standards the individual is being offered something less than the real thing: not a lucid joy but a sort of drugged peace for as long as the mind can be held in control; not knowledge but bare facts and information about things; not purified love for anything in particular, but a sensation akin to love without true subject or object, a ghost-town rather than a heaven. This, however, is still to take the dramatic side of things. Much Asian religion, particularly Buddhism, could strike one as rather smug, a pretext to feel good, to 'have' a tradition and not do much about it; its danger is less one of perverse doctrines and wickedness than of deadening indifference to anything vital, or (as used to be said of the Buddhists in franker, less religiously ecumenical days) 'they do nothing bad, but they do nothing especially good either'.[41] The same can be said of much Hinduism, and by Christian standards, priests and self-deifying gurus who continue to support this kind of faith from tradition, convenience and love of authority alone need to be set beside those Pharisees who receive condemnation for not entering the kingdom, and hindering those who would.

But judgments of this kind made about religions raise two further problems. If Christianity rather than Asia's 'natural' mysticism is intrinsically the most universal faith, on the terms given it would need to have more than Radhakrishnan's minimal requirements, which are (*a*) a basis in profound personal experience of the Ultimate and the ideal possibilities of life, and (*b*) consistency in its philosophical elaboration. Christianity would additionally need to be historically and scientifically true, or at least capable of some harmonization with history and science in support of its controversial affirmations concerning reality and human development. It would further require a credible scheme of salvation, that is, a concept of last things somewhat more satisfying than Augustine's, with its superstitious damnation of unbaptized infants, or the traditional Hindu alternative of almost endless reincarnations.

On the whole, post-Darwinian, post-liberal Christianity has been content to pass over precisely this objective truth in favour of existential truth, so that Genesis is cheerfully dismissed as myth, which happens to convey that God is Creator and that life is not arbitrary. Early in this century, with an almost iconoclastic zeal which thinly veiled an idolatry of science, whole passages of Old Testament history which were subsequently authenticated by archaeology and historical research were likewise consigned to oblivion. While I am not in sympathy with those fundamentalist scientists and exegetes of California who spend their days trying to prove that the Bible is as literally true as Euclid or Gray's *Anatomy*, I agree that its objective truth, its harmony with science, is not irrelevant. It should be more than 'myth', even 'true' myth; it should be able to supply clues and indications about where we come from, who we are, and where we are going, at least sufficient to be consistent with a world-affirming doctrine.

I am inclined to feel that the Bible has this character, and that dismissal of this aspect of revelation has been excessive and premature. One is reminded of Voltaire's mockery of the biblical statement that light was the first thing God created, whereas now we know that light was the first element. It is also true that while the earth was not created in six days, the development of species recorded in the Bible is in harmony with accepted patterns of evolution. In comparison with speculations like the Japanese, that humanity developed from the sweat of the gods, or the Indian, that it came from Brahma's urination, clearly the creation story is both exalted and comparatively 'scientific'. Its peculiar and unique telescoping of the time factor into days (though the Hebrew permits 'time' as an alternative translation) suggests a deliberate attempt to humanize a process: man is not to consider himself an exile in time and eternity, irrelevant to the aeons, as in the Hindu tradition. Altogether, it seems likely that a measure of understanding of the Bible as science will make a return, like the herbal remedies so long despised by the medical establishment, which is beginning to admit its limitations.

Much more crucial for a religion with exclusivist claims is its account of salvation and its conditions. In discussing Christian attitudes towards ultimate salvation and other faiths, two issues are usually confused: the credibility of the specifically Augustinian-Calvinistic interpretation of salvation and the credibility of a doctrine of judgment and damnation. These two are quite separate, since the former, though considered classic and typical by many advocates of religious ecumenism, are in fact constructions only. Nowhere in the New Testament is it stated that ignorance or even the state of being unbaptized (which is admittedly disapproved) is a ground for damnation; even St Paul implies the opposite (Rom. 2.14), while the fact that Christ descended into 'Hades' and preached to the dead (I Peter 3.19) in itself gives little ground for the doctrine of limbo held by the Catholics, which suggests that those living before Christ can never be fully saved.

This notwithstanding, a doctrine of judgment and hell appears well developed in Christian teaching, and even so radical a liberal theologian as John Hick insists that a presentation of the gospel which does not take account of this 'dark' and urgent side is not an honest one.[42] No matter how much one may disagree on *how* this aspect of doctrine should be interpreted, it must be acknowledged that Jesus envisaged a judgment; he also placed the final responsibility for salvation of both believers and the ignorant on his own shoulders: 'No one comes to the Father but by me', a statement which in reality is not so unreasonable if one reflects that in so many faiths God is not in fact believed to be personal.

Despite this, ever since Bishop Irenaeus in the second century, the question has been raised how a good God could consent to the creation of people who he foreknew would suffer eternally, their alleged evil thwarting the divine purpose and ability to bring good from evil. Would this discredit Christian doctrine and claims, especially to be a true and universal faith? The question scarcely seems to have interested the early Christians; their main concern was simply to obey and be delivered. Historically, salvation, even with the help of grace, has been considered a prize and not a right, as it has tended to become in modern thought. Only reflection on the Christian doctrine of love (or middle-class sentimentality) has made notions of judgment somewhat foreign to us. The Greeks and Romans believed in an eternal hell for some (the myths of Tantalus, Sisyphus, etc.), and in traditional Hinduism and Buddhism only a fraction, an elite, could seriously hope to attain salvation: for the rest, transmigration was more or less eternal. Madhva positively states that evil people will endure reincarnation for ever. Possibly influenced by Christianity's urgent idea of salvation, the Bhagavad Gita promises the believer cessation from reincarnation and protection at the end of the cycle and rebirth in the world of Brahman, but considering Krishna's status and the concept of periodic emanations from God, it is hard to see how the hope of such protection could be considered 'sure'. The ultimate sense of the soul's bondage, short of a dramatic deliverance, is everywhere projected upon the infinite, making endless suffering a possibility in any scheme which assumes the inalienable immortality of the spirit.

Conservative missionary thinking has been specifically loathe to review the question, not simply on scriptural grounds, but of the belief that there can be no true missionary impulse or advance without it. While it is true that complete disbelief in judgment appears to stultify Christian action, the most successful evangelists, at least in Asia, have been those like Sundar Singh, Kagawa and Fr Matteo Ricci who took judgment as a serious possibility. The solidity of their work depended upon the lack of mere haste which distinguished those of Hudson Taylor's kind. The latter scarcely founded a well organized church because of their attempt to save millions by a sentence or a tract. Moreover, in nervous pessimistic Asia, hell-fire preaching is self-defeating, being either completely dismissed or assuming the status of an obsession. Thus, in India, preaching like that of Paul Vankateswami only leaves Hindus beseeching Christians to pray for them to their god to deliver them from the Christian hell, or making offerings to Christ images with the same purpose, yet without the slightest feelings of repentance or attraction to the faith.

Precisely what Jesus intended when he spoke of hell, cannot be, and perhaps was not intended to be, known; the function of the allusions was primarily existential rather than to satisfy curiosity. However seriously and generally this teaching is to be taken, there is no question that its *prime* target was Jesus' religious contemporaries who rejected the Messiah, and also the rich and the hypocritical. (Later New Testament writing, like that of St John, added the followers of the latter-day Antichrist to the list of those in special danger of judgment.) Even the sayings of Jesus in their transcendent wisdom have a social context of sorts. If we did not know from contemporary records how vicious and demoralized the times of Jesus were, we might guess from the extent of degeneration which had overtaken the theoretically righteous Jewish society. It was an age for which there could be no answer but salvation by a kind of flight, mutilation and abandonment of a lot of philosophical and social dead wood. Divine mercy might be infinite, but human capacity to receive it is not so at any time, and as the Sermon on the Mount indicated about the fundamental relations of life, the measure a person gives will be the measure they receive, and it will be the merciful who receive mercy. One must therefore be at least 'human' in order to be spiritual, so that especially in a vicious age when mercy and human feeling were in short supply, the offer of salvation would be delivered with many a severe qualification and warning. Subsequent hell-fire evangelism which, in less cruel times and places, made God the wrathful enemy of everything from childish lies to onanism, discredited the teaching, making it something traumatic with God less loved than feared as a cruel monster. Even granted that many disqualifications do surround the gospel message, the *scope* of their application must remain an open question; it is not at all clear whether salvation is understood to have one or two levels, whether few are saved and most eternally lost, or whether an elite achieve full salvation and many are saved later. On the one hand, sayings like 'straight is the gate' and 'many are called but few are chosen' point to a limited hope of salvation, while other statements suggest that even if some are in danger of never being saved, others might have hope in the long run. The text, 'He who blasphemes the Holy Spirit never has forgiveness in this life or the next', by its phrase 'or the next' is suggestive in much the same way as the text 'You shall not come out till you have paid the last farthing'. Scholastic doctrine, however, reduced any forgiveness after death to bad Catholics who passed through purgatory, which they deduced from St Paul's words 'saved as by fire'. The Indian visionary, Sundar Singh, gave it the wider meaning, and this is obviously an attractive solution.

But the phrase 'attractive solution' in itself indicates the problem. Like sex, the subject of hell can never be treated with complete objectivity. If we have suffered much, or observed the abysses of human nature, as in those many 'good' German people who acquiesced in the evil of Hitler, we are ready, like Tertullian, to declare humanity evil and damn it all. If the sun shines, if we are among friends and witness deeds of charity, then like Irenaeus we believe that humanity is good, or at least redeemable. Only a total view could decide what was true here. To assume the worst but to hope for the best is perhaps the only sensible attitude, and I shall briefly review the possible arguments for the doctrine as it is generally felt to stand.

The greatest problem is why those foreordained to damnation should be created at all; which effectively means, why did God create the world at all, seeing that we were not necessary to the already infinite love enjoyed within the Trinity, which ought perhaps to have 'sacrificed' the desire to create rather than sacrificed itself for humanity later? Was God himself 'selfish' and 'imperfect' in creating the world? Many notable people, like Sophocles, Rousseau, Mozart, even Jeremiah, have cursed the day they were born, or regarded existence as not worth experiencing, without even considering a possible hell to pay for sins or unbelief at the end. The seriously deprived, the depressive, do of course present a special problem of values; all there is space to say here is that even if they cannot personally conceive of life as good or God as love, they are bound to place their conclusions against those of humanity at large. It may be true that God is *bound* to recompense *them* unconditionally, but they in turn would be bound to acknowledge that life is good for many people and who are also perfectly willing to enjoy it at the expense of others. The doctrine is defined in relation to the general human condition, not to purely personal or morbid experience of existence.

The first thing to recognize in the problem of the creation of the bad is that even God could not exactly foreknow the actions of individual beings who were not even possible. The decision to create the world would need to be prior to any such foreknowledge, and since evil was only a possibility to God, whose nature is free but good, although he might hypothesize failure, he would neither expect it nor imagine its extent. This is why he may well have 'regretted' his creation, with the misery it obliged him to tolerate, much as Jesus 'marvelled' at an unbelief which his nature could not really fathom. Since, as St Paul says, 'God desires that *all* men should be saved', it is unlikely that God *will* positively damn anyone; in reality they damn themselves, much as Judas committed suicide. This point is obscured by a Jewish tendency to render all passives in the active, saying that God will 'send' evil, when it means that God will not prevent some natural evil from falling on man. The danger of sin is precisely its self-destructive nature, its tendency to cause a drawing-away from God rather than a divine withdrawal from man. What can even God do for the type of soul, like the infamous de Sade, who described his depraved writings as 'dearer to me than life itself', and who, if that were possible, would like to have been completely evil.

The answer would perhaps be to allow evil to take its course and let the evil soul first torment itself, then dissolve, as Plato imagined it eventually would. This, however, is also problematic. Is there, or can there be, such a thing as *pure* nothingness in which there could be pure extinction? Asian philosophy has always described the void itself as 'full', the formless source of form, while many Christian mystics have seen hell and evil as in some way subsisting through (though separate from) God, and then, as I remarked earlier, the *ex nihilo* creation doctrine of traditional theology which assumes a void exists somewhere, needs to be questioned. Indeed, as Joseph Campbell has suggested, it may rest on a childish psychological impression.[43] This question apart, man is biblically described as created 'a living *soul*' and *for* God. Theoretically, it seems to be implied that he could have lived for ever, and in the bodily Edenic form ('Let them not eat of the fruit of the tree of life lest they live for ever'), so that the death which enters at the Fall must not be viewed simply as a punishment, but as deliverance from the resulting ills of continuing in the body, as opposed to being raised to a higher existence. It would seem, therefore, that once God had decided to create man, he could not rob him of the eternity to which his spirit, if not his body, was natural heir. If the species were capable of 'dissolving', then logically no 'good' souls could enjoy immortality either, in which case God would be doubly thwarted in creation, and if God is ultimately defeated in his purpose, he is no longer God. The soul, moreover, seems to demand its continuance. Though I cannot understand their views, there have been individuals, like the dying Renan, who admitted to thinking damnation preferable to extinction. Yet 'continuance' is perhaps not the word, nor is any conception of eternity as being for 'ever and ever', since time itself, as Augustine and Kant recognized, is a subjective notion dependent upon physical space (going from here to there in so many seconds), as opposed to the spiritual power of omnipresence or 'immediate' transference, so that logically announcing the judgment, the angel in Revelation declares that 'time will be no more'. Hence, hell would be more of an eternal present, a 'bottomless pit', in which evil withdraws into a nothingness it can never quite fathom, just as heaven is a moving to an unattainable fullness.

The dynamic nature of evil leads to our final consideration, which relates to the objection that God should patiently wait the aeons of the *bodhisattva* to redeem every soul, because every soul is redeemable. While I would agree with C. S. Lewis that if a thousand chances were of any use they would be given, they may not be of any use, the ultimate nature of sin may not permit an endless delay. In many souls, sins result chiefly from weakness and circumstance (though given scope and power they might be more sinful than they or the trusting would imagine), but in others it is a conscious or unconscious desire to destroy any good. In the Christian teaching this will to destruction is seen in heightened form on the spiritual front, where Satan or 'spiritual wickedness in high places' lures the soul to doom. Whether or not one cares, like Jeane Dixon, to identify the black holes of the universe with the operation of the forces of evil,[44] the fact remains that this world and probably the universe are doomed, and will end plunged into death and futility. God might wait even for the worst, but if Job and the gospels supply any insights into the beyond, it is that evil does not intend to wait, so that God's hand must be regarded as to some extent 'forced', to ring down the curtain first. Moreover, if repeated reincarnations were the answer, we might ask whether this would not repeat or even extend evil. As it is, the weak link of the theory of reincarnation is that the fortunate, the rich and powerful, are so immoral; at the present point in time they receive the benefit of the doubt, because it seems that their function is incidentally to help to purge the poor and weak of their former sins by making life hard for them. But as souls are saved, how will the sinners be purged? If the returning souls do not have evil masters, they would need to punish one another, and the more evil among them might only drag the remainder into greater corruption. One of the points about the most terrible of all Christ's parables, the parable of the poor man and Lazarus, is that some evil is so blind that it may not be able to repent. Lazarus still addresses Dives from hell as though he were his servant, not someone whom God has rewarded.

The metaphysics of why *unbelief* is included with sin, or is an expression of it, is a related issue which I can touch on only insofar as it helps us with considering the results for missions. Christianity has always demanded more than goodness, since goodness can never be sufficient for God, and something more than conscience may be needed for the performance of God's will. Social history, and even religion, is full of 'good' people who in good conscience have done harm. Obviously too, God, if he possesses the nature Christianity attributes to him, must claim human trust and a free response, or else the divine human reconciliation would become interested, even be resented to evil effect. Expressed in psychological or philosophical terms, the insistence on belief in Jesus could be considered the equivalent of stating that there can be so salvation without specific love and trust, the realization of God's children that they *are* his children, 'Except you become as little children you cannot enter the kingdom of heaven.' The possible intellectual difficulties of belief are thus scarcely in question; the belief and reconciliation is in any case a grace afforded by the Spirit; one less consents to a dogma than one is seized by it, or rather by the divine, when one recognizes one's situation and the nature of Jesus.

I am not thinking so much of Tillich's theology as of Watchman Nee's analysis of spiritual psychology and his insistence that the trouble with so much evangelism that he had witnessed among the Chinese was that it 'preached salvation' and condemned the many who refused it, when in fact, this involved only the presentation of a creed, something heard and intellected but not humanized or felt, the statement of belief and not of experience.[45] Had I not attended a Billy Graham rally in Hong Kong, I might not have appreciated the argument so much, or imagined how irrelevant a type of conservative evangelism can become within a non-Christian area. The entire address was filled with veiled threats, like 'You must die', 'Mao must die', 'Franco must die', 'the world's problems are becoming too great', leading up to the call to repent and turn to Christ. Since Christ was about the only person whose words and deeds had *not* been described and discussed, one was left wondering (as were Christians of various persuasions against whom I checked notes for that evening) precisely to whom, or to what, the Chinese enquirers imagined they were giving themselves, unless they were already the products of church schools, reasonably familiar with the New Testament.

So much evangelism today seems to be still fit for the first century, when Christians shook the dust from off their feet at a decadent, recalcitrant Jewry who should have known better and were, as events showed, courting national disaster religiously and politically by their behaviour. It should perhaps be noticed that Jesus says to St Thomas, 'Blessed are they who have not seen and yet have believed' (John 20.29), and also that the Holy Spirit did not prompt the disciples immediately to go into all the world in the sense of all religions at once, and anyhow, lest souls should be lost. Some regions were even forbidden to them. This signifies two things. First, that Christians should be generous enough to admit it was more easy for the first Christians to believe. The vivid memory of Christ, the Jewish education and expectation, the cultural homogeneity of the Roman world and the proto-church of Gentile synagogue-goers, were all conducive to the acceptance and diffusion of the gospel. Second, only due cultural and psychological preparation by a church and cultural and psychological readiness in those evangelized can produce that situation in which, as the

Catholic theologian Hans Küng has said, the gospel may be considered to be preached 'in its fullness' and properly decided for.[46]

The idea that preaching the Word means saturating whole towns and countries with tracts or revivalist formulas on all and sundry occasions discredits Christianity. (I myself am almost alarmed at the way in which the badgering techniques of American fundamentalists are making the population of America hostile to and blasé about religion. Religion is promoted like a business, on the media with commercials like so much soap, or shouted from the street corner until its 'mystery' is reduced to the cliché.) Hell may be within the logic of the faith, and judgment something certain classes of people need to reflect upon, but it takes little spiritual or theological insight to realize that God does not want or need 'converts'. As I replied to the Bali missionary, I believe conversion must be *honourable*.[47] To demand it at any cost, to insist persons must accept what one says and that those who do not are lost, as though one were the mouthpiece and perfect representative of God, when in fact one might be less than winsome and one's teaching obscure, can be a form of hidden arrogance. Some people's experience of religion and religious people can be so unfortunate that it might need a life-time and more to erase the impression, so that there must be some situations in which disbelief or ignorance cannot be judged in religious terms. The evangelist's concern should be simply to proclaim his message, not to satisfy his or researchers' curiosity into idiosyncratic or morbid reactions. In any case, even on religious terms, Christ is pictured as 'marrying' the church, so presumably he does not want terrorized or resentful souls. We do, however, gather that he wants his will to be done on earth as it is in heaven, and so, especially as worldwide life-expectancy increases and social issues impinge, it might be helpful to see evangelism not simply as some deliverance of lost heathen, but the bringing of persons from a measure of darkness into the light where they may realize their own and their societies' highest possibilities. Unless the religion concerned or its priesthood is locally perpetrating obvious evils, outright threats and condemnations are self-defeating, at least in Asia where, for example, the best Christians have been shown to have been the best Buddhists who saw the new faith as better fulfilling what they already sought, rather than some system of wickedness existing only to pervert their souls. Charges of that nature will only make them incredulous. With this human aspect in mind, I shall conclude the chapter with a summary of what extensive research has indicated to be the main conditions and factors of growth within missions.

IV

Perhaps because 'the Spirit blows where it will', there are no absolute and invariable rules in the patterns of mission growth, but in Asia, Africa and Latin America, the following principles frequently emerge. One of the most important errors of missions is to operate on the assumption that people are converted (or consciously change their religion) for rational or theological reasons which the missionary must not fail to supply in detail. Only a type of educated person is argued into any faith. The chief motivation appears nearly always to be self-betterment. This may be expressed in terms of moral improvement, religious improvement (as when, for example, the individual cannot 'relate' to Krishna, who demands chastity but played with the *gopis*) or improvement in intellectual knowledge, or social or family standing (a relative may have been converted), though the social reasons may be pretexts, since it has been found that in the long run conversion from 'mercenary' motives does not necessarily produce the inferior Christian: indeed, sometimes the opposite (one thinks of the parable of the two sons, in which the one who originally refused was the one who did his father's bidding). Christianity is thus associated with excellence and idealism, and one might say (though the mission sociologists do not) that the preaching of the word at first simply arouses the Christ archetype which is arguably universal.

The biggest movements into the church are of the group variety, whether as in the Catholic mass baptisms in South India under St Francis Xavier, or the Protestant revivalism in Korea. These group movements, however, have to fulfil certain conditions. Most importantly, they will need to be directed to the tribal group, the uprooted or the melting-pot society, and/or the working class sector. All available evidence points to the truth of Toynbee's thesis about the acceptance of new religions by the 'internal proletariat'.[48] Save in exceptional circumstances (as in traditional China, where contact with the mandarins was obligatory), all missions directed other than to the working classes fail, or enjoy limited success. The wealthy and the professional classes simply rationalize whatever religion is accepted by the mass, but personally exhibit little personal will to change or to diffuse the faith.

Any mission in which the decision to change religion bears additional racial or political implications is greatly slowed down or blocked altogether. Thus, if a rival tribe or nation, or a conquering nation, is Christian, and especially if conversion involves foreign education, de-culturization or enforced worship across ethnic and tribal lines (the conglomerate church), the mission fares so much the worse. Inconvenient though it can be, it is best, at least while the faith is being discovered, for each tribal or ethnic group to worship separately (e.g. Thais and Chinese Thais work best separately). The melting-pot situation should never be striven for, and American missionaries originating from the classic melting-pot society commit serious errors here. Converts should also communicate in their own language. Loss of a language, such as Irish to English, is nearly always a disaster, culturally and religiously. Ethnic groups like the American Indians have been shown to be much less responsive to religious appeals when addressed in a language other than the 'heart' language; there are also problems where, as among the Chinese, the Bible is so imperfectly rendered that it is preferably read in another tongue. American laymen who go on missionary holidays to distribute tracts and talk to people in English are mostly wasting time and also money, better spent upon the work of qualified missionaries.

In difficult areas, or unresponsive ones, where there are great complications of race and culture, insistence and saturation treatment are fatal and only create further hostility. The missionary should be satisfied, if need be, to maintain a presence and provide assistance, allowing the community opportunity to establish trust, and the mission itself to learn the problems of the area. One of the least effective instruments of mission is church school education, since it brings no adults into the church structure, and often inoculates the young, especially in hostile areas, against a faith with which they grow familiar from a purely school-room or examination aspect. The snob value of church-school education is also a hindrance to ecclesiastical reputation. Free education of the peasantry or working classes of the Third World is more appreciated and more effective. Brahmins, for instance, have always been pleased to send their children to the schools of a religion they told their offspring to reject. Higher education, therefore, does much more credit to the faith. So does health work, provided it does not become too conditional, or the sick are not badgered (this is very rarely the case). More effective everywhere is every kind of practical involvement in community and agricultural projects with adults. Radio work is usually very ineffective, though not necessarily so.

Basically, because of its intangible, distant quality, it must strive for relevance and appropriate cultural tone, more perhaps, than even a local church. This it does not currently do. English and American dominated as it is, it tends to use the Anglo-American format and proclaims rather than explains or compares; trying to reach every group, it often fails to touch any one group in particular. Thus, in India, its listeners and enquirers are mainly nominal Indian Christians and Muslims who need less explanation of the Christian concepts of God.

Missions in responsive areas have been hampered and blocked most by long and difficult catechumenates of churches, like the Catholic, and the excessively high standards demanded by some Protestant churches. Some churches have even refused to baptize illiterates, making education a condition of church membership. Fundamentalists who discourage enquirers by making issues out of smoking, drinking, or polygamy, lose converts unnecessarily because records show that in most cases, if the person genuinely demonstrated faith in the first place, these problems are nearly always resolved with time, and some personal and moral improvement is noted. Any delay with an enquirer, or a refusal to accept group decisions to be converted by tribes, is disastrous. It has been shown that where tribal groups have enquired about or decided for Christianity, and then came up against doubts concerning the sincerity of group conversion, or demands for lengthy educations, by the time the terms had been thrashed out or everyone educated, hurt feelings led to changed minds, whereas those who were quickly accepted and taught afterwards normally 'grew' even in the group.

I feel bound to say that all of this is very much a matter of common sense and ought not to have required elaborate statistics and research to make it apparent. Long questionnaires asking converts everything from their academic qualifications to their first impressions of Jesus seem too calculating to be nice, and though research like McGavren's serves a useful function as a corrective, there is something altogether too militaristic about the approach and aims, especially for Asia. Full implementation of Californian church growth schemes would merely place the church in the hands of the most hard-headed, whereas in Asia, it is the flowing water, bending bamboo and feminine endurance rather than the fire, organization and masculine force which wins in the long run. Zeal is no substitute for wisdom, or perhaps, as Jesus put it, one needs to be 'as wise as serpents but harmless as doves' (and as we have seen, 'harmful as serpents and silly as doves' might apply to many a past mission venture). These failures by persons supposedly guided by the Word also raises again the issue (which was alluded to in the first chapter) of just how much the Bible itself should be used and interpreted. In the light of all that has been considered so far, this must be one of the topics in the final chapter.

7

The Age of Aquarius

Now that I have given some indications of the conditions of church growth, it is possible, first, to forecast the future of the churches in Asia, and then to consider where religion and Christianity at large are heading. In this chapter I shall review some of the leading problems of the Christian position in the light of the new or undeveloped principles within the faith to which I have already drawn attention.

What will be the outcome for Christian outreach in Asia? Of the places specifically considered in this book, I am inclined to feel that Japan holds most promise, despite its poor formal response so far. Both Uchimura and Kagawa reported visions, or at least premonitory dreams, in which they saw Japan awakened to Christianity and its vision of the faith spreading out to influence the world.[1] Whether or not these can be considered 'revelations', I would feel the expectations, at any rate, to be within the bounds of possibility. As Toynbee would emphasize, there comes a point at which a country cannot accept the techniques and trade of another society without absorbing the basis of its ideas.[2] Japan has tried more than most to do just this for a full century, but is reaching a stage where, as the post-war literature and its crisis of identity demonstrates, the compromise is wearing thin because the native introversion is assuming the form of a more Western individualism and is requiring justification and explanation. No amount of Buddhist revivalism, however appealing and well organized, can counter this trend indefinitely. While it is true that the secularism and materialism of the modern West may satisfy many, there remains a strong vein of spirituality and a traditional prejudice against egoism and materialism which is unlikely to remain satisfied with it.

The almost fashionable status of Christianity, whether as personal faith or as a talking-point among the intelligentsia, could be symptomatic of an approaching religious crisis, and given the surprise patterns in Japanese social development, there is nothing to stop this diversely religious and agnostic country from suddenly turning more Christian. A good deal depends on how well the religion can be de-intellectualized and popularized by theologians, and how far Protestantism and Catholicism can temper certain traditional styles and thought-patterns in the way I have indicated. Assuming a Christian advance, it is likely that any popular movement would be divided between revivalists and ritualists, for this is a division historically natural to Japanese spirituality; under American and fundamentalist influence, however, it could be allowed to develop into an unnecessary ground for contention. The continued growth of the lively Korean church might also become a factor in making Christianity a serious popular alternative for Japan.

Korean influence might also prove crucial for China, as it becomes increasingly open towards East Asia and America. Some measure of rebirth for the Chinese church seems almost likely, even if only on a small scale. Atheism, as the theologian Paul Tillich has forcibly argued, is always most fervent when it has something to react against: terrible superstition or intolerant priesthoods.[3] Once triumphant, it produces a vacuum which serves as a breeding-ground for the metaphysical longings in the suppressed spirituality of the average man. Because China is under increasing pressure to allow more human rights, and because it cannot possibly return to discredited superstitions like Taoism, Christianity will obviously present the most viable and rational option for those seeking religion, provided that it can appear sufficiently Chinese. It is, moreover, unlikely that all of the hundreds of future students to be sent to America will wish to ignore the religious dimensions of the society they visit, though it would be unfortunate if (as seems quite likely) they were to be pestered by over-zealous individuals less concerned with them as persons than as potential missionaries for a narrow form of Christianity. On the other hand, after such a very long period of seclusion from the world and from ordinary freedoms, curiosity about the world and a desire for freedom will not encourage the acceptance of added commitments, while in a society offering little opportunity for individual advancement, there will be those who are happy to advance themselves by being more zealously atheistic. Scarcely had plans for the new Institute for the Study of World Religions been inaugurated than a new society for atheism was formed.

Altogether, any revival of Christian religion in China could cause great problems, and it could turn into a damp squib, reacting upon Chinese Christians generally. If after such a long period of separation from Rome, the Catholic church, never very skilled in coping with Chinese nationalism, tried to put its wandering sheep too exactly back into line, it would be bitterly resented, if not by Catholics, at least by all observers. Evangelical Protestants, who are also seemingly incorrigible about China, could occasion much resentment if they push Sungist revivalism as the only true faith, insisting on emotionalism which could only give rise to gossip, and if they encourage preaching without respect for the Chinese group soul, which easily gives rise to accusations of subversion. While it is unlikely that Western people will ever be allowed to enter China to preach and evangelize again, there is no doubt that many would like to do so, and such enthusiasts as the China watcher Leslie Lyall have moved from the view expressed in *Red Sky at Night*[4], that prayers should be offered for native pastors, to promoting the 'Love China' meetings of 1976, which anticipated the day, now dawning, when Americans and others could enter China to spend holidays, teach and trade, carrying the Word, Bibles and tracts with them. One dreads to think of the freaks, religious and otherwise, who, ignorant of China and its ways, may soon descend upon it, advocating their versions of religion or democracy. The least freedom accorded them will lead to the usual noisy presumption in Asia, which in the Chinese context could be punished overnight and without warning. I think that there is little question that restoration of national glory, nationalism rather than internationalism, is China's main concern (and this is natural enough), and it will only tolerate compromise with the West for as long as it contributes to its aims of rapid development. Thus those who fraternize too recklessly today may become the national enemies of tomorrow. 'China lovers' need to remember this, and any church should be encouraged to be thoroughly Chinese, even (I still insist) down to its religious pictures. I have been impressed at the way in which the walls of farmers' houses are filled, even plastered, with Chinese pictures, and the old religious icons have been replaced by posters of current leaders and colourful propagandist pictures of Chinese history.

It is not possible to be so optimistic for the churches in Thailand, despite the greater liberty. In this langorous tropical country, more haste often means less speed, and with so many opportunities lost and mistakes made, the problem now is not to spoil the venture entirely by mere saturation treatment, inspired in particular by fears of Communist take-over. It is possible that further Communist advance may create a wave of panic conversions, as happened in Cambodia in the last two years before its fall, but apart from this, major Christian movements do not seem likely, and perhaps are not really deserved. Missionary work needs to become more personalized (to become more aesthetic, for example) before it can hope to claim conversions with honour or real depth.

Politics is becoming an unavoidable issue. In most mission fields today, even those missionaries who would like to be more politically vocal are often denied the liberty to be so, or prefer to leave politics to their converts, who are nationals; but in Thailand, where missionaries have been taken into a degree of government confidence, it would seem only just that they should voice some protest against corruption and those reactionary elements of the society which have consistently jeopardized democracy and blindly continue on a selfish course which positively foments and facilitates student and Communist revolt. Of course, it will not help the churches under any possibly future Communist regime if they fail to do this now. Thailand is the domino which need not and certainly must not fall, because in view of events in Vietnam and Cambodia, the consequences for the rest of South East Asia would be unthinkable. However, the remarkable native capacity for diplomacy and recuperation cannot be relied on indefinitely. The hold on democracy, which dates only from 1932, is weak. The discontent of ethnic and fringe groups, failure of reform to keep pace with rapid development, and the serious division thus caused between the prosperous and rather decadent city and the poor and alert countryside affords an excellent opportunity for all kinds of subversion. In the days of media and development, political and urban centralization, formerly so necessary to this divided country, is now a liability causing envy in the countryside and slums and crime in the city. Decentralization would be a cure, if it is not too late. I hope, too, that protagonists of the view that all a country needs to solve its ills is for the leadership to accept Christianity will not advance in their plan to attack the body of the bureaucracy as yet unreached, or if they do, that they will not prejudice the church's position by demanding that converts should not attend the official Buddhist functions required of them. Basically there is no need for Thailand to fall to its Communists, because there are really no glaring wrongs and hardships which require total reorganization, as in a society like that of China. The so-called Communists should be revealed for what they often are, power-greedy malcontents who want to have their will even at the cost of plunging societies into savagery and backwardness, as in Cambodia. At present, the feud between pro-Soviet and pro-Chinese cliques among Thai communists and popular horror at events in Cambodia may lessen the force of this movement.

If the Thai prospects are not hopeful, it is even harder to think of India becoming authentically Christian, despite the presence of the Bible in many orthodox homes as yet another scripture to be read for edification. On the other hand, India is so fundamentally religious that it is more likely to show advances in Christianity than in Communism; it will surely be the last nation to do that. Its poverty and problems are such that not even Soviet imperialism will be especially interested in adding it to its conquests. The Indian church has scarcely begun to come to terms with social, cultural and religious realities, and as I have remarked, when it is not indifferent, it is either excessively intellectual, or evangelical in situations which cannot warrant it. Sociologically speaking, the biggest opportunity for the churches will arise simply from the growing disenchantment with Hinduism. When I have discussed what I believe to be the Spenglerian decline of the West and Christianity, I have usually received a reply to the effect that the decline was global and was also affecting Hinduism. The masses, while still dedicated to Hinduism, are becoming more fatalistic, stoical rather than genuinely pious in accepting their fate, which in some areas is actually becoming worse rather than better. The worsening is attributed to the forces of change. Urbanization, and the terrible evils which are accompanying it, cause a decline in fervour among formerly devout rural people, if not exactly a loss of faith. Massive political corruption and the failures of the national and Gandhian revolution to live up to expectations, particularly those of the depressed and untouchable classes, for whom altered laws have not brought improved conditions, nor pacifist protest a conquest of the prejudice and cruelty of the rich, have taken their toll of Hindu moral consciousness.

The labours of at least Mother Teresa and her associates have testified louder than any words that Christianity demands something more morally noble than contemporary Hinduism can supply, despite its tolerance and its mysticism. Nevertheless, strong resistance towards Christianity of a passive, eclectic kind can still be expected. Formally, Hinduism may discourage selfhood and egoism, but collectively its national ego is enormous (I have even visited a Mother India temple where the object of worship was a large sculptured map). Thus among the educated, there is a resistance to any non-indigenous faith, and perhaps even a half-realized desire to revert to the old exclusiveness which prevented Annie Besant from becoming a full Hindu, so as to be the new bearer of truth and the messiahs to a godless world. While it may be sincerely hoped that Indian Christianity will become more meaningfully Indian, there can be no answer to such aspirations. Neo-Hinduism is probably one of the most unexpected and significant challenges to Christianity today.

II

It is now possible to consider the future of Christianity at large. It should be evident that I feel that in the West, the future of Christianity much depends on how it responds to the challenge of the East, and on whether it is able to achieve an unprecedented revision of doctrinal statements, with a new emphasis on the feminine values of wholeness and feeling and a new ritual and organization. Because it is insufficiently related to the world beyond the West, Christianity currently seems to be sharing the general decline of the West in the Spenglerian sense, having become either excessively rationalistic or rabidly, unintellectually fundamentalist. Both these are signs of death and allow room for the trend towards the occult and mystery religions which, as Spengler so accurately forecast, is now overtaking the West. The situation is, of course, akin to that of Roman imperial society, whose materialism and poor religious life made it vulnerable to the various mystery religions. In the modern world, though much of the occult trend involves pure superstition and inferior thinking, it finds a measure of justification in the somewhat 'demoralizing' discovery of Einsteinian relativity, wrongly assumed to rule out the possibility of any certainty.

Until the 1970s it used to be imagined that religion in the twentieth century and the foreseeable future would be engaged in some desperate struggle with atheism, materialism or Communism. Today, as a result of the occult explosion and of a feminism which demands a mysticism 'beyond God the Father', it seems more likely that the battle could be between formal religions and a whole variety of occult-oriental variations, between Christianity and – in the broad sense – gnosticism. Since these variations will need justification, or even seek new gods and messiahs, the inclusiveness of Neo-Hinduism will become the covering philosophy – indeed to some extent it already plays this role. Thus is could be said that the religious question can be reduced to the competing claims of Christianity and Hinduism; we have almost come full circle and returned to the situation of two thousand years ago, when Christianity stood against mystery cults and gnostic philosophy, with which modern Hinduism, though more Puritanical, has much in common.

It is true that iconoclastic Islam is in the throes of a revival of missionary zeal because of political events since 1973, and its dogmatics may make a serious appeal to those who look for absolute certainties in an age of radical uncertainty. But there is something inglorious in a revival that has had to await mere economic power, and Islam is too political for its own good; it cannot satisfy the 'occult' cravings of the age, while the flirtations of its adherents with Soviet communism as in Iran and Palestine can almost be guaranteed in time to rebound on them both politically and spiritually. For this reason, I would not consider Islam a serious contender in the coming religious controversy which philosophically, if not practically, is between the Christian variety of exclusiveness and Hindu inclusiveness. (With Hinduism I include Buddhism, which is mystically similar, but which as a religion is seriously declining and is threatened by Communism in its South East Asian strongholds.)

At the present time, Christianity must appear rather less well equipped to defend and propagate its position than in the first few centuries of its existence. This is perhaps because Christianity is an historical religion which at its inception erupted on to the historical scene, challenging the Hinduistic claim of opponents like Celsus that 'truth is changeless' and God does not innovate, whereas now it has acquired a history, sometimes an imperfect one, which does not represent a dynamic development. It has adapted rather than evolved. While this adaptation has been sociologically and philosophically more significant than adaptation in most other faiths, it has perhaps been inadequate to the intrinsic nature of the religion itself and the revolutions of consciousness which such world-shaking faith was bound to instigate. For example, having committed itself to history and reform, Protestantism in particular has encouraged democracy to an extent to which the politics of St Paul, his view of authority and the social order, can only be an embarrassment. Having launched the revolutionary doctrine of the supremacy of love and softened human nature, it cannot but feel the incongruity of the New Testament views of almsgiving and the Pauline attitude to widows, which is only a few degrees more humane than that of traditional Hinduism. Having established the integrity of the individual and created unprecedented individualism, Christians may feel troubled by the seemingly inflexible, dismissive treatment of delicate sexual issues like, say, divorce, thus weakening the church's legitimate opposition to radical sex reform movements on spiritual and psychological grounds. It is not so much that early Christianity was wrong for its time, as that it has bequeathed us remarkably different needs, sensibilities and values, and that instead of acknowledging this development, Christians have largely ignored it: their treatment of doctrine and the Bible is not always sufficient to cover the alterations of consciousness. Furthermore, failure to take adequate stock of scientific and psychological advances renders this communications gap more serious. The conservative view that humanity, being fallen and sinful, is always basically the same and that biblical rulings are therefore always applicable, is not entirely true. Human character does change for both good and ill, and the very statement that Christ came 'in the fullness of time' is an affirmation of human evolution or change, while the concepts of the growth of the body of Christ and the procession of the Holy Spirit from the Father imply that the church should and indeed will strive to be different from what it was in the first few centuries. Besides, it is fairly obvious that in certain respects we have become more Christian. Leaving aside the fact that we have become more sentimental about children, animals and so on, St Francis seems more Christ-like than St Paul, the pictures of Fra Angelico more spiritual than the half-pagan images of the catacombs. The range of feeling and insight behind the *St Matthew Passion* and *The Brothers Karamazov* far exceeds the finicky considerations of some early Christian fathers.

What Christianity now requires is something more than the literalistic affirmations of conservatives or the rationalizing denial of liberals, or even the quasi-scientific reconciliations of a Teilhard. Given the demise of substance theory and the great fixed metaphysical systems it supported, these trends are not altogether helpful in terms of achieving a new inclusive view of the religion and making the philosophical restatements about its underlying principles. In relation to consciousness as it has developed and the new organic picture of reality, those trends would tend to be too sub-jective, too objective, and too deterministic respectively. Christ-ianity, like the world, is involved in a process, and so that the changes which have and will take place may be seen as the natural outcome rather than the contradiction of the origins, not only will the old mechanical views of natural law, inspiration and the like need to be discarded, but a new dynamic framework will have to be adopted in which the tension is between a philosophical monism on the one hand, and human free will, newly understood, on the other. As I intimated at the start, to answer to both modern and Asian needs, Christianity, at present reduced to a sort of existen-tialism, must give structure to its subjectivity and doctrine of wholeness through a unitive philosophy, while distinguishing itself from the Asian determinism to which monism lends itself, by sup-plying a new description of individualism.

All the reflections and conclusions in this book have been ex-pressed in relation to Asia, which means that I have perhaps given more thought to the mysticism of oneness than to free will; how-ever, we are forced back to that issue just as, if we approached the modern spiritual crisis from the standpoint of free will and indi-vidualism, we would be thrown back on monism. Western and Asian problems all lead to the same point.

In *Dr Faustus*, Thomas Mann's rather obscure novel about the Nietzschean complex and the development of modern European culture, there is a criticism of post-Renaissance culture and religion from a primarily psychological angle which, if I understand it aright (the novel is the despair of some critics), would support my views and is very relevant to the kind of theme we have considered.[5] Conservative Protestantism is criticized as being hostile to the cul-tural and scientific impulse, and running the risk of becoming pure subjectivity, self-laceration or 'demonology' which threatens the sense of wholeness. Liberal Protestantism is criticized because, al-though it is more cultured, it strives for an impossible reconciliation of religion with reason and is less true to human nature than the affirmations of sin, heaven and hell in traditional faith. Theology, Mann states, cannot be 'modern' like science because the psyche is not 'modern'.[6] On the other hand, both psyche and intellect properly resist the type of theological teaching on evil which Prot-estantism inherits from Catholicism and which can make even evil necessary for the glorification of virtue.

The important conclusions from a psychological perspective are (a) that as it has developed, the religious impulse which, as the

Protestant theologian Schleiermacher rightly affirmed, rests most fundamentally on a 'taste and feeling for the infinite', a desire for wholeness, is being intercepted by a host of secondary emotional and intellectual considerations; and (*b*) that man's free will is insufficiently respected in the system. As a result of increasingly convoluted philosophical definitions under the scholastics, Christian 'freedom' has ceased to be real 'freedom' because within the system free will has been reduced to a supposed choice between life and death, salvation and damnation. One might even exercise a purer freedom in choosing the latter, since evil is necessary to supply positive characteristics to God and virtue, and once one is committed to God and virtue, one's so-called 'freedom' is no more than accepting the absolute deterministic principles which God represents. In that case, the difference between God and the devil is nominal, a matter of feeling and opinion (Jung arrived at the same conclusion through criticism of the theory of the nothingness of evil, rather than that of the principle of plenitude, with which Mann is concerned). Thus psychologically popular Christianity has ceased to offer either authentic wholeness or peace, and has ceased to perform an adequate religious function.

I do not see how Christians can escape this criticism short of saying that God desires our good, so that we may as well do whatever he commands, and of course there must be circumstances regarding which the devout will claim that if God had not commanded them to do something against common reason, they would never have done things subsequently deemed worthwhile. But it is true that this does not settle the question whether a life of unthinking submission is desirable. As we saw in Chapter 1, it hardly seems so. Though Mann developed his religious reflections against his own German and Lutheran background, he composed his novel in America in the late 1940s, when evangelism was at a peak and the star of Billy Graham was rising, and there is no question that Graham's theology (of which Asia receives so much through missionaries) abounds in statements to the effect that God created us 'because he was lonely', set down the rules of friendship and said that if a man would not obey them, he would be sent to hell. This is a credo which makes God sound like a petulant child who punishes those who won't play, and in Asia, which already considers God to be basically cruel, is simply confused with existing views.

One day, perhaps, it will dawn upon Christians who can actually throw off the scholastic shackles, read St Paul in historical context and accept what the gospels actually say, that what God wanted was less our obedience than a discipline of trust; not our conformity to the death of absolute rules, but the exertion of our free will. The sin of Eden was a failure to fulfil the trust which makes freedom possible, the breaking of the *only* rule that was intended. Self-expression was desired. Notice that God brings the animals to Adam for him to invent the names! All rules are historically necessary expedients, and the result of original sin. God is sovereign, but he does not especially wish to be so; he prefers associates to servants and gives commands more to avert disasters than to express his being. Anything forced, even on the best pretexts is usually spiritually unsatisfactory. The introspective mind has always intuited this. One can obey rules and yet not submit to them mentally, and if those who do submit are at all philosophically minded, they will acknowledge how they do so only out of expediency or recognizing the higher idea which the law represents. One notices the emphasis on free will again and again throughout the gospels. So little does God wish to impose on man, that even the Lord's Prayer requests the coming of God's kingdom as though the only reason that God will intervene in human affairs is because he is asked to do so. God forces no one; evil and the 'prince of this world' are the ones who impose their will. If the gospels are not completely clear instructions for posterity, it is precisely because Jesus did not force even his words upon the disciples. The error they made when they consistently refused to absorb his forecasts of impending death has almost certainly led to the less than perfectly consistent treatment of the doctrine of kingdom and apocalypse, which a more human guru, drilling reluctant followers, would never have permitted. That would be the more purely human way of St Paul, and the results are evident for all to see. Though St Paul is not *directly* responsible for what has happened to Christian doctrine, there is little doubt that by preaching, not only mainly in terms of divine wrath, but in terms of 'law' as understood by Jews and Stoics, he made possible a degree of regression from Christian liberty to the deterministic scholastic view of God considered earlier, where the divine mind was made equal and identical with intellect. In former times, when Christianity was novel, society authoritarian and Western man the audience, there may have been value in the approach taken. Indeed, there probably was, because if I am right about collective individuation, this 'masculine' intellectual impulse was necessary for both spiritual beginnings and the social and scientific progress which required emphasis on the idea of precise

laws; if they are not stated with sophistication, monism and relativity are the most primitive and unscientific of world views, common even to tribal cultures.

We do, however, live in very different times, and in relation both
to the West and Asia the church needs to acknowledge what has
taken place in the human psyche since St Paul, and to recognize
that no scripture, no religion, is equally relevant to everyone all
the time in all its parts. Today it is high time that the church
looked at the gospels again, even at the expense of St Paul, who in
the hands of the evangelistically minded has certainly been emphasized to their detriment. Without denying that God can have
'wrath' and must judge, church missionaries surely need to remember that at best they are using words of a being beyond 'wrath'
and 'judgment' in the inferior human sense, and that there are
alternative (and, in the modern and Asian context, more helpful)
ways of describing the subject of salvation to speaking of the
'vessels of grace and vessels of wrath'. The psychological centre
which modern introversion and relativity demands will simply be
the distinction between those who are attuned or in harmony with
God and those who are not. Modern Western man has acquired
that 'taste and feeling for the infinite' which much of Asia has long
possessed; he has also been largely released by modern psychology
from the more morbid and trivial forms of sex guilt which has long
confused the question of sin, because devil figures are automatically
and universally associated with the *libido*. This means that the
Westerner's approach to religion, like that of Asian man, has become more pragmatic and existential. While questions like sin,
guilt and church organization can never be irrelevant, they cease
to be of interest in themselves to many believers and unbelievers.
St Paul might relate his faith to Jewish law, mediaeval philosophers
to laws of nature and necessity, and Protestants to the varieties of
morality, but interest and emphasis of this kind is culturally and
psychologically speaking 'extravert'. If he is sincere, modern and
Asian man may be persuaded to repent of certain ways and adopt
others if they can be seen in the long run to heighten his spiritual
effectiveness and peace of mind, or because they agree with the
truest 'way of things' – but not simply because some biblical and
ecclesiastical authority happens to command them. Rules and doctrines for their own sake or for the sake of argument belong to a
different social and intellectual order.

I am not surprised that even the greatest Asian Christians have
shown a lack of enthusiasm for Pauline doctrine which contrasts

with the almost obsessive role that it assumes in scholastic and missionary philosophy. In the third world generally, Jesus and the prophets, rather than Jesus and St Paul, seems to describe the spectrum of theological interest, and the kind of emphasis on free will and disciplined individualism which is required in Asia is likely to mean that the Asianization of Christianity will involve a reinterpretation of St Paul which reduces his influence philosophically, while it may discover him anew as regards his activity, his techniques of outreach and indigenization of the message generally. Unfortunately, I see little prospect of this happening yet, and in the light of the kind of problems I have been considering, the leading expressions of contemporary Christianity do not seem overwhelmingly relevant. They are:

1. *Catholicism.* Its response seems to be mainly negative, conservative and currently preoccupied with sex. Indeed, so concerned is it with birth control and abortion that the man in the street finds it hard to think of the religion other than as a sexual policy, and is in danger of ignoring all Christian values as a consequence. Moreover, because of the poor Catholic record in defending the Jews during the last war, opposition to abortion as a defence of life and human dignity rings hollowly in the ears of sceptics, no matter how sincerely it is intended. However, since such campaigns provide a cause for those who want causes, and since Catholicism offers certainties in an age of uncertainty and is Europe's symbol of continuity with a historical unity it is trying to revive, a measure of Catholic revival, however short-lived, seems likely. The almost fashionable evolutionist philosophy of Teilhard could help here, though its underlying totalitarianism and its refusal to think of God in terms of ultimate liberty is controversial. Moreover, even those who resort to Catholicism for certainities may become disillusioned when the esoteric or mystical tradition which I mentioned earlier comes to the fore. It will then become a virtual theosophy and a hard form of it at that, demanding everything from members and nothing from associates in other faiths; preaching dogma to one and ineffable truth to the rest. I have become aware that this contradiction is already beginning to annoy Asian Catholics.

2. *Episcopalian churches.* These have a strong ecumenical interest, which primarily means a movement towards reconciliation with the Roman communion. Though the very idea of Rome conjures up aesthetic and almost imperial associations of great appeal to Anglo-Saxon people who have not experienced the agonies of

clerical and anti-clerical politics in the continental countries, the episcopalian churches and those akin to them do not necessarily represent a dynamic movement. The Roman ideal is no longer a viable option for many in the West, and where the organization of Christian outreach is concerned, it has to be realized that Asians are too interested in an ecumenism of faiths to be impressed by any united fronts; they appreciate a variety of religious forms, provided that there are not so many it confuses them and leads to disputes. As it is, rapprochment of the churches entails a drift towards uniformity, especially in liturgy. The essentially mediaeval mass is becoming the focus of cultus at the moment when fewer than ever, even of Catholics, believe in transubstantiation or the sacerdotal powers of the priesthood. If the object is to convey the mystery and solemnity of belief to a materialistic society, many forms of ceremony could serve this purpose as well.

3. *Liberal theology.* In its advanced form, liberal theology has ended up in contradiction. Denying the possibility of sufficient knowledge both of Jesus as a historical figure and of Christ as a resurrected, eternal one, the theology of authors like Albert Schweitzer, Paul Tillich, John Robinson, John Hick and Rudolf Bultmann leaves the church with a Christ archetype, with psychological realizations rather than salvation in any traditional sense.[7] At the same time, such theologians, particularly Bultmann, are rationalists, anxious to dissociate the faith from anything resembling the Hindu suggestion that Christ 'came down' or was 'incarnated', like Krishna and the Hindu gods, and blissfully ignoring the fact that philosophically and psychologically they themselves have taken precisely the Hindu Buddhist position, virtually making Christ a *bodhisattva* among many others, albeit a more humanistic one. It is, however, precisely the affirmation of a resurrection and a resurrection body retaining the marks of a redemption made through the material realm which assures Christ both his individuality, as opposed to no-self, and his place and ours within an ongoing cosmic process to be realized positively, rather than in a world of illusion to be negated. Moreover, as Jung emphasized in criticizing Bultmann, liberal theology is based on a rationalism of science and philosophy which is already quite dated. Far from enlightening us, its demythologization has only given us the irreverent *Jesus Christ Superstar* of theatre and cinema. It is a discouraging factor for missions, confusing converts who insist on a measure of certainty.

4. *Fundamentalist and/or 'charismatic' religion.* This, with

Catholicism, is at present the most significant sociological and missionary phenomenon because of its American roots and underlying apocalypticism. Harold Falding maintains that 'it is upon the eschatological hope that most of the lingering ambiguity of Christianity centres'.[8] He believes that a new religion or renewed Christianity will have to clarify this issue and the faith generally in the light of advances in science and society which demanded more developed religious affirmations about man and the world. Despite the great claims of Christianity which, he believes, cannot be bettered by any other faith, an attitude of other-worldly Pauline self-denial in the expectation of a second coming cannot be maintained indefinitely. Though Toynbee would hold that church history has only just begun, I am inclined to agree with Falding's judgment, and so unconsciously are many Christians, with the result that they feel that Christ must come soon to straighten out the world and justify their faith before both are quite lost. Particularly among those who are unaware of, or opposed to, the kind of doctrinal elaboration I have outlined, the apocalypse will become a matter of obsession.

In making this statement I am neither defending nor denying the church's eschatological hope, but making a sociological observation. That the church was intended to have this hope would seem hard to deny; it is also apparent that at the least the present era is a disturbed apocalyptic axial period and if traditional Christian prophetic interpretations are valid, some of its events (like the rebirth of Israel and increasing natural disturbances) could be regarded as presaging the second coming. What must concern us here are the vastly different attitudes and social and missionary consequences of the apocalypticism of the church's unofficial 'prophets', most notably Jeane Dixon and David Wilkerson, which are already beginning to have their effect.

For the Catholic Jeane Dixon, our relationship with the future is dynamic. Present and future trials are a preparation for the unprecedented science and spirituality of the millennial Aquarius, and after the Antichrist and Second Coming a new and more sophisticated form of Christian religion will be inaugurated. Like the religion of the Antichrist, which will be a form of worship of men's fallen self, the new Christianity will be more individualized, more oriental, and avail itself of more techniques (like yoga) than the present form. Astrology will become an integral part of its psychology and organization. The conversion of the Jews and those of other faiths will finally be achieved by the direct intervention of God.[9]

By contrast, the Protestant Wilkerson is imprisoned in a static view of authority, sees nothing good within the present on which to build for the future, and anticipates only judgment except on those busy saving their souls and those of others. In his frenzied hatred of the contemporary world and most Christians who are not dedicated charismatics, we can see the unconscious frustration of the fundamentalist mind, which must have a complete end to things because it cannot hope to restore a first-century Christianity. The American church is about to suffer persecution, the harmless beginnings of which will be heralded by taxation and the examination of church organizations (which, in the case of some churches, might be thought long overdue, seeing that it has been common in Europe for two centuries or more). Astrology is evil, oriental religion is evil, science is virtually irrelevant to present and future needs, and only biblical faith has any real answers to anything.[10]

Already there have been two major, serious responses to this prophesying among a once-Christian nation, so dedicated to success that recent failures have rendered it half-drunk with doom fever. First, millions of dollars are being poured into organizations committed to evangelizing the world by AD 2000, and one dreads to think of the consequences as China, Thailand and Japan get bombarded with poorly translated tracts and garbled bits of the Bible proclaiming alarming news. Second, the obsessions of the historically misinformed Wilkerson have provided scapegoats, especially of homosexuals, for the doomstruck, and one can imagine (there is nothing like making one's own prophecies come true!) that the active intolerance associable with this scapegoating could, in some day of economic or other distress, react upon American churches justifying calls to discrimination against them. Wilkerson subscribes to the untenable thesis that homosexuality was the downfall of the ancient world (homosexuals are a minority at any time, and one is reminded of Gauquelin's thesis that astrology destroyed Rome), also that homosexual rape constituted the wickedness of Sodom, though Ezekiel does not even list it as a sin of that city, so that America is endangered by tolerating the homosexual who may soon make the parks and streets of America unsafe. Though as far as can be seen the parks and streets of America are already unsafe without the help from gays, this opinion seems to be at the back of the anti-gay campaign led by Anita Bryant, who seeks to deliver America from disintegration by abrogating homosexual rights, recommending job and housing discrimination and even, if possible, the jailing of the homosexual. This campaign is furthered by individuals who righteously proclaim, like former inquisitors to heretics, that they 'love' the homosexual very much but must not tolerate him. One wonders how continental Europe, permissive in this area for 200 years, has survived. Though I feel bound to agree that there is an unacceptable potentially dangerous side to America's gay revolution, as to its women's movement, the church damages its own cause in the twentieth century if it cannot sustain a measure of basic tolerance. On what basis will the church argue for the rights of the victims of religious persecution in the world? On the grounds that they *think* they should not be persecuted? Unless checked, such intolerance has no end.

Wilkerson's prophecies and the noisy campaign they have occasioned reveal the bankruptcy of much American religion in that they attack the symptoms rather than the causes. If more people 'live in sin' in America than formerly, it is not simply from lust, but because the terms of marriage and divorce are becoming so absurdly expensive; if prostitution is increasing, it is because the materialism which the church has insufficiently criticized is demanding that businessmen should not marry, while indifference towards the underprivileged who are everywhere indoctrinated to succeed has produced the urge to enrichment by any means, prostitution included. Extreme mobility, a further result of careerism and materialism, has also compromised marriage. If more men are homosexual, it is, as Jess Stearn's *The Sixth Man* indicated, also due to the liberation or masculinization of the women.[11] This, however, is a trend which evangelical churches, with their aggressive women evangelists, have long encouraged; the blatancy of gay advocacy is less an assault on society from Sodom than a result of the entire American system which, with its dating pins for twelve-year-olds, unnaturally forces the young into premature sexual identities.

The Chinese maintain that 'coming events cast their shadow'. I feel sure that, like the producers of certain disaster films, Wilkerson has seen some of these shadows, dipping into the collective unconscious and deducing the rest (compared with visions in the biblical account, his own scarcely suggest divine revelation), and if these visions of world recessions and natural disasters materialize, one can only hope that the church and missions of the future will not suffer as a result of the obsessions he will bequeath them.

So it is that Christianity is now approaching Aquarius somewhat empty handed, and *Luciferi vires accendit Aquarius acres* (Aquarius sets alight the forces of Satan) threatens to become true. Jung, no less than the prophetic Jeane Dixon, feared the advent of Antichrist, or some dark, violent, spiritual crisis approximating to it, as the West collapses in a worship of self, impossibly appropriating to itself the archetype of God. During the past four hundred years, the failure of the West to break away from scientific and philosophical dualism and of missions to relate to Asia with theological creativity has blocked the natural evolution of Western consciousness under Christianity towards monism and a doctrine of theosis, turning post-Reformation interiority into pure subjectivity, while at the same time producing revolutions of consciousness to which it has not responded. There were, of course, other factors in the observable decline of Christianity as such, for example the identification of the churches with the privileged classes during the class-alienating eras of industrial revolution and urbanization, and the blow dealt to literalistic religion by Darwinism, but these failures can in turn be referred to the improper treatment of the individualism which Protestantism had instigated, and the holism it did not admit.

In the present context, as I have already implied, it is not exactly the case that Christians and Christianity need another New Testament. In some usually secondary areas, scriptures always become old-fashioned as soon as the ink dries on their pages. For example, in Ezekiel the prophet denies in the name of the Lord the Mosaic doctrine that the children suffer for the sins of the parents. Yet despite the obviously dated nature of aspects of the Jewish Law, it still inspired an impressively enlightened humane society, as in modern Israel. Christians ought not to labour under nearly so great a handicap over interpretation as the Jews. The entire New Testament ethical system could be seen as having been reduced or demythologized in advance by Jesus' declaration that the whole of the law and the prophets hung on the two commandments to love God and one's neighbour (Matt. 22.37–39). Yet two things are lacking in modern hermeneutics, and quite seriously. First, an ability or sense of freedom really to generalize from New Testament ethics, which has meant that the church as an institution and Christians as individuals have often been held back from reform movements of personal liberty by the fact that the New Testament happens to say, 'Slaves be obedient to your masters', or 'Whoever marries a divorced woman commits adultery,' etc. Second, Christians in the age of psychology have also been in need of something more individualized and 'scientific' than the emotional generalizations intended originally to warn them against evil or to liberate them from the finicky laws of men. Thus while statements like, 'but immortality and all impurity or covetousness must not even be named among you ... for it is a shame even to speak of the things they do in secret,' must be seen in the context of resistance to the religious orgies of the gnostics and as a condemnation of mere muck-rating, *as they stand*, centuries later, the words can only seem to be a wonderful prescription for every form of sexual condemnation, repression and ignorance. No Christian psychiatrist, for example, could justify his studies if he took this passage literally; the most unhealthy Victorian prudery might seem much more orthodox. The trouble with this uncompromising purity is that, like the greed of the licentious, it seems to have no limits; the Victorians covered even table legs in case these suggested indecency.

Excepting certain common cruelties of man in which the Old Testament has acquiesced, like beating children, or abusing certain animals, like dogs (customs which may have been necessary in violent or unhygienic times), today many statements of the New Testament, read out of context and without discrimination, could cause misunderstanding or distress. Historically some Christians attributed all mental and physical illness to demonic possession or sin and opposed medicine because of Christ's healing ministry. This has had alarming consequences for the sick. The Chinese were told to *hate* their parents by some missionaries because of the text 'Whoever does not hate father and mother', which in fact means 'does not prefer me to ...'; the Aramaic of Christ imprisoned every statement in a black and white love/hate. It is suggestive of a lack of freedom towards the Bible that even today it has never really been paraphrased, still less summarized, on a cultural basis. The most literal translation, even where it stands to betray the sense and confuse, seems to be preferred. By implication, the original words contain a magical value. Fundamentalists can be so convinced of their power that they want a Bible, Leviticus, Numbers and all, in the hands of every individual, regardless of the fact that there have been believers and martyrs to the faith from ancient Rome to feudal Japan who never possessed a Bible. Granted there is every advantage in possessing the Scriptures, but knowing the facts and principles of the faith is more important, even preferable in certain illiterate societies or where adequate translations await greater learning. No scripture can be considered transcendent of the experiential structures to which it directs, and statements about these are always necessary. The power of the word which struck the Reformers was most essentially its power to release the experience from a description of its structures that had become mechanical; but misuse or mistranslation of the same words has sometimes had the same effect.

Something which impressed me in comparing religions is that while holding to the superiority of the Bible as a scripture, educated Asians' interpretation of their less tractable scriptures was often nearer the mark, more essential. In the first chapter I discussed a text from Hebrews concerning God 'chastening' those he loves and from which Toynbee derived great significance in terms of the psychology of historical and personal development. His interpretation is of the kind which a Hindu might well apply. The liberal commentator, with the possible exception of Tillich, would probably not do so, as he would too easily dismiss the text as a historical curio (and to some extent rightly), as too dangerous to assimilate. He would point out that in the days when brutal corporal punishments were the unquestioned prerogative of all authority figures from fathers to monarchs, such thinking was not harmful, but is unedifying today. This could, however, prevent in him a certain openness to experience. At the opposite end the fundamentalist, in his concern to hear God speaking, could distort the significance by over personalizing it. Instead of grasping the transcendental psychological-spiritual point that all the difficulties of life are not divinely spared even the righteous, and can provide a chance for growth and a review of priorities, the text may be seized upon to supply reasons for every incident from the uncomfortable to the tragic. 'I have not forgotten the sting of your lash . . . you let me suffer the agony of toothache,' writes St Augustine,[12] probably thinking of the Hebrews text. Even if one accepts, according to the 'illuminist' view of inspiration, that God can speak with a special message through the scriptures,[13] the obvious danger is that the vessel is mistaken for the message, and the unedifying result in the case of a verse like Heb. 12.6 can be admittance to the picture of a Cosmic Sadist manipulating situations to punish his own with the chastened soul, more ready themselves, like St Augustine, next time to be the scourge of society. Among the hyper-suggestible, the effect can even be a kind of mental paralysis in which individuals, as though under a psychic ometra, hardly dare think or act for themselves lest any negative word presage divine wrath.

The compromise between these two views is the standard Catholic one which has long summarized biblical faith in terms of some fixed law or principle. Here the principle would be penitence, and if we were always penitent, we would not need such texts to warn us, or even really need to read them. But as it happens, we do need them, or something like them, because life and the psyche are unpredictable, and hence God and events, though they may not be positively scourging people to reduce them to penitence, do exist to evince from them deeper or more creative responses. Religious psychological development contains both predictable and unpredictable elements, and the element of surprise (or what feels like it) is important.

It is nonetheless true that the predictable psychological elements constitute the essence, the ultimate 'law', in so far as there is one to any faith, and this essence must be more closely studied. While everything which distinguishes the Judaeo-Christian revelation as something more than perennial mysticism requires that it be mediated through patterns of history, thus to some extent entrapping it in local concerns and feelings, with the rise of modern psychology and anthropology, it is easier to effect a detachment; this detachment may even be necessary if these disciplines are not to take the lead in the interpretation for their own ends. My feeling is that the days of religious doctrine, as of secular philosophy, are largely over. They can be, and will be, seen as early forms of psychological and anthropological description, and if this is the case, Christianity, provided that it does not delay in absorbing the change, or like Tillich, limit the religion to mystical ontology,[14] has nothing to fear from this. It will still emerge in its uniqueness – indeed, it will be freed from the ever-increasing need for historical and social commentary, since it would no longer need to enquire of ancient customs to see precisely what a particular text meant to their writers, but will ask what transcendent psychological or historical principle was involved in their experience.

At the present time, if the differences between modern Christianity and that of the first century are not explained in some measure as 'the expansion of God', Christian or non-Christian, we shall only increase the pressure upon us. Catholic and Protestant conservatives will be in knots trying to accommodate themselves to impossible social or moral views, while non-Christians influenced by or reacting against Christianity will increasingly appropriate the God-archetype to themselves on some Hinduizing basis, precipitating serious spiritual or psychological crisis because, as

Jung insisted, the mental structure of Western man is not such that he can ever completely assimilate the oriental religions without harm to himself. Nietzsche, Crowley and Manson are extreme but nonetheless serious warnings of the kind of crisis which can be precipitated in the long run. Ultimately, Western man is marked by Christianity and tied to it whether he wants it or not.

In its social, moral aspect, the early formulation of Christianity as a doctrine presents two main difficulties: (a) a complex treatment of the doctrine of the Second Coming which has reacted upon its ethical values; and (b) a somewhat inconclusive view by logical Western standards of the status of the Old Testament, which has reacted on church politics. The controversy over the first topic raises doubts as to whether Christian morality is to be considered interim or as an expression of natural law; the confusion over the second has led to doubts as to how far the Old Testament was transcended, and how far it was intended as a valid guide to moral and social policy; partisans of the view that it was such a guide could justify crusades, witch-hunts and the imposition of Jewish sexual laws.

Apocalypse, with its implications for the Christian value-system, is a serious issue. While the ethics of the gospels have wide implications and extend even to economics, where Jesus seems 'heretically' to approve dealing in the usury forbidden by Jewish law (Matt. 25.27), under St Paul, as I have indicated, ethics has two major poles: on the one hand completely conservative obedience to authority and the powers that be, and on the other hand chastity. True, the apostle speaks of 'the flesh' or 'the lower nature' as the fount of most sins, and does not adopt the Greek dualism of good spirit and evil matter; however, he usually introduces the subject of sin with a reference to sexual sin, which appears to be treated more intolerantly than all other failings. In view of the terrible evils of the age, so vividly described by Juvenal, Suetonius and others, the slavery, the exploitation, the cruelties and tortures from which the Christians themselves would soon suffer, the omissions must appear rather surprising. It looks like a virtual negation of the social implications of the 'Your will be done on earth as in heaven' of the Lord's Prayer. However, this extreme personalization of Christianity strongly suggests two things: first, the 'pragmatism' of St Paul and church leaders who felt that the least admission of social criticism or suggestion of rebellion among poor Christians would be the complete undoing of the new church; and second, the fact that because of the Christian understanding of redemption and the church's expectations of a second coming, the need for exceptions, or considerations of psychological factors, did not have to be considered in judgments on sexual matters. Christians were to be 'above reproach'. Tactically, and St Paul was a master of tactics, there was and always has been a necessity for this approach, because it is a curious feature of mission history that in practically every civilized society into which Christianity has been introduced, the Roman objections would be repeated to fuel persecution. Christians, as we noted in the case of China and Japan, would be regarded as either dangerous revolutionaries, impudently challenging time-honoured authority, or libertines given to cannibalism, incest, child molestation and the like. Humanly, of course, after the crisis of the ancient world had passed in those areas where Christianity was established, other considerations would not fail to impinge, and the strain of imposing and justifying the original values became more intense; an automatic rigorism might as easily undermine by its mechanical nature what it had originally been devised to nurture.

Modern liberal theology mostly follows Schweitzer in claiming that New Testament morality is a crisis morality and that Jesus and the disciples made a mistake about the apocalypse,[15] or that it was only a metaphor for death and moral decision. This must appear questionable, and it certainly tends to ignore as much as it explains. Although Mark's gospel (currently assumed to be the earliest) reports Jesus as saying in the course of the prophecies of the parousia, 'Truly I say to you, this generation will not pass away before all these things take place' (Mark 13.30), the forecasts appear to have several foci of reference. 'But in those days. . . .', 'but of that day and hour', appear to refer to an ultimate apocalypse, anticipated by the downfall of Jerusalem within a generation. Moreover, the statement that the disciples will not have gone through all the cities of Israel before the kingdom has come in power would have given even the dullest disciple opportunity for disenchantment with apocalyptic expectations were only one form and manifestation of the kingdom implied. Even if, at worst, Mark be considered careless as a compiler, common sense itself would suggest that 'and the gospel must first be preached in all nations', or, 'wars and rumours of wars, nation will arise against nation' would not refer to events likely to be achieved within thirty or forty years. In Matthew, the impression of delay is enhanced by the parable of the talents, in which the master goes away a long time to a distant country, expecting his servants to get on with the business of living and investing. In Luke, the mention of a whole 'times of the Gentiles' to be lived through again militates against the belief that Christ taught a speedy Second Coming.[16] Despite its 'Lo, I come quickly', the Book of Revelation, whether composed as early as Nero or late as Diocletian, must cast doubt on the idea of very speedy return, since the situations envisaged, such as the whole world gazing upon the streets of Jerusalem, were impossibilities for the time. The 'quickly' is obviously relative to history, and it seems likely that the early Christians did not expect apocalypse in a generation, or in thousands of years, but in a few hundred.

The complexity of apocalyptic doctrine may in large measure be due to two factors: 1. The natural impatience of the Jewish mind, which first caused the disciples to try to force Christ's hand in the foundation of a kingdom, and which persisted in an unbelief about the nature and coming of the kingdom rebuked by the angels at the ascension. This impatience, which causes St John to say, 'Children, it is the last hour', is as distinctive as the weary Hindu tendency to call one mile a million and one year a billion. 2. The mostly non-logical style of Jewish thought, which by Western standards blends reality and symbol, historical event with historical principle or cycle. Notable examples of this are Ezekiel's lament over the king of Tyre, which suddenly blends with a lament over the fallen angel, Lucifer, and the confusing overlaps of person and principle in the description of Antiochus Epiphanes and some eschatological persecutor of the Jews (the Antichrist of Christian interpretation) in the Book of Daniel. Jesus also speaks in this manner at the Transfiguration (Matt. 7.11–13), when 'Elijah' is someone who both will come (like the Elijah of Revelation) and has come in John the Baptist, who repeats the work of the first Elijah.

Had the early church been more Jewish than it was, it is possible that the apocalyptic question would have been settled in the Jewish way, like that of the status of the Old Testament and its implications for public and private morality, beyond logic and beyond arguments from natural law, namely, prophetically, by inspiration, in terms of divine will in relation to a particular time and situation. As it is, despite St Paul's basic clarifications, the relationship between Old and New Testaments was still not perfectly consistent by logical Western standards, with the result that Christians would tend either to deny the Old Testament completely, like Marcion and Harnack, or let Aristotle's logic loose on it, like the scholastics, with some alarming consequences for society and individuals alike. Since St Paul gave so little indication of how society should be run, the unnecessary assumption made by an established church from St Augustine onwards was that its guidance should come from Jewish Law rather than prophetic leadership and Christian principles. Since even liberal Jewry rates the more inspiring prophets above the Law, the prescription was doubly conservative.

For many Christians, as for the highly legalistic reformer Calvin (he was, in fact, a lawyer), the Old Testament enjoyed complete authority, on the grounds that by implication Jesus accepted its authority by quoting from it, unless its provisions were specifically annulled by New Testament statements. Yet exactly what Christ believed about the Old Testament is hard to say. The only certainty is that he believed that the Law and the Prophets referred to his mission (Luke 24.45). At one time he appears to accept the absolute inspiration of the Old Testament, as when he states, 'Not one jot or tittle shall pass from the Law till all be fulfilled': at another, he seems to attribute even the Law to man, 'Moses gave you this commandment for the hardness of your heart' (i.e. not God), or 'You heard it said of old time. . . .' (as though only the customs of men were in question). Christ's refusals to observe the law about the sabbath, which he describes as only made for man anyway, or to punish adultery as required, have to be set against the injunction to the people to do what the Pharisees say (Matt. 23.2), or even more perplexing, the statement that 'God commanded, "Honour your father and your mother" ', and 'He who speaks evil of father or mother, let him die' (Matt. 15.4f.). Having waived or criticized other laws, it is problematic that he should have approved this particular provision, which is so open to cruel misuse. Granted that the gospels supply the barest paraphrase of Jesus' ministry, as St John's Gospel frankly admits (John 21.25), so that the 'God commanded' almost certainly refers to 'Honour thy father and mother' as one of the Ten Commandments and the 'Greater Law', and not the lesser provision, we may still feel uncomfortable at this possible contradiction. But it is perhaps at this point that we begin to see the forces involved, and only a Catholic authoritarianism on the one hand and a Protestant democracy of feeling on the other will hesitate to admit the likely solution. The élitist and 'political' answer is that Jesus simply adjusted the message to what his hearers were able to receive and argued *ad hominem*. Any reformer who has ever lived has been caught between the demands of those for whom self and liberty are the main guide and aspiration, and those for whom rules and society are the necessary and final authority. Both of these are limiting attitudes, harmful to true progress, and both are liable to set traps to destroy reformer and reform. Jesus was far from expecting his hearers always to understand him literally. 'How is it you fail to perceive that I did not speak about bread?', he asks his disciples (Matt. 16.11). . . . 'Then they understood that he did not tell them to beware of the leaven of bread but of the teaching of the Pharisees and Sadducees.' All the parables of the kingdom are in effect said to be a secret, a mystery open only to those able to receive them. The story of the tribute money which Christ commands Peter to take from the fish to give in tax (Matt. 18.20–28), with the words, 'Then the sons are free. However, not to give offence to them (the authorities) take that (the shekel) and give it to them for me and yourself', indicates the real situation.

The Hindus frequently ask in surprise whether Christianity has no esoteric tradition. The answer is yes, but not in the sense of a gnosis for the select, highly evolved few who are above all the laws to the point of pure licence. Laws exist because many people need and demand them, and although those who do not need them should act in a free manner, they may need to accept some submission to the Law for the greater good. The Sermon on the Mount certainly makes us ask how far it is a blueprint for the behaviour of the new Christian community, and how far it is a Zen-like exercise in pulling the carpet from beneath the feet of those who are self-satisfied and self-righteous before God in the keeping of laws. My feeling is that the Sermon is so extremely idealistic, so close to calculated hyperbole, as in 'if anyone strikes you on the right cheek, turn to him the other' (something that few Christians, including St Paul, who protested his rights of Roman citizenship have ever literally done), that it would be a trifle rash to assume that the teaching on, say, marriage and divorce within the same sermon could not be waived in any circumstances. Jesus certainly saw his teaching in terms of a development and concession to weak understanding. That is why he did not approach the Gentiles, for whom he ultimately intended his message. It was not that he did not care for them (his attitude to those he met shows the opposite), but that his Jewish followers who would have to found the church could never have accepted such openness which would have jeopardized the entire movement. It needed years to assimilate the doctrine before it could widen its horizons.

St Paul is generally considered to have resolved the question of law and grace, especially in Galatians and Romans, but he did so in relation to specific controversies rather than exhaustively, so there is no need to assume that he had said the last word on the question. If anything, the apostle still leaves the churches with problems to resolve and points to develop. In Galatians he writes, 'For freedom Christ has set you free; stand fast and do not submit to the law of slavery' (i.e., the Jewish Law); he himself dismissed Jewish sabbath-keeping, food-laws, etc., but even in Romans there is another aspect: 'I was once alive apart from the Law, but when the commandment came, sin revived and I died. . . . For sin, finding opportunity in the commandment, deceived me, and by it killed me. So the Law is holy and the commandment is holy and just and good' (Rom. 7.9–12). Such words could not fail to be an invitation to those Christians of the time who had been influenced by Judaism and were enamoured of the idea of keeping laws, and it was surely a rather specialized rabbinical view of the Law to regard its imposition as a divine attempt to make people feel guilty. Even assuming that this is correct, the Law also represented a socialization of religion, the means to give direction to the enlarging circle of Judaism. If Abraham and the patriarchs appear to have been holier and nearer to God *without* the Law, that is because they were acting before God as individuals, like Christians who may feel nearer to them than to the children of Israel. Furthermore, while it is true that all laws exist to arouse an awareness of responsibility and guilt, one cannot help wondering whether the sense of rebellion and guilt which St Paul experienced before the Law was not in part a natural psychological consequence of Pharisaism at large, which tried to interiorize and give a subtle significance to a cataract of laws, many of them purely social in function.

Thus the Pauline freedom from law, so newly discovered, was perhaps inevitably not total. It is unlikely that all the implications of the faith could be grasped by one man in one generation. In any case, Paul's was a legalistic mind, and not only does he see common situations in legal terms, Roman if not Jewish (Rom. 7.1–3), but he almost imposes the Christian life-style on Jewish precedent, pursuing the less than perfect with a legal zeal. Thus, in a particularly harsh moment, he proclaims (I Cor. 5.11): 'You are not to associate with any who bears the name of brother if he is guilty of immorality or greed. . . . Drive out the wicked person from among you.' One wonders how it would be possible (or kind) to determine whether someone was 'greedy' (gluttonous?). To gather from Tacitus, it may not have been so difficult; gluttony is said to have reached 'fantastic heights' during the period, with feasts punctuated by visits to the vomitorium. Unfortunately for posterity, St Paul is not specific in this way, so that even if we admit, given the times and the church's situation, that this intolerance was necessary, it does not sound well today, and was the kind of teaching which later would be a gift to fanatics who placed church and institutions before people.

Regardless of the attitudes of Jesus and St Paul, it seems that it was the perverse obsessions of the Gnostics which chiefly tilted the balance in the value accorded to Jewish Law in the early church. Since their theory of the soul and matter involved them in the position that a Creator God was evil, they twisted the gospel message to mean that Jesus was a rebel against the evil Yahweh, and all the sinners and rebels of the Old Testament were his true forbears at the expense of Moses and the prophets. This prompted severe reaction in favour of Moses and the Law, especially among Jewish converts, even when they were not legalists, so that by 147 and the *Apology* of Aristides, the Christian flock has become a second little Judaism striving to live a righteous life with the Ten Commandments, the true Law, engraved on their hearts. That could hardly be a bad thing in a society like Rome's, but the attitude which underlay the equation of Christian righteousness with the uncritical observance of those laws was more questionable, and was a concession to that trend of thinking within the church which, by the time of Constantine, led to calls for the imposition of Jewish laws and punishment for those not observing them. Since 'Thou shalt not kill' or 'Thou shalt not steal' have to be assessed in the light of war or extreme hardship, as even the Jews realized, the legalistic tendency was basically retrograde, and the spectacle of theoretically Christian societies hanging children for stealing sheep (proving more severe than even Jewish Law) did not prove edifying.

III

So far, we have highlighted two problem areas of Christian teaching which, by force of history and circumstance, have arguably suffered a more Europeanized interpretation than was strictly warranted by their Jewish origin with its emphasis on prophecy and inspiration. It is now possible to focus on the practical consequences for Christianity, which have been considerable in politics and ethics, and to see whether what has happened can in any way be reviewed in the light of a doctrine of 'the expansion of God' and the necessary reinterpretation of Christianity over against Asian faiths.

Since the contemporary world, both Asian and Western, is less rationally sceptical in its approach to Christianity than it used to be, it would currently see two major weaknesses in it, legal (or political) and sexual. These are intimately related problems which critics are liable to resolve in *gnostic* fashion, reducing the religion to nothing but a doctrine of being within love, denying its exclusiveness. Historically, gnostics tended to deny the legal and Jewish facets of Christianity altogether in order to justify licence, and their behaviour could be so extreme that the church was more anxious to suppress gnosticism than to reply to its more serious charges. In any case, it was hardly in an intellectual position to do this, given existing philosophical understanding of substance, evil, etc. Today, faced with the more restrained and intellectual gnosticism of the Asian faiths and Jungian psychology, Christianity has more hope of arriving at some solution.

First, then, there is the political record of Christianity in the crusades, heresy hunts, acquisition of church lands and tithes, priestly authority and punishment of sexual misdemeanours, which the most self-seeking persons could justify in terms either of divine authority or of the natural laws presumed to underlie Old Testament regulations. This aspect of church history tends to trouble Asians and Asian Christians in particular; some of them, who were brought up to believe that even the killing of animals is sin, are appalled at the wars and executions perpetrated in the name of Christianity. The second issue, sexual ethics, more nearly troubles the West in the post-Freudian era, including many Christians who, while basically committed to the sexual teachings of their faith and desiring higher standards than modern permissiveness has bequeathed us, feel that they can never quite return to, or recommend, the kind of Pauline severity and inflexibility on this issue which the mediaeval and Victorian experience appears to have discredited for all time. However, it is also an issue of some importance for missionary outreach and the reputation of existing overseas churches, like the Coptic, whose ruling on marriage and divorce is so unrealistic in the context of the sensual and impulsive Egyptian society, that the church is constantly disgraced by Christians being nominally converted to Islam in order to obtain a divorce and then being converted back again to marry Christians.

There are, of course, many reasons for the rise of political intolerance within Christianity, for example the way in which it suddenly – and unfortunately – became established under Constantine and its resistance to Islam. St Augustine's theory of the 'just war' in his *City of God* was particularly crucial. Many of the churches of the East held strictly to pacifism, believing this to be Christ's will, but in the West the relinquishment of the pacifist principle (an issue on which Christian values clearly run counter to Old Testament ones) left the door open to unprecedented reconciliation with the Old Testament.

In effect, this reconciliation was very simple because, as I have said, the Pauline treatment of the function and purpose of the Old Testament was not exhaustive, but was naturally couched in terms of the experience of the apostles and the requisites of salvation. The Jewish Law was seen in terms not of history, sociology or anthropology, but of its value in acquiring salvation. Those who, Pharisee-like, want to be justified before God and freed from guilt, see the Law as a hindrance and a frustration, so that it must be cancelled or transcended in favour of a life in the spirit by faith. This was the fundamental concern, but just where did it leave all the numerous commandments, ranging from tithes and the status of lepers to the punishment of robbery, irreligion and incest, some of them more or less relevant to Christians and Roman society? To what extent had they represented God's will, natural law, historical necessity, ignorance or tradition? Was there any binding factor? Since Jewish religious development was more inspirational and situational than logical or philosophical, these questions were scarcely answered, but for those looking for a principle, something like one suggested itself.

Although St Paul remarks in Galatians, 'For the whole Law is fulfilled in one word, you shall love your neighbour as yourself' (Gal. 5.14), he also writes, against the legalists, 'Why then the Law? It was added because of transgressions' (Gal. 3.19), and 'All who rely on works of the Law are under a curse, for it is written, cursed be every one who does not abide by all things written in the book of the Law.' This may be so, but if God gave laws to arouse guilt and doomed those not fulfilling them, then it was reasonable to assume that the Law was still valid wherever it was not specifically abrogated. The rhetoric of Hebrews (Heb. 2.2), expressing the most Jewish standpoint, all but affirms this. God the Father thus becomes God of unmitigated holiness and wrath whose anger against sin is only temporarily restrained by Jesus. Thus, we find Christians, like David Wilkerson today, who maintain that American Christians who do not give their tithes in accordance with Judaic laws are *robbing* God,[17] or the kind of missionary who told me that they were 'not exactly for tearing down heathen altars' but seemed to think, like the Conquistadores in South America, that if Christians were in power, or in a majority, some species of intolerance towards non-Christians might be justified. In this thinking, Jesus becomes God's mercy, but Yahweh is the true measure of man's duties and God's holiness and judgment, and it only needs theologians to add that the Law was mostly 'natural' in Aristotle's sense for them to secure a divine right to impose Jewish laws anywhere, anyhow, regardless of Christ's mercy or human liberty. Christianity has not so much abrogated the Law as merely lived beyond it, whereas sinners, heretics, etc., ought ideally to be subject to its severities, and in effect have no right even to live.

I believe that a balanced view can only be reached when, as far as is possible, Christians regard Judaism as a phenomenon in its own right, or at least in its complementary relation to Christianity as a total system. In so far as God is infinite, but also the God of history, revelation within history must be seen as a limitation subjecting even God to historical necessity. Perhaps only Barth and the neo-orthodox school has glimpsed this principle. Liberals will tend to say that before the prophets and Christ, man guided by conscience was merely groping for God, that Yahweh was a tribal god who became idealized like the Zeus of myth within Greek tragedy. However, this is to compromise God's capacity to take the initiative in religion, and seek mankind. By contrast, many conservatives will say that God gave man as much as he was able to receive of this truth, but that all the same this was a pure reflection of God's will. What I am saying is that to some extent the 'injustice' and 'cruelty' of Jewish Law (measured by Christian and modern standards) may have been at divine behest, not as a perfect reflection of God's wish or nature, but because historically there was no other option. As in the incarnation, God had to limit himself if he was to be manifested at all. In order to reveal himself in the context of existing religious belief, God could not have appeared otherwise than as he did, as a demanding, threatening God. Existing gods were usually cruel and wrathful; the need was for a God whose wrath and cruelty were consistent, 'just' and dependable. That is not to say that God can possess no righteous displeasure or did not intend societies to have laws to punish offenders. Nor is it to doubt whether there is an ultimate sense in which 'lawlessness' is death which the holiness of God cannot tolerate without the risk of befouling heaven itself, as Augustine had put it. However, the penalty for sin is theologically covered by the Christian doctrine of original sin and the necessity of death which is implied even in Genesis; thus surely God was never compelled to desire the death and punishment of sinners for individual sins (except perhaps as a deterrent against the most grave of them), especially as the heart of the problem is *sin* generally, not sins, as even St Paul realized. No law can cover this in relation to divine or human will: stealing, killing, dishonouring parents may occasionally and situationally be justified.

I suggest, then, that Jewish law be seen first and foremost as a definition of God and Judaism, the people of God, over against other religions and societies, and that to be credible it was made fierce. Almost more of a taboo system than a moral code in the modern sense, it can be viewed as a kind of divine white magic set up against the underlying shamanism of other religions. In these, the gods could be so fierce and demanding that had Yahweh been less so in the cause of righteousness, he would have been ignored or despised. Although I shall not pursue the hypothesis here, for those who have ever studied the matter (and most theologians have not) there are astonishing similarities between this taboo-law, albeit inverted, and the Grimoire, Tibetan and other Asian magical rites. The statement 'Go down and warn the people lest they break forth to the Lord to gaze and many of them perish' (Ex. 19.20) is redolent of commands not to step out of the magic circle lest the brightness of the spirits kill the magician. The intensely physical nature of the laws, the preparation in dress, fasting, washing, drinking, recall the magical preliminaries. I would suggest that a helpful way for Asians and many moderns to begin a reading of the Pentateuch would be to see it in terms of holiness within a magical framework, directed against an existing system of shamanistic magic, a point highlighted by the total prohibition of witchcraft.

But what is it beyond that? There appear to be three aspects. 1. As I have said, the 'occult' laws were the original means of conveying who and what God and man is. 2. The laws of hygiene can be seen as variously reflecting desert experience and God's protection of pre-scientific man by laws he did not understand. 3. The laws governing society (specifically tribal society) and interpersonal relationship present the greatest problem. Some of them, like the prohibition of incest, are fairly natural, eternal and general to most civilized societies; others, like taking usury, are dispensable according to time and place and one's views (mediaeval Catholicism adhered to it; Calvinism, with its capitalism, disregarded it). I think that the answer lies in the distinction between 'natural law' in absolute philosophical terms and nature itself. Nature knows laws, but no absolute ones. There is a law of gravity which seemed fairly absolute for mankind until the laws of aerodynamics challenged it. We can certainly affirm that the Old Testament does not contain natural laws and that even if it had something approximating to them, this would still not be indispensable. This can be inferred from cases from such widely divergent fields as sexual and dietary laws. Here are two instances. First, the Old Testament prohibits homosexuality. Even allowing that unlimited toleration is always controversial because marked deviation is a social danger, today the absolutist Mosaic ruling can only be taken to be an injustice. It concerns a practice which many tribes and civilized societies, like that of ancient Greece, have been proved to survive without undue harm. However, male rather than female homosexuality is penalized (whatever is not expressly forbidden is always understood to be permitted under Jewish law) and is regarded as an 'abomination', i.e., primarily as a religious offence, because of its association with cult prostitution in surrounding societies. Needless to say, this would be an illogical situation if we were concerned with natural law, because in that case particular behaviour should be penalized in both sexes. In this instance the ruling is perhaps closer to the Platonic demand that artists should be excluded from the Republic because of their susceptibility to low morals.

If a total ban on homosexuality now seems unjust, by contrast, dietary laws which included prohibition of the consumption of pork might appear by informed modern standards as the best possible ruling. Historically, the pig has always been a bearer of disease, and while this may no longer be the case today, pork has been found to be detrimental to heart and circulation; furthermore, if fattening and slaughtering pigs were not a profitable trade, vast amounts of cereal crop could be diverted for general consumption in a world of shortages. The case against the consumption of pork, indeed, against the consumption of any flesh, is strong, seeing that man as a species is not 'naturally' adapted to this. Yet despite the sympathy with this aspect of the dietary laws implied by the story of the Gadarene swine, both Jesus and St Paul firmly discard them. As is implied in I Corinthians, the reason can only be pragmatic; human weakness being what it is, such bans would prove insuperable barriers to Gentile acceptance of the faith. This is a fact that need not be doubted, considering that to this day missionaries to the Chinese are asked by the elderly if they will be allowed to eat pork in heaven, thus revealing the incredible attachment of some Gentile peoples to this food.

Given that there is no natural or indispensable law here, there is no reason why we should not speak of the natural, the normal, the healthy, the beneficial, and even the probable. Thus, though the definition and nature of religious 'laws' may have to be varied according to the needs of the age, society or the individual, it is still reasonable to maintain that generally speaking, marriage and the family were divinely intended, and that promiscuity, incest and so on, were not and are not 'natural', not only for reasons of health, but probably also for spiritual reasons. Similarly, it will be obvious that whether or not a Christian society can agree on the use of interest or the land distribution envisaged by Jewish law, it was clearly never meant to tolerate unbridled *laissez-faire*. The Jewish Law may not be an absolute law, but it provides edifying and reasonable patterns of law that may be considered basic. Christians will appreciate this and benefit most when they neither keep to one principle nor adhere to random provisions blindly in deference to the soteriological relationship of the Old Testament to the New. Such a system of law should be a form of culture, a way of evaluating things, as it has become for modern Judaism, rather than an exclusive norm.

It only remains to highlight qualities of the original Jewish Law which show that in its original context it is far from being the kind of imperialistic phenomenon which Christians can make it seem.

Execution for legal offences must be seen in the light of the tribal society in which, because imprisonment was unknown and psychiatry unthinkable, every undesirable or disturbed person (including fractious children) could be executed. In tribal societies, affirmation of group values over against the individual is always the prime consideration. Beyond this, however, the Law was full of humane provisions for the protection of the weak, of servants, and even animals;[18] of course, the '*lex talionis*', 'an eye for an eye', was an advance upon the existing rights to a life for an eye. The somewhat socialistic economics of Jewish law, like the law of Jubilees, were also designed to prevent those forms of exploitation against which the prophets later inveighed. In its social conscience, Jewish law must seem very advanced, even where its tolerance of individual rights is less pronounced.

Generally speaking, Jewish law was decidedly progressive and can lay some claim to being the basis of law as we know it. The requirement that the accused is not to be condemned without the firm evidence of at least two witnesses in a public trial was far in advance of systems of judgment like the Asian, which could depend upon probability, hearsay and the opinions of single mandarins holding trials in camera, it also made capital punishment rare. Torture was unknown to the system. Unless subject to the ultimate penalty, offenders were fined or flogged, and at that, much more mercifully than happened centuries later under the Romans. Many of the secondary, practical provisions of the Law, like those concerned with boundary making, can be paralleled in contemporary law codes, and could only be considered divinely given in the sense that existing custom was claimed to be the divine will; the greater humanity of the Law and its underlying moral purpose are the features which distinguish it from all previous systems and explain how, say, the Psalmists could meditate on it.

Less easy to understand today, even for those who would oppose permissiveness, is the early church's treatment of sex. At the beginning of the century the Satanist Aleister Crowley, who has enjoyed a minor revival because of the Beatles and their interest in the occult and Asian religions, forecast that the church's sexual teachings would be the downfall of Christianity by the end of the century. One suspects that unless some new clarifications or modifications are forthcoming, this could almost prove true. Radical feminism has been allowed to become almost a movement directed against God or the church ('the Antichrist and the Second Coming of Women are synonymous', declares Mary Daly),[19] while the less extreme who oppose the more absolute kinds of laws against abortion and divorce, or laws discriminating against homosexuals, cannot but feel disturbed and alienated by the near mediaevalism of campaigns of the Wilkerson variety. Ordinary Christians suddenly find themselves caught between the claims of libertines and fanatics, and as a result of the Freudian revolution and the individualism born of Protestant influence, even the early Christian attitude itself, long taken as normative, suddenly seems inflexibly narrow and at variance with the broader tendency of Christian ethics to achieve a golden and charitable mean.

The modern sense of alienation from the early Christian position is likely to be enhanced if the subject is approached in terms of comparative religion. This would incline anyone to say that the Pauline attitude is typical of the extremism of all religious beginnings which can never be reproduced and simply has to be modified. In early Confucianism, unascetic though it was, for a husband to make love to his wife during the three years mourning for a parent soon became a punishable crime, which was only revoked under the Mings. In Early Buddhism, women themselves and therefore contact with them were regarded as hopelessly base, and no holy person was to look at or touch women lest they be distracted or defiled. In the Yoga movement of Patanjali, because sex and control of sex were equated with occult energy, the adept was not to lose a drop of semen lest he lose his powers or increase his *karma*. These trends (and there have been others in Asian religions), are willingly followed at first, but as in Christian history, they later produce dangerous repression or permissive reactions. The psychiatrist Medard Boss, who has studied hysterical patterns of behaviour among Hindus, has observed the difficulties of adjustment the religion's notion of chastity can entail; neurosis can even result from common adolescent masturbation.[20]

Although I am extremely loath to acknowledge the significance of astrology in anything other than delineation of character, I cannot but be struck by a significant correlation between astrological ages. Puritanism of the kind I have discussed first begins to become a general social concern from about 250 BC onwards as history leaves the Aries-Libra age (conquest and law making) for the Pisces-Virgo age (mysticism and chastity); it begins to fall into disrepute during the last century, as the world begins to approach the Aquarius-Leo age which, if Aquarian qualities are at all understood, may be expected to take a somewhat more individualized and scientific approach to sexual ethics than the emotional and mystical one now waning. This era, as 'mutable' as its designation, was content to swing from absolute purity to absolute abandon, from the heights to the dregs, rather than to strive for any humanistic means. For those unsympathetic in such speculations this might seem a broad generalization were it not for other factors. As Jung noticed, the early Christian messianic symbol of the fish soon gave way to the astrological symbol of the two fishes, as though identifying the dispensation of the church with the Piscean age.[21] In any case, the Epistle of Barnabas (*c.* AD 90?) already envisages a dispensation of around two thousand years. I realize how offensive it will seem to some Christians to suggest that any Pauline attitudes we shall review are in the slightest degree an expression of the *Zeitgeist* (astrological or otherwise), and that early Christian reaction to them is influenced in the same way, yet if they deny this they are still left with a nagging problem. The amazing thing is that despite all the legalistic and heretical opposition to the apostles and all the wrangling about church organization during the first centuries of the era, precisely those elements that we would consider most controversial in relation to modern times, to the Old Testament and even the gospels, were accepted with least argument and even with a zeal outdoing St Paul. These were an absolute, or purely emotional, treatment of the issue of sexual relations, and a demand for almost abject submission to authority, both of which are Piscean-Virgo virtues. Not only would the supremacy of the spiritual and the chaste tend to be required by the incoming astrological age, but both signs are known as those of the servant, of service and obedience. Certainly in the Pauline world, chastity begins to be pursued gratuitously and Paul's advice to the single, to wives and widows, and his attitude to lesbians has no specific warrant from either Old Testament or gospels, while the New Testament attitude towards authority, although strategically needed in a young church, is at some variance with the prophetic tradition of the Bible and seems to go beyond necessary submission to make almost a new virtue out of it. 'Therefore, he who resists the authorities resists what God has appointed, and those who resist will incur judgment' (Rom. 13.2). Sad to recall, his statement would be used by priests and authorities against black slaves and starving, dispossessed Irish, who, unless God is completely unjust, had excellent reason to resist authorities.

It may be thought that I am being severe on St Paul, attacking him over what were only generalizations, or even duplicating an Irish attitude towards him (from the first, Irish Christianity is notable for its tendency to dismiss or exclude him from its considerations). However, let us examine the evidence. By way of introduction I must insist that my remarks are not intended to call in question Christian sexual morality as such, like the sanctity of marriage and the family, or the value of chastity, but rather to criticize the zealous romanticism or intolerance of St Paul which, closer to Buddha than to Jesus, appear to go beyond this, valuing only virginity, refusing to tolerate any failure or deviation from the rule, and making purity the *sine qua non* of religion and the only true measure of a person, with all the consequences in psychological misery and social problems that this would entail. Even if it be argued that St Paul's attitude is not perfectly consistent, that his severity is directed towards immoral or potentially immoral congregations (Rome, Corinth), and that he does display a psychologically more positive and generous attitude even for the age (Eph. 5.21–33), we do read a Bible and not a commentary, and live in the twentieth century. There is enough here to cause misunderstanding or mischief. So I shall put the case for the opposition before putting one for the defence, or at least, making an attempt to understand and reconcile.

An an example of harshness, I would cite the attitude to widows (I Tim. 5). These women are to receive no charity unless they are sixty (sixty must have been like eighty in Roman times!), have only been married once, and are approved as holy souls, spending day and night in prayer and humble deeds of charity, because younger widows are hussies and 'when they grow *wanton against Christ* they desire to marry'. Though today the worldly might consider that what widowed women past childbearing age did could hardly be very important, one could understand the condemnation if it were that 'they wish to live like harlots'; to suppose that 'a wish to marry' amounts to wantonness against God, staggers the mind. St Paul, in fact, concludes that young widows should remarry because they cannot be trusted to control their tongues or their selves rather than because they might find love or reasonable self-fulfilment. At least he did not demand that, hidden from the world, they fast and sleep on the floor, as did the Hindus.

Statements like 'It is better to marry than to burn' (I Cor. 7.8), which has long offended many Protestants (though see below on this), and 'if they cannot exercise self control they should marry', which could be considered as making the spouse a kind of prostitute, would suggest that sex is nothing but lust. In the circumstances the condemnation of prostitution (I Cor. 6.15) might seem superfluous, and one can well understand its near restitution in the minds of Augustine and Aquinas who, perhaps more realistically, appreciated that worse things than going to a prostitute (such as rape) could happen in a society of chaste and protected women. The role of women appears to be limited to childbearing; indeed in virtual denial of every biblical statement about salvation being unearned, it seems that wives must *earn* salvation by childbearing (I Tim. 2.15)! This sounds like the Buddha doubting whether women should be permitted to become even nuns because of their inability to reach salvation.

Needs, problems, exceptions, do not cross the horizon. 'Do not be deceived, neither the immoral . . . nor adulterers, nor homosexuals (or the effeminate or catamites?)[22] . . . will inherit the kingdom of God' (I Cor. 6.9). Even if, as is likely, this is to be understood to refer to hardened adulterers, after the manner of Christ's 'adulterous generation' or the 'spirit of adultery' in the prophetic denunciations, this is still harsh. The individual is sacrificed to the policy and reputation of a church. Historically, the generalization has put an intolerable burden upon all those who can plead extenuating circumstances and for whom what is technically speaking infidelity is likely or understandable, as in the case of desertion, the permanent injury or insanity of the spouse, arranged marriages, and so on. It has also placed burdens of guilt, anxiety and suspicion on especially chaste homosexuals who by reason of birth, physical appearance or peculiar upbringing have been under permanent suspicion of the community. In Spain, under Catholic influence, even suspicion of effeminacy has led to years in jail, and all that this homophobia has achieved is encouragement of the appalling *machismo* of the Spanish male. Despite the fact that St Paul, who disapproved of current asceticism, told Christians to love and respect their own bodies (Eph. 5.28), one is not entirely surprised that Origen castrated himself for fear of the loving Jesus or of losing his salvation. St Paul, in following his maxim to try to save people at any cost, hammered the message home to the rather insensitive Mediterranean peoples with their easy sensuality in a way that has probably been harmful to the sensitive and neurotic ever since. Where do such attitudes place Pauline affirmations, 'for freedom Christ has made you free', or 'act as free men'? Sexually, it might appear more like freedom to sit under some sword of Damocles, freedom to repent when demanded to do so by inquisitorial priests.

In any case this easy dismissal of the immoral can be said to trivialize the notions of both sin and divine mercy. Not so long before, Judaism had tolerated polygamy, for customs always undergo change, so that this sudden severity towards the monogamous contributed to the famous 'sex is sin' equation of the West, which has often given religion an obsessional rather than a constructive frame of mind. This unintentional trivialization of sin must, I think, constitute the chief criticism of Pauline Christianity.

Earlier, I gave some indication of the evils and injustices of Hong Kong, few of which are particularly sexual; even those of ancient Rome and Corinth could not have been exclusively sexual, yet St Paul ignores them, although they would have aroused the Hebrew prophets as they troubled St James. Thus, in Ephesians we read, 'They (the Gentiles) are darkened in their understanding . . . they have given themselves up to licentiousness, greedy to practise every kind of uncleanness. . . . It is because of such things that wrath of God comes upon the sons of disobedience.' Like most people, I have a concept of decadence (for example, bored, over-fed, over-paid Americans engaging in wife-swapping parties), but is the judgment of God really nothing but a judgment on adultery and orgies? Is not all but the most greedy and violent sexual behaviour more excusable, more psychologically explicable than the injustices and cruelty which moved the prophets? In effect, despite St Paul, even the Catholic church has traditionally believed this, which is why in Dante's *Inferno* the poet, influenced by scholastic teaching, rates the tragic romantic adultery of Francesca da Rimini among the least grave of mortal sins.[23] Two thousand years of social oppression later, and in a world of psychiatry and contraceptives, how relevant to us are the Pauline ethics which stand at the beginning of Christianity?

I must now try to sympathize with Paul's austere and difficult position, but first, I shall make some specific comments about St Paul. To argue in his defence, he was evidently more loved and lovable in person than subsequent readers have found him to be in the written word (otherwise Acts 20.37 would be unthinkable). His description of himself is likely to be valid. 'I who am humble when face to face with you but bold when I am away' (II Cor. 10.1). His letters rarely smile, and his typically Jewish abruptness (in Israel I found this quite offensive until I realized that the Jew's bark is worse than his bite and is the product of resistance to the world) is exaggerated by his evident difficulty in expressing himself in Greek. On the other hand, the fatherly geniality suggested by the epistles of Peter and John is completely lacking, and grace apart, the character of the apostle and former church persecutor was not naturally attractive. He was the man of steel, the intellectual driven by ideas, a prime representative of the Pharisee-ism Christ had opposed, and obviously it was these characteristics which on conversion made him the ideal founder of a church and the regulator of doctrine against almost insuperable odds. He could not be the sweetest and meekest of men at the same time, and despite the misunderstandings he might cause, his vocation could be regarded as yet another example of divine willingness 'to live dangerously',[24] to allow oneself to be forced. At least St Paul had the humility to say that the divine Word was contained in earthen vessels, so perhaps this should be taken into consideration. It is fairly apparent that in his case former cruelty has become bossiness, and former persecuting zeal is reduced to a horror of any situation he cannot personally control and an inability to be emotionally free and generous until he is in command. Nothing in II Corinthians can quite hide the fact that in I Corinthians St Paul hit the unfortunate Corinthians rather harder than the situation warranted, that he knew it himself, and that he had behaved as he did partly from a desire to have everything his own way. 'For this is why I wrote, that I might test and know whether you are obedient in everything' (II Cor. 2.9).

If St Paul suffered a complex, it was not a sexual one, as his modern critics have suggested, but more of the will-to-power complex which the Jewish psychologist Adler made the basis of his analysis. He needed to dominate out of fear of failure. After all, he had been married, since this was compulsory for membership of the Sanhedrin, but his wife had probably demanded a divorce on his conversion: 'I suffered the loss of all things' (Phil. 3.8), which would account for his note of bitterness in speaking of women. Though some of his attitudes could be regarded as pre-psychological or Semitic,[25] for a man of religion, a crusader, an intellectual to dismiss sex was not necessarily the cover for serious disturbance. The nearest he comes to this is in his very Jewish aversion to effeminacy, long hair, etc.; here he could be repressing his own feminine nature betrayed in sayings like I Cor. 11.14. However, only the extent to which he imposed his own value system on converts is controversial. His harsh treatment of sex can be said to be just one aspect of the will to dominate, since all life and experience is viewed intellectually and metaphysically in terms of conflict: light and darkness, freedom and liberty, mastery and slavery, cleanness and uncleanness, etc., and despite mention of the natural, there seems, in fact, very little time for the natural, the ordinary, the real. Sexual abstinence may be necessary or useful, but if nature (fallen nature) is any guide, it is not especially 'natural'. With St Paul, one feels that sex and natural affections sometimes have been lost to the satisfaction of a dialectic; there can only be sex yet no sex, complete mastery, complete subjugation to it. St Paul does not want to be subject to the common feelings or needs of mankind. In fact, he scarcely seems to appreciate them, just as he does not really observe the nature to which he appeals; in contrast to the almost hallucinatory clarity of Jesus' portrayals of religious hypocrisy or Juvenal's panoramas of worldly vice, St Paul's descriptions of the world and his advice to converts come in vague, sweeping generalizations. Dealing as they do with metaphysical realities, sin and righteousness, old self and new self,

freedom and liberty, are legitimate opposites, whereas the opposition of clean to unclean (a distinction borrowed from Jewish
ritualism, interiorized and applied to sex) is relative and questionable.[26] By and large, St Paul's basic teaching seems to me to be not
so much wrong as excessively spiritual. Luther was appalled that
the 'worldly' epistle of St James, which appears to contradict Paul's
spirituality and emphasis on faith, was ever included in the Bible.
We might differ and reflect that the Holy Spirit was obliged to
intervene to make a modification to such otherworldliness, to demonstrate that Christianity is not just a looking to the unseen, or
to a striving for salvation in a hereafter, but to a practical redemption within the present and this world. However, St Paul did not
exist in isolation from his age, and one must not overemphasize
possible weaknesses of psychology or argumentation, because
seeing him in context, there is something to be said for the view
that he could hardly have said other than he did.

The ultimate basis of St Paul's teaching is Christ's beatitude,
'Blessed are the pure in heart, for they shall see God.' In the final
analysis, purity is sincerity, and it is the undivided mind which
alone can reach God. Any mind which lives off deceptions and
divided loves, or is clouded by sensuality like a drunkard by drink,
is obviously not suited to any spiritual good thing. All religions are
agreed on this point, and we might consider it as much 'occult' or
'yogic' as moral. Single-mindedness is a spiritual technique, while
spiritual gifts, like healing and prophecy, almost certainly demand
a sublimation and transformation of sexual energy. In addition,
Christianity had given a significant new dimension to religion, the
physical. Emphasizing the unnaturalness of death,[27] it affirmed the
necessity of a physical immortality and the achievement of the first
stage of salvation within this world, through divine incarnation
and the body of the believer, who was the 'temple' of the Holy
Spirit and capable of possessing him. Thus, responsible physical
behaviour was the symbol of redeemed life and the proof of wor-
thiness for a future one. True love and marriage was also a symbol
of the spiritual union of Christ and the church (not primarily a
way of 'owning' spouses, as socialist critics of the ideal have
suggested).

All this was logical and reasonable enough, but other considerations almost certainly intervened to give a great emphasis to sexual
purity. Ever since Plato, despite its decadence the ancient world
(or at least its educated class) was inordinately attracted to asce-
tism; 'better to marry than to burn' is really an ironic retort to

those who desired to be ascetics, but were fitfully promiscuous. Even more than among the Jews, monogamy was the official ideal, legally sealed (a man could divorce his wife but not a wife her husband), and a good widow, like a Chinese widow today, would not remarry out of respect for her husband. The arranged marriage was common in many circles, with the consequence that to claim the right to virginity was the equivalent of claiming sexual liberty today, so that the church could not afford to be too tolerant, short of complete notoriety. The insecurity, even persecution, of the early church made it desirable that converts should not marry and produce offspring to become orphans, of which the Roman world was already too full. The politics of church founding virtually ruled out social criticism; emphasis on personal morality and the expectation of a speedy second coming would have further emphasized this. Exploitation of the Christian ethic of love by the gnostics must have settled the matter, and highlighted the theme of judgment.

Thus, even had St Paul privately been willing to be more lenient, it would have been almost impossible to countenance exceptions. Like Luther, caught between the outrage of Protestants and Catholics, when he proposed to sanction polygamy for Philip of Hesse because of his wife's barrenness, St Paul, caught between the nutcrackers of legalists and gnostics, had virtually no room for manoeuvre. The same thing must have applied to Jesus before him. It can be imagined that had Jesus dared permit exceptions to his ruling on divorce, say, because of desertion or insanity, history would have been full of spouses who disappeared or were driven insane.

This does not mean, however, that discretion was never meant to be used; indeed, if Jesus' ruling on divorce really implies what some churches have maintained, it effectively makes the divorced woman a permanent leper, more of an outcast than a repentant prostitute who can marry anyone with impunity because she never had a ring on her finger. Altogether, it is unlikely that we have more here than the greatest good for the greatest number (who often do not know what is good for them). It is true that Jesus connects marriage with the perfect order of Eden, but in Genesis all God actually *says* is that 'It is not good for man to be alone,' and that he will make him a helper. The argument of the church that indissoluble monogamy is absolutely natural to man and essential to society is weakened by the fact that the situation of the first family would also require incest, that monogamy was not required of the patriarchs, and that it is not universal throughout nature. Nor is it a reflection of any heavenly situation, for despite the 'bride of Christ' imagery, it is said there is *no* marriage in heaven, while the irreverent have pointed out that in a sense God 'cuckolded' Joseph.

Interpretation of Christianity in the light of Asian faiths thus forces us to realize anew, or for the first time, that God does and declares what he wills because what he wills is good. In relation to marriage or anything else, we may not speak of something as invariably good or good in itself. Things are only good in relation to the *whole*, in relation to God. Confronted with absolutist statements, one he cannot but recall sayings like, 'Why do you call me good, only God is good?', and, 'The Lord commended the *unjust steward.*' God's will can be sufficiently expressed, and we may assume it has been, where marriage is concerned, but no law can completely express the divine will in an imperfect world, which is why I think we should now even go so far as to ask whether Christ's teaching on marriage and divorce is achieving its evident purpose, and whether if he were here today he would not modify it.

The 'hardness of your hearts' which was the reason why Jesus criticized the Mosaic divorce law, was obviously directed towards the wife (and to some extent, to children), who could be easily cast off. Jesus tried to enhance the status of the wife, while St Paul's 'to the married I give charge, not I but the Lord ... that the husband should not divorce his wife' serves the same function against the cruel Roman custom in divorcing women. Now, as a result of changes in Western economics, education and society, the tables have almost been turned. Consequently, understanding of Christian marriage may need some revision. Despite the inconveniences of marriage highlighted by feminists, there can be little question that historically, it has existed more for the emotional benefit of women and children than for men, who have dictated the terms precisely because of the inconvenience they have felt. Jung's understanding of the psychology of marriage makes it fairly plain that marriage is the nadir of male identity,[28] though he shows the couple prey to inescapable patterns of psychological response which colour moral and spiritual attitudes. In men, for whom sex is closer to instinct, *anima* is soul, one woman, idealism; while in women, for whom sex is more related to personal attraction, *animus* is men in general, instinct, crooked rationalization. This situation leads to the demand of so many promiscuous men that their wife be a virgin before, and faithful after, marriage. If a man is unfaithful, he interprets his infidelities as satisfying nature, but his wife's liberties insult his being. By contrast, even the most moral women have an unconscious sympathy for the gigolo, which accounts for the tolerance which many women will display to the more outrageously unfaithful husbands. One infidelity may be taken as an insult, but many infidelities mean that the husband is virile and that by returning to his wife he announces her superiority to all contenders. It often happens especially in Protestant marriages that once the wife has 'captured' her man, if she is not herself captive to male authority, as St Paul demanded (and especially if the husband is actually faithful) the *animus*, unsatisfied, grows contemptuous of the husband and at the same time loses opportunities for spiritual integration, for as Jung recognized, the male should act psychologically as Logos to the female Eros. This explains the inharmonious religious marriage (which even John Wesley suffered) where the husband wrongly assumes his wife can be a soul mate, and, the more holy or loving he becomes, the more his wife degenerates into a shrew or a neurotic, imagining that if she were freer, she would achieve personhood (which is a half truth). Unless the husband is positively saintly, he withers and becomes embittered at his self-righteous wife who, taking her husband's fidelity as his duty and not something to be worked for, frequently tries him with everything from neglected appearance to sexual indifference, threatening divorce or separation at the first slip. All of this reminds us that the demand for chastity alone does not automatically solve all social and psychological problems. As the psychiatrist Leslie Weatherhead once observed, infidelity can sometimes save, rather than break, a certain type of inharmonious marriage; indeed, I am convinced that the 'hypocrisy' of many American clergy in the aftermath of the 'new morality' is attributable less to pure immorality (of which some accuse them) than to demoralization by the impossibly informal patterns of American Protestant courtship and marriage.

Thus, from the spiritual as much as from the moral point of view, it is possible that Christian marriage laws need to be redefined from the masculine rather than from the feminist standpoint, from which they appear to have begun. However, just as Jesus and St Paul appear to have dealt with the marriage laws in relation to existing practice, so must we, and it is controversial that the only reply to the times should be *semper idem* in this realm; indeed, it may be self deception to believe that one standard has applied till now; in the early church it was the Montanist heretics who sought to prevent Christian remarriage. It is no use lamenting what has happened socially, however unconducive to spirituality and good morals it may be. It must be dealt with as it stands. Conservatives still consider it reasonable even in this age when relationships are easily broken up that for the greater good of society and family, or even the soul, a partner to a match should not be remarried when, say, a spouse, casual about vows, has drifted off to pursue a career. However, the morality of countries like Greece and Germany, whose churches have been rather easy on divorce in comparison with Italy's, which has been uncompromising, must raise doubts over whether sacrificing the individual in fact serves the intended purposes. Unusual or unprecedented circumstances may require new and original solutions.

In any case we can no longer remain blind to psychological fact and history now that assimilation of Christianity has required that people should be considered as individuals, a change first clearly signalled by late mediaeval and Renaissance art, where man has acquired soul and individuality in contrast to the impersonalities of antique art. Sexual demands and problems are not just removed by grace, as St Augustine discovered, tormented all his life by sex dreams. It is one thing to repent and cease from the seducer's vanity or the sensualist's greed (and today many think themselves starved when, satiated like gluttons they are merely denied); another to ignore the natural physical demands of the body which have determined that some will be more highly sexed than others, just as some have larger appetites. As I write I think of religious marriages that I know, one of a theologian, one of a clergyman, and one of a devout lay woman. Though I would never have guessed it, and only discovered it accidentally, all are falling apart, or have fallen apart, on hopeless incompatibility, mainly sexual. The strain is exaggerated by the fact that the parties involved, believing that this ought not to be the case, do not like to admit it and seek help, or do not believe they ought to be divorced, though in one case, where the marriage is recent, childless, and the result of impulse on the part of a highly sexed but moral and sexually 'inexperienced' person, divorce would be the best solution before it destroys any children. (I may say that I am in favour of Pearl Buck's view that youthful first marriages should be fairly easy to dissolve, second ones much harder.)[29] In I Thessalonians 4.5, St Paul, less pragmatically than in I Corinthians, with its 'better to marry than to burn', states that every Christian should 'know how to take a wife for himself in holiness, not in the passion of lust like heathen. . . . ' It may be argued that unions of lust or convenience are dishonourable, but this does not alter the fact that psychology shows that there are two classes of people which do not respect the religious and irreligious: those who relate to the opposite sex primarily through the emotions, and those who relate in the broad sense 'erotically', their love growing out of some indelible impression. If such people, more accident prone than the former, are not free to experiment, then at least they need more guidance, and some objective means of determining what their sexual compatibilities are such as the new astrology appears to provide.

As we see persons psychologically as individuals, we come to realize how some persons quite unconsciously project themselves sexually, and others not at all, and how some appear to need love and eros for their inspiration and their work. Many female authors, like the novelists Pearl Buck, George Sand and George Eliot, could scarcely produce work without the help of a man, a love affair if not a sexual involvement. Many of the greatest Christian artists, like Michelangelo, Leonardo, Rembrandt, Raphael, Milton, Dostoyevsky and Tolstoy, had imperfect morals, as almost a condition of their creativity. Then there are classes of persons, from sailors to entertainers, for whom both marriage and total abstinence during much of their lives could be difficult or inadvisable, both for themselves and others (one thinks of the offspring of actors' marriages).

None of this means that Christians need to relinquish their cherished ideals, still less merely capitulate to some new morality which, exploiting concepts of Christian love and tolerance (as in America), virtually blesses spoiled co-eds or indulges the whims of husbands with the seven-year itch who want to end a marriage. Generally speaking, the flesh does war against the spirit, as St Paul claims, and single-mindedness is the invariable condition of all spirituality. However, as I hope has been shown, we are now perhaps in a better position than before to understand and act upon the Christian doctrine of growth, which could be the basis of a new ethic. Thus we may still believe in holy wedlock, but respecting the individual and observing individual need, we should not feel obliged to maintain it to the point of holy deadlock, in the belief that society, religion or family will collapse if the churches make compromises. Permissiveness is not the aim, which is rather, to help those who have come to the point where their situation, whatever it is, is intolerable, where their being is restricted and they say, to borrow Luther's phrase, 'So help me God, I can do no other'. Chastity and fidelity may be good, but their religious and social purpose need to be more 'scientifically' understood and applied; they are rarely so indispensable that they should be demanded of all at any cost. Such factors as sexual disease and the dangers of adolescent childbirth indicate beyond passing fashion that God and nature did not intend promiscuous abandon or adolescent experiment, but at the same time, in the context of a religion which claims that it can bring good out of evil, one cannot believe that perfect morals are always better than a reasonable compromise, or a mistake that can be learned from. Leaving aside the nervous breakdowns which chastity has been known to cause, history evidences fates sadder than death, like those of Origen, or of Emily Blatchley, Hudson Taylor's missionary assistant, who practically died of chastity and a broken heart in a situation in which a *ménage à trois* would have been agreeable to all three concerned, and not offensive to the Chinese society of the time.

Whether individually or socially, Christians cannot any longer apply their morality inflexibly and insensitively. Priorities have to be decided somewhere in relation to an imperfect world. Those who seek to outlaw prostitution and discourage pre-marital sex should tolerate easy first divorces to those who will marry on impulse. If women are to be inviolate or 'liberated' (which usually means masculinized), then homosexuality can hardly be banned and some prostitution needs to be accepted. Even the moralist Gladstone considered that some pornography or nudity was essential as a safety valve to a society like the Victorian. To seek to set limits on pornography, prostitution, divorce, etc., would seem to be more realistic than the current backlash attempts to outlaw them completely. Even while they criticize current permissiveness, Christian moralists also have to recall that our age is not an entirely bad one (despite all the comparisons with Rome, I fail to see evidence of the gladiatorial fights and sadistic orgies of Nero), and that by working on its better characteristics, they may help reform its worse ones, rather than alienating the public with unrelieved and discouraging condemnation. They are bound to recognize that the life-styles within which many children are being raised are as exotic and remote from all civilized norms as those of traditional Tahiti. The reason, at least in America, is, I believe, the same as in Tahiti; it is not always the decadence of the satiated, but the result of a highly permissive matriarchal psychology which, I would maintain, has long been gathering force and is resurgent within feminism. While it is possible that many children will renounce their parents and their indulgence – a 'hate parents' mood seems to be in the air – these persons who are technically immoral, by Christian standards, are still somebody's parents and many of the rising generation will feel only resentment at the moralists who seem to condemn arbitarily those from whom, presumably, they will have received most in life.

Having made these observations, I recognize that they will carry little weight for those who believe firmly in what they cáll grace, a subject which, though not pursued here, will become yet another major issue as conservatives and charismatics press their claims, and modern and oriental psychology challenges their definitions. As was made clear from Pope John Paul II's visit to America, orthodox response to broken marriages and other problems will always be the Pauline one of I Cor. 10.13, that as no one will be tempted above their ability and a way of escape will be provided, no one has a claim. In one sense they do not. Where there is a will, not to mention grace, there is usually a way, but one is obliged to consider the quality of existence being demanded and whether all remedies for anything less than the dangerous and vile are to be mutilations. Many people are probably too weak or foolish even to perceive ways of escape, in which case life must go on, and without dismissing the Pauline claim, it must be put against his own mention of being 'pressed against measure' and of great faith being a gift. If that is not conceded, one could finish condemning everyone who fell ill or suffered a nervous breakdown for demonstrating lack of faith. This charge has been made, as in Christian Science and other fringe groups. Only the individual can finally know and be responsible for his or her own situation. Prayers for healing can be answered spectacularly when little faith is involved, or seemingly ignored when much faith is involved. Since such matters cannot be regulated, the church has little right to demand that God *must* patch up marital situations (particularly where the free will of several people is involved) or complexes seemingly innate or beyond the stage of help. In this respect one thinks especially of inversion; despite St Paul's implicit suggestion (I Cor. 6.11) that it could be cured (after all, he would not have approved sexual experiment to determine whether it had been, and so could only speak in terms of a person's chastity over a short period), this is known to be curable only in cases where the young have been seduced into the disposition and are in a state of arrested development in adolescence. Otherwise, religionists are in danger of falling into the presumption which has caused priests, as in

Ireland, to tell women with thrombosis that they should not use contraceptives because 'God will give you strength'. To demand that God should perform miracles to that extent is arguably to 'tempt' him, or to suggest that one is sure that the answer must follow certain pre-ordained lines. If the 'darkness' which God sent St Thérèse of Lisieux, Simone Weil, C. S. Lewis and Bonhoeffer signifies anything, it is perhaps again that God is beholden to no one, not even those who believe in him, and that he does what he wills, refusing to be restricted by man's description, and to some extent willing his independence, his 'coming of age'. This 'coming of age' will possibly be the religious theme of Aquarius, seeing that it derives particularly from Aquarians like Bonhoeffer and Simone Weil.

Thus as regards the vexed modern problem of sex, while Christianity will never become merely permissive, it is possible that its answers will become less fixed and conventional. It may make modifications to its definitions of chastity, just as modifications are made to the connotations of 'decent'. With the advance of new disciplines, such as psychology and astrology, and Christianity's involvement with other religions, it may happen that, as in Hinduism, types of sexual and social character will eventually be distinguished and moral duties defined accordingly. Furthermore, if (as scientists project and the Bible prophesies) the time comes when to die at a hundred is to die young, it may also be that ages appropriate to marriage and childbearing and so on will be defined. In so far as the homosexual (or certain homosexuals) appear to represent not just a behavioural pattern but a temperament or class of individuals like the psychic or actor, their purpose may become clearer to us (despite St Paul, Jesus envisaged the unmarriageability of some men); the type of theology I have anticipated might well involve a restatement of their position in relation to the natural.[30] At any rate, we may be sure that, however eternal the spirit of Christian morals may be, it awaits a more scientific description in terms of an ethic of growth, and that the de-Westernization of the religion will facilitate this.

IV

An ethic of growth, a 'coming of age'. . . . This must introduce my final conclusions, because by now, I hope that I have succeeded in pointing a way towards a theological reinterpretation of Christianity which is more relevant to Asian needs, and which also provides the basis for a new kind of Christian culture or aesthetic. I have also tried to show that this work of reinterpretation is inseparable from the problems of the development and communication of Christianity in the modern West, and that its true problem and destiny is de-Westernization and all that that involves, rather than quasi-rationalist de-mythologization.

Interpreting Christianity against the Asian religions shows up inadequacies of past interpretation and brings to light little explored aspects of the faith. Reinterpretation suggests that some people above all need to see Bible and faith philosophically and psychologically *as a whole* (in contrast to the piecemeal analytical treatment which is liable to make issues and denominations out of a single verse), discovering truth in the balance of statements, in the feeling and sense of the whole, perceiving a unity which does not solely or merely formally hinge upon a soteriological theme, as some have thought. Grasping the religion as a whole will also call for an examination of it in terms of what distinguishes Christianity from the 'timeless' Eastern religions, namely its basis in growth and its understanding of Spirit, the implications of which Christians have only partially realized.

Traditional dogmatic interpretation of scripture owes much to the Greek concept of dogma, and even Greek aesthetics and science, in which 'eternal' static principles were perceived to exist in themselves, rather than organically in relation to God and the whole. Thus, the Bible has sometimes been read with excessive literalism or searched through for eternal laws, while the difference between Old and New Testaments was conceived of as two distinct levels of dispensations as opposed to the continuous development, modifications, 'expansion of God' which was involved. Naturally, there was an abrupt transition between Old and New Testament, but it also depended upon a more hidden gradual development, just as the concept of linear history, so characteristic of the Judaeo-Christian position, is modified by its cyclic aspect. Psalm 19.7 tells us that 'The Law of the Lord is perfect, reviving the heart', and God tells Joshua that the book of the Law shall not pass from his mouth, that he must meditate on it day and night, do *everything* that it says (Josh. 2.8), yet we know that in no time God and the prophets were modifying this 'perfect' law, and that Christ abolished it. What is really 'perfect' is God's will and intentions at any given time. At the wrong moment of history, the 'perfect' law could be a curse, as Christian misuse of it would demonstrate. Laws may be socially necessary, but religiously speaking, any kind of law partakes of *maya*, the *koan*, the veil to be pierced. When the religious mind says that the Law of the Lord is perfect, what is really meant is that any law, word or symbol in which God's eternity imposes itself upon the temporal situation, revealing his will, is perfect. As I have emphasized, God does what he wills, subject to no completely definable laws, and eventually, purged of the old Adam, as man 'partakes of the divine nature' (II Peter 1.4), so eventually he too will do what he wills ('love God and do what you like'). Ultimately, his duty will be to be himself, to expand and develop what God has given him. This means that while the essence of the scheme of salvation remains unchanged, it is the divine will that man and society should continue to undergo permutations, so that the faith will always require prophets to modify and redefine it, especially in its practical and ethical aspects. The capital importance attached to accredited prophets in Judaism and early Christianity ('earnestly desire the spiritual gifts, especially that you may prophesy') is really quite logical. Here is the possibility of change and the preparation for change. I am not, of course, thinking in terms of theological adjustment (which is a function of ecclesiastical 'teaching', or is just intellectual adjustment), but rather of original pronouncements like those of Jeane Dixon (we cannot argue over her credentials here) when she tells Catholics to prepare for the demise of the Papacy or to accept that henceforward God intends Christians to make use of astrology.

Divine will being what it is, while Bible or church are indispensable guides, they cannot be considered infallible in the context of an ongoing scheme of salvation with a redeemer who proclaims that he himself *is* the Way, the Truth and the Life. The historical failures of the church and the occasional weaknesses of the Bible, like the vindictiveness of some psalms or the injustices of St Paul, ought to make this fairly obvious. What, then, is seen in the Bible? In my view, neither the divine 'dictation' of fundamentalism nor the human gropings posited by the liberals, but an exemplification of what the Eastern (i.e. Orthodox) churches call 'synergy', the co-operation of God and man in which the mistakes, the injustices, bear their own special significance as part of that fallenness and evil out of which God is bringing good. The very applicability of the psalms to generations of readers, despite their obvious weaknesses, is part of the miracle of transformation to which the faith lays claim. However, a new way of reading the Bible needs to be established. I have suggested that those from Asian and modern culture, to whom the legal terminology of the Bible will signify little, could read the Old Testament in terms not just of law, but 'occult' variation, an anti-shamanism, a theory of virtue and ritual cleanliness as power which is then complemented in the New Testament by the 'yogic' treatment of sex and the occult theory of power in church unity and purity. This theme could be developed a good deal, since even the parables of Christ have 'shamanistic' magical overtones, as in the symbolization of the kingdom as a great tree in which the birds of the air lodge; this is not only archetypal but bears a similarity to the world tree ascended by the shaman who becomes a 'bird'. In general, however, the Bible should be read, not primarily as an oracle – we have observed the dangers to missions of reading the Bible as though it were written yesterday to give directives how to treat peoples and cultures today – but as a spiritual culture, the assimilation of whose variety imparts a spiritual way of acting and looking at things. It does not reveal a succession of incarnations, like the Puranic myths of Hinduism,[31] or describe so many 'masks' of God, like the comparative mythology of Joseph Campbell, but rather presents the account of one incarnation and many epiphanies. Hebrew rightly has several names for God, the force of which is lost in translation. Polytheism and Theosophy are corruptions of the truth (a realization produced from the archetype within man) that God discloses aspects of himself or modes of his being, so as to draw forth the individualism in man which permits his own expansion within the finite. If one reads Job, Ecclesiastes and Isaiah as literature, just as they are, not colouring them with traditional theological associations, one can see how, while Yahweh is a recognizable being who is not comparable to, say, Buddha, he clearly has different sides which evoke different responses. One must try to avoid both the purely devotional and purely academic Christian approaches to scripture in order to achieve a position similar to, but improving upon, the Hindu one, where it is possible to embrace the vast organic scheme at any point for one's spiritual enrichment. The objectivity of liberalism, its 'scientific' textual analyses and criticism, place argument and intellectual barriers between the reader and the living poetic, archetypal and spiritual content which should be beyond that. At the same time, despite the perhaps providential clarity of biblical literature, which has made it vivid and relatively easy to translate, one must not fall into the pietistic subjectivity that so waits to hear God's voice through the Word that, forgetful of time and self, it hears the words in terms of a permanent yesterday into which it slips, refusing to interpret the words through the medium of one's individuality and distance in time from the events concerned. Thus David Wilkerson, instead of being content to deduce that sacrilegious conduct can incur divine judgment, actually says that the doomed modern world should have heeded the fall of Shiloh.[32] This clearly shows that he lives in a dream world, unaware that the specific sacrilege of Shiloh is quite unrepeatable, and that not even most Christians know what it was. The idea that one does not simply give undivided devout attention to the proclamation of the Word, but self-consciously interposes oneself between God and his word, could seem an egotistical impiety to the orthodox, or even theologians like Bultmann, who believes that we should submit to the power of the Word. Yet such self-consciousness seems necessary especially in the Asian context, where the self is denigrated and obedience is mechanical, if indeed it is not the 'Aquarian' answer to the 'Piscean' emotionalism which has occasioned such unfortunate miscalculations of policy within recent mission ventures. While there must always be faith and faith will always be a matter of the heart within an increasingly complex world, a religion of psychology, calculation and technique must to some extent take the place of the emotional faiths, the pietisms and bhaktis of the outgoing age.

Since every religion must begin somewhere and proceed from some cultural matrix, Judaeo-Christian religion bears the stamp of its Middle Eastern, Semitic origins; it has the local tendency to think in terms of the book, the Law, the elemental, the perfect cube, the fixed hieratic image, at the expense of both the more humanistic, rationalist and logical considerations of the West and the organic, aesthetic and archetypal ones of the East. The Catholic and liberal experience has tended to become assimilated to the West and the fundamentalist experience to retain the Semitic element, which is why an American free church is aesthetically half way to the starkness of a mosque, and David Wilkerson a few steps removed from the fierceness of the Ayatollah Khomeini. What Christianity has not adjusted to is the spirit of the East, yet it is the mark of its universal capacity and destiny that, as I have shown, in philosophical terms it is intrinsically capable of doing so and, in so doing, of putting the other elements into a more balanced perfect perspective. Such a capacity is more than could be claimed of Hinduism, whose diverse pretensions are not satisfyingly consistent; or Buddhism, whose system has insufficient room for the real, for form, and those patterns of recurrence called 'laws' in the West; or Islam, which is effectively a political religion denying the aspiration to liberty. The question is, then, not whether Christianity can grow, and is capable of being a universal faith, but whether its adherents are genuinely willing to let it become that, to fulfil its potential.

It is to be doubted whether the kind of synthesis which I have indicated would be currently acceptable to most church and mission leadership in the West. Since, however, what I have written is more or less 'anthropological', derived from a study of what is and an awareness of what is coming into being in Asia and the Asian churches, it is possible that with time, the objections may be swept away by a popular consensus, much as popular feeling really proved the watershed of the iconoclastic movement in the church. For the foreseeable future, however, unless Christianity can respond to this new trend, it is likely that despite the temporary revivals to be expected, it will continue to decline as a religion if not fall into contradiction (as with the remains of the wealth of an increasingly Socialistic Catholicism and the legal intolerance of a theoretically democratic fundamentalism). This could be its undoing in times of stress, when the population feels itself more than ever alienated from the faith under the decline of religious education, and the force of occult revivalism. The church has also to decide whether it is to face the Western decline, apocalyptic expectation, or whatever name it gives to the catastrophic element of our times, solely as a collapse to be resisted or as a necessary death promising resurrection; whether to condemn the times outright or to perceive within them constructive elements out of which a new civilization could be born.

As most political philosophers realize, the future lies, not with the West but with the renascent East, and Aquarius will be fulfilled there and not in California. Slowly but surely the sun is setting on the long dominant West, the often unworthy guardian of the Christian faith and idealism, and we find ourselves on the shores of different seas. With or without the return of Christ, with or without astrology, a new, higher, more individualized form of Christian faith succeeding to the emotionalized asexual religion of the Pisces-Virgo age is one of the few certainties which lie beyond the storm clouds preparing for us. Universal spiritual renewal *on earth* has always constituted an aspiration of the church, as in the hope for the time when a new Law would go out from Zion. As the pace of change accelerates, however, it appears likely that in the confusion of the times, believers and unbelievers alike, instead of preparing for the new, will fall back upon imprisoning conservatism or, growing impatient, run after false gods and become victims of a premature Aquarianism and of those religions of the Antichrist (the Greek term anti– here meaning rival or substitute) which, as religions of the self and purely human wisdom, entail a spiritual ruin.

No religion has ever contacted another, reasoned with and appealed to it, without becoming more like it. Hinduism has become more Christian and acquired a greater sense of history and practical morality as a result of missionary activity; now Christianity stands to become more like Hinduism and Buddhism unless it is to collapse into itself or be absorbed by those religions and the new gnosticism which they protect. The reluctance of the church to enter into dynamic relation with Asia is evidently part of an old syndrome. St Thomas, as the apocryphal Acts of Thomas inform us, was chosen by lot to go East, but he refused the Lord's bidding. The Lord then appeared to him in a vision by night, telling him not to fear to take the gospel to India. Thomas still refused to go, until the Lord forced him through circumstances and the intervention of the Indian merchant, Abbanes. All things considered, it is surprising that two thousand years later, the church still appears almost frightened of Asia and its culture. By now there is so much less excuse than for St Thomas, and if Christianity does go to Asia in the proper spirit, it hardly stands to lose, though whatever the results, it seems they could well be momentous for everyone.

Select Bibliography

(a) General

Anderson, Gerald H. (ed.), *Asian Voices in Christian Theology*, Orbis Books, Maryknoll, New York 1976

Bary, Theodore de (ed.), *The Buddhist Tradition*, Vintage Books, New York 1969

Campbell, Joseph, *The Masks of God*, Secker and Warburg and Viking Press, New York 1962

Campbell, Joseph (ed.), *The Portable Jung*, Viking Press, New York 1971

Capra, Fritjof, *The Tao of Physics*, Wildwood House 1975

Cox, Harvey, *Turning East*, Simon and Schuster, New York 1977

Dechanet, J. M., *Christian Yoga*, Burns and Oates 1960

Eliade, Mircea, *The Myth of Eternal Return*, Routledge and Bollingen Press, New York 1954

—, *Shamanism*, Routledge and Bollingen Press, New York 1964

Enoch, H., *Evolution or Creation*, Evangelical Press 1976

Evans-Wentz, W. Y., *The Tibetan Book of the Dead*, Oxford University Press 1960

Exley, Richard and Helen, *The Missionary Myth*, Lutterworth Press 1973

Falding, Harold, *The Sociology of Religion*, McGraw-Hill, New York 1974

Gerth, H. H., and C. Wright Mills (eds), *From Max Weber. Essays in Sociology*, Routledge 1948

Govinda, Lama Anagarika, *The Way of the White Clouds. A*

Buddhist Pilgrim in Tibet, Shambhala Publications, Berkeley, California 1966

Graham, Dom Aelred, *Zen Catholicism*, Harcourt, Brace and World, New York 1963

—, *The End of Religion*, Harcourt, Brace and World, New York 1971

Griffiths, Michael, *Changing Asia*, Anzea Books 1977

Hick, John, *God and the Universe of Faiths*, Revised Edition, Fontana Books 1977

Jung, Carl, *Man and His Symbols*, Aldus Books 1964

—,*The Structure and Dynamics of the Psyche, Collected Works* 8, Routledge 1960

—, *The Archetypes and the Collective Unconscious, Collected Works* 9 i, Routledge ²1968

—, *Aion: Researches into the Phenomenology of the Self, Collected Works* 9 ii, Routledge 1959

Kelsey, Morton, *The Other Side of Silence*, SPCK 1976

Johnston, William, *The Inner Eye of Love*, Collins 1978

Koller, John M., *Oriental Philosophies*, Scribner 1970

Kraemer, Hendrik, *World Cultures and World Religions*, Lutterworth Press 1960

Kuhn, Isobel, *By Searching*, China Inland Mission 1957

—, *In the Arena*, China Inland Mission 1958

Lee, Sherman, E., *A History of Far Eastern Art*, Revised Edition, Thames and Hudson 1975

'Levi' (Levi Dowling), *The Aquarian Gospel of Jesus the Christ*, L. N. Fowler 1964

Lyall, Leslie, *Urgent Harvest*, Lutterworth Press 1961

Macourt, Malcolm (ed.), *Towards a Theology of Gay Liberation*, SCM Press 1977

McGavren, Donald, *Understanding Church Growth*, Eerdmans, Grand Rapids 1970

Menninger, Karl, *Whatever Became of Sin?*, Hawthorn Books, New York 1973

Merton, Thomas, *Zen and the Birds of Appetite*, New Directions 1968

Nasr, Seyyed Hossein, *Man and Nature*, Allen and Unwin 1968

Needleman, Jacob, *The New Religions*, Doubleday 1970

Neill, Stephen, *A History of Christian Missions*, Penguin Books 1964

Northrop, F. S. C., *The Meeting of East and West*, Macmillan, New York 1960

Noss, John B., *Man's Religions*, Macmillan, New York 1963

O'Connor, Patrick (ed.), *Buddhists Find Christ*, Charles E. Tuttle, Tokyo and Vermont 1975

Radhakrishnan, S., *Eastern Religions and Western Thought*, Oxford University Press 1939

Roszak, Theodore, *Unfinished Animal*, Faber 1975

Schilling, Harold K., *The New Consciousness in Science and Religion*, SCM Press and United Church Press, Philadephia 1973

Siu, R. G. M., *The Tao of Science*, MIT Press, Cambridge, Mass. 1957

Steadman, John, *The Myth of Asia*, Simon and Schuster, New York 1969

Stiskin, Nahum, *The Looking Glass God*, Autumn Press, Brookline, Mass. 1972

Toynbee, Arnold, *A Study of History*, Abridged Edition, Thames and Hudson 1972

Tucci, Giuseppe, *The Theory and Practice of Mandala*, Rider 1961

Van Alstyne, Richard W., *The United States and East Asia*, Thames and Hudson 1973

Velikovsky, Immanuel, *Ages in Chaos*, Sidgwick and Jackson 1953

Watts, Alan W., *In My Own Way*, Cape and Vintage Books, New York 1972

Weil, Simone, *Waiting on God*, Fontana Books 1959

West, J. A. and J. G. Toonder, *The Case for Astrology*, Penguin Books 1973

Zaehner, R. C., *Drugs, Mysticism and Makebelieve*, Collins 1972

(b) China

Barr, Pat, *To China with Love*, Hodder and Stoughton 1974

Bary, Theodore de (ed.) *Sources of Chinese Tradition* (two vols.), Columbia University Press, New York 1964

Blofeld, John, *Compassion Yoga*, Mandala Books, Amherst, Mass. 1977

—, *The Secret and Sublime*, Allen and Unwin 1973

Cameron, Nigel, *Mandarins and Barbarians*, Weatherhill, Rutland, Vermont 1970

Cao, Xuequin, *The Story of the Stone* (two vols.), Penguin Books 1973, 1977

Creel, H. G., *Chinese Thought*, University of Chicago Press 1953

Dawson, Raymond, *The Legacy of China*, Oxford University Press 1964

Hsia, C. T., *The Classic Chinese Novel*, Columbia University Press, New York 1968

Humane, Charles, and Wang Wu, *The Ying Yang*, Avon Books, New York 1971

Kinnear, Angus, *Against the Tide*, Victory Press 1973

Lyall, Leslie, *Flame for God: John Sung*, Overseas Missionary Fellowship 1954

Moore, Charles A. (ed.), *The Chinese Mind*, East West Centre Press, Hawaii 1967

Pollock, J. C., *Hudson Taylor and Maria*, Hodder and Stoughton 1962

Taylor, Dr and Mrs Howard, *Hudson Taylor – Early Years*, China Inland Mission 1911

Teng, Ssu-Yu and John Fairbank, *China's Response to the West*, Atheneum, New York 1973

Varg, Paul A., *Missionaries, Chinese and Diplomats*, Princeton University Press 1958

Wu, John C. H., *Chinese Humanism and Christian Spirituality*, St John's University Press, New York 1965

Yang, C. K., *Religion in Chinese Society*, University of California Press 1970

(c) Japan

Bary, Theodore de (ed.), *Sources of Japanese Tradition* (two vols.), Columbia University Press, New York 1964

Boxer, C. R., *The Christian Century in Japan*, University of California Press 1951

Ebizawa, Norimichi, *Japanese Witnesses for Christ*, Lutterworth Press 1957

Endo, Shusaku, *Silence*, Charles E. Tuttle, Tokyo and Vermont 1969

Iglehart, Charles W., *A Century of Protestant Christianity in Japan*, Charles E. Tuttle, Tokyo and Vermont 1959

Kagawa, Toyohiko, *The Challenge of Redemptive Love*, Abingdon Press, Nashville 1940

Lee, Robert, *Stranger in the Land. A Study of the Church in Japan*, Lutterworth Press 1967

Maloney, James C., *Understanding the Japanese Mind*, Charles E. Tuttle, Tokyo and Vermont 1954

Michalson, Carl, *Japanese Contributions to Christian Theology*, Westminster Press, Philadephia 1960

Miura, Ayako, *The Wind is Howling*, Hodder and Stoughton 1971

—, *Shiokari Pass*, Overseas Mission Fellowship 1974

Moore, Charles A. (ed.), *The Japanese Mind*, East West Centre Press, Hawaii 1967

Niwa, Fumio, *The Buddha Tree*, Charles E. Tuttle, Tokyo and Vermont 1959

Nyoiti, Sakurazawa, *Macrobiotics*, Tandem 1972

(d) *Thailand*

Blandford, Carl E., *Chinese Churches in Thailand*, Suriyaban Publishers, Bangkok nd

Cady, John F., *Southeast Asia: Its History and Development*, McGraw-Hill, New York 1966

Chaiwan, Saad, *The Christian Approach to Buddhists in Thailand*, Suriyaban Publishers, Bangkok 1975

Draskau, Jennifer (ed.), *Taw and Other Thai Stories*, Heinemann Educational (Asia) 1976

Hollinger, Carol, *Mai Pen Rai Means Never Mind*, Houghton Mifflin, Boston 1965

Koyama, Kosuke, *Waterbuffalo Theology*, SCM Press and Orbis Books, Maryknoll, New York 1974

Smith, Alex. S., *Strategy to Multiply Rural Churches*, Overseas Mission Fellowship, Bangkok 1977

Srinawk, Khamsing, *The Politician and Other Stories*, Oxford University Press 1973

Tambiah, S. J., *World Conqueror and World Renouncer*, Cambridge University Press 1976

—, *Buddhism and Spirit Cults in Northeast Thailand*, Cambridge University Press 1970

(e) *India*

Appasamy, A. J., *Sundar Singh. A Biography*, Christian Literature Society, Madras 1958

Bary, Theodore de (ed.), *Sources of Indian Tradition* (two vols.), Columbia University Press 1964

Brent, Peter, *Godmen of India*, Penguin Books 1972

Brunton, Paul, *A Search in Secret India*, Rider 1970

Chaudhuri, Nirad C., *Continent of Circe*, Chatto and Windus 1965

Hayward, Victor E. W. (ed.), *Church as Christian Community: Three Studies of North Indian Churches*, Lutterworth Press 1966

Hunt, Dave, *The God of the Untouchables*, Fleming Revell, New York 1976

Klostermaier, Klaus, *Hindu and Christian in Vrindaban*, SCM Press 1969

Luke, P. Y. and John B. Carman, *Village Christians and Hindu Culture*, Lutterworth Press 1968

Matthew, C. P. and M. M. Thomas, *The Indian Churches of St Thomas*, ISPCK 1967

Moore, Charles A. (ed.), *The Indian Mind*, East West Centre Press, Hawaii 1967

Prabhavananda, Swami, *The Sermon on the Mount according to Vedanta*, New American Library 1972

Raju, P. T., *The Philosophical Traditions of India*, Allen and Unwin 1971

Radhakrishnan, S., and Charles A. Moore, *A Sourcebook in Indian Philosophy*, Princeton University Press 1957

Vivekananda, Swami, *Teachings of Swami Vivekananda*, Advaita Ashrama, Calcutta, nd

Notes

NB: Page numbers of books are given from editions available to me. Where more than one edition has been published, further details appear in the Select Bibliography.

Chapter 1

1. In certain respects the trend, at least in America, is comparable to that of the decadent writer Huysmen, and the French *literati* of the 1890s who went in search of the mystical out of boredom and exhaustion and treated it like a refinement of sense pleasure.

2. Alan Watts, *In My Own Way*, Vintage Books, New York 1973, pp. 83, 305.

3. Philippe Aries, *Centuries of Childhood*, Cape 1962.

4. Harvey Cox, *Turning East*, Simon and Schuster, New York 1977. See especially Chapter 7.

5. Cox goes so far as to claim that the Asian doctrine has been so misunderstood as to be unrecognizable, and maintains that most Asian cults in America might need to be regarded as a new form of Western religion.

6. One thinks, for example, of the way in which Theosophy, which has tried to align Christianity with Buddhism and Hinduism, is unable to accept the prophetic status of Mohammed.

7. See Alvin Toffler, *Future Shock*, Bodley Head 1970, Chapter 12, 'The Origins of Overchoice'.

8. Anne Bancroft, *Modern Mystics and Sages*, Granada Publishing 1978, pp. 101, 201f.

9. Reinhold Niebuhr, *Does Civilization need Religion?*, Macmillan 1938, p. 12.

10. Donald Hoke, *The Church in Asia*, Moody Press, Chicago 1975, p. 198.

11. Michael Griffiths, *Changing Asia*, Anzea Books 1977.

12. Arnold Toynbee, *A Study of History*, Thames and Hudson 1972, p. 316; *The World and the West*, Oxford University Press 1952, p. 443.

13. F. S. C. Northrop, *The Meeting of East and West*, Macmillan, New York 1960, p. 430.

14. A variant Greek text runs, 'No variation due to shadow of turning'; this suggests, rather, that there is no wavering once a purpose has been established.

15. Klaus Klostermaier, *Hindu and Christian in Vrindaban*, SCM Press 1969.

16. Id., *Kristvidya: A Sketch of an Indian Christology*, CISRS, Bangalore 1967.

17. Swami Vivekananda, *Complete Works*, VII 29, Advaita Ashrama, Calcutta, p. 111.

18. This motion is not to be considered an assimilation of the doctrine of creation as emanation, which Christian dogma rejects; it would be closer to the idea of 'procession' from God. This will be considered in another section.

19. Klostermaier, *Kristvidya*, p. 38; *Hindu and Christian in Vrindaban*, p. 117.

20. It must, however, be admitted that the ethical emphasis is valid even where it is an improper philosophical distinction. The danger of not thinking of God as good is to worship God or the gods as in average Hinduism, simply as any species of superior *power*, and it is this which bestows on so much Asian religion its 'dark' quality and accounts for its unofficial association with demonologies.

21. The tradition of meticulous commentary which is typical at least of Protestantism is one of the ways in which Western man has overcome the cultural divide separating him from biblical man. Many who say that they love their Bibles might never have done so without the help of commentaries and could scarcely imagine reading the biblical text just as it stands. One reason why I have emphasized liturgy in indigenization is because I believe that to the more practical yet aesthetic Asian mentality, doctrine and details of commentary will seem less important as a way of overcoming the separation between biblical man and modern Christian than art. Art may well be the doctrine and commentary of the East. Certainly most Buddhists relate to their difficult doctrines less from scriptures than from art and ritual, and Buddhism originated in Asia.

22. Joseph Campbell, *The Masks of God*, Viking Press, New York 1962, see Chapters 1 and 5.

23. A. Stanley Bishop, *Gautama or Jesus?*, Kollupitiya Press, Colombo, 1907; D. T. Niles, *Eternal Life Now*, Ceylon Printers, Colombo, 1946.

24. Kazoh Kitamori, *The Theology of the Pain of God*, SCM Press 1966.

25. In the light of contemporary knowledge, relativity theory, sub-atomic physics and modern biology, we should have to say that there is only *one* law, namely the one to which the parts of the whole conform from the very fact that they are parts of a whole; the properties of any part are determined not by a fundamental law, but by the properties of all other parts. The trouble with ultimate relativity, though it is not contrary to Christian doctrine, is that it is all too giddily liberating for Western man who, without the interiority or self-discipline of the East, regularly confuses liberty with licence.

26. Aelred Graham, *Zen Catholicism*, Harcourt, Brace and World, New York 1963.

27. William Johnston, *The Inner Eye of Love*, Collins 1978.

28. In a modified form, these abuses still exist. Carl E. Blandford, *Chinese Churches in Thailand*, Suriyaban Publishers, Bangkok, p. 108, recommends that no household be given baptism without *publicly destroying* all household idols! One fails to see why the missionary in a brief ceremony cannot visit the house and receive the idols, which he disposes of, or gives to the appropriate persons, should there be something ancient or of cultural value. It is true that Blandford quotes the practice of a Chinese evangelist in Taiwan in support of this, but it is self-deception not to see the Chinese evangelist as merely repeating Victorian practice.

29. Lin Yutang, *From Pagan to Christian*, World Publishing Co, Cleveland 1959.

30. Pat Barr, *To China with Love*, Secker and Warburg 1972.

31. Quoted, id., p. 138.

32. Fletcher S. Brockman, *I Discover the Orient*, Harper and Brothers, New York 1935, pp. 14f., complained that missionary training did not let him get beyond St Paul.

33. Olin Stockwell, *With God in Red China*, Harper and Brothers, New York 1953, p. 182.

34. The real comparison of idol worship in the classic biblical sense would be less with the practices of Buddhism and Hinduism than with the worship of the invisible spirits, like the *nats* in Burma or the *phis* in Thailand (which in the past might involve human sacrifice and orgies), a worship which Buddhism itself, like Judaism, had at least periodically opposed. Buddhism and Hinduism worth the name stand in relation to Christianity more like Stoicism and the mystery religions of the New Testament period than idolatrous religion in the prophetic sense.

35. Aelred Graham, *The End of Religion*, Harcourt, Brace and World 1971, p. 38.

36. Stephen Neill, *A History of Christian Missions*, Penguin Books 1963, p. 575.

37. Though it is too early to draw conclusions, there is some evidence to suggest that Asians are more responsive – or at least, as in Bali, more tolerant – to missions when missionaries are more practically involved in their lives, as in agricultural projects, to which conservative missionaries

opposed to the 'social gospel' have been forced through despair or government pressure. Assistance of this kind is more generally available to the community than that of, say, the medical missionary, and gives its recipients more exposure to religion; trainees and assistants usually take part on condition that they attend Bible classes and religious services. Though this furthers religion in a manner common to many ideologies, especially Communist, it is somewhat interested and runs the risk of arousing a new resentment, making the convert feel obligated to God and the missionaries in a way that Mother Teresa of Calcutta, who is wary of exploiting gratitude, tries to avoid.

38. Richard and Helen Exley, *The Missionary Myth*, Lutterworth Press 1973, p. 144.

39. Quoted Pat Barr, *The Deer Cry Pavilion*, Macmillan 1968, p. 123.

40. See Paul Varg, *Missionaries, Chinese and Diplomats*, pp. 95, 99, 100, 181, 187. The *Chinese Christian Year Book* for 1926 reported a surge of nationalism running through the churches, demands for indigenization of clergy and message; in 1924, Christian-run colleges had been in riots against foreign influence.

41. D. Vaughan Rees, *The Jesus Family in Communist China*, Paternoster Press 1959.

42. For example, *The Story of the Stone*, Vol. I, Ch. 10. This novel is more familiarly known by the title *The Dream of the Red Chamber*, under which it was first translated in the West in an abridged version by Franz Kuhn, Pantheon Books 1958. The novel's fidelity to Chinese character and psychology is unparalleled, and no one wishing to understand China should fail to read it.

43. Shih Nai-an, *Water Margin* (two vols.), Commercial Press, Hong Kong 1963.

44. Dr and Mrs Howard Taylor, *Hudson Taylor and the China Inland Mission*, China Inland Mission 1918, pp. 175–177.

45. Colin Wilson, *The Outsider*, Pan Books 1970, p. 302.

46. See, for example, Colin Wilson, *The Origins of the Sexual Impulse*, Arthur Barker 1963, Chapter IX, 'The Theory of Symbolic Response'.

47. Arnold Toynbee, *A Study of History*, Thames and Hudson 1972.

48. C. G. Jung, *Aion, Collected Works*, Vol. 9 ii, Routledge 1959; *The Answer to Job*, Routledge 1959, para. 746.

49. Merlin Carothers, *Prison to Praise*, Logos International, Plainfield, New Jersey; 1972, *Praise Works*, Logos International, Plainfield, New Jersey, 1973.

50. Both Jung and Carothers finish with a rather hard God because they do not stress the fact that God did not *want* to chastise Job but rather allowed himself to be forced by Satan, the present world being a theatre of free will; even so, he was not the instrument of the chastisement.

51. Simone Weil, *Waiting on God*, Fontana Books 1959, pp. 76ff.

52. See *The Autobiography of St Thérèse of Lisieux*, Fontana Books 1960.

53. Søren Kierkegaard, *The Concept of Dread* and *Sickness Unto Death*, in *A Kierkegaard Anthology*, edited by Robert Bretall, Modern Library, New York 1959.

54. Dietrich Bonhoeffer, *Letters and Papers from Prison*, SCM Press 1971, pp. 360f.

55. C. S. Lewis, *A Grief Observed*, Faber 1966, p. 9.

56. Helen Roseveare, *He Gave Us This Valley*, Inter Varsity Press 1976.

57. Many remain optimists, seeing spring in one swallow and mistaking Asian politeness for interest; they will proclaim their field receptive or, noting how churches often begin slowly (witness the entry of Christianity into England), will assume that past labours were necessary and anticipate major changes in small improvement, all but inevitable given increased communications and a saturation approach. In 1973 Hoke records a twenty-year missionary veteran as claiming, 'The Thai people are ready to listen to Christianity. . . . There is the greatest opportunity ever for evangelical missions and missionaries. . . .' Of course this is possible, but one is reminded of Mrs Clara Mason, an early American Baptist missionary to Japan, joyfully declaring, 'Science also is undermining and divine fires of religious thought are consuming the ancient Japanese systems of idolatry . . . these marvels of force (steam cars) are teaching the Japanese the power of the one Lord who maketh the clouds his chariots and ministers a flaming fire,' whatever that means!

58. Aelred Graham, *The End of Religion*, Harcourt, Brace and World 1971, p. 100.

59. *The Myth of God Incarnate*, edited by John Hick, SCM Press 1977.

60. P. T. Forsyth, *The Person and Place of Jesus Christ*, Independent Press 1948, Lectures 10–12.

61. The modern need for a concept of divine growth and self-reflection was irreverently anticipated even by James Joyce in *Ulysses* when, mindful of the dynamic, idealist nature of Celtic thought and its similarity with Asian philosophy, he wrote the incantation 'Bloom Christ, Stephen Christ, Kitty Christ. . .' Someone less interested in reversing Christian values and defining the principle would have been obliged to write 'Christ Bloom', etc., to make the point with anything like theological correctness, but Joyce was aware of the direction European thought and the new psychology was taking. In his last writings Yeats foresaw the philosophical Celticization or orientalization of Christianity, the advent of the Druidic Christianity which he supposed the end of the age of Pisces and the dawn of Aquarius would witness.

62. Contemporary scientists, including Bounoure, Caullery, Lemoine, Dewar and Grant Watson have critized evolution. It is not necessarily reasonable because of the following considerations. The hypothesis of evolution is contrary to the law of entropy. The observed gradation of fauna is inadequate proof since each species of fauna has arisen suddenly with all essential characteristics. Both the categorization of species and the methods of dating them are much more open to question than scientists

officially admit. There is no explanation why some species have survived since the earliest geological age without evolution. Transformation of one species into another has never been achieved under any laboratory conditions. Demographic patterns would have to be very different. If men were as old as stated, even given war and natural disaster, population would be much higher. Philosophically, spirit and mind could not have evolved from matter unless anteriorly present to it, just as objects are not lifted against a gravitational field unless there is already a reserve of energy in the mover.

63. Theodore Roszak, *Unfinished Animal*, Faber 1976, p. 76.

64. The new feature consists of qualities like fluidity, solidity, electrical conductivity, etc., which are physical realities yet not of the kind with 'parts', and they appear randomly with material objects and are exhibited by systematic wholes only. There is no such thing as a fluid or electrically conducting molecule.

65. Fritjof Capra, *The Tao of Physics*, Wildwood House 1975.

66. Harold K. Schilling, *The New Consciousness in Science and Religion*, SCM Press 1973.

67. Hossein Nasr, *Man and Nature*, Allen and Unwin 1968, pp. 31–33.

68. Schilling, op. cit., pp. 223–5.

69. Ibid., pp. 199f.

70. Ibid., p. 247.

71. Edward Schillebeeckx, OP, *God the Future of Man*, Sheed and Ward 1968, pp. 35, 36, 53, 178.

72. The term 'the Aquarian gospel' which, as may be seen, I use in my own sense, was coined by Levi Dowling (1844–1911), a fundamentalist turned spiritualist who composed a revised gospel, 'The Aquarian Gospel of Jesus the Christ', from purported visions of the 'Akashic Record'. This gospel, which is currently popular with the occult set in the States, is doctrinally in large measure a return to the Ebionite heresy. The Christ is simply the divine principle which possessed the man Jesus, who, like Buddha, had purged himself through many reincarnations, and visited and converted almost every country worth visiting. In the Aquarian age, the Christ principle will establish love, peace and goodwill everywhere.

73. René Monod, *The Korean Revival*, Hodder and Stoughton 1971.

74. Jerrold Schechter, *The New Face of Buddha*, Gollancz 1967, p. 17.

75. L. H. Lee, *Why the Goodwill Failed*, Quoted by Varg, op. cit., pp. 307f.

76. Leslie D. Weatherhead, *Psychology, Religion and Healing*, Hodder and Stoughton 1957; Morton Kelsey, *The Other Side of Silence*, SPCK 1976.

77. C. G. Jung, 'Christ a Symbol of the Self', in *Aion, Collected Works*, Vol. 9 ii, Routledge 1959.

78. C. G. Jung, *The Answer to Job*, Routledge 1959.

79. C. G. Jung, *Memories, Dreams, Reflections*, Collins 1963, pp. 89, 136, 164.

80. Greek philosophy, being of the substance variety, put Christian theology in the awkward position of making Satan and evil a substance which, because it then seemed equal to God, as in Manichaeism, or something for which God was responsible, caused Christian philosophers to maintain that it was *nothing*. 'Evil does not subsist as a living being, nor can we set before our eyes any substantial essence thereof. . . . Evil does not inhere within its own substance but arises from the mutilation of the soul' (St Basil), or 'Evil in its nature is neither a thing nor does it bring anything forth' (Dionysios the Areopagite etc.) Quoted by Jung in 'Christ as a Symbol of the Self', paras. 85 and 88. According to Jung, psychological problems can only result, for this solution is unacceptable to the unconscious. It will not do to make Satan an illusion and evil a matter of intellectual opinion. He notes that the philosophy of Aquinas scarcely has room for evil; it renders it a subjective notion by maintaining that God created everything good and gave everything appetites which each tries to satisfy as it suits them, albeit some fail to see what is best for them. Jung feels that this would make it reasonable for the devil to do what suits him, and our opinion that it may be wrong is nothing but an opinion. Jung himself believed that it is dishonest and irresponsible to minimize evil, for Satan is as real as God and may be part of him; he challenges the idea that God cannot be evil. Omnipotence must be able to be evil if it so wishes.

81. C. G. Jung, *The Answer to Job*, para. 733. 'He (St John) thus outlined the programme for the whole aeon of Pisces with its dramatic enantiodromia and its dark end which we have still to experience.'

82. C. G. Jung, *Memories, Dreams, Reflections*, p. 311.

83. C. G. Jung, 'A Psychological Approach to the Dogma of the Trinity, Zosimus', *Collected Works*, Vol. XI, Routledge 1958, para. 127.

84. C. G. Jung, *Memories, Dreams, Reflections*, p. 49.

85. C. G. Jung, *Memories, Dreams, Reflections*, p. 207. The same acknowledgment can be found in the Asian drama. Despite the theoretical union of opposites in the mysticism, in the religious dramas right always wins until next time – albeit by a narrow margin.

86. Mary Daly, *Beyond God the Father*, Beacon Press 1973, pp. 95, 96, 140.

87. John Blofeld, *The Secret and Sublime*, Allen and Unwin 1973: for example, the epiphany of evil at the hermitage (p. 55), the comportment of the exorcists (p. 68), the way in which the bliss channelled by the master is withdrawn just before it should reach a climax (p. 204).

Chapter 2

1. John Steadman, *The Myth of Asia*, Simon and Schuster, New York 1969.

2. Aldous Huxley, *The Perennial Philosophy*, Chatto and Windus 1946.

3. Nirad Chaudhuri, *Continent of Circe*, Chatto and Windus 1965, p. 180.

4. Alan Watts, *In My Own Way*, Vintage Books, New York 1972.

5. Joseph Needleman, *The New Religions*, Pocket Books, New York 1970, p. 183.

6. John Blofeld, *Compassion Yoga,* Allen and Unwin 1977.

7. Pat Barr, *To China with Love*, Hodder and Stoughton 1974.

8. Paul Varg, *Missionaries, Chinese and Diplomats*, Princeton University Press 1958.

9. Carol Hollinger, *Mai Pen Rai Means Never Mind*, Houghton Mifflin, Boston 1965, p. 124: 'I feel that the east is incapable of proper footnotes and scholarly documentation. . .'

10. Arthur Waley, *The Way and Its Power*, Allen and Unwin 1934, *Tao Te Ching* XIII and XXXIX.

11. Many Chinese do, of course, read *Tao Te Ching* as a scripture, and much of it can be considered in that light, but even at that it is often read in conjunction with the work of Chung Tzu, which is generally considered more strictly mystical.

12. André Malraux, *The Voices of Silence*, Secker and Warburg 1954, Part III, Section VI. For example, Simone Weil in *Waiting on God*, Fontana Books 1959, (see 'Forms of the Implicit Love of God', pp. 94ff.) entertained reservations about missions and suggested that a great problem is that every religion possesses its exoteric and esoteric forms, and thus Christians will say on the basis of some classic philosophical statement that Hindus believe this while Hindus say that Christians believe something else, and both are often quite wrong. Still, this ought not to daunt us. It is true, for example, that Hinyana Buddhists strive for nirvana while Thai paintings emphasize paradise, that Christians hold to a view of concrete salvation, while the authors of *The Myth of God Incarnate* propose a purely psychological one of myth and symbols, but none of this is so representative that it can cancel out all generalization. These adjustments are only the more obvious reminders of the human element which modifies all traditions, but usually the modification is conscious; there is a notion of what is meant to be believed.

13. William and Kampan Klausner, *Conflict or Communication*, Bangkok 1978, which offers 'studies in Thai and Western cultures', begins by declaring that after a month's residence one imagines one knows something but that after twenty years one hesitates to be definite. Plainly, in Asia ordinary sociology, not to mention the sociology of religion, is in danger of becoming ineffable.

14. C. G. Jung, *Psychology and Religion: West and East, Collected Works*, Vol. 11, Routledge and Kegan Paul 1958.

15. C. G. Jung, 'The Difference Between Eastern and Western Thinking:

Psychological Commentary on The Tibetan Book of the Great Liberation', op. cit., para. 782.

16. J. M. Dechanet, *Christian Yoga*, Burns and Oates 1960.

17. S. Radhakrishnan, *Eastern Religions and Western Thought*, Oxford University Press 1939, p. 322.

18. George Mikes, *The Land of the Rising Yen*, Penguin Books 1973, pp. 116–20.

19. Paul Varg, *Missionaries, Chinese and Diplomats*, Princeton University Press 1958, p. 115.

20. John Blofeld, *The Tantric Mysticism of Tibet*, Allen and Unwin 1970; *The Secret and Sublime*, Allen and Unwin 1973; Count Hermann Keyserling, *The Travel Diary of a Philosopher*, Cape 1925, Vol. II.

21. Carol Hollinger, *Mai Pen Rai Means Never Mind*, Houghton Mifflin, Boston 1965.

22. F. S. C. Northrop, *The Meeting of East and West*, Macmillan, New York 1960.

23. Wu Ching Tzu, *The Scholars*, Foreign Languages Press, Pekin 1973, Chapters IV and V.

24. C. G. Jung, 'On the Psychology of the Trickster Figure', in *The Archetypes and the Collective Unconscious, Collected Works* Vol. 9 i, Routledge 1959.

25. Chi Chun-hsiang, 'The Orphan of Chao', in *Six Yuan Plays*, Penguin Books 1973.

26. *The Soga Brothers' Revenge*; this is a popular legend, like a Grimm's tale, familiar from prints.

27. Lama Anagarika Govinda, *The Way of the White Clouds*, Shambhala Publications Berkeley, California 1966, Part V, Chapter 15.

28. A. David-Neel, *Initiations and Initiates in Tibet*, Rider 1970.

29. Lama Anagarika Govinda, *The Way of the White Clouds*, Part I, Chapters 8, 9 and 12.

30. Pearl Buck, *My Several Worlds*, John Day 1954.

31. Verisa Seely McWilliams, *Lafcadio Hearn*, Houghton Mifflin, Boston 1946.

32. André Malraux, *Antimemoirs*, Penguin Books 1970, p. 225.

33. Wang Yang-Ming, *Source Book in Chinese Philosophy*, collected and translated by Wing-tsit Chan, Princeton University Press 1970, p. 402.

34. Bertrand Russell, *The Problem of China*, Allen and Unwin 1922.

35. Quoted by Paul A. Cohen, *China and Christianity*, Harvard University Press, Cambridge, Mass. 1963.

36. Nigel Cameron, *Barbarians and Mandarins*, p. 176. The chapter 'Matteo Ricci and the Reluctant Dragon' makes a good general introduction to his life and work.

37. Chou Men-hwa, *Preface to Establishing Chinese Theological Thought*; articles in the 1968 series of *Christian Tribune*, Taiwan.

38. James A. Pike, Interview in *Psychics* by Editors of Psychic Magazine, Berkeley Medallion, New York 1978; Leslie Weatherhead, *Psycho-*

logy, Religion and Healing, Hodder and Stoughton 1954, Chapter III, 'The Problem of Demon Possession'.

39. Pastor Andrew Gih, *The Church Behind the Bamboo Curtain*, Lakeland Publications 1976.

40. Leslie Lyall, *Flame for God*, Overseas Missionary Fellowship ³1961.

41. Quoted by Donald E. Hoke, *The Church in Asia*, Moody Press, Chicago 1975, p. 36.

42. Watchman Nee, *Re-thinking Missions*, Shanghai 1938. Precisely what constitutes the often mentioned, never read *Re-thinking Missions* is not clear. The original seems to have been published in Shanghai in 1938 under the title *Kung-tso Tsai-ssu* and *Re-thinking the Work*, though always subsequently referred to as Nee's *Re-thinking Missions*. In 1939 an altered *Concerning Our Missions* appeared, and then appeared later as *The Normal Christian Church Life*, then *The Normal Christian Life* which are the versions in which the study seems to be read today.

43. Watchman Nee, *What Shall This Man Do?*, Victory Press 1968, p. 9.

44. Ibid., p. 161.

45. Ibid., p. 142.

46. Ibid., p. 141.

47. C. K. Yang, *Religion in Chinese Society*, University of California Press 1961.

Chapter 3

1. Chairman Mao, *On the Ten Major Relationships*, 25 April 1956.

2. I cannot hope to justify this statement fully here. Jung would, of course, emphasize the role of the conscious over against the unconscious, rather than speak in terms of any Freudian super-ego, which is perhaps a weakness, though if one stresses the role of the super-ego, one might seem to support the old fallacy that Christianity is a moral, not a mystical faith. In fact, I am thinking more in terms of the metaphysical bias of the super-ego towards immaculate otherness.

3. That Chinese people, especially students and the working class, are genuinely busy or even overworked in Hong Kong, as in much of Asia, is practically ignored by some churches which favour long sermons, long catechism classes, long prayer and Bible study meetings, where all the ordinary person would like is a more 'formal' religion with a bit of relaxing socializing. Unless missionary religion is to be harnessed to a critique of Asian socio-economic values generally, which it surely ought to be, Christian religion, as presented, will hardly be considered other than a form of social privilege for the leisure it requires. 'Good' Chinese Christians of the evangelical type can sometimes be exhausting to look at and listen to for their necessarily hyper-energetic style.

4. Probably too, because the rich never pay their taxes and it would cost the government too much in legal expenses, considering how much

already business tax involves the law. The Jockey Club never discloses its income.

5. Acceptance of homosexuality seems to have been variable with the region and ethnic group. The Manchu peoples portrayed in *The Dream* were certainly tolerant. A number of references to inversion have been made in this book, as it seems to be a rather vital, sensitive issue in Asia. Not only does the feeling between most Western and East Asian men tend to be of mutual, physical revulsion, with the Occidental tending to regard the Asian as effeminate, but unless I am seriously mistaken, the combined influences of Christian morality, feminism, and what appears to be a modern excess of males in the population, is disposing many men from a formally polygamous unascetical society, towards a measure of inversion. To whatever extent this is true one has to reckon with resentment towards any Christian severity on the matter, seeing its sexual reformism could indirectly have helped towards producing it.

6. Religious people, though likely to be considered second-class citizens, may enjoy more toleration, or feel more self respecting, in some regions more than others. The Chinese Church Research Centre, a branch of the China Graduate School of Theology, Hong Kong, which is one of the soberest and best informed on the situation, notes that Christians are strongest in certain rural areas they detail, and where Christianity has the longest history of presence, so that the religion is no longer felt, whether by Christians or others, to be a 'foreign faith'.

7. A Hong Kong doctor who has visited China several times in a professional and private capacity, has subsequently assured me they exist, but are nearly always kept indoors where a member of the family, especially retired members, can keep some check upon them.

8. Pearl Buck, *The Good Earth*, John Day 1931.

9. I am unable to account for the fact that despite an allegedly higher female than male population, men seemed to be 4:1 to women in most places. Were the women in the fields as opposed to factories, or just at home? No one could answer this.

10. Simone Weil, *Waiting on God*, Fontana Books 1959, p. 137.

11. Arnold Toynbee, *The Historian's Approach to Religion*, Oxford University Press 1956.

12. Stephen Neill, *A History of Christian Missions*, Penguin Books 1964, p. 28.

13. The nearest approach to this in Judaeo-Christian thought is Moses raising the serpent in the desert for the people to look at and be healed, or St Paul's talk of 'looking ever to Jesus'. Grace exists here not in a given force, but as the power of a manifestation one sees or introspects.

14. Shusaku Endo, *Wonderful Fool*, Peter Owen 1974.

15. Kukrit Pramoj, *Red Bamboo*, Progress Publishing, Bangkok 1961.

16. Most homes possess a God-shelf in a place of honour, or wherever it can be fitted, with a red icon of a favoured deity and the ancestral tablets or photos beside it. Christian families are liable to replace the icon

with an aesthetically incongruous crucifix or plaster image and not quite know what to do about their ancestors save dust the tablets and sometimes feel guilty and anxious at festivals that they are not feeding the spirits, who they may see returning to them in dreams requesting their dues. This applies less to the young who try to live apart from parents on marriage, but they are not necessarily less superstitious and may put up a God of Money poster for luck. Hence a ceremony is not irrelevant; it may even help to reaffirm the better side of the Chinese family idea.

17. A service without Cantonese hymns and music is a real deprivation considering how musical the Cantonese in fact are. So-called Chinese hymns exist, but they are mostly translations and very artificial, the words and phrases so forced to fill the music that Western hymns are often preferred. What is needed is Chinese composed lyrics, interchangeable between Cantonese and Mandarin, with the actual tones of the words fitted to the rhythms of the music and to Chinese harmony, something which has never really been attempted. Some persons whom I have encouraged to work on this, however, consider it will be necessary to use the less-known folk music. This avoids any complaint that if one uses any religious chant, one spoils the hymns by association with, say, Buddhist ceremony (though I feel that if there is to be a mystical note at all, it will be necessary to risk this sometimes). In the church at large, opposition to adapting native religious music has been over-influenced by places where there has been little tradition of secular music, and what exists recalls spirit possession and the old gods, as in Indonesia.

18. Privacy is a peculiar thing in the Asian setting. Visitors to Hong Kong remind me of something I have ceased to notice, and which is much more pronounced in Japan, namely, the way people are detached and create space between themselves within the crowd, refuse to notice certain things from politeness. Ensuring oneself privacy is a safety valve against the neurosis and breakdown to which overcrowding leads many. At the same time it favours heartlessness; one refuses to notice the child or animal being beaten, or even the pickpocket at work. Striking a true balance between letting people live their lives and proper moral concern has yet to be made.

Chapter 4

1. G. B. Sanson, *Japan: A Short Cultural History*, Cresset Press 1931, p. 13.

2. Hendrik Kraemer, *World Cultures and World Religions*, Lutterworth Press 1960, p. 201.

3. For Yukio Mishima and Yusanari Kawabata and the significance of other modern writers, see Arthur G. Kimball, *Crisis in Identity and Contemporary Japanese Novels*, Charles E. Tuttle, Tokyo and Vermont 1973; Edwin McClellan, *Two Japanese Novelists: Soseki and Toson*,

Charles E. Tuttle, Tokyo and Vermont 1973; Donald Keene, *Modern Japanese Literature*, Grove Press, New York 1956.

4. Robert Lee, *Stranger in the Land*, Lutterworth Press 1967, pp. 17f.

5. Ruth Benedict, *The Chrysanthemum and The Sword*, Routledge and Kegan Paul 1967.

6. Sei Shonagen, *The Pillow Book*, Allen and Unwin 1928; Murasaki Shikibu, *The Tale of Genji*, Allen and Unwin nd; Kagero Nikki, *The Gossamer Years*, Charles E. Tuttle, Tokyo and Vermont 1964.

7. C. G. Jung, 'General Description of the Types', in *Psychological Types, Collected Works*, 6 ii, Routledge 1923.

8. Ruth Benedict, op. cit., p. 112.

9. Ibid., p. 114.

10. James Clark Maloney, *Understanding the Japanese Mind*, Charles E. Tuttle, Tokyo and Vermont 1954.

11. Philip Kapleau, *The Three Pillars of Zen*, Harper & Row, New York 1967, p. 228.

12. Count Hermann Keyserling, *Travel Diary of a Philosopher*, Vol. II, Cape 1925, p. 217.

13. There is a terrible one-sidedness and an inhuman quality to some Japanese values which has given rise to much self-deception in the leadership. It is hard to credit the austerity of statements like that of Muro Kyuso in *Conversations at Suruga Dai* (quoted in *Sources of Japanese Tradition* Vol. I, edited by Theodore de Bary, Columbia University Press, New York, p. 428) that, 'When faced with however unpleasant a duty, the way of the samurai consists in regarding his own wishes, even his life itself, as of less value than rubbish', or of Yamago Soko in *Takkyo Domon* (quoted ibid., p. 393) that, 'To him (the sage) personal gain and a fat salary are more fleeting attractions than a snow flake on a red hot stove.' The result of such dismissal of feeling is seen in Odo Nobunaga's slaughter of the twenty thousand monks at Hiei. Raging out of control, he declared against all appeals that he was not the destroyer of the monastery. It was its own destroyer; what he was doing was only for the good of Japan and peace – he meant that he was doing it to advance his power. Japanese business management today reproduces the same enormous self-deception when it judges Western industry inhuman because it lacks its own paternal solicitude towards the 'family' of employees, a family which in fact would not dare to criticize or complain.

14. Sei Shonagen, *The Pillow Book*, Allen and Unwin 1928, p. 62.

15. Fumio Niwa, *The Buddha Tree*, Charles E. Tuttle, Tokyo and Vermont 1959.

16. See Dom Aelred Graham, *Conversations Buddhist and Christian*, Collins 1969; Thomas Merton, *Zen and the Birds of Appetite*, New Directions 1969.

17. Eisai, see *Sources of Japanese Tradition*, pp. 235–40.

18. Zenda Watanabe, see Carl Michalson's *Japanese Contributions to Christian Theology*, Westminster Press, Philadelphia 1960.

19. All these books cited are mentioned or described either in Michalson, op. cit., or in Gerald H. Anderson, *Asian Voices in Christian Theology*, Orbis Books, Maryknoll 1976, though the latter does not reference them or even state whether they are translated, which most are probably not. Further details are available in the *Japanese Christian Year Book*, for the period 1945–1973. Also, 'A Selected Bibliography of Christology in Japan', in *The North Asian Journal of Theology 2*, March 1969, pp. 117–34.

20. Kazoh Kitamori, *Theology of the Pain of God*, SCM Press and John Knox Press, Richmond, Va 1964.

21. Toyohiko Kagawa, *Christ and Japan*, SCM Press 1928, p. 112.

22. Ibid., p. 113.

23. In an interview recorded in Dom Aelred Graham, *Conversations Christian and Buddhist*, Collins 1969, p. 184.

24. Murasaki Shikibu, *The Tale of Genji, Sources of Japanese Tradition*, p. 178.

25. Aiyko Miura, *The Wind is Howling*, Hodder and Stoughton 1970, pp. 89f.

26. Donald McGavren, *Understanding Church Growth*, Eerdmans, Grand Rapids, Michigan 1970.

27. Robert Lee, *Stranger in the Land*, Lutterworth Press 1967, Chapter 6, 'Uptown Church'.

28. The notion of the creative response is important in Gogarten's work, but especially in his *Politische Ethik*, Diederichs, Jena 1932.

29. This is still the case in India with its tantric rites and erotic temples, where the eroticism is obviously closest to that of the West. Pure pleasure or a mystical union of persons is not the end, which is rather yogic, the acquiring of magical powers of union with the divine by control of the act.

30. Leslie T. Lyall, *Urgent Harvest*, Lutterworth Press 1962, p. 30.

31. See, for example, Saikaku Ihara, *Comrade Loves of the Samurai*, Charles E. Tuttle, Tokyo and Vermont 1972.

32. Junichiro Tanizaki, *Some Prefer Nettles*, Knopf, New York 1955; Yukio Mishima, *The Temple of the Golden Pavilion*, Knopf 1959; Yukio Mishima, *Forbidden Colours*, Knopf 1968; Yasunari Kawabata, *House of the Sleeping Beauties*, Kodansha International, Tokyo 1969; Akiyuki Nozaka, *The Pornographers*, Secker & Warburg 1969.

33. Toyohiko Kagawa, *Christ and Japan*, p. 29.

34. Pearl S. Buck, *China as I See It*, Methuen 1971, p. 70.

35. Karl Menninger, *Whatever Happened To Sin?*, Hawthorn Books, New York 1973, pp. 39–43.

36. Emil Brunner, *The Divine Imperative*, Lutterworth Press 1937; for marriage and divorce, see especially chapters XXXI and XXXII.

THE EXPANSION OF GOD

Chapter 5

1. To the point of violence, which has suddenly become one of the country's leading problems and the most radical mark of departure from traditional values. 11,300 people were killed in criminal acts in 1975 alone, according to the Bangkok correspondent of the *South China Morning Post*, 8 March 1976 (perhaps 1,300 ought to be the number). Factors have been the serious lack of legal control over possession of arms, very rapid urbanization and disruption to traditional life-styles with little change to the gap between rich and poor, political instability, and mounting rents. The right wing likes to blame post-Sarit democracy, but the shocking disappearance of critics of corruption or the status quo ('contracts' can be placed against personal and political enemies in Bangkok for 2,000 – 5,000 Baht) rather belies this.

2. Carol Hollinger, *Mai Pen Rai Means Never Mind*, Houghton Mifflin, Boston 1965, p. 61.

3. Buddhadasa Bhikku, *Buddhadhamma for Students*, Sublime Life Mission, Bangkok (no date), pp. 5f.

4. The Jatakas are folk stories of the previous lives of Buddha, very influential in Thai culture, and many monks build their sermons for the laity on them. They take for granted the existence of a quasi-soul which supplies identity. It is an assumption that can be compared with the theory of *pudgala*, a spark of personality postulated by the Sammitiya sect of Buddhism in India.

5. Kosuke Koyama, 'Will the Monsoon Rain Make God Wet?', *Waterbuffalo Theology*, SCM Press 1974, pp. 27–42.

6. Upasika Nacb Maharuranonda, *The Development of Insight*, Buddhist University, Bangkok 1965, p. 79.

7. Cf. the *Analects*, for example XII 21. In Confucianism one may admonish inferiors and 'remonstrate' with the rest, but never attack anyone, though in contrast to the theoretically universal Buddhist charity (and, one imagines, psychologically more injurious) one should hate certain people privately (XXIV 17).

8. In reality, one main meal a day of this fare (there is a light breakfast) is insufficient for the monks, which is why so many are seen (incongruously) smoking. On the whole, I am inclined to regard Asian vegetarianism as a curse. In regions of India where it is strictly observed, I have seen labourers hardly able to carry three bricks for fatigue. In Thailand, however, the national casuistry permits a monk to eat meat on the basis that if it is positively given to him (which it should not be, but often is), the more important rule is to eat whatever is presented.

9. Carol Hollinger, *Mai Pen Rai Means Never Mind*, p. 237.

10. Like Dr Elizabeth Langley, who gradually became aware of corruptions in one government department where she was advising on the education of blind children, and from which she was dismissed in mys-

terious circumstances (see *Mission Thailand*, Vantage Press, New York 1977).

11. Carol Hollinger, *Mai Pen Rai Means Never Mind*, Chapter IX, 'Invigilation'.

12. *Wetsandon Chadok* is the story of the Great Birth. The Buddha underwent 550 births according to the Jatakas, of which the last ten, known as 'Thotsachat' in Thailand, are the most significant, and the Great Birth is the last of these. From hearing, reading or sponsoring reading of *Wetsandon Chadok*, great merit accrues to popular religion. For the lore surrounding this tale, see Phya Anuman Rajadhon, *Thet Maha Chet*, Thai Culture New Series No. 21, Fine Arts Dept, Bangkok 1974, and Elizabeth Wray, Clare Rosenfield and Dorothy Bailey, *Ten Lives of the Buddhas*, Weatherhill, New York 1972. This book is also a study of Thai art and culture.

13. Danit Yupho, *The Custom and Rite of Paying Homage to Teachers*, Thai Culture New Series no. 11, Fine Arts Dept, Bangkok 1970.

14. S. J. Tambiah, *World Conqueror and World Renouncer*, Cambridge University Press 1976.

15. For instance, the logic and conservatism which forbade Burmese medical authorities to make full use of modern medicine and attack agents of disease, like rats and cockroaches, has never troubled Thailand, which has never been as intellectually Buddhist as Burma.

16. In 1970, they composed 12.6% of total church membership with a 5.1% growth rate (as opposed to 2.1%).

17. The Jews are more inspirational and individualistic, their materialism perhaps less ingrained than acquired in bitter experiences of insecurity and persecution. The Chinese, by comparison, are more bureaucratically inclined, and concerned, like the French, to make a formal show, if need be at the expense of imagination and individualism, though they are undoubtedly more moralistic than the French.

18. In view of Chinese involvement in Communism in Malaysia and drug-trafficking in Thailand, it is slightly controversial that Blandford's *Chinese Churches in Thailand* is so concerned with Chinese needs, and emphasizes Chinese restrictions in Thailand (pp. 12–15): they have been forced to use Thai in schools, adopt Thai names and cannot buy land unless married to a Thai (this represents an attempt to keep land in Thai hands because the business is in Chinese hands). There is some anti-Chinese prejudice in South East Asia, and in Indonesia some real injustice and persecution, but Thailand is minimally to blame. Moreover, considering how elsewhere missionaries acquiesced in imposition of Western culture and language, one is surprised at this particular sympathy.

19. Kosuke Koyama, *Waterbuffalo Theology*, SCM Press 1974; Daniel McGilvary, *A Half Century among the Siamese and the Lao*, Fleming H. Revell, New York 1912.

20. However, this judgment cannot be considered certain. Serious historical doubt attaches to the mixture of 'enlightened' policy-making and

the religious conservatism which characterized this monarch. The 'enlightenment' was very relative and much caused by fears of Western encroachment and popular discontent, and also a temperamental disposition to scepticism in all spheres, and this arguably gives a slightly Machiavellian caste to the Buddhist revivalism and corresponding rejection of Christianity. In a monarch who believed so little, and who, despite his long monastic career, was hardly an exemplar of Buddhist virtues (one thinks of his tempers, his diet, his sensuality, his despotism, often held in check only by fears of Western protest) there seems something interested in the thoroughness of his religious reformism, especially in the emphasis on the need for monks to reach and teach the common people. It seems possible that corruption and change had produced the crisis situation in which Christianity might well have entered Siamese society, especially had the monarch been converted or shown himself more positively favourable. Unfortunate though the missionary approach was, monarchical self-interest must be weighed strongly against it.

21. Saad Chaiwan, *The Christian Approach to Buddhists in Thailand*, Suriyaban Publishers, Bangkok 1975.

22. Alex S. Smith, *Strategy to Multiply Local Churches*, OMF Publishers, Bangkok 1977, p. 237.

23. Consider, for example, Dr Lert Srichandra's story of how his Protestant school refused him baptism because his mother could not afford the term's school fees. See *Buddhists Find Christ*, ed. Patrick O'Connor, Charles E. Tuttle, Tokyo and Vermont 1975, p. 15.

24. *The Proclamation of the Christian Message in a Buddhist Environment*, Federation of Asian Bishops' Conference No. 5, 1977.

25. This translation is from Montri Umavijani, *The Domain of Thai Literature*, Bangkok 1978, p. 20. Suntorn Phu (or Sunthorn Bhu) (1788–1855) is one of Thailand's greatest and personally most colourful poets, chiefly remembered for his fantastic epic of adventure Phra Abhai Mani. For an English retelling, see Prem Chaya, *The Story of Phra Abhai Mani*, Chatra Books, Bangkok 1952.

26. Kosuke Koyama, *Waterbuffalo Theology*, SCM Press 1974, chapters 7 and 13.

27. I see no objection to this last idea. It is clearly stated in the Old Testament, in the laws about kosher food, that the blood of meat is not to be eaten because 'the blood is the life'. There are therefore no grounds for revelling in a mystique of blood, as in morbid hymns like 'There is a fountain filled with blood drawn from Emmanuel's veins'. Blood equals life, so 'without the shedding of blood there is no remission of sins' meant that without the sacrifice of a life there is no forgiveness.

28. Kosuke Koyama, 'Bangkok and Wittenberg', *Waterbuffalo Theology*, pp. 73–6.

29. Shusaku Endo, *A Life of Christ*, Paulist Press, New York 1978.

30. Emil Brunner, *The Divine Imperative*, Lutterworth Press 1937; in *Waterbuffalo Theology*, p. 92.

31. Donald McGavren, *Understanding Church Growth*, Eerdmans, Grand Rapids, Michigan 1970.

32. Anthropologically, this particular treatment of spirit cultus is practically unforgivable, and Smith is the victim of a one-sidedly religious emphasis. While the dangerous and superstitious nature cult cannot be overlooked, it is absurd to assume that the people always believe that real spirits are involved, still more absurd to believe that where spirits are widely believed in, there must be demons at work. There is a general anthropological consensus that the Thai spirit cult often serves the social function of permitting protest and abuse within a non-confrontationist social etiquette. Trance and hysteria supply the rural person with a face-saving protest device comparable to the function of drunkenness among city people. Thus not only is superstition being attacked, but a particular form of redress. The moral is surely that the missionary should not attack what he has not first endeavoured to understand, and is not willing to replace with something better. I also feel that theologically, the 'wrath' often unconsciously projected through the *phi* could be examined to demonstrate the religious necessity of the wrath and protest which Thai society and religion try to suppress.

33. The novels of Dokmai Sod are not available in English, nor is most modern Thai fiction, which is not usually considered of sufficiently wide interest to merit it. Her work is discussed in Montri Umavijani, *Dimensions of Thai Literature*, Bangkok 1978, pp. 29–31. Among translated fiction, essential and representative work would be Kukrit Pramoj, *Red Bamboo*, Progress Publishing, Bangkok 1961, and Khamsing Srinawk, *The Politician and Other Stories*, Oxford in Asia 1973.

34. Within the socially accepted code, as when in North Thailand young men are fined for touching women, or persons are attacked (like a teacher who was recently shot dead by someone outraged at his offence to public morals by having an affair with a female member of staff). However, as in Japan, where the nation possesses a more exotic moral and legal situation by Western standards because it has never been colonized, the subject of morals is very complex. Ultimately, modern prostitution is traceable to the abolition of polygamy (1925), which has only been legally effective among the elite; while they are absolutely required to have only one wife, often they took women of pleasure, with the wife's permission. Lower down the social scale, polygamy is still common, and the society could be regarded as unofficially polygamous, a matter of some consequence for church membership, especially in relation to the men, who are much less religious than the women, at least in terms of 'Buddhism', if not 'animism'.

35. Vincent Monteil, *Indonésie*, Editions du Seuil, Paris 1972, pp. 17f.

36. According to McGavren, who represents a typical Puritan view, in Jamaica the church is filled almost exclusively with the young and old, because of the very loose moral atmosphere, in which people take lovers every few months, or even weeks. Yet these people consider themselves

Christian and bring their illegitimate children for blessing. McGavren says that nothing can be done about this, and that all their appeals to become church members must be refused. Deplorable though the situation is, surely something could be done? If it encouraged them to better moral standards and stopped them drifting into black magic and other cults, could they not at least be baptized and confirmed and admitted to communion at a once- or twice-yearly repentance service, say at Christmas or Easter? What they did after that would be their own responsibility, but the ignorance of the people and universal custom, however bad, must be taken into account in judging and dealing with the question.

Chapter 6

1. Shusaku Endo, *Silence*, Charles E. Tuttle, Tokyo and Vermont 1969.

2. Nirad Chaudhuri, *Continent of Circe*, Chatto and Windus, 1965.

3. Some leading distinctions between Christian and Hindu doctrines were made in Chapter 1.

4. Wendy Doniger O'Flaherty, *Hindu Myths*, Penguin 1975, pp. 11–13.

5. Vedantic philosophy is that branch of philosophy which arose in commentary on the sacred Vedas, the scriptures comprising the Vedic hymns and Upanishads.

6. Sri Ramakrishna, quoted by Swami Vivekenanda, *Collected Works* III, 18, Mayavati Memorial Edition, Calcutta 1955.

7. Swami Vivekenanda, *Collected Works*, II, pp. 33f.

8. Sheila Cassidy, *Audacity to Believe*, Collins 1977.

9. In the Sankhya philosophy of evolution, a passive evolution subject to cycles, there is a combination of mind and matter for change, but it sounds dreadful; the comparison is of a lame man of good vision mounted on the shoulders of a blind man of sure foot!

10. Mark Sunder Rao, *Ananyatva: Realization of Christian Non Duality* (Indian Christian Thought Series No. 2), CISRS, Bangalore 1964.

11. Surgit Singh, *Preface to Personality*, Christian Literature Society, Madras 1952.

12. V. P. Chenchiah (and others), *Rethinking Christianity in India*, A. N. Sudarisanam, Madras 1938.

13. P. Y. Luke and John B. Carman, *Village Christians and Hindu Culture*, Lutterworth Press 1968.

14. A. J. Appasamy, *Christianity as Bhaktimarga*, Macmillan 1927; *The Gospel and India's Heritage*, SPCK 1942.

15. For his life and views see D. Hunt, *The God of the Untouchables*, Fleming H. Revell, New York 1976.

16. K. T. Paul, *The British Connection with India*, SCM 1928.

17. Alexander Duff, *The New Era of the English Language and English Literature in India*, 1837; William Miller, *The Christian Conception of*

God's Dealing with Mankind, 1890; *The Place of Hinduism in the Story of the World*, 1895; John Wilson, *The Evangelization of India*, 1849; *The British Sovereignty in India* (an address), 1835.

18. Nicol MacNicol, *Is Christianity Unique?* SCM Press 1936.

19. Peter Brent, *Godmen of India*, Penguin Books 1972, p. 61.

20. Save perhaps recently in a unique example of that creative symbolism, the gift which Jung believed Christianity had lost, when in the allegories of C. S. Lewis the lion Aslan becomes a God image.

21. A concept to be taken seriously and not associated only with the most primitive myth. Even Krishna devotees would affirm that his incarnation was the expression of a divine 'sport', not as in the case of Christ a terrible and serious necessity, for even though Krishna might be said to be 'saving the world' and 'restoring the balance', the world is not really that important and depends upon how one regards it.

22. Jeane Dixon, *Yesterday, Today and Tomorrow*, William Morrow, New York 1975, p. 268.

23. See Denis Brian, *Jeane Dixon: The Witnesses*, Doubleday, New York 1976, p. 9.

24. Andre Barbault, *Le Zodiaque*, Editions du Seuil, Paris 1958.

25. Cheiro (Count Louis Hamon), *You and Your Hand*, Sphere Books 1974, p. xv.

26. There was considerable hostility to Buddhism, some say persecution, and until the English conquest, no good Hindu was supposed to leave the borders of mother India.

27. John Hick, *God and the Universe of Faiths*, revised edition Collins 1977; W. E. Hocking, *The Coming World Civilization,* Allen and Unwin 1958; F. S. C. Northrop, *The Meeting of East and West*, Macmillan, New York 1946; Wilfred Cantwell Smith, *Questions of Religious Truth*, Scribner, New York 1967; Arnold Toynbee, *Christianity among the Religions of the World*, Oxford University Press 1958.

28 Arnold Toynbee, *A Study of History*, pp. 328, 333, 348.

29. Arnold Toynbee, *Christianity among the Religions of the World*, p. 110.

30. Richard and Helen Exley, *The Missionary Myth*, Lutterworth Press 1973, p. 162.

31. S. Radhakrishnan, *Eastern Religions and Western Philosophies*, Oxford University Press 1939, pp. 324, 293; Paul Arthur Schilpp, *The Philosophy of Sarvapelli Radhakrishnan*, Tudor Publishing House, New York 1932, p. 810 and footnote. For Radhakrishnan, doctrine is dangerous in motive and consequence, and he quotes Huxley: 'Because Christianity believed that they had only one Avatar, Christian history has been disgraced by more and bloodier crusades ... than has the history of Hinduism or Buddhism.' It can be understood how Radhakrishnan, as a member of a conquered society, would perceive Christianity as perpetrating through dogma a 'jealous God' syndrome, and average missionary glorification of the more warlike figures, like David and Joshua, does not

always help. As regards the Jews and their character it must be understood that while God may be seen as using certain traits, he does not necessarily approve them, or if he does so, only in relation to something surrounding them, which is less good. That God wholly supported the Jewish aggression or Jewish perception of being chosen is challenged by statements like Josh. 5.13f., where the angel is neither for nor against Israel at Jericho, or Amos 9.7, where after admitting that God has only revealed himself to Israel (Amos 3.2), it is said that Jews are only like the Ethiopians and Philistines whom God also 'brought out' of other lands. Provided that this is remembered, it is natural that Christians should draw spiritual and moral lessons from the Jewish wars. Even Hindus and Buddhists have national epics of wars from which they do the same.

32. John Hick, *God and the Universe of Faiths*, Revised Edition, Collins 1977, p. 136; Huston Smith, *The Religions of Man*, Harper and Row, New York 1958, p. 312; Arnold Toynbee, *Christianity among the Religions of the World*, p. 96.

33. Hick, op. cit., p. 135.

34. S. Radhakrishnan, *Eastern Religions and Western Philosophers*, chapter 5.

35. Watchman Nee, *What Shall This Man Do?*, p. 41.

36. Arnold Toynbee, *Christianity among the Religions of the World*, p. 96.

37. F. S. C. Northrop, *The Meeting of East and West*.

38. S. Radhakrishnan, *Eastern Religions and Western Philosophies*, Clarendon Press 1939, Chapter 8.

39. R. C. Zaehner, *Drugs, Mysticism and Makebelieve*, Collins 1978, Chapter 5.

40. George Bernanos, *Monsieur Ouine*, see *Oeuvres Romanesques*, Bibliotheque de la Pléïade, Gallimard, Paris 1961.

41. I feel sure that the author of *The Dream of the Red Chamber* intuited this in the nightmarishly tragic finale of his novel, and that the book is not just a criticism of the traditional society but a protest by a Buddhist believer of the final cruelty of his faith. The paradise from which in a vision the hero is cast out is one in which persons for whom he cared have become shadows who cannot acknowledge his possessive affection, yet it is to this 'heaven' that he must still strive in order to attain release from the torment of existence on earth. In the end, when he leaves his household for ever to achieve enlightenment, the ordeal is so terrible for him and members of his household that he can only break away by laughing the crazy laughter of the Zen masters, mocking sorrow and denying love altogether. The author shows an uncharacteristic logic in the treatment of the Buddhist theme.

42. John Hick, *Evil and the God of Love*, Fontana Books 1968, p. 382.

43. Joseph Campbell, *The Masks of God: Primitive Mythology*, Revised Edition, Penguin Books, 19xx, p. 86.

44. Jeane Dixon, *The Call to Glory*, Morrow, New York, 1971.

45. Watchman Nee, *What Shall This Man Do?*, pp. 37, 41.

46. Hans Küng, in *Christian Revelation and World Religions*, ed. J. Neusner, Burns and Oates 1967, p. 56.

47. See above, pp. 19f.

48. Arnold Toynbee, *The Historian's Approach to Religion*, Oxford University Press 1956, pp. 37, 99; *A Study of History*, p. 229.

Chapter 7

1. Carl Michalson, *Japanese Contributions to Christian Theology*, Westminster Press, Philadelphia 1960; Toyhiko Kagawa, *Christ and Japan*, SCM Press 1928, pp. 99f.

2. Arnold Toynbee, *A Study of History*, Thames and Hudson 1972, chapters 46 and 48.

3. Paul Tillich, *Systematic Theology*, Vol. 1, SCM Press 1978 (University of Chicago Press 1951).

4. Leslie T. Lyall, *Red Sky at Night*, Hodder and Stoughton 1969.

5. Thomas Mann, *Dr Faustus*, Penguin Books 1971, chapters 11, 12, 13.

6. Ibid., pp. 89f., 96.

7. See Rudolf Bultmann, *Jesus Christ and Mythology*, SCM Press 1960; John Hick, *God and the Universe of Faiths*, revised edition, Fontana Books 1977; John A. T. Robinson, *Honest to God*, SCM Press 1963; Paul Tillich, *The New Being*, SCM Press 1956; Albert Schweitzer, *The Quest of the Historical Jesus*, A. and C. Black [3]1954. The implications of this kind of theology have been exposed in Trevor Ling, *Buddha, Marx and God*, Macmillan 1966. Ling's opinion is that if modern theology, like Bultmann's, can be considered Christianity, then Buddhism can be considered a religion (as opposed to a philosophy).

8. Harold Falding, *The Sociology of Religion*, McGraw-Hill, New York 1974. p. 233.

9. Jeane Dixon, *My Life and Prophecies*, Morrow, New York 1969, pp. 49f.; *The Call to Glory*, Morrow, New York 1971.

10. David Wilkerson, *The Vision*, Fleming H. Revell, New York 1974; *Racing towards Judgment*, Fleming H. Revell, New York 1976.

11. Jess Stearn, *The Sixth Man*, Doubleday, New York 1961.

12. Augustine, *Confessions*, Book IX 4.

13. Lutheran teaching from Luther to Barth takes the view that the Bible is inspired, not in the sense that every sentence is dictated by God, but that it was made clear under divine influence, and as such, is able to become the vehicle through which God speaks to us in a way that we will recognize. An example might be the Asia missionary Isobel Kuhn (See *In the Arena*, Lutterworth Press 1959, p. 185), who tells how when she read in the Psalms 'and so he gives his beloved sleep', she knew she would die of cancer (as she did). The problematic feature of this kind of 'illuminist' experience is that though the sense of the message can be so different from

the literal sense, it will be used to support claims to the literal power and truth of the same scripture used. Strictly speaking, illuminist reading would only prove that God can use anything to speak, and the Bible would normally be the best vehicle. Thus Isadora Duncan was overcome with supernatural terror of imminent judgment when, before her children died, her book opened at a poem about proud Niobe whom the gods punished by taking her children from her.

14. Paul Tillich, *The Shaking of the Foundations*, SCM Press 1949. This work, which gives the flavour of his huge opus, also betrays its limitations. If anything, shaking the foundations of what it defends seems to be a feature. While I am sympathetic to the psychologization of religion which Tillich attempted, and am impressed by his many insights, by reducing original sin to what is called most fundamentally a sense of separation inherent in conscious being itself and by making freedom rather than its misuse the major problem, one is left with a Hindu doctrine of ignorance or duality as the root of suffering and individualism of accidental value.

15. Albert Schweitzer, *The Quest of the Historical Jesus*.

16. The claim of Bultmann, Schweitzer and others that Jesus' warning to the high priest that he would see him coming in messianic glory proves that Jesus expected his speedy return in fact proves no more than the nature of the belief of those making the claim. Obviously, if Jesus was who he claimed to be, the behaviour and attitude of the high priest would be so culpable that, whether returning within one generation or ten thousand, God might be expected to ensure his awareness of his crime.

17. David Wilkerson, *Racing towards Judgment*, p. 126.

18. Prohibitions, such as those against seething a kid in its mother's milk, eating carrion and not muzzling the ox treading corn, led to considerable respect for animals. There was no forcing of premature deliveries to acquire the tender meat or skins of young animals, and no animal could be used as a beast of burden until weaned. Since carrion was interpreted to include any animals dying in pain, death of animals, whether for Jewish sacrifice or common consumption, had to be instantaneous, which meant that only one clear cut of the jugular vein and carotid artery was permissible rather than clubbing, puncturing, etc. By contrast, the Hindu and Buddhist preservation of life allows much cruelty to animals, who can die the most painful slow deaths on the way to becoming edible carrion if they are not positively ill-treated during life. I was appalled at the ill-treatment of animals in India, where sacred cows roam free but half-starved, and the bullocks drawing carts are struck without mercy.

19. Mary Daly, *Beyond God the Father*, Beacon Press, Boston 1973, p. 96.

20. Medard Boss, *A Psychiatrist Discovers India*, Oswald Wolff 1965; see the chapter, 'A Psychological Prejudice of the West', pp. 46–88, esp. 54f., 75.

21. C. G. Jung, 'The Sign of the Fishes', in *Aion*, Collected Works, Vol. IX, part 2, Routledge 1959.

22. 'Catamite' is believed by many theologians to be the best translation; the reference is probably to the custom whereby Greek husbands shared their favours with kept men, male prostitutes. This translation would put a very different complexion on the text, but one is obliged to treat the Bible and St Paul here, not as they ought perhaps to be translated, but in the light of the impression that current reading must produce.

23. Dante, *The Divine Comedy*, Canto V. See also the commentary on this Canto in the translation by Dorothy L. Sayers, Penguin Books 1969.

24. Arnold Toynbee, *A Study of History*, p. 103.

25. For St Paul, morality is an abstract passion, like many Semitic passions, one in which under the influence of desert culture details and causes are often ignored. One has only to read the *Satires* of Juvenal, with their comments on Roman morals, to realize that lust for lust's sake was rarer than lust for profit, as in modern America, and that the insight that money is the root of many evils could usefully have been developed further. Sex was an industry, a way of securing jobs, of rising in society, of inheriting. 'Cash always wins in the end', Juvenal declares, commenting on the morals of the well-raised young. It was also unrealistic of St Paul to claim that incest was a sin unknown even to the surrounding pagans. St Columba said the same thing when incest was far from unknown among the Celts. In the working classes, or in matriarchally inclined societies, incest is unfortunately more common than is supposed. Catullus was shocked by the incest of Clodius, but his poem expresses an upper-class view. In the Old Testament, Ammon violated his half-sister Tamar (II Samuel 9), but although the relationship was forbidden by Jewish law, king David suggested that, in view of Ammon's desperation, had he requested Tamar, David would have given him to her. True, it was the case of a half-sister only, and not sister or mother, but without condoning incest, which is as undesirable biologically as it is morally, one might point out that this highlights the narrowness of St Paul's judgments and reminds us that discretion should be used in most situations.

26. There are, of course, forms of conduct that may be termed indecent or 'vile', but as we saw in Chapter 1, it is impossible to refuse the earthy or 'unclean' character of sex. Emil Brunner, in *The Divine Imperative* (ch. XXXII), maintains from experience that the religious marriage is most insecure when entered upon or maintained in denial of 'eros' through supposed obligations of friendship or spirituality. (I assume 'eros' here to be intended in the general Jungian sense of a certain attunement to what is symbolized by the earth gods, since obviously not everyone is or needs to be the erotic personality type to be fulfilled.)

27. Living cells are potentially immortal. Under optimum test conditions, pieces of animal tissue, muscle and nerve cells can be kept alive indefinitely. It is only the relationship to the whole organism which in-

volves them in death, the body being like the proverbial chain, only as strong as its weakest link.

28. C. G. Jung, for example in *Man and His Symbols*, Aldus Books 1964, p. 127.

29. Pearl Buck, *My Several Worlds*, Bantam Books, New York 1954, p. 361.

30. It is doubtful whether religious prejudice against homosexuality can ever be justified entirely on the basis of natural law; the consequences of its role as a 'discontent of civilization' might be more pertinent. Emotional feeling apart, logically there can be little that is 'unnatural' about most expressions of inversion unless one maintains that the sex act is exclusively to engender offspring. Homosexuality, though like heterosexuality a form of expression for many different types of people, does appear to lend itself to association with the hysterical magical or mediumistic function, and homosexuals do appear somewhat easily influenced, if not corruptible, and allies of the regressive or highly permissive matriarchal culture. In certain African tribes, homosexuals have been feared for their magical powers.

31. Puranic myths are those which deal specifically with incarnations. There are Shivapurana, Krishnapurana and so on. For myth generally see J. E. B. Gray, *Indian Folk Tales and Legends*, Oxford University Press 1961.

32. David Wilkerson, *Racing towards Judgement*, pp. 41f.

Index

445

INDEX